Encyclopedia of
World War II
A Political, Social, and Military History

Encyclopedia of
World War II

A Political, Social, and Military History

VOLUME V: DOCUMENTS

Dr. Priscilla Mary Roberts

Editor, Documents Volume

Dr. Spencer C. Tucker

Editor

A B C ● C L I O

Santa Barbara, California   Denver, Colorado   Oxford, England

Library of Congress Cataloging-in-Publication Data
Encyclopedia of World War II : a political, social, and military history /
Spencer C. Tucker, editor, Priscilla Mary Roberts, editor.
    p. cm.
  Includes bibliographical references and index.
   ISBN 1-57607-999-6 (hardcover : alkaline paper) — ISBN 1-57607-095-6 (e-book)
1. World War, 1939–1945—Encyclopedias. 2. History, Modern—20th century—Encyclopedias. I. Title: Encyclopedia of World War Two. II. Title: Encyclopedia of World War 2. III. Tucker, Spencer, 1937– IV. Roberts, Priscilla Mary.
   D740.E516 2004
   940.53'03—dc22   2004023745

10 09 08 07 06 05   10 9 8 7 6 5 4 3 2 1

This book is also available on the World Wide Web as an ebook.
Visit abc-clio.com for details.

ABC-CLIO, Inc.
130 Cremona Drive, P.O. Box 1911
Santa Barbara, California 93116–1911

This book is printed on acid-free paper ∞.
Manufactured in the United States of America

Contents

List of Documents

Introduction

Documents are the raw materials of history. The historian must recognize their unique properties and exercise great caution in handling them. The story the documents tell may or may not be true, and each type of document has its own advantages and disadvantages. One distinguished World War II historian, Sir John Wheeler-Bennett, edited collections of German documents on interwar foreign policy and termed documents "the bare bones of history." He recalled, as "a young and budding historian I had a thing about documents. I believed that in documents lay the real truth of history." He nonetheless confessed that, though never losing his basic interest in documents, he later

> discovered . . . that historical truth—in that it exists at all—lies not in documents alone, nor in memoirs, diaries, biographies or oral history. All these are essential and invaluable factors in the historian's armoury but, when the chips are down, the final result depends on the historian himself alone, on his ability to weigh, assay and analyse the accumulated material at his disposal and to come up with his own honest opinions and conclusions. There are no answers at the back of the book. (Wheeler-Bennett 1976, 58)

The further back we go in the historical record, the fewer documents we normally have at our disposal. This is due in part to the loss or destruction of many documents over time and to the fact that mass literacy has been largely a phenomenon of the nineteenth and twentieth centuries. When fewer people were able to read or write, the written record was less extensive. Those who lacked the ability to leave any written record of their own were underrepresented in historical accounts, which relied heavily on written sources.

The documents in this volume are only a tiny fraction of the millions of documents World War II generated. In a few cases, tracking down these documents presented a challenge demanding persistence and ingenuity. In assembling this collection, the editor was fortunate in having at her disposal the outstanding resources of the libraries of the University of Hong Kong, George Washington University and its associated consortium, and the Library of Congress. Perhaps the hardest task, however, was not simply locating these documents but making the final selection.

Quite a number of documents chose themselves. One important priority was to provide reasonably full coverage of both the diplomatic and the military courses of the war. Another was to give some sense of its geographical extent and implications. Whether actual fighting took place on its soil, for every country involved in World War II, the political, social, and economic impact was profound. The documents included here were chosen to convey some sense of the wider domestic consequences of the experience of total war.

World War II did not have tidy temporal limits. Powers entered the war at different times: Great Britain, Germany, and France in 1939, Italy in 1940, the Soviet Union in mid-1941, and the United States at the end of 1941. In a broader perspective, the causes of World War II can be traced back at least to World War I, which fragmented and weakened the existing international system, creating a set of problems it would take another war to resolve. Nor did the consequences of World War II end when the fighting ended in 1945. The power vacuum it created in large parts of the world was effectively filled by the Cold War, which evolved out of the balance of forces that existed when the war ended and from ideological and geopolitical conflicts, the ancestry of which was far more venerable. The documents in this volume therefore cover the rise of Benito Mussolini and Adolf Hitler, the development of the Sino-Japanese conflict, the

Italo-Ethiopian War, the Spanish Civil War, and the reaction of the large Western democracies, including the United States, to these events.

Although the formal time-frame for this volume ends in 1945, one can already discern in the documents the burgeoning Cold War, as tensions mounted between the Soviet Union and the Western Allies over control of Eastern Europe and the treatment of Germany. From early in the war, liberal Europeans demonstrated a real wish to integrate their continent so as to prevent future wars resembling the two of the previous thirty years. The rise of nationalist and communist political forces in Asia was also clearly apparent even before World War II began, but the war enormously enhanced the position of both and ultimately ended formal Western colonialism there. Significantly, by 1945, top American political and military leaders were urging that their country indefinitely maintain a strong and modern military capable of responding immediately to international challenges and also an overseas intelligence capability.

Politicians, diplomats, and generals made—or tried to make—the war's biggest decisions, but their ultimate success in implementing these decisions depended on their ability to win support or at least acquiescence from their populations. Tens of millions of ordinary people fought in the war, as soldiers or irregular partisans. At least as many worked in the war industries and hundreds of millions lived in territories that were fought over, bombed, or occupied. Tens of millions of soldiers and civilians died, in combat, as prisoners of war or as the victims of bombing, atrocities, concentration camps, exposure, starvation, and disease. From small children to the elderly, even among those fortunate enough to escape the war's worst ravages, its effects were still felt long after the actual fighting ceased. For many, the war was a period of brutal hardship; of battles and experiences they would rather forget. For others more fortunate, the war was a period of camaraderie and excitement, of using their skills and living their lives with an intensity they would never again attain, and of shared effort in a common and uplifting cause. And for many, maybe even the majority, the war and its effects were simply to be endured. Some, of course, left no records behind.

For many years, newspapers reported the war in detail, from the level of high policy down to human interest stories of its impact on individuals who might or might not be typical. Official government broadcasting operations and private broadcasting stations also kept extensive collections of transcripts and recordings of radio broadcasts. Official government records in the political, military, diplomatic, economic, and domestic spheres record the information that the government wanted to share with its citizens.

Less official materials were also abundant, their survival in many cases dependent upon the vagaries of chance. Private organizations, business or philanthropic, often maintained what were effectively their own archives, and some individuals saved large collections of personal papers. Many of those involved in the war kept diaries—those in prominent or interesting positions perhaps in the hope of enshrining their claims to historical recognition, many ordinary people in the expectation that their wartime experiences would be among the high points of their lives. After the war ended, new technology, especially light and easily operable recording machines, contributed to the development of the new field of oral history, whose practitioners made dedicated efforts to collect, transcribe, and make available the recollections of all levels of wartime participants, from those who were children at the time to high-ranking officials. The growing interest in family history likewise impelled individuals to set down their recollections for future generations.

One must always, however, approach every source with what will often prove to be well-warranted skepticism. Documents are never simply neutral records of events. Every document is written for a purpose, even if it is simply to record one's own private experiences and feelings. In no circumstances can one treat a document in a vacuum; the more one knows about its context, the better one can appreciate it.

What, then, is the value of documents to historians? Should we conclude that, since every document is inherently problematic, it is impossible to make any credible use of them? To that, the dedicated historian would undoubtedly answer: Certainly not. Historians regard documents as treasures and devote much effort and ingenuity to tracking down new and previously overlooked sources. The interpretation of written sources, while overwhelming at times, is not a task requiring superhuman talents. It merely demands the fundamental qualifications of any good historian: knowledge, skill, discernment, and critical abilities.

No single collection of documents could ever hope to encapsulate the vast range of individual experiences in and responses to World War II. Even though several were chosen at least in part because each seemed broadly representative of a particular type of wartime experience, the small selection of personal letters and memoirs included here perhaps suggests how very differently the same war could be felt for each man, woman, or child involved.

— Priscilla Mary Roberts

Reference
Wheeler-Bennett, John. *Friends, Enemies and Sovereigns*. London: Macmillan, 1976.

Encyclopedia of

World War II

A Political, Social, and Military History

Documents Prior to 1938

1. The Quest for Lebensraum: Extract from Adolf Hitler, *Mein Kampf* (1924)

In 1924 Adolf Hitler, then a rising young politician, published his memoirs and political program, a volume named Mein Kampf (My Struggle). *He claimed that Germany needed and was entitled to* Lebensraum *[living space] to fulfill its national ambitions and potential and that such territory could only be found in the lands east of Germany, especially Communist Russia, a state he claimed was dominated by Jews. Hitler flatly declined to be satisfied with the restoration of the pre–World War I German boundaries of 1914.*

If under foreign policy we must understand the regulation of a nation's relations with the rest of the world, the manner of this regulation will be determined by certain definite facts. As National Socialists we can, furthermore, establish the following principle concerning the nature of the foreign policy of a folkish state:

The foreign policy of the folkish state must safeguard the existence on this planet of the race embodied in the state, by creating a healthy, viable natural relation between the nation's population and growth on the one hand and the quantity and quality of its soil on the other hand.

As a healthy relation we may regard only that condition which assures the sustenance of a people on its own soil. Every other condition, even if it endures for hundreds, nay, thousands of years, is nevertheless unhealthy and will sooner or later lead to the injury if not annihilation of the people in question.

Only an adequately large space on this earth assures a nation freedom of existence.

Moreover, the necessary size of the territory to be settled cannot be judged exclusively on the basis of present requirements, not even in fact on the basis of the yield of the soil compared to the population. . . . If a nation's sustenance as such is assured by the amount of its soil, the safeguarding of the existing soil itself must also be borne in mind. This lies in the general power-political strength of the state, which in turn to no small extent is determined by geomilitary considerations.

Hence, the German nation can defend its future only as a world power. . . .

Germany today is no world power. Even if our momentary military impotence were overcome, we should no longer have any claim to this title. What can a formation, as miserable in its relation of population to area as the German Reich today, mean on this planet? In an era when the earth is gradually being divided up among states, some of which embrace almost entire continents, we cannot speak of a world power in connection with a formation whose political mother country is limited to the absurd area of five hundred thousand square kilometers.

From the purely territorial point of view, the area of the German Reich vanishes completely as compared with that of the so-called world powers. . . .

Thus, in the world today we see a number of power states, some of which not only far surpass the strength of our German nation in population, but whose area above all is the chief support of their political power. Never has the relation of the German Reich to other existing world states been as unfavorable as at the beginning of our history two thousand years ago and again today. Then we were a young people, rushing headlong into a world of great crumbling state formations, whose last giant, Rome, we ourselves helped to fell. Today we find ourselves in a world of great power states in process of formation, with our own Reich sinking more and more into insignificance.

We must bear this bitter truth coolly and soberly in mind. We must follow and compare the German Reich through the centuries in its relation to other states with regard to population and area. I know that everyone will then come to the dismayed conclusion which I have stated at the beginning of this discussion: *Germany is no longer a world power, regardless whether she is strong or weak from the military point of view.*

We have lost all proportion to the other great states of the earth, and this thanks only to the positively catastrophic leadership of our nation in the field of foreign affairs, thanks to our total failure to be guided by what I should almost call a testamentary aim in foreign policy, and thanks to the loss of any healthy instinct and impulse of self-preservation.

If the National Socialist movement really wants to be consecrated by history with a great mission for our nation, it must be permeated by knowledge and filled with pain at our true situation in this world; boldly and conscious of its goal, it must take up the struggle against the aimlessness and incompetence which have hitherto guided our German nation in the line of foreign affairs. Then, without consideration of "traditions" and prejudices, it must find the courage to gather our people and their strength for an advance along the road that will lead this people from its present restricted living space to new land and soil, and hence also free it from the danger of vanishing from the earth or of serving others as a slave nation.

The National Socialist movement must strive to eliminate the disproportion between our population and our area—viewing this latter as a source of food as well as a basis for power politics—between our historical past and the hopelessness of our present impotence. And in this it must remain aware that we, as guardians of the highest humanity on this earth, are bound by the highest obligation, and the more it strives to bring the German people to racial awareness so that, in addition to breeding dogs, horses, and cats, they will have mercy on their own blood, the more it will be able to meet this obligation. . . .

I still wish briefly to take a position on the question as to what extent the demand for soil and territory seems ethically and morally justified. This is necessary, since unfortunately, even in so-called folkish circles, all sorts of unctuous

bigmouths step forward, endeavoring to set the rectification of the injustice of 1918 as the aim of the German nation's endeavors in the field of foreign affairs, but at the same time find it necessary to assure the whole world of folkish brotherhood and sympathy.

I should like to make the following preliminary remarks: The demand for restoration of the frontiers of 1914 is a political absurdity of such proportions and consequences as to make it seem a crime. Quite aside from the fact that the Reich's frontiers in 1914 were anything but logical. For in reality they were neither complete in the sense of embracing the people of German nationality, nor sensible with regard to geomilitary expediency. They were not the result of a considered political action, but momentary frontiers in a political struggle that was by no means concluded; partly, in fact, they were the results of chance. With equal right and in many cases with more right, some other sample year of German history could be picked out, and the restoration of the conditions at that time declared to be the aim of an activity in foreign affairs. . . .

The boundaries of the year 1914 mean nothing at all for the German future. Neither did they provide a defense of the past, nor would they contain any strength for the future.

Through them the German nation will neither achieve its inner integrity, nor will its sustenance be safeguarded by them, nor do these boundaries, viewed from the military standpoint, seem expedient or even satisfactory, nor finally can they improve the relation in which we at present find ourselves toward the other world powers, or, better expressed, the real world powers. The lag behind England will not be caught up, the magnitude of the Union will not be achieved; not even France would experience a material diminution of her world-political importance. . . .

And so we National Socialists consciously draw a line beneath the foreign policy tendency of our pre-War period. We take up where we broke off six hundred years ago. We stop the endless German movement to the south and west, and turn our gaze toward the land in the east. At long last we break off the colonial and commercial policy of the pre-War period and shift to the soil policy of the future.

If we speak of soil in Europe today, we can primarily have in mind only Russia and her vassal border states.

Here Fate itself seems desirous of giving us a sign. By handing Russia to Bolshevism, it robbed the Russian nation of that intelligentsia which previously brought about and guaranteed its existence as a state. For the organization of a Russian state formation was not the result of the political abilities of the Slavs in Russia, but only a wonderful example of the state-forming efficacy of the German element in an inferior race. Numerous mighty empires on earth have been created in this way. Lower nations led by Germanic organizers and overlords have more than once grown to be mighty state formations and have endured as long as the racial nucleus of the creative state race maintained itself. For centuries Russia drew nourishment from this Germanic nucleus of its upper leading strata. Today it can be regarded as almost totally exterminated and extinguished. It has been replaced by the Jew. Impossible as it is for the Russian by himself to shake off the yoke of the Jew by his own resources, it is equally impossible for the Jew to maintain the mighty empire forever. He himself is no element of organization, but a ferment of decomposition. The Persian empire in the east is ripe for collapse. And the end of Jewish rule in Russia will also be the end of Russia as a state. We have been chosen by Fate as witnesses of a catastrophe which will be the mightiest confirmation of the soundness of the folkish theory.

Our task, the mission of the National Socialist movement, is to bring our own people to such political insight that they will not see their goal for the future in the breathtaking sensation of a new Alexander's conquest, but in the industrious work of the German plow, to which the sword need only give soil. . . .

If the National Socialist movement frees itself from all illusions with regard to this great and all-important task, and accepts reason as its sole guide, the catastrophe of 1918 can some day become an infinite blessing for the future of our nation. Out of this collapse our nation will arrive at a complete reorientation of its activity in foreign relations, and, furthermore, reinforced within by its new philosophy of life, will also achieve outwardly a final stabilization of its foreign

policy. Then at last it will acquire what England possesses and even Russia possessed, and what again and again induced France to make the same decisions, essentially correct from the viewpoint of her own interests, to wit: A political testament.

The political testament of the German nation to govern its outward activity for all time should and must be:

Never suffer the rise of two continental powers in Europe. Regard any attempt to organize a second military power on the German frontiers, even if only in the form of creating a state capable of military strength, as an attack on Germany, and in it see not only the right, but also the duty, to employ all means up to armed force to prevent the rise of such a state, or, if one has already arisen, to smash it again. See to it that the strength of our nation is founded, not on colonies, but on the soil of our European homeland. Never regard the Reich as secure unless for centuries to come it can give every scion of our people his own parcel of soil. Never forget that the most sacred right on this earth is a man's right to have earth to till with his own hands, and the most sacred sacrifice the blood that a man sheds for this earth.

[Italics as in original]

2. Benito Mussolini (and Giovanni Gentile), "What Is Fascism?" Article for the *Italian Encyclopedia* (1932)

Italy was the first European state to embrace fascism after the First World War. The former socialist journalist Benito Mussolini, who fought as a corporal in the war, attacked the peace settlement as giving far too little to Italy and organized right-wing opposition to the existing government. In 1922 King Victor Emanuel appointed him prime minister. Fascist doctrine, as expounded by Mussolini, glorified military action and heroism in the interests of the state, to which individual rights were to be subordinated, and looked back to an idealized mythological past—in Italy's case the Roman empire. Mussolini called for military expansion and the acquisition of overseas colonies.

. . . [A]s regards the future development of mankind—and quite apart from all present political considerations—Fascism does not, generally speaking, believe in the possibility of utility of perpetual peace. It therefore discards pacifism as a cloak for cowardly supine renunciation in contradistinction to self-sacrifice. War alone keys up all human energies to their maximum tension and sets the seal of nobility on those people who have the courage to face it. All

other tests are substitutes which never place a man face to face with himself before the alternative of life or death. . . . The Fascist accepts and loves life; he rejects and despises suicide as cowardly. Life as he understands it means duty, elevation, conquest; life must be lofty and full, it must be lived for oneself but above all for others, both near by and far off, present and future. . . .

Such a conception of life makes Fascism the resolute

negation of the doctrine underlying so-called scientific and Marxian socialism, the doctrine of historic materialism which would explain the history of mankind in terms of the class struggle and by changes in the processes and instruments of production, to the exclusion of all else.

... Fascism believes now and always in sanctity and heroism, that is to say in acts in which no economic motive—remote or immediate—is at work. Having denied historic materialism, which sees in men mere puppets on the surface of history, appearing and disappearing on the crest of the waves while in the depths the real directing forces move and work, Fascism also denies the immutable and irreparable character of the class struggle which is the natural outcome of this economic conception of history; above all it denies that the class struggle is the preponderating agent in social transformations. . . .

After socialism, Fascism trains its guns on the whole block of democratic ideologies, and rejects both their premises and their practical applications and implements. Fascism denies that numbers, as such, can be the determining factor in human society; it denies the right of numbers to govern by means of periodical consultations; it asserts the irremediable and fertile and beneficent inequality of men who cannot be leveled by any such mechanical and extrinsic device as universal suffrage. . . .

... In rejecting democracy Fascism rejects the absurd conventional life of political equalitarianism, the habit of collective irresponsibility, the myth of felicity and indefinite progress. . . .

... Granted that the XIXth century was the century of socialism, liberalism, democracy, this does not mean that the XXth century must also be the century of socialism, liberalism, democracy. Political doctrines pass; nations remain. We are free to believe that this is the century of authority, a century tending to the "right," a Fascist century. If the XIXth century was the century of the individual (liberalism implies individualism) we are free to believe that this is the "collective" century, and therefore the century of the State. . . .

The key-stone of the Fascist doctrine is its conception of the State, of its essence, its functions, and its aims. For Fascism the State is absolute, individuals and groups relative. Individuals and groups are admissable insofar as they come within the State. Instead of directing the game and guiding the material and moral progress of the community, the liberal State restricts its activities to recording results. The Fascist State is wide awake and has a will of its own. For this reason it can be described as "ethical." . . .

The Fascist State organises the nation, but it leaves the individual adequate elbow room. It has curtailed useless or harmful liberties while preserving those which are essential. In such matters the individual cannot be the judge, but the State only.

... Fascism sees in the imperialistic spirit—i.e., in the tendency of nations to expand—a manifestation of their vitality. In the opposite tendency, which would limit their interests to the home country, it sees a sign of decadence. Peoples who rise or rearise are imperialistic; renunciation is characteristic of dying peoples. The Fascist doctrine is that best suited to the tendencies and feelings of a people which, like the Italian, after lying fallow during centuries of foreign servitude, is now reasserting itself in the world.

But imperialism implies discipline, the coordination of efforts, a deep sense of duty and a spirit of self-sacrifice. This explains many aspects of the practical activity of the State, as also the severity which has to be exercised towards those who would oppose this spontaneous and inevitable movement of XXth century Italy by agitating outgrown ideologies of the XIXth century, ideologies rejected wherever great experiments in political and social transformations are being dared.

Never before have the peoples thirsted for authority, direction, order, as they do now. If each age has its doctrine, then innumerable symptoms indicate that the doctrine of our age is the Fascist. That it is vital is shown by the fact that it has aroused a faith; that this faith has conquered souls is shown by the fact that Fascism can point to its fallen heroes and its martyrs.

Fascism has now acquired throughout the world that universality which belongs to all doctrines which by achieving self-expression represent a moment in the history of human thought.

Source: Benito Mussolini (and Giovanni Gentile), "What Is Fascism?" *Enciclopedia Italiana di scienze, lettere ed arti.* 36 vols. (Rome, Italy: Istituto Giovanni Treccani, 1929–1939). Vol. 14 (1932), 847–851. Reprinted in Benito Mussolini, *Fascism: Doctrine and Institutions* (Rome: Ardita Publishers, 1935), 7–42; this excerpt is 18–31.

3. Japan Withdraws from the League of Nations: Count Yasuya Ichida, Japanese Minister of Foreign Affairs, Telegram to the Secretary-General of the League of Nations, 27 March 1933

In September 1931 Japanese troops provoked an armed clash over the railroad in Mukden, Manchuria (present-day Shenyang, China). The League of Nations protested against Japan's actions and passed resolutions ordering the withdrawal of Japanese troops, which Japan ignored. The following year this incident became the pretext for Japan to establish a puppet regime in Manchuria, the nominally independent state of Manzhouguo, headed by the former Chinese emperor, Aisin Gioro Pu Yi. The League of Nations and many of its member nations, together with the United States, refused to recognize Manzhouguo as a independent country, which soon caused Japan to withdraw entirely from the League. In March 1933, shortly before President Franklin D. Roosevelt took office in the United States, the Japanese emperor issued a rescript proclaiming Japan's decision to leave. Japan's foreign minister informed the League immediately of Japan's withdrawal. A sense that Japan enjoyed special rights in East Asia informed both documents.

The Japanese Government believe that the national policy of Japan, which has for its aim to ensure the peace of the Orient and thereby contribute to the cause of peace throughout the world, is identical in spirit with the mission of the League of Nations, which is to achieve international peace and security. It has always been with pleasure, therefore, that this country has for thirteen years past, as an original Member of the League and a permanent member of its Council, extended a full measure of co-operation with her fellow members towards the attainment of its high purpose. It is indeed a matter of historical fact that Japan has continuously participated in the various activities of the League with a zeal not inferior to that exhibited by any other nation. At the same time, it is, and has always been, the conviction of the Japanese Government that in order to render possible the maintenance of peace in various regions of the world, it is necessary in existing circumstances to allow the operation of the Covenant of the League to vary in accordance with the actual conditions prevailing in each of those regions. Only by acting on this just and equitable principle can the League fulfill its mission and increase its influence.

Acting on this conviction, the Japanese Government have, ever since the Sino-Japanese dispute was, in September 1937–38, submitted to the League, at meetings of the League, and on other occasions, continually set forward a consistent view. This was, that if the League was to settle the issue fairly and equitably, and to make a real contribution to the promotion of peace in the Orient, and thus enhance its prestige, it should acquire a complete grasp of the actual conditions in this quarter of the globe, and apply the Covenant of the League in accordance with these conditions.

They have repeatedly emphasized and insisted upon the absolute necessity of taking into consideration the fact that China is not an organized State—that its internal conditions and external relations are characterized by extreme confusion and complexity, and by many abnormal and exceptional features—and that, accordingly, the general principles and usages of international law which govern the ordinary relations between nations are found to be considerably modified in their operation so far as China is concerned, resulting in the quite abnormal and unique international practices which actually prevail in that country.

However, the majority of the Members of the League evinced in the course of its deliberations during the past seventeen months a failure either to grasp these realities or else to face them and take them into proper account. Moreover, it has frequently been made manifest in these deliberations that there exist serious differences of opinion between Japan and these Powers concerning the application and even the interpretation of various international engagements and obligations, including the Covenant of the League and the principles of international law. As a result, the Report adopted by the Assembly at the Special Session of February 24 last, entirely misapprehending the spirit of Japan, pervaded as it is by no other desire than the maintenance of peace in the Orient, contains gross errors both in the ascertainment of facts and in the conclusions deduced. In asserting that the action of the Japanese army at the time of the incident of September 18, and subsequently, did not fall within the just limits of self-defence, the Report assigned no reasons and came to an arbitrary conclusion, and in ignoring alike the state of tension which preceded, and the various aggravations which succeeded, the incident—for all of which the full responsibility is incumbent upon China—the Report creates a source of fresh conflict in the political arena of the Orient. By refusing to acknowledge the actual circumstances that led to the foundation of Manchukuo, and by attempting to challenge the position taken up by Japan in recognizing the new State, it cuts away the ground for the stabilisation of the Far Eastern situation.

Nor can the terms laid down in its recommendations—as was fully explained in the Statement issued by this Government on February 25 last—ever be of any possible service in securing enduring peace in these regions.

The conclusion must be that, in seeking a solution of the question, the majority of the League have attached greater importance to upholding inapplicable formulae than to the real task of assuring peace, and higher value to the vindica-tion of academic theses than to the eradication of the sources of future conflict. For these reasons, and because of the profound differences of opinion existing between Japan and the majority of the League in their interpretation of the Covenant and of other treaties, the Japanese Government have been led to realize the existence of an irreconcilable divergence of views, dividing Japan and the League on policies of peace, and especially as regards the fundamental principles to be followed in the establishment of a durable peace in the Far East. The Japanese Government, believing that in these circumstances there remains no room for further co-operation, hereby give notice, in accordance with the provisions of Article 1, Paragraph 3, of the Covenant, of the intention of Japan to withdraw from the League of Nations.

Source: Website: History of the League of Nations. Available at http://www.unog.ch/library/archives/lon/library/Docs/kjap-out.html.

4. Adolf Hitler, Proclamation and Address to the German People, 14 October 1933

Shortly after coming to power in Germany, Hitler announced his intention to withdraw from the League of Nations and also from the European disarmament conference then in progress. The League, he argued, was merely an instrument to enforce the unjust peace settlement of the Treaty of Versailles. He appealed to the German people to endorse these actions in a referendum, and by a large majority, they were approved.

Adolf Hitler, Proclamation, 14 October 1933

Filled with the sincere desire to accomplish the work of the peaceful internal reconstruction of our nation and of its political and economic life, former German Governments, trusting in the grant of a dignified equality of rights, declared their willingness to enter the League of Nations and to take part in the Disarmament Conference.

In this connection Germany suffered a bitter disappointment.

In spite of our readiness to carry through German disarmament . . . other Governments could not decide to redeem the pledges signed by them in the Peace Treaty.

By the deliberate refusal of real moral and material equality of rights to Germany, the German nation and its Governments have been profoundly humiliated.

After the German Government had declared, as a result of the equality of rights expressly laid down on December 11, 1932, that it was again prepared to take part in the Disarmament Conference, the German Foreign Minister and our delegates were informed . . . that this equality of rights could no longer be granted to present-day Germany.

As the German Government regards this action as an unjust and humiliating discrimination against the German na-tion, it is not in a position to continue, as an outlawed and second-class nation, to take part in negotiations which could only lead to further arbitrary results.

While the German Government again proclaims its unshaken desire for peace, it declares to its great regret that, in view of these imputations, it must leave the Disarmament Conference. It will also announce its departure from the League of Nations.

It submits this decision . . . to the judgment of the German people.

Source: John W. Wheeler-Bennett, ed., *Documents on International Affairs 1933* (London: Oxford University Press, 1934), 287–289. Reprinted with permission of Chatham House.

Adolf Hitler, Address to the German People, 14 October 1933

My German Nation!

In November 1918, when the German nation laid down its arms trusting implicitly in the assurances contained in President Wilson's 14 Points, this marked the end of a disastrous struggle for which some individual statesmen could be blamed but certainly not the people of the warring nations. The German People fought so heroically only because they were completely convinced that they had been wrongfully attacked and were therefore justified in fighting. The other nations had hardly any idea of the immense sacrifice which Germany, almost entirely without allies, was forced to make at that time. If in those months the rest of the world had held out its hand to its defeated enemy in a spirit of fairness, mankind would have been spared a great deal of suffering and countless disappointments.

The German People suffered the most profound disappointment. Never had a defeated nation tried more sincerely to assist in healing the wounds of its former enemy than the German People did in the long years when it complied with the dictates imposed upon it. The fact that all these sacrifices could not genuinely pacify the other nations was due to a treaty which, by attempting to perpetuate the status of victor and vanquished, could only perpetuate hatred and enmity. The nations of the world had a right to expect that people would have learned from the greatest war in history that the sacrifices—particularly those of the European nations—far exceed any potential gain. So when this treaty forced the German People to destroy all its armaments in order to achieve world-wide general disarmament, many people believed that this was merely a sign that an awareness capable of saving the world was spreading.

The German nation destroyed its weapons. Counting on its former enemies to honor the terms of the treaty, it complied with their demands with almost fanatical conscientiousness. On land, air and sea an enormous quantity of war material was deactivated, destroyed and scrapped. In accordance with the wishes of the powers which were dictating the terms, the former army of millions was replaced by a small professional army equipped with weapons of no military significance. At that time the political leaders of the nation were men whose intellectual roots were entirely within the world of the victorious powers. For this very reason the German People were entitled to expect that the rest of the world would keep its word, for the German People were trying to fulfill their treaty obligations by the sweat of their brow under immense hardship and indescribable deprivation.

No war can remain a permanent human condition. No peace can be the perpetuation of war. At some point the victor and the vanquished must find a way to join in mutual understanding and trust. For fifteen years the German People have waited and hoped that the end of the war would also bring an end to the hatred and enmity. But it seemed that the aim of the Treaty of Versailles was not to bring mankind lasting peace but instead to keep it in a state of permanent hatred.

The consequences were unavoidable. When right finally yields to might a state of permanent uncertainty disturbs and inhibits the course of normal international relations. In concluding this treaty it was completely forgotten that the world could not be rebuilt by the slave labor of a violated nation; that this could be ensured only by the cooperation of all nations in mutual trust; that the basic prerequisite for such cooperation is the removal of the war psychosis; that historical clarification of the problematical question of war guilt cannot be achieved by the victor forcing the defeated nation to sign a peace treaty which begins with a confession of the defeated nation's war guilt. On the contrary, for then the ultimate responsibility for the war emerges most clearly from the contents of a dictate like this!

The German People are utterly convinced that they are not responsible for the war. The other participants in this tragic disaster may well be equally convinced of their innocence. This makes it all the more urgent to ensure that this situation, in which all sides are convinced that they are not to blame, does not become a state of permanent enmity. We must also ensure that the memories of this world-wide catastrophe are not artificially kept alive, and that, by unnaturally perpetuating the idea of a "victor" and a "vanquished," a permanent state of inequality is not created, causing on the one side understandable arrogance and on the other bitter resentment.

It is no coincidence that after such a protracted and artificially prolonged sickness of the human race certain consequences must manifest themselves. A shattering collapse of the economy was followed by a no less dangerous general political decline. But what possible meaning did the World War have, if the consequences were an endless series of economic disasters not only for the vanquished but also for the victors? The well-being of the nations is not greater, nor has there been a genuine improvement in their political fortunes or a profound increase in human happiness! Armies of unemployed have formed a new social class and the disintegration of the economic structure of the nations is accompanied by the gradual collapse of their social structure.

It is Germany which suffered the most from the consequences of this peace treaty and the general uncertainty which it has created. The number of unemployed rose to one third of the normal national work force. That, however, meant that, including all family members, approximately twenty million out of sixty-five million people in Germany were without any livelihood and faced a hopeless future. It was only a question of time before this host of economically disenfranchised people would become an army of politically and socially alienated fanatics.

One of the oldest civilized countries in the contemporary human community with over six million Communists was on the brink of a disaster which only the indifferent and ignorant could ignore. If the red menace had spread like a raging fire throughout Germany, the Western civilized nations would have been forced to recognize that it does matter whether the banks of the Rhine and the North Sea coast are guarded by the advance troops of a revolutionary expansionist Asiatic empire, or by peaceful German farmers and working men who, genuinely conscious of a common bond with the other civilized European nations, are struggling to earn their daily bread by honest labor. The National Socialist movement, in rescuing Germany from this imminent catastrophe, saved not only the German nation but rendered the rest of Europe a historic service.

This National Socialist revolution has but one goal, namely to restore order within its own nation, to give our hungry masses work and bread, to champion the concepts of honor, loyalty and decency as the basis of a moral code which cannot harm other nations but only contribute to their general welfare. If the National Socialist movement did not represent a body of ideas and ideals, it could never have succeeded in saving our People from ultimate disaster. It remained true to these ideals not only in the course of its struggle to obtain power but also after it came to power! We have waged war on all the depravity, dishonesty, fraud and corruption which had festered and spread within our nation since the disastrous Treaty of Versailles. This movement is dedicated to the task of restoring loyalty, faith and decency without regard to person.

For the last eight months we have been engaged in a heroic struggle against the Communist threat to our nation, against the subversion of our culture, the destruction of our art and the corruption of our public morality. We have put an end to atheism and blasphemy. We humbly thank Providence for granting us success in our struggle to alleviate the distress of the unemployed and to save the German farmer. In just under eight months, in the course of a program which we calculated would require four years, more than two and a quarter million of the six million unemployed have been returned to useful production.

The most persuasive evidence of this enormous achievement is provided by the German People themselves. They will show the world how firmly they support a regime which has no other goal than—through peaceful labor and acts of civilized morality—to assist in the reconstruction of a world which is anything but happy today. . . . In claiming without reservation the rights granted us in the treaties themselves, I wish to state without reservation that as far as Germany is concerned no further territorial conflicts exist between the two countries [Germany and France]. After the return of the Saar only a madman could conceive of a war between the two states, for which from our point of view there would then no longer be any moral or rational justification. For no one could demand the extermination of millions of young lives in order to achieve a correction of the present frontiers which would be questionable both in its extent and value.

When the French Premier asks why German youth are marching in rank and file, our reply is that this is not to demonstrate against France. It is to display and document the political will required to defeat Communism and which will be necessary to keep Communism in check. In Germany only the army bears arms. And the National Socialist organizations have only one enemy and that is Communism. But the world must accept the fact that when the German People organize themselves so as to protect our Nation from this danger, they select the only forms which can guarantee success. While the rest of the world is digging in behind indestructible fortifications, building vast fleets of aircraft, enormous tanks, huge pieces of artillery, it cannot speak of a threat when German National Socialists bearing absolutely no arms march in columns of four, thus providing visible evidence and effective protection of the German national community!

When, however, the French Premier asks why Germany is demanding weapons which would have to be destroyed later, this is an error. The German People and the German Government never demanded weapons but only equal rights. If the world decides that all weapons down to the last machine gun are to be destroyed, we are prepared to sign a convention to this effect immediately. If the world decides that specific weapons are to be destroyed, we are prepared to forgo them. If, however, the world approves of certain weapons for every nation, we are not prepared to be excluded as a nation deprived of the same rights.

If we fight for the things in which we sincerely believe, we shall be more honorable partners within the family of nations than if we were prepared to accept humiliating and dishonorable conditions. . . .

The former German Governments confidently joined the League of Nations hoping to find there a forum where they could achieve a just resolution of conflicting national interests, and above all genuine reconciliation with their former enemies. This presupposed, however, the ultimate recognition of equal rights for the German nation. Their participation in the disarmament conference was based on the same assumption. Demotion to the status of membership without equal rights in an institution or conference of this nature is an intolerable humiliation for a nation of 65 million people which values its honor and for a government which attaches no less importance to its honor!

The German People more than fulfilled its obligation to disarm. It should now be the turn of the nations who are armed to show no less willingness to fulfill the same obligations. In taking part in this conference the German Government's goal is not to negotiate for a few cannons or machine guns for the German People, but to work towards universal world peace as an equal partner. Germany has no less a right to security than any other nation. . . . The deliberate demotion of our nation, by granting every nation of the world an automatic right which we alone are denied, is in our view a perpetuation of intolerable discrimination. In my speech about peace in May I already stated that under these circumstances, to our great regret, we would not be able to remain within the League of Nations or to participate in international conferences.

Germany's current leaders have nothing in common with the paid traitors of November 1918. All of us—like every decent Englishman and Frenchman—have risked our lives to do our duty to our fatherland. We are not responsible for the war, we are not responsible for what happened in it. We feel responsible only for what every man of honor had to do, and we did, at a time of national crisis. The boundless love we feel for our nation is matched by our ardent desire to reach an understanding with the other nations and we will attempt to achieve this wherever possible. It is impossible for us, as the representatives of an honest nation and as honest people, to participate in institutions under conditions which would be acceptable only to a dishonest person. In the past men may well have existed who even under such intolerable conditions may have believed that they could be party to international agreements. There is no point in examining whether they were the best elements in our nation, but beyond any doubt the best elements in our nation did not support them. The world can only be interested in negotiating with the honest men rather than the questionable elements within a nation, and in signing treaties with the former rather than the latter. The world must, however, in turn make allowance for the sense of honor of a regime of this nature, just as we in turn are grateful that we are able to deal with honest men. This is all the more vital, because only in this kind of atmosphere can the solution be found which will lead to genuine peace between the nations. Unless a confer-

ence of this nature is conducted in a spirit of sincere understanding it is doomed to failure. Having gathered from the statements of the official representatives of a number of major powers that they have no intention of granting Germany equal rights at the present time, Germany at this time and in such a humiliating position finds it impossible to impose its presence upon other nations. The implementation of the threats to use force can only constitute violations of international law.

The German Government is absolutely convinced that its appeal to the entire German nation will prove to the world that the Government's desire for peace and its concept of honor are shared by the entire nation. In order to document this claim I have decided to request the President of the Reich (Reichspräsident) to dissolve the German Parliament (Reichstag) and in new elections and a plebiscite provide the German People with the chance to make a historical statement, not merely by approving of their government's principles but by showing total solidarity with them.

May this statement convince the world that the German People have expressed their total solidarity with their government in this struggle for equal rights and honor; that both sincerely desire only to play their part in ending an epoch of tragic human error, regrettable discord and strife between the nations which dwell in the most civilized continent in the world and have a common mission to accomplish for all mankind. May this powerful demonstration of our People's desire for peace and honor succeed in providing the relationships between the European states with the necessary basis not only for an end to a century of discord and strife but for the foundation for a new and better community: namely, the recognition of a common higher duty based on equal rights for all!

Source: Adolf Hitler. WS: An Apolitical Web Site. Available at http://www.adolfhitler.ws/lib/speeches/text/331014.html. Reprinted with permission of the web site.

5. The Appeal of Adolf Hitler: Diary of William Shirer, 5–10 September 1934

In 1934 the strongly antifascist American journalist William Shirer attended the Nuremberg rallies. Despite his profound personal distaste for Hitler and the Nazis, he was able to appreciate the spell that Hitler's use of pageantry and oratory exerted upon the watching audience.

Excerpts from William Shirer's *Berlin Diary*
ENTRY, 5 SEPTEMBER 1934
I'm beginning to comprehend, I think, some of the reasons for Hitler's astounding success. Borrowing a chapter from the Roman [Catholic] Church, he is restoring pageantry and

colour and mysticism to the drab lives of twentieth-century Germans. This morning's opening meeting in the Luitpold Hall on the outskirts of Nuremberg was more than a gorgeous show; it also had something of the mysticism and religious fervour of an Easter or Christmas Mass in a great

Gothic cathedral. The hall was a sea of brightly coloured flags. Even Hitler's arrival was made dramatic. The band stopped playing. There was a hush over the thirty thousand people packed in the hall. Then the band struck up the *Badenweiler March,* a very catchy tune, and used only, I'm told, when Hitler makes his big entries. Hitler appeared in the back of the auditorium, and followed by his aides, Göring, Goebbels, Hess, Himmler, and the others, he strode slowly down the long centre aisle while thirty thousand hands were raised in salute. It is a ritual, the old-timers say, which is always followed. Then an immense symphony orchestra played Beethoven's *Egmont* Overture. Great Klieg lights played on the stage, where Hitler sat surrounded by a hundred party officials and officers of the army and navy. Behind them the "blood flag," the one carried down the streets of Munich in the ill-fated putsch. Behind this, four or five hundred S.A. standards. When the music was over, Rudolf Hess, Hitler's closest confidant, rose and slowly read the names of the Nazi "martyrs"—brown-shirts who had been killed in the struggle for power—a roll-call of the dead, and the thirty thousand seemed very moved.

In such an atmosphere no wonder, then, that every word dropped by Hitler seemed like an inspired Word from on high. . . .

ENTRY, 6 SEPTEMBER 1934

Hitler sprang his *Arbeitdienst,* his Labour Service Corps, on the public for the first time today and it turned out to be a highly trained, semimilitary group of fanatical Nazi youths. Standing there in the early morning sunlight which sparkled on their shiny spades, fifty thousand of them, with the first thousand bared above the waist, suddenly made the German spectators go mad with joy when, without warning, they broke into a perfect goose-step. Now, the goose-step has always seemed to me to be an outlandish exhibition of the human being in his most undignified and stupid state, but I felt for the first time this morning what an inner chord it strikes in the strange soul of the German people. Spontaneously they jumped up and shouted their applause. There was a ritual even for the Labour Service boys. They formed an immense *Sprechchor*—a chanting chorus—and with one voice intoned such words as these: "We want one Leader! Nothing for us! Everything for Germany! *Heil Hitler!*" . . .

ENTRY, 7 SEPTEMBER 1934

Another great pageant tonight. Two hundred thousand party officials packed in the Zeppelin Wiese with their twenty-one thousand flags unfurled in the searchlights like a forest of weird trees. "We are strong and will get stronger," Hitler shouted at them through the microphone, his words echoing across the hushed field from the loud-speakers. And there, in the flood-lit night, jammed together like sardines, in one mass formation, the little men of Germany who have made Nazism possible achieved the highest state of being the Germanic man knows: the shedding of their individual souls and minds—with the personal responsibilities and doubts and problems—until under the mystic lights and at the sound of the magic words of the Austrian they were merged completely in the Germanic herd. Later they recovered enough—fifteen thousand of them—to stage a torchlight parade through Nuremberg's ancient streets, Hitler taking the salute in front of the station across from our hotel. . . .

ENTRY, 10 SEPTEMBER 1934

Today the army had its day, fighting a very realistic sham battle in the Zeppelin Meadow. It is difficult to exaggerate the frenzy of the three hundred thousand German spectators when they saw their soldiers go into action, heard the thunder of the guns, and smelt the powder. I feel that all those Americans and English (among others) who thought that German militarism was merely a product of the Hohenzollerns—from Frederick the Great to Kaiser Wilhelm II—made a mistake. It is rather something deeply ingrained in all Germans. They acted today like children playing with tin soldiers. The Reichswehr [German army] "fought" today only with the "defensive" weapons allowed them by Versailles, but everybody knows they've got the rest—tanks, heavy artillery, and probably airplanes.

LATER—After seven days of almost ceaseless goose-stepping, speech-making, and pageantry, the party rally came to an end tonight. And though dead tired and rapidly developing a bad case of crowd-phobia, I'm glad I came. You have to go through one of these to understand Hitler's hold on the people, to feel the dynamic in the movement he's unleashed and the sheer, disciplined strength the Germans possess. And now—as Hitler told the correspondents yesterday in explaining his technique—the half-million men who've been here during the week will go back to their towns and villages and preach the new gospel with new fanaticism.

Source: William L. Shirer, *Berlin Diary: The Journal of a Foreign Correspondent, 1934–1941* (New York: Alfred A. Knopf, 1941), 18–23. Reprinted with permission of Alfred A. Knopf.

6. Adolf Hitler, Proclamation Denouncing the Military Clauses of the Treaty of Versailles, 16 March 1935

Two years after he came to power, Adolf Hitler announced that Germany would no longer observe the military clauses of the Treaty of Versailles, which had imposed tight ceilings for personnel and armaments on German military, naval, and air forces. When the League of Nations passed resolutions condemning Germany's action, Hitler simply ignored that organization's pronouncements. After claiming that the Soviet army posed a serious threat to German security, he launched a massive German rearmament program, one major component of which was the creation of a huge air force. The same day, Germany passed a military service law, whereby all young German men had to undergo compulsory military training.

When in November 1918 the German people, trusting in the promises given in President Wilson's Fourteen Points, grounded arms after four and a half years' honourable resistance in a war whose outbreak they had never desired, they believed they had rendered a service not only to tormented humanity, but also to a great idea. . . .

Our people trustingly seized upon the idea of a new order in the relations between peoples, an order which was to be ennobled on one hand by doing away with the secrecy of diplomatic cabinet policies and on the other hand by abandoning the terrible methods of war. . . . The idea of the League of Nations has perhaps in no nation awakened more fervent acclaim than in Germany . . .

The German people, and especially their Governments of that time, were convinced that, by fulfillment of the conditions of disarmament laid down in the Versailles Treaty and in accordance with the promises of that Treaty, the beginning of international general disarmament would be marked and guaranteed.

For only in a two-sided fulfillment of the task by the Treaty could there lie a moral and sensible justification for a demand which, one-sidedly imposed and executed, had necessarily led to an eternal discrimination, and thereby to a declaration of inferiority of a great nation.

Under such conditions, however, a peace treaty of this sort could never create the conditions for a true inward reconciliation of peoples, nor for the pacification of the world achieved in this manner, but could only set up a hatred that would gnaw eternally.

Germany has, according to the investigation of the Inter-Allied Control Commission, fulfilled the disarmament conditions imposed upon her . . . the German people had the right to expect the redemption also by the other side of obligations undertaken. . . . But while Germany as one party to the Treaty had fulfilled its obligations, the redemption of the obligation on the part of the second partner to the Treaty failed to become a fact. That means: the High Contracting Parties of the former victor States have one-sidedly divorced themselves from the obligations of the Versailles Treaty. Not alone did they refrain from disarming. . . . No. Not even was there a halt in the armaments race, on the contrary, the increase of armaments . . . became evident. . . .

The world . . . has again resumed its cries of war, just as though there never had been a World War nor the Versailles Treaty. In the midst of these highly armed warlike States . . . Germany was, militarily speaking, in a vacuum, defencelessly at the mercy of every threatening danger.

The German people recall the misfortune and suffering of fifteen years' economic misery and political and moral humiliation. It was, therefore, understandable that Germany began loudly to demand the fulfillment of the promises made by other States to disarm. . . .

[Hitler gave a lengthy review of these negotiations.]

The German Government must, however, to its regret, note that for months the rest of the world has been rearming continuously and increasingly. It sees in the creation of a Soviet Russian Army of 101 divisions, that is, in an admitted peace strength of 960,000 men, an element that at the time of the conclusion of the Versailles Treaty could not have been divined. It sees in the forcing of similar measures in other States further proofs of the refusal to accept the disarmament ideas as originally proclaimed. . . .

In these circumstances the German Government, as the guardian of the honour and interests of the German nation, desires to make sure that Germany possesses sufficient instruments of power not only to maintain the integrity of the German Reich, but also to command international respect and value as co-guarantor of general peace.

For in this hour the German Government renews before the German people, before the entire world, its assurance of its determination never to proceed beyond the safeguarding of German honour and the freedom of the Reich, and especially does it not intend in rearming Germany to create any instrument for warlike attack but, on the contrary, exclusively for defence and thereby for the maintenance of peace.

In so doing, the German Reich's Government expresses the confident hope that the German people, having again reverted to their own honour, may be privileged in independent equality to make their contribution for the pacification of the world in free and open co-operation with other nations and their Governments. . . .

Source: John W. Wheeler-Bennett, ed., *Documents on International Affairs 1935* (London: Oxford University Press, 1936), 58–64. Reprinted with permission of Chatham House.

7. German Law on Military Service, 16 March 1935

To support Hitler's denunciation of the military restraints of the Treaty of Versailles, the Reichstag immediately passed legislation to subject all young German men to compulsory military training and expand the size of the army.

1. Service in the Armed Forces is predicated upon university military service.
2. The German peace army, including police units which have been incorporated in the army, shall comprise twelve corps command and thirty-six divisions.
3. The Reich Minister of War is charged with the duty of submitting immediately to the Reich Ministry detailed laws on compulsory military duty.

Source: Web site: The Nizkor Project. Available at http://www.nizkor.org/hweb/imt/nca/nca–01/nca–01–09–aggression–02–10.html.

8. The Soviet Union Embraces the Popular Front: Resolution of the Seventh World Congress of the Communist International, August 1935

Until the mid-1930s, Soviet Communists generally fiercely condemned any other leftists or socialists who did not share precisely their own political views. The rise of fascism in Germany and the increasingly bellicose behavior of Benito Mussolini's Italy alarmed Soviet leader Josef Stalin into switching to a popular front policy. In the interests of opposing fascism, Soviet leaders were now prepared to ally themselves with non-Communist leftists of every political complexion, and the Communist International promptly endorsed such "popular front" policies. Popular Front governments briefly held power in both France and Spain. Simultaneously, the Soviet Union attempted to form alliances within the international state system it had once rejected, joining the League of Nations in 1934 and signing a mutual security treaty with France the following year.

In face of the towering menace of fascism to the working class and all the gains it has made, to all toilers and their elementary rights, to the peace and liberty of the peoples, the Seventh Congress of the Communist International declares that *at the present historical stage it is the main and immediate task of the international labor movement to establish the united fighting front of the working class.* For a successful struggle against fascism, the bitterest enemy of all the toilers, who, without distinction of political views, have been deprived of all rights and liberties, it is imperative that unity of action be established between all sections of the working class, irrespective of what organization they belong to, even before the majority of the working class unites on a common fighting platform for the overthrow of capitalism and the victory of the proletarian revolution. But it is precisely for this very reason that this task makes it the duty of the Communist Parties to take into consideration the changed circumstances and to apply the united front tactics *in a new manner,* by seeking to reach agreements with the organizations of the toilers of various political trends for joint action on a factory, local, district, national and international scale.

With this as its point of departure, the Seventh Congress of the Communist International enjoins the Communist Parties to be guided by the following instructions when carrying out the united front tactics.

1. *The defense of the immediate economic and political interests of the working class, the defense of the latter against fascism,* must be the starting point and form the main content of the workers' united front in all capitalist countries. In order to set the broad masses in motion, such slogans and forms of struggle must be put forward as arise from the vital needs of the masses and from the level of their fighting capacity at the given stage of development. Communists must not limit themselves to merely issuing appeals to struggle for proletarian dictatorship, but must show the masses *what they are to do today* to defend themselves against capitalist plunder and fascist barbarity. They must strive, through the joint action of the labor organizations, to mobilize the masses around *a program of demands that are calculated to really shift the burden of the consequences of the crisis on to the shoulders of the ruling class; demands, the fight to realize which, disorganizes fascism, hampers the preparations for imperialist war, weakens the bourgeoisie and strengthens the positions of the proletariat. . . .*

2. Without for a moment giving up their independent work in the sphere of Communist education, organization and mobilization of masses, the Communists, in order to render the road to unity of action easier for the workers, *must strive to secure joint action with the Social-Democratic Parties,* reforming trade unions and other organizations of the toilers against the class enemies of the proletariat, on the basis of short or long-term agreements. . . .

5. Joint action with the Social-Democratic Parties and organizations not only does not preclude, but on the contrary, *renders still more necessary the serious and well-founded criticism of* reformism, of Social-Democracy as the ideology and practice of class collaboration with the bourgeoisie, and the patient exposition of the principles and program of Communists to the Social-Democratic workers. . . .

6. *Election campaigns* must be utilized for the further development and strengthening of the united fighting front of the proletariat. While coming forward independently in the elections and unfolding the program of the Communist Party before the masses, the Communists must seek to establish a united front with the Social-Democratic Parties and the trade unions (also with the organizations of the toiling peasants, handicraftsmen, etc.), and exert every effort to prevent the election of reactionary and fascist candidates. In face of fascist danger, the Communists may, *while reserving for themselves freedom of political agitation and criticism,* participate in election campaigns on *a common platform and with a common ticket of the antifascist front,* depending on the growth and success of the united front movement, also depending on the electoral system in operation. . . .

Emphasizing the special importance of forming a united front in the sphere of the economic struggle of the workers and the establishment of the unity of the trade union movement as a most important step in consolidating the united front of the proletariat, the Congress makes it a duty of the Communists to adopt all practical measures for the realization of the unity of the trade unions by industries and on a national scale.

Source: Robert V. Daniels, *A Documentary History of Communism and the World: From Revolution to Collapse,* 3rd ed. (Hanover, NH: University Press of New England, 1994), 74–75. Reprinted with permission of University Press of New England.

9. The United States Neutrality Act, 31 August 1935

As the international situation in both Europe and Asia deteriorated, many members of the U. S. Congress feared disputes arising over American arms trade with belligerents or the deaths of Americans traveling on belligerent ships might draw the United States into another war. Seeking to avoid this, in 1935, both houses of Congress passed legislation whereby once the president proclaimed that a state of war existed between two or more countries, Americans were forbidden to trade in munitions with any belligerent government, and only at their own risk could American citizens travel on belligerent ships.

Joint Resolution Providing for the prohibition of the export of arms, ammunition, and implements of war to belligerent countries; the prohibition of the transportation of arms, ammunition, and implements of war by vessels of the United States for the use of belligerent states; for the registration and licensing of persons engaged in the business of manufacturing, exporting, or importing arms, ammunition, or implements of war; and restricting travel by American citizens on belligerent ships during war.

Resolved by the Senate and House of Representatives of

the United States of America in Congress assembled, That upon the outbreak or during the progress of war between, or among, two or more foreign states, the President shall proclaim such fact, and it shall thereafter be unlawful to export arms, ammunition, or implements of war from any place in the United States, or possessions of the United States, to any port of such belligerent states, or to any neutral port for transshipment to, or for the use of, a belligerent country.

The President, by proclamation, shall definitely enumerate the arms, ammunition, or implements of war, the export of which is prohibited by this Act.

The President may, from time to time, by proclamation, extend such embargo upon the export of arms, ammunition, or implements of war to other states as and when they may become involved in such war.

Whoever, in violation of any of the provisions of this section, shall export, or attempt to export, or cause to be exported, arms, ammunition, or implements of war from the United States, or any of its possessions, shall be fined not more than $10,000 or imprisoned not more than five years, or both, and the property, vessel, or vehicle containing the same shall be subject to the provisions of sections 1 to 8, inclusive, title 6, chapter 30, of the Act approved June 15, 1917. . . . In the case of the forfeiture of any arms, ammunition, or implements of war by reason of a violation of this Act, no public or private sale shall be required; but such arms, ammunition, or implements of war shall be delivered to the Secretary of War for such use or disposal thereof as shall be approved by the President.

When in the judgment of the President the conditions which have caused him to issue his proclamation have ceased to exist he shall revoke the same and the provisions hereof shall thereupon cease to apply.

Except with respect to prosecutions committed or forfeitures incurred prior to March 1, 1936, this section and all proclamations issued thereunder shall not be effective after February 29, 1936. . . .

SEC. 3. Whenever the President shall issue the proclamation provided for in section 1 of this Act, thereafter it shall be unlawful for any American vessel to carry any arms, ammunition, or implements of war to any port of the belligerent countries named in such proclamation as being at war, or to any neutral port for transshipment to, or for the use of, a belligerent country.

Whoever, in violation of the provisions of this section, shall take, attempt to take, or shall authorize, hire, or solicit another to take any such vessel carrying such cargo out of port or from the jurisdiction of the United States shall be fined not more than $10,000 or imprisoned not more than

five years, or both; and, in addition, such vessel, her tackle, apparel, furniture, equipment, and the arms, ammunition, and implements of war on board shall be forfeited to the United States.

When the President finds the conditions which have caused him to issue his proclamation have ceased to exist, he shall revoke his proclamation, and the provisions of this section shall thereupon cease to apply. . . .

SEC. 5. Whenever, during any war in which the United States is neutral, the President shall find that special restrictions placed on the use of the ports and territorial waters of the United States, or of its possessions, by the submarines of a foreign nation will serve to maintain peace between the United States and foreign nations, or to protect the commercial interests of the United States and its citizens, or to promote the security of the United States, and shall make proclamation thereof, it shall thereafter be unlawful for any such submarine to enter a port or the territorial waters of the United States or any of its possessions, or to depart therefrom, except under such conditions and subject to such limitations as the President may prescribe. When, in his judgment, the conditions which have caused him to issue his proclamation have ceased to exist, he shall revoke his proclamation and the provisions of this section shall thereupon cease to apply.

SEC. 6. Whenever, during any war in which the United States is neutral, the President shall find that the maintenance of peace between the United States and foreign nations, or the protection of the lives of citizens of the United States, or the protection of the commercial interests of the United States and its citizens, or the security of the United States requires that the American citizens should refrain from traveling as passengers on the vessels of any belligerent nation, he shall so proclaim, and thereafter no citizen of the United States shall travel on any vessel of any belligerent nation except at his own risk, unless in accordance with such rules and regulations as the President shall prescribe: Provided, however, That the provisions of this section shall not apply to a citizen traveling on the vessel of a belligerent whose voyage was begun in advance of the date of the President's proclamation, and who had no opportunity to discontinue his voyage after that date: And provided further, That they shall not apply under ninety days after the date of the President's proclamation to a citizen returning from a foreign country to the United States or to any of its possessions. When, in the President's judgment, the conditions which have caused him to issue his proclamation have ceased to exist, he shall revoke his proclamation and the provisions of this section shall thereupon cease to apply.

SEC. 7. In every case of the violation of any of the provisions of this Act where a specific penalty is not herein provided, such violator or violators, upon conviction, shall be fined not more than $10,000 or imprisoned not more than five years, or both. . . .

Source: U.S. Department of State, *Peace and War: United States Foreign Policy, 1931–1941* (Washington, DC: U.S. Government Printing Office, 1943), 265–271.

10. President Franklin D. Roosevelt, Message on the Neutrality Act, September 1935

A few days after the passage of the first United States Neutrality Act, President Franklin D. Roosevelt rather reluctantly signed the legislation. When doing so, he suggested that as it stood, certain aspects were too inflexible and it might require revision in the future, and that should the legislation be renewed when it expired, consideration might be given to modification of its terms.

I have given my approval to S. J. Resolution 173—the neutrality legislation which passed the Congress last week.

I have approved this Joint Resolution because it was intended as an expression of the fixed desire of the Government and the people of the United States to avoid any action which might involve us in war. The purpose is wholly excellent, and this Joint Resolution will to a considerable degree serve that end.

It provides for a licensing system for the control of carrying arms, etc., by American vessels; for the control of the use of American waters by foreign submarines; for the restriction of travel by American citizens on vessels of belligerent Nations; and for the embargo of the export of arms, etc., to both belligerent Nations.

The latter Section terminates at the end of February, 1936. This Section requires further and more complete consideration between now and that date. Here again the objective is wholly good. It is the policy of this Government to avoid being drawn into wars between other Nations, but it is a fact that no Congress and no Executive can foresee all possible future situations. History is filled with unforeseeable situations that call for some flexibility of action. It is conceivable that situations may arise in which the wholly inflexible provisions of Section I of this Act might have exactly the opposite effect from that which was intended. In other words, the inflexible provisions might drag us into war instead of keeping us out. The policy of the Government is definitely committed to the maintenance of peace and the avoidance of any entanglements which would lead us into conflict. At the same time it is the policy of the Government by every peaceful means and without entanglement to cooperate with other similarly minded Governments to promote peace.

In several aspects further careful consideration of neutrality needs is most desirable and there can well be an expansion to include provisions dealing with other important aspects of our neutrality policy which have not been dealt with in this temporary measure.

Source: Web site: ibiblio. Available at http://www.ibiblio.org/pha/7–2–188/188–03.html.

11. Benito Mussolini, "A Call to Arms," Speech to His Followers, 2 October 1935

In October 1935 Italy, seeking colonies of its own, ignored the strictures of the League of Nations and invaded Abyssinia (Ethiopia) in East Africa. Benito Mussolini, Italy's fascist leader (Duce), argued that Italy deserved her "place in the sun," especially because she had not received her just rewards for joining the Allies against Germany in 1915. He urged France and Britain to ignore any League of Nations call for sanctions upon Italy.

Black Shirts of the Revolution! Men and women of all Italy! Italians all over the world—beyond the mountains, beyond the sea! Listen!

A solemn hour is about to strike in the history of the country. Twenty million Italians are at this moment gathered in the squares of all Italy. It is the greatest demonstration that human history records. Twenty million! One heart alone! One will alone! One decision!

This manifestation signifies that the tie between Italy and Fascism is perfect, absolute, and unalterable. Only brains softened by puerile illusions, by sheer ignorance, can think differently, because they do not know what exactly is the Fascist Italy of 1935.

For many months the wheel of destiny and of the impulse of our calm determination moves toward the goal. In these last hours the rhythm has increased and nothing can stop it now. It is not only an army marching towards its goals, but as if 44,000,000 Italians were marching in unity behind this army because the blackest of injustices is being attempted against them, that of taking from them their place in the sun.

When, in 1915, Italy threw in her fate with that of the Allies, how many cries of admiration, how many promises! But after the common victory, which cost Italy 600,000 dead, 400,000 lost, 1,000,000 wounded, when peace was being discussed around the table only the crumbs of a rich colonial booty were left for us to pick up.

For thirteen years we have been patient while the circle tightened around us at the hands of those who wish to suffocate us. We have been patient with Ethiopia for forty years—it is enough now.

Instead of recognizing the rights of Italy, the League of Nations dares talk of sanctions. But until there is proof to the contrary I refuse to believe that the authentic people of France will join in supporting sanctions against Italy.

The 6,000 dead at the action of Boligny—whose devotion was so heroic that the enemy commander was forced to admire them—those fallen would now turn in their graves.

And until there is proof to the contrary, I refuse to believe that the authentic people of Britain will want to spill blood and send Europe into a catastrophe for the sake of a barbarian country unworthy of ranking among civilized nations.

Just the same, we cannot afford to overlook the possible developments of tomorrow. To economic sanctions, we shall answer with our discipline, our spirit of sacrifice, our obedience. To military sanctions, we shall answer with military measures. To acts of war, we shall answer with acts of war.

A people worthy of their past and their name cannot and never will take a different stand. Let me repeat, in the most categorical manner, the sacred pledge which I make at this moment before all the Italians gathered together today, that I shall do everything in my power to prevent a colonial conflict from taking on the aspect and weight of a European war.

This conflict may be attractive to certain minds, which hope to avenge their disintegrated temples through this new catastrophe. Never, as at this historical hour, have the people of Italy revealed such force of character, and it is against this people to which mankind owes its greatest conquest, this people of heroes, of poets and saints, of navigators, of colonizers, that the world dares threaten sanctions.

Italy! Italy! Entirely and universally Fascist! The Italy of the Black Shirt revolution, rise to your feet, let the cry of your determination rise to the skies and reach our soldiers in East Africa. Let it be a comfort to those who are about to fight. Let it be an encouragement to our friends and a warning to our enemies.

It is the cry of Italy, which goes beyond the mountains and the seas out into the great big world. It is the cry of justice and of victory.

Source: "Text of Premier Mussolini's Address to the Italian People on the War," United Press Dispatch to the *New York Times,* datelined 2 October 1935, official Italian government translation, published in the *New York Times,* 3 October 1935.

12. President Roosevelt, Statement Imposing an Arms Embargo on Ethiopia and Italy, 30 October 1935

Faced with the outbreak of war between Italy and Ethiopia, the U.S. president had no alternative but to impose an arms embargo upon both countries.

In view of the situation which has unhappily developed between Ethiopia and Italy, it has become my duty under the provisions of the Joint Resolution of Congress approved August 31, 1935, to issue, and I am to-day issuing, my proclamation making effective an embargo on the exportation from this country to Ethiopia and Italy of arms, ammunition, and implements of war. Notwithstanding the hope we entertained that war would be avoided, and the exertion of our influence in that direction, we are now compelled to rec-

ognize the simple and indisputable fact that Ethiopian and Italian armed forces are engaged in combat, thus creating a state of war within the intent and meaning of the Joint Resolution. In these specific circumstances I desire it to be understood that any of our people who voluntarily engage in transactions of any character with either of the belligerents do so at their own risk.

Source: The History of the League of Nations Web site. Available at http://www.unog.ch/library/archives/lon/library/Docs/kusneu.html.

13. The Nuremberg Laws on Citizenship and Race: The Reich Citizenship Law of 15 September 1935, and Supplementary Decree, 14 November 1935

The Nazi government soon passed legislation putting into effect its theories that Jews were inferior and were not entitled to German citizenship. Under the Nuremberg decrees of September–November 1935, German Jews were denied citizenship and could not hold public office. They were also forbidden to marry German nationals. The citizenship law came into force on 30 September 1935.

German Citizenship Law, 15 September 1935

1. (1) A national is a person who belongs to the protective association of the German Reich and as a result is under special obligations to it (2) Nationality is acquired in accordance with the provisions of the Reich and State nationality laws.
2. (1) Only a national of German or similar blood, who proves by his behaviour that he is willing and able loyally to serve the German people and Reich, is a citizen of the Reich (2) The right to citizenship is obtained by the grant of Reich citizenship papers (3) Only a citizen of the Reich may enjoy full political rights in consonance with the provisions of the laws.
3. The Reich Minister of the Interior, in conjunction with the Deputy to the *Fuehrer,* will issue the required legal and administrative decrees for the implementation and amplification of this law.

Source: Available at http://www.mtsu.edu/~baustin/nurmlaw2.html.

Law for the Protection of German Blood and German Honour, 15 September 1935

Inspired by the realization that the purity of German blood is the pre-requisite for the continued existence of the German people, and animated by the inflexible determination to assure the German nation for all time, the Reichstag has unanimously passed the following law, which is promulgated herewith:

1. Marriages between Jews and nationals of German or similar blood are forbidden. Marriages concluded in spite of this are invalid, even if they have been contracted with a view to circumventing this law. . . .
2. Extra-marital intercourse between Jews and nationals of German or similar blood is forbidden.
3. Jews may not employ in their households female nationals of German or similar blood under 45 years of age.
4. Jews are forbidden to hoist the Reich and national flags and to show the Reich colours. They are, on the other hand, allowed to show the Jewish colours. . . .

Source: Available at http://www.mtsu.edu/~baustin/nurmlaw2.html.

First Supplementary Decree of November 14, 1935

On the basis of Article III of the Reich Citizenship Law of September 15, 1935, the following is hereby decreed:

1. (1) Until further provisions concerning citizenship papers, all subjects of German or kindred blood who possessed the right to vote in the *Reichstag* elections when the Citizenship Law came into effect, shall, for the present, possess the rights of Reich citizens. The same shall be true of those upon whom the Reich Minister of the Interior, in conjunction with the Deputy to the *Fuehrer* shall confer citizenship (2) The Reich Minister of the Interior, in conjunction with the Deputy to the *Fuehrer,* may revoke citizenship.
2. (1) The provisions of Article I shall apply also to subjects who are of mixed Jewish blood (2) An individual of mixed Jewish blood is one who is descended from one or two grandparents who, racially, were full Jews, insofar that he is not a Jew according to Section 2 of Article 5. Full-blooded Jewish grandparents are those who belonged to the Jewish religious community.
3. Only citizens of the Reich, as bearers of full political rights, can exercise the right of voting in political matters, and have the right to hold public office. The Reich Minister of the Interior, or any agency he empowers, can make exceptions during the transition period on the matter of holding public office. The measures do not apply to matters concerning religious organizations.
4. (1) A Jew cannot be a citizen of the Reich. He cannot exercise the right to vote; he cannot hold public office (2) Jewish officials will be retired as of December 31, 1935. In the event that such officials served at the front in the World War either for Germany or her allies,

they shall receive as pension, until they reach the age limit, the full salary last received, on the basis of which their pension would have been computed. They shall not, however, be promoted according to their seniority in rank. When they reach the age limit, their pension will be computed again, according to the salary last received on which their pension was to be calculated (3) These provisions do not concern the affairs of religious organizations (4) The conditions regarding service of teachers in public Jewish schools remains unchanged until the promulgation of new laws on the Jewish school system.

5. (1) A Jew is an individual who is descended from at least three grandparents who were, racially, full Jews (2) A Jew is also an individual who is descended from two full-Jewish grandparents if:

(a) he was a member of the Jewish religious community when this law was issued, or joined the community later;

(b) when the law was issued, he was married to a person who was a Jew, or was subsequently married to a Jew;

(c) he is the issue from a marriage with a Jew, in the sense of Section I, which was contracted after the coming into effect of the Law for the Protection of German Blood and Honor of September 15, 1935;

(d) he is the issue of an extramarital relationship with a Jew, in the sense of Section I, and was born out of wedlock after July 31, 1936.

6. (1) Insofar as there are, in the laws of the Reich or in the decrees of the National Socialist German Workers' Party and its affiliates, certain requirements for the purity of German blood which extend beyond Article 5, the same remain untouched. . . .

7. The *Fuehrer* and Chancellor of the Reich is empowered to release anyone from the provisions of these administrative decrees.

Source: Available at http://www.mtsu.edu/~baustin/nurmlaw2.html.

First Ordinance for the Execution of the Law for the Protection of German Blood and German Honour, 14 November 1935

2. Marriages between Jews and nationals of mixed Jewish blood who have only one fully Jewish grandparent shall also belong to the category of marriages forbidden. . . .

3. (1) Nationals of mixed Jewish blood with two grandparents who are full Jews require the permission of the Reich Minister for the Interior and the deputy of the Leaders . . . in order to contract a marriage with nationals of German or similar blood or with nationals of mixed Jewish blood who have only one full Jewish grandparent . . .

4. A marriage shall not be contracted between nationals of mixed Jewish blood who have only one full Jewish grandparent. . . .

Source: Available at http://www.mtsu.edu/~baustin/nurmlaw2.html.

14. The United States Neutrality Act, 29 February 1936

The U.S. neutrality acts were only valid for a year and to remain in force, had to be extended on their expiration. On each occasion, Congress attempted to remedy flaws in the legislation that had become apparent in the preceding year. In 1936, Congress gave the president discretion whether or not to proclaim that a state of war existed between two or more countries. President Franklin D. Roosevelt had only invoked the act in connection with the conflict between Italy and Ethiopia, since he wished American arms to be available to Ethiopia, with the cause of which he sympathized. The new legislation also forbade Americans providing financing through loans or credits for trade in munitions with belligerents.

JOINT RESOLUTION Extending and amending the joint resolution (Public Resolution Numbered 67, Seventy-fourth Congress), approved August 31, 1935.

Resolved by the Senate and House of Representatives of the United States of America in Congress assembled, That section 1 of the joint solution (Public Resolution Numbered 67, Seventy-fourth Congress) approved August 31, 1935, be, and the same hereby is, amended by striking out in the first section, on the second line, after the word "assembled" the

following words: "That upon the outbreak or during the progress of war between," and inserting therefor the words: "Whenever the President shall find that there exists a state of war between"; and by striking out the word "may" after the word "President" and before the word "from" in the twelfth line, and inserting in lieu thereof the word "shall"; and by substituting for the last paragraph of said section the following paragraph: "except with respect to offenses committed, or forfeitures incurred prior to May 1, 1937, this section and all proclamations issued thereunder shall not be effective after May 1, 1937."

SEC. 2. There are hereby added to said joint resolution two new sections, to be known as sections la and lb, reading as follows:

"SEC. la. Whenever the President shall have issued his proclamation as provided for in section 1 of this Act, it shall thereafter during the period of the war be unlawful for any person within the United States to purchase, sell, or exchange bonds, securities, or other obligations of the government of any belligerent country, or of any political subdivision thereof, or of any person acting for or on behalf of such government, issued after the date of such proclamation, or to make any loan or extend any credit to any such government or person: Provided, That if the President shall find that such action will serve to protect the commercial or other interests of the United States or its nationals, he may, in his discretion, and to such extent and under such regulation as he may prescribe, except from the operation of this section ordinary commercial credits and short-time obligations in aid of legal transactions and of a character customarily used in normal peace-time commercial transactions.

"The provisions of this section shall not apply to a renewal or adjustment of such indebtedness as may exist on the date of the President's proclamation.

"Whoever shall violate the provisions of this section or of any regulations issued hereunder shall, upon conviction thereof, be fined not more than $50,000 or imprisoned for not more than five years, or both. Should the violation be by a corporation, organization, or association, each officer or agent thereof participating in the violation may be liable to the penalty herein prescribed.

"When the President shall have revoked his proclamation as provided for in section 1 of this Act, the provisions of this section and of any regulations issued by the President hereunder shall thereupon cease to apply.

"SEC. lb. This Act shall not apply to an American republic or republics engaged in war against a non-American state or states, provided the American republic is not cooperating with a non-American state or states in such war."

SEC. 3. Section 9 of said joint resolution is amended to read as follows:

"There is hereby authorized to be appropriated from time to time, out of any money in the Treasury not otherwise appropriated, such amounts as may be necessary to carry out the provisions and accomplish the purposes of this Act."

Approved, February 29, 1936.

Source: U.S. Department of State, Publication 1983, *Peace and War: United States Foreign Policy, 1931–1941* (Washington, DC: U.S. Government Printing Office, 1943), 312–314.

15. German Memorandum Respecting the Termination of the Treaty of Locarno and the Reoccupation of the Rhineland, 7 March 1936

In May 1935, the French government, alarmed by German rearmament, concluded a treaty of mutual assistance with the Soviet Union. In March 1936, this document was submitted to the French parliament for ratification. The German government, declaring the treaty constituted a breach of the 1923 Treaty of Locarno, promptly announced that it considered the latter treaty as ipso facto terminated. German troops would therefore re-occupy the Rhineland, which the Treaty of Versailles had stipulated should remain demilitarized. International protests ensued, but no country instituted concrete measures to reverse the German action. Although Germany stated its readiness to reenter the League of Nations, that event never took place.

. . . . The latest debates and decisions of the French Parliament have shown that France, in spite of the German representations, is determined to put the pact with the Soviet Union definitively into force. A diplomatic conversation has even revealed that France already regards herself as bound by her signature of this pact on the 2nd May 1935. In the face of such a development of European politics, the German Government, if they do not wish to neglect or to abandon the interests of the German people which they have duty of safeguarding, cannot remain inactive.

The German Government have continually emphasized during the negotiations of the last years their readiness to observe and fulfill all the obligations arising from the Rhine Pact (Locarno Agreements) as long as the other contracting parties were ready on their side to maintain the peace. This obvious and essential condition can no longer be regarded as fulfilled by France. France has replied to the repeated friendly offers and peaceful assurances made by Germany by infringing the Rhine Pact through a military alliance with the Soviet Union exclusively directed against Germany. In this manner, however, the Locarno Rhine Pact has lost its inner meaning and ceased in practice to exist. Consequently Germany regards herself for her part as no longer bound by this dissolved treaty. . . . In accordance with the fundamental right of a nation to secure its frontiers and ensure its possibilities of defence, the German Government have today restored the full and unrestricted sovereignty of Germany in the demilitarized zone of the Rhineland.

. . . . The German Government declare themselves ready to conclude new agreements for the creation of a system of peaceful security for Europe on the basis of the following proposals:

(1) The German Government declare themselves ready to enter into negotiations with France and Belgium with regard to the creation of a zone demilitarized on both sides. . . .

(2) The German Government propose . . . the conclusion of a non-aggression pact between Germany, France and Belgium. . . .

(3) The German Government desire to invite Great Britain and Italy to sign this treaty as guarantor Powers. . . .

(5) The German Government are prepared . . . to conclude an air pact calculated to prevent in an automatic and effective manner the danger of sudden air attacks.

(6) The German Government repeat their offer to conclude with the States bordering Germany in the east non-aggression pacts. . . .

(7) Now that Germany's equality of rights and the restoration of her full sovereignty over the entire territory of the German Reich have finally been attained, the German Government consider the chief reason for their withdrawal from the League of Nations removed. They are therefore willing to re-enter the League of Nations. In this connection they express the expectation that in the course of a reasonable period the question of colonial equality of rights and that of the separation of the League Covenant from its Versailles setting may be clarified through friendly negotiations.

Source: G. A. Kertesz, *Documents in the Political History of the European Continent 1815–1939* (Oxford, UK: Clarendon Press, 1968), 486–487.

16. The Anti-Comintern Pact: German-Japanese Agreement and Supplementary Protocol, Signed at Berlin, 25 November 1936

By the mid-1930s, nations increasingly aligned themselves with each other on ideological lines, with fascists presenting themselves as the sworn enemies of bolshevism or communism, and vice versa. In late 1936, two fascist states, Germany and Japan, signed the Anti-Comintern Pact, whereby each agreed to oppose the spread of communism at home and abroad.

Agreement Guarding against the Communistic International

The Imperial Government of Japan and the Government of Germany,

In cognizance of the fact that the object of the Communistic International (the so-called Comintern) is the disintegration of, and the commission of violence against, existing States by the exercise of all means at its command,

Believing that the toleration of interference by the Communistic International in the internal affairs of nations not only endangers their internal peace and social welfare, but threatens the general peace of the world,

Desiring to co-operate for defense against communistic disintegration, have agreed as follows.

ARTICLE I

The High Contracting States agree that they will mutually keep each other informed concerning the activities of the Communistic International, will confer upon the necessary measures of defense, and will carry out such measures in close co-operation.

ARTICLE II

The High Contracting States will jointly invite third States whose internal peace is menaced by the disintegrating work of the Communistic International, to adopt defensive measures in the spirit of the present Agreement or to participate in the present Agreement.

ARTICLE III

The Japanese and German texts are each valid as the original text of this Agreement. The Agreement shall come into force on the day of its signature and shall remain in force for the term of five years. The High Contracting States will, in a reasonable time before the expiration of the said term, come to an understanding upon the further manner of their co-operation. . . .

Source: U.S. Department of State, *Papers Relating to the Foreign Relations of the United States: Japan, 1931–1941,* Vol. 2 (Washington, DC: U.S. Government Printing Office, 1943).

17. Resolution of the League of Nations Council on Spain, 12 December 1936

In summer 1936 a civil war began in Spain, when fascist army officers led by Colonel Francisco Franco launched a Nationalist rebellion against the newly elected leftist Republican government. Franco and his supporters, who appealed to national pride and honor, were determined to thwart the left and impose a fascist government on Spain. They soon received recognition, together with encouragement and support in men and weaponry, from the sympathetic fascist governments of Germany and Italy. At the end of the year the indignant Spanish government appealed to the League of Nations to force those regimes to cease their assistance to the Nationalist rebels. In response, the League of Nations Council passed a resolution urging all nations to refrain from intervention in the civil conflict in that state and establishing a Non-Intervention Committee. All sides in the conflict ignored this resolution, together with several more to the same effect that the League promulgated over the next three years. With their own government's backing, Russian Communists likewise soon began to flock to the Republican cause, as did idealistic leftists from Europe and the United States. In 1939 the war, fought with great brutality by all parties, finally ended in a victory for Franco's forces.

The Council . . .

I

Noting that it has been requested to examine a situation which, in the terms of Article 11 of the Covenant (No. 206), is such as to affect international relations and to threaten to disturb international peace or the good understanding between nations upon which peace depends;

Considering that good understanding ought to be maintained irrespective of the internal régimes of States;

Bearing in mind that it is the duty of every State to respect the territorial integrity and political independence of other States, a duty which, for Members of the League of Nations, has been recognized by the Covenant:

Affirms that every State is under an obligation to refrain from intervening in the internal affairs of another State;

II

Considering that the setting-up of a Committee of Non-Intervention and the undertakings entered into in that connection arise out of the principles stated above;

Having been informed that new attempts are made in the Committee to make its action more effective, in particular by instituting measures of supervision, the necessity for which is becoming increasingly urgent:

Recommends the Members of the League represented on the London Committee to spare no pains to render the non-intervention undertakings as stringent as possible, and to take appropriate measures to ensure forthwith that the fulfillment of the said undertakings is effectively supervised; . . .

IV

Notes that there are problems of a humanitarian character in connexion with the present situation, in regard to which co-ordinated action of an international and humanitarian character is desirable as soon as possible;

Recognizes, further, that, for the reconstruction which Spain may have to undertake, international assistance may also be desirable;

And authorizes the Secretary-General to make available the assistance of the technical services of the League of Nations should a suitable opportunity occur.

Source: G. A. Kertesz, *Documents in the Political History of the European Continent 1815–1939* (Oxford, UK: Clarendon Press, 1968), 496–497.

18. Joint Congressional Resolution Prohibiting Exports of Arms to Spain, 8 January 1937

When the Spanish Civil War began, existing U.S. neutrality legislation did not cover internecine conflicts. The U.S. Congress nonetheless wished to keep its own country at a distance from this new crisis. In response to the intensifying civil war, in January 1937, Congress therefore prohibited all exports of arms to Spain, effectively preventing either side from obtaining munitions of war from the United States.

JOINT RESOLUTION

To prohibit the exportation of arms, ammunition, and implements of war from the United States to Spain.

Resolved by the Senate and House of Representatives of the United States of America in Congress assembled, That during the existence of the state of civil strife now obtaining in Spain it shall, from and after the approval of this Resolution be unlawful to export arms, ammunition, or implements of war from any place in the United States, or possessions of the United States, to Spain or to any other foreign country for transshipment to Spain or for use of either of the opposing forces in Spain. Arms, ammunition, or implements of war, the exportation of which is prohibited by this Resolution, are those enumerated in the President's Proclamation No. 2163 of April 10, 1936.

Licenses heretofore issued under existing law for the exportation of arms, ammunition, or implements of war to Spain shall, as to all future exportations thereunder, ipso facto be deemed to be cancelled.

Whoever in violation of any of the provisions of this Resolution shall export, or attempt to export, or cause to be exported either directly or indirectly, arms, ammunition, or implements of war from the United States or any of its possessions, shall be fined not more than ten thousand dollars or imprisoned not more than five years, or both.

When in the judgment of the President the conditions described in this Resolution have ceased to exist, he shall proclaim such fact, and the provisions hereof shall thereupon cease to apply.

Approved, January 8, 1937, at 12.30 P.M.

Source: U.S. Department of State, Publication 1983, *Peace and War: United States Foreign Policy, 1931–1941* (Washington, DC: U.S. Government Printing Office, 1943), 353–354.

19. The United States Neutrality Act, 1 May 1937

The U.S. neutrality legislation of 1937 extended the American arms embargo to countries in a state of civil war, and also to nations that were assisting one or another belligerent or party in a civil war. The new legislation clearly reflected the experience of the Spanish Civil War, in which each side received assistance from other European Communist or fascist powers. American ships were also forbidden to carry munitions of war to any belligerent state.

JOINT RESOLUTION To amend the joint resolution, approved August 31, 1935, as amended.

Resolved . . .

EXPORT OF ARMS, AMMUNITION, AND
IMPLEMENTS OF WAR

Section 1. (a) Whenever the President shall find that there exists a state of war between, or among, two or more foreign states, the President shall proclaim such fact, and it shall thereafter be unlawful to export, or attempt to export, or cause to be exported, arms, ammunition, or implements of war from any place in the United States to any belligerent state named in such proclamation, or to any neutral state for transshipment to, or for the use of, any such belligerent state.

(b) The President shall, from time to time, by proclamation, extend such embargo upon the export of arms, ammunition, or implements of war to other states as and when they may become involved in such war.

(c) Whenever the President shall find that such a state of civil strife exists in a foreign state and that such civil strife is of a magnitude or is being conducted under such conditions that the export of arms, ammunition, or implements of war from the United States to such foreign state would threaten or endanger the peace of the United States, the President shall proclaim such fact, and it shall thereafter be unlawful to export, or attempt to export, or cause to be exported, arms, ammunition, or implements of war from any place in the United States to such foreign state, or to any neutral state for transshipment to, or for the use of, such foreign state.

(d) The President shall, from time to time by proclamation, definitely enumerate the arms, ammunition, and implements of war, the export of which is prohibited by this section. The arms, ammunition, and implements of war so enumerated shall include those enumerated in the President's proclamation Numbered 2163, of April 10, 1936, but shall not include raw materials or any other articles or materials not of the same general character as those enumerated in the said proclamation, and in the Convention for the Supervision for the International Trade in Arms and Ammunition and in Implements of War, signed at Geneva June 17, 1925.

(e) Whoever, in violation of any of the provisions of this Act, shall export, or attempt to export, or cause to be exported, arms, ammunition, or implements of war from the United States shall be fined not more than $10,000, or imprisoned not more than five years, or both . . .

(f) In the case of the forfeiture of any arms, ammunition, or implements of war by reason of a violation of this Act, . . . such arms, ammunition, or implements of war shall be delivered to the Secretary of War for such use or disposal thereof as shall be approved by the President of the United States.

(g) Whenever, in the judgment of the President, the conditions which have caused him to issue any proclamation under the authority of this section have ceased to exist, he shall revoke the same, and the provisions of this section shall thereupon cease to apply with respect to the state or states named in such proclamation, except with respect to offenses committed, or forfeiture incurred, prior to such revocation.

EXPORT OF OTHER ARTICLES AND MATERIALS
Section 2. (a) Whenever the President shall have issued a proclamation under the authority of section 1 of this Act and he shall thereafter find that the placing of restrictions on the shipment of certain articles or materials in addition to arms, ammunition, and implements of war from the United States to belligerent states, or to a state wherein civil strife exists, is necessary to promote the security or preserve the peace of the United States or to protect the lives of citizens of the United States, he shall so proclaim, and it shall thereafter be unlawful, for any American vessel to carry such articles or materials to any belligerent state, or to any state wherein civil strife exists, named in such proclamation issued under the authority of section 1 of this Act, or to any neutral state for transshipment to, or for the use of, any such belligerent

states or any such state wherein civil strife exists. The President shall by proclamation from time to time definitely enumerate the articles and materials which it shall be unlawful for American vessels to so transport . . .

(c) The President shall from time to time by proclamation extend such restrictions as are imposed under the authority of this section to other states as and when they may be declared to become belligerent states under the authority of section 1 of this Act.

(d) The President may from time to time change, modify, or revoke in whole or in part any proclamations issued by him under the authority of this section.

(e) Except with respect to offenses committed, or forfeitures incurred, prior to May 1, 1939, this section and all proclamations issued thereunder shall not be effective after May 1, 1939.

FINANCIAL TRANSACTIONS
Section 3. (a) Whenever the President shall have issued a proclamation under the authority of section 1 of this Act, it shall thereafter be unlawful for any person within the United States to purchase, sell, or exchange bonds, securities, or other obligations of the government of any belligerent state or of any state wherein civil strife exists, named in such proclamation, or of any political subdivision of any such state, or of any person acting for or on behalf of the government of any such state, or of any faction or asserted government within any such state wherein civil strife exists, or of any person acting for or on behalf of any faction or asserted government within any such state wherein civil strife exists, issued after the date of such proclamation, or to make any loan or extend any credit to any such government, political subdivision, faction, asserted government, or person, or to solicit or receive any contribution for any such government, political subdivision, faction, asserted government, or person:

PROVIDED, That if the President shall find that such action will serve to protect the commercial or other interest of the United States or its citizens, he may, in his discretion, and to such extent and under such regulations as he may prescribe, except from the operation of this section ordinary commercial credits and short-time obligations in aid of legal transactions and of a character customarily used in normal peacetime commercial transactions. Nothing in this subsection shall be construed to prohibit the solicitation or collection of funds to be used for medical aid and assistance, or for food and clothing to relieve human suffering, when such solicitation or collection of funds is made on behalf of and for use by any person or organization which is not acting for or on behalf of any such government, political subdivision, faction, or asserted government, but all such solicitations and collections of funds shall be subject to the approval of the President and shall be made under such rules and regulations as he shall prescribe. . . .

(c) Whoever shall violate the provisions of this section or of any regulations issued hereunder shall, upon conviction thereof, be fined not more than $50,000 or imprisoned for not more than five years, or both. Should the violation be by a corporation, organization, or association, each officer or agent thereof participating in the violation may be liable to the penalty herein prescribed. . . .

EXCEPTIONS—AMERICAN REPUBLICS
Section 4. This Act shall not apply to an American republic or republics engaged in war against a non-American state or states, provided the American republic is not cooperating with a non-American state or states in such a war . . .

AMERICAN VESSELS PROHIBITED FROM CARRYING ARMS TO BELLIGERENT STATES
Section 6. (a) Whenever the President shall have issued a proclamation under the authority of section 1 of this Act, it shall thereafter be unlawful, until such proclamation is revoked, for any American vessel to carry any arms, ammunition, or implements of war to any belligerent state, or to any state wherein civil strife exists, named in such proclamation, or to any neutral state for transshipment to, or for the use of, any such belligerent state or any such state wherein civil strife exists.

(b) Whoever, in violation of the provisions of this section, shall take, or attempt to take, or shall authorize, hire, or solicit another to take, any American vessel carrying such cargo out of port or from the jurisdiction of the United States shall be fined not more than $10,000, or imprisoned not more than five years, or both; and in addition, such vessel, and her tackle, apparel, furniture, and equipment, and the arms, ammunition, and implements of war on board, shall be forfeited to the United States.

USE OF AMERICAN PORTS AS BASE OF SUPPLY
Section 7. (a) Whenever, during any war in which the United States is neutral, the President, or any person thereunto authorized by him, shall have cause to believe that any vessel, domestic or foreign, whether requiring clearance or not, is about to carry out of a port of the United States, fuel, men, arms, ammunition, implements of war, or other supplies to any warship, tender, or supply ship of a belligerent state, but the evidence is not deemed sufficient to justify forbidding the departure of the vessel as provided for by section 1, title V, chapter 30, of the Act approved June 15, 1917, and if, in the President's judgment, such action will serve to maintain peace between the United States and foreign states, or to protect the commercial interests of the United States and its cit-

izens, or to promote the security or neutrality of the United States, he shall have the power and it shall be his duty to require the owner, master, or person in command thereof, before departing from a port of the United States, to give a bond to the United States, with sufficient sureties, in such amount as he shall deem proper, conditioned that the vessel will not deliver the men, or any part of the cargo, to any warship, tender, or supply ship of the belligerent state.

(b) If the President, or any person thereunto authorized by him, shall find that a vessel, domestic or foreign, in a port of the United States, has previously cleared from a port of the United States during such war and delivered its cargo or any part thereof to a warship, tender, or supply ship of a belligerent state, he may prohibit the departure of such vessel during the duration of the war.

SUBMARINES AND ARMED MERCHANT VESSELS
Section 8. Whenever, during any war in which the United States is neutral, the President shall find that special restrictions placed on the use of the ports and territorial waters of the United States by the submarines or armed merchant vessels of a foreign state, will serve to maintain peace between the United States and foreign states, or to protect the commercial interests of the United States and its citizens, or to promote the security of the United States, and shall make proclamation therefore, it shall thereafter be unlawful for any such submarine or armed merchant vessel to enter a port or the territorial waters of the United States or to depart therefrom, except under such conditions and subject to such limitations as the President may prescribe. Whenever, in his judgment, the conditions which have caused him to issue his proclamation have ceased to exist, he shall revoke his proclamation and the provisions of this section shall thereupon cease to apply.

TRAVEL ON VESSELS OF BELLIGERENT STATES
Section 9. Whenever the President shall have issued a proclamation under the authority of section 1 of this Act it shall thereafter be unlawful for any citizen of the United States to travel on any vessel of the state or states named in such proclamation, except in accordance with such rules and regulations as the President shall prescribe. . . .

ARMING OF AMERICAN MERCHANT VESSELS PROHIBITED
Section 10. Whenever the President shall have issued a proclamation under the authority of section 1, it shall thereafter be unlawful, until such proclamation is revoked, for any American vessel engaged in commerce with any belligerent state, or any state wherein civil strife exists, named in such proclamation, to be armed or to carry any arma-

ment, arms, ammunition, or implements of war, except small arms and ammunition therefore which the President may deem necessary and shall publicly designate for the preservation of discipline aboard such vessels.

REGULATIONS
Section 11. The President may, from time to time, promul-gate such rules and regulations, not inconsistent with law, as may be necessary and proper to carry out any of the pro-visions of this Act; and he may exercise any power or au-thority conferred on him by this Act through such officer or officers, or agency or agencies, as he shall direct. . . .

Source: Web site: TeachingAmericanHistory.org. Available at http://teachingamericanhistory.org/library/inndex.asp?document=40.

20. The Sino-Japanese War Begins: The Japanese Embassy in Washington to the U.S. Department of State, 12 July 1937

Throughout World War II, Japan never formally declared war on China, and China left its formal declaration of war on Japan until December 1941, immediately after Pearl Harbor. The following note from the Japanese Embassy in Washington to the United States Department of State recounts the Japanese version of the incident of July 1937 at the Marco Polo Bridge, near Beijing in China, which precipitated full-scale hostilities between the two countries.

1. In the evening of July 7, 1937, a detachment of the Japanese troops stationed at Fengtai, near Peiping, was engaged in a night maneuver in the vicinity of Lukow Kiao. At 11:40 P.M. Chinese troops under the command of Feng Chih-an (29th Army) made an at-tack upon the Japanese soldiers for no cause at all.

    Thereupon the detachment stopped the maneuver and asked the command at Fengtai to send out rein-forcements.

2. At such maneuvers, the Japanese troops immediately carry a very small quantity of loaded shells for use in case of emergency. In point of fact the commanding officer of the said detachment had with him one box of loaded shells for the machine guns. In view of these facts, it is absolutely impossible for the Japa-nese soldiers to have challenged the Chinese.

3. The right of maneuver of the Japanese troops sta-tioned in North China is clearly stipulated in the China-Japanese Protocol of 1902 concerning the restoration of Tientsin to China. Moreover, the Japa-nese authorities had informed the Chinese in advance of the holding of the maneuver in question. It is en-tirely groundless to say that the recent maneuver of the Japanese troops is an unlawful act committed out-side the region stipulated in the said Protocol as re-ported in the newspapers.

4. Since the night of July 7, the Japanese authorities have made an earnest endeavor to localize the inci-dent and once succeeded in bringing the Chinese au-thorities to agree to a peaceful settlement. On the night of July 10, however, the 29th Army, in violation of the agreement, suddenly fired on the Japanese troops, causing considerable casualties. In addition, it is reported, China has been increasing the forces of the first line by ordering Suiyan troops to march south and by sending central forces and air corps to the front.

    Since the night of July 10, China not only has failed to manifest any sincerity toward a peaceful settle-ment but has flatly rejected the local negotiation at Peiping.

5. The presence of disorderly Chinese troops in the Peiping and Tientsin area not only disturbs peace and order in North China which is of vital impor-tance to Japan, but also endangers the lives and prop-erty of the Japanese nationals there.

    In the circumstances, the Japanese Government has decided to take precautionary steps to meet all situations, including the dispatch of additional mili-tary forces to North China.

6. The Japanese Government, desirous as ever to pre-serve peace in East Asia, has not abandoned hope that through peaceful negotiations the aggravation of the situation may yet be prevented.

An amicable solution can yet be attained if China agrees to offer apologies for the recent lawless action and to give adequate guarantees against such outrages in future.

In any case the Japanese Government is prepared to give full consideration to the rights and interests of the Powers in China.

Source: U.S. Department of State, *Papers Relating to the Foreign Relations of the United States: Japan: 1931–1941,* 2 vols. (Washington, DC: U.S. Government Printing Office, 1943), 1: 318–319.

21. President Franklin D. Roosevelt, Quarantine Speech, 5 October 1937

As the international situation deteriorated in both Asia and Europe, the U.S. president toyed with the idea that his country might join with others in taking action against aggressor nations. In a speech delivered in the city of Chicago, in the American isolationist heartland of the Midwest, he floated the idea that the United States might join with other "peace-loving" nations in subjecting aggressor nations to a "quarantine," presumably through the imposition of economic and other sanctions. The following day the U.S. government issued a public statement protesting against Japanese behavior in China and calling for the cessation of fighting. Although Roosevelt's speech, delivered the same day that the League of Nations adopted a report condemning Japanese behavior in China, was well received, at that time he took no further concrete action to implement the measures he had suggested.

. . . . The political situation in the world, which of late has been growing progressively worse, is such as to cause grave concern and anxiety to all the peoples and nations who wish to live in peace and amity with their neighbors.

Some 15 years ago the hopes of mankind for a continuing era of international peace were raised to great heights when more than 60 nations solemnly pledged themselves not to resort to arms in furtherance of their national aims and policies. The high aspirations expressed in the Briand-Kellogg Pact and the hopes for peace thus raised have of late given way to a haunting fear of calamity. The present reign of terror and international lawlessness began a few years ago.

It began through unjustified interference in the internal affairs of other nations or the invasion of alien territory in violation of treaties. It has now reached the stage where the very foundations of civilization are seriously threatened. The landmarks, the traditions which have marked the progress of civilization toward a condition of law and order and justice are being wiped away.

Without a declaration of war and without warning or justification of any kind, civilians, including vast numbers of women and children, are being ruthlessly murdered with bombs from the air. In times of so-called peace, ships are being attacked and sunk by submarines without cause or notice. Nations are fomenting and taking sides in civil warfare in nations that have never done them any harm. Nations claiming freedom for themselves deny it to others.

Innocent peoples, innocent nations are being cruelly sacrificed to a greed for power and supremacy which is devoid of all sense of justice and humane considerations.

To paraphrase a recent author, "perhaps we foresee a time when men, exultant in the technique of homicide, will rage so hotly over the world that every precious thing will be in danger, every book, every picture, every harmony, every treasure garnered through two millenniums, the small, the delicate, the defenseless—all will be lost or wrecked or utterly destroyed."

If those things come to pass in other parts of the world, let no one imagine that America will escape, that America may expect mercy, that this Western hemisphere will not be attacked and that it will continue tranquilly and peacefully to carry on the ethics and the arts of civilization.

No, if those days come, "there will be no safety by arms, no help from authority, no answer in science. The storm will rage until every flower of culture is trampled and all human beings are leveled in a vast chaos."

If those days are not to come to pass—if we are to have a world in which we can breathe freely and live in amity without fear—then the peace-loving nations must make a concerted effort to uphold laws and principles on which alone peace can rest secure.

The peace-loving nations must make a concerted effort in opposition to those violations of treaties and those ignorings of human instincts which today are creating a state of international anarchy and instability from which there is no escape through mere isolation or neutrality.

Those who cherish their freedom and recognize and respect the equal right of their neighbors to be free and live in peace, must work together for the triumph of law and moral principles in order that peace, justice, and confidence may prevail throughout the world. There must be a return to a belief in the pledged word, in the value of a signed treaty. There must be recognition of the fact that national morality is as vital as private morality.

A bishop wrote me the other day: "It seems to me that something greatly needs to be said in behalf of ordinary humanity against the present practice of carrying the horrors of war to helpless civilians, especially women and children. It may be that such a protest might be regarded by many, who claim to be realists, as futile, but may it not be that the heart of mankind is so filled with horror at the present needless suffering that that force could be mobilized in sufficient volume to lessen such cruelty in the days ahead. Even though it may take 20 years, which God forbid, for civilization to make effective its corporate protest against this barbarism, surely strong voices may hasten the day."

There is a solidarity and interdependence about the modern world, both technically and morally, which makes it impossible for any nation completely to isolate itself from economic and political upheavals in the rest of the world, especially when such upheavals appear to be spreading and not declining. There can be no stability or peace either within nations or between nations except under laws and moral standards adhered to by all. International anarchy destroys every foundation for peace. It jeopardizes either the immediate or the future security of every nation, large or small. It is, therefore, a matter of vital interest and concern to the people of the United States that the sanctity of international treaties and the maintenance of international morality be restored.

The overwhelming majority of the peoples and nations of the world today want to live in peace. They seek the removal of barriers against trade. They want to exert themselves in industry, in agriculture and in business, that they may increase their wealth through the production of wealth-producing goods rather than striving to produce military planes and bombs and machine guns and cannon for the destruction of human lives and useful property.

In those nations of the world which seem to be piling armament on armament for purposes of aggression, and those other nations which fear acts of aggression against them and their security, a very high proportion of their national income is being spent directly for armaments. It runs from 30 to as high as 50 per cent. The proportion that we in the United States spend is far less—11 or 12 per cent.

How happy we are that the circumstances of the moment permit us to put our money into bridges and boulevards, dams and reforestation, the conservation of our soil, and many other kinds of useful works rather than into huge standing armies and vast supplies of implements of war.

Nevertheless, my friends, I am compelled, as you are compelled, to look ahead. The peace, the freedom, and the security of 90 per cent of the population of the world is being jeopardized by the remaining 10 per cent who are threatening a breakdown of all international order and law. Surely the 90 per cent who want to live in peace under law and in accordance with moral standards that have received almost universal acceptance through the centuries, can and must find some way to make their will prevail.

The situation is definitely of universal concern. The questions involved relate not merely to violations of specific provisions of particular treaties; they are questions of war and of peace, of international law and especially of principles of humanity. It is true that they involve definite viola-tions of agreements, and especially of the Covenant of the League of Nations, the Briand-Kellogg Pact and the Nine Power Treaty. But they also involve problems of world economy, world security and world humanity.

It is true that the moral consciousness of the world must recognize the importance of removing injustices and well-founded grievances; but at the same time it must be aroused to the cardinal necessity of honoring sanctity of treaties, of respecting the rights and liberties of others and of putting an end to acts of international aggression.

It seems to be unfortunately true that the epidemic of world lawlessness is spreading.

AND MARK THIS WELL: When an epidemic of physical disease starts to spread, the community approves and joins in a quarantine of the patients in order to protect the health of the community against the spread of the disease.

It is my determination to pursue a policy of peace and to adopt every practicable measure to avoid involvement in war. It ought to be inconceivable that in this modern era, and in the face of experience, any nation could be so foolish and ruthless as to run the risk of plunging the whole world into war by invading and violating, in contravention of solemn treaties, the territory of other nations that have done them no real harm and are too weak to protect themselves adequately. Yet the peace of the world and the welfare and security of every nation are today being threatened by that very thing.

No nation which refuses to exercise forbearance and to respect the freedom and rights of others can long remain strong and retain the confidence and respect of other nations. No nation ever loses its dignity or its good standing by conciliating its differences, and by exercising great patience with, and consideration for, the rights of other nations.

War is a contagion, whether it be declared or undeclared. It can engulf states and peoples remote from the original scene of hostilities. We are determined to keep out of war, yet we cannot insure ourselves against the disastrous effects of war and the dangers of involvement. We are adopting such measures as will minimize our risk of involvement, but we cannot have complete protection in a world of disorder in which confidence and security have broken down.

If civilization is to survive, the principles of the Prince of Peace must be restored. Shattered trust between nations must be revived.

Most important of all, the will for peace on the part of peace-loving nations must express itself to the end that nations that may be tempted to violate their agreements and the rights of others will desist from such a course. There must be positive endeavors to preserve peace.

Source: Samuel I. Rosenman, ed., *The Public Papers and Addresses of Franklin D. Roosevelt, 1937* (New York: Macmillan, 1941), 406–411.

22. Italy Joins the German-Japanese Anti-Comintern Pact: Protocol Signed in Rome, 6 November 1937

At the end of 1937, Italy formally joined the Anti-Comintern Pact that Germany and Japan had signed one year earlier. This action formally aligned all three major fascist states together against communism, another indication of the degree to which international politics were increasingly organized on ideological lines.

The Government of the German Reich,

The Italian Government and

The Imperial Japanese Government

Considering that the Communist International continues consistently to endanger the civilized world in the West and East, and disturbs and destroys its peace and order,

Convinced that close co-operation between all States interested in maintaining peace and order can alone diminish and remove this danger,

Considering that Italy, which since the beginning of this Fascist Government has combated this danger with inflexible determination and has eradicated the Communist International in its territory, has decided to take its place against the common enemy side by side with Germany and Japan who, for their part, are animated by the same desire to guard against the Communist International,

Have agreed as follows, in accordance with Article II of the Agreement against the Communist International concluded on November 25, 1936, in Berlin between Germany and Japan:

Article 1.—Italy accedes to the Agreement against the Communist International together with the Additional Protocol, concluded between Germany and Japan on November 25, 1936, a copy of which is annexed.

Article 2.—The three Powers signing the present Protocol agree that Italy shall be considered as an original signatory of the Agreement and Additional Protocol mentioned in the preceding article, the signature of the present Protocol being equivalent to the signature of the above-mentioned Agreement and Additional Protocol.

Article 3.—The present Protocol is considered as an integral part of the above-mentioned Agreement and Additional Protocol. . . .

Source: Stephen Heald, ed., *Documents on International Affairs 1937* (Oxford, UK: Oxford University Press, 1939), 306–307. Reprinted with permission of Chatham House.

23. The Hossbach Memorandum, Berlin, 10 November 1937: Minutes of a Conference in the Reich Chancellery, Berlin, 5 November 1937, from 4:15 to 8:30 P.M.

In late 1937, German Chancellor Adolf Hitler met with his top military and diplomatic advisers to discuss their country's future strategy in international affairs. Notes of the meeting were taken by Colonel Hossbach, an aide who acted as secretary. Hitler discussed his plans to annex both Czechoslovakia and Austria in the near future, enterprises he believed could be accomplished without war with either Great Britain or France. He also argued that the latest possible dates for a major war must be 1943–1945, since after that date, the German military position in relation to that of potential enemies would begin to deteriorate.

Present:

The Fuehrer and Chancellor, Field Marshal von Blomberg, War Minister,

Colonel General Baron von Fritsch, Commander in Chief, Army,

Admiral Dr. H. C. Raeder, Commander in Chief, Navy,

Colonel General Göring, Commander in Chief, Luftwaffe,

Baron von Neurath, Foreign Minister,

Colonel Hossbach.

The Fuehrer began by stating that the subject of the present conference was of such importance that its discussion would, in other countries, certainly be a matter for a full Cabinet meeting, but he—the Fuehrer—had rejected the idea of making it a subject of discussion before the wider circle of the Reich Cabinet just because of the importance of the matter. His exposition to follow was the fruit of thorough deliberation and the experiences of his 4 1/2 years of power. He wished to explain to the gentlemen present his basic ideas concerning the opportunities for the development of our position in the field of foreign affairs and its requirements, and he asked, in the interests of a long-term German policy, that his exposition be regarded, in the event of his death, as his last will and testament.

The Fuehrer then continued:

The aim of German policy was to make secure and to preserve the racial community [*Volksmasse*] and to enlarge it. It was therefore a question of space.

The German racial community comprised over 85 million people and, because of their number and the narrow limits of habitable space in Europe, constituted a tightly packed racial core such as was not to be met in any other country and such as implied the right to a greater living space than in the case of other peoples. If, territorially speaking, there existed no political result corresponding to this German racial core, that was a consequence of centuries of historical development, and in the continuance of these political conditions lay the greatest danger to the preservation of the German race at its present peak. To arrest the decline of Germanism [*Deutschtum*] in Austria and Czechoslovakia was as little possible as to maintain the present level in Germany itself. Instead of increase, sterility was setting in, and in its train disorders of a social character must arise in course of time, since political and ideological ideas remain effective only so long as they furnish the basis for the realization of the essential vital demands of a people. Germany's future was therefore wholly conditional upon the solving of the need for space, and such a solution could be sought, of course, only for a foreseeable period of about one to three generations. . . .

The question for Germany ran: where could she achieve the greatest gain at the lowest cost.

German policy had to reckon with two hate-inspired antagonists, Britain and France, to whom a German colossus in the center of Europe was a thorn in the flesh, and both countries were opposed to any further strengthening of Germany's position either in Europe or overseas; in support of this opposition they were able to count on the agreement of all their political parties. Both countries saw in the establishment of German military bases overseas a threat to their own communications, a safeguarding of German commerce, and, as a consequence, a strengthening of Germany's position in Europe. . . .

Beside the British Empire there existed today a number of states stronger than she. The British motherland was able to protect her colonial possessions not by her own power, but only in alliance with other states. How, for instance, could Britain alone defend Canada against attack by America, or her Far Eastern interests against attack by Japan! . . .

France's position was more favorable than that of Britain. The French Empire was better placed territorially; the inhabitants of her colonial possessions represented a supplement to her military strength. But France was going to be confronted with internal political difficulties. In a nation's life about 10 percent of its span is taken up by parliamentary forms of government and about 90 percent by authoritarian forms. Today, nonetheless, Britain, France, Russia, and the smaller states adjoining them, must be included as factors [*Machtfaktoren*] in our political calculations.

Germany's problem could only be solved by means of force and this was never without attendant risk. The campaigns of Frederick the Great for Silesia and Bismarck's wars against Austria and France had involved unheard-of risk, and the swiftness of the Prussian action in 1870 had kept Austria from entering the war. If one accepts as the basis of the following exposition the resort to force with its attendant risks, then there remain still to be answered the questions "when" and "how." In this matter there were three cases [*Falle*] to be dealt with:

Case 1: Period 1943–1945.
After this date only a change for the worse, from our point of view, could be expected.

The equipment of the army, navy, and Luftwaffe [air force], as well as the formation of the officer corps, was nearly completed. Equipment and armament were modern; in further delay there lay the danger of their obsolescence. In particular, the secrecy of "special weapons" could not be preserved forever. The recruiting of reserves was limited to current age groups; further drafts from older untrained age groups were no longer available.

Our relative strength would decrease in relation to the rearmament which would by then have been carried out by the rest of the world. If we did not act by 1943–45 any year could, in consequence of a lack of reserves, produce the food crisis, to cope with which the necessary foreign exchange was not available, and this must be regarded as a "waning point of the regime." Besides, the world was expecting our attack and was increasing its counter-measures from year to year. It was while the rest of the world was still preparing its defenses [*sich abriegele*] that we were obliged to take the offensive.

Nobody knew today what the situation would be in the years 1943–45. One thing only was certain, that we could not wait longer.

On the one hand there was the great Wehrmacht [army], and the necessity of maintaining it at its present level, the aging of the movement and of its leaders; and on the other, the prospect of a lowering of the standard of living and of a limitation of the birth rate, which left no choice but to act. If the Fuehrer was still living, it was his unalterable resolve to solve Germany's problem of space at the latest by 1943–45. The necessity for action before 1943–45 would arise in cases 2 and 3.

Case 2:

If internal strife in France should develop into such a domestic crisis as to absorb the French Army completely and render it incapable of use for war against Germany, then the time for action against the Czechs had come.

Case 3:

If France is so embroiled by a war with another state that she cannot "proceed" against Germany.

For the improvement of our politico-military position our first objective, in the event of our being embroiled in war, must be to overthrow Czechoslovakia and Austria simultaneously in order to remove the threat to our flank in any possible operation against the West. In a conflict with France it was hardly to be regarded as likely that the Czechs would declare war on us on the very same day as France. The desire to join in the war would, however, increase among the Czechs in proportion to any weakening on our part and then her participation could clearly take the form of an attack toward Silesia, toward the north or toward the west.

If the Czechs were overthrown and a common German-Hungarian frontier achieved, a neutral attitude on the part of Poland could be the more certainly counted on in the event of a Franco-German conflict. Our agreements with Poland only retained their force as long as Germany's strength remained unshaken. In the event of German setbacks a Polish action against East Prussia, and possibly against Pomerania and Silesia as well, had to be reckoned with.

On the assumption of a development of the Situation leading to action on our part as planned, in the years 1943–45, the attitude of France, Britain, Italy, Poland, and Russia could probably be estimated as follows:

Actually, the Fuehrer believed that almost certainly Britain, and probably France as well, had already tacitly written off the Czechs and were reconciled to the fact that this question could be cleared up in due course by Germany. Difficulties connected with the Empire, and the prospect of being once more entangled in a protracted European war, were decisive considerations for Britain against participation in a war against Germany. Britain's attitude would certainly not be without influence on that of France. An attack by France without British support, and with the prospect of the offensive being brought to a standstill on our western fortifications, was hardly probable. Nor was a French march through Belgium and Holland without British support to be expected; this also was a course not to be contemplated by us in the event of a conflict with France,

because it would certainly entail the hostility of Britain. It would of course be necessary to maintain a strong defense [*eine Abriegelung*] on our western frontier during the prosecution of our attack on the Czechs and Austria. And in this connection it had to be remembered that the defense measures of the Czechs were growing in strength from year to year, and that the actual worth of the Austrian Army also was increasing in the course of time. Even though the populations concerned, especially of Czechoslovakia, were not sparse, the annexation of Czechoslovakia and Austria would mean an acquisition of foodstuffs for 5 to 6 million people, on the assumption that the compulsory emigration of 2 million people from Czechoslovakia and 1 million people from Austria was practicable. The incorporation of these two States with Germany meant, from the politico-military point of view, a substantial advantage because it would mean shorter and better frontiers, the freeing of forces for other purposes, and the possibility of creating new units up to a level of about 12 divisions, that is, 1 new division per million inhabitants.

Italy was not expected to object to the elimination of the Czechs, but it was impossible at the moment to estimate what her attitude on the Austrian question would be; that depended essentially upon whether the Duce were still alive.

The degree of surprise and the swiftness of our action were decisive factors for Poland's attitude. Poland, with Russia at her rear, will have little inclination to engage in war against a victorious Germany.

Military intervention by Russia must be countered by the swiftness of our operations; however, whether such an intervention was a practical contingency at all was, in view of Japan's attitude, more than doubtful.

Should case 2 arise—the crippling of France by civil war—the situation thus created by the elimination of the most dangerous opponent must he seized upon whenever it occurs for the blow against the Czechs.

The Fuehrer saw case 3 coming definitely nearer; it might emerge from the present tensions in the Mediterranean, and he was resolved to take advantage of it whenever it happened, even as early as 1938.

In the light of past experience, the Fuehrer did not see any early end to the hostilities in Spain. If one considered the length of time which Franco's offensives had taken up till now, it was fully possible that the war would continue another 3 years. On the other hand, a 100 percent victory for Franco was not desirable either, from the German point of view; rather were we interested in a continuance of the war and in the keeping up of the tension in the Mediterranean. Franco in undisputed possession of the Spanish Peninsula precluded the possibility of any further intervention on the part of the Italians or of their continued occupation of the

Balearic Islands. As our interest lay more in the prolongation of the war in Spain, it must be the immediate aim of our policy to strengthen Italy's rear with a view to her remaining in the Balearics. But the permanent establishment of the Italians on the Balearics would be intolerable both to France and Britain, and might lead to a war of France and England against Italy—a war in which Spain, should she be entirely in the hands of the Whites, might make her appearance on the side of Italy's enemies. The probability of Italy's defeat in such a war was slight, for the road from Germany was open for the supplementing of her raw materials. The Fuehrer pictured the military strategy for Italy thus: on her western frontier with France she would remain on the defensive, and carry on the war against France from Libya against the French North African colonial possessions.

As a landing by Franco-British troops on the coast of Italy could be discounted, and a French offensive over the Alps against northern Italy would be very difficult and would probably come to a halt before the strong Italian fortifications, the crucial point [*Schwerpunkt*] of the operations lay in North Africa. The threat to French lines of communication by the Italian Fleet would to a great extent cripple the transportation of forces from North Africa to France, so that France would have only home forces at her disposal on the frontiers with Italy and Germany.

If Germany made use of this war to settle the Czech and Austrian questions, it was to be assumed that Britain—herself at war with Italy—would decide not to act against Germany. Without British support, a warlike action by France against Germany was not to be expected.

The time for our attack on the Czechs and Austria must be made dependent on the course of the Anglo-French-Italian war and would not necessarily coincide with the commencement of military operations by these three States. Nor had the Fuehrer in mind military agreements with Italy, but wanted, while retaining his own independence of action, to exploit this favorable situation, which would not occur again, to begin and carry through the campaign against the Czechs. This descent upon the Czechs would have to be carried out with "lightning speed."

In appraising the situation Field Marshal von Blomberg and Colonel General von Fritsch repeatedly emphasized the necessity that Britain and France must not appear in the role of our enemies, and stated that the French Army would not be so committed by the war with Italy that France could not at the same time enter the field with forces superior to ours on our western frontier. General von Fritsch estimated the probable French forces available for use on the Alpine frontier at approximately twenty divisions, so that a strong French superiority would still remain on the western frontier, with the role, according to the German view, of invading the Rhineland. In this matter, moreover, the advanced state of French defense preparations [*Mobiolmachung*] must be taken into particular account, and it must be remembered apart from the insignificant value of our present fortifications—on which Field Marshal von Blomberg laid special emphasis—that the four motorized divisions intended for the West were still more or less incapable of movement. In regard to our offensive toward the southeast, Field Marshal von Blomberg drew particular attention to the strength of the Czech fortifications, which had acquired by now a structure like a Maginot Line and which would gravely hamper our attack.

General von Fritsch mentioned that this was the very purpose of a study which he had ordered made this winter, namely, to examine the possibility of conducting operations against the Czechs with special reference to overcoming the Czech fortification system; the General further expressed his opinion, that under existing circumstances he must give up his plan to go abroad on his leave, which was due to begin on November 10. The Fuehrer dismissed this idea on the ground that the possibility of a conflict need not yet be regarded as imminent. To the Foreign Minister's objection that an Anglo-French-Italian conflict was not yet within such a measurable distance as the Fuehrer seemed to assume, the Fuehrer put the summer of 1938 as the date which seemed to him possible for this. In reply to considerations offered by Field Marshal von Blomberg and General von Fritsch regarding the attitude of Britain and France, the Fuehrer repeated his previous statements that he was convinced of Britain's nonparticipation, and therefore he did not believe in the probability of belligerent action by France against Germany. Should the Mediterranean conflict under discussion lead to a general mobilization in Europe, then we must immediately begin action against the Czechs. On the other hand, should the powers not engaged in the war declare themselves disinterested, then Germany would have to adopt a similar attitude to this for the time being.

Colonel General Göring thought that, in view of the Fuehrer's statement, we should consider liquidating our military undertakings in Spain. The Fuehrer agrees to this with the limitation that he thinks he should reserve a decision for a proper moment.

The second part of the conference was concerned with concrete questions of armament.

HOSSBACH
Certified Correct:
Colonel (General Staff)

Source: Documents on German Foreign Policy 1918–1945, Series D Volume 1, From Neurath to Ribbentrop (September 1937–September 1938) (Washington, DC: U.S. Government Printing Office, 1949), 29–39.

24. President Franklin D. Roosevelt, Message to the Congress Recommending Increased Armament for National Defense, 28 January 1938

By the beginning of 1938, the international situation alarmed President Franklin D. Roosevelt sufficiently to impel him to recommend substantial increases in U.S. defense spending to Congress. He stated bluntly that "our national defense is, in the light of the increasing armaments of other Nations, inadequate for purposes of national security."

To the Congress:

The Congress knows that for many years this Government has sought in many Capitals with the leaders of many Governments to find a way to limit and reduce armaments and to establish at least the probability of world peace.

The Congress is aware also that while these efforts, supported by the hopes of the American people, continue and will continue they have nevertheless failed up to the present time.

We, as a peaceful Nation, cannot and will not abandon active search for an agreement among the nations to limit armaments and end aggression. But it is clear that until such agreement is reached—and I have not given up hope of it—we are compelled to think of our own national safety.

It is with the deepest regret that I report to you that armaments increase today at an unprecedented and alarming rate. It is an ominous fact that at least one-fourth of the world's population is involved in merciless devastating conflict in spite of the fact that most people in most countries, including those where conflict rages, wish to live at peace. Armies are fighting in the Far East and in Europe; thousands of civilians are being driven from their homes and bombed from the air. Tension throughout the world is high.

As Commander-in-Chief of the Army and Navy of the United States it is my constitutional duty to report to the Congress that our national defense is, in the light of the increasing armaments of other Nations, inadequate for purposes of national security and requires increase for that reason.

In spite of the well-known fact that the American standard of living makes our ships, our guns and our planes cost more for construction than in any other Nation and that the maintenance of them and of our Army and Navy personnel is more expensive than in any other Nation, it is also true that the proportion of the cost of our military and naval forces to the total income of our citizens or to the total cost of our Government is far lower than in the case of any other great Nation.

Specifically and solely because of the piling up of additional land and sea armaments in other countries, in such manner as to involve a threat to world peace and security, I make the following recommendations to the Congress:

(1) That there be authorized for the Army of the United States additions to anti-aircraft materiel in the sum of $8,800,000 and that of this sum $6,800,000 be appropriated for the fiscal year 1939.

(2) That there be authorized and appropriated for the better establishment of an Enlisted Reserve for the Army the sum of $450,000.

(3) That there be authorized the expenditure of $6,080,000 for the manufacture of gauges, dies and other aids to manufacture of Army materiel, the sum of $5,000,000 thereof to be expended during the fiscal year 1939.

(4) That the sum of $2,000,000 be authorized and appropriated toward the making up of deficiencies in ammunition for the Army.

(5) That the existing authorized building program for increases and replacements in the Navy be increased by 20 per cent.

(6) That this Congress authorize and appropriate for the laying down of two additional battleships and two additional cruisers during the calendar year 1938. This will call for the expenditure of a very small amount of Government funds during the fiscal year 1939.

(7) That the Congress authorize and appropriate a sum not to exceed $15,000,000 for the construction of a number of new types of small vessels, such construction to be regarded as experimental in the light of new developments among Navies; and to include the preparation of plans for other types of ships in the event that it may be necessary to construct such ships in the future.

I believe also that the time has come for the Congress to enact legislation aimed at the prevention of profiteering in time of war and the equalization of the burdens of possible war. Such legislation has been the subject for many years of full study in this and previous Congresses.

It is necessary for all of us to realize that the unfortunate world conditions of today have resulted too often in the discarding of those principles and treaties which underlie international law and order; and in the entrance of many new factors into the actual conduct of war.

Adequate defense means that for the protection not only of our coasts but also of our communities far removed from the coast, we must keep any potential enemy many hundred miles away from our continental limits.

We cannot assume that our defense would be limited to one ocean and one coast and that the other ocean and the other coast would with certainty be safe. We cannot be certain that the connecting link, the Panama Canal, would be safe. Adequate defense affects therefore the simultaneous defense of every part of the United States of America.

It is our clear duty to further every effort toward peace but at the same time to protect our Nation. That is the purpose of these recommendations. Such protection is and will be based not on aggression but on defense.

Source: Web site: ibiblio. Available at http://www.ibiblio.org/pha/7–2–188/188–08.html.

25. Broadcast by the Former Austrian Chancellor Dr. Kurt von Schuschnigg, 11 March 1938

Under the Treaty of Versailles, union between Austria and Germany was forbidden. After regaining the Rhineland, Adolf Hitler's next objective was Austria, where the Austrian Nazi party agitated for union (Anschluss) with Germany. As chancellor, the authoritarian Kurt von Schuschnigg headed a semifascist government, but he nonetheless opposed annexation. In early March 1938, German troops massed on the Austrian border, as the Austrian government organized a nationwide plebiscite on whether Austria should join Germany. Despite that pressure, Chancellor von Schuschnigg urged the defense of Austrian independence. On 11 March, under pressure from Germany, Arthur Seyss-Inquart, head of the German Nazi party, replaced von Schuschnigg as chancellor of Austria, and the plebiscite scheduled for 13 March was cancelled. German troops marched into Austria, and the two countries were forcibly united. Schuschnigg made a public broadcast to the Austrian people, protesting against these developments. Shortly afterward he was imprisoned and did not regain his freedom until Germany's defeat in 1945.

Men and women of Austria!

Today we have been confronted with a difficult and decisive situation. I am authorized to report to the Austrian people on the events of the day.

The Government of the German Reich presented the Federal President with an ultimatum with a time-limit, according to which he had to appoint as Federal Chancellor a prescribed candidate, and constitute a Government in accordance with the proposals of the Government of the German Reich. Otherwise it was intended that German troops should march into Austria at the hour named.

I declare before the world that the reports which have been spread in Austria that there have been labour troubles, that streams of blood have flowed, and that the Government was not in control of the situation and could not maintain order by its own means, are fabrications from A to Z.

The Federal President authorizes me to inform the Austrian people that we yield to force. Because we are not minded, at any cost and even in this grave hour, to shed German blood, we have ordered our armed forces, in case the invasion is carried out, to withdraw without resistance and to await the events of the next hours. . . .

So I take my leave of the Austrian people with a German word and a heartfelt wish—God protect Austria!

Source: Stephen Heald, ed., *Documents on International Affairs 1938* (Oxford, UK: Oxford University Press, 1939), 2: 64–66. Reprinted with permission of Chatham House.

26. President Franklin D. Roosevelt, Message Sent Directly to the President of Czechoslovakia and the Chancellor of Germany and through the Secretary of State to the Prime Ministers of Great Britain and France, Morning of 26 September 1938

In late September 1938, Adolf Hitler's demands that the Czech territory of the Sudetenland be incorporated in Germany came to a head. Great Britain, France, and the Soviet Union had all guaranteed Czechoslovakia's security, but the first two powers were reluctant to go to war. The Soviets stated their readiness to fight, but in reality they were in no position to do so. Hitler therefore refused to compromise on his demands for the Sudetenland. As negotiations continued and appeared deadlocked, the U.S. president sent a message to the leaders of all those nations concerned, urging them to make every effort to reach a settlement that would preserve European peace.

The fabric of peace on the continent of Europe, if not throughout the rest of the world, is in immediate danger. The consequences of its rupture are incalculable. Should hostilities break out the lives of millions of men, women and children in every country involved will most certainly be lost under circumstances of unspeakable horror.

The economic system of every country involved is certain to be shattered. The social structure of every country involved may well be completely wrecked.

The United States has no political entanglements. It is caught in no mesh of hatred. Elements of all Europe have formed its civilization.

The supreme desire of the American people is to live in peace. But in the event of a general war they face the fact that no nation can escape some measure of the consequences of such a world catastrophe.

The traditional policy of the United States has been the furtherance of the settlement of international disputes by pacific means. It is my conviction that all people under the threat of war today pray that peace may be made before, rather than after, war.

It is imperative that peoples everywhere recall that every civilized nation of the world voluntarily assumed the solemn obligations of the Kellogg-Briand Pact of 1928 to solve controversies only by pacific methods. In addition, most nations are parties to other binding treaties obligating them to preserve peace. Furthermore, all countries have today available for such peaceful solution of difficulties which may arise, treaties of arbitration and conciliation to which they are parties.

Whatever may be the differences in the controversies at issue and however difficult of pacific settlement they may be, I am persuaded that there is no problem so difficult or so pressing for solution that it cannot be justly solved by the resort to reason rather than by the resort to force.

During the present crisis the people of the United States and their Government have earnestly hoped that the negotiations for the adjustment of the controversy which has now arisen in Europe might reach a successful conclusion.

So long as these negotiations continue, so long will there remain the hope that reason and the spirit of equity may prevail and that the world may thereby escape the madness of a new resort to war.

On behalf of the 130 millions of people of the United States of America and for the sake of humanity everywhere I most earnestly appeal to you not to break off negotiations looking to a peaceful, fair, and constructive settlement of the questions at issue.

I earnestly repeat that so long as negotiations continue, differences may be reconciled. Once they are broken off reason is banished and force asserts itself.

And force produces no solution for the future good of humanity.

Source: Web site: ibiblio. Available at http://www.ibiblio.org/pha/7–2–188/188–10.html.

27. Agreement Concluded at Munich, between Germany, Great Britain, France, and Italy, 29 September 1938

In August 1938, German Chancellor Adolf Hitler demanded that Czechoslovakia cede to Germany the Sudetenland, a portion of that state's territory the population of which was largely of ethnically German origin. The Czechs proclaimed their willingness to fight Germany and sought assistance in doing so from Great Britain, France, and the Soviet Union. While the latter state proclaimed its own willingness to aid the Czechs, Britain and France were far more reluctant to contemplate war. Eventually Neville Chamberlain, the British prime minister, flew to meet Hitler at Berchtesgaden in Germany and, with French assistance, brokered an agreement whereby Czechoslovakia handed over the Sudetenland to Germany. Welcomed by many at the time and subsequently defended on the grounds that in September 1938 Britain was militarily too ill-equipped to face war against Germany, the controversial Munich Agreement nonetheless quickly came to symbolize the interwar irresolution of the Western democracies in dealing with any serious threat to international peace and order.

GERMANY, the United Kingdom, France and Italy, taking into consideration the agreement, which has been already reached in principle for the cession to Germany of the Sudeten German territory, have agreed on the following terms and conditions governing the said cession and the measures consequent thereon, and by this agreement they each hold themselves responsible for the steps necessary to secure its fulfilment:

1. The evacuation will begin on 1st October.
2. The United Kingdom, France and Italy agree that the evacuation of the territory shall be completed by the 10th October, without any existing installations having been destroyed, and that the Czechoslovak Government will be held responsible for carrying out the evacuation without damage to the said installations.
3. The conditions governing the evacuation will be laid down in detail by an international commission composed of representatives of Germany, the United Kingdom, France, Italy and Czechoslovakia.
4. The occupation by stages of the predominantly German territory by German troops will begin on 1st October. The four territories marked on the attached map will be occupied by German troops in the following order:

    The territory marked No. I on the 1st and 2nd of October; the territory marked No. II on the 2nd and 3rd of October; the territory marked No. III on the 3rd, 4th and 5th of October; the territory marked No. IV on the 6th and 7th of October. The remaining territory of preponderantly German character will be ascertained by the aforesaid international commission forthwith and be occupied by German troops by the 10th of October.

5. The international commission referred to in paragraph 3 will determine the territories in which a plebiscite is to be held. These territories will be occupied by international bodies until the plebiscite has been completed. The same commission will fix the conditions in which the plebiscite is to be held, taking as a basis the conditions of the Saar plebiscite. The commission will also fix a date, not later than the end of November, on which the plebiscite will be held.
6. The final determination of the frontiers will be carried out by the international commission. The commission will also be entitled to recommend to the four Powers, Germany, the United Kingdom, France and Italy, in certain exceptional cases, minor modifications in the strictly ethnographical determination of the zones which are to be transferred without plebiscite.
7. There will be a right of option into and out of the transferred territories, the option to be exercised within six months from the date of this agreement. A German-Czechoslovak commission shall determine the details of the option, consider ways of facilitating the transfer of population and settle questions of principle arising out of the said transfer.
8. The Czechoslovak Government will within a period of four weeks from the date of this agreement release from their military and police forces any Sudeten Germans who may wish to be released, and the Czechoslovak Government will within the same period release Sudeten German prisoners who are serving terms of imprisonment for political offences. . . .

ANNEX TO THE AGREEMENT
His Majesty's Government in the United Kingdom and the

French Government have entered into the above agreement on the basis that they stand by the offer, contained in Paragraph 6 of the Anglo-French Proposals of 19 September, relating to an international guarantee of the new boundaries of the Czechoslovak State against unprovoked aggression.

When the question of the Polish and Hungarian minorities in Czechoslovakia has been settled, Germany and Italy for their part shall give a guarantee to Czechoslovakia.

Source: J. Noakes and G. Pridham, eds., *Nazism: A Documentary Reader 1919–1945*, Vol. 3: *Foreign Policy, War and Racial Extermination* (Exeter, UK: University of Exeter Press, 1988), 110–111.

28. Neville Chamberlain, "Peace for Our Time," 30 September 1938

Only too soon, Chamberlain's public declaration on returning from Munich that the agreement represented "peace for our time" was discredited, making it synonymous in the future with a myopic determination to ignore at any price the threats that authoritarian dictatorships posed to democratic nations during the 1930s.

[Neville Chamberlain read this statement to a cheering crowd assembled outside 10 Downing Street, the British prime minister's official residence, on the evening of his return from Germany, where Britain, France, and Germany had signed the Munich Agreement.]

We, the German Führer and Chancellor, and the British Prime Minister, have had a further meeting today and are agreed in recognizing that the question of Anglo-German relations is of the first importance for the two countries and for Europe.

We regard the agreement signed last night and the Anglo-German Naval Agreement as symbolic of the desire of our two peoples never to go to war with one another again.

We are resolved that the method of consultation shall be the method adopted to deal with any other questions that may concern our two countries, and we are determined to continue our efforts to remove possible sources of difference, and thus to contribute to assure the peace of Europe.

[He then added:]

My good friends this is the second time in our history that there has come back from Germany to Downing Street peace with honor. I believe it is peace for our time. And now I recommend you to go home and sleep quietly in your beds.

Source: History of the United Kingdom Web site, Primary Documents. Available at http://www.lib.byu.edu/~rdh/eurodocs/uk/peace.html.

1939 Documents

29. President Franklin D. Roosevelt, Message to the U.S. Congress, 12 January 1939

Addressing Congress on 4 January 1939 in his annual State of the Union message, President Franklin D. Roosevelt warned that, despite the narrow escape from European war the previous September, the international situation was ominous. Besides calling for major increases in American defense spending, he urged national unity in the crisis as an essential component of U.S. security. Warning that time was pressing, just over a week later, he followed up with a message asking Congress to authorize specific, detailed, and substantial increases in the country's military budget, including a major program to enhance American aircraft production.

In my annual message to this Congress I have spoken at some length of the changing world conditions outside of the American Hemisphere which make it imperative that we take immediate steps for the protection of our liberties.

It would be unwise for any of us to yield to any form of hysteria. Nevertheless, regardless of political affiliations, we can properly join in an appraisal of the world situation and agree on the immediate defense needs of the Nation.

It is equally sensational and untrue to take the position that we must at once spend billions of additional money for building up our land, sea, and air forces on the one hand, or to insist that no further additions are necessary on the other.

What needs to be emphasized is the great change which has come over conflicts between nations since the World War ended, and especially during the past 5 or 6 years.

Those of us who took part in the conduct of the World War will remember that in the preparation of the American armies for actual participation in battle, the United States, entering the war on April 6 1917, took no part whatsoever in any major engagement until the end of May 1918. In other words, while other armies were conducting the actual fighting, the United States had more than a year of absolute peace at home, without any threat of attack on this continent to train men, to produce raw materials, to process them into munitions and supplies and to forge the whole into fighting forces. It is even a matter of record that as late as the autumn of 1918, American armies at the front used almost exclusively French or British artillery and aircraft.

Calling attention to these facts does not remotely intimate that the Congress or the President have any thought of taking part in another war on European soil, but it does show that in 1917 we were not ready to conduct large scale land or air operations. Relatively we are not much more ready to do so today than we were then—and we cannot guarantee a long period, free from attack, in which we could prepare.

I have called attention to the fact that "We must have armed forces and defenses strong enough to ward off sudden attack against strategic positions and key facilities essential to insure sustained resistance and ultimate victory." And I have said, "We must have the organization and location of those key facilities so that they may be immediately utilized and rapidly expanded to meet all needs without danger of serious interruption by enemy attack."

I repeat that "there is new range and speed to offense."

Therefore, it has become necessary for every American to restudy present defense against the possibilities of present offense against us.

Careful examination of the most imperative present needs leads me to recommend the appropriation at this session of the Congress, with as great speed as possible, of approximately $525,000,000, of which sum approximately $210,000,000 would be actually spent from the Treasury before the end of the fiscal year ending June 30, 1940.

The survey indicates that of this sum approximately $450,000,000 should be allocated for new needs of the Army, $65,000,000 for new needs of the Navy, and $10,000,000 for training of civilian air pilots. . . .

In the case of the Army, information from other nations leads us to believe that there must be a complete revision of our estimates for aircraft. The Baker board report of a few years ago is completely out of date. No responsible officer advocates building our air forces up to the total either of planes on hand or of productive capacity equal to the forces of certain other nations. We are thinking in the terms of necessary defenses and the conclusion is inevitable that our existing forces are so utterly inadequate that they must be immediately strengthened.

It is proposed that $300,000,000 be appropriated for the purchase of several types of airplanes for the Army. This should provide a minimum increase of 3,000 planes, but it is hoped that orders placed on such a large scale will materially reduce the unit cost and actually provide many more planes.

Military aviation is increasing today at an unprecedented and alarming rate. Increased range, increased speed, increased capacity of airplanes abroad have changed our requirements for defensive aviation. The additional planes recommended will considerably strengthen the air defenses of the continental United States, Alaska, Hawaii, Puerto Rico, and the Canal Zone. If an appropriation bill can be quickly enacted, I suggest that $50,000,000 of the $300,000,000 for airplanes be made immediately available in order to correct the present lag in aircraft production due to idle plants.

Of the balance of approximately $150,000,000 requested for the Army, I suggest an appropriation of $110,000,000 to provide "critical items" of equipment which would be needed immediately in time of emergency, and which cannot be obtained from any source within the time and quantity desired—materiel such as antiaircraft artillery, semiautomatic rifles, antitank guns, tanks, light and heavy artillery, ammunition, and gas masks. Such purchases would go far to equip existing units of the Regular Army and the National Guard.

I suggest approximately $32,000,000 for "educational orders" for the Army—in other words, to enable industry to prepare for quantity production in an emergency, of those military items which are noncommercial in character and are so difficult of manufacture as to constitute what are known as "bottlenecks" in the problem of procurement.

The balance should be used, I believe, for improving and strengthening the seacoast defenses of Panama, Hawaii, and the continental United States, including the construction of a highway outside the limits of the Panama Canal Zone, important to the defense of the zone.

The estimated appropriation of $65,000,000 for the Navy should be divided into (a) $44,000,000 for the creation or strengthening of Navy bases in both oceans in general agreement with the report of the special board which has already been submitted to the Congress, (b) about $21,000,000 for additional Navy airplanes and air material tests.

Finally, national defense calls for the annual training of additional air pilots. This training should be primarily directed to the essential qualifications for civilian flying. In cooperation with educational institutions, it is believed that the expenditure of $10,000,000 a year will give primary training to approximately 20,000 citizens.

In the above recommendations for appropriations totaling $525,000,000, I have omitted reference to a definite need, which, however, relates to the implementing of existing defenses for the Panama Canal. The security of the Canal is of the utmost importance. The peace garrison now there is inadequate to defend this vital link. This deficiency cannot be corrected with existing forces without seriously jeopardizing the general defense by stripping the continental United States of harbor defense and antiaircraft personnel. The permanent garrison in the Canal Zone should be increased to provide the minimum personnel required to man the antiaircraft and seacoast armament provided for the defense of the Canal. Such personnel cannot be increased until additional housing facilities are provided—and, in the meantime, additional personnel must be trained. I recommend, therefore, an appropriation of $27,000,000 to provide an adequate peace garrison for the Canal Zone and to house it adequately. Five million dollars of this sum should be made available immediately in order that work on necessary construction can be initiated.

All of the above constitutes a well-rounded program, considered by me as Commander in Chief of the Army and Navy, and by my advisors to be a minimum program for the necessities of defense. . . .

Devoid of all hysteria, this program is but the minimum of requirements.

I trust, therefore, that the Congress will quickly act on this emergency program for the strengthening of the defense of the United States.

Source: U.S. Department of State, Publication 1983, *Peace and War: United States Foreign Policy, 1931–1941* (Washington, DC: U.S. Government Printing Office, 1943), 450–453.

30. Text of Agreement between Adolf Hitler and President Emile Hácha of Czechoslovakia, 15 March 1939

President Eduard Beneš of Czechoslovakia resigned after the Munich crisis, to be replaced by the inexperienced Emile Hácha. Early in 1939, Adolf Hitler began to allege that Bohemia and Moravia, those portions of the Czech state that had escaped German annexation six months earlier at Munich, were in great disorder, since ethnic Germans were suffering intense persecution, and the Czech government could not prevent this. Germany therefore offered to take charge of these areas. Facing threats from Hitler that the German air force would bomb Prague, Hácha capitulated and allowed German troops to invade Bohemia and Moravia, which then became a German protectorate for the next six years.

The Führer and Reichskanzler to-day received in Berlin, at their own request, the President of the Czechoslovak State, Dr. Hácha, and the Czechoslovak Foreign Minister, Dr. Chvalkovský, in the presence of Herr von Ribbentrop, the Reich Foreign Minister. At this meeting the serious situation which had arisen, in consequence of the events of recent weeks, within the territory which had hitherto formed part of Czechoslovakia, was subjected to a completely frank examination. The conviction was unanimously expressed on both sides that the object of all their efforts must be to assure quiet, order and peace in this part of Central Europe. The President of the Czechoslovak State declared that, in order to serve this end and to reach a final pacification, he confidently placed the fate of the Czech people and of their country in the hands of the Führer of the German Reich. The Führer accepted this declaration and expressed his determination to take the Czech people under the protection of the German Reich and to assure to them the autonomous development of their national life in accordance with their special characteristics.

In witness whereof this document is signed in duplicate.
Berlin, 15 March 1939
(Signed) *ADOLF HITLER*
DR. HÁCHA
HERR VON RIBBENTROP
DR. CHVALKOVSKÝ

Source: Arnold J. Toynbee, *Documents on International Affairs 1939–1946, Volume I: March–September 1939* (London: Oxford University Press, 1951), 56. Reprinted with permission of Chatham House.

31. The Western Guarantee of Polish Independence: British Prime Minister Neville Chamberlain, Statement in the House of Commons, 31 March 1939

The German assumption in March 1939 of a protectorate over the remainder of Czechoslovakia, a move that effectively amounted to annexation of that country and also contravened the agreement reached at Munich six months earlier, finally impelled the Western powers to take a decisive stand against Germany. Speaking in the House of Commons, the British prime minister announced that both Britain and France had undertaken to guarantee Poland's security against outside aggression. Since Poland was known to be Germany's next contemplated target, if neither side backed down, this pledge was likely to precipitate war.

The Prime Minister (Mr. Chamberlain): The right hon. gentleman the leader of the Opposition asked me this morning whether I could make a statement as to the European situation. As I said this morning, His Majesty's Government have no official confirmation of the rumours of any projected attack on Poland and they must not, therefore, be taken as accepting them as true.

I am glad to take this opportunity of stating again the general policy of His Majesty's Government. They have constantly advocated the adjustment, by way of free negotiation between the parties concerned, of any differences that may arise between them. They consider that this is the natural and proper course where differences exist. In their opinion there should be no question incapable of solution by peaceful means, and they would see no justification for the substitution of force or threats of force for the method of negotiation.

As the House is aware, certain consultations are now proceeding with other Governments. In order to make perfectly clear the position of His Majesty's Government in the meantime before those consultations are concluded, I now have to inform the House that during that period, in the event of any action which clearly threatened Polish independence, and which the Polish Government accordingly considered it vital to resist with their national forces, His Majesty's Government would feel themselves bound at once to lend the Polish Government all support in their power. They have given the Polish Government an assurance to this effect.

I may add that the French Government have authorised me to make it plain that they stand in the same position in this matter as do His Majesty's Government.

Source: Great Britain, *Documents Concerning German-Polish Relations and the Outbreak of Hostilities between Great Britain and Germany on September 3, 1939.* Presented by the Secretary of State for Foreign Affairs to Parliament by Command of His Majesty, Misc. No. 9 (1939), Cmd. 6106 (London: His Majesty's Stationery Office, 1939), 36.

32. Adolf Hitler, Directive for "Operation WHITE," the Attack on Poland, 11 April 1939

In response to Adolf Hitler's pressure on Poland to cede the Danzig corridor to Germany, in March 1939, Great Britain and France gave Poland a guarantee that, should Poland be attacked, both nations would respond by declaring war on its aggressor. Believing that this action meant that Poland would not yield without war, in April, an infuriated Hitler issued a military directive that his armed forces should prepare themselves to attack Poland any time after 1 September 1939.

The present attitude of Poland requires, over and above the plan "Frontier Security East," the initiation of military preparations, to remove if necessary any threat from this direction for ever.

1.) *Political Requirements and Aims*
German relations with Poland continue to be based on the principles of avoiding any disturbances. Should Poland, however, change her policy towards Germany, which so far has been based on the same principles as our own, and adopt a threatening attitude towards Germany, a final settlement might become necessary in spite of the Treaty in force with Poland.

The aim will then be to destroy Polish military strength, and create in the East a situation which will satisfy the requirements of national defence. The Free State of Danzig will be proclaimed a part of the Reich territory at the outbreak of hostilities, at the latest.

The political leaders consider it their task in this case to isolate Poland if possible, that is to say, to limit the war to Poland only.

The development of increasing internal crises in France and resulting British restraint might produce such a situation in the not too distant future.

Intervention by Russia, if she were in a position to intervene, cannot be expected to be of any use to Poland, because this would mean Poland's destruction by Bolshevism.

The attitude of the Baltic States will be determined wholly by German military superiority. (In the course of further developments it may become necessary to occupy the Baltic states up to the border of the former Courland and to incorporate them in the Reich.)

Germany cannot count on Hungary as a certain ally. Italy's attitude is determined by the Rome-Berlin Axis.

2.) *Military Conclusions*
The great objections in the reconstruction of the German Wehrmacht will continue to be determined by the antagonism of the Western Democracies. "Operation WHITE" constitutes only a precautionary complement to these preparations. It is not to be looked upon in any way, however, as the necessary prerequisite for a military conflict with the Western opponents.

The isolation of Poland will be all the more easily maintained, even after the outbreak of hostilities, if we succeed in starting the war with sudden, heavy blows and in gaining rapid successes.

The overall situation will require, however, that in all cases precautions be taken to safeguard the western frontier and the German North Sea coast, as well as the air above them.

Against the Baltic States—Lithuania in particular—security measures are to be carried out in case of a Polish march through this country.

3.) *Tasks of the Wehrmacht*
The task of the Wehrmacht is to destroy the Polish Armed

Forces. To this end a surprise attack is to be aimed at and prepared. Camouflaged or open general mobilization will not be ordered earlier than the day before the attack and at the latest possible moment. The forces provided for "Frontier Security West" (section I, "Frontier Security") must not be employed for the time being for any other purpose.

All other frontiers are to be kept under observation only; the Lithuanian frontier is to be covered.

Source: J. Noakes and G. Pridham, eds., *Nazism 1919–1945: A Documentary Reader,* Volume 3: *Foreign Policy, War and Racial Extermination* (Exeter, UK: University of Exeter Press, 1988), 127–128.

33. Albert Einstein to President Franklin D. Roosevelt, 2 August 1939

Even before Germany was formally at war with the Allies, anti-Nazi scientists were well aware of the possibility that Germany might develop an atomic bomb. Albert Einstein, the renowned German physicist who had developed the theory of relativity, a man whose Jewish origins had forced him to flee to the United States, wrote to President Franklin D. Roosevelt on the subject. He urged that the United States should attempt to buy up international uranium stocks and encourage its scientists to develop atomic weapons before the Nazi regime succeeded in doing so. Roosevelt responded positively and quickly to Einstein's exhortations.

Some recent work by E. Fermi and L. Szilard, which has been communicated to me in manuscript, leads me to expect that the element uranium may be turned into a new and important source of energy in the immediate future. Certain aspects of the situation which has arisen seem to call for watchfulness and if necessary, quick action on the part of the Administration. I believe therefore that it is my duty to bring to your attention the following facts and recommendations.

In the course of the last four months it has been made probable through the work of Joliot in France as well as Fermi and Szilard in America that it may be possible to set up a nuclear chain reaction in a large mass of uranium, by which vast amounts of power and large quantities of new radium-like elements would be generated. Now it appears almost certain that this could be achieved in the immediate future.

This new phenomenon would also lead to the construction of bombs, and it is conceivable—though much less certain—that extremely powerful bombs of this type may thus be constructed. A single bomb of this type, carried by boat and exploded in a port, might very well destroy the whole port together with some of the surrounding territory. However, such bombs might very well prove too heavy for transportation by air.

The United States has only very poor ores of uranium in moderate quantities. There is some good ore in Canada and former Czechoslovakia, while the most important source of uranium is in the Belgian Congo.

In view of this situation you may think it desirable to have some permanent contact maintained between the Administration and the group of physicists working on chain reactions in America. One possible way of achieving this might be for you to entrust the task with a person who has your confidence and who could perhaps serve in an unofficial capacity. His task might comprise the following:

a) to approach Government Departments, keep them informed of the further development, and put forward recommendations for Government action, giving particular attention to the problem of securing a supply of uranium ore for the United States.

b) to speed up the experimental work, which is at present being carried on within the limits of the budgets of University laboratories, by providing funds, if such funds be required, through his contacts with private persons who are willing to make contributions for this cause, and perhaps also by obtaining co-operation of industrial laboratories which have necessary equipment.

I understand that Germany has actually stopped the sale of uranium from the Czechoslovakian mines which she has taken over. That she should have taken such early action might perhaps be understood on the ground that the son of the German Under-Secretary of State, von Weizsacker, is attached to the Kaiser-Wilhelm Institute in Berlin, where some of the American work on uranium is now being repeated.

Source: Web site: PBS: American Experience. Available at http://www.pbs.org/wgbh/amex/truman/psources/ps. Reprinted with permission of Israeli Archives and Princeton University Press.

34. British Prime Minister Neville Chamberlain to Adolf Hitler, 22 August 1939

As German troops moved to threaten Poland, and Adolf Hitler alleged Polish mistreatment of German minorities, the British prime minister wrote to Hitler. He warned that whatever Hitler might believe, Great Britain would regard it as a casus belli should Germany invade or declare war on Poland.

Your Excellency will have already heard of certain measures taken by His Majesty's Government, and announced in the press and on the wireless this evening.

These steps have, in the opinion of His Majesty's Government, been rendered necessary by the military movements which have been reported from Germany, and by the fact that apparently the announcement of a German-Soviet Agreement is taken in some quarters in Berlin to indicate that intervention by Great Britain on behalf of Poland is no longer a contingency that need be reckoned with. No greater mistake could be made. Whatever may prove to be the nature of the German-Soviet Agreement, it cannot alter Great Britain's obligation to Poland which His Majesty's Government have stated in public repeatedly and plainly, and which they are determined to fulfil.

It has been alleged that, if His Majesty's Government had made their position more clear in 1914, the great catastrophe would have been avoided. Whether or not there is any force in that allegation, His Majesty's Government are resolved that on this occasion there shall be no such tragic misunderstanding.

If the case should arise, they are resolved, and prepared, to employ without delay all the forces at their command, and it is impossible to foresee the end of hostilities once engaged. It would be a dangerous illusion to think that, if war once starts, it will come to an early end even if a success on any one of the several fronts on which it will be engaged should have been secured.

Having thus made our position perfectly clear, I wish to repeat to you my conviction that war between our two peoples would be the greatest calamity that could occur. I am certain that it is desired neither by our people, nor by yours, and I cannot see that there is anything in the questions arising between Germany and Poland which could not and should not be resolved without the use of force, if only a situation of confidence could be restored to enable discussions to be carried on in an atmosphere different from that which prevails to-day.

We have been, and at all times will be, ready to assist in creating conditions in which such negotiations could take place, and in which it might be possible concurrently to discuss the wider problems affecting the future of international relations, including matters of interest to us and to you.

The difficulties in the way of any peaceful discussion in the present state of tension are, however, obvious, and the longer that tension is maintained, the harder will it be for reason to prevail.

These difficulties, however, might be mitigated, if not removed, provided that there could for an initial period be a truce on both sides—and indeed on all sides—to press polemics and to all incitement.

If such a truce could be arranged, then, at the end of that period, during which steps could be taken to examine and deal with complaints made by either side as to the treatment of minorities, it is reasonable to hope that suitable conditions might have been established for direct negotiations between Germany and Poland upon the issues between them (with the aid of a neutral intermediary, if both sides should think that that would be helpful).

But I am bound to say that there would be slender hope of bringing such negotiations to successful issue unless it were understood beforehand that any settlement reached would, when concluded, be guaranteed by other Powers. His Majesty's Government would be ready, if desired, to make such contribution as they could to the effective operation of such guarantees.

At this moment I confess I can see no other way to avoid a catastrophe that will involve Europe in war.

In view of the grave consequences to humanity, which may follow from the action of their rulers, I trust that Your Excellency will weigh with the utmost deliberation the considerations which I have put before you.

Source: Web site: The Avalon Project at the Yale Law School. Available at http://www.yale.edu/lawweb/avalon/wwii/bluebook/blbk56.htm.

35. The Nazi-Soviet Non-Aggression Pact, Protocols, and Clarifications, 23 August 1939–10 January 1941

On 23 August 1939 Count Joachim von Ribbentrop, the German foreign minister, and V. M. Molotov, his Soviet counterpart, signed a nonaggression pact between their two countries, together with several secret protocols delineating the Soviet and German spheres of influence in Eastern Europe and the Baltic republics, including an understanding on the partitioning of Poland between the two signatory powers. Under the agreement, the Soviet Union also provided appreciable quantities of valuable war supplies to Germany. These agreements were subjected to further clarifications on 28 August 1939, 28 September 1939, and, in one case, also on 10 January 1941. They paved the way for Hitler to invade Poland one week later, the event that, in turn, impelled Great Britain and France to declare war on Germany, the beginning of general war in Europe.

Non-Aggression Pact between Germany and the Union of Soviet Socialist Republics, 23 August 1939

The Government of the German Reich and the Government of the Union of Soviet Socialist Republics, guided by the desire to strengthen the cause of peace between Germany and the Union of Soviet Socialist Republics, and taking as a basis the fundamental regulations of the Neutrality Agreement concluded in April 1926 between Germany and the Union of Soviet Socialist Republics, have reached the following agreement:

Article 1. The two Contracting Parties bind themselves to refrain from any act of force, any aggressive action and any attack on one another, both singly and also jointly with other Powers.

Article 2. In the event of one of the Contracting Parties becoming the object of warlike action on the part of a third Power, the other Contracting Party shall in no manner support this third Power.

Article 3. The Governments of the two Contracting Parties shall in future remain continuously in touch with one another, by way of consultation, in order to inform one another on questions touching their joint interests.

Article 4. Neither of the two Contracting Parties shall participate in any grouping of Powers which is directed directly or indirectly against the other Party.

Article 5. In the event of disputes or disagreements arising between the Contracting Parties on questions of this or that kind, both Parties would clarify these disputes or disagreements exclusively by means of friendly exchange of opinion or, if necessary, by arbitration committees.

Article 6. The present Agreement shall be concluded for a period of ten years on the understanding that, insofar as one of the Contracting Parties does not give notice of termination one year before the end of this period, the period of validity of this Agreement shall automatically be regarded as prolonged for a further period of five years.

Article 7. The present Agreement shall be ratified within the shortest possible time. The instruments of ratification shall be exchanged in Berlin. The Agreement takes effect immediately after it has been signed.

Source: U.S. Department of State, *Nazi-Soviet Relations 1939–1941: Documents from the Archives of the German Foreign Office,* eds. Raymond James Sontag and James Stuart Beddie (Washington, DC: U.S. Government Printing Office, 1948), 76–78, 105–107.

Secret Supplementary Protocol on the Border of the Spheres of Interest of Germany and the USSR, signed by V. M. Molotov and Joachim von Ribbentrop, 23 August 1939

In signing the nonaggression pact between Germany and the Union of Soviet Socialist Republics, the undersigned plenipotentiaries of the two sides discussed in strict confidentiality the issue of delimiting the spheres of mutual interest in Eastern Europe. This discussion led to the following result:

1. In the event of territorial-political reorganization of the districts making up the Baltic states (Finland, Estonia, Latvia, Lithuania), the northern border of Lithuania is simultaneously the border of the spheres of interest of Germany and the USSR. The interests of Lithuania with respect to the Vilnius district are recognized by both sides.

2. In the event of territorial-political reorganization of

the districts making up the Polish Republic, the border of the spheres of interest of Germany and the USSR will run approximately along the Pisa, Narew, Vistula, and San rivers.

The question of whether it is in the signatories' mutual interest to preserve the independent Polish State and what the borders of that state will be can be ascertained conclusively only in the course of future political development.

In any event, both governments will resolve this matter through friendly mutual agreement.

3. Concerning southeastern Europe, the Soviet side emphasizes the interest of the USSR in Bessarabia. The German side declares its complete political disinterest in these areas.

4. This protocol will be held in strict secrecy by both sides.

Source: U.S. Department of State, *Nazi-Soviet Relations 1939–1941: Documents from the Archives of the German Foreign Office,* eds. Raymond James Sontag and James Stuart Beddie (Washington, DC: U.S. Government Printing Office, 1948), 76–78, 105–107.

Clarification of the Secret Supplementary Protocol of 23 August 1939, signed in Moscow by V. M. Molotov and Count F. W. Schulenburg, 28 August 1939

In order to clarify the first paragraph of point 2 of the "Secret Supplementary Protocol" of 23 August 1939, this is to explain that said paragraph is to be read in the following final version, namely:

"2. In the event of the territorial-political reorganization of the districts making up the Polish State, the border of the spheres of interest of Germany and the USSR will run approximately along the Pisa, Narew, Vistula, and San rivers."

Source: U.S. Department of State, *Nazi-Soviet Relations 1939–1941: Documents from the Archives of the German Foreign Office,* eds. Raymond James Sontag and James Stuart Beddie (Washington, DC: U.S. Government Printing Office, 1948), 76–78, 105–107.

Confidential Protocol Concerning the Possibility of Resettling the Population Residing within the Spheres of Interest of the Governments of the USSR and Germany, signed by V. M. Molotov and Joachim von Ribbentrop, 28 September 1939

The Government of the USSR will not impede German citizens or other persons of German ancestry residing within its spheres of interest should they desire to move to Germany or to German spheres of interest. It agrees that this resettlement will be conducted by persons authorized by the Ger-

man Government in accordance with responsible local authorities and that in the process the property rights of the resettled persons will not be infringed.

The German Government assumes the same obligation with respect to persons of Ukrainian or Belorussian ancestry residing within its spheres of interest.

Source: U.S. Department of State, *Nazi-Soviet Relations 1939–1941: Documents from the Archives of the German Foreign Office,* eds. Raymond James Sontag and James Stuart Beddie (Washington, DC: U.S. Government Printing Office, 1948), 76–78, 105–107.

Secret Supplementary Protocol on Changing the Soviet-German Agreement of 23 August Concerning the Spheres of Interest of Germany and the USSR, signed by V. M. Molotov and Joachim von Ribbentrop, 28 September 1939

The undersigned plenipotentiaries state the concurrence of the German Government and the Government of the USSR in the following:

Point 1 of the secret supplementary protocol signed on 23 August 1939 is changed so that the territory of the Lithuanian state is included in the sphere of interest of the USSR because, on the other side, Lublin voivodeship and parts of Warsaw voivodeship are included in the sphere of interest of Germany (see map accompanying the Treaty on Friendship and the Border between the USSR and Germany, signed today). As soon as the Government of the USSR takes special measures on Lithuanian territory to protect its interests, the present German-Lithuanian border, with the objective of making it a natural and simple border, will be adjusted so that the Lithuanian territory that lies southwest of the line shown on the map goes to Germany.

It is further stated that economic agreements between Germany and Lithuania now in force must not be broken by the aforementioned measures by the Soviet Union.

Source: U.S. Department of State, *Nazi-Soviet Relations 1939–1941: Documents from the Archives of the German Foreign Office,* eds. Raymond James Sontag and James Stuart Beddie (Washington, DC: U.S. Government Printing Office, 1948), 76–78, 105–107.

Secret Supplementary Protocol on Preventing Polish Agitation on the Territory of the Other Treaty Signatory, signed by V. M. Molotov and Joachim von Ribbentrop, 28 September 1939

The undersigned plenipotentiaries, in concluding the Soviet-German treaty on the border and friendship, have stated their concurrence in the following:

Neither side will permit on their territories any sort of Polish agitation affecting the territory of the other country. They will abort such agitation on their own territories and will inform each other as to effective measures to accomplish this.

Source: U.S. Department of State, *Nazi-Soviet Relations 1939–1941: Documents from the Archives of the German Foreign Office,* eds. Raymond James Sontag and James Stuart Beddie (Washington, DC: U.S. Government Printing Office, 1948), 76–78, 105–107.

Secret Protocol of 10 January 1941, Clarifying the Agreements of August 1939

The Chairman of the Council of People's Commissars of the USSR V. M. Molotov, with the authorization of the Government of the USSR on one side, and German Ambassador Count von der Schulenburg, with the authorization of the Government of Germany on the other side, have concurred on the following:

1. The government of Germany renounces its claims to the part of the territory of Lithuania indicated in the Secret Supplementary Protocol of September 28, 1939, and shown on the map that is attached to this Protocol.
2. The Government of the USSR agrees to compensate the Government of Germany for the territory indicated in point 1 of the present Protocol with a payment to Germany in the amount of 7,500,000 gold dollars, the equivalent of 31,500,000 German marks.

Payment of the sum of 31.5 million German marks will be made as follows: one-eighth, i.e., 3,937,500 German marks, in deliveries of nonferrous metals over a three-month period beginning from the day of signing of the present Protocol, and the remaining seven-eighths, i.e., 27,562,500 German marks, in gold through deductions from German payments of gold that the German side has to make before February 11, 1941, based on an exchange of letters between the People's Commissar of Foreign Trade of the USSR A. I. Mikoyan and the Chairman of the German Economic Delegation Mr. Schnurre that took place in conjunction with the signing of the "Agreement of January l0, 1941, on Mutual Deliveries of Commodities for the Second Treaty Period according to the Economic Agreement of February 11, 1940, between the USSR and Germany."

3. The present Protocol . . . comes into force immediately upon signing.

Source: U.S. Department of State, *Nazi-Soviet Relations 1939–1941: Documents from the Archives of the German Foreign Office,* eds. Raymond James Sontag and James Stuart Beddie (Washington, DC: U.S. Government Printing Office, 1948), 76–78, 105–107.

36. President Franklin D. Roosevelt, Telegram to the Chancellor of Germany (Hitler), 24 August 1939

Despite Adolf Hitler's rejection of his earlier pleas for peace, as it seemed ever more likely that Great Britain and France would declare war on Germany over Poland, President Franklin D. Roosevelt appealed once more to the German chancellor to reach a negotiated settlement acceptable to the Western democracies. He also sent a message to the president of Poland, urging that he conclude a negotiated settlement with Germany, and one to King Victor Emmanuel of Italy, asking the latter to act as a mediator in the dispute. When President Ignacy Mościcki of Poland replied noncommittally the next day, Roosevelt was sufficiently encouraged to press negotiations once more upon Hitler, who remained unresponsive to all his suggestions.

In the message which I sent to you on last April 14 I stated that it appeared to me that the leaders of great nations had it in their power to liberate their peoples from the disaster that impended, but that unless the effort were immediately made with good will on all sides to find a peaceful and constructive solution of existing controversies, the crisis which the world was confronting must end in catastrophe. Today that catastrophe appears to be very near at hand indeed.

To the message which I sent to you last April I have received no reply, but because of my confident belief that the cause of world peace—which is the cause of humanity itself—rises above all other considerations, I am again addressing myself to you with the hope that the war which impends and the consequent disaster to all peoples everywhere may yet be averted.

I therefore urge with all earnestness—and I am likewise urging the President of the Republic of Poland—that the Governments of Germany and of Poland agree by common accord to refrain from any positive act of hostility for a reasonable and stipulated period, and that they agree likewise by common accord to solve the controversies which have arisen between them by one of the three following methods: first, by direct negotiation; second, by submission of these controversies to an impartial arbitration in which they can both have confidence; or, third, that they agree to the solution of these controversies through the procedure of conciliation, selecting as conciliator or moderator a national of one of the traditionally neutral states of Europe, or a national of one of the American republics which are all of them free from any connection with or participation in European political affairs.

Both Poland and Germany being sovereign governments, it is understood, of course, that upon resort to any one of the alternatives I suggest, each nation will agree to accord complete respect to the independence and territorial integrity of the other.

The people of the United States are as one in their opposition to policies of military conquest and domination. They are as one in rejecting the thesis that any ruler, or any people, possess the right to achieve their ends or objectives through the taking of action which will plunge countless millions of people into war and which will bring distress and suffering to every nation of the world, belligerent and neutral, when such ends and objectives, so far as they are just and reasonable, can be satisfied through processes of peaceful negotiation or by resort to judicial arbitration.

I appeal to you in the name of the people of the United States, and I believe in the name of peace-loving men and women everywhere, to agree to the solution of the controversies existing between your Government and that of Poland through the adoption of one of the alternative methods I have proposed. I need hardly reiterate that should the Governments of Germany and of Poland be willing to solve their differences in the peaceful manner suggested, the Government of the United States still stands prepared to contribute its share to the solution of the problems which are endangering world peace in the form set forth in my message of April 14.

FRANKLIN D. ROOSEVELT

Source: U.S. Department of State, Publication 1983, *Peace and War: United States Foreign Policy, 1931–1941* (Washington, DC: U.S. Government Printing Office, 1943), 476–477.

37. Agreement of Mutual Assistance between the United Kingdom and Poland, London, 25 August 1939

On 25 August, Great Britain and Poland signed a formal agreement of mutual assistance. In practice, the military support Britain could provide Poland against German attack was extremely limited. The agreement nonetheless bound Britain to go to war with any power that should attack Poland, a commitment that could easily precipitate a broad European war.

The Government of the United Kingdom of Great Britain and Northern Ireland and the Polish Government:

Desiring to place on a permanent basis the collaboration between their respective countries resulting from the assurances of mutual assistance of a defensive character which they have already exchanged:

Have resolved to conclude an Agreement for that purpose and have appointed as their Plenipotentiaries:

The Government of the United Kingdom of Great Britain and Northern Ireland:

The Rt. Hon. Viscount Halifax, K.G., G.C.S.I., G.C.I.E., Principal Secretary of State for Foreign Affairs;

The Polish Government:

His Excellency Count Edward Raczynski, Ambassador Extraordinary and Plenipotentiary of the Polish Republic in London;

Who, having exchanged their Full Powers, found in good and due form, have agreed [to the] following provisions:

ARTICLE I.

Should one of the Contracting Parties become engaged in hostilities with a European Power in consequence of aggression by the latter against that Contracting Party, the other Contracting Party will at once give the Contracting Party engaged in hostilities all the support and assistance in its power.

ARTICLE 2.

(1) The provisions of Article I will also apply in the event of any action by a European Power which clearly threatened, directly or indirectly, the independence of one of the Contracting Parties, and was of such a nature that the Party in question considered it vital to resist it with its armed forces.

(2) Should one of the Contracting Parties become engaged in hostilities with a European Power in consequence of action by that Power which threatened the

independence or neutrality of another European State in such a way as to constitute a clear menace to the security of that Contracting Party, the provisions of Article I will apply, without prejudice, however, to the rights of the other European State concerned.

ARTICLE 3.

Should a European Power attempt to undermine the independence of one of the Contracting Parties by processes of economic penetration or in any other way, the Contracting Parties will support each other in resistance to such attempts. Should the European Power concerned thereupon embark on hostilities against one of the Contracting Parties, the provisions of Article I will apply.

ARTICLE 4.

The methods of applying the undertakings of mutual assistance provided for by the present Agreement are established between the competent naval, military and air authorities of the Contracting Parties.

ARTICLE 5.

Without prejudice to the foregoing undertakings of the Contracting Parties to give each other mutual support and assistance immediately on the outbreak of hostilities, they will exchange complete and speedy information concerning any development which might threaten their independence and, in particular, concerning any development which threatened to call the said undertakings into operation.

ARTICLE 6.

(1) The Contracting Parties will communicate to each other the terms of any undertakings of assistance against aggression which they have already given or may in future give to other States.

(2) Should either of the Contracting Parties intend to give such an undertaking after the coming into force of the present Agreement, the other Contracting Party shall, in order to ensure the proper functioning of the Agreement, be informed thereof.

(3) Any new undertaking which the Contracting Parties may enter into in future shall neither limit their obligations under the present Agreement nor indirectly create new obligations between the Contracting Party not participating in these undertakings and the third State concerned.

ARTICLE 7.

Should the Contracting Parties be engaged in hostilities in consequence of the application of the present Agreement, they will not conclude an armistice or treaty of peace except by mutual agreement.

ARTICLE 8.

(1) The present Agreement shall remain in force for a period of five years.

(2) Unless denounced six months before the expiry of this period it shall continue in force, each Contracting Party having thereafter the right to denounce it at any time by giving six months' notice to that effect.

(3) The present Agreement shall come into force on signature.

Source: Web site: The Avalon Project at the Yale Law School. Available at http://www.yale.edu/lawweb/avalon/wwii/bluebook/blbk19.htm.

38. Benito Mussolini to Adolf Hitler, 25 August 1939

In late August, Adolf Hitler wrote to Italian dictator Benito Mussolini explaining that he intended to invade Poland even if it meant war with Britain and France. Mussolini replied immediately assuring Hitler of his sympathy but warning that, if other powers declared war on Germany over Poland, Italy was unlikely to come to Germany's assistance.

FÜHRER: I am replying to your letter which has just been delivered to me by Ambassador von Mackersen.

(1) Concerning the agreement with Russia, I approve of that completely. His Excellency Marshal Göring will tell you that in the discussion which I had with him last April I stated that a rapprochement between Germany and Russia was necessary to prevent encirclement by the democracies.

(2) I consider it desirable to try to avoid a break or any deterioration in relations with Japan, since that would result in Japan's return to a position close to the democratic powers. With this in mind, I have telegraphed to Tokyo and it appears that after the first surprise of public opinion passed, a better psychological attitude prevails.

(3) The Moscow treaty blockades Rumania and can alter the position of Turkey, which accepted the English

loan, but which has not yet signed the treaty of alliance. A new attitude on the part of Turkey would upset all the strategic plans of the French and English in the Eastern Mediterranean.

(4) As regards Poland I have complete understanding for the German position and for the fact that such strained relations cannot continue permanently.

(5) As for the practical position of Italy, in case of a military collision, my point of view is as follows:

If Germany attacks Poland and the conflict remains localized, Italy will afford Germany every form of political and economic assistance which is requested.

If Germany attacks, and Poland's allies open a counterattack against Germany, I want to let you know in advance that it would be better if I did not take the initiative in military activities in view of the present situation of Italian war preparations, which we have repeatedly previously explained to you, Führer, and to Herr von Ribbentrop.

Our intervention can, therefore, take place at once if Germany delivers to us immediately the military supplies and the raw materials to resist the attack which the French and English especially would direct against us.

At our meetings the war was envisaged for after 1942 and at such time I would have been ready on land, on sea, and in the air according to the plans which had been arranged.

I am also of the opinion that the purely military preparations which have already been undertaken and the others which will be entered upon in Europe and Africa will serve to immobilize important French and British forces.

I consider it my implicit duty as a true friend to tell you the whole truth and inform you about the actual situation in advance. Not to do so might have unpleasant consequences for us all. This is my point of view and since within a short time I must summon the highest governmental bodies of the realm, I ask you to let me know yours as well.

MUSSOLINI

Source: Web site: The Avalon Project at the Yale Law School. Available at http://www.yale.edu/lawweb/avalon/nazsov/ns058.htm.

39. Message Communicated to H.M. Ambassador in Berlin (Sir Nevile Henderson) by the State Secretary for Foreign Affairs (Joachim von Ribbentrop) on 31 August 1939, at 9:15 P.M.

Throughout late August, negotiations between Great Britain and Germany continued, serving, if nothing else, as a convenient smokescreen for Germany's military preparations to invade Poland. On the evening of 31 August, the German government informed the British government that Polish officials had refused to enter into the negotiations with Germany proposed by the British government. Germany once more stated its demands for Danzig and the Polish Corridor. Later that evening, the Polish government indicated its willingness to consider entering into direct talks with Germany, but by this time German troops had already been ordered to invade Poland.

His Majesty's Government informed the German Government, in a note dated the 28th August, 1939, of their readiness to offer their mediation towards direct negotiations between Germany and Poland over the problems in dispute. In so doing they made it abundantly clear that they, too, were aware of the urgent need for progress in view of the continuous incidents and the general European tension. In a reply dated the 28th August, the German Government, in spite of being sceptical as to the desire of the Polish Government to come to an understanding, declared themselves ready in the interests of peace to accept the British mediation or suggestion. After considering all the circumstances prevailing at the time, they considered it necessary in their note to point out that, if the danger of a catastrophe was to be avoided, then action must be taken readily and without delay. In this sense they declared themselves ready to receive a personage appointed by the Polish Government up to the evening of the 30th August, with the proviso that the latter was, in fact, empowered not only to discuss but to conduct and conclude negotiations.

Further, the German Government pointed out that they felt able to make the basic points regarding the offer of an understanding available to the British Government by the time the Polish negotiator arrived in Berlin.

Instead of a statement regarding the arrival of an authorised Polish personage, the first answer the Government of the Reich received to their readiness for an understanding was the news of the Polish mobilisation, and only towards 12 o'clock on the night of the 30th August, 1939, did they receive a somewhat general assurance of British readiness to help towards the commencement of negotiations.

Although the fact that the Polish negotiator expected by the Government of the Reich did not arrive removed the necessary condition for informing His Majesty's Government of the views of the German Government as regards possible bases of negotiation, since His Majesty's Government themselves had pleaded for direct negotiations between Germany and Poland, the German Minister for Foreign Affairs, Herr von Ribbentrop, gave the British Ambassador on the occasion of the presentation of the last British note precise information as to the text of the German proposals which would be regarded as a basis of negotiation in the event of the arrival of the Polish plenipotentiary.

The Government of the German Reich considered themselves entitled to claim that in these circumstances a Polish personage would immediately be nominated, at any rate retroactively.

For the Reich Government cannot be expected for their part continually not only to emphasise their willingness to start negotiations, but actually to be ready to do so, while being from the Polish side merely put off with empty subterfuges and meaningless declarations.

It has once more been made clear as a result of a démarche which has meanwhile been made by the Polish Ambassador that the latter himself has no plenary powers either to enter into any discussion, or even to negotiate.

The Führer and the German Government have thus waited two days in vain for the arrival of a Polish negotiator with plenary powers.

In these circumstances the German Government regard their proposals as having this time too been to all intents and purposes rejected, although they consider that these proposals, in the form in which they were made known to the British Government also, were more than loyal, fair and practicable.

The Reich Government consider it timely to inform the public of the bases for negotiation which were communicated to the British Ambassador by the Minister for Foreign Affairs, Herr von Ribbentrop.

The situation existing between the German Reich and Poland is at the moment of such a kind that any further incident can lead to an explosion on the part of the military forces which have taken up their position on both sides. Any peaceful solution must be framed in such a way as to ensure that the events which lie at the root of this situation cannot be repeated on the next occasion offered, and that thus not only the East of Europe, but also other territories shall not be brought into such a state of tension. The causes of this development lie in: (1) the impossible delineation of frontiers, as fixed by the Versailles dictate; (2) the impossible treatment of the minority in the ceded territories.

In making these proposals, the Reich Government are, therefore, actuated by the idea of finding a lasting solution which will remove the impossible situation created by frontier delineation, which may assure to both parties their vitally important line of communication, which may—as far as it is at all possible—remove the minority problem and, in so far as this is not possible, may give the minorities the assurance of a tolerable future by means of a reliable guarantee of their rights.

The Reich Government are content that in so doing it is essential that economic and physical damage done since 1918 should be exposed and repaired in its entirety. They, of course, regard this obligation as being binding for both parties.

These considerations lead to the following practical proposals:

(1) The Free City of Danzig shall return to the German Reich in view of its purely German character, as well as of the unanimous will of its population;

(2) The territory of the so-called Corridor which extends from the Baltic Sea to the line Marienwerder-Graudenz-Kulm-Bromberg (inclusive) and thence may run in a westerly direction to Schönlanke, shall itself decide as to whether it shall belong to Germany or Poland;

(3) For this purpose a plebiscite shall take place in this territory. The following shall be entitled to vote: all Germans who were either domiciled in this territory on the 1st January, 1918, or who by that date have been born there, and similarly of Poles, Kashubes, &c., domiciled in this territory on the above day (the 1st January, 1918) or born there up to that date. The Germans who have been driven from this territory shall return to it in order to exercise their vote with a view to ensuring an objective plebiscite, and also with a view to ensuring the extensive preparation necessary therefor. The above territory shall, as in the case of the Saar territory, be placed under the supervision of an international commission to be formed immediately, on which shall be represented the four Great Powers—Italy, the Soviet Union, France and England. This commission shall exercise all the rights of sovereignty in this territory. With this end in view, the territory shall be evacuated within a period of the utmost brevity, still to be agreed upon, by the Polish armed forces, the Polish police, and the Polish authorities;

(4) The Polish port of Gdynia, which fundamentally constitutes Polish sovereign territory so far as it is confined territorially to the Polish settlement, shall be excluded from the above territory. The exact frontiers of this Polish port should be determined between Germany and Poland, and, if necessary, delimited by an international committee of arbitration;

(5) With a view to assuring the necessary time for the execution of the extensive work involved in the carrying out of a just plebiscite, this plebiscite shall not take place before the expiry of twelve months;

(6) In order to guarantee unrestricted communication between Germany and East Prussia and between Poland and the sea during this period, roads and railways shall be established to render free transit traffic possible. In this connexion only such taxes as are necessary for the maintenance of the means of communication and for the provision of transport may be levied;

(7) The question as to the party to which the area belongs is to be decided by simple majority of the votes recorded;

(8) In order to guarantee to Germany free communication with her province of Danzig-East Prussia, and to Poland her connexion with the sea after the execution of the plebiscite—regardless of the results thereof—Germany shall, in the event of the plebiscite area going to Poland, receive an extra-territorial traffic zone, approximately in a line from Butow to Danzig or Dirschau, in which to lay down an autobahn and a 4-track railway line. The road and the railway shall be so constructed that the Polish lines of communication are not affected, i.e., they shall pass either over or under the latter. The breadth of this zone shall be fixed at 1 kilometre, and it is to be German sovereign territory. Should the plebiscite be favourable to Germany, Poland is to obtain rights, analogous to those accorded to Germany, to a similar extra-territorial communication by road and railway for the purpose of free and unrestricted communication with her port of Gdynia;

(9) In the event of the Corridor returning to the German Reich, the latter declares its right to proceed to an exchange of population with Poland to the extent to which the nature of the Corridor lends itself thereto;

(10) Any special rights desired by Poland in the port of Danzig would be negotiated on a basis of territory against similar rights to be granted to Germany in the port of Gdynia;

(11) In order to remove any feeling in this area that either side was being threatened, Danzig and Gdynia would have the character of exclusively mercantile towns, that is to say, without military installations and military fortifications;

(12) The peninsula of Hela, which as a result of the plebiscite might go either to Poland or to Germany, would in either case have similarly to be demilitarised;

(13) Since the Government of the German Reich has the most vehement complaints to make against the Polish treatment of minorities, and since the Polish Government for their part feel obliged to make complaints against Germany, both parties declare their agreement to have these complaints laid before an international committee of enquiry, whose task would be to examine all complaints as regards economic or physical damage, and any other acts of terrorism. Germany and Poland undertake to make good economic or other damage done to minorities on either side since the year 1918, or to cancel expropriation as the case may be, or to provide complete compensation to the persons affected for this and any other encroachments on their economic life;

(14) In order to free the Germans who may be left in Poland and the Poles who may be left in Germany from the feeling of being outlawed by all nations, and in order to render them secure against being called upon to perform actions or to render services incompatible with their national sentiments, Germany and Poland agree to guarantee the rights of both minorities by means of the most comprehensive and binding agreement, in order to guarantee to these minorities the preservation, the free development and practical application of their nationality (Volkstum), and in particular to permit for this purpose such organisation as they may consider necessary. Both parties undertake not to call upon members of the minority for military service;

(15) In the event of agreement on the basis of these proposals, Germany and Poland declare themselves ready to decree and to carry out the immediate demobilisation of their armed forces;

(16) The further measures necessary for the more rapid execution of the above arrangement shall be agreed upon by both Germany and Poland conjointly.

Source: Web site: The Avalon Project at the Yale Law School. Available at http://www.yale.edu/lawweb/avalon/wwii//bluebook/blbk98.htm.

40. Clare Hollingworth, The German Invasion of Poland, 30 August–1 September 1939

On 30 August 1939, Clare Hollingworth, who had just begun working for the British newspaper The Daily Telegraph, *beginning what would become a renowned career as a war correspondent, was staying with friends in Katowice, Poland, on the border with Germany. War was generally considered imminent. She decided to cross the frontier into Germany, borrowing the British Consul's official car for the purpose. During this brief day-trip Hollingworth saw German tanks massed on the border in readiness to attack Poland, and one night later, after she had returned to Katowice, the invasion began. Hollingworth became the first reporter to file a dispatch on the outbreak of the European war. In a book published in 1940 she described at greater length these events and her experiences.*

Clare Hollingworth on the German Invasion of Poland: Excerpts from *The Three Weeks' War in Poland* (1940)

Since all British correspondents had been expelled from Berlin some days before, I decided to have a look round in German Silesia. Katowice was too quiet for news. I crossed the frontier at Beuthen without trouble. (Though news of my crossing so upset the Polish Foreign Office that the British Embassy were required to vouch for me.) The German frontier town was nearly deserted. It was open to enfilading fire from Polish batteries, and the Germans evidently thought it prudent to evacuate civilians. Those who remained looked depressed and unhappy. I spoke to old acquaintances and found increased trust in Hitler, even among those who had been critical—but, linked with this, a refusal to believe in war.

"It won't come to that, liebes Fraülein, don't you worry. The Führer will get Germany her rights without war this time, just as he did before."

They told me stories of the "atrocities" committed by Poland against her German minority, and asked me if I had seen such things. I had not.

"Ah, you don't see them, but they happen every day. Why do you suppose our people come across the frontier to escape the Poles?" Then I learned an interesting thing. German "refugees" from Poland were not being allowed into the Reich. They were being kept for use on the frontier. We were to hear much of them before the end of the war.

I found a noticeable shortage of supplies in Beuthen. There was no soap for foreigners, while even for Germans it was strictly rationed. Aspirin itself, the German product par excellence, was unobtainable. A friendly butcher showed the meat ration, the weekly allowance for a family with two children; it was enough for three meals, I reckoned, and your German is no vegetarian. The family's tea ration would have made a good "mash" (as they say in the Midlands) for six English tea-drinkers; and the coffee, which tasted like burnt toast, and *was* burnt maize, could perhaps serve twelve. Oils and fats could be bought with a special permit only. Butter, cream and milk had been unobtainable for five weeks. I found it impossible to get meals in restaurants, and should have gone hungry, had not a waiter, well tipped in the past, produced a partridge from nowhere. What kind of victualling is this, I wondered, on which to begin a major war?

I drove along the fortified frontier road via Hindenburg (which in the nineteen-twenties the townsfolk voted to call "Leninburg") to Gleiwitz, which had become a military town. On the road were parties of motor-cycle despatch-riders, bunched together and riding hard. As we came over the little ridge into the town, sixty-five of them burst past us, each about ten yards behind the other. From the road I could see bodies of troops, and at the roadside hundreds of tanks, armoured cars and field guns stood or moved off toward the frontier. Here and there were screens of canvas or planking, concealing the big guns; they seemed not to be camouflaged against air-attack. I guessed that the German Command was preparing to strike to the north of Katowice and its fortified lines: the advance which was to reach Czestochowa in two days of war.

In the middle of all this I bought odd things—wine, electric torches—and drove back peacefully. Now and then a trooper would spot the Union Jack on my car and give a sudden, astonished gape. As we reached a length of road which lies parallel with the frontier, I looked across a hollow, some wire and tank-barricades, and watched the peasant-women moving about the Polish fields, a few hundred yards away. In the evening I returned to Poland, without trouble, the feverish preparations of the German military uppermost in my mind.

[The next day, Hollingworth learned that in her absence the Polish authorities had uncovered and, so they believed, squelched various plots by German-Polish nationals, activities in which the

German Consul was openly implicated, a fact that "showed me again that we stood on the edge of war." She nonetheless retired to bed, but was awoken in the early hours of 1 September 1939.]

Slam! Slam! . . . a noise like doors banging. I woke up. It could not be later than five in the morning. Next, the roar of airplanes and more doors banging. Running to the window I could pick out the planes, riding high, with the guns blowing smoke-rings below them. There was a long flash into the town park, another, another. Incendiary bombs? I wondered. As I opened my door I ran against the friends with whom I was staying, in their dressing-gowns.

"What is all this about?"

"We aren't sure. A big air-raid practice was announced for to-day. Or it may be something more. We are trying to reach Zoltaszek" (my old friend the Chief of Police). Just then the Polish maid appeared.

"Only Mrs. Zoltaszek is at home."

"Then ask her what's going on. Is this an air-raid practice? What does she know?" they pressed the girl. She spoke into the telephone for a moment and then turned, her eyes wide open.

"She . . . she says it's the beginning of war! . . ."

I grabbed the telephone, reached the *Telegraph* correspondent in Warsaw and told him my news. I heard later that he rang straight through to the Polish Foreign Office, who had had no word of the attack. The *Telegraph* was not only the first paper to hear that Poland was at war—it had, too, the odd privilege of informing the Polish Government itself.

I had arranged for a car to come on the first hint of alarm, but it did not arrive. We stood, drank coffee, walked about the rooms and waited; I was alternately cursing my driver and wondering whether the *Telegraph* would produce a Special Edition for my news. The war, as a tragic disaster, was not yet a reality. When my driver came at last, he met my fury with a pitying smile.

"It's only an air-raid practice," he said.

We ran down to the British Consulate, which I knew well. On our way I noticed smiles on the faces turned up to the sky. "Well," they seemed to be saying, "so this is the air-raid practice."

"But of course it's an air-raid practice, Herr Konsul," the Secretary of the Consulate was saying as I arrived. My own reaction, for the moment, was actual fear: fear that I had made the *gaffe* of my life by reporting a non-existent war.

However, official confirmation of the war came soon enough. At once the Secretary—one of the German minority, who had worked at the Consulate since its opening in 1920—burst into tears.

"This is the end of poor Germany," she wept.

Just then my sympathy with "poor Germany" was not all that it might have been.

Everyone at the Consulate was working furiously. Papers were being stuffed into the big, old-fashioned stoves until ashes fluffed under one's feet. The Consul was whipping round by telephone to ensure the departure of those British subjects who remained.

Source: Clare Hollingworth, *The Three Weeks' War in Poland* (London: Duckworth, 1940), 11–17. Courtesy Clare Hollingworth.

41. British Prime Minister Neville Chamberlain, Speech in the British House of Commons, 1 September 1939

British diplomats soon learned of the German invasion of Poland on the night of 31 August– 1 September 1939. On the morning of 1 September, the British and French governments delivered an ultimatum to Germany, stating that if German troops were not withdrawn within forty-eight hours, they would both declare war on Germany. Neville Chamberlain addressed the House of Commons, giving an account of the negotiations of the previous days, which made it clear that Hitler had throughout intended war with Poland.

. . . . Only last night the Polish Ambassador did see the German Foreign Secretary, Herr von Ribbentrop. Once again he expressed to him what, indeed, the Polish Government had already said publicly, that they were willing to negotiate with Germany about their disputes on an equal basis. What was the reply of the German Government? The reply was that without another word the German troops crossed the Polish frontier this morning at dawn and are since reported to be bombing open towns. [An Hon. Member: "Gas?"] In these circumstances there is only one course open to us. His Majesty's Ambassador in Berlin and the French Ambassador have been instructed to hand to the German Government the following document:

"Early this morning the German Chancellor issued a proclamation to the German Army which indicated clearly that he was about to attack Poland. Information which has reached His Majesty's Government in the United Kingdom and the French Government indicates that German troops have crossed the Polish frontier and that attacks upon Polish towns are proceeding. In these circumstances it appears to the Governments of the United Kingdom and France that by their action the German Government have created conditions, namely, an aggressive act of force against Poland threatening the independence of Poland, which call for the implementation by the Governments of the United Kingdom and France of the undertaking to Poland to come to her assistance. I am accordingly to inform your Excellency that unless the German Government are prepared to give His Majesty's Government satisfactory assurances that the German Government have suspended all aggressive action against Poland and are prepared promptly to withdraw their forces from Polish territory, His Majesty's Government in the United Kingdom will without hesitation fulfil their obligations to Poland."

[An Hon. Member: "Time limit?"] If a reply to this last warning is unfavourable, and I do not suggest that it is likely to be otherwise, His Majesty's Ambassador is instructed to ask for his passports. In that case we are ready. Yesterday, we took further steps towards the completion of our defensive preparations. This morning we ordered complete mobilisation of the whole of the Royal Navy, Army and Royal Air Force. We have also taken a number of other measures, both at home and abroad, which the House will not perhaps expect me to specify in detail. Briefly, they represent the final steps in accordance with prearranged plans. These last can be put into force rapidly, and are of such a nature that they can be deferred until war seems inevitable. Steps have also been taken under the powers conferred by the House last week to safeguard the position in regard to stocks of commodities of various kinds.

. . . . As regards the immediate man-power requirements, the Royal Navy, the Army and the Royal Air Force are in the fortunate position of having almost as many men as they can conveniently handle at this moment. There are, however, certain categories of service in which men are im-

mediately required, both for Military and Civil Defence. These will be announced in detail through the Press and the B.B.C. . . .

So much for the immediate present. Now we must look to the future. It is essential in the face of the tremendous task which confronts us, more especially in view of our past experiences in this matter, to organise our man-power this time upon as methodical, equitable and economical a basis as possible. We, therefore, propose immediately to introduce legislation directed to that end. A Bill will be laid before you which for all practical purposes will amount to an expansion of the Military Training Act. Under its operation all fit men between the ages of 18 and 41 will be rendered liable to military service if and when called upon. It is not intended at the outset that any considerable number of men other than those already liable shall be called up, and steps will be taken to ensure that the man-power essentially required by industry shall not be taken away. . . .

It now only remains for us to set our teeth and to enter upon this struggle, which we ourselves earnestly endeavoured to avoid, with determination to see it through to the end. We shall enter it with a clear conscience, with the support of the Dominions and the British Empire, and the moral approval of the greater part of the world. We have no quarrel with the German people, except that they allow themselves to be governed by a Nazi Government. As long as that Government exists and pursues the methods it has so persistently followed during the last two years, there will be no peace in Europe. We shall merely pass from one crisis to another, and see one country after another attacked by methods which have now become familiar to us in their sickening technique. We are resolved that these methods must come to an end. If out of the struggle we again re-establish in the world the rules of good faith and the renunciation of force, why, then even the sacrifices that will be entailed upon us will find their fullest justification.

Source: Web site: The Avalon Project at the Yale Law School. Available at http://www.yale.edu/lawweb/avalon/wwii/bluebook/blbk105.htm.

42. Telegram from the British Foreign Secretary to the British Ambassador at Berlin, 3 September 1939, 5 A.M.

Early in the morning of 3 September 1939, the British foreign secretary dispatched what was effectively an ultimatum to Germany. It stated that unless Germany ceased its military operations against Poland by 11 A.M. that day, Great Britain would consider itself at war with Germany.

Please seek interview with [German] Minister for Foreign Affairs at 9 A.M. today, Sunday, or, if he cannot see you then, arrange to convey at that time to representative of German Government the following communication:

"In the communication which I had the honour to make to you on 1st September I informed you, on the instructions of His Majesty's Principal Secretary of State for Foreign Affairs, that, unless the German Government were prepared to give His Majesty's Government in the United Kingdom satisfactory assurances that the German Government had suspended all aggressive action against Poland and were prepared promptly to withdraw their forces from Polish Territory, His Majesty's Government in the United Kingdom would, without hesitation, fulfill their obligations to Poland.

"Although this communication was made more than twenty-four hours ago, no reply has been received but German attacks upon Poland have been continued and intensified. I have accordingly the honour to inform you that, unless not later than 11 A.M., British Summer Time, today 3rd September, satisfactory assurances to the above effect have been given by the German Government and have reached His Majesty's Government in London, a state of war will exist between the two countries as from that hour."

If the assurance referred to in the above communication is received, you should inform me by any means at your disposal before 11 A.M. today 3rd September. If no such assurance is received here by 11 A.M., we shall inform the German representative that a state of war exists as from that hour.

Source: G. A. Kertesz, *Documents in the Political History of the European Continent 1815–1939* (Oxford, UK: Clarendon Press, 1968), 504.

43. German Reply to the British Ultimatum, 3 September 1939, 11:20 A.M.

Twenty minutes after the deadline of the British ultimatum expired, the German government issued its reply. As was anticipated, Germany refused to alter its policy toward Poland, which effectively meant that the two countries would shortly be at war.

The German Government have received the British Government's ultimatum of the 3rd September, 1939. They have the honour to reply as follows:

1. The German Government and the German people refuse to receive, accept, let alone to fulfill, demands in the nature of ultimata made by the British Government.

2. On our eastern frontier there has for many months already reigned a condition of war. Since the time when the Versailles Treaty first tore Germany to pieces, all and every peaceful settlement was refused to all German Governments. The National Socialist Government also has since the year 1933 tried again and again to remove by peaceful negotiations the worst rapes and breaches of justice of this treaty. The British Government have been among those who, by their intransigent attitude, took the chief part in frustrating every practical revision. Without the intervention of the British Government—of this the German Government and the German people are fully conscious—a reasonable solution doing justice to both sides would certainly have been found between Germany and Poland. For Germany did not have the intention nor had she raised the demands of annihilating Poland. The Reich demanded only the revision of those articles of the Versailles Treaty which already at the time of the formulation of that dictate had been described by understanding statesmen of all nations as being in the long run unbearable, and therefore impossible for a great nation and also for the entire political and economic interests of Eastern Europe. British statesmen, too, declared the solution in the East which was then forced upon Germany as

containing the germ of future wars. To remove this danger was the desire of all German Governments and especially the intention of the new National Socialist People's Government. The blame for having prevented this peaceful revision lies with the British Cabinet policy.

3. The British Government have—an occurrence unique in history—given the Polish State full powers for all actions against Germany which that State might conceivably intend to undertake. The British Government assured the Polish Government of their military support in all circumstances, should Germany defend herself against any provocation or attack. Thereupon the Polish terror against the Germans living in the territories which had been torn from Germany immediately assumed unbearable proportions. The Free City of Danzig was, in violation of all legal provisions, first threatened with destruction economically and by measures of customs policy, and was finally subjected to a military blockade and its communications strangled. All these violations of the Danzig Statute, which were well known to the British Government, were approved and covered by the blank cheque given to Poland. The German Government, though moved by the sufferings of the German population which was being tortured and treated in an inhuman manner, nevertheless remained a patient onlooker for five months, without undertaking even on one single occasion any similar aggressive action against Poland. They only warned Poland that these happenings would in the long run be unbearable, and that they were determined, in the event of no other kind of assistance being given to this population, to help them themselves. All these happenings were known in every detail to the British Government. It would have been easy for them to use their great influence in Warsaw in order to exhort those in power there to exercise justice and humaneness and to keep to the existing obligations. The British Government did not do this. . . . The British Government, therefore, bear the responsibility for all the unhappiness and misery which have now overtaken and are about to overtake many peoples.

4. After all efforts at finding and concluding a peaceful solution had been rendered impossible by the intransigence of the Polish Government covered as they were by England, after the conditions resembling civil war, which had existed already for months at the eastern frontier of the Reich, had gradually developed into open attacks on German territory, without the British Government raising any objections, the German Government determined to put an end to this continual threat, unbearable for a great Power, to the external and finally also to the internal peace of the German people, and to end it by those means which, since the Democratic Governments had in effect sabotaged all other possibilities of revision, alone remained at their disposal for the defence of the peace, security and honour of the Germans. The last attacks of the Poles threatening Reich territory they answered with similar measures. The German Government does not intend, on account of any sort of British intentions or obligations in the East, to tolerate conditions which are identical with those conditions which we observe in Palestine which is under British protection. The German people, however, above all do not intend to allow themselves to be ill-treated by the Poles.

5. The German Government, therefore, reject the attempt to force Germany, by means of a demand, having the character of an ultimatum, to recall its forces which are lined up for the defence of the Reich, and thereby to accept the old unrest and the old injustice. The threat that, failing this, they will fight Germany in the war, corresponds to the intention proclaimed for years past by numerous British politicians. The German Government and the German people have assured the English people countless times how much they desire an understanding, indeed close friendship, with them. If the British Government hitherto always refused these offers and now answer them with an open threat of war, it is not the fault of the German people and of their Government, but exclusively the fault of the British Cabinet or of those men who for years have been preaching the destruction and extermination of the German people. The German people and their Government do not, like Great Britain, intend to dominate the world, but they are determined to defend their own liberty, their independence, and above all their life. The intention . . . of carrying the destruction of the German people even further than was done through the Versailles Treaty is taken note of by us, and we shall therefore answer any aggressive action on the part of England with the same weapons and in the same form.

Source: G. A. Kertesz, *Documents in the Political History of the European Continent 1815–1939* (Oxford, UK: Clarendon Press, 1968), 504–507.

44. French Premier Édouard Daladier, Statement to the Nation, 3 September 1939

On 3 September 1939, the French prime minister announced to his countrymen that Germany had ignored a last-minute appeal from France and Britain to withdraw from Poland. France and Britain were therefore at war with Germany.

Men and Women of France.

Since daybreak on September 1, Poland has been the victim of the most brutal and most cynical of aggression. Her frontiers have been violated. Her cities are being bombed. Her army is heroically resisting the invader.

The responsibility for the blood that is being shed falls entirely upon the Hitler Government. The fate of peace is in Hitler's hands. He chose war.

France and England have made countless efforts to safeguard peace. This very morning they made a further urgent intervention in Berlin in order to address to the German Government a last appeal to reason and request it to stop hostilities and to open peaceful negotiations.

Germany met us with a refusal. She had already refused to reply to all the men of goodwill who recently raised their voices in favor of the peace of the world.

She therefore desires the destruction of Poland, so as to be able to dominate Europe quickly and to enslave France.

In rising against the most frightful of tyrannies, in honoring our word, we fight to defend our soil, our homes, our liberties.

I am conscious of having worked unremittingly against the war until the last minute.

I greet with emotion and affection our young soldiers, who now go forth to perform the sacred task which we ourselves did perform before them. They can have full confidence in their chiefs, who are worthy of those who have previously led France to victory.

The cause of France is identical with that of Righteousness. It is the cause of all peaceful and free nations. It will be victorious.

Men and Women of France!

We are waging war because it has been thrust on us. Every one of us is at his post, on the soil of France, on that land of liberty where respect of human dignity finds one of its last refuges. You will all co-operate, with a profound feeling of union and brotherhood, for the salvation of the country.

Vive la France!

Source: Web site: The Avalon Project at Yale Law School. Available at http://www.yale.edu/lawweb/avalon/wwii/fr3.htm.

45. President Franklin D. Roosevelt, Radio Address, 3 September 1939

As war began in Europe, President Roosevelt addressed the American people. He stated that he hoped to preserve peace in the United States and that within a few days the government would issue an official proclamation of neutrality. He pointedly stated that he would not, however, ask Americans to remain neutral in their thoughts, an indication of where his own sympathies and those of most of his countrymen lay.

Tonight my single duty is to speak to the whole of America.

Until 4:30 this morning I had hoped against hope that some miracle would prevent a devastating war in Europe and bring to an end the invasion of Poland by Germany.

For 4 long years a succession of actual wars and constant crises have shaken the entire world and have threatened in each case to bring on the gigantic conflict which is today unhappily a fact.

It is right that I should recall to your minds the consistent

and at times successful efforts of your Government in these crises to throw the full weight of the United States into the cause of peace. In spite of spreading wars I think that we have every right and every reason to maintain as a national policy the fundamental moralities, the teachings of religion, and the continuation of efforts to restore peace—for some day, though the time may be distant, we can be of even greater help to a crippled humanity.

It is right, too, to point out that the unfortunate events of these recent years have been based on the use of force or the threat of force. And it seems to me clear, even at the outbreak of this great war, that the influence of America should be consistent in seeking for humanity a final peace which will eliminate, as far as it is possible to do so, the continued use of force between nations. . . .

You must master at the outset a simple but unalterable fact in modern foreign relations. When peace has been broken anywhere, peace of all countries everywhere is in danger.

It is easy for you and me to shrug our shoulders and say that conflicts taking place thousands of miles from the continental United States, and, indeed, the whole American hemisphere, do not seriously affect the Americas—and that all the United States has to do is to ignore them and go about our own business. Passionately though we may desire detachment, we are forced to realize that every word that comes through the air, every ship that sails the sea, every battle that is fought does affect the American future.

Let no man or woman thoughtlessly or falsely talk of America sending its armies to European fields. At this moment there is being prepared a proclamation of American neutrality. This would have been done even if there had been no neutrality statute on the books, for this proclamation is in accordance with international law and with American policy.

This will be followed by a proclamation required by the existing Neutrality Act. I trust that in the days to come our neutrality can be made a true neutrality. It is of the utmost importance that the people of this country, with the best information in the world, think things through. The most dangerous enemies of American peace are those who, without well-rounded information on the whole broad subject of the past, the present, and the future, undertake to speak with authority, to talk in terms of glittering generalities, to give to the Nation assurances or prophecies which are of little present or future value. . . .

I cannot prophesy the immediate economic effect of this new war on our Nation, but I do say that no American has the moral right to profiteer at the expense either of his fellow citizens or of the men, women, and children who are living and dying in the midst of war in Europe.

Some things we do know. Most of us in the United States believe in spiritual values. Most of us, regardless of what church we belong to, believe in the spirit of the New Testament—a great teaching which opposes itself to the use of force, of armed force, of marching armies, and falling bombs. The overwhelming masses of our people seek peace—peace at home, and the kind of peace in other lands which will not jeopardize peace at home.

We have certain ideas and ideals of national safety, and we must act to preserve that safety today and to preserve the safety of our children in future years.

That safety is and will be bound up with the safety of the Western Hemisphere and of the seas adjacent thereto. We seek to keep war from our firesides by keeping war from coming to the Americas. For that we have historic precedent that goes back to the days of the administration of President George Washington. It is serious enough and tragic enough to every American family in every State in the Union to live in a world that is torn by wars on other continents. Today they affect every American home. It is our national duty to use every effort to keep them out of the Americas.

And at this time let me make the simple plea that partisanship and selfishness be adjourned, and that national unity be the thought that underlies all others.

This Nation will remain a neutral nation, but I cannot ask that every American remain neutral in thought as well. Even a neutral has a right to take account of facts. Even a neutral cannot be asked to close his mind or his conscience.

I have said not once but many times that I have seen war and that I hate war. I say that again and again.

I hope the United States will keep out of this war. I believe that it will. And I give you assurances that every effort of your Government will be directed toward that end.

As long as it remains within my power to prevent, there will be no blackout of peace in the United States.

Source: U.S. Department of State, Publication 1983, *Peace and War: United States Foreign Policy, 1931–1941* (Washington, DC: U.S. Government Printing Office, 1943), 483–485.

46. Declaration of the Government of the German Reich and the Government of the U.S.S.R., 28 September 1939

After defeating Poland and dividing its territory between them, the German and Soviet governments appealed to Britain and France to end the war, a course that would have left those governments suggesting it in undisturbed enjoyment of their new acquisitions.

After the Government of the German Reich and the Government of the U.S.S.R. have, by means of the treaty signed today, definitively settled the problems arising from the collapse of the Polish state and have thereby created a sure foundation for a lasting peace in Eastern Europe, they mutually express their conviction that it would serve the true interest of all peoples to put an end to the state of war existing at present between Germany on the one side and England and France on the other. Both Governments will therefore direct their common efforts, jointly with other friendly powers if occasion arises, toward attaining this goal as soon as possible.

Should, however, the efforts of the two Governments remain fruitless, this would demonstrate the fact that England and France are responsible for the continuation of the war, whereupon, in case of the continuation of the war, the Governments of Germany and of the U.S.S.R. shall engage in mutual consultations with regard to necessary measures.

Source: Web site: The Avalon Project at the Yale Law School. Available at http://www.yale.edu/lawweb/avalon/nazsov/dec939.htm.

47. The Declaration of Panama, Adopted at the Meeting of the Ministers of Foreign Affairs of the American Republics in Panama, 3 October 1939

One month after war began in Europe, representatives of all the various American states met in Panama. The United States was instrumental in the passage of a resolution that imposed a "hemisphere defense zone" around both American continents, stretching several hundred miles into the Atlantic and Pacific. Only Canadian waters were excluded. Although all belligerents were supposedly banned from undertaking hostilities within this zone, in practice its intention was to prevent German naval operations in the area. The enforcement of this zone would depend largely upon the U.S. Navy.

The governments of the American republics meeting at Panamá, have solemnly ratified their neutral status in the conflict which is disrupting the peace of Europe, but the present war may lead to unexpected results which may affect the fundamental interests of America and there can be no justification for the interests of the belligerents to prevail over the rights of neutrals causing disturbances and suffering to nations which by their neutrality in the conflict and their distance from the scene of events, should not be burdened with its fatal and painful consequences.

During the World War of 1914–1918 the Governments of Argentina, Brazil, Chile, Columbia, Ecuador and Peru advanced, or supported, individual proposals providing in principle a declaration by the American republics that the belligerent nations must refrain from committing hostile acts within a reasonable distance from their shores.

The nature of the present conflagration, in spite of its already lamentable proportions, would not justify any obstruction to inter-American communications which, engendered by important interests, call for adequate protection. This fact requires the demarcation of a zone of security including all the normal maritime routes of communication and trade between the countries of America.

To this end it is essential as a measure of necessity to adopt immediately provisions based on the above-mentioned precedents for the safeguarding of such interests, in order to avoid a repetition of the damages and sufferings sustained by the American nations and by their citizens in the war of 1914–1918.

There is no doubt that the governments of the American republics must foresee those dangers and as a measure of self-protection insist that the waters to a reasonable distance from their coasts shall remain free from the commission of hostile acts or from the undertaking of belligerent activities by nations engaged in a war in which the said governments are not involved.

For these reasons the governments of the American republics

RESOLVE AND HEREBY DECLARE

1. As a measure of continental self-protection, the American republics, so long as they maintain their neutrality, are as of inherent right entitled to have those waters adjacent to the American Continent, which they regard as of primary concern and direct utility in their relations, free from the commission of any hostile act by any non-American belligerent nation, whether such hostile act be attempted or made from land, sea, or air.

   Such waters shall be defined as follows. All waters comprised within the limits set forth hereafter except the territorial waters of Canada and of the undisputed colonies and possessions of European countries within these limits . . . [details omitted].

2. The governments of the American republics agree that they will endeavor, through joint representation to such belligerents as may now or in the future be engaged in hostilities, to secure the compliance by them with the provisions of this declaration, without prejudice to the exercise of the individual rights of each state inherent in their sovereignty.

3. The governments of the American republics further declare that whenever they consider it necessary they will consult together to determine upon the measures which they may individually or collectively undertake in order to secure the observance of the provisions of this declaration.

4. The American republics, during the existence of a state of war in which they themselves are not involved, may undertake, whenever they may determine that the need therefore exists, to patrol, either individually or collectively, as may be agreed upon by common consent, and in so far as the means and resources of each may permit, the waters adjacent to their coasts within the area above defined.

Source: James W. Gantenbein, *Documentary Background of World War II 1931 to 1941* (New York: Columbia University Press, 1948), 994–996.

48. Franklin D. Roosevelt to Albert Einstein, 19 October 1939

Six weeks after war began in Europe, President Franklin D. Roosevelt replied affirmatively to Albert Einstein's earlier suggestion that the United States should mount a major initiative to develop atomic weapons. From this seed would grow the MANHATTAN Project and the bombings of Hiroshima and Nagasaki.

I want to thank you for your recent letter and the most interesting and important enclosure.

I found this data of such import that I have convened a Board consisting of the head of the Bureau of Standards and a chosen representative of the Army and Navy to thoroughly investigate the possibilities of your suggestion regarding the element of uranium.

I am glad to say that Dr. Sachs will cooperate and work with this Committee and I feel this is the most practical and effective method of dealing with the subject.

Please accept my sincere thanks.

Source: Web site: PBS: American Experience. Available at http://www.pbs.org/wgbh/amex/truman/psources/ps.

49. Heinrich Himmler, Order to the Members of the German SS and Police, 28 October 1939

National Socialist racial theory urged all "Aryan" men to father as many children as possible to carry on the race. At the beginning of the war, Heinrich Himmler, head of the German SS and Police, directed all members of those two organizations to father as many children as possible, whether legitimate or not. He was concerned that otherwise they might die in battle with no offspring to perpetuate their genetic heritage.

To all men of the SS and Police

The old proverb that only he can die in peace who has sons and children must again hold good in this war, particularly for the SS. He can die in peace who knows that his clan and everything that his ancestors and he himself have wanted and striven for will be continued in his children. The greatest gift for the widow of a man killed in battle is always the child of the man she has loved.

Beyond the limits of bourgeois laws and conventions, which are perhaps necessary in other circumstances, it can be a noble task for German women and girls of good blood to become even outside marriage, not light-heartedly but out of a deep moral seriousness, mothers of the children of soldiers going to war of whom fate alone knows whether they will return or die for Germany. . . .

During the last war, many a soldier decided from a sense of responsibility to have no more children during the war so that his wife would not be left in need and distress after his death. You SS men need not have these anxieties; they are removed by the following regulations:

1. Special delegates, chosen by me personally, will take over in the name of the *Reichsführer SS* [head of the SS], the guardianship of all legitimate and illegitimate children of good blood whose fathers were killed in the war. We will support these mothers and take over the education and material care of these children until they come of age, so that no mother and widow need suffer want.

2. During the war, the SS will take care of all legitimate and illegitimate children born during the war and of expectant mothers in cases of need. After the war, when the fathers return, the SS will in addition grant generous material help to well-founded applications by individuals.

SS-Men and you mothers of these children which Germany has hoped to show that you are ready, through your faith in the Führer and for the sake of the life of our blood and people, to regenerate life for Germany just as bravely as you know how to fight and die for Germany.

Source: Jeremy Noakes, ed., *Nazism 1919–1945, Volume 4: The Home Front in World War II* (Exeter, UK: University of Exeter Press, 1998), 368–369. Reprinted with permission of University of Exeter Press.

50. General Hans Frank, Decree for the Combating of Violent Acts in the General Government [of Poland], 31 October 1939

In all the conquered territories, the feared security force, the SS (Schutzstaffel), exerted heavy influence upon the German occupation authorities, pressuring them to emphasize security and racial considerations. Two months after German forces invaded Poland, General Hans Frank, who remained governor general of Poland from 1939 to spring 1945, issued a decree imposing the death penalty for numerous acts of resistance to the German occupation forces. By this decree, Frank also permitted the SS to operate their own courts-martial to deal with offenses committed under its provisions.

1. Anyone who commits a violent act against the German Reich or the German sovereign authority in the General Government will receive the death penalty.
2. Anyone who willfully damages equipment belonging to the German authorities, objects which serve the work of the authorities, or installations which are for the benefit of the public will receive the death penalty.

3. Anyone who encourages or incites disobedience to the decrees or regulations issued by the German authorities will receive the death penalty.

4. Anyone who commits a violent act against a German because of his membership of the German nation will receive the death penalty.

5. Anyone who willfully commits arson and thereby damages the property of a German will receive the death penalty.

6. Those who incite or aid such acts will be punished in the same way as the persons who commit them. Attempted acts will be punished in the same way as those which have been committed. . . .

8. Anyone who conspires to commit such a crime as those contained in Sections 1–5, enters into serious discussion of such crimes, offers to commit such a crime, or anyone who accepts such an offer will receive the death penalty.

9. Anyone who receives information about the intention to commit a crime such as those contained in Sections 1–5 and fails to report it to the authorities, or to the person who is threatened at once, or in time for the crime to be prevented, will receive the death penalty. . . .

10. (2) Anyone who receives information about the unauthorized possession of a weapon by another person and fails to inform the authorities immediately will receive the death penalty.

Source: J. Noakes and G. Pridham, eds., *Nazism 1919–1945: Volume 3: Foreign Policy, War and Racial Extermination: A Documentary Reader* (Exeter, UK: University of Exeter Press, 1988), 367. Reprinted with permission of University of Exeter Press.

51. The "Cash-and-Carry" United States Neutrality Act: 76th Congress, 2nd Session, Public Resolution No. 54, 4 November 1939

In fall 1939, the U.S. neutrality legislation came up for renewal. On 21 September, President Roosevelt asked Congress for major revisions in the existing neutrality legislation. He would undoubtedly have preferred to repeal it entirely, but at this juncture, that option was almost certainly still politically impossible. A compromise was reached whereby belligerent nations, in effect the Allies, could now purchase munitions of war in the United States, but only if they paid in cash and transported the goods in their own vessels. Americans were still forbidden either to finance such war trade or to provide shipping for munitions of war. The new legislation reflected prevailing American sympathy for the Allies, even as many Americans still hoped their country would avoid intervention in the war.

JOINT RESOLUTION To preserve the neutrality and the peace of the United States and to secure the safety of its citizens and their interests.

Whereas the United States, desiring to preserve its neutrality in wars between foreign states and desiring also to avoid involvement therein, voluntarily imposes upon its nationals by domestic regulation the restrictions set out in this joint resolution; and

Whereas by so doing the United States waives none of its own rights or privileges, or those of any of its nationals, under international law, and expressly reserves all the rights and privileges to which it and its nationals are entitled under the law of nations; and

Whereas the United States hereby expressly reserves the right to appeal, change or modify this joint resolution in the interests of the peace, security or welfare of the United States and its people: Therefore be it Resolved,

PROCLAMATION OF A STATE OF WAR
BETWEEN FOREIGN STATES
Section 1. (a) That whenever the President, or the Congress by concurrent resolution, shall find that there exists a state of war between foreign states, and that it is necessary to promote the security or preserve the peace of the United States or to protect the lives of citizens of the United States, the President shall issue a proclamation naming the states involved; and he shall, from time to time, by proclamation, name other states as and when they may become involved in the war.

(b) Whenever the state of war which shall have caused the President to issue any proclamation under the authority of this section shall have ceased to exist with respect to any state named in such proclamation, he shall revoke such proclamation with respect to such state.

COMMERCE WITH STATES ENGAGED IN ARMED CONFLICT

Sec. 2. (a) Whenever the President shall have issued a proclamation under the authority of section 1 (a) it shall thereafter be unlawful for any American vessel to carry any passengers or any articles or materials to any state named in such proclamation.

(b) Whoever shall violate any of the provisions of subsection (a) of this section or of any regulations issued thereunder shall, upon conviction thereof, be fined not more than $50,000 or imprisoned for not more than five years, or both. Should the violation be by a corporation, organization, or association, each officer or director thereof participating in the violation shall be liable to the penalty herein prescribed.

(c) Whenever the President shall have issued a proclamation under the authority of section 1 (a) it shall thereafter be unlawful to export or transport, or attempt to export or transport, or cause to be exported or transported, from the Untied States to any state named in such proclamation, any articles or materials (except copyrighted articles or materials) until all right, title, and interest therein shall have been transferred to some foreign government, agency, institution, association, partnership, corporation, or national . . .

(g) The provisions of subsections (a) and (c) of this section shall not apply to transportation by American vessels (other than aircraft) of mail, passengers, or any articles or materials (except articles or materials listed in a proclamation referred to in or issued under the authority of section 12 [i])

1. to any port in the Western Hemisphere south of thirty-five degrees north latitude,
2. to any port in the Western Hemisphere north of thirty-five degrees north latitude and west of sixty-six degrees west longitude,
3. to any port on the Pacific or Indian Oceans, including the China Sea, the Tasman Sea, the Bay of Bengal, and the Arabian Sea, and any other dependent waters of either of such oceans, seas, or bays or,
4. to any port on the Atlantic Ocean or its dependent waters south of thirty degrees north latitude.

The exceptions contained in this subsection shall not apply to any such port which is included within a combat area as defined in section 3 which applies to such vessels . . .

(i) Every American vessel to which the provisions of subsections (g) and (h) apply, and every neutral vessel to which the provisions of subsection (l) apply, shall, before departing from a port or from the jurisdiction of the United States, file with the collector of customs of the port of departure, or if there is no such collector at such port then with the nearest collector of customs, a sworn statement (1) containing a complete list of all the articles and materials carried as cargo by such vessel, and the names and addresses of the consignees of all such articles and materials, and (2) stating the ports at which such articles and materials are to be unloaded and the ports of call of such vessel. All transportation referred to in subsections (f), (g), (h), and (l) of this section shall be subject to such restrictions, rules, and regulations as the President shall prescribe; but no loss incurred in connection with any transportation excepted under the provisions of subsections (g), (h), and (l) of this section shall be made the basis of any claim put forward by the Government of the United States . . .

(l) The provisions of subsection (c) of this section shall not apply to the transportation by a neutral vessel to any port referred to in subsection (g) of this section of any articles or materials (except articles or materials listed in a proclamation referred to in or issued under the authority of section 12 [i]) so long as such port is not included within a combat area as defined in section 3 which applies to American vessels.

COMBAT AREAS

Sec. 3. (a) Whenever the President shall have issued a proclamation under the authority of section 1 (a), and he shall thereafter find that the protection of citizens of the United States so requires, he shall, by proclamation, define combat areas, and thereafter it shall be unlawful, except under such rules and regulations as may be prescribed, for any citizen of the United States or any American vessel to proceed into or through any such combat area. The combat areas so defined may be made to apply to surface vessels or aircraft, or both.

(b) In case of the violation of any of the provisions of this section by any American vessel, or any owner or officer thereof, such vessel, owner, or officer shall be fined not more than $50,000 or imprisoned for not more than five years, or both. Should the owner of such vessel be a corporation, organization, or association, each officer or director participating in the violation shall be liable to the penalty hereinabove prescribed. In case of the violation of this section by any citizen traveling as a passenger, such passenger may be fined not more than $10,000 or imprisoned for not more than two years, or both.

(c) The President may from time to time modify or extend any proclamation issued under the authority of this section, and when the conditions which shall have caused him to issue any such proclamation shall have ceased to exist he shall revoke such proclamation and the provisions of this section shall thereupon cease to apply, except as to offenses committed prior to such revocation. . . .

TRAVEL ON VESSELS OF BELLIGERENT STATES

Sec. 5. (a) Whenever the President shall have issued a proclamation under the authority of section 1 (a) it shall thereafter be unlawful for any citizen of the United States to travel on any vessel of any state named in such proclamation, except in accordance with such rules and regulations as may be prescribed.

(b) Whenever any proclamation issued under the authority of section 1 (a) shall have been revoked with respect to any state the provisions of this section shall thereupon cease to apply with respect to such state, except as to offenses committed prior to such revocation.

ARMING OF AMERICAN MERCHANT VESSELS PROHIBITED

Sec. 6. Whenever the President shall have issued a proclamation under the authority of section 1 (a), it shall thereafter be unlawful until such proclamation is revoked, for any American vessel engaged in commerce with any foreign state to be armed, except with small arms and ammunition therefor, which the President may deem necessary and shall publicly designate for the preservation of discipline aboard any such vessel.

FINANCIAL TRANSACTIONS

Sec. 7. (a) Whenever the President shall have issued a proclamation under the authority of section 1 (a), it shall thereafter be unlawful for any person within the United States to purchase, sell, or exchange bonds, securities, or other obligations of the government of any state named in such proclamation, or of any political subdivision of any such state, or of any person acting for or on behalf of the government of any such state, or political subdivision thereof, issued after the date of such proclamation, or to make any loan or extend any credit (other than necessary credits accruing in connection with the transmission of telegraph, cable, wireless and telephone services) to any such government, political subdivision, or person. The provisions of this subsection shall also apply to the sale by any person within the United States to any person in a state named in any such proclamation of any articles or materials listed in a proclamation referred to in or issued under the authority of section 12 (i). . . .

SOLICITATION AND COLLECTION OF FUNDS AND CONTRIBUTIONS

Sec. 8. (a) Whenever the President shall have issued a proclamation under the authority of section 1 (a), it shall thereafter be unlawful for any person within the United States to solicit or receive any contribution for or on behalf of the government of any state named in such proclamation

or for or on behalf of any agent or instrumentality of any such state. . . .

AMERICAN REPUBLICS

Sec. 9. This joint resolution (except section 12) shall not apply to any American republic engaged in war against a non-American state or states, provided the American republic is not cooperating with a non-American state or states in such war. . . .

NATIONAL MUNITIONS CONTROL BOARD

Sec. 12. . . . (d) It shall be unlawful for any person to export, or attempt to export, from the United States to any other state, any arms, ammunition, or implements of war listed in a proclamation referred to in or issued under the authority of subsection (i) of this section, or to import, or attempt to import, to the United States from any other state, any of the arms, ammunition, or implements of war listed in any such proclamation, without first having submitted to the Secretary of State the name of the purchaser and the terms of sale and having obtained a license therefore. . . .

(i) The President is hereby authorized to proclaim upon recommendation of the Board from time to time a list of articles which shall be considered arms, ammunition, and implements of war for the purposes of this section; but the proclamation Numbered 2237, of May 1, 1937 (50 Stat. 1834) defining the term "arms, ammunition, and implements of war" shall, until it is revoked, have full force and effect as if issued under the authority of this subsection. . . .

GENERAL PENALTY PROVISION

Sec. 15. In every case of the violation of any of the provisions of this joint resolution or of any rule or regulation issued pursuant thereto where a specific penalty is not herein provided, such violator or violators, upon conviction, shall be fined not more than $10,000, or imprisonment not more than two years, or both. . . .

REPEALS

Sec. 19. The joint resolution of August 31, 1935, as amended and the joint resolution of January 8, 1937, are hereby repealed; but offenses committed and penalties, forfeitures, or liabilities incurred under either of such joint resolutions prior to the date of enactment of this joint resolution may be prosecuted and punished, and suits and proceedings for violations of either of such joint resolution or any rule or regulation issued pursuant thereto may be commenced and prosecuted, in the same manner and with the same effect as if such joint resolution had not been repealed.

Source: Web site: Documents of the Interwar Period. Available at http://www.mtholyoke.edu/acad/intrel/WorldWar2/neutrality.htm.

52. Address of Finland's Prime Minister, A. K. Cajander, at Helsinki Fair Hall, at a National Defense Celebration Arranged by Finnish Private Enterprise Owners, 23 November 1939

On 30 November 1939, the Soviet Union invaded Finland, a small country on its borders in the far northwest of Europe, which until 1918 had been under Russian rule. Josef Stalin, the Soviet president, alleged that Finland might otherwise pose a potential threat to Russia and proposed an exchange of territory which the Finns found unacceptable. The Finns publicly defied all the Soviet Union's demands and, once war broke out, appealed for Western aid, declaring their determination to fight on to the bitter end. Finland's plight attracted much sympathy from the Western powers. Ironically, after Germany's June 1941 invasion of Russia, the Finns allied themselves with Germany against the Soviet Union.

The people of Finland stand in front of an unexpected incident. The events followed in quick succession and the total sequence of events emerged as a total surprise for the majority of the Finnish people. . . .

A little bit over two months ago the Soviet Union approached the Finnish Cabinet making certain propositions which were explained as aiming at improvement of the security of St. Petersburg or Leningrad and at strengthening of the friendly relationship between Finland and the Soviet Union.

These proposals were not completely unexpected. The forthcoming talks concerning required improvements of Leningrad's security were anticipated in private conversations with some members of the Finnish Cabinet a considerable time ago. . . .

A new decisive turn of events in Europe and even in the whole world took place when Germany and the Soviet Union concluded a non-aggression pact which in some respects even exceeded the regular scope of such agreements.

The pact came like a bolt from the blue. In Finland it, however, was not a complete surprise. As early as 1937 a remark was made by a prominent foreign authority about a possibility of the Soviet Union and Germany to conclude a pact perhaps in the near future. But the very timing of this non-aggression pact was, I guess, a complete surprise to all of us. . . .

The non-aggression pact between Germany and the Soviet Union was immediately followed by a war between Germany and Poland from which again a new war between the Western Powers and Germany ensued. A universal conflagration was ignited.

The Oslo countries, Finland included, declared themselves to be absolutely neutral in this campaign between the great powers. Despite their neutrality Finland and other Oslo countries suffer continuously and heavily from the economic consequences of the great war. Furthermore, especially Holland, Belgium and Finland but Switzerland, too, have been able to keep to their neutrality only by maintaining an extremely efficient guard for their defense.

In the opposite case their declaration of neutrality would scarcely have been respected.

When Poland was near to collapse the Soviet Union marched its troops into eastern Poland and occupied it. Simultaneously the Soviet People's Commissar for Foreign Affairs made it known to the governments of Finland and the Baltic countries, as well as to other countries, that it will conduct a policy of neutrality towards them. . . .

The only great power which could have earlier been a potential threat to Leningrad—well, in that case presumably along the southern coast of the Gulf of Finland—namely Germany, has concluded a non-aggression pact with the Soviet Union, which means that there exists no threat against the Soviet Union and Leningrad from there—without considering the overall present importance of Leningrad to the Soviet Union. And the new Soviet naval and air bases in Liepaja (Libau), Ventpils (Windau), Hiiumaa, Saaremaa and Paldiski permit, as disclosed by the Soviets, the Soviet Union to rule the Baltic Sea and thus the Gulf of Finland and up to the Gulf's farthest recess in front of Leningrad.

Judging from the present facts, all arguments about threats to Leningrad from the Finnish territory are very difficult to understand.

A request for negotiations with the Soviet government was received on the 5th of October. For over a month friendly discussions were carried out between the Finnish and Soviet Cabinets concerning concrete political issues of certain territorial exchanges to improve the security of Leningrad.

The Cabinet of Finland, after discussing with representatives of parliamentary groups and after consulting the highest military command, yielded to Soviet demands in order to maintain good neighborly relations so far as it could, as a representative of an independent nation, to increase the security of a foreign metropolis but without sacrificing Finland's own national security.

However, the Soviets have made propositions which are very far away from those which can be considered as prerequisites in securing Leningrad. If they were accepted it would have offended Finland's neutrality and damaged her opportunities to self-defence: it would have meant severing the southern defence line of Finland at two of its most important points and handing over its first-class fortifications to a foreign power. Thus it had resulted in severe decrease in the security of Finland. Such proposals were unacceptable to the Finnish government. . . .

Finland will not submit herself to a role of a vassal country. We will not yield to this by someone waging a nerve war or trying to exhaust us or doing the contrary, by offering temptations. Finland will peacefully, with open eyes and determined mind, observe the events in the west and in the east, and as a peace loving country, which always appreciates good neighborly relations, is at any time ready to continue the negotiations on a basis which does not risk the vital interests of Finland or her national values. No further concessions can be attained especially now when Finland herself gains nothing from these territorial exchanges.

Finland is convinced that it is advantageous to the real interests of the Soviet Union that it has as a neighbor a nation, whose loyalty it can trust in all circumstances.

The global situation continues tense, and this makes Finland among many other neutral countries to keep a considerable amount of men in arms as protectors of neutrality and also be otherwise prepared. . . .

We have to keep together—as a unified nation—like we did at the time of our first challenge, as unanimous as a democratic nation relying on its free will can ever be. The spirits born from our ordeals should and will stand the hardships, too. But even at that moment when an immediate danger is over we have to stay together. All in all we are a small nation and the stability of our international status depends decisively on our unanimity.

The world attention has focused on us without our own active influence. We have been met with a large scale sympathy of nations. This state of affairs obliges us. Let us make it known that we are worthy of the sympathy the world both in speeches and deeds has shown to us.

Source: Web site: History of Finland: A Selection of Events and Documents. Available at http://www.histdoc.net/history/cajander.html. Copyright by Paul Kruhse. Reprinted with permission.

53. President Franklin D. Roosevelt, Statement on Finland, 1 December 1939

On hearing the news of the Soviet invasion of Finland, President Franklin D. Roosevelt took the occasion of one of his regular press conferences to express shock and condemnation. That same month the League of Nations also expelled the Soviet Union, citing its attacks on Poland and Finland as the reasons for taking this action.

The news of the Soviet naval and military bombings within Finnish territory has come as a profound shock to the Government and people of the United States. Despite efforts made to solve the dispute by peaceful methods to which no reasonable objection could be offered, one power has chosen to resort to force of arms. It is tragic to see the policy of force spreading, and to realize that wanton disregard for law is still on the march. All peace-loving peoples in those nations that are still hoping for the continuance of relations throughout the world on the basis of law and order will unanimously condemn this new resort to military force as the arbiter of international differences.

To the great misfortune of the world, the present trend to force makes insecure the independent existence of small nations in every continent and jeopardizes the rights of mankind to self-government. The people and government of Finland have a long, honorable and wholly peaceful record which has won for them the respect and warm regard of the people and Government of the United States.

Source: Web site: History of Finland: A Selection of Events and Documents. Available at http://www.histdoc.net/history.roosevelt.html.

1940 Documents

54. Plans for a United Europe: Proposals of Jacques Maritain, Spring 1940

As early as spring 1940 the French intellectual and philosopher Jacques Maritain, who went into American exile after the fall of France, was proposing European federation as the only means of preventing further European conflicts. In part, Maritain's proposals represented a response to German claims to represent a "new order" in Europe. His later writings and lectures on the subject were clandestinely published and distributed in occupied France, and helped to inspire the postwar movement for European unity.

The war in which the peoples of France and Britain have been involved is a just war on their part. The peace for which they are fighting must be a just peace. That means that Europe will have to be refashioned, taking into account the real, natural and historical conditions of its component peoples; all ideas of empire and domination must give way to a spirit of cooperation, while guarding against any reawakening of aggressive powers. Only thus can we prevent the recurrence of general war every twenty-five years.

As far as one can speak today of a future peace which will have to be framed in circumstances that cannot yet be foreseen, it is vital to avoid basing the discussion on a false conception of the problem. A large section of British opinion rightly urges the need for a federal solution which would respect the natural aspirations of the Germanic peoples as well as the other peoples of Europe, and would do away with the apparatus of humiliation and vindictive coercion that vitiated the last peace and prepared the way for Hitler. A large part of French opinion rightly insists on the need—not only for French security, but in order that a lasting European regime may be established—to prevent large-scale German rearmament and extirpate Prussian imperialism, while avoiding the political mistakes and weakness which also vitiated the last peace and prepared the way for Hitler. These

two attitudes are perfectly compatible, and it would be absurd to treat them as opposites. . . .

We must not tire of repeating that sooner or later, when the present convulsions and perhaps other sufferings are over, a federal solution will be seen as the only way out for Europe, and also for Germany herself. With an imperialist Germany formed by Prussia and the Prussian spirit into an iron unity, a kind of monstrous giantism, a European federation would soon turn into a European servitude with no hope of redemption except by more savage wars. With an inorganic Europe of rival states jealously guarding all the privileges of their sovereignty, a Germany kept down by force in a state of guilt and division would inevitably devote its energy and tenacity to pressing embittered claims which would once more involve the world in ruin. What we must have, once the Hitlerian dream has been drowned in blood, is a federal solution with the assent of Europe and the German peoples delivered from Nazism and the Prussian spirit; in other words, a political plurality of German states reflecting the diversity of their cultural heritage and integrated in a European federation whose members would all agree to the diminution of sovereignty necessary for the purpose of organic institutional cooperation. No doubt there will be many a profound and terrible upheaval before we reach that goal, but we believe it is the only hope for Europe and Western civilization. . . .

Of course any ideal can be betrayed, and the idea of European federation, like any other great idea, can be ruined by egoism and blind ambition seeking to exploit it to its own advantage. Men of good will must be vigilant to avert this evil. But everything leads us to think that post-war conditions in the world will be such that any attempt to subject it to imperialist designs will be doomed to failure.

We should also note that, whereas the Prussian mind cannot conceive of a federal Europe except as a Europe enslaved to Germany, Britain is now alive to the idea of re-making Europe and France has become more aware of the interdependence of all nations. Between them these two are strong enough to raise the idea of a European federation above any imperialistic design and to make it conform to the essential purpose of cooperation and the common weal. A great deal of moral purification is here needed, and is possible. Britain can purify her sense of empire, retaining only the idea of a free commonwealth based on political friendship; France can purify her sense of the nation state, retaining only the organic and political unity of the motherland, which will not be weakened but enhanced by entry into a federal structure. On both sides there must be acceptance of the diminution of state sovereignty required for the sake of a genuine international organization. If this surrender is conceived in the name of liberty, it will lead finally to the establishment of what may rightfully be called a new Christendom.

Source: Jacques Maritain, *De la justice politique. Notes sur la presente guerre* (Paris, 1940). Quoted and translated in Walter Lipgens, ed., *Documents on the History of European Integration:* Series B, Vol. I: *Continental Plans for European Union 1939–1945* (Berlin and New York: de Gruyter, 1984), 274–277. Reprinted with permission of Walter de Gruyter, Co.

55. "Blood, Toil, Tears, and Sweat": Winston Churchill, Speech in the British House of Commons, 13 May 1940

In May 1940, as German forces launched a blitzkrieg attack on Western Europe, Winston Churchill, a veteran politician who had been a longtime critic of the Chamberlain administration's appeasement policies, became British prime minister. Taking power when Great Britain faced a grim war situation, in his first speech as prime minister, Churchill stated that all he could offer the British people was "blood, toil, tears, and sweat."

On Friday evening last I received from His Majesty the mission to form a new administration. It was the evident will of Parliament and the nation that this should be conceived on the broadest possible basis and that it should include all parties . . .

To form an administration of this scale and complexity is a serious undertaking in itself. But we are in the preliminary phase of one of the greatest battles in history. We are in action at many other points—in Norway and in Holland—and we have to be prepared in the Mediterranean. The air battle is continuing, and many preparations have to be made here at home.

In this crisis I think I may be pardoned if I do not address the House at any length today, and I hope that any of my friends and colleagues or former colleagues who are affected by the political reconstruction will make all allowances for any lack of ceremony with which it has been necessary to act.

I say to the House as I said to ministers who have joined this government, I have nothing to offer but blood, toil, tears, and sweat. We have before us an ordeal of the most grievous kind. We have before us many, many months of struggle and suffering.

You ask, what is our policy? I say it is to wage war by land, sea, and air. War with all our might and with all the strength God has given us, and to wage war against a monstrous tyranny never surpassed in the dark and lamentable catalogue of human crime. That is our policy.

You ask, what is our aim? I can answer in one word. It is victory. Victory at all costs—Victory in spite of all terrors—Victory, however long and hard the road may be, for without victory there is no survival.

Let that be realized. No survival for the British Empire, no survival for all that the British Empire has stood for, no survival for the urge, the impulse of the ages, that mankind shall move forward toward his goal.

I take up my task in buoyancy and hope. I feel sure that our cause will not be suffered to fail among men. I feel entitled at this juncture, at this time, to claim the aid of all and to say, "Come then, let us go forward together with our united strength."

Source: Winston S. Churchill, *The Complete Speeches,* 8 vols., ed. Robert Rhodes James (New York: Chelsea House Publishers, 1974), 6: 6218–6220.

56. "We Shall Never Surrender": Winston Churchill, Speech in the British House of Commons, 4 June 1940

By early June 1940, it was clear that the British Expeditionary Force in France had suffered a serious defeat. Britain launched a desperate evacuation effort from the Dunkirk beaches, sending every type of vessel across the Channel to bring its troops home. Most of Britain's military equipment was lost in France. Speaking not just for his British audience but also to the government and people of the United States, the only possible source of outside aid for his country, Winston Churchill promised that his country would fight on and would never surrender.

In a long series of very fierce battles, now on this front, now on that, fighting on three fronts at once, battles fought by two or three divisions against an equal or sometimes larger number of the enemy, and fought very fiercely on old ground so many of us knew so well, our losses in men exceed 30,000 in killed, wounded and missing. . . .

In the confusion of departure it is inevitable that many should be cut off. Against this loss of over 30,000 men we may set the far heavier loss certainly inflicted on the enemy, but our losses in material are enormous. We have perhaps lost one-third of the men we lost in the opening days of the battle on March 21, 1918, but we have lost nearly as many guns—nearly 1,000—and all our transport and all the armored vehicles that were with the army of the north.

These losses will impose further delay on the expansion of our military strength. That expansion has not been proceeding as fast as we had hoped. The best of all we had to give has been given to the B. E. F., and although they had not the number of tanks and some articles of equipment which were desirable they were a very well and finely equipped army. They had the first fruits of all our industry had to give. That has gone and now here is further delay.

How long it will be, how long it will last depends upon the exertions which we make on this island. An effort, the like of which has never been seen in our records, is now being made. Work is proceeding night and day, Sundays, and week days. Capital and labor have cast aside their interests, rights and customs and put everything into the common stock. Already the flow of munitions has leaped forward. There is no reason why we should not in a few months overtake the sudden and serious loss that has come upon us without retarding the development of our general program.

Nevertheless, our thankfulness at the escape of our army with so many men, and the thankfulness of their loved ones, who passed through an agonizing week, must not blind us to the fact that what happened in France and Belgium is a colossal military disaster.

The French Army has been weakened, the Belgian Army has been lost and a large part of those fortified lines upon which so much faith was reposed has gone, and many valuable mining districts and factories have passed into the enemy's possession.

The whole of the Channel ports are in his hands, with all the strategic consequences that follow from that, and we must expect another blow to be struck almost immediately at us or at France. . . .

We must never forget the solid assurances of sea power and those which belong to air power if they can be locally exercised. I have myself full confidence that if all do their duty and if the best arrangements are made, as they are being made, we shall prove ourselves once again able to defend our island home, ride out the storms of war, outlive the menace of tyranny, if necessary for years, if necessary, alone.

At any rate, that is what we are going to try to do. That is the resolve of His Majesty's Government, every man of them. That is the will of Parliament and the nation. The British Empire and the French Republic, linked together in their cause and their need, will defend to the death their native soils, aiding each other like good comrades to the utmost of their strength, even though a large tract of Europe and many old and famous States have fallen or may fall into the grip of the Gestapo and all the odious apparatus of Nazi rule.

We shall not flag nor fail. We shall go on to the end. We shall fight in France and on the seas and oceans; we shall fight with growing confidence and growing strength in the air. We shall defend our island whatever the cost may be; we shall fight on beaches, landing grounds, in fields, in streets and on the hills. We shall never surrender and even if, which I do not for a moment believe, this island or a large part of it were subjugated and starving, then our empire beyond the seas, armed and guarded by the British Fleet, will carry on the struggle until, in God's good time, the New World with all its power and might, sets forth to the liberation and rescue of the Old.

Source: Winston S. Churchill, *The Complete Speeches,* 8 vols., ed. Robert Rhodes James (New York: Chelsea House Publishers, 1974), 6: 6225–6231.

57. Benito Mussolini, "Speech on War Entry," 10 June 1940

Although Italy was an ally of Germany, both ideologically and by treaty, Italy's fascist dictator Benito Mussolini initially hesitated to join the European war. In August 1939, he told Hitler: "If Germany attacks Poland and the conflict is localized, Italy will give Germany every form of political and economic aid which may be required." He warned, however, that Italy would not participate in a wider war, stating: "If Germany attacks Poland and the allies of the latter counter-attack Germany, I must emphasize to you that I cannot assume the initiative of warlike operations, given the actual conditions of Italian military preparations which have been repeatedly and in timely fashion pointed out to you." Germany's stunning military successes of May and June 1940 and the impending defeat of France impelled the opportunistic Mussolini to reverse his stance, declare war on both France and Britain, and invade France.

Fighters of land, sea and air, Blackshirts of the revolution and of the legions, men and women of Italy, of the empire and of the Kingdom of Albania, listen!

The hour destined by fate is sounding for us. The hour of irrevocable decision has come. A declaration of war has already been handed to the Ambassadors of Great Britain and France.

We take the field against the plutocratic and reactionary democracies who always have blocked the march and frequently plotted against the existence of the Italian people.

Several decades of recent history may be summarized in these words: Phrases, promises, threats of blackmail, and finally, crowning that ignoble edifice, the League of Nations of fifty-two nations.

Our conscience is absolutely clear.

With you, the entire world is witness that the Italy of fascism has done everything humanly possible to avoid the tempest that envelops Europe, but all in vain.

It would have sufficed to revise treaties to adapt them to changing requirements vital to nations and not consider them untouchable for eternity.

It would have sufficed not to begin the stupid policy of guarantees, which proved particularly deadly for those who accepted them.

It would have sufficed not to reject the proposal the Fuehrer made last Oct. 6 after the campaign in Poland ended.

Now all that belongs to the past.

If today we have decided to take the risks and sacrifices of war, it is because the honor, interests and future firmly impose it since a great people is truly such if it considers its obligations sacred and does not avoid the supreme trials that determine the course of history.

We are taking up arms, after having solved the problem of our continental frontiers, to solve our maritime frontiers. We want to break the territorial and military chains that confine us in our sea because a country of 45,000,000 souls is not truly free if it has not free access to the ocean.

This gigantic conflict is only a phase of the logical development of our revolution. It is the conflict of poor, numerous peoples who labor against starvers who ferociously cling to a monopoly of all riches and all gold on earth.

It is a conflict of fruitful, useful peoples against peoples who are in a decline. It is a conflict between two ages, two ideas.

Now the die is cast and our will has burned our ships behind us.

I solemnly declare that Italy does not intend to drag other peoples bordering on her by sea or land into the conflict. Switzerland, Yugoslavia, Greece, Turkey and Egypt, take note of these words of mine. It depends on them and only on them if these words are rigorously confirmed or not.

Italians, in a memorable mass meeting in Berlin, I said that according to the rules of Fascist morals, when one has a friend one marches with him to the end. This we have done and will continue to do with Germany, her people and her victorious armed forces.

On this eve of an event of import for centuries, we turn our thoughts to His Majesty, the King and Emperor, who always has understood the thought of this country. Lastly, we salute the new Fuehrer, the chief of great allied Germany.

Proletarian, Fascist Italy has arisen for the third time, strong, proud, compact as never before.

There is only one order. It is categorical and obligatory to every one. It already wings over and enflames hearts from the Alps to the Indian Ocean: Conquer!

And we will conquer in order, finally, to give a new world of peace with justice to Italy, to Europe and to the universe.

Italian people, rush to arms and show your tenacity, your courage, your valor.

Source: Official Italian government translation published in the *New York Times,* 11 June 1940.

58. "Their Finest Hour": Winston Churchill, Speech in the British House of Commons, 18 June 1940

As the last of the British forces escaped from France and the French government neared surrender, Winston Churchill again reiterated Great Britain's determination to fight on alone for as long as might be necessary. He also offered France common citizenship with Great Britain, a proposal that in some ways anticipated the later European Union. Churchill's government believed that a German invasion of the British Isles was the next item on Hitler's military agenda. The prime minister therefore sought to persuade the British people that, even though the military situation was desperate, any such undertaking would fail, provided the British could find the resolution to endure the air bombing that would precede it. Churchill's stirring rhetoric not only heartened his own countrymen but also caught the imagination of the rest of the world. As with earlier speeches, his speech was intended to win the support not only of his own population but also of the American president and people.

. . . . The disastrous military events which have happened during the past fortnight have not come to me with any sense of surprise. Indeed, I indicated a fortnight ago as clearly as I could to the House that the worst possibilities were open; and I made it perfectly clear then that whatever happened in France would make no difference to the resolve of Britain and the British Empire to fight on, "if necessary for years, if necessary alone." . . .

I have thought it right upon this occasion to give the House and the country some indication of the solid, practical grounds upon which we base our inflexible resolve to continue the war. There are a good many people who say, "Never mind. Win or lose, sink or swim, better die than submit to tyranny—and such a tyranny." And I do not dissociate myself from them. But I can assure them that our professional advisers of the three Services unitedly advise that we should carry on the war, and that there are good and reasonable hopes of final victory. . . .

If Hitler can bring under his despotic control the industries of the countries he has conquered, this will add greatly to his already vast armament output. On the other hand, this will not happen immediately, and we are now assured of immense, continuous and increasing support in supplies and munitions of all kinds from the United States; and especially of airplanes and pilots from the Dominions and across the oceans, coming from regions which are beyond the reach of enemy bombers. . . .

We do not yet know what will happen in France or whether the French resistance will be prolonged, both in France and in the French Empire overseas. The French Government will be throwing away great opportunities and casting adrift their future if they do not continue the war in accordance with their Treaty obligations, from which we have not felt able to release them. The House will have read the historic declaration in which, at the desire of many Frenchmen—and of our own hearts—we have proclaimed our willingness at the darkest hour in French history to conclude a union of common citizenship in this struggle. However matters may go in France or with the French Government, or other French Governments, we in this island and in the British Empire will never lose our sense of comradeship with the French people. If we are now called upon to endure what they have been suffering, we shall emulate their courage, and if final victory rewards our toils they shall share the gains, aye, and freedom shall be restored to all. We abate nothing of our just demands; not one jot or tittle do we recede. Czechs, Poles, Norwegians, Dutch, Belgians have joined their causes to our own. All these shall be restored.

What General Weygand called the Battle of France is over. I expect that the Battle of Britain is about to begin. Upon this battle depends the survival of Christian civilization. Upon it depends our own British life, and the long continuity of our institutions and our Empire. The whole fury and might of the enemy must very soon be turned on us. Hitler knows that he will have to break us in this island or lose the war. If we can stand up to him, all Europe may be free and the life of the world may move forward into broad, sunlit uplands. But if we fail, then the whole world, including the United States, including all that we have known and cared for, will sink into the abyss of a new Dark Age made more sinister, and perhaps more protracted, by the lights of perverted science. Let us therefore brace ourselves to our duties and so bear ourselves that, if the British Empire and its Commonwealth last for a thousand years, men will still say, "This was their finest hour."

Source: Winston S. Churchill, *The Complete Speeches,* 8 vols., ed. Robert Rhodes James (New York: Chelsea House Publishers, 1974), 6: 6231–6238.

59. Armistice Agreement between the German High Command of the Armed Forces and French Plenipotentiaries, Compiègne, 22 June 1940

Facing overwhelming military defeat, on 22 June 1940, French military leaders signed an armistice with Germany. Under its terms, a large portion of France, including Paris, the capital city, was to be under German military occupation. All French military armaments were to be surrendered to Germany. The armistice left Great Britain the only power still fighting against Germany.

Between the chief of the High Command of the armed forces, Col. Gen. [Wilhelm] Keitel, commissioned by the Fuehrer of the German Reich and Supreme Commander in Chief of the German Armed Forces, and the fully authorized plenipotentiaries of the French Government, General [Charles L. C.] Huntziger, chairman of the delegation; Ambassador [Léon] Noel, Rear Admiral [Maurice R.] LeLuc, Army Corps General [Georges] Parisot and Air Force General [Jean-Marie Joseph] Bergeret, the following armistice treaty was agreed upon:

ARTICLE I.

The French Government directs a cessation of fighting against the German Reich in France as well as in French possessions, colonies, protectorate territories, mandates as well as on the seas.

It [the French Government] directs the immediate laying down of arms of French units already encircled by German troops.

ARTICLE II.

To safeguard the interests of the German Reich, French State territory north and west of the line drawn on the attached map will be occupied by German troops.

As far as the parts to be occupied still are not in control of German troops, this occupation will be carried out immediately after the conclusion of this treaty.

ARTICLE III.

In the occupied parts of France the German Reich exercises all rights of an occupying power The French Government obligates itself to support with every means the regulations resulting from the exercise of these rights and to carry them out with the aid of French administration.

All French authorities and officials of the occupied territory, therefore, are to be promptly informed by the French Government to comply with the regulations of the German military commanders and to cooperate with them in a correct manner.

It is the intention of the German Government to limit the occupation of the west coast after ending hostilities with England to the extent absolutely necessary.

The French Government is permitted to select the seat of its government in unoccupied territory, or, if it wishes, to move to Paris. In this case, the German Government guarantees the French Government and its central authorities every necessary alleviation so that they will be in a position to conduct the administration of unoccupied territory from Paris.

ARTICLE IV.

French armed forces on land, on the sea, and in the air are to be demobilized and disarmed in a period still to be set. Excepted are only those units which are necessary for maintenance of domestic order. Germany and Italy will fix their strength. The French armed forces in the territory to be occupied by Germany are to be hastily withdrawn into territory not to be occupied and be discharged. These troops, before marching out, shall lay down their weapons and equipment at the places where they are stationed at the time this treaty becomes effective. They are responsible for orderly delivery to German troops.

ARTICLE V.

As a guarantee for the observance of the armistice, the surrender, undamaged, of all those guns, tanks, tank defense weapons, war planes, anti-aircraft artillery, infantry weapons, means of conveyance, and munitions can be demanded from the units of the French armed forces which are standing in battle against Germany and which at the time this agreement goes into force are in territory not to be occupied by Germany.

The German armistice commission will decide the extent of delivery.

ARTICLE VI.

Weapons, munitions, and war apparatus of every kind remaining in the unoccupied portion of France are to be stored and/or secured under German and/or Italian control—so far as not released for the arming allowed to French units.

The German High Command reserves the right to direct all those measures which are necessary to exclude unauthorized use of this material. Building of new war apparatus in unoccupied territory is to be stopped immediately.

ARTICLE VII.

In occupied territory, all the land and coastal fortifications, with weapons, munitions, and apparatus and plants of every kind are to be surrendered undamaged. Plans of these fortifications, as well as plans of those already conquered by German troops, are to be handed over.

Exact plans regarding prepared blastings, land mines, obstructions, time fuses, barriers for fighting, etc., shall be given to the German High Command. These hindrances are to be removed by French forces upon German demand.

ARTICLE VIII.

The French War Fleet is to collect in ports to be designated more particularly, and under German and/or Italian control to demobilize and lay up—with the exception of those units released to the French Government for protection of French interests in its colonial empire.

The peacetime stations of ships should control the designation of ports.

The German Government solemnly declares to the French Government that it does not intend to use the French War Fleet which is in harbors under German control for its purposes in war, with the exception of units necessary for the purposes of guarding the coast and sweeping mines.

It further solemnly and expressly declares that it does not intend to bring up any demands respecting the French War Fleet at the conclusion of a peace.

All warships outside France are to be recalled to France with the exception of that portion of the French War Fleet which shall be designated to represent French interests in the colonial empire.

ARTICLE IX.

The French High Command must give the German High Command the exact location of all mines which France has set out, as well as information on the other harbor and coastal obstructions and defense facilities. Insofar as the German High Command may require, French forces must clear away the mines.

ARTICLE X.

The French Government is obligated to forbid any portion of its remaining armed forces to undertake hostilities against Germany in any manner.

The French Government also will prevent members of its armed forces from leaving the country and prevent armaments of any sort, including ships, planes, etc., being taken to England or any other place abroad.

The French Government will forbid French citizens to fight against Germany in the service of States with which the German Reich is still at war. French citizens who violate this provision are to be treated by German troops as insurgents.

ARTICLE XI.

French commercial vessels of all sorts, including coastal and harbor vessels which are now in French hands, may not leave port until further notice. Resumption of commercial voyages will require approval of the German and Italian Governments.

French commercial vessels will be recalled by the French Government or, if return is impossible, the French Government will instruct them to enter neutral harbors.

All confiscated German commercial vessels are, on demand, to be returned [to Germany] undamaged.

ARTICLE XII.

Flight by any airplane over French territory shall be prohibited. Every plane making a flight without German approval will be regarded as an enemy by the German Air Force and treated accordingly.

In unoccupied territory, air fields and ground facilities of the air force shall be under German and Italian control.

Demand may be made that such air fields be rendered unusable. The French Government is required to take charge of all foreign airplanes in the unoccupied region to prevent flights. They are to be turned over to the German armed forces.

ARTICLE XIII.

The French Government obligates itself to turn over to German troops in the occupied region all facilities and properties of the French armed forces in undamaged condition.

It [the French Government] also will see to it that harbors, industrial facilities, and docks are preserved in their present condition and damaged in no way.

The same stipulations apply to transportation routes and equipment, especially railways, roads, and canals, and to the whole communications network and equipment, waterways and coastal transportation services.

Additionally, the French Government is required on demand of the German High Command to perform all necessary restoration labor on these facilities.

The French Government will see to it that in the occupied region necessary technical personnel and rolling stock of the railways and other transportation equipment, to a degree normal in peacetime, be retained in service.

ARTICLE XIV.

There is an immediate prohibition of transmission for all wireless stations on French soil. Resumption of wireless connections from the unoccupied portion of France requires a special regulation.

ARTICLE XV.

The French Government obligates itself to convey transit freight between the German Reich and Italy through unoccupied territory to the extent demanded by the German Government.

ARTICLE XVI.

The French Government, in agreement with the responsible German officials, will carry out the return of population into occupied territory.

ARTICLE XVII.

The French Government obligates itself to prevent every transference of economic valuables and provisions from the territory to be occupied by German troops into unoccupied territory or abroad.

These valuables and provisions in occupied territory are to be disposed of only in agreement with the German Government. In that connection, the German Government will consider the necessities of life of the population in unoccupied territory.

ARTICLE XVIII.

The French Government will bear the costs of maintenance of German occupation troops on French soil.

ARTICLE XIX.

All German war and civil prisoners in French custody, including those under arrest and convicted who were seized and sentenced because of acts in favor of the German Reich, shall be surrendered immediately to German troops.

The French Government is obliged to surrender upon demand all Germans named by the German Government in France as well as in French possessions, colonies, protectorate territories, and mandates.

The French Government binds itself to prevent removal of German war and civil prisoners from France into French possessions or into foreign countries. Regarding prisoners already taken outside of France, as well as sick and wounded German prisoners who cannot be transported, exact lists with the places of residence are to be produced. The German

High Command assumes care of sick and wounded German war prisoners.

ARTICLE XX.

French troops in German prison camps will remain prisoners of war until conclusion of a peace.

ARTICLE XXI.

The French Government assumes responsibility for the security of all objects and valuables whose undamaged surrender or holding in readiness for German disposal is demanded in this agreement or whose removal outside the country is forbidden. The French Government is bound to compensate for all destruction, damage or removal contrary to agreement.

ARTICLE XXII.

The Armistice Commission, acting in accordance with the direction of the German High Command, will regulate and supervise the carrying out of the armistice agreement. It is the task of the Armistice Commission further to insure the necessary conformity of this agreement with the Italian-French armistice.

The French Government will send a delegation to the seat of the German Armistice Commission to represent the French wishes and to receive regulations from the German Armistice Commission for executing [the agreement].

ARTICLE XXIII.

This armistice agreement becomes effective as soon as the French Government also has reached an agreement with the Italian Government regarding cessation of hostilities.

Hostilities will be stopped six hours after the moment at which the Italian Government has notified the German Government of conclusion of its agreement. The German Government will notify the French Government of this time by wireless.

ARTICLE XXIV.

This agreement is valid until conclusion of a peace treaty. The German Government may terminate this agreement at any time with immediate effect if the French Government fails to fulfill the obligations it assumes under the agreement.

Source: U.S. Department of State, Publication No. 6312, *Documents on German Foreign Policy 1918–1945, Series D, IX* (Washington, DC: U.S. Government Printing Office, 1956), 671–676.

60. Memorandum from Assistant Secretary of State Breckinridge Long to U.S. State Department Officials Adolf A. Berle and James Dunn, 26 June 1940, Describing Methods of Obstructing the Granting of U.S. Visas to Applicants

Some influential diplomats sought to impede the entry of Jewish would-be emigrants into the United States. In summer 1940, just after the fall of France, Assistant Secretary of State Breckinridge Long explained to two of his colleagues methods whereby it could be made almost impossible for Jews to obtain visas to enter the United States. Long displayed no concern for the fact that this decision might well mean death or, at best, internment in a concentration camp for those Jews refused entry.

Attached is a memorandum from [Long's assistant] Mr. [Avra] Warren. I discussed the matter with him on the basis of this memorandum. There are two possibilities and I will discuss each category briefly.

NON-IMMIGRANTS

Their entry into the United States can be made to depend upon prior authorization by the Department [of State]. This would mean that the consuls would be divested of discretion and that all requests for non-immigrant visas (temporary visitor and transit visas) be passed upon here. It is quite feasible and can be done instantly. It will permit the Department to effectively control the immigration of persons in this category and private instructions can be given to the Visa Division as to nationalities which should not be admitted as well as to individuals who are to be excluded.

This must be done for universal application and could not be done as regards Germany, for instance, or Russia, for instance, or any other one government because it would first, invite retaliation and second, would probably be a violation of some of our treaty arrangements. The retaliation clause is in connection with Germany because it could mean the closing of our offices in almost all of Europe.

IMMIGRANTS

We can delay and effectively stop for a temporary period of indefinite length the number of immigrants into the United States. We could do this by simply advising our consuls to put every obstacle in the way and to require additional evidence and to resort to various administrative devices which would postpone and postpone and postpone the granting of the visas. However, this could only be temporary. In order to make it more definite it would have to be done by suspension of the rules under the law by the issuance of a proclamation of emergency—which I take it we are not yet ready to proclaim.

SUMMING UP

We can effectively control non-immigrants by prohibiting the issuance of visas unless the consent of the Department to this be obtained in advance for universal application.

We can temporarily prevent the number of immigrants from certain localities such as Cuba, Mexico and other places of origin of German intending immigrants by simply raising administrative obstacles.

The Department will be prepared to take these two steps immediately upon the decision but emphasis must be placed on the fact that discrimination must not be practiced and with the additional thought that in case a suspension of the regulations should be proclaimed under the need of an emergency, it would be universally applicable and would affect refugees from England.

The Canadian situation and travel across that border we can handle through an exception to the general rule and so advise our consuls in Canada.

Source: Assistant Secretary of State Breckinridge Long, Memorandum to State Department Officials Adolf A. Berle and James Dunn, 26 June 1940, Describing Methods of Obstructing the Granting of U.S. Visas to Applicants. Available at Public Broadcasting Service. http://www.pbs.org/wgbh/amex/holocaust/filmmore/reference/primary/barmemo.html.

61. President Franklin D. Roosevelt, Message to the Congress Recommending Additional Appropriations for National Defense, 10 July 1940

In summer 1940, the stunning recent German successes in Europe impelled President Franklin D. Roosevelt to ask Congress for greatly increased funding for defense. As he himself pointed out, it was the third such request he had submitted in slightly under two months, an index of just how grave he considered the international situation to be.

. . . . On May 16, in a message to the Congress, I pointed out that the swift and shocking developments of that time forced every neutral nation to look to its defenses in the light of new factors loosed by the brutal force of modern offensive war. I called attention to the treacherous use of the "fifth column," by which persons supposed to be peaceful visitors were actually a part of an enemy unit of occupation, and called especial attention to the necessity for the protection of the whole American Hemisphere from control, invasion or domination. I asked at that time for a sum totaling $1,182,000,000 for the national defense.

On May 31, 1940, I again sent a message to the Congress, to say that the almost incredible events of the then past two weeks in the European conflict had necessitated another enlargement of our military program, and at that time I asked for $1,277,741,170 for the acceleration and development of our military and naval needs as measured in both machines and men.

Again today, in less than two months' time, the changes in the world situation are so great and so profound that I must come once again to the Congress to advise concerning new threats, new needs, and the imperative necessity of meeting them. Free men and free women in the United States look to us to defend their freedom against all enemies, foreign and domestic. Those enemies of freedom who hate free institutions now deride democratic Governments as weak and inefficient.

We, the free men and women of the United States, with memories of our fathers to inspire us and the hopes of our children to sustain us, are determined to be strong as well as free. The apologists for despotism and those who aid them by whispering defeatism or appeasement, assert that because we have not devoted our full energies to arms and to preparation for war that we are now incapable of defense.

I refute that imputation.

We fully understand the threat of the new enslavement in which men may not speak, may not listen, may not think. As these threats become more numerous and their dire meaning more clear, it deepens the determination of the American people to meet them with wholly adequate defense.

We have seen nation after nation, some of them weakened by treachery from within, succumb to the force of the aggressor. We see great nations still gallantly fighting against aggression, encouraged by high hope of ultimate victory.

That we are opposed to war is known not only to every American, but to every government in the world. We will not use our arms in a war of aggression; we will not send our men to take part in European wars.

But, we will repel aggression against the United States or the Western Hemisphere. The people and their representatives in the Congress know that the threats to our liberties, the threats to our security, the threats against our way of life, the threats to our institutions of religion, of democracy, and of international good faith, have increased in number and gravity from month to month, from week to week, and almost from day to day.

It is because of these rapid changes; it is because of the grave danger to democratic institutions; and above all, it is because of the united will of the entire American people that I come to ask you for a further authorization of $4,848,171,957 for the national defense.

Let no man in this country or anywhere else believe that because we in America still cherish freedom of religion, of speech, of assembly, of the press; that because we maintain our free democratic political institutions by which the nation after full discussion and debate chooses its representatives and leaders for itself—let no man here or elsewhere believe that we are weak.

The United States is the greatest industrial nation in the world. Its people, as workers and as business men, have proved that they can unite in the national interest and that they can bring together the greatest assembly of human skills, of mechanical production, and of national resources, ever known in any nation.

The principal lesson of the war up to the present time is that partial defense is inadequate defense.

If the United States is to have any defense, it must have total defense.

We cannot defend ourselves a little here and a little there. We must be able to defend ourselves wholly and at any time.

Our plans for national security, therefore, should cover total defense. I believe that the people of this country are willing to make any sacrifice to attain that end.

After consultation with the War and Navy Departments and the Advisory Commission to the Council of National Defense, I recommend a further program for the national defense. This contemplates the provision of funds and authorizations for the materiel requirements without which the manpower of the nation, if called into service, cannot effectively operate, either in the production of arms and goods, or their utilization in repelling attack.

In broad outline our immediate objectives are as follows:

1. To carry forward the Naval expansion program designed to build up the Navy to meet any possible combination of hostile naval forces.
2. To complete the total equipment for a land force of approximately 1,200,000 men, though of course this total of men would not be in the Army in time of peace.
3. To procure reserve stocks of tanks, guns, artillery, ammunition, etc., for another 800,000 men or a total of 2,000,000 men if a mobilization of such a force should become necessary.
4. To provide for manufacturing facilities, public and private, necessary to produce critical items of equipment for a land force of 2,000,000 men, and to produce the ordnance items required for the aircraft program of the Army and Navy—guns, bombs, armor, bombsights and ammunition.
5. Procurement of 15,000 additional planes for the Army and 4,000 for the Navy, complete with necessary spare engines, armaments, and the most modern equipment.

The foregoing program deals exclusively with materiel requirements. The Congress is now considering the enactment of a system of selective training for developing the necessary manpower to operate this materiel and manpower to fill army non-combat needs. In this way we can make certain that when this modern materiel becomes available, it will be placed in the hands of troops trained, seasoned, and ready, and that replacement materiel can be guaranteed....

The total amount which I ask of the Congress in order that this program may be carried out with all reasonable speed is $2,161,441,957, which it is estimated would be spent out of the Treasury between now and July 1, 1941, and an additional $2,686,730,000 for contract authorizations.

So great a sum means sacrifice. So large a program means hard work—the participation of the whole country in the total defense of the country. This nation through sacrifice and work and unity proposes to remain free.

Source: Web site: ibiblio. Available at http://www.ibiblio.org/pha/7–2–188/188–18.html.

62. Declaration on "Reciprocal Assistance and Cooperation for the Defense of the Nations of the Americas," Adopted at the Meeting of the Ministers of Foreign Affairs of the American Republics in Havana, 30 July 1940

Meeting in Havana, Cuba, the foreign ministers of the United States and the various Latin American nations joined in a statement that an attack by a non-American nation on any one of them would be regarded as an attack on all.

The Second Meeting of the Ministers of Foreign Affairs of the American Republics

DECLARES

That any attempt on the part of a non-American state against the integrity or inviolability of the territory, the sovereignty or the political independence of an American state shall be considered as an act of aggression against the states which sign this declaration.

In case acts of aggression are committed or should there be reason to believe that an act of aggression is being prepared by a non-American nation against the integrity or inviolability of the territory, the sovereignty or the political independence of an American nation, the nations signatory to the present declaration will consult among themselves in order to agree upon the measure it may be advisable to take.

All the signatory nations, or two or more of them, according to circumstances, shall proceed to negotiate the necessary complementary agreements so as to organize co-operation for defense and the assistance that they shall lend each other in the event of aggressions such as those referred to in this declaration.

Source: James W. Gantenbein, *Documentary Background of World War II 1931 to 1941* (New York: Columbia University Press, 1948), 997.

63. German Foreign Minister (Count Joachim von Ribbentrop), Authority of Nazi Ambassador to Vichy France Otto Abetz, 3 August 1940

After the armistice with Germany, part of France was occupied, while until 1943 the remaining portion was ruled by a government based at Vichy and largely subservient to Germany. Otto Abetz, the Nazi ambassador to France, effectively functioned as a proconsul, supervising the nominally independent Vichy regime.

In answer to a question of the Quartermaster General, addressed to the High Command of the Armed Forces and transmitted by the latter to the Ministry of Foreign Affairs, the Führer has appointed Abetz, until now Minister, as Ambassador, and on my report has decreed the following:

I. Ambassador Abetz has the following functions in France:

1. To advise the military agencies on political matters.
2. To maintain permanent contact with the Vichy Government and its representatives in the occupied zone.
3. To influence the important political personalities in the occupied zone and in the unoccupied zone in a way favorable to our intentions.
4. To guide from the political point of view the press, the radio, and the propaganda in the occupied zone and to influence the responsible elements engaged in the molding of public opinion in the unoccupied zone.
5. To take care of the German, French, and Belgian citizens returning from internment camps.
6. To advise the secret military police and the Gestapo on the seizure of politically important documents.
7. To seize and secure all public art treasures and private art treasures, and particularly art treasures belonging to Jews, on the basis of special instructions relating thereto.

II. The Führer has expressly ordered that only Ambassador Abetz shall be responsible for all political questions in Occupied and Unoccupied France. Insofar as military interests are touched by his duties, Ambassador Abetz shall act only in agreement with the Military Command in France.

III. Ambassador Abetz will be attached to the Military Commander in France as his deputy. His domicile shall continue to be in Paris as hitherto. He will receive from me instructions for the accomplishment of his tasks and will be responsible solely to me. I shall greatly appreciate it if the High Command of the Armed Forces will give the necessary orders to the military agencies concerned as quickly as possible.

Source: Trial of the Major War Criminals before the International Military Tribunal, Nuremberg, 14 November 1945–1 October 1946, 42 vols. (Nuremberg, 1948), 6: 560–561 (Doc. RF-1061). The text in German may be found in ibid., 32: 432–433 (Doc. 3614-PS).

64. Reich Economics Minister Walter Funk, Memorandum for Hermann Göring, Proposals for a "New Order" in Europe, 6 August 1940

In late June 1940, Hermann Göring, Adolf Hitler's deputy, instructed Walter Funk, the Reich's economics minister, to prepare and submit to him proposals for a "New Order" in Europe. These were to focus upon the economic integration of the occupied territories with Germany proper, economic measures that might be taken against enemy states, and the eventual economic reconstruction of continental Europe. The proposals Funk submitted focused primarily upon the first of these mandates, envisaging effective German control of all the major sectors of the European economy.

The question of what form the European economy will finally take cannot of course be answered definitively at the present time.

I am working on the assumption that the integration of the occupied territories in the economy of Greater Germany and the reconstruction of a continental European economy under German leadership will not occur through a single political act such as the conclusion of a customs or currency union, but that this goal will be achieved through a series of individual measures which will begin at once and to some extent have already begun. The decisive factor must be to link the European economies as completely and as closely as possible with the economy of Greater Germany. In the process, all measures which are designed to improve the satisfaction of German needs and to strengthen German economic influence in the various countries concerned must be given priority, while vice versa all measures which, from the standpoint of our greater German interests, are unimportant must be prevented or be postponed until later. From this point of view, at the moment the following measures are important and have priority:

1. The securing of as large a proportion as possible of European production for German requirements.
2. The extension of European production with a view to a further improvement in the possibilities of satisfying German needs from within Europe, i.e., the application of the principles of the Four Year Plan and the German Battle of Production to the European economy.
3. The creation of a European payments system (Central Clearing) on the basis of the *Reichsmark,* which in the first instance will provide the technical means for paying for the influx of German goods onto the German market and, secondly, will deal with the gold and credit aspects of the exchange of goods within Europe.
4. The control of international trade within Europe as well as European trade with overseas countries through inter-state agreements involving the exercise of German power and influence. The control of the economic and financial policy of the European states with the aim of aligning the economic-political methods and form of economic activity practiced by them as far as possible with the German norms.

   These questions are being dealt with at this moment in the territories occupied by the German Wehrmacht [army]; it must be our next task gradually to create a similar state of affairs in the other countries which are dependent on us.
5. The linking of the European economies with the greater German economy under German leadership in the following spheres:
   (a) The organization of the economy: the creation of organizational forms such as those represented in Germany by the Organization of Business [*Organisation der gewerblichen Wirtschaft*] and the Reich Food Estate and the fusion of these organizations into a combined European organization under German leadership.
   (b) The inclusion of the relevant branches of European business in the German market-regulating associations (Cartells) at the same time ensuring that German leadership is firmly secured (iron, coal, metals, chemicals, electricity etc.).
   (c) Securing control of the capital of the most important European industrial undertakings (armaments industry, iron and metal industries, etc.).
   (d) The infiltration of the decisive posts in European business with suitable German experts.
6. Simplification of the practice of granting permits for international trade within Europe, the removal of restrictive regulations, the adaptation of the customs arrangements to the need for an intensification of

trade and cooperation in the industrial, raw material, and agrarian spheres.

As far as point 2 of your commission, "Economic conflict with the enemy states," is concerned, I consider it premature to make you any suggestions at present. Preparations are, however, underway in house. In this connection, I would like to reiterate my view that in order to construct a unified European *Grossraumwirtschaft* [new economic order] under German leadership it is vital to take over the leading business posts in Europe which at the moment are all in possession of Englishmen and Frenchmen. Similarly, we need a reserve of foreign exchange and raw materials for the transitional period in order to be able to remove the restrictions on German consumption as soon as possible. I am thinking in terms of a sum of circa ten billion gold marks which represents the equivalent of the value of the German private property stolen by the Allies.

I would be grateful if you would inform me of your approval of the proposed work programme and of any further wishes you may have in connection with it. The relevant Ministries, in particular the Reich Ministry of Food and Agriculture and the Foreign Ministry, have expressed their approval of the programme.

Source: J. Noakes and G. Pridham, eds., *Nazism 1919–1945,* Volume 3: *Foreign Policy, War and Racial Extermination: A Documentary Reader* (Exeter, UK: University of Exeter Press, 1988), 281–282. Reprinted with permission of University of Exeter Press.

65. British Prime Minister Winston Churchill to General Charles de Gaulle, Enclosing Memorandum of Agreement, 7 August 1940

Not all French soldiers surrendered when the French government signed an armistice with Germany. A number of them, of whom the most prominent was a tank commander then fifty years of age, General Charles de Gaulle, fled to Great Britain, where they claimed to represent the "Free French" who wished to continue to fight against Germany. De Gaulle, a difficult personality, enjoyed notoriously poor relations with both British Prime Minister Winston Churchill and U.S. President Franklin D. Roosevelt, both of whom wished that the Free French had turned to a less prickly leader. Nonetheless, the Allied governments had little alternative but to support him. In August 1940, Churchill sent de Gaulle a memorandum of agreement, which became the basic document governing the relationship between the Free French and the British government.

You were good enough to give me your ideas as to the organization, employment and conditions of service of the French volunteer force now being assembled under your command, in your capacity, in which you are recognized by His Majesty's Government in the United Kingdom, of leader of all free Frenchmen, wherever they may be, who rally to you in support of the Allied Cause.

I now send you a memorandum which, if you concur, will be agreed between us as governing the organization, employment and conditions of service of your force.

I would take this opportunity of stating that it is the determination of His Majesty's Government, when victory has been gained by the Allied arms, to secure the full restoration of the independence and greatness of France.

MEMORANDUM OF AGREEMENT.

I.

(1) General de Gaulle is engaged in raising a French force composed of volunteers. This force, which includes naval, land and air units and scientific and technical personnel, will be organized and employed against the common enemies.

(2) This force will never be required to take up arms against France.

II.

(1) This force will, as far as possible, retain the character of a French force in respect of personnel, particularly as regards the discipline, language, promotion and duties.

(2) So far as may be necessary for their equipment, this force will have priority of allocation as regards property in and the use of material (particularly weapons, aircraft, vehicles, ammunition, machinery and supplies) which has already been brought by French armed forces from any quarter, or which

may so be brought in the future by such French forces, into territory under the authority of His Majesty's Government in the United Kingdom or into territory where the British High Command exercises authority. In the case of French forces, the command of which has been delegated by agreement between General de Gaulle and the British High Command, no transfer, exchange or reallocation of equipment, property, and material in possession of these forces will be made by order of General de Gaulle without prior consultation and agreement with the British High Command.

(3) His Majesty's Government will, as soon as practicable, supply the French force with the additional equipment which may be essential to equip its units on a scale equivalent to that of British units of the same type.

(4) Naval vessels from the French fleet will be allocated as follows:

The French force will commission and operate as many vessels as it is able to man.

The allocation of the vessels to be commissioned and operated by the French force under (a) will be a matter for agreement from time to time between General de Gaulle and the British Admiralty.

Vessels not allocated under (b) to the French force will be available for commissioning and operating under the direction of the British Admiralty.

Of the vessels mentioned under (c) some may be operated under direct British control and some may be operated by other allied naval forces.

Vessels operated under British control will when possible include in their complement a proportion of French officers and men.

All vessels concerned will remain French property.

(5) The possible use of French merchant ships and of their crews, in so far as this is for the purpose of military operations by General de Gaulle's force, will be the subject of arrangements between General de Gaulle and the British departments concerned. Regular contact will be maintained between the Ministry of Shipping and General de Gaulle as regards the use of the rest of the ships and the employment of the merchant seamen.

(6) General de Gaulle, who is in supreme command of the French force, hereby declares that he accepts the general direction of the British High Command. When necessary, he will delegate, in agreement with the British High Command, the immediate command of any part of his force to one or more British officers of appropriate rank, subject to what is stated at the end of Article I above.

III.

The status of French volunteers will be established in the following manner:

(1) Volunteers will enroll for the duration of the war for the purpose of fighting against the common enemies.

(2) They will receive pay on a basis to be settled separately by agreement between General de Gaulle and the Departments concerned. The period of time during which such rates will apply will be a matter for settlement between General de Gaulle and His Majesty's Government in the United Kingdom.

(3) The volunteers and their dependants will be granted pensions and other benefits in respect of the disablement or death of the volunteers on a basis to be settled by separate agreement between General de Gaulle and the Department concerned.

(4) General de Gaulle will be entitled to form a civil establishment containing the administrative services required for the organization of his force, the numbers and emoluments of the members of this establishment being settled in consultation with the British Treasury.

(5) The General will also be entitled to recruit technical and scientific staff for war work. The numbers, manner of remuneration and method of employment of this staff will be settled in consultation with the Department of His Majesty's Government concerned.

(6) His Majesty's Government in the United Kingdom will use their best endeavours, at the time of the conclusion of peace, to help the French volunteers to regain any rights, including national status, of which they may have been deprived as a result of their participation in the struggle against the common enemies. His Majesty's Government are willing to afford special facilities to such volunteers to acquire British nationality, and will seek any necessary powers.

IV.

(1) Any expenditure incurred for the purpose of the constitution and maintenance of the French force under the provisions of this agreement will be met, in the first instance, by the appropriate Departments of His Majesty's Government in the United Kingdom, which will be entitled to exercise any necessary examination and audit.

(2) The sums required will be regarded as advances and specially recorded; all questions relating to the ultimate settlement of these advances, including any credits which may be set off by agreement, will be a matter for subsequent arrangements.

V.

This agreement shall be regarded as having come into force [retroactively] on the 1st July, 1940.

Source: Margaret Carlyle, ed., *Documents on International Affairs 1939–1946,* Volume II: *Hitler's Europe* (London: Oxford University Press, 1954), 167–170. Reprinted with permission of Chatham House.

66. "The Few": Winston Churchill, Speech in the British House of Commons, 20 August 1940

At the height of the Battle of Britain, when German air raids sought to pulverize British industrial towns and eliminate the British air force, Winston Churchill once more addressed the House of Commons. As always, he reiterated British determination to continue fighting against Germany and updated the progress made in British rearmament since the disaster of Dunkirk. Churchill defended Britain's policy of refusing to allow supplies into Europe even to feed civilians in the occupied countries of the continent. The British premier described the "destroyers for bases" deal with the United States then under negotiation, whereby the United States would obtain base rights in various British Caribbean islands in return for providing fifty overage destroyers and other war supplies. He expressed his confidence that the United States and Britain would work ever more closely together against Hitler. Churchill also paid moving and memorable tribute to the British airmen, "the few," who were holding off Hitler's forces.

Almost a year has passed since the war began, and it is natural for us, I think, to pause on our journey at this milestone and survey the dark, wide field. It is also useful to compare the first year of this second war against German aggression with its forerunner a quarter of a century ago. Although this war is in fact only a continuation of the last, very great differences in its character are apparent. In the last war millions of men fought by hurling enormous masses of steel at one another. "Men and shells" was the cry, and prodigious slaughter was the consequence. In this war nothing of this kind has yet appeared. It is a conflict of strategy, of organization, of technical apparatus, of science, mechanics and morale. The British casualties in the first 12 months of the Great War amounted to 365,000. In this war, I am thankful to say, British killed, wounded, prisoners and missing, including civilians, do not exceed 92,000, and of these a large proportion are alive as prisoners of war. Looking more widely around, one may say that throughout all Europe, for one man killed or wounded in the first year perhaps five were killed or wounded in 1914–15.

The slaughter is only a small fraction, but the consequences to the belligerents have been even more deadly. We have seen great countries with powerful armies dashed out of coherent existence in a few weeks. We have seen the French Republic and the renowned French Army beaten into complete and total submission with less than the casu-

alties which they suffered in any one of half a dozen of the battles of 1914–18. The entire body—it might almost seem at times the soul—of France has succumbed to physical effects incomparably less terrible than those which were sustained with fortitude and undaunted will power 25 years ago. . . .

There is another more obvious difference from 1914. The whole of the warring nations are engaged, not only soldiers, but the entire population, men, women and children. The fronts are everywhere. The trenches are dug in the towns and streets. Every village is fortified. Every road is barred. The front line runs through the factories. The workmen are soldiers with different weapons but the same courage. These are great and distinctive changes from what many of us saw in the struggle of a quarter of a century ago. There seems to be every reason to believe that this new kind of war is well suited to the genius and the resources of the British nation and the British Empire; and that, once we get properly equipped and properly started, a war of this kind will be more favorable to us than the somber mass slaughters of the Somme and Passchendaele. If it is a case of the whole nation fighting and suffering together, that ought to suit us, because we are the most united of all the nations, because we entered the war upon the national will and with our eyes open, and because we have been nurtured in freedom and individual responsibility and are the products, not of totalitarian uniformity, but of tolerance and variety. If all these qualities are turned, as they are being turned, to the arts of war, we may be able to show the enemy quite a lot of things that they have not thought of yet. Since the Germans drove the Jews out and lowered their technical standards, our science is definitely ahead of theirs. Our geographical position, the command of the sea, and the friendship of the United States enable us to draw resources from the whole world and to manufacture weapons of war of every kind, but especially of the superfine kinds, on a scale hitherto practiced only by Nazi Germany.

Hitler is now sprawled over Europe.... It is our intention to maintain and enforce a strict blockade, not only of Germany, but of Italy, France, and all the other countries that have fallen into the German power.... There have been many proposals, founded on the highest motives, that food should be allowed to pass the blockade for the relief of these populations. I regret that we must refuse these requests. The Nazis declare that they have created a new unified economy in Europe. They have repeatedly stated that they possess ample reserves of food and that they can feed their captive peoples.... Many of the most valuable foods are essential to the manufacture of vital war material. Fats are used to make explosives. Potatoes make the alcohol for motor spirit. The plastic materials now so largely used in the construction of aircraft are made of milk. If the Germans use these commodities to help them to bomb our women and children, rather than to feed the populations who produce them, we may be sure that imported foods would go the same way, directly or indirectly, or be employed to relieve the enemy of the responsibilities he has so wantonly assumed. Let Hitler bear his responsibilities to the full, and let the peoples of Europe who groan beneath his yoke aid in every way the coming of the day when that yoke will be broken. Meanwhile, we can and we will arrange in advance for the speedy entry of food into any part of the enslaved area, when this part has been wholly cleared of German forces, and has genuinely regained its freedom. We shall do our best to encourage the building up of reserves of food all over the world, so that there will always be held up before the eyes of the peoples of Europe, including—I say deliberately—the German and Austrian peoples, the certainty that the shattering of the Nazi power will bring to them all immediate food, freedom and peace.

Rather more than a quarter of a year has passed since the new Government came into power in this country. What a cataract of disaster has poured out upon us since then! The trustful Dutch overwhelmed; their beloved and respected Sovereign driven into exile; the peaceful city of Rotterdam the scene of a massacre as hideous and brutal as anything in the Thirty Years' War; Belgium invaded and beaten down; our own fine Expeditionary Force, which King Leopold called to his rescue, cut off and almost captured, escaping as it seemed only by a miracle and with the loss of all its equipment; our Ally, France, out; Italy in against us; all France in the power of the enemy, all its arsenals and vast masses of military material converted or convertible to the enemy's use; a puppet Government set up at Vichy which may at any moment be forced to become our foe; the whole western seaboard of Europe from the North Cape to the Spanish frontier in German hands; all the ports, all the airfields on this immense front employed against us as potential springboards of invasion. Moreover, the German air power, numerically so far outstripping ours, has been brought so close to our Island that what we used to dread greatly has come to pass and the hostile bombers not only reach our shores in a few minutes and from many directions, but can be escorted by their fighting aircraft. Why, Sir, if we had been confronted at the beginning of May with such a prospect, it would have seemed incredible that at the end of a period of horror and disaster, or at this point in a period of horror and disaster, we should stand erect, sure of ourselves, masters of our fate and with the conviction of final victory burning unquenchable in our hearts. Few would have believed we could survive; none would have believed that we should today not only feel stronger but should actually be stronger than we have ever been before.

Let us see what has happened on the other side of the scales. The British nation and the British Empire, finding themselves alone, stood undismayed against disaster. No one flinched or wavered; nay, some who formerly thought of peace, now think only of war. Our people are united and resolved, as they have never been before. Death and ruin have become small things compared with the shame of defeat or failure in duty. We cannot tell what lies ahead. It may be that even greater ordeals lie before us. We shall face whatever is coming to us. We are sure of ourselves and of our cause, and that is the supreme fact which has emerged in these months of trial.

Meanwhile, we have not only fortified our hearts but our Island. We have rearmed and rebuilt our armies in a degree which would have been deemed impossible a few months ago. We have ferried across the Atlantic, in the month of July, thanks to our friends over there, an immense mass of munitions of all kinds: cannon, rifles, machine guns, cartridges and shell, all safely landed without the loss of a gun or a round. The output of our own factories, working as they have never worked before, has poured forth to the troops. The whole British Army is at home. More than 2,000,000 determined men have rifles and bayonets in their hands tonight, and three-quarters of them are in regular military formations. We have never had armies like this in our Island in time of war. The whole Island bristles against invaders, from the sea or from the air. . . .

Our Navy is far stronger than it was at the beginning of the war. The great flow of new construction set on foot at the outbreak is now beginning to come in. We hope our friends across the ocean will send us a timely reinforcement to bridge the gap between the peace flotillas of 1939 and the war flotillas of 1941. There is no difficulty in sending such aid. The seas and oceans are open. The U-boats are contained. The magnetic mine is, up to the present time, effectively mastered. The merchant tonnage under the British flag, after a year of unlimited U-boat war, after eight months of intensive mining attack, is larger than when we began. We have, in addition, under our control at least 4,000,000 tons of shipping from the captive countries which has taken refuge here or in the harbors of the Empire. Our stocks of food of all kinds are far more abundant than in the days of peace, and a large and growing program of food production is on foot.

Why do I say all this? Not, assuredly, to boast; not, assuredly, to give the slightest countenance to complacency. The dangers we face are still enormous, but so are our advantages and resources. I recount them because the people have a right to know that there are solid grounds for the confidence which we feel, and that we have good reason to believe ourselves capable, as I said in a very dark hour two months ago, of continuing the war "if necessary alone, if necessary for years." . . .

The great air battle which has been in progress over this Island for the last few weeks has recently attained a high intensity. It is too soon to attempt to assign limits either to its scale or to its duration. We must certainly expect that greater efforts will be made by the enemy than any he has so far put forth. . . .

On the other hand, the conditions and course of the fighting have so far been favorable to us. I told the House two months ago that, whereas in France our fighter aircraft were wont to inflict a loss of two or three to one upon the Germans, and in the fighting at Dunkirk, which was a kind of no-man's-land, a loss of about three or four to one, we expected that in an attack on this Island we should achieve a larger ratio. This has certainly come true. . . .

A vast and admirable system of salvage, directed by the Ministry of Aircraft Production, ensures the speediest return to the fighting line of damaged machines, and the most provident and speedy use of all the spare parts and material. At the same time the splendid—nay, astounding—increase in the output and repair of British aircraft and engines which Lord Beaverbrook has achieved by a genius of organization and drive, which looks like magic, has given us overflowing reserves of every type of aircraft, and an ever-mounting stream of production both in quantity and quality. The enemy is, of course, far more numerous than we are. But our new production already, as I am advised, largely exceeds his, and the American production is only just beginning to flow in. It is a fact, as I see from my daily returns, that our bomber and fighter strength now, after all this fighting, are larger than they have ever been. We believe that we shall be able to continue the air struggle indefinitely and as long as the enemy pleases, and the longer it continues the more rapid will be our approach, first towards that parity, and then into that superiority, in the air upon which in a large measure the decision of the war depends.

The gratitude of every home in our Island, in our Empire, and indeed throughout the world, except in the abodes of the guilty, goes out to the British airmen who, undaunted by odds, unwearied in their constant challenge and mortal danger, are turning the tide of the World War by their prowess and by their devotion. Never in the field of human conflict was so much owed by so many to so few. All hearts go out to the fighter pilots, whose brilliant actions we see with our own eyes day after day; but we must never forget that all the time, night after night, month after month, our bomber squadrons travel far into Germany, find their targets in the darkness by the highest navigational skill, aim their attacks, often under the heaviest fire, often with serious loss, with deliberate careful discrimination, and inflict shattering blows upon the whole of the technical and war-making structure of the Nazi power. On no part of the Royal Air Force does the weight of the war fall more heavily than on the daylight bombers, who will play an invaluable part in the case of invasion and whose unflinching zeal it has been necessary in the meanwhile on numerous occasions to restrain.

We are able to verify the results of bombing military targets in Germany, not only by reports which reach us through many sources, but also, of course, by photography. I have no hesitation in saying that this process of bombing the military industries and communications of Germany and the air bases and storage depots from which we are attacked, which process will continue upon an ever-increasing scale until the end of the war, and may in another year attain dimensions hitherto undreamed of, affords one at least of the most certain, if not the shortest, of all the roads to victory. Even if the Nazi legions stood triumphant on the Black Sea, or indeed upon the Caspian, even if Hitler was at the gates of India, it would profit him nothing if at the same time the entire economic and scientific apparatus of German war power lay shattered and pulverized at home. . . .

The defection of France has, of course, been deeply damaging to our position. . . .

Most of the other countries that have been overrun by

Germany for the time being have persevered valiantly and faithfully. The Czechs, the Poles, the Norwegians, the Dutch, the Belgians are still in the field, sword in hand, recognized by Great Britain and the United States as the sole representative authorities and lawful Governments of their respective States.

That France alone should lie prostrate at this moment is the crime, not of a great and noble nation, but of what are called "the men of Vichy." We have profound sympathy with the French people. Our old comradeship with France is not dead. In General de Gaulle and his gallant band, that comradeship takes an effective form. These free Frenchmen have been condemned to death by Vichy, but the day will come, as surely as the sun will rise tomorrow, when their names will be held in honor, and their names will be graven in stone in the streets and villages of a France restored in a liberated Europe to its full freedom and its ancient fame. . . .

A good many people have written to me to ask me to make on this occasion a fuller statement of our war aims, and of the kind of peace we wish to make after the war, than is contained in the very considerable declaration which was made early in the autumn. Since then we have made common cause with Norway, Holland and Belgium. We have recognized the Czech Government of Dr. Beneš, and we have told General de Gaulle that our success will carry with it the restoration of France. I do not think it would be wise at this moment, while the battle rages and the war is still perhaps only in its earlier stage, to embark upon elaborate speculations about the future shape which should be given to Europe or the new securities which must be arranged to spare mankind the miseries of a third World War. The ground is not new, it has been frequently traversed and explored, and many ideas are held about it in common by all good men, and all free men. But before we can undertake the task of rebuilding we have not only to be convinced ourselves, but we have to convince all other countries that the Nazi tyranny is going to be finally broken. The right to guide the course of world history is the noblest prize of victory. We are still toiling up the hill; we have not yet reached the crest-line of it; we cannot survey the landscape or even imagine what its condition will be when that longed-for morning comes. The task which lies before us immediately is at once more practical, more simple and more stern. I hope—indeed, I pray—that we shall not be found unworthy of our victory if after toil and tribulation it is granted to us. For the rest, we have to gain the victory. That is our task.

There is, however, one direction in which we can see a little more clearly ahead. We have to think not only for ourselves but for the lasting security of the cause and principles for which we are fighting and of the long future of the British Commonwealth of Nations. Some months ago we came to the conclusion that the interests of the United States and of the British Empire both required that the United States should have facilities for the naval and air defense of the Western Hemisphere against the attack of a Nazi power which might have acquired temporary but lengthy control of a large part of Western Europe and its formidable resources. We had therefore decided spontaneously, and without being asked or offered any inducement, to inform the Government of the United States that we would be glad to place such defense facilities at their disposal by leasing suitable sites in our Transatlantic possessions for their greater security against the unmeasured dangers of the future. The principle of association of interests for common purposes between Great Britain and the United States had developed even before the war. Various agreements had been reached about certain small islands in the Pacific Ocean which had become important as air fueling points. In all this line of thought we found ourselves in very close harmony with the Government of Canada.

Presently we learned that anxiety was also felt in the United States about the air and naval defense of their Atlantic seaboard, and President Roosevelt has recently made it clear that he would like to discuss with us, and with the Dominion of Canada and with Newfoundland, the development of American naval and air facilities in Newfoundland and in the West Indies. There is, of course, no question of any transference of sovereignty—that has never been suggested—or of any action being taken without the consent or against the wishes of the various Colonies concerned; but for our part, His Majesty's Government are entirely willing to accord defense facilities to the United States on a 99 years' leasehold basis, and we feel sure that our interests no less than theirs, and the interests of the Colonies themselves and of Canada and Newfoundland, will be served thereby. These are important steps. Undoubtedly this process means that these two great organizations of the English-speaking democracies, the British Empire and the United States, will have to be somewhat mixed up together in some of their affairs for mutual and general advantage. No one can stop it. Like the Mississippi, it just keeps rolling along. Let it roll. Let it roll on full flood. Let us not view the process with any misgivings. I could not stop it if I wished; no one can stop it. Like the Mississippi, it just keeps rolling along. Let it roll. Let it roll on full flood, inexorable, irresistible, benignant, to broader lands and better days.

Source: Winston S. Churchill, *The Complete Speeches,* 8 vols., ed. Robert Rhodes James (New York: Chelsea House Publishers, 1974), 6: 6260–6268.

67. United States National Defense Advisory Commission Directive, 31 August 1940 (as Reported in the *New York Times*, 14 September 1940)

This government directive on wartime labor was largely written by Sidney Hillman, one of the top leaders of the Committee on Industrial Organization, which in the later 1930s had spearheaded the drive to unionize such major industries as steel and automobile production. In May 1940, as German forces appeared likely to defeat France, President Franklin D. Roosevelt announced a huge new program to increase American military and naval production, and appointed a seven-man National Defense Advisory Commission to oversee this effort. Hillman, a longtime Roosevelt ally, was entrusted with coordinating defense labor. As the New York Times reported, on 13 September 1940 Roosevelt sent this directive to the United States Congress.

Primary among the objectives of the Advisory Commission to the Council of National Defense is the increase in production of materials required by our armed forces and the assurance of adequate future supply of such materials with the least possible disturbance to production of supplies for the civilian population. The scope of our present program entails bringing into production many of our unused resources of agriculture, manufacturing and man power.

This program can be used in the public interest as a vehicle to reduce unemployment and otherwise strengthen the human fiber of our nation. In the selection of plant locations for new production, in the interest of national defense, great weight must be given to this factor.

In order that surplus and unemployed labor may be absorbed . . . all reasonable efforts should be made to avoid hours in excess of 40 per week. However, in emergencies or where the needs of the national defense cannot be otherwise met, exceptions to this standard should be permitted. When the requirements of the defense program make it necessary to work in excess of these hours, or where work is required on Saturdays, Sundays or holidays, overtime should be paid in accordance with the recognized local practices.

All work carried on as part of the defense program should comply with Federal statutory provisions affecting labor wherever such provisions are applicable. This applies to the Walsh-Healey Act, Fair Labor Standards Act, the National Labor Relations Act, etc. There should be compliance with State and local statutes affecting labor relations, hours of work, wages, Workmen's Compensation, safety, sanitation, etc.

Adequate provision should be made for the health and safety of employes.

As far as possible, the local employment or other agencies designated by the United States Employment Service should be utilized.

Workers should not be discriminated against because of age, sex, race, or color.

Adequate housing facilities should be made available for employees.

The commission reaffirms the principles enunciated by the Chief of Ordnance of the United States Army in his order of Nov. 15, 1917, relative to the relation of labor standards to efficient production:

"Industrial history proves that reasonable hours, fair working conditions, and a proper wage scale are essential to high production. Every attempt should be made to conserve in every way possible all our achievements in the way of social betterment. But the pressing argument for maintaining industrial safeguards in the present emergency is that they actually contribute to efficiency."

Source: Associated Press Dispatch, "Roosevelt Statement on Contracts," Dateline Washington, DC, 13 September 1940, published in the *New York Times*, 14 September 1940, p. 9.

68. The Destroyers-for-Bases Deal: The Secretary of State (Cordell Hull) to the British Ambassador (Lord Lothian), 2 September 1940

After negotiations lasting all summer, in September 1940, Great Britain and the United States reached an agreement whereby Great Britain accorded the United States basing rights in Newfoundland, Bermuda, the Caribbean, and British Guiana. In return, the United States supplied 50 surplus destroyers to the British, to augment its naval forces in the battle against Hitler.

I have received your note of September 2, 1940, of which the text is as follows:

I have the honour under instructions from His Majesty's Principal Secretary of State for Foreign Affairs to inform you that in view of the friendly and sympathetic interest of His Majesty's Government in the United Kingdom in the national security of the United States and their desire to strengthen the ability of the United States to cooperate effectively with the other nations of the Americas in the defence of the Western Hemisphere, His Majesty's Government will secure the grant to the Government of the United States, freely and without consideration, of the lease for immediate establishment and use of naval and air bases and facilities for entrance thereto and the operation and protection thereof, on the Avalon Peninsula and on the southern coast of Newfoundland, and on the east coast and on the Great Bay of Bermuda.

Furthermore, in view of the above and in view of the desire of the United States to acquire additional air and naval bases in the Caribbean and in British Guiana, and without endeavouring to place a monetary or commercial value upon the many tangible and intangible rights and properties involved, His Majesty's Government will make available to the United States for immediate establishment and use naval and air bases and facilities for entrance thereto and the operation and protection thereof, on the eastern side of the Bahamas, the southern coast of Jamaica, the western coast of St. Lucia, the west coast of Trinidad in the Gulf of Paria, in the island of Antigua and in British Guiana within fifty miles of Georgetown, in exchange for naval and military equipment and material which the United States Government will transfer to His Majesty's Government.

All the bases and facilities referred to in the preceding paragraphs will be leased to the United States for a period of ninety-nine years, free from all rent and charges other than such compensation to be mutually agreed on to be paid by the United States in order to compensate the owners of private property for loss by expropriation or damage arising out of the establishment of the bases and facilities in question.

His Majesty's Government, in the leases to be agreed upon, will grant to the United States for the period of the leases all the rights, power, and authority within the bases leased, and within the limits of the territorial waters and air spaces adjacent to or in the vicinity of such bases, necessary to provide access to and defence of such bases, and appropriate provisions for their control.

Without prejudice to the above-mentioned rights of the United States authorities and their jurisdiction within the leased areas, the adjustment and reconciliation between the jurisdiction of the authorities of the United States within these areas and the jurisdiction of the authorities of the territories in which these areas are situated, shall be determined by common agreement.

The exact location and bounds of the aforesaid bases, the necessary seaward, coast and anti-aircraft defences, the location of sufficient military garrisons, stores and other necessary auxiliary facilities shall be determined by common agreement. His Majesty's Government are prepared to designate immediately experts to meet with experts of the United States for these purposes. Should these experts be unable to agree in any particular situation, except in the case of Newfoundland and Bermuda, the matter shall be settled by the Secretary of State of the United States and His Majesty's Secretary of State for Foreign Affairs.

I am directed by the President to reply to your note as follows: The Government of the United States appreciates the declarations and the generous action of His Majesty's Government as contained in your communication which are destined to enhance the national security of the United States and greatly to strengthen its ability to cooperate effectively with the other nations of the Americas in the defense of the Western Hemisphere. It therefore gladly accepts the proposals.

The Government of the United States will immediately designate experts to meet with experts designated by His Majesty's Government to determine upon the exact location of the naval and air bases mentioned in your communication under acknowledgment.

In consideration of the declarations above quoted, the Government of the United States will immediately transfer to His Majesty's Government fifty United States Navy destroyers generally referred to as the twelve hundred-ton type.

Source: Private Laws, Concurrent Resolutions, Treaties, International Agreements Other than Treaties, and Proclamations. Part 2, United States *Statutes at Large Containing the Laws and Concurrent Resolutions Enacted During the Second and Third Sessions of the Seventy-Sixth Congress of the United States of America, 1939–1941, and Treaties, International Agreements Other Than Treaties, Proclamations, and Reorganization Plans.* Vol. 54. (Washington, DC: U.S. Government Printing Office, 1941), 2406–2408.

69. Speech of Dr. Robert Ley, Director of the German Labor Front, as Reported in the Swedish Press, 15 September 1940

In February 1940, Adolf Hitler instructed Robert Ley, head of the German Labor Front, a government agency the aim of which was to further the welfare of the German people, to prepare a scheme for comprehensive old-age pensions. Ley apparently persuaded Hitler to endorse this proposal on the grounds that it would encourage all Germans to remain loyal to the state while enduring wartime difficulties and deprivation. Pensions would also be conditional on individuals' support for the National Socialist regime. Ley clearly intended that his pension scheme would constitute only one part of a wide-ranging social welfare program. The Finance and Labor Ministries opposed Ley's plans as impracticable. They were, however, symptomatic of the degree to which, to win popular support for the war effort, most governments at war felt obliged to promise their citizenry the reward of future social benefits.

The German people are going to be rewarded for their wartime sacrifices with an old age free from cares.

In eighteen years Germany will not be recognizable. A proletarian nation will have become a master nation.

In ten years' time the German worker will live better than an English lord.

The meeting started late because the Reich Chancellor, Hitler, was spending the evening with Dr. Ley as his guest. Hitler regularly rings up his closest colleagues and invites himself for a few hours. This evening he told Dr. Ley among other things that house construction methods were completely out of date. We are still building in exactly the same way as a thousand years ago by putting brick upon brick. Building technology has never been modernized or rationalized. Germany will have the task of reforming the construction industry. Prefabricated materials will have to be used. If in the future everything has been standardized and prefabricated then later on it will only be necessary to put the materials together at the building site so that a house can be built in a few days. According to Dr. Ley, this type of building will be 50 per cent cheaper than hitherto.

The starting point of the interview was the creation of a new old age pensions scheme which has been in preparation for a year. And which is apparently now ready. It is intended to be the reward for the wartime sacrifices made by the German people. I asked Dr. Ley if it would be based on some kind of insurance scheme. His reply was:

It will be based on completely new principles, since the whole nation will guarantee that the old age pensions are paid for by the national community. A social contribution will be paid as part of income tax and it is now my task through rationalization to achieve a more effective use of the same amount of money. I rejected an insurance-based scheme; it creates too large an administrative apparatus and, in any case, is a compulsory savings system to which the poor do not have access. The financial apparatus of the state will take over responsibility for collecting the money for the old age pensions and also for payment. In this way there will be no administrative costs. The pensions will be three times higher than hitherto because the administrative costs will have been saved. Thus, invalidity pensions will be increased from RM [reichsmarks] 33 to RM 90 per month. The old age pension will increase from the current minimum of RM 60 to a maximum of RM 250. In addition to the normal pensions, there will be an honorarium for the victims of the war and for those injured at work, for example for miners who have become invalids through their work. Mothers who have at least four children will receive an equivalent subsidy. They will not only be decorated with the Mothers' Cross but will get their honorarium in old age.

All in all, we will need 8 billion for the new old age pension scheme. Up to now this sum has been spent on insurance schemes. Thus, no new burden will be placed on the nation. The administrative costs will now be completely eliminated since the tax system will take over the scheme. This will save 2 billion. Furthermore, I have devised a scheme to utilize the unemployment insurance for the old age pensions, which will bring in another 2 billion. As is well known, the former will no longer be needed, since there will not be any unemployment in Germany.

In future, the workers will not receive their long wage slips as they do now with the numerous deductions for insurance and unemployment benefit. All these figures made the workers suspicious; now this will all be done via taxation.

If we take over the insurance capital, Dr. Ley continued, then we hope that we can reduce interest rates to 2 or 1.5 per cent and, when this is achieved, it will benefit the individual consumer. We will no longer need the insurance companies' money, since the housing construction industry, for which it was needed hitherto, is going to be financed by the state.

The health insurance offices will also disappear and be replaced by a health service. The party will build Community Houses in all towns. Doctors and dentists will work there. The health of every German will be examined once a year just like a car engine is serviced once a year. There will be three groups of doctors:

1. General practitioners, who know the genetic history of every single family and who have the families' trust.
2. Company doctors who are employed in the factories.
3. Specialists who will be treated as artists and, as a result, will have a special position in the national community.

The practice of medicine will be licensed. Its economic basis will be secured and, in addition, there will be the opportunity for private practice.

The post-war national socialist reforms will revolutionize social conditions, continued Dr. Ley, in that in future there would be no difference in the payment of workers of the hand and workers of the brain. Hitler wants payment in future to be made in accordance with three principles: the danger involved in the work (for this reason miners will be paid the most), the difficulty of the occupation, and, finally, according to performance. In future, the piecework rates will be set not by the plant managers but by independent agencies. The wages principle will be radically reformed.

The wage will be divided into a tied and a free sum. In future, people will not be able to buy just what they want. Just as at the moment the rationing system prevents many people from buying more than a certain amount of many goods, the same will be true in the future. The goods which Germany has to import will be controlled by the state. The use of wages will be directed in accordance with the interests of the state. Since Germany has too little wool, it is not on for certain people to buy ten suits and hang them in their wardrobes. Similarly, it is not on for people to drink twenty-five cups of coffee when one is enough. The demand for imported goods will be restricted, whereas people will gladly purchase what we ourselves produce in quantity, such as, for example, the Volkswagen from German steel. It is Hitler's plan to pay wages in coupons so that people can have wage rises but only on condition that they use the higher wages to buy a Volkswagen or a house on an estate. So the state will say: OK you can have more money but you must invest the extra income in a house.

In future there will be an eight-hour working day in Germany. The laws which currently prevent workers from freely choosing their place of work will be repealed. The weekend will go from Saturday midday until Monday morning. Everybody will have holidays and over the next ten years Dr. Ley intends to build ten spa hotels, as well as the new large complex in Rügen with 20,000 beds, and finally KdF [the Nazi leisure program, Strength Through Joy] hotels with 2,400 beds in each city.

The training period for young people will be shortened. The apprentice period will be reduced through rationalization from four years to two.

Finally, a major building programme will be carried out. Very shortly Hitler will sign a decree to this effect. Three rooms with a large kitchen and bathroom will become the norm. They will cost RM 30 per month since the rents are going to be halved and it will be 50 per cent cheaper to build prefabricated houses.

During the course of the press conference, Dr. Ley repeatedly emphasized that power means money. After the war the role of London will have been played out and Germany will have the power. Then Germany will be rich enough to realize its programme so that in ten years' time the German worker will be better off than an English lord.

Source: Original article appeared in *Berlinske Tikende,* 15 September 1940 (translated into German in Bundesarchiv Berlin). Jeremy Noakes, ed., *Nazism 1919–1945, Volume 4: The Home Front in World War II* (Exeter, UK: University of Exeter Press, 1998), 289–291. Reprinted with permission of University of Exeter Press.

70. The Selective Service Act, 16 September 1940

Selective service legislation was eventually passed in September 1940, at the height of a presidential election campaign. All American men aged between 21 and 36 were required to register for the draft and, if called up, to serve for one year. Should Congress declare that the national interest was endangered, their term of service might be extended. No more than 900,000 men could be trained under the act at any one time, and inductees could not serve outside the Western Hemisphere. More than 16 million men signed up on 16 October 1940, the day selected for implementation of the legislation, which—although later greatly expanded—provided the basis for the system of conscription in operation throughout World War II. The act also empowered the president to compel private businesses to give priority to the production of goods for the war effort.

Public Law 783, 76 Cong., 2d Sess., An Act to Provide for the Common Defense by Increasing the Personnel of the Armed Forces of the United States and Providing for Its Training.

. . . Be it enacted by the Senate and House of Representatives of the United States of America in Congress assembled, that (a) the Congress hereby declares that it is imperative to increase and train the personnel of the armed forces of the United States.

(b) The Congress further declares that in a free society the obligation and privileges of military training and service should be shared generally in accordance with a fair and just system of selective compulsory military training and service.

(c) The Congress further declares, in accordance with our traditional military policy as expressed in the National Defense Act of 1916, as amended, that it is essential that the strength and organization of the National Guard, as an integral part of the first-line defenses of this Nation, be at all times maintained and assured. To this end, it is the intent of the Congress that whenever the Congress shall determine that troops are needed for the national security in excess of those of the Regular Army and those in active training and service under section 3(b), the National Guard of the United States, or such part thereof as may be necessary, shall be ordered to active Federal service and continued therein so long as such necessity exists.

Sec. 2. Except as otherwise provided in this Act, it shall be the duty of every male citizen of the United States, and of every male alien residing in the United States, who, on the day or days fixed for the first or any subsequent registration, is between the ages of twenty-one and thirty-six, to present himself for and submit to registration at such time or times and place or places, and in such manner and in such age group or groups, as shall be determined by rules and regulations prescribed hereunder.

Sec. 3. (a) Except as otherwise provided in the Act, every male citizen of the United States, and every male alien residing in the United States who has declared his intention to become such a citizen, between the ages of twenty-one and thirty-six at the time fixed for his registration, shall be liable for training and service in the land or naval forces of the United States. The President is authorized from time to time, whether or not a state of war exists, to select and induct into the land and naval forces of the United States for training and service, in the manner provided in this Act, such number of men as in his judgment is required for such forces in the national interest: *Provided,* That within the limits of the quota determined under section 4 (b) for the subdivision in which he resides, any person, regardless of race or color, between the ages of eighteen and thirty-six, shall be afforded an opportunity to volunteer for induction into the land or naval forces of the United States for the training and service prescribed in subsection (b), but no person who so volunteers shall be inducted for such training so long as he is deferred after classification: *Provided further,* That no men shall be inducted for such training and service until adequate provision shall have been made for such shelter, sanitary facilities, water supplies, heating and lighting arrangements, medical care, and hospital accommodations, for such men, as may be determined by the Secretary of War or the Secretary of the Navy, as the case may be, to be essential to public and personal health: *Provided further,* That except in time of war there shall not be in active training or service in the land forces of the United States at any one time under subsection (b) more than nine hundred thousand men inducted under the provisions of this Act. The men inducted into the land or naval forces for training and service under this Act shall be assigned to camps or units of such forces.

(b) Each man inducted under the provisions of subsection (a) shall serve for a training and service period of twelve consecutive months, unless sooner discharged, except that whenever the Congress has declared that the national interest is imperiled, such twelve-month period may be extended by the President to such time as may be necessary in the interests of national defense.

(c) Each such man, after the completion of his period of training and service under subsection (b), shall be transferred to a reserve component of the land or naval forces of the United States; and until he attains the age of forty-five, or until the expiration of a period of ten years after such transfer, or until he is discharged from such reserve component, whichever occurs first, he shall be deemed to be a member of such reserve component and shall be subject to such additional training and service as may now or hereafter be prescribed by law: *Provided,* That any man who completes at least twelve months' training and service in the land forces under subsection (b), and who thereafter serves satisfactorily in the Regular Army or in the active National Guard for a period of at least two years, shall, in time of peace, be relieved from any liability to serve in any reserve component of the land or naval forces of the United States and from further liability for the training and service under subsection (b), but nothing in this subsection shall be construed to prevent any such man, while in a reserve component of such forces, from being ordered or called to active duty, in such forces.

(d) With respect to the men inducted for training and service under this Act there shall be paid, allowed, and extended the same pay, allowances, pensions, disability and death compensation, and other benefits as are provided by law in the case of other enlisted men of like grades and length of service of that component of the land or naval forces to which they are assigned, and after transfer to a reserve component of the land or naval forces as provided in subsection (c) there shall be paid, allowed and extended with respect to them the same benefits as are provided by law in like cases with respect to other members of such reserve component. Men in such training and service and men who have been so transferred to reserve components shall have an opportunity to qualify for promotion.

(e) Persons inducted into the land forces of the United States under this Act shall not be employed beyond the limits of the Western Hemisphere except in the Territories and possessions of the United States, including the Philippine Islands. . . .

Sec. 4. (a) The selection of men for training and service under section 3 (other than those who are voluntarily inducted pursuant to this Act) shall be made in an impartial manner, under such rules and regulations as the President may prescribe, from the men who are liable for such training and service and who at the time of selection are registered and classified but not deferred or exempted: *Provided,* That in the selection and training of men under this Act, and

in the interpretation and execution of the provisions of this Act, there shall be no discrimination against any person on account of race or color. . . .

[Following sections exempted ministers of religion and theology students, occupations the president determined to be of national importance, college students, and conscientious objectors on grounds of religion.]

Sec. 9. The President is empowered, through the head of the War Department or the Navy Department of the Government, in addition to the present authorized methods of purchase or procurement, to place an order with any individual, firm, association, company, corporation, or organized manufacturing industry for such product or material as may be required, and which is of the nature and kind usually produced or capable of being produced by such individual, firm, company, association, corporation, or organized manufacturing industry.

Compliance with all such orders for products or material shall be obligatory on any individual firm, association, company, corporation, or organized manufacturing industry or the responsible head or heads thereof and shall take precedence over all other orders and contracts theretofore placed with such individual, firm, company, association, corporation, or organized manufacturing industry, and any individual, firm, association, company, corporation, or organized manufacturing industry or the responsible head or heads thereof owning or operating any plant equipped for the manufacture of arms or ammunition or parts of ammunition, or any necessary supplies or equipment for the Army or Navy, and any individual firm, association, company, corporation, or organized manufacturing industry or the responsible head or heads thereof owning or operating any manufacturing plant, which, in the opinion of the Secretary of War or the Secretary of the Navy shall be capable of being readily transformed into a plant for the manufacture of arms or ammunition, or parts thereof, or other necessary supplies or equipment, who shall refuse to give to the United States such preference in the matter of the execution of orders, or who shall refuse to manufacture the kind, quantity, or quality of arms or ammunition, or the parts thereof, or any necessary supplies or equipment, as ordered by the Secretary of War or the Secretary of the Navy, or who shall refuse to furnish such arms, ammunition, or parts of ammunition, or other supplies or equipment, at a reasonable price as determined by the Secretary of War or the Secretary of the Navy, as the case may be, then and in either such case, the President, through the head of the War or Navy Departments of the Government, in addition to the present authorized methods of purchase or procurement, is hereby authorized to take immediate possession of any such plant or plants, and through the appropriate branch, bureau, or department of the Army or Navy to manufacture therein such product or material as may be required, and any individual firm, company, association, or corporation, or organized manufacturing industry or the responsible head or heads thereof, failing to comply with the provision of this section shall be deemed guilty of a felony, and upon conviction shall be punished by imprisonment for not more than three years and a fine not exceeding $50,000. . . .

[Following sections provided for the establishment of local selective service boards to implement the legislation, and provided penalties for evading the law.]

Source: John O'Sullivan and Alan M. Meckler, eds., *The Draft and Its Enemies: A Documentary History* (Urbana: University of Illinois Press, 1974), 176–186.

71. Three-Power (Tripartite) Pact between Germany, Italy, and Japan, Signed in Berlin, 27 September 1940

In September 1940, the governments of Germany, Italy, and Japan formally allied themselves with each other, to establish a "new order" in both Europe and Asia. This alignment effectively linked all the various opponents of the Western democracies, intensifying the ideological aspects of the international conflict.

The governments of Germany, Italy and Japan, considering it as a condition precedent of any lasting peace that all nations of the world be given each its own proper place, have decided to stand by and co-operate with one another in regard to their efforts in greater East Asia and regions of Europe respectively wherein it is their prime purpose to establish and maintain a new order of things calculated to promote the mutual prosperity and welfare of the peoples concerned.

Furthermore, it is the desire of the three governments to extend co-operation to such nations in other spheres of the world as may be inclined to put forth endeavours along lines similar to their own, in order that their ultimate aspirations for world peace may thus be realized.

Accordingly, the governments of Germany, Italy and Japan have agreed as follows:

ARTICLE ONE

Japan recognizes and respects the leadership of Germany and Italy in establishment of a new order in Europe.

ARTICLE TWO

Germany and Italy recognize and respect the leadership of Japan in the establishment of a new order in greater East Asia.

ARTICLE THREE

Germany, Italy and Japan agree to co-operate in their efforts on aforesaid lines. They further undertake to assist one another with all political, economic and military means when one of the three contracting powers is attacked by a power at present not involved in the European war or in the Chinese-Japanese conflict.

ARTICLE FOUR

With the view to implementing the present pact, joint technical commissions, members which are to be appointed by the respective governments of Germany, Italy and Japan will meet without delay.

ARTICLE FIVE

Germany, Italy and Japan affirm that the aforesaid terms do not in any way affect the political status which exists at present as between each of the three contracting powers and Soviet Russia.

ARTICLE SIX

The present pact shall come into effect immediately upon signature and shall remain in force 10 years from the date of its coming into force. At the proper time before expiration of said term, the high contracting parties shall at the request of any of them enter into negotiations for its renewal.

Source: Web site: The Avalon Project at the Yale Law School. Available at http://www.yale.edu/lawweb/avalon/wwii/triparti/htm.

72. Undated Statement Handed to the Secretary of State by the Japanese Ambassador, 8 October 1940

From the beginning of outright war between Japan and China in 1937, the U.S. government gradually imposed trade embargoes of increasing severity on goods and materials that might assist the Japanese war effort. At the end of September 1940, the regulations on iron and steel scrap were tightened dramatically. One week later, the Japanese ambassador delivered a formal protest on the matter to the secretary of state.

Since iron and steel scrap classified as No. 1 heavy melting scrap was placed under export-licensing system on July 26, 1940, permission of the United States Government was obtained up to August 19 of the same year for 99 percent of applications for shipments to Japan.

In the light of this fact, the sudden enlargement of the iron and steel scrap licensing system to include all grades of these materials is hardly explicable from the standpoint of national defense, on which the regulation of September 30, 1940, is purported to be based.

The discriminatory feature of the announcement, that licenses will be issued to permit shipments to the countries of the Western Hemisphere and Great Britain only, has created a widespread impression in Japan that it was motivated by a desire to bring pressure upon her.

The fact that the majority of essential articles and materials that Japan desires to import from America is placed under licensing system is causing a feeling of tension among the people of Japan, who naturally presume that the system is intended to be a precursor of severance of economic relations between Japan and the United States.

In view of the high feeling in Japan it is apprehended that, in the event of continuation by the United States Government of the present attitude toward Japan in matters of trade restriction, especially if it leads to the imposition of further measures of curtailment, future relations between Japan and the United States will be unpredictable.

It is a matter of course that the Governments of both Japan and the United States should endeavor as best they can to preclude such an eventuality. To this endeavor the Japanese Government will devote itself and trusts that it may have the full cooperation of the United States Government.

Source: U.S. Department of State, Publication 1983, *Peace and War: United States Foreign Policy, 1931–1941* (Washington, DC: U.S. Government Printing Office, 1943), 579.

73. "Plan Dog": Harold R. Stark, U.S. Chief of Naval Operations, Memorandum for the Secretary [of the Navy, Frank Knox], 12 November 1940

In November 1940, the chief of U.S. naval operations, Harold R. Stark, sent the secretary of the navy a memorandum arguing that British and U.S. strategic interests were highly interdependent. He therefore argued that the existing naval strategic Plan Orange directed primarily against Japan should be modified in favor of Plan Dog (Plan D), which would involve a major Atlantic naval commitment together with primarily defensive measures in the Pacific. This "Atlantic first" strategy would ultimately govern the entire American prosecution of the war.

Referring to my very brief touch in a recent conference as to the desirability of obtaining at once some light upon the major decisions which the President may make for guiding our future naval effort in the event of war, and in further immediate preparation for war, you may recall my remarks the evening we discussed War Plans for the Navy. I stated then that if Britain wins decisively against Germany we could win everywhere; but that if she loses the problems confronting us would be very great; and, while we might not lose everywhere, we might, possibly, not win anywhere.

As I stated last winter on the Hill, in these circumstances we would be set back upon our haunches. Our war effort, instead of being widespread, would then have to be confined to the Western Hemisphere.

I now wish to expand my remarks, and to present to you my views concerning steps we might take to meet the situation that will exist should the United States enter war either alone or with allies. In this presentation, I have endeavored to keep in view the political realities in our own country.

The first thing to consider is how and where we might become involved.

The immediate war alternatives seem to be:

(a) War with Japan in which we have no allies. This might be precipitated by Japanese armed opposition should we strongly reinforce our Asiatic Fleet or the Philippines Garrison, should we start fortifying Guam, or should we impose additional important economic sanctions; or it might be precipitated by ourselves in case of overt Japanese action against us, or by further extension of Japanese hegemony.

(b) War with Japan in which we have the British Empire, or the British Empire and Netherlands East Indies, as allies. This might be precipitated by one of the causes mentioned in (a), by our movement of a naval reinforcement to Singapore, or by Japanese attack on British or Netherlands territory.

(c) War with Japan in which she is aided by Germany and Italy, and in which we are or are not aided by allies. To the causes of such a war, previously listed, might be added augmented American material assistance to Great Britain, our active military intervention in Britain's favor, or our active resistance to German extension of military activities to the Western Hemisphere.

(d) War with Germany and Italy in which Japan would not be initially involved, and in which we would be allied with the British. Such a war would be initiated by American decision to intervene for the purpose of preventing the disruption of the British Empire, or German capture of the British Isles.

(e) We should also consider the alternative of now remaining out of war, and devoting ourselves exclusively to building up our defense of the Western Hemisphere, plus the preservation by peaceful means of our Far Eastern interests, and plus also continued material assistance to Great Britain.

As I see it, our major national objectives in the immediate future might be stated as preservation of the territorial, economic, and ideological integrity of the United States, plus that of the remainder of the Western Hemisphere; the prevention of the disruption of the British Empire, with all

that such a consummation implies; and the diminution of the offensive military power of Japan, with a view to the retention of our economic and political interests in the Far East. It is doubtful, however, that it would be in our interest to reduce Japan to the status of an inferior military and economic power. A balance of power in the Far East is to our interest as much as is a balance of power in Europe.

The questions that confront me are concerned with the preparation and distribution of the naval forces of the United States, in cooperation with its military forces, for use in war in the accomplishment of all or part of these national objectives.

I can only surmise as to the military, political, and economic situation that would exist in the Atlantic should the British Empire collapse. Since Latin-America has rich natural resources, and is the only important area of the world not now under the practical control of strong military powers, we can not dismiss the possibility that, sooner or later, victorious Axis nations might move firmly in that direction. For some years they might remain too weak to attack directly across the sea; their effort more likely would first be devoted to developing Latin American economic dependence, combined with strongly reinforced internal political upheavals for the purpose of establishing friendly regimes in effective military control.

The immediacy of danger to us may depend upon the security of the Axis military position in Eastern Europe and the Mediterranean, the degree of our own military preoccupation in the Pacific, and the disturbing influence of unsatisfied economic needs of Latin-America.

The present situation of the British Empire is not encouraging. I believe it easily possible, lacking active American military assistance, for that empire to lose this war and eventually be disrupted.

It is my opinion that the British are over-optimistic as to their chances for ultimate success. It is not at all sure that the British Isles can hold out, and it may be that they do not realize the danger that will exist should they lose in other regions.

Should Britain lose the war, the military consequences to the United States would be serious.

If we are to prevent the disruption of the British Empire, we must support its vital needs.

Obviously, the British Isles, the "Heart of the Empire," must remain intact. But even if the British Isles are held, this does not mean that Britain can win the war. To win, she must finally be able to effect the complete, or, at least, the partial collapse of the German Reich.

This result might, conceivably, be accomplished by bombing and by economic starvation through the agency of the blockade. It surely can be accomplished only by military successes on shore, facilitated possibly by over-extension and by internal antagonisms developed by the Axis conquests.

Alone, the British Empire lacks the manpower and the material means to master Germany. Assistance by powerful allies is necessary both with respect to men and with respect to munitions and supplies. If such assistance is to function effectively, Britain must not only continue to maintain the blockade, but she must also retain intact geographical positions from which successful land action can later be launched.

Provided England continues to sustain its present successful resistance at home, the area of next concern to the British Empire ought to be the Egyptian Theater. Should Egypt be lost, the Eastern Mediterranean would be opened to Germany and Italy; the effectiveness of the sea blockade would be largely nullified; Turkey's military position would be fully compromised; and all hope of favorable Russian action would vanish. Any anti-German offensive in the Near East would then become impossible.

The spot next in importance to Egypt, in my opinion, is Gibraltar, combined with West and Northwest Africa. From this area an ultimate offensive through Portugal, Spain, and France, with the help of populations inimical to Germany, might give results equal to those which many years ago were produced by Wellington. The western gate to the Mediterranean would still be kept closed, provided Britain holds this region.

This brief discussion naturally brings into question the value to Britain of the Mediterranean relative to that of Hong Kong, Singapore, and India. Were the Mediterranean lost, Britain's strength in the Far East could be augmented without weakening home territory.

Japan probably wants the British out of Hong Kong and Singapore; and wants economic control, and ultimately military control, of Malaysia.

It is very questionable if Japan has territorial ambitions in Australia and New Zealand.

But does she now wish the British out of India, thus exposing that region and Western China to early Russian penetration or influence? I doubt it.

It would seem more probable that Japan, devoted to the Axis alliance only so far as her own immediate interests are involved, would prefer not to move military forces against Britain, and possibly not against the Netherlands East Indies, because, if she can obtain a high degree of economic control over Malaysia, she will then be in a position to improve her financial structure by increased trade with Britain and America.

Her economic offensive power will be increased. Her military dominance will follow rapidly or slowly, as seems best at the time.

The Netherlands East Indies has 60,000,000 people, under the rule of 80,000 Dutchmen, including women and children. This political situation cannot be viewed as in permanent equilibrium. The rulers are unsupported by a home country or by an alliance. Native rebellions have occurred in the past, and may recur in the future. These Dutchmen will act in what they believe is their own selfish best interests.

Will they alone resist aggression, or will they accept an accommodation with the Japanese?

Will they resist, if supported only by the British Empire?

Will they firmly resist, if supported by the British Empire and the United States?

Will the British resist Japanese aggression directed only against the Netherlands East Indies?

Should both firmly resist, what local military assistance will they require from the United States to ensure success?

No light on these questions has been thrown by the report of the proceedings of the recent Singapore Conference.

The basic character of a war against Japan by the British and Dutch would be the fixed defense of the Malay Peninsula, Sumatra, and Java. The allied army, naval, and air forces now in position are considerable, and some future reenforcement may be expected from Australia and New Zealand. Borneo and the islands to the East are vulnerable. There is little chance for an allied offensive. Without Dutch assistance, the external effectiveness of the British bases at Hong Kong and Singapore would soon disappear.

The Japanese deployment in Manchukuo and China requires much of their Army, large supplies and merchant tonnage, and some naval force. It is doubtful if Japan will feel secure in withdrawing much strength from in front of Russia, regardless of non-aggression agreements. The winter lull in China will probably permit the withdrawal of the forces they need for a campaign against Malaysia. The availability of ample supplies for such a campaign is problematical.

Provided the British and Dutch cooperate in a vigorous and efficient defense of Malaysia, Japan will need to make a major effort with all categories of military force to capture the entire area. The campaign might even last several months. Whether Japan would concurrently be able successfully to attack Hong Kong and the Philippines, and also strongly to support the fixed positions in the Mid-Pacific, seems doubtful. During such a campaign, due to her wide dispersion of effort, Japan would, unquestionably, be more vulnerable to attack by the United States (or by Russia) than she would be once Malaysia is in her possession.

This brings us to a consideration of the strategy of an American war against Japan, that is, either the so-called "Orange Plan," or a modification. It must be understood that the Orange Plan was drawn up to govern our operations when the United States and Japan are at war, and no other nations are involved.

You have heard enough of the Orange Plan to know that, in a nutshell, it envisages our Fleet's proceeding westward through the Marshalls and the Carolines, consolidating as it goes, and then on to the recapture of the Philippines. Once there, the Orange Plan contemplates the eventual economic starvation of Japan, and, finally, the complete destruction of her external military power. Its accomplishment would require several years, and the absorption of the full military, naval, and economic energy of the American people.

In proceeding through these Mid-Pacific islands, we have several subsidiary objectives in mind. First, we hope that our attack will induce the Japanese to expose their Fleet in action against our Fleet, and lead to their naval defeat. Second, we wish to destroy the ability of the Japanese to use these positions as air and submarine bases from which to project attacks on our lines of communication to the mainland and Hawaii. Third, we would use the captured positions for supporting our further advance westward.

Most of the island positions are atolls. These atolls, devoid of natural sources of water other than rainfall, and devoid of all supplies, are merely narrow coral and sand fringes around large shallow areas where vessels may anchor. Alone, they are undefendable against serious attack, either by one side or the other. They do, however, afford weak positions for basing submarines and seaplanes. Our Fleet should have no difficulty in capturing atolls, provided we have enough troops, but we could not hold them indefinitely unless the Fleet were nearby.

We know little about the Japanese defenses in the Mid-Pacific. We believe the real islands of Truk and Ponape in the Carolines are defended with guns and troops, and we believe that some of the atolls of the Marshalls may be equipped as submarine and air bases, and be garrisoned with relatively small detachments of troops.

The Marshalls contain no sites suitable for bases in the absence of the Fleet, though there are numerous good anchorages. With the Fleet at hand, they can be developed for use as seaplane and submarine bases for the support of an attack on real islands such as Ponape and Truk. With the Fleet permanently absent, they will succumb to any serious thrust.

Our first real Marshall-Caroline objective is Truk, a magnificent harbor, relatively easily defended against raids, and capable of conversion into an admirable advanced base. When we get this far in the accomplishment of the "Orange Plan," we have the site for a base where we can begin to assemble our ships, stores, and troops, for further advance toward the Philippines. It would also become the center of the defense system for the lines of communications against flank attack from Japan.

Getting to Truk involves a strong effort. We would incur losses from aircraft, mines, and submarines, particularly as the latter could be spared from the operations in Malaysia.

We would lose many troops in assaulting the islands. Going beyond Truk initiates the most difficult part of the Orange Plan, would take a long time, and would require the maximum effort which the United States could sustain.

Truk is not looked upon as a satisfactory final geographical objective. It is too far away to support useful operations in the China Sea. It can not be held in the absence of fairly continuous Fleet support. No matter what gains are made in the Mid-Pacific, they would undoubtedly be lost were the Fleet to be withdrawn to the Atlantic. We would have then to choose between a lengthy evacuation process, and a major loss of men, material, and prestige.

In advancing to the capture of Ponape and Truk, the Orange Plan contemplates proceeding promptly, delaying in the Marshalls only long enough to destroy Japanese shore bases, to capture the atolls neccessary to support the advance, and to deny future bases to Japan.

We have little knowledge as to the present defensive strength of the Marshall and Caroline groups, considered as a whole. If they are well defended, to capture them we estimate initial needs at 25,000 thoroughly trained troops, with another 50,000 in immediate reserve. If they are not well defended, an early advance with fewer troops might be very profitable. Several months must elapse from the present date before 75,000 troops could be made ready, considering the defense requirements of Alaska, Hawaii, and Samoa, and our commitments with respect to the internal political stability of the Latin-American countries.

We should consider carefully the chances of failure as well as of success. An immediate success would be most important morally, while a failure would be costly from the moral viewpoint. Before invading Norway, Germany trained for three months the veterans of the Polish campaign. Remembering Norway, we have the example of two methods of overseas adventure. One is the British method; the other is the German method.

The question of jumping directly from Hawaii to the Philippines has often been debated, but, so far as I know, this plan has always been ruled out by responsible authorities as unsound from a military viewpoint. Truk is 1,900 miles from Yokohama, 5,300 miles from San Francisco, 3,200 miles from Honolulu, and 2,000 miles from Manila. I mention this to compare the logistic problem with that of the Norway incident. An enormous amount of shipping would be required. Its availability under present world conditions would be doubtful.

Of course the foregoing, (the Orange Plan), is a major commitment in the Pacific, and does not envisage the cooperation of allies. Once started the abandonment of the offensive required by the plan, to meet a threat in the Atlantic, would involve abandoning the objectives of the war, and also great loss of prestige.

A totally different situation would exist were the Philippines and Guam rendered secure against attack by adequate troops, aircraft, and fortifications. The movement of the Fleet across the Pacific for the purpose of applying direct pressure upon Japan, and its support when in position, would be less difficult than in the existing situation.

Should we adopt the present Orange Plan today, or any modification of that plan which involves the movement of very strong naval and army contingents to the Far East, we would have to accept considerable danger in the Atlantic, and would probably be unable to augment our material assistance to Great Britain.

We should, therefore, examine other plans which involve a war having a more limited objective than the complete defeat of Japan, and in which we would undertake hostilities only in cooperation with the British and Dutch, and in which these undertake to provide an effective and continued resistance in Malaysia.

Our involvement in war in the Pacific might well make us also an ally of Britain in the Atlantic. The naval forces remaining in the Atlantic, for helping our ally and for defending ourselves, would, by just so much, reduce the power which the United States Fleet could put forth in the Pacific.

The objective in a limited war against Japan would be the reduction of Japanese offensive power chiefly through economic blockade. Under one concept, allied strategy would comprise holding the Malay Barrier, denying access to other sources of supply in Malaysia, severing her lines of communication with the Western Hemisphere, and raiding communications to the Mid-Pacific, the Philippines, China, and Indo-China. United States defensive strategy would also require army reinforcement of Alaska and the Hawaiian Islands, the establishment of naval bases in the Fiji-Samoan and Gilbert Islands areas, and denial to Japan of the use of the Marshalls as light force bases. We might be able to reenforce the Philippine garrison, particularly with aircraft. I do not believe that the British and Dutch alone could hold the Malay Barrier without direct military assistance by the United States. In addition to help from our Asiatic Fleet, I am convinced that they would need further reenforcement by ships and aircraft drawn from our Fleet in Hawaii, and possibly even by troops.

Besides military aid for the allied defense forces, our intervention would bring them a tremendous moral stimulus.

An alternative concept of the suggested limited war would be to provide additional support from the main body of the Fleet either by capturing the Marshalls, or by capturing both the Marshalls and Carolines. This, or a similar Fleet activity, would be for the purpose of diverting away from Malaysia important Japanese forces to oppose it, and thus reducing the strength of their assault against the Dutch and British.

But we should consider the prospect that the losses which we would incur in such operations might not be fruitful of compensating results. Furthermore, withdrawal of the Fleet from captured positions for transfer to the Atlantic would be more difficult.

It is out of the question to consider sending our entire Fleet at once to Singapore. Base facilities are far too limited, the supply problem would be very great, and Hawaii, Alaska, and our coasts would be greatly exposed to raids.

One point to remember, in connection with a decision to adopt a limited offensive role, as in both of the alternative plans just mentioned, is that, in case of reverses, public opinion may require a stronger effort. For example, should Japanese success in the Far East seem imminent, there would be great pressure brought to bear to support our force there, instead of leaving it hanging in the air. Thus, what we might originally plan as a limited war with Japan might well become an unlimited war; our entire strength would then be required in the Far East, and little force would remain for eventualities in the Atlantic and for the support of the British Isles.

Let us now look eastward, and examine our possible action in the Atlantic.

In the first place, if we avoid serious commitment in the Pacific, the purely American Atlantic problem, envisaging defense of our coasts, the Caribbean, Canada, and South America, plus giving strong naval assistance to Britain, is not difficult so long as the British are able to maintain their present naval activity. Should the British Isles then fall we would find ourselves acting alone, and at war with the world. To repeat, we would be thrown back on our haunches.

Should we enter the war as an ally of Great Britain, and not then be at war with Japan, we envisage the British asking us for widespread naval assistance. Roughly, they would want us, in the Western Atlantic Ocean from Cape Sable to Cape Horn, to protect shipping against raiders and submarine activities. They would also need strong reenforcements for their escort and minesweeping forces in their home waters; and strong flying boat reconnaissance from Scotland, the Atlantic Islands, and Capetown. They might ask us to capture the Azores and the Cape Verde Islands. To their home waters they would have us send submarines and small craft, and to the Mediterranean assistance of any character which we may be able to provide. They would expect us to take charge of allied interests in the Pacific, and to send a naval detachment to Singapore.

This purely naval assistance, would not, in my opinion, assure final victory for Great Britain. Victory would probably depend upon her ability ultimately to make a land offensive against the Axis powers. For making a successful land offensive, British manpower is insufficient. Offensive troops from other nations will be required. I believe that the United States, in addition to sending naval assistance, would also need to send large air and land forces to Europe or Africa, or both, and to participate strongly in this land offensive. The naval task of transporting an army abroad would be large.

To carry out such tasks we would have to exert a major naval and military effort in the Atlantic. We would then be able to do little more in the Pacific than remain on a strict defensive.

Were we to enter the war against Germany and Italy as an ally of Great Britain, I do not necessarily anticipate immediate hostile action by Japan, whatever may be her Axis obligation. She may fear eventual consequences and do nothing. We might be faced with demands for concessions as the price of her neutrality. She might agree to defer her aggressions in the Netherlands East Indies for the time being by a guarantee of ample economic access to the Western Hemisphere and to British and Dutch possessions. But she might even demand complete cessation of British and American assistance to China.

The strong wish of the American government and people at present seems to be to remain at peace. In spite of this, we must face the possibility that we may at any moment become involved in war. With war in prospect, I believe our every effort should be directed toward the prosecution of a national policy with mutually supporting diplomatic and military aspects, and having as its guiding feature a determination that any intervention we may undertake shall be such as will ultimately best promote our own national interests. We should see the best answer to the question: "Where should we fight the war, and for what objective?" With the answer to this question to guide me, I can make a more logical plan, can more appropriately distribute the naval forces, can better coordinate the future material preparation of the Navy, and can more usefully advise as to whether or not proposed diplomatic measures can adequately be supported by available naval strength.

That is to say, until the question concerning our final military objective is authoritatively answered, I can not de-termine the scale and the nature of the effort which the Navy may be called upon to exert in the Far East, the Pacific, and the Atlantic.

It is a fundamental requirement of our military position that our homeland remain secure against successful attack. Directly concerned in this security is the safety of other parts of the Western Hemisphere. A very strong pillar of the defense structure of the Americas has, for many years, been the balance of power existing in Europe. The collapse of Great Britain or the destruction or surrender of the British Fleet will destroy this balance and will free European military power for possible encroachment in this hemisphere.

I believe that we should recognize as the foundation of adequate armed strength the possession of a profitable foreign trade, both in raw materials and in finished goods. Without such a trade, our economy can scarcely support heavy armaments. The restoration of foreign trade, particularly with Europe, may depend upon the continued integrity of the British Empire.

It may be possible for us to prevent a British collapse by military intervention.

Our interests in the Far East are very important. The economic effect of a complete Japanese hegemony in that region is conjectural. But regardless of economic considerations, we have heretofore strongly opposed the further expansion of Japan.

We might temporarily check Japanese expansion by defeating her in a war in the Far East, but to check her permanently would require that we retain possession of, and militarily develop, an extensive and strategically located Asiatic base area having reasonably secure lines of communication with the United States. Retaining, and adequately developing, an Asiatic base area would mean the reversal of long-standing American policy.

Whether we could ensure the continued existence of a strong British Empire by soundly defeating Japan in the Far East is questionable, though continuing to hold on there for the present is a definite contribution to British strength.

Lacking possession of an Asiatic base area of our own, continued British strength in the Far East would doubtless prove advantageous to us in checking Japan permanently.

The military matters discussed in this memorandum may properly receive consideration in arriving at a decision on the course that we should adopt in the diplomatic field.

An early decision in this field will facilitate a naval preparation which will best promote the adopted course. As I see affairs today, answers to the following broad questions will be most useful to the Navy:

(A) Shall our principal military effort be directed toward hemisphere defense, and include chiefly those activities within the Western Hemisphere which contribute directly to security against attack in either or both oceans? An affirmative answer would indicate that the United States, as seems now to be the hope of this country, would remain out of war unless pushed into it. If and when forced into war, the greater portion of our Fleet could remain for the time being in its threatening position in the Pacific, but no major effort would be exerted overseas either to the east or the west; the most that would be done for allies, besides providing material help, would be to send detachments to assist in their defense. It should be noted here that, were minor help to be given in one direction, public opinion might soon push us into giving it major support, as was the case in the World War.

Under this plan, our influence upon the outcome of the European War would be small.

(B) Shall we prepare for a full offensive against Japan, premised on assistance from the British and Dutch forces in the Far East, and remain on the strict defensive in the Atlantic? If this course is selected, we would be placing full trust in the British to hold their own indefinitely in the Atlantic, or, at least, until after we should have defeated Japan decisively, and thus had fully curbed her offensive power for the time being. Plans for augmenting the scale of our present material assistance to Great Britain would be adversely affected until Japan had been decisively defeated. The length of time required to defeat Japan would be very considerable.

If we enter the war against Japan and then if Great Britain loses, we probably would in any case have to reorient towards the Atlantic. There is no dissenting view on this point.

(C) Shall we plan for sending the strongest possible military assistance both to the British in Europe, and to the British, Dutch, and Chinese in the Far East? The naval and air detachments we would send to the British Isles would possibly ensure their continued resistance, but would not increase British power to conduct a land offensive. The strength we could send to the Far East might be enough to check the southward spread of Japanese rule for the duration of the war. The strength of naval forces remaining in Hawaii for the defense of the Eastern Pacific, and the strength of the forces in the Western Atlantic for the defense of that area, would be reduced to that barely sufficient for executing their tasks. Should Great Britain finally lose, or should Malaysia fall to Japan, our naval strength might then be found to have been seriously reduced, relative to that of the Axis powers. It should be understood that, under this plan, we would be operating under the handicap of fighting major wars on two fronts.

Should we adopt Plan (C), we must face the consequences that would ensue were we to start a war with one plan, and then, after becoming heavily engaged, be forced

greatly to modify it or discard it altogether, as, for example, in case of a British fold up. On neither of these distant fronts would it be possible to execute a really major offensive. Strategically, the situation might become disastrous should our effort on either front fail.

(D) Shall we direct our efforts toward an eventual strong offensive in the Atlantic as an ally of the British, and a defensive in the Pacific? Any strength that we might send to the Far East would, by just so much, reduce the force of our blows against Germany and Italy. About the least that we would do for our ally would be to send strong naval light forces and aircraft to Great Britain and the Mediterranean. Probably we could not stop with a purely naval effort. The plan might ultimately require capture of the Portuguese and Spanish Islands and military and naval bases in Africa and possibly Europe; and thereafter even involve undertaking a full scale land offensive. In consideration of a course that would require landing large numbers of troops abroad, account must be taken of the possible unwillingness of the people of the United States to support land operations of this character, and to incur the risk of heavy loss should Great Britain collapse. Under Plan (D) we would be unable to exert strong pressure against Japan, and would necessarily gradually reorient our policy in the Far East. The full national offensive strength would be exerted in a single direction, rather than be expended in areas far distant from each other. At the conclusion of the war, even if Britain should finally collapse, we might still find ourselves possessed of bases in Africa suitable for assisting in the defense of South America.

Under any of these plans, we must recognize the possibility of the involvement of France as an ally of Germany.

I believe that the continued existence of the British Empire, combined with building up a strong protection in our home areas, will do most to ensure the status quo in the Western Hemisphere, and to promote our principal national interests. As I have previously stated, I also believe that Great Britain requires from us very great help in the Atlantic, and possibly even on the continents of Europe or Africa, if she is to be enabled to survive. In my opinion Alternatives (A), (B), and (C) will most probably not provide the necessary degree of assistance, and, therefore, if we undertake war, that Alternative (D) is likely to be the most fruitful for the United States, particularly if we enter the war at an early date.

Initially, the offensive measures adopted would, necessarily, be purely naval. Even should we intervene, final victory in Europe is not certain. I believe that the chances for success are in our favor, particularly if we insist upon full equality in the political and military direction of the war.

The odds seem against our being able under Plan (D) to check Japanese expansion unless we win the war in Europe. We might not long retain possession of the Philippines. Our political and military influence in the Far East might largely disappear, so long as we were fully engaged in the Atlantic. A preliminary to a war in this category would be a positive effort to avoid war with Japan, and to endeavor to prevent war between Japan and the British Empire and the Netherlands East Indies. The possible cost of avoiding a war with Japan has been referred to previously.

I would add that Plan (D) does not mean the immediate movement of the Fleet into the Atlantic. I would make no further moves until war should become imminent, and then I would recommend redistribution of our naval forces as the situation then demanded. I fully recognize the value of retaining strong forces in the Pacific as long as they can profitably be kept there.

Until such time as the United States should decide to engage its full forces in war, I recommend that we pursue a course that will most rapidly increase the military strength of both the Army and the Navy, that is to say, adopt Alternative (A) without hostilities.

Under any decision that the President may tentatively make, we should at once prepare a complete Joint Plan for guiding Army and Navy activities. We should also prepare at least the skeletons of alternative plans to fit possible alternative situations which may eventuate. I make the specific recommendation that, should we be forced into a war with Japan, we should, because of the prospect of war in the Atlantic also, definitely plan to avoid operations in the Far East or the Mid-Pacific that will prevent the Navy from promptly moving to the Atlantic forces fully adequate to safeguard our interests and policies in the event of a British collapse. We ought not now willingly engage in any war against Japan unless we are certain of aid from Great Britain and the Netherlands East Indies.

No important allied military decision should be reached without clear understanding between the nations involved as to the strength and extent of the participation which may be expected in any particular theater, and as to a proposed skeleton plan of operations.

Accordingly, I make the recommendation that, as a preliminary to possible entry of the United States into the conflict, the United States Army and Navy at once undertake secret staff talks on technical matters with the British military and naval authorities in London, with Canadian military authorities in Washington, and with British and Dutch authorities in Singapore and Batavia. The purpose would be to reach agreements and lay down plans for promoting unity of allied effort should the United States find it necessary to enter the war under any of the alternative eventualities considered in this memorandum.

Source: Folder Navy Department "Plan Dog," Box 4, Presidential Safe Files, Franklin D. Roosevelt Papers, Franklin D. Roosevelt Presidential Library, Hyde Park, NY.

74. The British Blitz: "Coventry's Ordeal: Ruthless Bombing: Dusk-to-Dawn Attacks," Article in *The Manchester Guardian*, 16 November 1940

After the fall of France, Hitler decided to go ahead with an invasion of Britain, in preparation for which he sought to win German air superiority. In July 1940 the Luftwaffe, the German air force, began intensive raids on British airfields, factories, and radar stations, in purported retaliation for British air attacks on German towns. On 7 September German air commanders switched tactics and targets to the civilian population, mounting massive bombing raids on most major British cities, including London, Britain's capital and symbolic heart. Between then and May 1941 the Luftwaffe made 127 large-scale nighttime attacks on British cities, 71 on London, the others against other major industrial centers. The objective was both to break the morale of the civilian population and to damage or destroy Britain's industrial capacity. The blitz did not, however, succeed in breaking the British will to resist, but became part of British national mythology of the war, enshrined as a time when all Britons, whatever their class, sex, or age, held together in a spirit of national unity and determination and endured heavy punishment rather than submit to German demands. In late autumn 1940 Hitler formally postponed his projected invasion, but raids against British cities nonetheless continued for several months. One of the most devastating was that on Coventry, the German "Moonlight Sonata" raid of 14–15 November 1940, which destroyed much of the city, including the famous cathedral, leaving somewhere between 380 and 550 people dead and several hundred others seriously injured.

The spire of Coventry Cathedral today stood as a sentinel over the grim scene of destruction below following a dusk-to-dawn raid on the town which the Nazis claimed was the biggest attack in the history of air war. Casualties are officially estimated as being in the region of 1,000.

Some fires were still alight when, with the coming of dawn, the German bombers flew off to terminate a night of merciless, indiscriminate bombing. The Luftwaffe, carrying through the raid (which Berlin, claiming that 500 'planes took part, described as reprisal for the R.A.F. attack on Munich), used terror-bombing tactics. From dusk to dawn there was seldom a period of more than two minutes when a bomb could not be heard falling. The centre of the city bears witness to the savagery of their attack.

In the first six hours of the attack wave upon wave of 25 or more bombers in quick succession scattered hundreds of bombs of all types over a wide area. Brilliant moonlight was not sufficient for the German airmen, who dropped flares and incendiary bombs to light up the scene soon to be bathed in a great red glow. The barrage from the ground defences never slackened and for most of the night the raiders were kept at a great height from which accurate bombing was impossible.

The famous Cathedral is little more than a skeleton, masses of rubble forming huge mounds within its bare walls, while other targets included two hospitals, two churches, hotels, clubs, cinemas, public shelters, public baths, police station, and post office.

The Provost (the Very Rev. R. T. Howard) and a party of cathedral watchers attempted to deal with twelve incendiary bombs. They tackled them with sand and attempted to smother them, until a shower of other incendiaries, accompanied this time by high explosives, rendered impossible their efforts to save the cathedral, only the tower and steeple of which remain. "The cathedral," said the Provost, "will rise again, will be rebuilt, and it will be as great a pride to future generations as it has been to generations in the past."

Tonight the Cathedral was a reeking shell. Blackened arches and window faces of fretted stone, still stately for all their disfigurement, framed a picture of hideous destruction. Blocks of masonry, heavy pieces of church furniture, and plaques commemorating famous men were merged into a common dust. In addition to the two churches, a Methodist chapel was wrecked, as well as a library (with thousands of volumes and treasured manuscripts), a hall, a ward and operating theatre of one hospital, the outbuildings of an isolation hospital, two hotels, and a newspaper office. Some retail shops, large stores, and office buildings were destroyed by fire or damaged by high-explosive bombs.

With some of the gas, electricity, and water mains damaged, shortage of water handicapped the firemen, and in some cases it was necessary to use dynamite to prevent neighbouring property from being involved in the flames.

In the city and suburbs it was impossible to walk down many streets without seeing some kind of damage. The centre of the town has been seriously damaged by fire and high-explosive bombs. Groups of refugees thronged the roads from the town, making their way from their devastated homes in the hope of reaching country billets before to-night's blackout.

Few shops were open, but throughout the day shopkeepers and businessmen have been salvaging what remained of their possessions. The amazing thing about them was that they could still smile. They were grubbing about among shattered timber and bricks, rescuing stock-in-trade, type-writers, files of business papers, and the like, and putting the best face upon calamity. Some shopkeepers whose shops had gone sold their recovered wares on the pavement, while businessmen went about the job of setting themselves up in new premises. Together with this private enterprise went official action. The Ministry of Food had promptly stepped in to make sure that the people should have their quota of goods in spite of damage to shops. An Official was instructed to check the food position and, if necessary, to draw upon emergency stocks. He found, however, that the town's supplies were not materially affected. The Mayor (Alderman J. A. Moseley) also gave the assurance that "everything possible will be done for the sufferers and the homeless."

Mobile canteens are doing magnificent work in helping to feed the homeless people, and this evening private cars, loaded to capacity with comforts, were pouring into the city.

Within a few hours of the raid taking place, Mr. Herbert Morrison, Minister of Home Security, was on the scene conferring with civic heads and making emergency arrangements. Following a conference with the mayor and other civic officials at which Lord Dudley, Regional Commissioner, was present, Mr. Morrison said: "We have cleared up many details and settled the policy to be adopted. The National Service units of the city have stood up to their duty magnificently. They have displayed great courage and determination under exceptional strain. I am very grateful to them for their devotion to duty in the service of their country. The local authority is taking full and prompt measures to deal with the emergency."

Of the people of Coventry, to whose spirit of cheerfulness he paid a high tribute, Mr. Morrison said: "They regarded it as a nasty business, but realised that it will be a thousand times worse if Hitler ever came to them. Such actions as this can only lead to a determination by this country's people to put everything they possibly can into the war effort."

Source: "Coventry's Ordeal: Ruthless Bombing: Dusk-to-Dawn Attacks," *The Manchester Guardian,* 16 November 1940. Available at Guardian Unlimited: Guardian Century; http://century.guardian.co.uk/1940–1949/Story/0,6051,127361,00.html.

75. Winston Churchill to Franklin D. Roosevelt, 7 December 1940

Winston Churchill thought this the most important letter he ever wrote to President Franklin D. Roosevelt. As 1940 drew to an end, British dollar reserves were exhausted, and the prospect loomed that before long Britain would be unable to pay for any further American war supplies. This letter, drafted by Churchill with advice from other government officials, including Lord Lothian, the British ambassador in Washington, frankly set out the desperate British position of high shipping losses and inadequate naval defenses and merchant tonnage and asked the United States, in its own interests, to make up these deficiencies. Although still arguing that such assistance represented the best means of keeping the United States itself out of war, Churchill was clearly suggesting that the United States take measures that would place it even more clearly on the side of Great Britain and that, should the Axis object to them, had the potential to make the country an active rather than passive belligerent. Churchill's appeal was the genesis of the Lend-Lease program, which Roosevelt proposed to Congress and the American people early in 1941, and of the expansion of hemispheric defense zone, which he extended ever farther into the Atlantic during that year.

As we reach the end of this year I feel that you will expect me to lay before you the prospects for 1941. I do so strongly and confidently because it seems to me that the vast majority of American citizens have recorded their conviction that the safety of the United States as well as the future of our two democracies and the kind of civilization for which they stand are bound up with the survival and independence of the British Commonwealth of Nations. Only thus can those bastions of sea power, upon which the control of the Atlantic and the Indian Oceans depends, be preserved in faithful and friendly hands. The control of the Pacific by the United States Navy and of the Atlantic by the British Navy is indispensable to the security of the trade routes of both our countries and the surest means to preventing the war from reaching the shores of the United States. . . .

2. There is another aspect. It takes between three and four years to convert the industries of a modern state to war purposes. Saturation point is reached when the maximum industrial effort that can be spared from civilian needs has been applied to war production. Germany certainly reached this point by the end of 1939. We in the British Empire are now only about halfway through the second year. The United States, I should suppose, was by no means so far advanced as we. Moreover, I understand that immense programs of naval, military and air defence are now on foot in the United States, to complete which certainly two years are needed. It is our British duty in the common interest as also for our own survival to hold the front and grapple with Nazi power until the preparations of the United States are complete. Victory may come before the two years are out; but we have no right to count upon it to the extent of relaxing any effort that is humanly possible. Therefore I submit with very great respect for your good and friendly consideration that there is a solid identity of interest between the British Empire and the United States while these conditions last. It is upon this footing that I venture to address you.

3. The form which this war has taken and seems likely to hold does not enable us to match the immense armies of Germany in any theatre where their main force can be brought to bear. We can however by the use of sea power and air power meet the German armies in the regions where only comparatively small forces can be brought into action. We must do our best to prevent German domination of Europe spreading into Africa and into Southern Asia. We have also to maintain in constant readiness in this Island armies strong enough to make the problem of an overseas invasion insoluble. For these purposes we are forming as fast as possible, as you are already aware, between fifty and sixty divisions. Even if the United States was our ally instead of our indispensable partner we should not ask for a large American expeditionary army. Shipping, not men, is the limiting factor and the power to transport munitions and supplies claims priority over the movement by sea of large numbers of soldiers.

4. The first half of 1940 was a period of disaster for the Allies and for the Empire. The last five months have witnessed a strong and perhaps unexpected recovery by Great Britain; fighting alone but with invaluable aid in munitions and in destroyers placed at our disposal by the great Republic of which you are for the third time chosen Chief.

5. The danger of Great Britain being destroyed by a swift overwhelming blow has for the time being very greatly receded. In its place there is a long, gradually maturing danger, less sudden and less spectacular but equally deadly. This

mortal danger is the steady and increasing diminution of our sea tonnage. We can endure the shattering of our dwellings and the slaughter of our civilian population by indiscriminate air attacks and we hope to parry these increasingly as our science develops and to repay them upon military objectives in Germany as our Air Force more nearly approaches the strength of the enemy. The decision for 1941 lies upon the seas; unless we can establish our ability to feed this Island, to import munitions of all kinds which we need, unless we can move our armies to the various theatres where Hitler and his confederate Mussolini must be met, and maintain them there and do all this with the assurance of being able to carry it on till the spirit of the continental dictators is broken, we may fall by the way and the time needed by the United States to complete her defensive preparations may not be forthcoming. It is therefore in shipping and in the power to transport across the oceans, particularly the Atlantic Ocean, that in 1941 the crunch of the whole war will be found. If on the other hand we are able to move the necessary tonnage to and fro across the salt water indefinitely, it may well be that the application of superior air power to the German homeland and the rising anger of other Nazi-gripped populations will bring the agony of civilization to a merciful and glorious end. But do not let us underrate the task.

6. Our shipping losses, the figure[s] for which in recent months are appended, have been on a scale quite comparable to that of the worst years of the first war. In the 5 weeks ending November 3rd the figures reached a total of 420,500 tons. Our estimation of the annual tonnage which ought to be imported in order to maintain our war effort at full strength is 43,000,000 tons; the tonnage entering in September was only at the rate of 37,000,000 tons and in October at 38,000,000 tons. Were the diminution to continue at this rate it would be fatal, unless indeed immensely greater replenishment than anything at present in sight could be achieved in time. Although we are doing all we can to meet this situation by new methods, the difficulty of limiting the losses is obviously much greater than in the last war. We lack the assistance of the French Navy, the Italian Navy and the Japanese Navy, and above all the United States Navy, which was of such vital help to us during the culminating years. The enemy commands the ports all around the northern and western coast of France. He is increasingly basing his submarines, flying boats and combat planes on these ports and on the islands off the French coast. We lack the use of ports or territory in Eire in which to organize our coastal patrols by air and sea. In fact, we have now only one effective passage of entry to the British Isles, namely the northern approach, against which the enemy is increasingly concentrating, reaching ever farther out by U-boat action

and long distance bombing. In addition, there have for some months been merchant ship raiders both in the Atlantic and in the Indian Oceans. And now we have powerful warship raiders to contend with as well. We need ships both to hunt down and to escort. Large as are our resources and preparations, we do not possess enough.

7. The next six or seven months bring the relative battleship strength in home waters to a smaller margin than is satisfactory. . . .

9. There is a second field of danger: the Vichy Government may either by joining Hitler's new order in Europe or through some maneuver such as forcing us to attack an expedition dispatched by sea against free French Colonies, find an excuse for ranging with the Axis Powers the very considerable undamaged naval forces still under its control. If the French Navy were to join the Axis, the control of West Africa would pass immediately into their hands with the gravest consequences to our communication between the northern and southern Atlantic, and also affect Dakar and of course thereafter South America.

10. A third sphere of danger is in the Far East. Here it seems clear that the Japanese are thrusting Southward through Indo China to Saigon and other naval and air bases, thus bringing them within a comparatively short distance of Singapore and the Dutch East Indies. It is reported that the Japanese are preparing five good divisions for possible use as an overseas expeditionary force. We have today no forces in the Far East capable of dealing with this situation should it develop.

11. In the face of these dangers, we must try to use the year 1941 to build up such a supply of weapons, particularly aircraft, both by increased output at home in spite of bombardment, and through ocean-borne supplies, as will lay the foundation of victory. In view of the difficulty and magnitude of this task, as outlined by all the facts I have set forth to which many others could be added, I feel entitled, nay bound, to lay before you the various ways in which the United States could give supreme and decisive help to what is, in certain aspects, the common cause.

12. The prime need is to check or limit the loss of tonnage on the Atlantic approaches to our Islands. This may be achieved both by increasing the naval forces, which cope with attacks, and by adding to the number of merchant ships on which we depend. For the first purpose there would seem to be the following alternatives:

1. The reassertion by the United States of the doctrine of the freedom of the seas from illegal and barbarous warfare in accordance with the decisions reached after the late Great War, and as freely accepted and

defined by Germany in 1935. From this, the United States ships should be free to trade with countries against which there is not an effective legal blockade.

2. It would, I suggest, follow that protection should be given to this lawful trading by United States forces, i.e., escorting battleships, cruisers, destroyers and air flotillas. Protection would be immediately more effective if you were able to obtain bases in Eire for the duration of the war. I think it is improbable that such protection would provoke a declaration of war by Germany upon the United States though probably sea incidents of a dangerous character would from time to time occur. Hitler has shown himself inclined to avoid the Kaiser's mistake. He does not wish to be drawn into war with the United States until he has gravely undermined the power of Great Britain. His maxim is "one at a time." The policy I have ventured to outline, or something like it, would constitute a decisive act of constructive non-belligerency by the United States, and more than any other measure would make it certain that British resistance could be effectively prolonged for the desired period and victory gained.

3. Failing the above, the gift, loan or supply of a large number of American vessels of war, above all destroyers already in the Atlantic, is indispensable to the maintenance of the Atlantic route. Further, could not United States naval forces extend their sea control over the American side of the Atlantic, so as to prevent molestation by enemy vessels of the approaches to the new line of naval and air bases which the United States is establishing in British islands in the Western Hemisphere. The strength of the United States naval forces is such that the assistance in the Atlantic that they could afford us, as described above, would not jeopardize control over the Pacific. . . .

13. The object of the foregoing measures is to reduce to manageable proportions the present destructive losses at sea. In addition it is indispensable that the merchant tonnage available for supplying Great Britain and for the waging of the war by Great Britain with all vigour, should be substantially increased beyond the one and a quarter million tons per annum which is the utmost we can now build. The convoy system, the detours, the zig zags, the great distances from which we now have to bring our imports, and the congestion of our western harbours, have reduced by about one third the value of our existing tonnage. To ensure final victory, not less than three million tons of additional merchant shipbuilding capacity will be required. Only the

United States can supply this need. . . . Moreover we look to the industrial energy of the Republic for a reinforcement of our domestic capacity to manufacture combat aircraft. Without that reinforcement reaching us in a substantial measure, we shall not achieve the massive preponderance in the air on which we must rely to loosen and disintegrate the German grip on Europe. . . . I invite you then, Mr. President, to give earnest consideration to an immediate order on joint account for a further 2,000 combat aircraft a month. Of these aircraft I would submit that the highest possible proportion should be heavy bombers, the weapon on which above all others we depend to shatter the foundations of German military power. I am aware of the formidable task that this would impose upon the industrial organization of the United States. Yet, in our heavy need, we call with confidence to the most resourceful and ingenious technicians in the world. We ask for an unexampled effort believing that it can be made. . . .

15. You have also received information about our armies. In the munitions sphere, in spite of enemy bombing, we are making steady progress. Without your continued assistance in supply of machine tools and in the further release from stock of certain articles we could not hope to equip as many as 50 divisions in 1941. I am grateful for the arrangements already practically completed for your aid in the equipment of the army which we have already planned and for the provision of American-type weapons for an additional 10 divisions in time for the campaign of 1942. But when the tide of dictatorship begins to recede, many countries, trying to regain their freedom, may be asking for arms, and there is no source to which they can look except to the factories of the United States. I must therefore also urge the importance of expanding to the utmost American productive capacity for small arms, artillery and tanks.

16. I am arranging to present you with a complete program of munitions of all kinds which we seek to obtain from you, the greater part of which is of course already agreed. An important economy of time and effort will be produced if the types selected for the United States Services should, whenever possible, conform to those which have proved their merit under actual conditions of war. In this way reserves of guns and ammunition and of airplanes become inter-changeable and are by that very fact augmented. This is however a sphere so highly technical that I do not enlarge upon it.

17. Last of all I come to the question of finance. The more rapid and abundant the flow of munitions and ships, which you are able to send us, the sooner will our dollar credits be exhausted. They are already as you know very heavily drawn upon by payments we have made to date. Indeed as you know orders already placed or under negotiation, including

expenditure settled or pending for creating munitions factories in the United States, many times exceed the total exchange resources remaining at the disposal of Great Britain. The moment approaches when we shall no longer be able to pay cash for shipping and other supplies. While we will do our utmost and shrink from no proper sacrifice to make payments across the exchange, I believe that you will agree that it would be wrong in principle and mutually disadvantageous in effect if, at the height of this struggle, Great Britain were to be divested of all saleable assets so that after victory was won with our blood, civilization saved and time gained for the United States to be fully armed against all eventualities, we should stand stripped to the bone. Such a course would not be in the moral or economic interests of either of our countries. We here would be unable after the war to purchase the large balance of imports from the United States over and above the volume of our exports, which is agreeable to your tariffs and domestic economy. Not only should we in Great Britain suffer cruel privations but widespread unemployment in the United States would follow the curtailment of American exporting power.

18. Moreover I do not believe the Government and people of the United States would find it in accordance with the principles which guide them, to confine the help which they have so generously promised only to such munitions of war and commodities as could be immediately paid for. You may be assured that we shall prove ourselves ready to suffer and sacrifice to the utmost for the Cause, and that we glory in being its champion. The rest we leave with confidence to you and to your people, being sure that ways and means will be found which future generations on both sides of the Atlantic will approve and admire.

19. If, as I believe, you are convinced, Mr. President, that the defeat of the Nazi and Fascist tyranny is a matter of high consequence to the people of the United States and to the Western Hemisphere, you will regard this letter not as an appeal for aid, but as a statement of the action necessary to the achievement of our common purpose.

Source: Winston Churchill to Franklin D. Roosevelt, 7 December 1940, enclosed in Lord Lothian to Roosevelt, 8 December 1940. Folder Diplomatic Correspondence Great Britain: Military Situation: December 1940, Box 34, Presidential Safe Files, Franklin D. Roosevelt Papers, Franklin D. Roosevelt Presidential Library, Hyde Park, NY. Available at http://www.fdrlibrary.marist.edu/psf/box34/a311s08.html.

76. Adolf Hitler, Military Directive No. 21 for "Operation BARBAROSSA," the Invasion of Russia, 18 December 1940

By the end of 1940, disputes with the Soviet Union over Finland and Bulgaria had led Adolf Hitler to conclude that Russia would not acquiesce indefinitely in German domination of Europe. These developments only reinforced Hitler's long-cherished ambition of mounting an invasion of Russia. In December 1940, he instructed the German military to prepare to launch such an operation the following spring, a campaign Hitler anticipated would be swift and decisive.

TOP SECRET

BY OFFICER ONLY

The German Wehrmacht must be prepared *to crush Soviet Russia in a quick campaign* (Operation Barbarossa) even before the conclusion of the war against England.

For this purpose the *Army* will have to employ all available units, with the reservation that the occupied territories must be secured against surprises.

For the *Luftwaffe* it will be a matter of releasing such strong forces for the Eastern campaign in support of the Army that a quick completion of the ground operations can be counted on and that damage to eastern German territory by enemy air attacks will be as slight as possible. This concentration of the main effort in the east is limited by the requirement that the entire combat and armament area dominated by us must remain adequately protected against enemy air attacks and that the offensive operations against England, particularly against her supply lines, must not be permitted to break down.

The main effort of the *Navy* will remain unequivocally directed against England, even during an Eastern campaign.

I shall order the *concentration* against Soviet Russia possibly eight weeks before the intended beginning of operations.

Preparations requiring more time to get under way are to be started now, if this has not yet been done, and are to be completed by 15 May 1941.

It is of decisive importance, however, that the intention to attack does not become apparent.

The preparations of the High Commands are to be made on the following basis:

I.

General Purpose

The mass of the Russian *Army* in western Russia is to be destroyed in daring operations, by driving forward deep armoured wedges; and the retreat of units capable of combat into the vastness of Russian territory is to be prevented.

In quick pursuit a line is then to be reached from which the Russian *Air Force* will no longer be able to attack the territory of the German Reich. The ultimate objective of the operation is to establish a cover against Asiatic Russia from the general line Volga-Archangel. Then, in case of necessity, the last industrial area left to Russia in the Urals can be eliminated by the Luftwaffe.

In the course of these operations the Russian *Baltic Sea Fleet* will quickly lose its bases and thus will no longer be able to fight.

Effective intervention by the Russian *Air Force* is to be prevented by powerful blows at the very beginning of operations. . . .

IV.

All orders to be issued by the commanders-in-chief on the basis of this directive must clearly indicate that they are *precautionary measures* for the possibility that Russia should change her present attitude toward us. The number of officers to be assigned to the preparatory work at an early date is to be kept as small as possible; additional personnel should be briefed as late as possible and only to the extent required for the activity of each individual. Otherwise, through the discovery of our preparations—the date of their execution has not even been fixed—there is danger that most serious political and military disadvantages may arise. . . .

Source: Margaret Carlyle, ed., *Documents on International Affairs 1939–1946,* Volume II: *Hitler's Europe* (London: Oxford University Press, 1954), 68–72. Reprinted with permission of Chatham House.

77. "The Arsenal of Democracy": Franklin D. Roosevelt, Fireside Chat on National Security and the Common Cause, 29 December 1940

As 1940 came to an end, Franklin D. Roosevelt responded to Winston Churchill's appeal for assistance with a public "fireside chat" to the American people. He urged that the United States must become the world's "arsenal of democracy," mounting a major rearmament effort of its own while supplying the Allies. His speech laid the groundwork for the Lend-Lease legislation passed early the next year, under which the United States government, though still formally neutral, provided massive military assistance to the Allies.

This is not a fireside chat on war. It is a talk on national security; because the nub of the whole purpose of your President is to keep you now, and your children later, and your grandchildren much later, out of a last-ditch war for the preservation of American independence and all the things that American independence means to you and to me and to ours. . . .

Never before since Jamestown and Plymouth Rock has our American civilization been in such danger as now.

For, on September 27, 1940, by an agreement signed in Berlin, three powerful nations, two in Europe and one in Asia, joined themselves together in the threat that if the United States of America interfered with or blocked the expansion program of these three nations—a program aimed at world control—they would unite in ultimate action against the United States.

The Nazi masters of Germany have made it clear that they intend not only to dominate all life and thought in their own country, but also to enslave the whole of Europe, and then to use the resources of Europe to dominate the rest of the world.

It was only three weeks ago their leader stated this: "There are two worlds that stand opposed to each other." And then in defiant reply to his opponents, he said this: "Others are correct when they say: With this world we cannot ever reconcile ourselves. . . . I can beat any other power in the world." So said the leader of the Nazis.

In other words, the Axis not merely admits but proclaims that there can be no ultimate peace between their philosophy of government and our philosophy of government.

In view of the nature of this undeniable threat, it can be asserted, properly and categorically, that the United States has no right or reason to encourage talk of peace, until the day shall come when there is a clear intention on the part of the aggressor nations to abandon all thought of dominating or conquering the world.

At this moment, the forces of the states that are leagued against all peoples who live in freedom, are being held away from our shores. The Germans and the Italians are being blocked on the other side of the Atlantic by the British, and by the Greeks, and by thousands of soldiers and sailors who were able to escape from subjugated countries. In Asia, the Japanese are being engaged by the Chinese nation in another great defense.

In the Pacific Ocean is our fleet.

Some of our people like to believe that wars in Europe and in Asia are of no concern to us. But it is a matter of most vital concern to us that European and Asiatic war-makers should not gain control of the oceans which lead to this hemisphere. . . .

If Great Britain goes down, the Axis powers will control the continents of Europe, Asia, Africa, Australasia, and the high seas—and they will be in a position to bring enormous military and naval resources against this hemisphere. It is no exaggeration to say that all of us, in all the Americas, would be living at the point of a gun—a gun loaded with explosive bullets, economic as well as military.

We should enter upon a new and terrible era in which the whole world, our hemisphere included, would be run by threats of brute force. To survive in such a world, we would have to convert ourselves permanently into a militaristic power on the basis of war economy.

Some of us like to believe that even if Great Britain falls, we are still safe, because of the broad expanse of the Atlantic and of the Pacific. But the width of those oceans is not what it was in the days of clipper ships. At one point between Africa and Brazil the distance is less than from Washington to Denver, Colorado—five hours for the latest type of bomber. And at the North end of the Pacific Ocean America and Asia almost touch each other.

Even today we have planes that could fly from the British Isles to New England and back again without refueling. And remember that the range of the modern bomber is ever being increased. . . .

There are those who say that the Axis powers would never have any desire to attack the Western Hemisphere. That is the same dangerous form of wishful thinking which has destroyed the powers of resistance of so many conquered peoples. The plain facts are that the Nazis have proclaimed, time and again, that all other races are their inferiors and therefore subject to their orders. And most important of all, the vast resources and wealth of this American Hemisphere constitute the most tempting loot in all the round world.

Let us no longer blind ourselves to the undeniable fact that the evil forces which have crushed and undermined and corrupted so many others are already within our own gates.

Your Government knows much about them and every day is ferreting them out.

Their secret emissaries are active in our own and in neighboring countries. They seek to stir up suspicion and dissension to cause internal strife. They try to turn capital against labor, and vice versa. They try to reawaken long slumbering racial and religious enmities which should have no place in this country. They are active in every group that promotes intolerance. They exploit for their own ends our natural abhorrence of war. These trouble-breeders have but one purpose. It is to divide our people into hostile groups and to destroy our unity and shatter our will to defend ourselves.

There are also American citizens, many of them in high places, who, unwittingly in most cases, are aiding and abetting the work of these agents. I do not charge these American citizens with being foreign agents. But I do charge them with doing exactly the kind of work that the dictators want done in the United States.

These people not only believe that we can save our own skins by shutting our eyes to the fate of other nations. Some of them go much further than that. They say that we can and should become the friends and even the partners of the Axis powers. Some of them even suggest that we should imitate the methods of the dictatorships. Americans never can and never will do that.

The experience of the past two years has proven beyond doubt that no nation can appease the Nazis. . . . We know now that a nation can have peace with the Nazis only at the price of total surrender. . . .

The history of recent years proves that shootings and chains and concentration camps are not simply the transient tools but the very altars of modern dictatorships. They may talk of a "new order" in the world, but what they have in mind is only a revival of the oldest and the worst tyranny. In that there is no liberty, no religion, no hope.

The proposed "new order" is the very opposite of a United States of Europe or a United States of Asia. It is not a Government based upon the consent of the governed. It is not a union of ordinary, self-respecting men and women to protect themselves and their freedom and their dignity from oppression. It is an unholy alliance of power and pelf to dominate and enslave the human race.

The British people and their allies today are conducting an active war against this unholy alliance. Our own future security is greatly dependent on the outcome of that fight. Our ability to "keep out of war" is going to be affected by that outcome.

Thinking in terms of today and tomorrow, I make the direct statement to the American people that there is far less chance of the United States getting into war, if we do all we can now to support the nations defending themselves against attack by the Axis than if we acquiesce in their defeat, submit tamely to an Axis victory, and wait our turn to be the object of attack in another war later on.

If we are to be completely honest with ourselves, we must admit that there is risk in any course we may take. But I deeply believe that the great majority of our people agree that the course that I advocate involves the least risk now and the greatest hope for world peace in the future.

The people of Europe who are defending themselves do not ask us to do their fighting. They ask us for the implements of war, the planes, the tanks, the guns, the freighters which will enable them to fight for their liberty and for our security. Emphatically we must get these weapons to them in sufficient volume and quickly enough, so that we and our children will be saved the agony and suffering of war which others have had to endure.

Let not the defeatists tell us that it is too late. It will never be earlier. Tomorrow will be later than today.

Certain facts are self-evident.

In a military sense Great Britain and the British Empire are today the spearhead of resistance to world conquest. They are putting up a fight which will live forever in the story of human gallantry.

There is no demand for sending an American Expeditionary Force outside our own borders. There is no intention by any member of your Government to send such a force. You can, therefore, nail any talk about sending armies to Europe as deliberate untruth.

Our national policy is not directed toward war. Its sole purpose is to keep war away from our country and our people.

Democracy's fight against world conquest is being greatly aided, and must be more greatly aided, by the rearmament of the United States and by sending every ounce and every ton of munitions and supplies that we can possibly spare to help the defenders who are in the front lines. It is no more unneutral for us to do that than it is for Sweden, Russia and other nations near Germany, to send steel and ore and oil and other war materials into Germany every day in the week.

We are planning our own defense with the utmost urgency; and in its vast scale we must integrate the war needs of Britain and the other free nations which are resisting aggression.

This is not a matter of sentiment or of controversial personal opinion. It is a matter of realistic, practical military policy, based on the advice of our military experts who are in close touch with existing warfare. These military and naval experts and the members of the Congress and the Administration have a single-minded purpose—the defense of the United States. . . .

We must be the great arsenal of democracy. For us this is an emergency as serious as war itself. We must apply ourselves to our task with the same resolution, the same sense of urgency, the same spirit of patriotism and sacrifice as we would show were we at war. . . .

I believe that the Axis powers are not going to win this war. I base that belief on the latest and best information.

We have no excuse for defeatism. We have every good reason for hope—hope for peace, hope for the defense of our civilization and for the building of a better civilization in the future.

I have the profound conviction that the American people are now determined to put forth a mightier effort than they have ever yet made to increase our production of all the implements of defense, to meet the threat to our democratic faith.

As President of the United States I call for that national effort. I call for it in the name of this nation which we love and honor and which we are privileged and proud to serve. I call upon our people with absolute confidence that our common cause will greatly succeed.

Source: Franklin D. Roosevelt, Speech, "The Arsenal of Democracy," 29 December 1940. Fireside Chat Files: State Department, 1940, Franklin D. Roosevelt Library Digital Archives.

78. United States Industrial and Economic Mobilization: Recollections of Joe Marcus, Head of the Civilian Requirements Division, National Defense Advisory Committee

World War II pulled the American economy out of depression, brought full employment and full production, and was the beginning of several decades of prosperity and economic growth in the United States. Joe Marcus, a New Deal economist who became head of the Civilian Requirements Division of the National Defense Advisory Committee in 1940, reflected later on his experiences with American economic mobilization during the Second World War and the growth of a military-industrial complex.

Most of my time was spent fighting with representatives of industry. Did we have the capacity to make enough steel, enough copper, for military as well as civilian needs? Our reports showed we didn't. The top industrial boys resisted this very strongly. They had gone through the Depression and, from their standpoint, there was an excess of capacity. They weren't going to fiddle around, increasing the capacity just because some screwball kids tell them they don't have enough.

What happens in a severe depression is that your consumption goes down, say, twenty percent. With a decrease in construction and in the demand for machinery by about eighty percent, it's devastating. From '32 to '39, there is recovery. But there are still ten or eleven million unemployed. The production of consumer goods is still low. All they're doing is replacing worn-out equipment. Why add more machinery? Why build more factories? Let's say they have the capacity to produce 80 million tons of steel and the demand is for only 70 million. Why should they listen to some screwballs in Washington who say, If there's a war, you're going to need 150 million tons?

We were young New Dealers who found the military in their planning stodgy and backward. They thought we didn't have the industrial capacity to produce more than, say, 5 billion dollars worth of military goods. So a group of us wrote a memorandum showing that there were so many unemployed, so much machine-tool capacity, that it was possible to produce 75 billion dollars worth. It flew in the face of the military statements.

Roosevelt had that memo on his desk on the day of Pearl Harbor. When he reorganized the War Production Board, with Donald Nelson on board, he insisted that the boys who wrote the memo watch the program. He set up two committees on the board. One was planning. The other was program progress control. I was yanked out of my previous job and made program progress control officer. (Laughs.)

When we got into the war, everything was a mess. Suddenly you've got to produce an enormous number of planes, tanks, build an eleven-million-man army, supply the British and, soon afterwards, the Russians. And the Free French. We needed an enormous jump in production. There was a bottleneck: machine tools.

Nelson got on the radio and said the machine-tool producers were not doing their job. They were not working around the clock, not working three shifts. The Machinery and Allied Products Institute, the trade association, says to Nelson, We can't run three shifts. Nelson tells them not to bother him, to talk to the guy who wrote the speech. So they came to see me.

Now my studies were based on statistics. I don't know how to build a machine tool. I barely knew one machine tool from another. (Laughs.) They insisted I make a tour of the machine-building industries. I accepted the invitation. I came back with my report: the Machinery and Allied Products Institute was wrong. I had visited factories across the street from each other, one working three shifts, one working one shift. Now they wanted me to take over planning and controls for the tool industry. (Laughs.)

I hesitated. It was a challenge: I was a critic, now I had to do something. It was a question of the war, too. I felt it was important. I was young. I was Jewish. I had never met a payroll. So I accepted the challenge.

Here I was, an outsider, reorganizing the whole goddamn thing. It was insane the way they were operating. You take government people: they don't know where the hell the factories are, don't know the possibilities. You take the industry people: they're concerned about their business after the war, doing things the way they have traditionally done it. They had no sense of the war needs and planning.

The heads of these divisions were dollar-a-year men. They kept their company salaries. They were the leaders of industry. Now, down below, you had heads of companies who actually knew their business. You also had guys the industry wanted to get rid of, executives they didn't know what to do with. Washington wants someone in charge of ball bearings? Send this clown there.

The first job I tackled was machine tools. Say an auto factory, an airplane factory, had all the lathes it needed but didn't have milling machines. Another factory, making tanks, was all ready to go with milling machines but didn't have lathes. I looked into it: how did they distribute these machines? I discovered it was done on the basis of conflicts within the military forces themselves. The army wanted machine tools for army products, the navy wanted theirs, the air force theirs. Ten percent went to one, five to another, three to a third. It made no sense. It had no connection to what the actual needs were. Someone had to take over, to allocate machine tools on a priority system. So I did. I couldn't have done it without support from some of the top people who really understood. It was a way of thinking different from what they'd been accustomed to. Others, well . . .

They all were patriotic, but in different ways. Many worried about how their regular customers would react. If I said, Send this abrasive to such and such a firm which was not their standard customer and wouldn't be after the war, don't send it to one which had been their customer, they were bothered—and how! Many fights took place.

In the early days, some of these industrialists wouldn't sign major military contracts until they had the right kind. The right kind? When the war ends, who's stuck with the supplies? What payment do we get when you terminate? Who's gonna pay when we move it out? They wanted to make sure of every cent of profit.

The concessions in these contracts was the biggest thing of all. The war had to be won. Dr. New Deal—with all of FDR's talk about economic royalists—goodbye. Dr. Win The War, hello. The government gives in. The military, of course, is much more sympathetic to business. They feel more comfortable with them. They're the same kind of boys. (Laughs.)

The railroad industry didn't like what I was doing. They brought in their own people with Dun & Bradstreet reports. Everything, they said, was fine. My report remained downstairs. One day, Bernard Baruch shows up. He starts to yell at the top guys of the War Production Board: "You guys aren't doing anything. You're not prepared. There's not enough steel, not enough copper, not enough aluminum." So they rushed down and got me to come up with my report. To show him they were thinking about it. (Laughs.) That's the only time they ever paid any attention to my reports.

One of my early reports showed that there won't be enough railroad cars to move the wheat, the iron ore, the coal because an awful lot of cars were in disuse, needed repairs. We must build more cars. Otherwise, when push comes to shove, there'll be no way to move things around unless we have government controls. Well, do you know that my report, an internal report, was used by the Association of American Railroads in full-page ads in the *Washington Post,* all over? Scare headlines: Socialism proposed by the government.

Pearl Harbor comes along. We're at war. A system of controls of raw material is set up. According to priorities. At that point, guys from the Association of American Railroads come to see me. They want to wine and dine me. They say, "You understand our problem. Will you help us get our allocation of steel? Otherwise, we can't repair the cars." I did help them. But do you know they were so stupid, they never really did it right, as far as I'm concerned. There's resistance in industry to the idea of planning. Comes the big crisis, they'll learn.

We were a group of young people, idealistic, who came in with the New Deal. We were not career-minded. When it came to the New Deal, we carried out its basic principles. When it came to the war, it was to win it. That meant getting production out. It was as simple as that. Though we worked with big industrialists, we were not subservient to them. We understood their problems, but we had the nerve to fight 'em on policy matters. . . .

The most single important legacy of the war is what Eisenhower warned us about in his farewell speech: the military-industrial complex. In the past, there were business representatives in Washington, but now they are Washington. And with the military buildup beyond all our imagination, we have a new fusion of power. It has become a permanent feature of American life.

Source: "Recollections of Joe Marcus, Head of the Civilian Requirements Division, National Defense Advisory Committee," in Studs Terkel, ed., *The Good War: An Oral History of World War Two* (New York: Pantheon Books, 1984), 325–329. Reprinted by permission of Donadio and Olsen. Copyright 1984 by Studs Terkel.

1941 Documents

79. "The Four Freedoms": President Franklin D. Roosevelt, State of the Union Address Delivered to Congress, 6 January 1941

In his annual State of the Union address to Congress in January 1941, President Franklin D. Roosevelt highlighted the international situation. He pledged that the United States would assist those countries that were "resisting aggression" and that it would defend the Western hemisphere against all incursions. To do so, he argued, the United States must immediately mount a huge rearmament program. He also committed the country to the defense at home and abroad of the "four freedoms": freedom of speech, freedom of religion, freedom from want, and freedom from fear.

I address you, the Members of the Seventy-seventh Congress, at a moment unprecedented in the history of the Union. I use the word "unprecedented," because at no previous time has American security been as seriously threatened from without as it is today.

Our national policy is this:

First, by an impressive expression of the public will and without regard to partisanship, we are committed to all-inclusive national defense.

Second, by an impressive expression of the public will and without regard to partisanship, we are committed to full support of all those resolute peoples, everywhere, who are resisting aggression and are thereby keeping war away from our hemisphere. By this support, we express our determination that the democratic cause shall prevail; and we strengthen the defense and security of our own Nation.

Third, by an impressive expression of the public will and without regard to partisanship, we are committed to the proposition that principles of morality and considerations for our own security will never permit us to acquiesce in a peace dictated by aggressors and sponsored by appeasers.

We know that enduring peace cannot be bought at the cost of other people's freedom.

In the recent national election there was no substantial difference between the two great parties in respect to that national policy. No issue was fought out on this line before the American electorate. Today, it is abundantly evident that American citizens everywhere are demanding and supporting speedy and complete action in recognition of obvious danger.

Therefore, the immediate need is a swift and driving increase in our armament production. . . .

I also ask this Congress for authority and for funds sufficient to manufacture additional munitions and war supplies of many kinds, to be turned over to those nations which are now in actual war with aggressor nations.

Our most useful and immediate role is to act as an arsenal for them as well as for ourselves. They do not need manpower. They do need billions of dollars worth of the weapons of defense.

The time is near when they will not be able to pay for them in ready cash. We cannot, and will not, tell them they must surrender, merely because of present inability to pay for the weapons which we know they must have. . . .

For what we send abroad, we shall be repaid, within a reasonable time following the close of hostilities, in similar materials, or, at our option, in other goods of many kinds which they can produce and which we need.

Let us say to the democracies: "We Americans are vitally concerned in your defense of freedom. We are putting forth our energies, our resources, and our organizing powers to give you the strength to regain and maintain a free world. We shall send you, in ever-increasing numbers, ships, planes, tanks, guns. This is our purpose and our pledge."

In fulfillment of this purpose we will not be intimidated by the threats of dictators that they will regard as a breach of international law and as an act of war our aid to the democracies which dare to resist their aggression. Such aid is not an act of war, even if a dictator should unilaterally proclaim it so to be. . . .

In the future days, which we seek to make secure, we look forward to a world founded upon four essential human freedoms.

The first is freedom of speech and expression—everywhere in the world.

The second is freedom of every person to worship God in his own way—everywhere in the world.

The third is freedom from want—which, translated into world terms, means economic understandings which will secure to every nation a healthy peacetime life for its inhabitants—everywhere in the world.

The fourth is freedom from fear—which, translated into world terms, means a world-wide reduction of armaments to such a point and in such a thorough fashion that no nation will be in a position to commit an act of physical aggression against any neighbor—anywhere in the world.

That is no vision of a distant millennium. It is a definite basis for a kind of world attainable in our own time and generation. That kind of world is the very antithesis of the so-called new order of tyranny which the dictators seek to create with the crash of a bomb.

To that new order we oppose the greater conception—the moral order. A good society is able to face schemes of world domination and foreign revolutions alike without fear.

Since the beginning of our American history we have been engaged in change—in a perpetual peaceful revolution—a revolution which goes on steadily, quietly adjusting itself to changing conditions without the concentration camp or the quick-lime in the ditch. The world order which we seek is the cooperation of free countries, working together in a friendly, civilized society.

This Nation has placed its destiny in the hands and heads and hearts of its millions of free men and women; and its faith in freedom under the guidance of God. Freedom means the supremacy of human rights everywhere. Our support goes to those who struggle to gain those rights or keep them. Our strength is in our unity of purpose.

To that high concept there can be no end save victory.

FRANKLIN D. ROOSEVELT

Source: U.S. Department of State, Publication 1983, *Peace and War: United States Foreign Policy, 1931–1941* (Washington, DC: U.S. Government Printing Office, 1943), 608–610.

80. Admiral Yamamoto Isoroku to Japanese Navy Minister Oikawa Koshiro, 7 January 1941

From the beginning of 1941 Admiral Yamamoto Isoroku, commander of the Japanese Combined Pacific Fleet, formulated and began to advocate plans for an unannounced attack on American naval forces at Pearl Harbor. He drew on Japan's past historical experience in successfully launching such an attack against the Russian Pacific Fleet in 1904, the opening of the Russo-Japanese War. The eventual attack on Pearl Harbor closely followed Yamamoto's plans and was directed by him.

(CORDIALLY REQUEST THAT YOUR MINISTER ALONE READ THIS.)

(IT IS ALSO REQUESTED THAT THIS LETTER BE BURNED AFTER READING.)

OPINIONS ON WAR PREPARATIONS

Although a precise outlook on the international situation is hard for anyone to make, it is needless to say that now the time has come for the Navy, especially the Combined Fleet, to devote itself seriously to war preparations, training and operational plans with a firm determination that a conflict with the U.S. and Great Britain is inevitable.

Therefore, I dare say here generally what I have in mind, to which your kind consideration is cordially invited. (This generally corresponds to what I verbally said to you roughly late in last November.)

1. *War Preparations:* Views on war preparations of the

Combined Fleet have already been conveyed to the central authorities in Tokyo, and I believe the central authorities have been exerting the utmost efforts for their completion.

As the aforementioned request covers general major points alone, however, I think more detailed requests will be made when a real war is sure to come. Preparations are required to be made by all means will be marked as such, to which your special consideration is cordially invited. Especially, in view of the fact that satisfaction can never be attained in air strength, whether aircraft or personnel, your special encouragement is kindly requested to promote their production whenever opportunities arise.

2. *Training:* Most of the training that has so far been planned and carried out deal with normal and with normal and fundamental circumstances, under which each unit is assigned a mission with the "*yogei sakusen*" [decisive engagement] as its main aim. Needless to say, the utmost efforts should be made to master it, as by so doing sufficient capabilities will be made so as to meet requirements needed in varied scenes of an engagement and a battle.

Considering a case in which this country goes to war with the U.S. and Great Britain as a practical problem, however, I think there may be no such case happening throughout the whole period of an expected war as all of the Combined Fleet closing in an enemy force, deploy, engage in a gunnery and torpedo duel, and finally charge into the enemy force in as gallant a way as possible. On the other hand, there may be cases in which various problems that have been somehow neglected in peace-time training in spite of their importance actually happen. In view of the current situation, therefore, I think earnest studies should be made of those problems.

Even when aforementioned normal and fundamental training is carried out, instead of being engrossed in overall tactical movements lacking precise consideration, unremitting studies should be made as to whether his fleet, squadron, division and ship display its fighting power to the utmost degree in every phase of maneuvers. (It will be an effective way for that end to let deviate shell firing and actual torpedo firing be included in every maneuver, and designate units at random during the maneuver to practice this training.)

If either of the British and Italian Fleets, which encountered in the Mediterranean sea last year, had been fully trained from peace time to rouse up in the fighting spirit of "attacking enemy whenever it is sighted" and accustomed to a sudden firing, there ought not to have been a case in which none was sunk on either side in spite of the fact that the duel took place for 25 minutes. It should be regarded as a blunder that could not be allowed in our Navy.

3. *Operational Policy:* Studies on operational policy, too, have so far been based on one big "*yogei sakusen*" to be fought in a formal way. Review of numerous maneuvers held in the past, however, shows that the Japanese Navy has never won an overwhelming victory even once; they used to be suspended under such a situation that, if by letting things take their own course, there was much fear that our Navy might be dragged into gradual defeat.

It might be of some use only when collecting reference materials for determining whether we should go to war or not, but it should not be repeated by all means if and when a decision is made to go to war.

The most important thing we have to do first of all in a war with the U.S., I firmly believe, is to fiercely attack and destroy the U.S. main fleet at the outset of the war, so that the morale of the U.S. Navy and her people goes down to such an extent that it cannot be recovered.

Only then shall we be able to secure an invincible stand in key positions in East Asia, thus being able to establish and keep the East Asia Co-Prosperity Sphere.

Well, then, what policy should we take to accomplish this?

4. *Operational Plan That Should Be Adopted at the Outset of War:*

We learned many lessons in the Russo-Japanese War. Among them, those concerning the outset of war are as follows:

a. Japan had a chance to launch a surprise attack upon the enemy main force at the outset of war.
b. The morale of our destroyer force at the outset of war was not necessarily high (there being exceptions) and their skill was insufficient. This was most regrettable, about which serious reflection should be made.
c. Both the planning and execution of the blockade operation were insufficient.

In view of these successes and failures in the Russo-Japanese War, we should do our very best at the outset of a war with the U.S., and we should have a firm determination of deciding the fate of the war on its first day.

The outline of the operational plan is as follows:

a. In case of the majority of the enemy main force being in Pearl Harbor, to attack it thoroughly with our air force and to blockade the harbor.
b. In case they are staying outside of the harbor, too, to apply the same attack method as the above.

The strength to be used in the aforementioned operation and their assignments:

a. 1st and 2nd Carrier Divisions (2nd Carrier Division alone in an unavoidable case) to launch a forced or surprise attack with all of their air strength, risking themselves on a moonlit night or at dawn.

b. One destroyer squadron to rescue survivors of carriers sunken by an enemy counterattack.

c. One submarine squadron to attack the enemy fleeing in confusion after closing in on Pearl Harbor (or other anchorages), and, if possible, to attack them at the entrance of Pearl Harbor so that the entrance may be blocked by sunken ships.

d. Supply force to assign several tankers with the force for refueling at sea.

In case the enemy comes out from Hawaii before our attack and keeps on coming at us, to encounter it with all of our decisive force and destroy it in one stroke.

It is not easy to succeed in either case, but I believe we could be favored by God's blessing when all officers and men who take part in this operation have a firm determination of devoting themselves to their task, even sacrificing themselves.

The above is an operation with the U.S. main force as a main target, and an operation of launching a forestalling and surprise attack on the enemy air forces in the Philippines and Singapore should definitely be made almost at the same time of launching attacks on Hawaii. However, if and when the U.S. main force is destroyed, I think, those untrained forces deploying in those southern districts will lose morale to such an extent that they could hardly be of much use in actual bitter fighting.

On the other hand, when we take a defensive stand toward the east and await the enemy coming on out of fear that such an operation against Hawaii is too risky, we cannot rule out the possibility that the enemy would dare to launch an attack upon our homeland to burn our capital city and other cities.

If such happens, our Navy will be subject to fierce attacks by the public, even when we succeed in the southern operation. It is evidently clear that such a development will result in lowering the morale of the nation to such an extent that it cannot be recovered. (It is not a laughing matter at all to recall how much confusion our nation was thrown into when the Russian fleet appeared in the Pacific in the Russo-Japanese War.)

I sincerely desire to be appointed C-in-C of an air fleet to attack Pearl Harbor so that I may personally command that attack force.

I firmly believe that there is a more suitable man to command the normal operations of the Grand Combined Fleet after that operation, as I previously stated my view verbally to your Minister.

Sincerely hoping that you will pass a clear judgment on my request to shift me to that post, so that I may be able to devote myself exclusively to my last duty to our country. . . .

Source: Donald M. Goldstein and Katherine V. Dillon, *The Pearl Harbor Papers: Inside the Japanese Plans* (Washington, DC: Brassey's, 1993), 115–118. Reprinted with permission of Brassey's.

81. Japanese Foreign Minister Matsuoka Yōsuke, Cable Number 44 to the Washington Embassy (Koshi), 30 January 1941

In 1940, U.S. naval intelligence deciphered the Japanese secret Foreign Office codes. Although German intelligence informed the Japanese foreign minister in May 1941 that they believed such code-breaking was taking place, American officials retained the ability to decipher much of Japan's official cable traffic. Among the messages decoded was one from the Foreign Ministry in Tokyo to the embassy in Washington, instructing Japanese diplomats in the United States to determine American military capabilities and to launch a campaign of propaganda and subversion in collaboration with Italy and Germany.

(Foreign Office secret)

(1) Establish an intelligence organ in the Embassy which will maintain liaison with private and semi-official intelligence organs. (See my messages to Washington #591 and #732 from New York to Tokyo, both of last year's series.) With regard to this, we are holding discussions with the various circles involved at the present time.

(2) The focal point of our investigations shall be the determination of the total strength of the U.S. Our investigations shall be divided into three general classi-

fications: political, economic, and military, and definite course of action shall be mapped out.

(3) Make a survey of all persons or organizations which either openly or secretly oppose participation in the war.

(4) Make investigations of all anti-Semitism, communism, movements of Negroes, and labor movements.

(5) Utilization of U.S. citizens of foreign extraction (other than Japanese), aliens (other than Japanese), communists, Negroes, labor union members, and anti-Semites, in carrying out the investigations described in the preceding paragraph would undoubtedly bear the best results.

These men, moreover, should have access to governmental establishments, (laboratories?), governmental organizations of various characters, factories, and transportation facilities.

(6) Utilization of our "Second Generations" and our resident nationals. (In view of the fact that if there is any slip in this phase, our people in the U.S. will be subjected to considerable persecution, the utmost caution must be exercised.)

(7) In the event of U.S. participation in the war, our intelligence set-up will be moved to Mexico, making that country the nerve center of our intelligence net. Therefore, will you bear this in mind and in anticipation of such an eventuality, set up facilities for a U.S.-Mexico international intelligence net. This net which will cover Brazil, Argentina, Chile, and Peru will also be centered in Mexico.

(8) We shall cooperate with the German and Italian intelligence organs in the U.S. This phase has been discussed with the Germans and the Italians in Tokyo, and it has been approved....

Source: Web site: National Counterintelligence Center: Counter Intelligence in World War II. Available at http://www.fas.org/irp/ops/ci/docs/ci2/2ch2_a.htm.

82. Reverend Arle Brooks, Statement upon His Conviction for Draft Evasion, January 1941

The United States Selective Service Act of 1940 contained provisions for exemption for conscientious objection on religious grounds. Members of some American denominations, however, considered even registering for the draft unacceptable. One of these was the Reverend Arle Brooks of the Disciples of Christ Church, who was convicted of draft evasion in January 1941. Although Brooks could have used his status as a minister to avoid military service, he preferred to make a public issue of his pacifist beliefs. Before his sentencing, he made the following public statement justifying his stance.

My conscience forbade me to register under the Selective Service Training Act of 1940.

The present wars are the natural product of our economic system and our way of living. Preparation for war is easier than going through the painful process of reconstructing our social and economic system and improving our own lives.

Wars destroy human lives. Individuals have the right to give their lives for a cause. They have no right to take the life of another. Wars are destructive, futile and immoral. Wars have failed to solve the basic problems of the world. Participation in war to settle international or national differences does not do justice to man's intelligence.

The people of America are filled with fear of an invasion. Are we so morally weak that the power of one man could control 130,000,000 free people? Free people cannot be enslaved unless they allow it. Are we too lethargic to find a better method of settling international affairs? The people of India have almost won their freedom from Great Britain without firing a shot. They are willing to give their lives but refuse to take the lives of the British soldiers.

Democracy does not mean a blind following of the will of the majority. In a democracy the minority has a right and a duty to follow its ideals. Sometimes the ideals of the minority have eventually been adopted by the majority. Gandhi said, "We are sunk so low that we fancy that it is our duty and our religion to do what the law lays down. If man will only realize that it is unmanly to obey laws that are unjust no man's tyranny will enslave him.... It is a superstition and an ungodly thing to believe that an act of a majority binds a minority." I believe in and have worked for the brotherhood of man, which is the highest form of democracy and which recognizes no national boundaries. I have worked with children of the slums of Chicago, with transients, relief people, prisoners in Texas, and with sharecroppers in Mississippi.

Conscription is a denial of the democracy for which I have worked. Under conscription the individual is required blindly to obey his superior officer even when the superior officer is wrong. Hitler could not wage his war if the people of Germany had not granted him the power to conscript them. The United States is adopting a system of conscription which may produce tyranny instead of freedom.

I cannnot agree with those who believe that registration is a mere census. Registration is the first and necessary step in conscription. My conscience will not permit me to take this first step.

As a minister I could have received complete exemption.

I felt it my moral duty to do all within my power to protest against conscription which will eventually weaken and destroy democracy. I am not evading the draft. I am opposing it. I am defending democracy.

Source: *Christian Century* 58 (5 February 1941), 181. Reprinted in John O'Sullivan and Alan M. Meckler, eds., *The Draft and Its Enemies: A Documentary History* (Urbana: University of Illinois Press, 1974), 174–176.

83. Henry R. Luce, "The American Century," February 1941

In February 1941, as the United States moved steadily closer to war with Germany, the leading American magazine publisher Henry R. Luce, the son of a Chinese missionary, wrote an influential essay, "The American Century," envisaging an enormous postwar expansion of his country's international role. Luce's article later came to seem an almost emblematic statement prophesying the rise of the United States to world power from the mid-twentieth century onward.

There is one fundamental issue which faces America as it faces no other nation. It is an issue peculiar to America and peculiar to America in the 20th Century—now. It is deeper even than the immediate issue of War. If America meets it correctly, then, despite hosts of dangers and difficulties, we can look forward and move forward to a future worthy of men, with peace in our hearts.

If we dodge the issue, we shall flounder for ten or 20 or 30 bitter years in a chartless and meaningless series of disasters. . . .

Where are we? We are in the war. All this talk about whether this or that might or might not get us into the war is wasted effort. We are, for a fact, in the war. . . .

Now that we are in this war, how did we get in? We got in on the basis of defense. Even that very word, defense, has been full of deceit and self-deceit.

To the average American the plain meaning of the word defense is defense of the American territory. Is our national policy today limited to the defense of the American homeland by whatever means may seem wise? It is not. We are now in a war to promote, encourage and incite so-called democratic principles throughout the world. The average American begins to realize now that's the kind of war he's in. And he's halfway for it. But he wonders how he ever got there, since a year ago he had not the slightest intention of getting into any such thing. Well, he can see now how he got there. He got there via "defense."

Behind the doubts in the American mind there were and are two different picture-patterns. One of them stressing the appalling consequences of the fall of England leads us to a war of intervention. As a plain matter of the defense of

American territory is that picture necessarily true? It is not necessarily true. For the other picture is roughly this: while it would be much better for us if Hitler were severely checked, nevertheless regardless of what happens in Europe it would be entirely possible for us to organize a defense of the northern part of the Western Hemisphere so that this country could not be successfully attacked. . . . No man can say that that picture of America as an impregnable armed camp is false. No man can honestly say that as a pure matter of defense—defense of our homeland—it is necessary to get into or be in this war.

The question before us then is not primarily one of necessity and survival. It is a question of choice and calculation. The true questions are: Do we want to be in this war? Do we prefer to be in it? And, if so, for what? . . .

This questioning reflects our truest instincts as Americans. But more than that. Our urgent desire to give this war its proper name has a desperate practical importance. If we know what we are fighting for, then we can drive confidently toward a victorious conclusion and, what's more, have at least an even chance of establishing a workable Peace.

Furthermore—and this is an extraordinary and profoundly historical fact which deserves to be examined in detail—America and only America can effectively state the war aims of this war. . . .

The big, important point to be made here is simply that the complete opportunity of leadership is ours. . . . [I]f our trouble is that we don't know what we are fighting for, then it's up to us to figure it out. Don't expect some other country to tell us. Stop this Nazi propaganda about fighting somebody else's war. We fight no wars except our wars.

"Arsenal of Democracy?" We may prove to be that. But today we must be the arsenal of America and of the friends and allies of America. . . .

In the field of national policy, the fundamental trouble with America has been, and is, that whereas their nation became in the 20th Century the most powerful and the most vital nation in the world, nevertheless Americans were unable to accommodate themselves spiritually and practically to their fate. Hence they have failed to play their part as a world power—a failure which has had disastrous consequences for themselves and for all mankind. And the cure is this: to accept wholeheartedly our duty and our opportunity as the most powerful and vital nation in the world, and in consequence exert upon the world the full impact of our influence, for such purposes as we see fit and by such means as we see fit. . . .

Consider the 20th Century. It is ours not only in the sense that we happen to live in it but ours also because it is America's first century as a dominant power in the world. So far, this century of ours has been a profound and tragic disappointment. No other century has been so big with promise for human progress and happiness. And in no one century have so many men and women and children suffered such pain and anguish and bitter death. . . .

What can we say about an American Century? It is meaningless merely to say that we reject isolationism and accept the logic of internationalism. What internationalism? Rome had a great internationalism. So had the Vatican and Genghis Khan and the Ottoman Turks and the Chinese Emperors and 19th Century England. After the first World War, Lenin had one in mind. Today Hitler seems to have one in mind—one which appeals strongly to some American isolationists whose opinion of Europe is so low that they would gladly hand it over to anyone who would guarantee to destroy it for ever. But what internationalism have we Americans to offer?

Ours cannot come out of the vision of any one man. It must be the product of the imaginations of many men. It must be a sharing with all peoples of our Bill of Rights, our Declaration of Independence, our Constitution, our magnificent industrial products, our technical skills. It must be an internationalism of the people, by the people and for the people. . . .

Once we cease to distract ourselves with lifeless arguments about isolationism, we shall discover that there is already an immense American internationalism. American jazz, Hollywood movies, American slang, American machines and patented products, are in fact the only things that every community in the world, from Zanzibar to Hamburg, recognizes in common. Blindly, unintentionally, accidentally and really in spite of ourselves, we are already a world power in all the trivial ways—in very human ways. But

there is a great deal more than that. America is already the intellectual, scientific and artistic capital of the world. Americans—Midwestern Americans—are today the least provincial people in the world. They have traveled the most and they know more about the world than the people of any other country. America's worldwide experience in commerce is also far greater than most of us realize.

Most important of all, we have that indefinable, unmistakable sign of leadership: prestige. And unlike the prestige of Rome or Genghis Khan or 19th Century England, American prestige throughout the world is faith in the good intentions as well as in the ultimate intelligence and ultimate strength of the whole American people. We have lost some of that prestige in the last few years. But most of it is still there. . . .

No narrow definition can be given to the American internationalism of the 20th Century. It will take shape, as all civilizations take shape, by the living of it, by work and effort, by trial and error, by enterprise and adventure and experience.

And by imagination!

As America enters dynamically upon the world scene, we need most of all to seek and to bring forth a vision of America as a world power which is authentically American and which can inspire us to live and work and fight with vigor and enthusiasm. And as we come now to the great test, it may yet turn out that in all of our trials and tribulations of spirit during the first part of this century we as a people have been painfully apprehending the meaning of our time and now in this moment of testing there may come clear at last the vision which will guide us to the authentic creation of the 20th Century—our Century. . . .

Consider four areas of life and thought in which we may seek to realize such a vision:

First, the economic. It is for America and for America alone to determine whether a system of free economic enterprise—an economic order compatible with freedom and progress—shall or shall not prevail in this century. We know perfectly well that there is not the slightest chance of anything faintly resembling a free economic system prevailing in this country if it prevails nowhere else. What then does America have to decide? Some few decisions are quite simple. For example: we have to decide whether or not we shall have for ourselves and our friends freedom of the seas—the right to go with our ships and our ocean-going airplanes where we wish, when we wish and as we wish. The vision of Americas [sic] as the principal guarantor of the freedom of the seas, the vision of America as the dynamic leader of world trade, has within it the possibilities of such enormous human progress as to stagger the imagination. Let us not be staggered by it. Let us rise to its tremendous possibilities. Our thinking of world trade today is on ridiculously small terms. For example, we think of Asia as being worth only a few hundred million a year to us. Actually, in the decades to come Asia will be worth to us exactly zero—or else it will be worth to us four, five, ten billions of dollars a year. And the latter are the terms we must think in, or else confess a pitiful impotence.

Closely akin to the purely economic area and yet quite different from it, there is the picture of an America which will send out through the world its technical and artistic skills. Engineers, scientists, doctors, movie men, makers of entertainment, developers of airlines, builders of roads, teachers, educators. Throughout the world, these skills, this training, this leadership is needed and will be eagerly welcomed, if only we have the imagination to see it and the sincerity and good will to create the world of the 20th Century.

But now there is a third thing which our vision must immediately be concerned with. We must undertake now to be the Good Samaritan of the entire world. It is the manifest duty of this country to undertake to feed all the people of the world who as a result of this worldwide collapse of civilization are hungry and destitute—all of them, that is, whom we can from time to time reach consistently with a very tough attitude toward all hostile governments. For every dollar we spend on armaments, we should spend at least a dime in a gigantic effort to feed the world—and all the world should know that we have dedicated ourselves to this task. Every farmer in America should be encouraged to produce all the crops he can, and all that we cannot eat—and perhaps some of us could eat less—should forthwith be dispatched to the four quarters of the globe as a free gift, administered by a humanitarian army of Americans, to every man, woman and child on this earth, who is really hungry. . . .

But all this is not enough. All this will fail and none of it will happen unless our vision of America as a world power includes a passionate devotion to great American ideals. We have some things in this country which are infinitely precious and especially American—a love of freedom, a feeling for the equality of opportunity, a tradition of self-reliance and independence and also of co-operation. In addition to ideals and notions which are especially American, we are the inheritors of all the great principles of Western civilization—above all Justice, the love of Truth, the ideal of Charity. The other day Herbert Hoover said that America was fast becoming the sanctuary of the ideals of civilization. For the moment it may be enough to be the sanctuary of these ideals. But not for long. It now becomes our time to be the powerhouse from which the ideals spread throughout the world and do their mysterious work of lifting the life of mankind from the level of the beasts to what the Psalmist called a little lower than the angels.

America as the dynamic center of ever-widening spheres of enterprise, America as the training center of the skillful servants of mankind, America as the Good Samaritan, really believing again that it is more blessed to give than to receive, and America as the powerhouse of the ideals of Freedom and Justice—out of these elements surely can be fashioned a vision of the 20th Century to which we can and will devote ourselves in joy and gladness and vigor and enthusiasm. . . .

It is in this spirit that all of us are called, each to his own measure of capacity, and each in the widest horizon of his vision, to create the first great American Century.

Source: Henry R. Luce, "The American Century," *Life,* February 1941. Reprinted in Michael J. Hogan, ed., *The Ambiguous Legacy: U.S. Foreign Relations in the "American Century"* (Cambridge: Cambridge University Press, 1999), 11–29. Reprinted with permission of Time, Inc.

84. German Führer Adolf Hitler, Order on Collaboration with Japan, Issued by General Wilhelm Keitel, Chief of the Armed Forces High Command, 5 March 1941

Germany sought to persuade Japan to move aggressively against British and American interests in East and Southeast Asia. From the German perspective, such policies would divert Anglo-American attention from the war with Germany. In anticipation of a forthcoming visit by Japanese Foreign Minister Matsuoka Yōsuke, Hitler ordered his military to collaborate closely with their Japanese counterparts in developing a joint strategy.

The Führer has issued the following order regarding collaboration with Japan:

1. It must be the aim of the collaboration based on the Three-Power Pact to induce Japan as soon as possible to take active measures in the Far East. Strong British forces will thereby be tied down, and the center of gravity of the interests of the United States of America will be diverted to the Pacific.

The sooner it intervenes, the greater will be the prospects of success for Japan in view of the still undeveloped preparedness for war on the part of its adversaries. The "Barbarossa" operation will create particularly favorable political and military prerequisites for this.

2. To prepare the way for collaboration it is essential to strengthen the Japanese military potential with all means available.

For this purpose the High Commands of the branches of the Armed Forces will comply in a comprehensive and generous manner with Japanese desires for assistance in military economics and in technical matters. Reciprocity is desirable but this factor should not stand in the way of negotiations. Priority should naturally be given to those Japanese proposals which would have the most immediate application in waging war.

In special cases the Führer reserves the decision to himself.

3. The harmonizing of the operational plans of the two parties is the responsibility of the Navy High Command.

This will be subject to the following guiding principles:

a. The common aim of the conduct of war is to be stressed as forcing England to the ground quickly and thereby keeping the United States out of the war. Beyond this Germany has no political, military, or economic interests in the Far East which would give occasion for any reservations with regard to Japanese intentions.

b. The great successes achieved by Germany in mercantile warfare make it appear particularly suitable to employ strong Japanese forces for the same purpose. In this connection every opportunity to support German mercantile warfare must be exploited.

c. The raw material situation of the pact powers demands that Japan should acquire possession of those territories which it needs for the continuation of the war, especially if the United States intervenes. Rubber shipments must be carried out even after the entry of Japan into the war, since they are of vital importance to Germany.

d. The seizure of Singapore as the key British position in the Far East would mean a decisive success for the entire conduct of war of the Three Powers.

In addition, attacks on other systems of bases of British naval power—extending to those of American naval power only if the entry of the United States into the war cannot be prevented—will result in weakening the enemy's system of power in that region and also, just like the attack on sea communications, in tying down substantial forces of all kinds (Australia).

A date for the beginning of operational discussions cannot yet be fixed.

4. In the military commissions to be formed in accordance with the Three-Power Pact, only such questions are to be dealt with as equally concern the three participating powers. These will include primarily the problems of economic warfare.

The working out of the details is the responsibility of the "Main Commission" with the cooperation of the Armed Forces High Command.

5. The Japanese must not be given any intimation of the Barbarossa operation.

Source: Margaret Carlyle, ed., *Documents on International Affairs 1939–1946,* Volume II: *Hitler's Europe* (London: Oxford University Press, 1954), 82–83. Reprinted with permission of Chatham House.

85. The Lend-Lease Act, 11 March 1941

In March 1941, the U.S. Congress passed the Lend-Lease Act. This act became the basis under which, throughout the war, the United States supplied its numerous allies with massive quantities of military supplies designed to assist them in their efforts to wage war upon Germany, Italy, and Japan.

AN ACT Further to promote the defense of the United States, and for other purposes.

Be it enacted by the Senate and House of Representatives of the United States of America in Congress assembled, That this Act may be cited as "An Act to Promote the Defense of the United States." . . . SEC. 3. (a) Notwithstanding the provisions of any other law, the President may, from time to time, when he deems it in the interest of national defense, authorize the Secretary of War, the Secretary of the Navy, or the head of any other department or agency of the Government—

(1) To manufacture in arsenals, factories, and shipyards under their jurisdiction, or otherwise procure, to the extent to which funds are made available therefor, or contracts are authorized from time to time by the

Congress, or both, any defense article for the government of any country whose defense the President deems vital to the defense of the United States.

(2) To sell, transfer title to, exchange, lease, lend, or otherwise dispose of, to any such government any defense article, but no defense article not manufactured or procured under paragraph (1) shall in any way be disposed of under this paragraph, except after consultation with the Chief of Staff of the Army or the Chief of Naval Operations of the Navy, or both. The value of defense articles disposed of in any way under authority of this paragraph, and procured from funds heretofore appropriated, shall not exceed $1,300,000,000. The value of such defense articles shall be determined by the head of the department or agency concerned or such other department, agency, or officer as shall be designated in the manner provided in the rules and regulations issued hereunder. Defense articles procured from funds hereafter appropriated to any department or agency of the Government, other than from funds authorized to be appropriated under this Act, shall not be disposed of in any way under authority of this paragraph except to the extent hereafter authorized by the Congress in the Acts appropriating such funds or otherwise.

(3) To test, inspect, prove, repair, outfit, recondition, or otherwise to place in good working order, to the extent to which funds are made available therefor, or contracts are authorized from time to time by the Congress, or both, any defense article for any such government, or to procure any or all such services by private contract.

(4) To communicate to any such government any defense information pertaining to any defense article furnished to such government under paragraph (2) of this subsection.

(5) To release for export any defense article disposed of in any way under this subsection to any such government.

(b) The terms and conditions upon which any such foreign government receives any aid authorized under subsection (a) shall be those which the President deems satisfactory, and the benefit to the United States may be payment or repayment in kind or property, or any other direct or indirect benefit which the President deems satisfactory.

(c) After June 30, 1943, or after the passage of a concurrent resolution by the two Houses before June 30, 1943, which declares that the powers conferred by or pursuant to subsection (a) are no longer necessary to promote the defense of the United States, neither the President nor the head of any department or agency shall exercise any of the powers conferred by or pursuant to subsection (a) except that until July 1, 1946, any of such powers may be exercised to the extent necessary to carry out a contract or agreement with such a foreign government made before July 1,1943, or before the passage of such concurrent resolution, whichever is the earlier.

(d) Nothing in this Act shall be construed to authorize or to permit the authorization of convoying vessels by naval vessels of the United States.

(e) Nothing in this Act shall be construed to authorize or to permit the authorization of the entry of any American vessel into a combat area in violation of section 3 of the Neutrality Act of 1939. . . .

SEC. 8. The Secretaries of War and of the Navy are hereby authorized to purchase or otherwise acquire arms, ammunition, and implements of war produced within the jurisdiction of any country to which section 3 is applicable, whenever the President deems such purchase or acquisition to be necessary in the interests of the defense of the United States. . . .

Source: Public Laws. Part 1, *United States Statutes at Large Containing the Laws and Concurrent Resolutions Enacted During the First Session of the Seventy-Seventh Congress of the United States of America, 1941–1942, and Treaties, International Agreements Other than Treaties, and Proclamations.* Vol. 55 (Washington, DC: U.S. Government Printing Office, 1942), 31–33.

86. "Draft Understanding," Paper Presented to the Department of State through the Medium of Private American and Japanese Individuals, 9 April 1941

By 1941, the United States and Japan were seriously at odds over Japanese policy in Asia, especially toward China. Private Americans, notably two Catholic missionary fathers, working in collaboration with the Japanese ambassador to the United States and various Japanese military figures, developed a draft of what they hoped might become an understanding between Japan and the United States. Although many of its proposals were unacceptable to the United States, to start the ball rolling on talks, Secretary of State Cordell Hull agreed to discuss it. This proposal marked the beginning of eight months of intensive but ultimately fruitless negotiations over the possibility of reconciling the differences dividing Japan and the United States.

The Governments of the United States and of Japan accept joint responsibility for the initiation and conclusion of a general agreement disposing the resumption of our traditional friendly relations.

Without reference to specific causes of recent estrangement, it is the sincere desire of both Governments that the incidents which led to the deterioration of amicable sentiment among our peoples should be prevented from recurrence and corrected in their unforeseen and unfortunate consequences.

It is our present hope that, by a joint effort, our nations may establish a just peace in the Pacific; and by the rapid consummation of an *entente cordiale,* arrest, if not dispel, the tragic confusion that now threatens to engulf civilization.

For such decisive action, protracted negotiations would seem ill-suited and weakening. We, therefore, suggest that adequate instrumentalities should be developed for the realization of a general agreement which would bind, meanwhile, both Governments in honor and in act.

It is our belief that such an understanding should comprise only the pivotal issues of urgency and not the accessory concerns which could be deliberated at a Conference and appropriately confirmed by our respective Governments.

We presume to anticipate that our Governments could achieve harmonious relations if certain situations and attitudes were clarified or improved: to wit:

1. The concepts of the United States and of Japan respecting international relations and the character of nations.
2. The attitudes of both governments toward the European War.
3. The relations of both nations toward the China Affair.
4. Naval, aerial, and mercantile marine relations in the Pacific.
5. Commerce between both nations and their financial cooperation.
6. Economic activity of both nations in the Southwestern Pacific area.
7. The policies of both nations affecting political stabilization in the Pacific.

Accordingly, we have come to the following mutual understanding, subject, of course, to modifications by the United States Government and subject to the official and final decision of the Government of Japan.

I.

The Concepts of the United States and of Japan Respecting International Relations and the Character of Nations

The Governments of the United States and of Japan might jointly acknowledge each other as equally sovereign states and contiguous Pacific powers.

Both Governments assert the unanimity of their national policies as directed toward the foundation of a lasting peace and the inauguration of a new era of respectful confidence and cooperation among our peoples.

Both Governments might declare that it is their traditional, and present, concept and conviction that nations and races compose, as members of a family, one household; each equally enjoying rights and admitting responsibilities with a mutuality of interests regulated by peaceful processes and directed to the pursuit of their moral and physical welfare, which they are bound to defend for themselves as they are bound not to destroy for others.

Both Governments are firmly determined that their respective traditional concepts on the character of nations and the underlying moral principles of social order and national life will continue to be preserved and never transformed by foreign ideas or ideologies contrary to those moral principles and concepts.

II.

The Attitudes of Both Governments Toward the European War

The Government of Japan maintains that the purpose of its Axis Alliance was, and is, defensive and designed to prevent the extension of military grouping among nations not directly affected by the European War.

The Government of Japan, with no intention of evading its existing treaty obligation, desires to declare that its military obligations under the Axis Alliance come into force only when one of the parties of the Alliance is aggressively attacked by a power not at present involved in the European War.

The Government of the United States maintains that its attitude toward the European War is, and will continue to be, determined by no aggressive alliance aimed to assist any one nation against another. The United States maintains that it is pledged to the hate of war, and accordingly its attitude toward the European War is, and will continue to be, determined solely and exclusively by considerations of the protective defense of its own national welfare and security.

III.

China Affairs

The President of the United States, if the following terms are approved by His Excellency and guaranteed by the Government of Japan, might request the Chiang Kai-shek regime to negotiate peace with Japan:

a. Independence of China.
b. Withdrawal of Japanese troops from Chinese territory, in accordance with an agreement to be reached between Japan and China.
c. No acquisition of Chinese territory.
d. No imposition of indemnities.
e. Resumption of the "Open Door"; the interpretation and application of which shall be agreed upon at some future, convenient time between the United States and Japan.
f. Coalescence of the Governments of Chiang Kai-shek and of Wang Ching-wei.
g. No large-scale or concentrated immigration of Japanese into Chinese territory.
h. Recognition of Manchukuo.

With the acceptance of the Chiang Kai-shek regime of the aforementioned Presidential request, the Japanese Government shall commence direct peace negotiations with the newly coalesced Chinese Government, or constituent elements thereof.

The Government of Japan shall submit to the Chinese concrete terms of peace, within the limits of aforesaid general terms and along the line of neighborly friendship, joint defense against communistic activities, and economic cooperation.

Should the Chiang Kai-shek regime reject the request of President Roosevelt, the United States Government shall discontinue assistance to the Chinese.

IV.

Naval, Aerial, and Mercantile Marine Relations in the Pacific

a. As both the Americans and the Japanese are desirous of maintaining the peace in the Pacific, they shall not resort to such disposition of their naval forces and aerial forces as to menace each other. Detailed, concrete agreement thereof shall be left for determination at the proposed joint Conference.
b. At the conclusion of the projected Conference, each nation might dispatch a courtesy naval squadron to visit the country of the other and signalize the new era of Peace in the Pacific.
c. With the first ray of hope for the settlement of China affairs, the Japanese Government will agree, if desired, to use its good offices to release for contract by Americans a certain percentage of their total tonnage of merchant vessels, chiefly for the Pacific service, so soon as they can be released from their present commitments. The amount of such tonnage shall be determined at the Conference.

V.

Commerce Between Both Nations, and Their Financial Cooperation

When official approbation to the present understanding has been given by both Governments, the United States and Japan shall assure each other to mutually supply such commodities as are respectively available or required by either of them. Both Governments further consent to take necessary steps to the resumption of normal trade relations as formerly established under the Treaty of Navigation and Commerce between the United States and Japan. If a new commercial treaty is desired by both Governments, it could be elaborated at the proposed Conference and concluded in accordance with usual procedures.

For the advancement of economic cooperation between both nations, it is suggested that the United States extend to Japan a gold credit in amounts sufficient to foster trade and industrial development directed to the betterment of Far Eastern economic conditions and to the sustained economic cooperation of the Governments of the United States and of Japan.

VI.

Economic Activity of Both Nations in the Southwestern Pacific Area

On the pledged basis of guarantee that Japanese activities in the Southwestern Pacific shall be carried on by peaceful means, without resorting to arms, American cooperation and support shall be given in the production and procurement of natural resources (such as oil, rubber, tin, nickel) which Japan needs.

VII.

The Policies of Both Nations Affecting Political Stabilization in the Pacific

a. The Government of the United States and of Japan will not acquiesce in the future transfer of territories or the relegation of existing States within the Far East and in the Southwestern Pacific to any European Power.

b. The Government of the United States and of Japan jointly guarantee the independence of the Philippine Islands and will consider means to come to their assistance in the event of unprovoked aggression by any third power.

c. The Government of Japan requests the friendly and diplomatic assistance of the Government of the United States for the removal of Hong Kong and Singapore as doorways to further political encroachment by the British in the Far East.

d. Japanese immigration to the United States and to the Southwestern Pacific shall receive amicable consideration—on a basis of equality with other nationals and freedom from discrimination.

CONFERENCE

a. It is suggested that a Conference between delegates of the United States and of Japan be held at Honolulu and that this Conference be opened for the United States by President Roosevelt and for Japan by Prince Konoye. The delegates could number less than five each, exclusive of experts, clerks, etc.

b. There shall be no foreign observers at the Conference.

c. This Conference could be held as soon as possible (May 1941) after the present understanding has been reached.

d. The present agenda of the Conference would not include a reconsideration of the present understanding but would direct its efforts to the specification of the prearranged agenda and drafting of instruments to effectuate the understanding. The precise agenda could be determined upon by mutual agreement between the two Governments.

AGENDA

The present understanding shall be kept as a confidential memorandum between the Governments of the United States and of Japan.

The scope, character, and timing of the announcement of this understanding will be agreed upon by both Governments.

Source: U.S. Department of State, *Papers Relating to the Foreign Relations of the United States: Japan, 1931–1941,* 2 vols. (Washington, DC: U.S. Government Printing Office, 1943), 2: 398–402.

87. Text of the U.S.-Danish Agreement on Greenland, 9 April 1941

In April 1941, the United States announced that it would construct air and naval bases on Greenland, a huge island far out in the Atlantic, which was under Danish sovereignty. Germany had occupied Denmark in spring 1940, so the United States reached this agreement with the government in exile. The Roosevelt administration feared that, unless it took this measure and effectively assumed responsibility for Greenland's defense, the territory might easily fall under German control.

Whereas:

ONE. After the invasion and occupation of Denmark on April 9, 1940 by foreign military forces, the United Greenland Councils at their meeting at Godhavn on May 3, 1940 adopted in the name of the people of Greenland a resolution reiterating their oath of allegiance to King Christian X of Denmark and expressing the hope that, for as long as Greenland remains cut off from the mother country, the Government of the United States of America will continue to hold in mind the exposed position of the Danish flag in Greenland, of the native Greenland and Danish population, and of established public order; and

TWO. The Governments of all of the American Republics have agreed that the status of regions in the Western Hemisphere belonging to European powers is a subject of deep concern to the American Nations, and that the course of military events in Europe and the changes resulting from them may create the grave danger that European territorial possessions in America may be converted into strategic centers of aggression against nations of the American Continent; and

THREE. Defense of Greenland against attack by a non-American power is essential to the preservation of the peace and security of the American Continent and is a subject of vital concern to the United States of America and also to the Kingdom of Denmark; and

FOUR. Although the sovereignty of Denmark over Greenland is fully recognized, the present circumstances for the time being prevent the Government in Denmark from exercising its powers in respect of Greenland.

Therefore,

The undersigned, to wit: CORDELL HULL, Secretary of State of the United States of America, acting on behalf of the Government of the United States of America, and HENRIK DE KAUFFMANN, Envoy Extraordinary and Minister Plenipotentiary of His Majesty the King of Denmark at Washington, acting on behalf of His Majesty the King of Denmark in His capacity as sovereign of Greenland, whose authorities in Greenland have concurred herein, have agreed as follows:

ARTICLE I

The Government of the United States of America reiterates its recognition of and respect for the sovereignty of the Kingdom of Denmark over Greenland. Recognizing that as a result of the present European war there is danger that Greenland may be converted into a point of aggression against nations of the American Continent, the Government of the United States of America, having in mind its obligations under the Act of Habana signed on July 30, 1940, accepts the responsibility of assisting Greenland in the maintenance of its present status.

ARTICLE II

It is agreed that the Government of the United States of America shall have the right to construct, maintain and operate such landing fields, seaplane facilities and radio and meteorological installations as may be necessary for the accomplishment of the purposes set forth in Article I.

ARTICLE III

The grants of the rights specified in Article II shall also include the right to improve and deepen harbors and anchorages and the approaches thereto, to install aids to navigation by air and by water, and to construct roads, communication services, fortifications, repair and storage facilities, and housing for personnel, and generally, the right to do any and all things necessary to insure the efficient operation, maintenance and protection of such defense facilities as may be established.

ARTICLE IV

The landing fields, seaplane, harbor and other defense facilities that may be constructed and operated by the Government of the United States of America under Articles II and III will be made available to the airplanes and vessels of all the American Nations for purposes connected with the common defense of the Western Hemisphere.

ARTICLE V

It is agreed that the Government of the United States of America shall have the right to lease for such period of time as this Agreement may be in force such areas of land and water as may be necessary for the construction, operation and protection of the defense facilities specified in Articles II and III. In locating the aforesaid defense areas, the fullest consideration consistent with military necessity shall be given to the welfare, health and economic needs of the native population of Greenland. It is agreed, however, that since the paramount objective sought is the early attainment of an adequate defense establishment in Greenland, the utilization of any area deemed by the Government of the United States of America to be needed for this purpose shall not be delayed pending the reaching of an agreement upon the precise terms of a formal lease. A description of such areas, by metes and bounds, and a statement of the purpose for which they are needed shall in each case be communicated to the Danish authorities in Greenland as soon as practicable, and the negotiation of a formal lease shall be undertaken within a reasonable period of time thereafter.

ARTICLE VI

The Kingdom of Denmark retains sovereignty over the defense areas mentioned in the preceding articles. So long as this Agreement shall remain in force, the Government of the United States of America shall have exclusive jurisdiction over any such defense area in Greenland and over military and civilian personnel of the United States and their families, as well as over all other persons within such areas except Danish citizens and native Greenlanders, it being understood, however, that the Government of the United States may turn over to the Danish authorities in Greenland for trial and punishment any person committing an offense within a defense area, if the Government of the United States shall decide not to exercise jurisdiction in such case. The Danish authorities in Greenland will take adequate measures to insure the prosecution and punishment in case of conviction of all Danish citizens, native Greenlanders, and other persons who may be turned over to them by the authorities of the United States, for offenses committed within the said defense areas.

ARTICLE VII

It is agreed that the Government of the United States of America shall have the right to establish and maintain postal facilities and commissary stores to be used solely by military and civilian personnel of the United States, and their families, maintained in Greenland in connection with the Greenland defense establishment. If requested by the Danish authorities in Greenland, arrangements will be made to enable persons other than those mentioned to purchase necessary supplies at such commissary stores as may be established.

ARTICLE VIII

All materials, supplies and equipment for the construction, use and operation of the defense establishment and for the personal needs of military and civilian personnel of the United States, and their families, shall be permitted entry into Greenland free of customs duties, excise taxes, or other charges, and the said personnel and their families, shall also be exempt from all forms of taxation, assessments or other levies by the Danish authorities in Greenland.

ARTICLE IX

The Government of the United States of America will respect all legitimate interests in Greenland as well as all the laws, regulations and customs pertaining to the native population and the internal administration of Greenland. In exercising the rights derived from this Agreement the Government of the United States will give sympathetic consideration to all representations made by the Danish authorities in Greenland with respect to the welfare of the inhabitants of Greenland.

ARTICLE X

This Agreement shall remain in force until it is agreed that the present dangers to the peace and security of the American Continent have passed. At that time the modification or termination of the Agreement will be the subject of consultation between the Government of the United States of America and the Government of Denmark. After due consultation has taken place, each party shall have the right to give the other party notice of its intention to terminate the Agreement, and it is hereby agreed, that at the expiration of twelve months after such notice shall have been received by either party from the other this Agreement shall cease to be in force.

Source: U.S. Department of State, Publication 1983, *Peace and War: United States Foreign Policy, 1931–1941* (Washington, DC: U.S. Government Printing Office, 1943), 641–647.

88. Pact of Neutrality between the Union of Soviet Socialist Republics and Japan and Declaration Regarding Mongolia, 13 April 1941

In April 1941, the Soviet Union and Japan, the past relations of which had often been difficult, signed a formal agreement that they would remain neutral toward each other. Russia also agreed to respect Japan's interests in Manchuria, in exchange for reciprocal pledges from Japan on Mongolia. Later that year, Germany invaded the Soviet Union and Japan declared war on both the United States and Britain. Even so, these agreements remained in effect until the summer of 1945, shortly before Japan's surrender.

The Presidium of the Supreme Soviet of the Union of Soviet Socialist Republics and His Majesty the Emperor of Japan, guided by a desire to strengthen peaceful and friendly relations between the two countries, have decided to conclude a pact on neutrality, for which purpose they have appointed as their Representatives: [names omitted]

Who, after an exchange of their credentials, which were found in due and proper form, have agreed on the following:

ARTICLE ONE

Both Contracting Parties undertake to maintain peaceful and friendly relations between them and mutually respect the territorial integrity and inviolability of the other Contracting Party.

ARTICLE TWO

Should one of the Contracting Parties become the object of

hostilities on the part of one or several third powers, the other Contracting Party will observe neutrality throughout the duration of the conflict.

ARTICLE THREE
The present Pact comes into force from the day of its ratification by both Contracting Parties and remains valid for five years. In case neither of the Contracting Parties denounces the Pact one year before the expiration of the term, it will be considered automatically prolonged for the next five years.

ARTICLE FOUR
The present Pact is subject to ratification as soon as possible. The instruments of ratification shall be exchanged in Tokyo, also as soon as possible. . . .

Declaration Regarding Mongolia, 13 April 1941
In conformity with the spirit of the Pact on neutrality concluded on April 13, 1941, between the U.S.S.R. and Japan, the Government of the U.S.S.R. and the Government of Japan, in the interest of insuring peaceful and friendly relations between the two countries, solemnly declare that the U.S.S.R. pledges to respect the territorial integrity and inviolability of Manchukuo and Japan pledges to respect the territorial integrity and inviolability of the Mongolian People's Republic.

Source: Web site: The Avalon Project at the Yale Law School. Available at http://www.yale.edu/lawweb/avalon/wwii/s1.htm.

89. Opposition to American Intervention in World War II: Charles A. Lindbergh, Radio Address, 23 April 1941

While President Franklin D. Roosevelt and his chief advisers were strongly interventionist in World War II, taking measures that effectively made American entry into the conflict more likely, opposition to the war also existed. The private group America First was established in 1940 to organize those forces who believed that the best way the United States could meet the ever-more-serious international crisis was by building up American defenses while holding itself aloof from Europe. Its most celebrated member was the aviator Charles Lindbergh, the first person to make a solo flight across the Atlantic, whose personal inspections of German military forces during the later 1930s had convinced him that Germany had gained irreversible airpower superiority over Britain and France.

There are many viewpoints from which the issues of this war can be argued. Some are primarily idealistic. Some are primarily practical. One should, I believe, strive for a balance of both. But, since the subjects that can be covered in a single address are limited, tonight I shall discuss the war from a viewpoint which is primarily practical. It is not that I believe ideals are unimportant, even among the realities of war; but if a nation is to survive in a hostile world, its ideals must be backed by the hard logic of military practicability. If the outcome of war depended upon ideals alone, this would be a different world than it is today.

I know I will be severely criticized by the interventionists in America when I say we should not enter a war unless we have a reasonable chance of winning. That, they claim, is far too materialistic a viewpoint. They will advance again the same arguments that were used to persuade France to declare war against Germany in 1939. But I do not believe that our American ideals, and our way of life, will gain through an unsuccessful war. And I know that the United States is not prepared to wage war in Europe successfully at this time. We are no better prepared today than France was when the interventionists in Europe persuaded her to attack the Siegfried line.

I have said it before, and I will say it again, that I believe it will be a tragedy to the entire world if the British Empire collapses. That is one of the main reasons why I opposed this war before it was declared and why I have constantly advocated a negotiated peace. I did not feel that England and France had a reasonable chance of winning. France has now been defeated; and, despite the propaganda and confusion of recent months, it is now obvious that England is losing the war. I believe this is realized even by the British Government. But they have one last desperate plan remaining. They hope that they may be able to persuade us to send another American Expeditionary Force to Europe, and to share with England militarily, as well as financially, the fiasco of this war.

I do not blame England for this hope, or for asking for our assistance. But we now know that she declared a war under circumstances which led to the defeat of every nation that sided with her from Poland to Greece. We know that in the desperation of war England promised to all those nations armed assistance that she could not send. We know that she misinformed them, as she has misinformed us, concerning her state of preparation, her military strength, and the progress of the war.

In time of war, truth is always replaced by propaganda. I do not believe that we should be too quick to criticize the actions of a belligerent nation. There is always the question whether we, ourselves, would do better under similar circumstances. But we in this country have a right to think of the welfare of America first, just as the people in England thought first of their own country when they encouraged the smaller nations of Europe to fight against hopeless odds. When England asks us to enter this war, she is considering her own future and that of her Empire. In making our reply, I believe we should consider the future of the United States and that of the Western Hemisphere.

It is not only our right, but it is our obligation as American citizens, to look at this war objectively and to weigh our chances for success if we should enter it. I have attempted to do this, especially from the standpoint of aviation; and I have been forced to the conclusion that we cannot win this war for England, regardless of how much assistance we extend.

I ask you to look at the map of Europe today and see if you can suggest any way in which we could win this war if we entered it. Suppose we had a large army in America, trained and equipped. Where would we send it to fight? The campaigns of the war show only too clearly how difficult it is to force a landing, or to maintain an army, on a hostile coast.

Suppose we took our Navy from the Pacific and used it to convoy British shipping. That would not win the war for England. It would, at best, permit her to exist under the constant bombing of the German air fleet. Suppose we had an air force that we could send to Europe. Where could it operate? Some of our squadrons might be based in the British Isles, but it is physically impossible to base enough aircraft in the British Isles alone to equal in strength the aircraft that can be based on the continent of Europe.

I have asked these questions on the supposition that we had in existence an Army and an air force large enough and well enough equipped to send to Europe; and that we would dare to remove our Navy from the Pacific. Even on this basis, I do not see how we could invade the continent of Europe successfully as long as all of that continent and most of Asia is under Axis domination. But the fact is that none of these suppositions are correct. We have only a one-ocean Navy. Our Army is still untrained and inadequately equipped for foreign war. Our air force is deplorably lacking in modern fighting planes.

When these facts are cited, the interventionists shout that we are defeatists, that we are undermining the principles of democracy, and that we are giving comfort to Germany by talking about our military weakness. But everything I mention here has been published in our newspapers and in the reports of congressional hearings in Washington. Our military position is well known to the governments of Europe and Asia. Why, then, should it not be brought to the attention of our own people.

I say it is the interventionists in America as it was in England and in France, who give aid and comfort to the enemy. I say it is they who are undermining the principles of democracy when they demand that we take a course to which more than 80 percent of our citizens are opposed. I charge them with being the real defeatists, for their policy has led to the defeat of every country that followed their advice since this war began. There is no better way to give comfort to an enemy than to divide the people of a nation over the issue of foreign war. There is no shorter road to defeat than by entering a war with inadequate preparation. Every nation that has adopted the interventionist policy of depending upon someone else for its own defense has met with nothing but defeat and failure. . . .

There is a policy open to this Nation that will lead to success—a policy that leaves us free to follow our own way of life and to develop our own civilization. It is not a new and untried idea. It was advocated by Washington. It was incorporated in the Monroe Doctrine. Under its guidance the United States became the greatest Nation in the world.

It is based upon the belief that the security of a nation lies in the strength and character of its own people. It recommends the maintenance of armed forces sufficient to defend this hemisphere from attack by any combination of foreign powers. It demands faith in an independent American destiny. This is the policy of the America First Committee today. It is a policy not of isolation, but of independence; not of defeat, but of courage. It is a policy that led this Nation to success during the most trying years of our history, and it is a policy that will lead us to success again. . . .

The United States is better situated from a military standpoint than any other nation in the world. Even in our present condition of unpreparedness no foreign power is in a position to invade us today. If we concentrate on our own defenses and build the strength that this Nation should maintain, no foreign army will ever attempt to land on American shores.

War is not inevitable for this country. Such a claim is defeatism in the true sense. No one can make us fight abroad unless we ourselves are willing to do so. No one will attempt to fight us here if we arm ourselves as a great nation should be armed. Over a hundred million people in this Nation are opposed to entering the war. If the principles of democracy mean anything at all, that is reason enough for us to stay out. If we are forced into a war against the wishes of an overwhelming majority of our people, we will have proved democracy such a failure at home that there will be little use fighting for it abroad.

The time has come when those of us who believe in an independent American destiny must band together and organize for strength. We have been led toward war by a minority of our people. This minority has power. It has influence. It has a loud voice. But it does not represent the American people. During the last several years I have traveled over this country from one end to the other. I have talked to many hundreds of men and women, and have letters from tens of thousands more, who feel the same way as you and I.

Most of these people have no influence or power. Most of them have no means of expressing their convictions, except by their vote which has always been against this war. They are the citizens who have had to work too hard at their daily jobs to organize political meetings. Hitherto, they have re-

lied upon their vote to express their feelings; but now they find that it is hardly remembered except in the oratory of a political campaign. These people, the majority of hardworking American citizens, are with us. They are the true strength of our country. And they are beginning to realize, as you and I, that there are times when we must sacrifice our normal interests in life in order to insure the safety and the welfare of our Nation.

Such a time has come. Such a crisis is here. That is why the America First Committee has been formed—to give voice to the people who have no newspaper, or newsreel, or radio station at their command; to the people who must do the paying, and the fighting, and the dying if this country enters the war.

Source: Charles A. Lindbergh, Radio Address, 23 April 1941. Reprinted in T. H. Breen, ed., *The Power of Words: Documents in American History*, Vol. 2, *From 1865* (New York: HarperCollins, 1996), 172–174. Reprinted with permission of Manuscripts and Archives, Yale University Library.

90. President Franklin D. Roosevelt, Proclamation of Unlimited National Emergency, 27 May 1941

In May 1941, President Franklin D. Roosevelt declared that due to the war in Europe and Asia, a state of national emergency was necessary in the United States. This measure authorized him to take such action as he felt desirable to safeguard American security. It represented another important step bringing the United States closer to outright war.

BY THE PRESIDENT OF THE UNITED STATES OF AMERICA

A Proclamation

(Proclaiming That an Unlimited National Emergency Confronts This Country, Which Requires That Its Military, Naval, Air and Civilian Defenses Be Put on the Basis of Readiness to Repel Any and All Acts or Threats of Aggression Directed Toward any Part of the Western Hemisphere.)

WHEREAS on September 8, 1939 because of the outbreak of war in Europe a proclamation was issued declaring a limited national emergency and directing measures "for the purpose of strengthening our national defense within the limits of peacetime authorizations,"

WHEREAS a succession of events makes plain that the objectives of the Axis belligerents in such war are not confined to those avowed at its commencement, but include overthrow throughout the world of existing democratic order, and a worldwide domination of peoples and economies through the destruction of all resistance on land and sea and in the air, AND

WHEREAS indifference on the part of the United States

to the increasing menace would be perilous, and common prudence requires that for the security of this nation and of this hemisphere we should pass from peacetime authorizations of military strength to such a basis as will enable us to cope instantly and decisively with any attempt at hostile encirclement of this hemisphere, or the establishment of any base for aggression against it, as well as to repel the threat of predatory incursion by foreign agents into our territory and society,

NOW, THEREFORE, I, FRANKLIN D. ROOSEVELT, President of the United States of America, do proclaim that an unlimited national emergency confronts this country, which requires that its military, naval, air and civilian defences be put on the basis of readiness to repel any and all acts or threats of aggression directed toward any part of the Western Hemisphere.

I call upon all the loyal citizens engaged in production for defense to give precedence to the needs of the nation to the end that a system of government that makes private enterprise possible may survive.

I call upon all our loyal workmen as well as employers to

merge their lesser differences in the larger effort to insure the survival of the only kind of government which recognizes the rights of labor or of capital.

I call upon loyal state and local leaders and officials to co-operate with the civilian defense agencies of the United States to assure our internal security against foreign directed subversion and to put every community in order for maximum productive effort and minimum of waste and unnecessary frictions.

I call upon all loyal citizens to place the nation's needs first in mind and in action to the end that we may mobilize and have ready for instant defensive use all of the physical powers, all of the moral strength and all of the material resources of this nation. . . .

Source: Department of State Bulletin, 31 May 1941 (Washington, DC: U.S. Government Printing Office, 1941).

91. Ho Chi Minh, Letter from Abroad, May or June 1941

The European war encouraged nationalist forces within Asian colonies. In mid-May 1941, the Eighth Plenum of the Communist Party of Indochina decided to launch an armed uprising against the Vichy-oriented French colonial administration of Indochina and the Japanese with whom the French were collaborating. The rebellion proved abortive, but before it took place, the party's leader, Ho Chi Minh, still in exile, sent this letter of encouragement.

Elders!

Prominent personalities!

Intellectuals, peasants, workers, traders, and soldiers!

Dear compatriots!

Since the French were defeated by the Germans, their forces have been completely disintegrated. However, with regard to our people, they continue to plunder us pitilessly, suck all our blood, and carry out a barbarous policy of all-out terrorism and massacre. Concerning their foreign policy, they bow their heads and kneel down, shamelessly cutting our land for Siam; without a single word of protest, they heartlessly offer our interests to Japan. As a result, our people suffer under a double yoke: they serve not only as buffaloes and horses to the French invaders but also as slaves to the Japanese plunderers. Alas! What sin have our people committed to be doomed to such a wretched plight!

Living in such painful and lamentable conditions, can our people bind their own hands to doom themselves to death? No! Certainly not! More than 20 million sons and daughters of Lac Hong are resolute to do away with slavery. For nearly eighty years under the French invaders' iron heels we have unceasingly sacrificed ourselves and struggled for national independence and freedom. . . .

Now, the opportunity has come for liberation. France itself is unable to dominate our country. As to the Japanese, on the one hand they are bogged in China, on the other they are hamstrung by the British and American forces and certainly cannot use all their forces to contend with us. If our entire people are united and single-minded, we are certainly able to smash the picked French and Japanese armies.

Compatriots throughout the country! Rise up quickly!

Let us follow the heroic example of the Chinese people! Rise up quickly to organize the Association for National Salvation to fight the French and the Japanese.

Elders!

Prominent personalities!

Some hundreds of years ago, when our country was endangered by the Mongolian dynasty, our elders under the Tran dynasty rose up indignantly and called on their sons and daughters throughout the country to rise as one in order to kill the enemy. Finally they saved their people from danger, and their good name will be carried into posterity for all time. The elders and prominent personalities of our country should follow the example set by our forefathers in the glorious task of national salvation.

Rich people, soldiers, workers, peasants, intellectuals, employees, traders, youth, and women who warmly love your country! At the present time national liberation is the most important problem. Let us unite together! As one in mind and strength we shall overthrow the Japanese and French and their jackals in order to save people from the situation between boiling water and burning heat.

Dear compatriots!

National salvation is the common cause to the whole of our people. Every Vietnamese must take part in it. He who has money will contribute his money, he who has strength will contribute his strength, he who has talent will contribute his talent. I pledge to use all my modest abilities to follow you and am ready for the last sacrifice.

Revolutionary fighters!

The hour has struck! Raise aloft the insurrectionary banner and guide the people throughout the country to overthrow the Japanese and French! The sacred call of the Fatherland is resounding in your ears; the blood of our heroic predecessors who sacrificed ther lives is stirring in your hearts! The fighting spirit of the people is displayed everywhere before you! Let us rise up quickly! Unite with each other, unify your action to overthrow the Japanese and the French.

Victory to Viet-Nam's Revolution!
Victory to the World's Revolution!

Source: Bernard B. Fall, ed., *Ho Chi Minh on Revolution: Selected Writings, 1920–66* (London: Pall Mall Press, 1967), 132–134. Reprinted with permission of the family of Bernard Fall.

92. William J. Donovan, Memorandum for President Franklin D. Roosevelt, "Memorandum of Establishment of Service of Strategic Information," 10 June 1941

In summer 1941, William J. Donovan, a Buffalo lawyer and vehemently pro-Allied former U.S. attorney general who won the Congressional Medal of Honor in World War I, proposed to President Franklin D. Roosevelt the creation of a U.S. foreign intelligence service. He prepared this memorandum after discussions with Secretary of the Navy Frank Knox, Secretary of War Henry L. Stimson, Assistant Secretary of War John J. McCloy, several British intelligence operatives, and various others close to Roosevelt.

Strategy without information upon which it can rely is helpless. Likewise, information is useless unless it is intelligently directed to the strategic purpose. Modern warfare depends upon the economic base—upon the supply of raw materials, on the capacity and performance of the industrial plant, on the scope of agricultural production, and upon the character and efficiency of communications. Strategic reserves will determine the strength of the attack and the resistance of the defense. Steel and gasoline constitute these reserves as much as do men and powder. The width and depth of terrain occupied by the present-day Army exacts an equally wide and deep network of operational lines. The "depth of strategy" depends upon the "depth of armament."

The commitment of all the resources of a nation, moral as well as material, constitutes what is called total war. To anticipate every intention as to the mobilization and employment of these forces is a difficult task. General von Bernhardi says, "We must try by correctly foreseeing what is coming, to anticipate developments and thereby to gain an advantage which our opponents cannot overcome on the field of battle. That is what the future expects us to do."

Although we are facing imminent peril, we are lacking in effective services for analyzing, comprehending, and appraising such information as we might obtain (or in some cases have obtained) relative to the intention of potential enemies and the limit of the economic and military resources of these enemies. Our mechanism of collecting information is inadequate. It is true we have intelligence units in the Army and Navy. We can assume that through these units our fighting services can obtain technical information in time of peace, have available immediate operation information in time of war, and, on certain occasions, obtain "spot" news as to enemy movements. But these services cannot, out of the very nature of things, obtain that accurate, comprehensive, long-range information without which no strategic board can plan for the future. And we have arrived at the moment when there must be plans laid down for the spring of 1942.

We have, scattered throughout the various departments of our Government, documents and memoranda concerning military and naval and air and economic potentials of the Axis which, if gathered together and studied in detail by carefully selected trained minds, with a knowledge both of the related languages and techniques, would yield valuable and often decisive results.

Critical analysis of this information is as presently important for our supply program as if we were actually engaged in armed conflict. It is unimaginable that Germany would engage in a $7 billion supply program without first studying in detail the productive capacity of her actual and potential enemies. It is because she does exactly this that she displays such mastery in the secrecy, timing and effectiveness of her attacks.

Even if we participate to no greater extent than we do now, it is essential that we set up a central enemy intelligence organization which would itself collect, either directly or through existing departments of Government, at home and abroad, pertinent information concerning potential enemies, the character and strength of their armed forces, their internal economic organization, their principal channels of supply, the morale of their troops and their people and their relations with their neighbors or allies.

For example, in the economic field there are many weapons that can be used against the enemy. But in our Government, these weapons are distributed through several different departments. How and when to use them is of vital interest not only to the Commander-in-Chief but to each of the departments concerned. All departments should have the same information upon which economic warfare could be determined.

To analyze and interpret such information by applying to it not only the experience of Army and Naval officers, but also of specialized, trained research officials in the relative scientific fields (including technological, economic, financial and psychological scholars), is of determining influence in modern warfare.

Such analysis and interpretation must be done with immediacy and speedily transmitted to the intelligence services of those departments which, in some cases, would have been supplying the essential raw materials of information.

But there is another element in modern warfare, and that is the psychological attack against the moral and spiritual defenses of a nation. In this attack, the most powerful weapon is radio. The use of radio as a weapon, though effectively employed by Germany, is still to be perfected. But this perfec-

tion can be realized only by planning, and planning is dependent upon accurate information. From this information, action could be carried out by appropriate agencies.

The mechanism of this service to the various departments should be under the direction of a Coordinator of Strategic Information, who would be responsible directly to the President. This Coordinator could be assisted by an advisory panel consisting of the Director of FBI, the Directors of the Army and Navy Intelligence Service, with corresponding officials from other Governmental departments principally concerned.

The attached chart shows the allocation of and the interrelation between the general duties to be discharged under the appropriate directors. Much of the personnel would be drawn from the Army and Navy and other departments of the Government, and it will be seen from the chart that the proposed centralized unit will neither displace nor encroach upon the FBI, Army and Navy Intelligence, or any other department of the Government.

The basic purpose of this Service of Strategic Information is to constitute a means by which the President, as Commander-in-Chief, and his Strategic Board would have available accurate and complete enemy intelligence reports upon which military operational decisions could be based.

Source: File Coordinator of Information 1941, Box 141, Subject Files, President's Secretary's File, Papers of Franklin D. Roosevelt, Franklin D. Roosevelt Presidential Library, Hyde Park, NY.

93. Hitler's Decision to Invade the Soviet Union: Adolf Hitler to Benito Mussolini, 21 June 1941

One of Hitler's greatest mistakes was his decision to invade the Soviet Union in June 1941, a war that would bleed Germany white of men and resources. Writing to his fellow dictator, Benito Mussolini, on 21 June 1941, Hitler explained his decision to invade the Soviet Union in terms that made it clear that he ultimately expected victory there. It seems that he had in all probability always intended to break the Nazi-Soviet Non-Aggression Pact whenever this might seem most convenient to him.

Duce!

I am writing this letter to you at a moment when months of anxious deliberation and continuous nerve-racking waiting are ending in the hardest decision of my life. I believe—after seeing the latest Russian situation map and after appraisal of numerous other reports—that I cannot take the responsibility for waiting longer, and above all, I believe that there is no other way of obviating this danger—unless it be further waiting, which, however, would necessarily lead to disaster in this or the next year at the latest.

The situation: England has lost this war. With the right of the drowning person, she grasps at every straw which, in her

imagination, might serve as a sheet anchor. Nevertheless, some of her hopes are naturally not without a certain logic. England has thus far always conducted her wars with help from the Continent. The destruction of France—in fact, the elimination of all west-European positions—is directing the glances of the British warmongers continually to the place from which they tried to start the war: to Soviet Russia.

Both countries, Soviet Russia and England, are equally interested in a Europe fallen into ruin, rendered prostrate by a long war. Behind these two countries stands the North American Union goading them on and watchfully waiting. Since the liquidation of Poland, there is evident in Soviet

Russia a consistent trend, which, even if cleverly and cautiously, is nevertheless reverting firmly to the old Bolshevist tendency to expansion of the Soviet State. The prolongation of the war necessary for this purpose is to be achieved by tying up German forces in the East, so that—particularly in the air—the German Command can no longer vouch for a large-scale attack in the West. I declared to you only recently, Duce, that it was precisely the success of the experiment in Crete that demonstrated how necessary it is to make use of every single airplane in the much greater project against England. It may well happen that in this decisive battle we would win with a superiority of only a few squadrons. I shall not hesitate a moment to undertake such a responsibility if, aside from all other conditions, I at least possess the one certainty that I will not then suddenly be attacked or even threatened from the East. The concentration of Russian forces—I had General Jodl submit the most recent map to your Attaché here, General Maras—is tremendous. Really, all available Russian forces are at our border. Moreover, since the approach of warm weather, work has been proceeding on numerous defenses. If circumstances should give me cause to employ the German air force against England, there is danger that Russia will then begin its strategy of extortion in the South and North, to which I would have to yield in silence, simply from a feeling of air inferiority. It would, above all, not then be possible for me without adequate support from an air force, to attack the Russian fortifications with the divisions stationed in the East. If I do not wish to expose myself to this danger, then perhaps the whole year of 1941 will go by without any change in the general situation. On the contrary, England will be all the less ready for peace, for it will be able to pin its hopes on the Russian partner. Indeed, this hope must naturally even grow with the progress in preparedness of the Russian armed forces. And behind this is the mass delivery of war material from America which they hope to get in 1942.

Aside from this, Duce, it is not even certain whether I shall have this time, for with so gigantic a concentration of forces on both sides—for I also was compelled to place more and more armored units on the eastern border, also to call Finland's and Rumania's attention to the danger—there is the possibility that the shooting will start spontaneously at any moment. A withdrawal on my part would, however, entail a serious loss of prestige for us. This would be particularly unpleasant in its possible effect on Japan. I have, therefore, after constantly racking my brains, finally reached the decision to cut the noose before it can be drawn tight. I believe, Duce, that I am hereby rendering probably the best possible service to our joint conduct of the war this year. For my overall view is now as follows:

1. France is, as ever, not to be trusted. Absolute surety that North Africa will not suddenly desert does not exist.

2. North Africa itself, insofar as your colonies, Duce, are concerned, is probably out of danger until fall. I assume that the British, in their last attack, wanted to relieve Tobruk. I do not believe they will soon be in a position to repeat this.

3. Spain is irresolute and—I am afraid—will take sides only when the outcome of the war is decided.

4. In Syria, French resistance can hardly be maintained permanently either with or without our help.

5. An attack on Egypt before autumn is out of the question altogether. I consider it necessary, however, taking into account the whole situation, to give thought to the development of an operational unit in Tripoli itself which can, if necessary, also be launched against the West. Of course, Duce, the strictest silence must be maintained with regard to these ideas, for otherwise we cannot expect France to continue to grant permission to use its ports for the transportation of arms and munitions.

6. Whether or not America enters the war is a matter of indifference, inasmuch as she supports our opponent with all the power she is able to mobilize.

7. The situation in England itself is bad; the provision of food and raw materials is growing steadily more difficult. The martial spirit to make war, after all, lives only on hopes. These hopes are based solely on two assumptions: Russia and America. We have no chance of eliminating America. But it does lie in our power to exclude Russia. The elimination of Russia means, at the same time, a tremendous relief for Japan in East Asia, and thereby the possibility of a much stronger threat to American activities through Japanese intervention.

I have decided under these circumstances as I already mentioned, to put an end to the hypocritical performance in the Kremlin. I assume, that is to say, I am convinced, that Finland, and likewise Rumania, will forthwith take part in this conflict, which will ultimately free Europe, for the future also, of a great danger. General Maras informed us that you, Duce, wish also to make available at least one corps. If you have that intention, Duce—which I naturally accept with a heart filled with gratitude—the time for carrying it out will still be sufficiently long, for in this immense theater of war the troops cannot be assembled at all points at the same time anyway. You, Duce, can give the decisive aid, however, by strengthening your forces in North Africa, also, if possible, looking from Tripoli toward the West, by proceeding further to build up a group which, though it be small at first, can march into France in case of a French violation of the treaty; and finally, by carrying the air war and, so far as it is possible, the submarine war, in intensified degree, into the Mediterranean.

So far as the security of the territories in the West is concerned, from Norway to and including France, we are strong enough there—so far as army troops are concerned—to meet any eventuality with lightning speed. So far as air war on England is concerned, we shall for a time remain on the defensive—but this does not mean that we might be incapable of countering British attacks on Germany; on the contrary, we shall, if necessary, be in a position to start ruthless bombing attacks on British home territory. Our fighter defense, too, will be adequate. It consists of the best squadrons that we have.

As far as the war in the East is concerned, Duce, it will surely be difficult, but I do not entertain a second's doubt as to its great success. I hope, above all, that it will then be possible for us to secure a common food-supply base in the Ukraine for some time to come, which will furnish us such additional supplies as we may need in the future. I may state at this point, however, that, as far as we can tell now, this year's German harvest promises to be a very good one. It is conceivable that Russia will try to destroy the Rumanian oil region. We have built up a defense that will—or so I think—prevent the worst. Moreover, it is the duty of our armies to eliminate this threat as rapidly as possible.

I waited until this moment, Duce, to send you this information, because the final decision itself will not be made until 7 o'clock tonight. I earnestly beg you, therefore, to refrain, above all, from making any explanation to your Ambassador at Moscow, for there is no absolute guarantee that our coded reports cannot be decoded. I, too, shall wait until the last moment to have my own Ambassador informed of the decisions reached.

The material that I now contemplate publishing gradually, is so exhaustive that the world will have more occasion to wonder at our forbearance than at our decision, except for that part of the world which opposes us on principle and for which, therefore, arguments are of no use.

Whatever may now come, Duce, our situation can become no worse as a result of this step; it can only improve. Even if I should be obliged at the end of this year to leave 60 or 70 divisions in Russia, that is only a fraction of the forces that I am now continually using on the eastern front. Should England nevertheless not draw any conclusions from the hard facts that present themselves, then we can, with our rear secured, apply ourselves with increased strength to the dispatching of our opponent. I can promise you, Duce, that what lies in our German power, will be done.

Any desires, suggestions, and assistance of which you, Duce, wish to inform me in the contingency before us, I would request that you either communicate to me personally or have them agreed upon directly by our military authorities.

In conclusion, let me say one more thing, Duce. Since struggling through to this decision, I again feel spiritually free. The partnership with the Soviet Union, in spite of the complete sincerity of the efforts to bring about a final conciliation, was nevertheless often very irksome to me, for in some way or other it seemed to me to be a break with my whole origin, my concepts, and my former obligations. I am happy now to be relieved of these mental agonies.

Source: U.S. Department of State, *Nazi-Soviet Relations 1939–1941. Documents from the Archives of the German Foreign Office* (Washington, DC: U.S. Government Printing Office), 349–353.

94. A. Philip Randolph and the March on Washington, January–June 1941

The stated values of the United States, as proclaimed in its war aims, made the Roosevelt administration vulnerable to demands by African Americans for legal equality and the end of segregation and discrimination. In the first half of 1941, A. Philip Randolph, leader of the trade union the Brotherhood of Sleeping Car Porters, a traditionally black occupation, took advantage of the crisis to put pressure on Washington to end racial discrimination by planning a march on Washington by 100,000 African Americans to protest racial segregation. Given professed American support for democracy and equality and opposition to Nazi racialism, such an event would have been a damaging propaganda blow. It also provided the seed for the 1963 March on Washington headed by the black activist the Reverend Martin Luther King Jr., a gathering largely organized by Randolph and at which he himself also spoke. In the shorter term, the threatened 1941 march was called off when the Roosevelt administration issued Executive Order 8802, outlawing discrimination in any industrial plant awarded government defense contracts and establishing an enforcement agency, the Fair Employment Practices Commission. Although these measures often proved ineffective in practice, they marked the beginning of government efforts toward racial equality in the United States.

Philip Randolph, Statement Made on the Proposed March on Washington, 15 January 1941

Negro America must bring its power and pressure to bear upon the agencies and representatives of the Federal Government to exact their rights in National Defense employment and the armed forces of the country. I suggest that ten thousand Negroes march on Washington, D. C. with the slogan: "We loyal Negro American citizens demand the right to work and fight for our country." No propaganda could be whipped up and spread to the effect that Negroes seek to hamper defense. No charge could be made that Negroes are attempting to mar national unity. They want to do none of these things. On the contrary, we seek the right to play our part in advancing the cause of national defense and national unity. But certainly there can be no national unity where one tenth of the population are denied their basic rights as American citizens.

Source: Spartacus Web Site. Available at http://www.spartacus.schoolnet.co.uk/USAmarchW.htm. Reprinted with permission of Spartacus Web Site.

Extract from Transcript of 18 June 1941 White House Meeting between Franklin D. Roosevelt, Philip Randolph, Walter White of the National Association for the Advancement of Colored People, and Fiorello La Guardia, Mayor of New York

Philip Randolph: Mr. President, time is running on. You are quite busy, I know. But what we want to talk with you about is the problem of jobs for Negroes in defense industries. Our people are being turned away at factory gates because they are colored. They can't live with this thing. Now, what are you going to do about it?

Franklin D. Roosevelt: Well, Phil, what do you want me to do?

Philip Randolph: Mr. President, we want you to do something that will enable Negro workers to get work in these plants.

Franklin D. Roosevelt: Why, I surely want them to work, too. I'll call up the heads of the various defense plants and have them see to it that Negroes are given the same opportunity to work in defense plants as any other citizen in the country.

Philip Randolph: We want you to do more than that. We want something concrete, something tangible, definite, positive, and affirmative.

Franklin D. Roosevelt: What do you mean?

Philip Randolph: Mr. President, we want you to issue an executive order making it mandatory that Negroes be permitted to work in these plants.

Franklin D. Roosevelt: Well Phil, you know I can't do that. If I issue an executive order for you, then there'll be no end to other groups coming in here and asking me to issue executive orders for them, too. In any event, I couldn't do anything unless you called off this march of yours. Questions like this can't be settled with a sledge hammer.

Philip Randolph: I'm sorry, Mr. President, the march cannot be called off.

Franklin D. Roosevelt: How many people do you plan to bring?

Philip Randolph: One hundred thousand, Mr. President.

Franklin D. Roosevelt: Walter, how many people will really march?

    Walter White: One hundred thousand, Mr. President.

    Fiorello La Guardia: Gentlemen, it is clear that Mr. Randolph is not going to call off the march, and I suggest we all begin to seek a formula.

    Source: Spartacus Web Site. Available at http://www.spartacus. schoolnet.co.uk/USAmarchW.htm. Reprinted with permission of Spartacus Web Site.

Philip Randolph, Statement on the Cancellation of the March on Washington, 25 June 1941

The march has been called off because its main objective, namely the issuance of an Executive Order banishing discrimination in national defense, was secured. The Executive Order was issued upon the condition that the march be called off.

    Source: Spartacus Web Site. Available at http://www.spartacus. schoolnet.co.uk/USAmarchW.htm. Reprinted with permission of Spartacus Web Site.

95. President Franklin D. Roosevelt, Executive Order 8802, Reaffirming Policy of Full Participation in the Defense Program by All Persons, Regardless of Race, Creed, Color, or National Origin, and Directing Certain Action in Furtherance of Said Policy, 25 June 1941

In June 1941, under pressure from African Americans, Franklin D. Roosevelt issued an executive order that supposedly banned discrimination in connection with all defense program contracts. In practice, the U.S. Congress refused to provide the funding to enforce decisions made under this executive order, and those who sought to evade its provisions often argued that winning the war must take priority over ending discrimination.

WHEREAS it is the policy of the United States to encourage full participation in the national defense program by all citizens of the United States, regardless of race, creed, color, or national origin, in the firm belief that the democratic way of life within the Nation can be defended successfully only with the help and support of all groups within its borders; and

    WHEREAS there is evidence that available and needed workers have been barred from employment in industries engaged in defense production solely because of considerations of race, creed, color, or national origin, to the detriment of workers' morale and of national unity:

    NOW, THEREFORE, by virtue of the authority vested in me by the Constitution and the statutes, and as a prerequisite to the successful conduct of our national defense production effort, I do hereby reaffirm the policy of the United States that there shall be no discrimination in the employment of workers in defense industries or government because of race, creed, color, or national origin, and I do hereby declare that it is the duty of employers and of labor organizations, in furtherance of said policy and of this order, to provide for the full and equitable participation of all workers in defense industries, without discrimination because of race, creed, color, or national origin;

And it is hereby ordered as follows:

1. All departments and agencies of the Government of the United States concerned with vocational and training programs for defense production shall take special measures appropriate to assure that such programs are administered without discrimination because of race, creed, color, or national origin;

2. All contracting agencies of the Government of the United States shall include in all defense contracts hereafter negotiated by them a provision obligating the contractor not to discriminate against any worker because of race, creed, color, or national origin;

3. There is established in the Office of Production Management a Committee on Fair Employment Practice, which shall consist of a chairman and four other members to be appointed by the President. The Chairman and members of the Committee shall serve as such without compensation but shall be entitled to actual and necessary transportation, subsistence and other expenses incidental to performance of their duties. The Committee shall receive and investigate complaints of discrimination in violation

of the provisions of this order and shall take appropriate steps to redress grievances which it finds to be valid. The Committee shall also recommend to the several departments and agencies of the Government of the United States and to the President all measures which may be deemed by it necessary or proper to effectuate the provisions of this order.

Source: Samuel I. Rosenman, ed., *The Public Papers and Addresses of Franklin D. Roosevelt, 1941* (New York: Harper Brothers, 1950), 233–235. Also available at http://www.eeoc.gov/35th/thelaw/eo–8802.html.

96. "Outline of National Policies in View of the Changing Situation": Policy Document Approved by the Imperial Conference, Japanese Government, 2 July 1941

After lengthy and heated discussions among top Japanese military and political leaders, a full-scale Japanese Imperial Conference met on 2 July 1941 to approve a document guiding Japanese policy. Foreign Minister Matsuoka Yōsuke had argued forcefully but unsuccessfully for a "Northern policy" of war against Soviet Russia rather than a "Southern policy" of moving into French Indochina. The army and navy received permission to annex bases in southern French Indochina, even at the risk of war with the United States and Britain; no final decision was made on war against the Soviet Union, though military units in Manchuria were instructed to prepare themselves for potential involvement in such a conflict; and, though admitting the possibility of war with the United States and Britain, the participants hoped to avert such an outcome by means of diplomatic negotiations.

Policy

1. Our Empire is determined to follow a policy that will result in the establishment of the Greater East Asia Co-prosperity Sphere and will thereby contribute to world peace, no matter what change may occur in the world situation.

2. Our Empire will continue its efforts to effect a settlement of the China Incident, and will seek to establish a solid basis for the security and preservation of the nation. This will involve taking steps to advance south, and, depending on changes in the situation, will involve a settlement of the Northern Question as well.

3. Our Empire is determined to remove all obstacles in order to achieve the above-mentioned objectives.

Summary

1. Pressure applied from the southern regions will be increased in order to force the capitulation of the Chiang regime. At the appropriate time, depending on future developments, the rights of a belligerent will be exercised against the Chungking regime, and hostile Foreign Settlements will be taken over.

2. In order to guarantee the security and preservation of the nation, our Empire will continue all necessary diplomatic negotiations with reference to the southern regions, and will also take such other measures as may be necessary.

In order to achieve the following objectives, preparations for war with Great Britain and the United States will be made. First of all, on the basis of "Outline of Policies Toward French Indochina and Thailand" and "Acceleration of Policies Concerning the South," various measures relating to French Indochina and Thailand will be taken, with the purpose of strengthening our advance into the southern regions. In carrying out the plans outlined above, our Empire will not be deterred by the possibility of being involved in a war with Great Britain and the United States.

3. Our attitude with reference to the German-Soviet war will be based on the spirit of the Tripartite Pact. However, we will not enter the conflict for the time being. We will secretly strengthen our military preparedness vis-à-vis the Soviet Union, and we will deal with this matter independently. In the meantime, we will conduct diplomatic negotiations with great care. If the German-Soviet war should develop to the advantage of our Empire, we will, by resorting to armed force, settle the Northern Question and assure the security of the northern borders.

4. In carrying out the various policies mentioned above [in Section 3], and especially in deciding on the use of

armed force, we will make certain that there will be no great obstacles to the maintenance of our basic posture with respect to war with Great Britain and the United States.

5. In accordance with established policy, we will strive to the utmost, by diplomatic and other means, to prevent the entry of the United States into the European war. But if the United States should enter the war, our Empire will act in accordance with the Tripartite Pact. However, we will decide independently as to the time and method of resorting to force.

6. We will immediately turn our attention to putting the nation on a war footing. In particular, the defense of the homeland will be strengthened.

7. Concrete plans covering this program will be drawn up separately.

Source: Nobutaka Ike, ed., *Japan's Decision for War: Records of the 1941 Policy Conferences* (Stanford, CA: Stanford University Press, 1967), 78–79. Reprinted with permission of Stanford University.

97. President Franklin D. Roosevelt, Message to Congress, Relating to the Dispatch of Naval Forces to Iceland, 7 July 1941

The U.S. hemisphere defense zone stretched increasingly farther into the Atlantic. In July 1941, President Franklin D. Roosevelt announced that the United States had dispatched naval forces to Iceland to prevent that country's potential use as a German naval base and, if necessary, to defend Iceland against outside attack. By doing so, the United States also enhanced its own military capabilities.

To the Congress of the United States:

I am transmitting herewith for the information of the Congress a message I received from the Prime Minister of Iceland on July 1, and the reply I addressed on the same day to the Prime Minister of Iceland in response to this message.

In accordance with the understanding so reached, forces of the United States Navy have today arrived in Iceland in order to supplement, and eventually to replace, the British forces which have until now been stationed in Iceland in order to insure the adequate defense of that country.

As I stated in my message to the Congress of September 3 last regarding the acquisition of certain naval and air bases from Great Britain in exchange for certain overage destroyers, considerations of safety from overseas attack are fundamental.

The United States cannot permit the occupation by Germany of strategic outposts in the Atlantic to be used as air or naval bases for eventual attack against the Western Hemisphere. We have no desire to see any change in the present sovereignty of those regions. Assurance that such outposts in our defense frontier remain in friendly hands is the very foundation of our national security and of the national security of every one of the independent nations of the New World.

For the same reason substantial forces of the United States have now been sent to the bases acquired last year from Great Britain in Trinidad and in British Guiana in the south in order to forestall any pincers movement undertaken by Germany against the Western Hemisphere. It is essential that Germany should not be able successfully to employ such tactics through sudden seizure of strategic points in the South Atlantic and in the North Atlantic.

The occupation of Iceland by Germany would constitute a serious threat in three dimensions:

The threat against Greenland and the northern portion of the North American Continent, including the islands which lie off it.

The threat against all shipping in the North Atlantic.

The threat against the steady flow of munitions to Britain—which is a matter of broad policy clearly approved by the Congress.

It is, therefore, imperative that the approaches between the Americas and those strategic outposts, the safety of which this country regards as essential to its national security and which it must therefore defend, shall remain open and free from all hostile activity or threat thereof.

As Commander in Chief I have consequently issued orders to the Navy that all necessary steps be taken to insure the safety of communications in the approaches between Iceland and the United States, as well as on the seas between the United States and all other strategic outposts.

This Government will insure the adequate defense of

Iceland with full recognition of the independence of Iceland as a sovereign state.

In my message to the Prime Minister of Iceland I have given the people of Iceland the assurance that the American forces sent there would in no way interfere with the internal and domestic affairs of that country, and that immediately upon the termination of the present international emergency all American forces will be at once withdrawn, leaving the people of Iceland and their Government in full and sovereign control of their own territory.

Source: Web site: ibiblio. Available at http://www.ibiblio.org/pha/7–2–188/188–27.html.

98. Agreement between the United Kingdom and the Union of Soviet Socialist Republics, 12 July 1941

Three weeks after Germany invaded the Soviet Union, the British and Soviet governments signed an agreement whereby they promised to act as allies in their common war against Germany, and that neither would conclude a separate peace.

His Majesty's Government in the United Kingdom and the Government of the Union of Soviet Socialist Republics have concluded the present Agreement and declare as follows:

(1) The two Governments mutually undertake to render each other assistance and support of all kinds in the present war against Hitlerite Germany.

(2) They further undertake that during this war they will neither negotiate nor conclude an armistice or treaty of peace except by mutual agreement. . . .

Source: Department of State Bulletin, 27 September 1941 (Washington, DC: U.S. Government Printing Office, 1941).

99. Memorandum by the Acting Secretary of State (Welles) on a Meeting between President Franklin D. Roosevelt and the Japanese Ambassador on the Japanese Occupation of Indochina, 24 July 1941

After Japanese forces, with the sanction of the German-dominated Vichy government, occupied bases in southern French Indochina, the United States issued a formal protest against this action, on the grounds that it could not be justified in terms of Japanese national security. That same day, President Franklin D. Roosevelt met with the Japanese ambassador, to protest against Japanese policies toward French Indochina. Roosevelt warned that if these policies were not modified, the United States might cut off all gasoline exports to Japan. Roosevelt asked Japan to consider a solution whereby Indochina might be neutralized during the war.

At the request of the Japanese Ambassador, the President received the Ambassador for an off-the-record conference in the Oval Room at the White House at five o'clock this afternoon. At the President's request, Admiral Stark and I were present.

At the outset of the conference the President made approximately the following statement to the Ambassador. The President said, referring to a talk which he had made this morning to a home defense group under the leadership of Mayor La Guardia, that for more than two years the United States had been permitting oil to be exported from the United States to Japan. He said that this had been done because of the realization on the part of the United States that if these oil supplies had been shut off or restricted the Japanese Government and people would have been furnished with an incentive or a pretext for moving down upon the Netherlands East Indies in order to assure themselves of a greater oil supply than that which, under present conditions, they were able to obtain. The United States had been pursuing this policy primarily for the purpose of doing its utmost to play its full part in making the effort to preserve peace in the Pacific region. At the present time, the President said, the Ambassador undoubtedly knew that there was a very considerable shortage in the oil supply in the eastern part of the United States and the average American man and woman were unable to understand why, at a time when they themselves were asked to curtail their use of gasoline oil, the United States Government should be permitting oil supplies to continue to be exported to Japan when Japan during these past two years had given every indication of pursuing a policy of force and conquest in conjunction with the policy of world conquest and domination which Hitler was carrying on. The average American citizen could not understand why his Government was permitting Japan to be furnished with oil in order that such oil might be utilized by Japan in carrying on her purposes of aggression. The President said that if Japan attempted to seize oil supplies by force in the Netherlands East Indies, the Dutch would, without the shadow of a doubt, resist, the British would immediately come to their assistance, war would then result between Japan, the British and the Dutch, and, in view of our own policy of assisting Great Britain, an exceedingly serious situation would immediately result. It was with all of these facts in mind, the President said, that notwithstanding the bitter criticism that had been leveled against the Administration and against the Department of State, the President up to now had permitted oil to be shipped by Japan from the United States.

The President then went on to say that this new move by Japan in Indochina created an exceedingly serious problem for the United States. He said that, as I had stated to the Ambassador yesterday, insofar as assuring itself that it could obtain foodstuffs and raw materials from Indochina, Japan, of course, had it reached an agreement with the United States along the terms of the discussions between Secretary Hull and the Ambassador, would have been afforded far greater assurances of obtaining such supplies on equal terms with any other nation. More than that, the President said, the cost of any military occupation is tremendous and the occupation itself is not conducive to the production by civilians in occupied countries of food supplies and raw materials of the character required by Japan. Had Japan undertaken to obtain the supplies she required from Indochina in a peaceful way, she not only would have obtained larger quantities of such supplies, but would have obtained them with complete security and without the draining expense of a military occupation. Furthermore, from the military standpoint, the President said, surely the Japanese Government could not have in reality the slightest belief that China, Great Britain, the Netherlands or the United States had any territorial designs on Indochina nor were in the slightest de-

gree providing any real threats of aggression against Japan. This Government, consequently, could only assume that the occupation of Indochina was being undertaken by Japan for the purpose of further offense and this created a situation which necessarily must give the United States the most serious disquiet.

The President said that he had been following in complete detail the conversations which had been progressing between Secretary Hull and the Ambassador and that he was confident that the Ambassador would agree that the policies now undertaken in Indochina by the Japanese Government were completely opposed to the principles and the letter of the proposed agreement which had been under discussion.

At this point the Ambassador took out of his pocket two sheets of notes which he had prepared and asked the President's permission to refer to them in order to make a statement of his Government's position.

In this exposition the Ambassador covered exactly the same ground which he had covered in his conversation with me last night.

The only points of difference were that at the outset of the conversation, the Ambassador very clearly and emphatically stated that the move by Japan into Indochina was something which he personally deplored and with which he personally was not in agreement. . . .

The President then said that he had a proposal to make to the Ambassador which had occurred to him just before the Ambassador had come in and which he had not had time to talk over with me before making his proposal to the Ambassador.

The President said that it might be too late for him to make this proposal but he felt that no matter how late the hour might be, he still wished to seize every possible opportunity of preventing the creation of a situation between Japan and the United States which could only give rise to serious misunderstandings between the two peoples. The President stated that if the Japanese Government would refrain from occupying Indochina with its military and naval forces, or, had such steps actually been commenced, if the Japanese Government would withdraw such forces, the President could assure the Japanese Government that he would do everything within his power to obtain from the Governments of China, Great Britain, the Netherlands, and of course the United States itself a binding and solemn declaration, provided Japan would undertake the same commitment, to regard Indochina as a neutralized country in the same way in which Switzerland had up to now been regarded by the powers as a neutralized country. He stated that this would imply that none of the powers concerned would undertake any military act of aggression against Indochina and would refrain from the exercise of any military control within or over Indochina. He would further endeavor to procure from Great Britain and the other pertinent powers a guarantee that so long as the present emergency continued, the local French authorities in Indochina would remain in control of the territory and would not be confronted with attempts to dislodge them on the part of de Gaullist or Free French agents or forces.

If these steps were taken, the President said, Japan would be given solemn and binding proof that no other power had any hostile designs upon Indochina and that Japan would be afforded the fullest and freest opportunity of assuring herself of the source of food supplies and other raw materials in Indochina which she was seeking to secure.

The Ambassador then reiterated concisely and quite clearly what the President had suggested. He then made some statement which was not quite clear to the effect that such a step would be very difficult at this time on account of the face-saving element involved on the part of Japan and that only a very great statesman would reverse a policy at this time.

The President then mentioned the fact that in the United States the belief was apparent that such policies as those which Japan was now pursuing were due to German pressure upon Japan. To this the Ambassador reacted by saying that Japan was, of course, an independent country and that while such pressure might be exercised, decisions on the policy she was pursuing were solely her own and no one else had any responsibility for them.

The President then said that one thing the Japanese Government did not understand as clearly as this Government was the fact that Hitler was bent upon world domination and not merely the domination of Europe or of Africa. The President said that if Germany succeeded in defeating Russia and dominating Europe and then dominating Africa, there wasn't the slightest question in his mind that Germany thereafter would turn her attention to the Far East and likewise to the Western Hemisphere, and, that while such a development might not take place for many years, perhaps even ten years, the laws of chance made it easily possible that in such contingency, the navies of Japan and of the United States would be cooperating together against Hitler as the common enemy. The President reemphasized his belief that what Hitler had in mind was complete domination of the entire world.

To this the Ambassador replied that he would like to quote an old Chinese proverb in which he had great faith, namely, "He who continuously brandishes the sword eventually kills himself."

The Ambassador said that he would immediately report his conversation to his Government in Tokyo. He seemed to be very much impressed with what the President had said but I did not gather from his reactions that he was in any sense optimistic as to the result.

Source: U.S. Department of State, Publication 1983, *Peace and War: United States Foreign Policy, 1931–1941* (Washington, DC: U.S. Government Printing Office, 1943), 699–702.

100. President Franklin D. Roosevelt's Executive Order Freezing Japanese and Chinese Assets in the United States: White House Statement, 26 July 1941

Two days after meeting with the Japanese ambassador, President Roosevelt issued an executive order freezing Japanese assets in the United States. This decree effectively blocked trade between the U.S. and Japan. The State Department simultaneously imposed a complete embargo on all U.S. exports to Japan, including gasoline, which was essential to Japan's continuation of its war against China. The imposition of these measures marked a substantial hardening in American policy toward Japan, in response to Japan's occupation of Indochinese bases.

In view of the unlimited national emergency declared by the President, he has today issued an Executive Order freezing Japanese assets in the United States in the same manner in which assets of various European countries were frozen on June 14, 1941. This measure, in effect, brings all financial and import and export trade transactions in which Japanese interests are involved under the control of the government, and imposes criminal penalties for violation of the order.

This Executive Order, just as the order of June 14, 1941, is designed among other things to prevent the use of the financial facilities of the United States and trade between Japan and the United States in ways harmful to national defense and American interests, to prevent the liquidation in the United States of assets obtained by duress or conquest and to curb subversive activities in the United States.

At the specific request of Generalissimo Chiang Kai-shek,

and for the purpose of helping the Chinese Government, the President has, at the same time, extended the freezing control to Chinese assets in the United States. The administration of the licensing system with respect to Chinese assets will be conducted with a view to strengthening the foreign trade and exchange position of the Chinese Government.

The inclusion of China in the Executive Order, in accordance with the wishes of the Chinese Government, is a continuation of this government's policy of assisting China.

Source: U.S. Department of State, *Peace and War: United States Foreign Policy, 1931–1941* (Washington, DC: U.S. Government Printing Office, 1943), 704–705.

101. Agreement between Japan and France Pledging Military Cooperation in Defense of Indochina, Tokyo, 29 July 1941

Undeterred by warnings from the United States and Great Britain, at the end of July 1941, Japan and the Vichy government signed an agreement whereby they pledged to cooperate together to defend Indochina. Under German pressure, the Vichy government effectively acquiesced in Japan's takeover of bases in its Asian colony.

The Imperial Japanese Government and the Government of France,

Taking into consideration the present international situation, And recognizing as the result, that there exist reasons for Japan to consider that, in case the security of French Indo-China should be threatened, general tranquillity in East Asia and her own security would be exposed to danger,

And renewing at this opportunity the promise made by Japan, on the one hand, to respect the rights and interests of France in East Asia, especially the territorial integrity of French Indo-China and the French sovereignty over the whole of the Union of French Indo-China; and the promise made by France, on the other hand, not to conclude with any third Power or Powers any agreement or understanding regarding Indo-China envisaging political, economic or military co-operation which is directly or indirectly aimed against Japan.

Have agreed upon the following provisions:

(1) The two Governments mutually promise military co-operation for joint defence of French Indo-China.
(2) Measures to be taken for such co-operation shall be the object of special arrangements.
(3) The above stipulations shall be valid only so long as the situation which has motivated their adoption exists.

Source: Unofficial translation, *Contemporary Japan,* October 1941.

102. Japanese Foreign Minister, Tokyo, Cable to Japanese Embassy, Berlin, 31 July 1941

By the end of July 1941, after a cabinet meeting earlier that month decided on policies likely to result in war, the Japanese government in Tokyo was effectively convinced that war with the United States was probably inevitable. The Japanese foreign minister cabled the Japanese ambassador in Berlin, asking him to bear this decision in mind and to make Japan's sympathies clear to the German government. American code-breakers intercepted and deciphered this cable, a copy of which was also sent to the Japanese ambassador in Washington.

From time to time you have been sending us your various opinions about what we ought to do to help Germany who desires our assistance now that she is at war with Russia. After a conference with the military, at the risk of a certain amount of repetition which may cause you some ennui, I am wiring you the Imperial Government's policy and views. Hereafter, will you please act accordingly.

1. In a cabinet meeting during the forenoon of July 2, the broad outlines of our decision concerning our

future policy were drawn. You were informed of it by Circular #1390[a]. Ever since then the Government has been and is devoting every effort to bring about the materialization of that policy.

2. The China incident has already extended over a period of four years, and the Imperial Government's general trend, particularly its military trend, has hitherto been to expend the greater part of its energies in an endeavor to bring a conclusion to the incident, and now a new situation faces us from the north and from the south. In order to meet it, there is more reason than ever before for us to arm ourselves to the teeth for all-out war.

   It seems that Germany also understands this position of ours fairly well. The German embassy people here in Tokyo are already quite aware of it. And yet I fear that their homeland is not yet as well informed as they are on our position.

3. Commercial and economic relations between Japan and third countries, led by England and the United States, are gradually becoming so horribly strained that we cannot endure it much longer. Consequently, our Empire, to save its very life, must take measures to secure the raw materials of the South Seas. Our Empire must immediately take steps to break asunder this ever-strengthening chain of encirclement which is being woven under the guidance and with the participation of England and the United States, acting like a cunning dragon seemingly asleep. That is why we decided to obtain military bases in French Indo-China and to have our troops occupy that territory.

   That step in itself, I dare say, gave England and the United States, not to mention Russia, quite a setback in the Pacific that ought to help Germany, and now Japanese-American relations are more rapidly than ever treading the evil road. This shows what a blow it has been to the United States.

4. Needless to say, the Russo-German war has given us an excellent opportunity to settle the northern question, and it is a fact that we are proceeding with our preparations to take advantage of this occasion. Not only will we have to prepare, however, but we must choose well our chance. In view of the real situation facing our Empire, this should be easily understood. If the Russo-German war proceeds too swiftly, our Empire would inevitably not have time to take any effective symmetrical action.

5. I know that the Germans are somewhat dissatisfied over our negotiations with the United States, but we wished at any cost to prevent the United States from getting into the war, and we wished to settle the Chinese incident. We were working toward those objectives. Let him who will gainsay the fact that as a result we have indelibly impressed upon the United States the profoundness of the determination of the Empire of Japan and restrained her from plunging into the conflict against Germany.

   It should be understood that we started these talks at a time which seemed opportune to us, and on the assumption that there was complete trust between Japan and Germany. For that matter, did not Germany start a war with Russia because of her own military expediency when it was least desirable on our part? Now we have not only to settle the Chinese incident but have to meet a new challenge in the north as well as in the south, and this is quite inconvenient.

   We are expending our best efforts to cooperate with Germany. She knows it and ought to understand our actions.

6. Well, the formula for cooperation between Tokyo and Berlin, in order to realize the fundamental spirit of the Tripartite Pact, should be for each country to have a certain flexibility in its conduct. What I mean to say is that each should understand that real cooperation does not necessarily mean complete symmetry of action. In other words, we should trust each other and while striving toward one general objective, each use our own discretion within the bounds of good judgment.

Thus, all measures which our Empire shall take will be based upon a determination to bring about the success of the objectives of the Tripartite Pact. That this is a fact is proven by the promulgation of an Imperial rescript. We are ever working toward the realization of those objectives, and now during this dire emergency is certainly no time to engage in any light unpremeditated or over-speedy action.

Source: United States, 79th Congress, 2nd Session, Joint Committee on the Pearl Harbor Attack, *Hearings,* 39 pts. (Washington, DC: U.S. Government Printing Office, 1946) J, Pt. 12: 8–10. Exhibits of Joint Committee, Exhibit No. 1 Intercepted Diplomatic Messages Sent by the Japanese Government between 1 July and 8 December 1941. Available at www.ibiblio.org/pha/timeline/410731a.htm.

103. The Atlantic Charter, 14 August 1941

The Atlantic Charter was signed after President Franklin D. Roosevelt and British Prime Minister Winston Churchill met secretly at sea, at Argentia Harbor, off Placentia Bay on the Newfoundland coast, from 8 to 11 August 1941. It represented the first formal statement of the principles and objectives for which the United States and Great Britain were fighting. Roosevelt and Churchill both signed this statement. One week later, on 21 August 1941, in a message to the United States Congress enclosing the text of this statement, Roosevelt stated that there could be no compromise or negotiated peace with Nazism, and added the interpretive comment that the charter's " declaration of principles includes of necessity the world need for freedom of religion and freedom of information. No society of the world organized under the announced principles could survive without these freedoms which are a part of the whole freedom for which we strive."

The President of the United States of America and the Prime Minister, Mr. Churchill, representing His Majesty's Government in the United Kingdom, being met together, deem it right to make known certain common principles in the national policies of their respective countries on which they base their hopes for a better future for the world.

First, their countries seek no aggrandizement, territorial or other;

Second, they desire to see no territorial changes that do not accord with the freely expressed wishes of the peoples concerned;

Third, they respect the right of all peoples to choose the form of government under which they will live; and they wish to see sovereign rights and self-government restored to those who have been forcibly deprived of them;

Fourth, they will endeavor, with due respect for their existing obligations, to further the enjoyment by all States, great or small, victor or vanquished, of access, on equal terms, to the trade and to the raw materials of the world which are needed for their economic prosperity;

Fifth, they desire to bring about the fullest collaboration between all nations in the economic field with the object of securing, for all, improved labor standards, economic advancement and social security;

Sixth, after the final destruction of the Nazi tyranny, they hope to see established a peace which will afford to all nations the means of dwelling in safety within their own boundaries, and which will afford assurance that all the men in all lands may live out their lives in freedom from fear and want;

Seventh, such a peace should enable all men to traverse the high seas and oceans without hindrance;

Eighth, they believe that all of the nations of the world, for realistic as well as spiritual reasons must come to the abandonment of the use of force. Since no future peace can be maintained if land, sea or air armaments continue to be employed by nations which threaten, or may threaten, aggression outside of their frontiers, they believe, pending the establishment of a wider and permanent system of general security, that the disarmament of such nations is essential. They will likewise aid and encourage all other practicable measures which will lighten for peace-loving peoples the crushing burden of armaments.

Source: U.S. Department of State, A Decade of American Foreign Policy: Basic Documents, 1941–1949 (Washington, DC: U.S. Government Printing Office, 1950), 2.

104. White House Press Release, Statement on Sending a Military Mission to China, 26 August 1941

In August 1941, the U.S. government announced that it would send a military mission to China and that China would receive Lend-Lease assistance in its war against Japan.

This Government is preparing to send a military mission to China. The mission will be sent for the purpose of assisting in carrying out the purposes of the Lend-Lease Act. It is being organized and it will operate under the direction of the Secretary of War. Its chief will be Brigadier General John Magruder.

The function of the mission will be to study, in collaboration with Chinese and other authorities, the military situation in China, the need of the Chinese Government for materiel and materials; to formulate recommendations regarding types and quantities of items needed; to assist in procurement in this country and in delivery in China of such materiel and materials; to instruct in the use and maintenance of articles thus provided; and to give advice and suggestions of appropriate character toward making Lend-Lease assistance to China as effective as possible in the interest of the United States, of China, and of the world effort in resistance to movements of conquest by force.

The sending of this mission is in keeping with and is on parallel lines to the sending of a similar mission to the Soviet Union. The purposes of the two missions are identical.

General Magruder has had long experience in China where he twice served as Military Attaché. He, therefore, will be working on familiar ground, among people he knows well and to whom he is well known. An adequate staff of thoroughly qualified officers will accompany General Magruder.

Source: Samuel I. Rosenman, ed., *The Public Papers and Addresses of Franklin D. Roosevelt, 1941* (New York: Harper and Brothers, 1950), 343–344.

105. "The Essentials for Carrying out the Empire's Policies": Document Adopted by the Japanese Imperial Conference, 6 September 1941

By September 1941, continuing negotiations between Japan and the United States to reach a modus vivendi in the Pacific had proved fruitless. In early September, the Japanese government approved a policy document that effectively set a time limit to negotiations with the United States and Great Britain, after which Japan would embark on war. Before this document was adopted, the visibly unhappy Japanese emperor interrogated his top military men as to the prospects that they were about to involve Japan in a lengthy and unwinnable war. He also insisted on presenting the participants with a lengthy list of questions on the current military and diplomatic situation. Though the advocates of war admitted that this would be risky, and that victory was by no means certain, they apparently never considered making significant concessions to the United States but preferred to argue that the circumstances would never be more favorable for war.

In view of the current critical situation, in particular, the offensive attitudes that such countries as the United States, Great Britain, and the Netherlands are taking towards Japan, and in view of the situation in the Soviet Union and the condition of the Empire's national power, we will carry out our policy toward the South, which is contained in the "Outline of National Policies in View of the Changing Situation," as follows:

I. Our Empire, for the purposes of self-defense and self-preservation, will complete preparations for war, with the last ten days of October as a tentative deadline, resolved to go to war with the United States, Great Britain, and the Netherlands if necessary.

II. Our Empire will concurrently take all possible diplomatic measures vis-à-vis the United States and Great Britain, and thereby endeavor to attain our objectives. The minimum objectives of our Empire to be attained through negotiations with the United States and Great Britain and the maximum concessions therein to be made by our Empire are noted in the attached documents.

III. In the event that there is no prospect of our demands being met by the first ten days of October through the diplomatic negotiations mentioned above, we will immediately decide to commence hostilities against the United States, Britain, and the Netherlands.

Policies other than those toward the South will be based on established national policy; and we will especially try to prevent the United States and the Soviet Union from forming a united front against Japan.

[Attached Document]

The Minimum Demands of Our Empire to Be Attained Through Diplomatic Negotiations with the United States (and Great Britain), and the Maximum Concessions to Be Made by Our Empire

ITEM ONE:
The minimum demands of our Empire to be attained through diplomatic negotiations with the United States and Great Britain.

1. The United States and Great Britain shall neither inter-

fere with nor obstruct the settlement of the China Incident by our Empire.

(a) They shall not obstruct our efforts to settle the Incident on the basis of the Fundamental Treaty between Japan and China, and the Joint Declaration of Japan, Manchukuo, and China.

(b) They shall close the Burma Road and cease to assist the Chiang Kai-shek regime militarily, politically, and economically.

Note: This does not prejudice the position that our Empire has been taking in relation to the settlement of the China Incident in the [Japanese ambassador to the United States] Nomura operation. We should particularly insist on stationing our troops under a new agreement between Japan and China. However, we have no objection to affirming that we are in principle prepared to withdraw our troops following the settlement of the Incident, except for those that are dispatched to carry out the purposes of the Incident. We have no objection to affirming that the economic activities of the United States and Great Britain in China will not be restricted, insofar as they are carried out on an equitable basis.

2. The United States and Great Britain shall refrain from actions that may threaten the defense of our Empire in the Far East.

(a) They shall not secure any military rights in the territories of Thailand, the Netherlands East Indies, China, and the Far Eastern section of the Soviet Union.

(b) They shall not increase their military forces in the Far East beyond the present strength [of those forces].

Note: Any demand to dissolve the special relations between Japan and French Indochina based on the agreement between Japan and France shall not be accepted.

3. The United States and Great Britain shall cooperate in the acquisition of goods needed by our Empire.

(a) They shall restore commercial relations with our Empire and supply those goods from their territories in the Southwest Pacific that our Empire urgently needs to sustain herself.

(b) They shall amicably contribute to the economic cooperation between Japan, Thailand, and the Netherlands East Indies.

ITEM TWO:

The maximum concessions to be made by our Empire:

If the demands indicated in Item One are met,

1. Our Empire will not advance militarily from the bases in French Indochina to the neighboring areas other than China.

Note: If we are asked about our attitude toward the Soviet Union, we will reply that we will not resort to military force unilaterally unless the Soviet Union violates the Japanese-Soviet Neutrality Pact and acts against the spirit of the pact in such a way as to menace Japan and Manchukuo.

2. Our Empire is prepared to withdraw its forces from French Indochina after a just peace has been established in the Far East.

3. Our Empire is prepared to guarantee the neutrality of the Philippine Islands.

APPENDIX:

Japan's attitude toward the European war will be governed by the ideas of protection and self-defense. Japan's interpretation of the Tripartite Pact and her actions therein in the event that the United States should enter the European war will be made by herself acting independently.

Note: The above does not alter our obligations under the Tripartite Pact.

Source: Nobutaka Ike, ed., *Japan's Decision for War: Records of the 1941 Policy Conferences* (Stanford, CA: Stanford University Press, 1967), 135–136. Reprinted with permission of Stanford University.

106. The "Shoot-on-Sight" Policy: President Franklin D. Roosevelt, Radio Address Concerning the German Attack on the Destroyer *Greer*, 11 September 1941

By autumn 1941, American naval vessels were escorting convoys of merchant ships bound for Great Britain and Russia well over halfway across the Atlantic. This practice meant that they were increasingly likely to clash with German submarines and other naval vessels. In September 1941, the U.S. destroyer Greer *was the subject of a German torpedo attack. In indignant terms, President Roosevelt described this incident to Congress, carefully omitting to mention that the* Greer *had in fact been following the submarine and radioing its whereabouts to a British military airplane equipped with antisubmarine torpedoes. Roosevelt also rightly noted that American merchant vessels increasingly were targets for German submarine attacks. Roosevelt used this episode to authorize American naval vessels to shoot on sight should they encounter any German ship. In effect, an undeclared naval war between Germany and the United States was now under way in Atlantic waters. Four weeks later, Roosevelt would also request Congress to permit the arming of merchant vessels carrying goods bound for nations at war.*

My fellow Americans:

The Navy Department of the United States has reported to me that on the morning of September 4 the U. S. Destroyer GREER, proceeding in full daylight toward Iceland, had reached a point southeast of Greenland. She was carrying American mail to Iceland. She was flying the American flag. Her identity as an American ship was unmistakable.

She was then and there attacked by a submarine. Germany admits that it was a German submarine. The submarine deliberately fired a torpedo at the GREER, followed later by another torpedo attack. In spite of what Hitler's propaganda bureau has invented, and in spite of what any American obstructionist organization may prefer to believe, I tell you the blunt fact that the German submarine fired first upon this American destroyer without warning, and with deliberate design to sink her.

Our destroyer, at the time, was in waters which the Government of the United States had declared to be waters of self-defense surrounding outposts of American protection in the Atlantic.

In the north, outposts have been established by us in Iceland, Greenland, Labrador, and Newfoundland. Through these waters there pass many ships of many flags. They bear food and other supplies to civilians and they bear materiel of war, for which the people of the United States are spending billions of dollars, and which, by congressional action, they have declared to be essential for the defense of their own land.

The United States destroyer, when attacked, was proceeding on a legitimate mission.

If the destroyer was visible to the submarine when the torpedo was fired, then the attack was a deliberate attempt by the Nazis to sink a clearly identified American warship. On the other hand, if the submarine was beneath the surface and, with the aid of its listening devices, fired in the direction of the sound of the American destroyer without even taking the trouble to learn its identity—as the official German communiqué would indicate—then the attack was even more outrageous. For it indicates a policy of indiscriminate violence against any vessel sailing the seas, belligerent or non-belligerent.

This was piracy—legally and morally. It was not the first nor the last act of piracy which the Nazi government has committed against the American flag in this war. Attack has followed attack. . . .

It would be unworthy of a great nation to exaggerate an isolated incident, or to become inflamed by some one act of violence. But it would be inexcusable folly to minimize such incidents in the face of evidence which makes it clear that the incident is not isolated, but part of a general plan.

The important truth is that these acts of international lawlessness are a manifestation of a design which has been made clear to the American people for a long time. It is the Nazi design to abolish the freedom of the seas, and to acquire absolute control and domination of the seas for themselves.

For with control of the seas in their own hands, the way can become clear for their next step—domination of the United States and the Western Hemisphere by force. Under Nazi control of the seas, no merchant ship of the United States or of any other American republic would be free to carry on any peaceful commerce, except by the condescending grace of this foreign and tyrannical power. The Atlantic Ocean, which has been and which should always be, a free and friendly highway for us would then become a deadly menace to the commerce of the United States, to the coasts of the United States, and to the inland cities of the United States.

The Hitler government, in defiance of the laws of the sea and of the recognized rights of all other nations, has presumed to declare, on paper, that great areas of the seas—even including a vast expanse lying in the Western Hemisphere—are to be closed, and that no ships may enter them for any purpose, except at peril of being sunk. Actually they are sinking ships at will and without warning in widely separated areas both within and far outside of these far-flung pretended zones.

This Nazi attempt to seize control of the oceans is but a counterpart of the Nazi plots now being carried on throughout the Western Hemisphere, all designed toward the same end. For Hitler's advance guards—not only his avowed agents but also his dupes among us—have sought to make ready for him footholds and bridgeheads in the New World, to be used as soon as he has gained control of the oceans.

His intrigues, his plots, his machinations, his sabotage in this New World are all known to the Government of the United States. Conspiracy has followed conspiracy. . . .

To be ultimately successful in world mastery Hitler knows that he must get control of the seas. He must first destroy the bridge of ships which we are building across the Atlantic, over which we shall continue to roll the implements of war to help destroy him and all his works in the end. He must wipe out our patrol on sea and in the air. He must silence the British Navy.

It must be explained again and again to people who like to think of the United States Navy as an invincible protection that this can be true only if the British Navy survives. That is simple arithmetic.

For if the world outside the Americas falls under Axis domination, the shipbuilding facilities which the Axis Powers would then possess in all of Europe, in the British Isles, and in the Far East would be much greater than all the shipbuilding facilities and potentialities of all the Americas—not only greater but two or three times greater. Even if the United States threw all its resources into such a situation, seeking to double and even redouble the size of our Navy, the Axis Powers, in control of the rest of the world, would have the manpower and the physical resources to out-build us several times over.

It is time for all Americans of all the Americas to stop being deluded by the romantic notion that the Americas can go on living happily and peacefully in a Nazi-dominated world. Generation after generation America has battled for the general policy of the freedom of the seas. That policy is a very simple one, but a basic, fundamental one. It means that no nation has the right to make the broad oceans of the world at great distances from the actual theater of land war unsafe for the commerce of others.

That has been our policy, proved time and time again, in all our history.

Our policy has applied from time immemorial—and still applies—not merely to the Atlantic but to the Pacific and to all other oceans as well.

Unrestricted submarine warfare in 1941 constitutes a defiance—an act of aggression—against that historic American policy. . . .

This attack on the GREER was no localized military operation in the North Atlantic. This was no mere episode in a struggle between two nations. This was one determined step toward creating a permanent world system based on force, terror, and murder.

And I am sure that even now the Nazis are waiting to see whether the United States will by silence give them the green light to go ahead on this path of destruction.

The Nazi danger to our western world has long ceased to be a mere possibility. The danger is here now—not only from a military enemy but from an enemy of all law, all liberty, all morality, all religion. . . .

One peaceful nation after another has met disaster because each refused to look the Nazi danger squarely in the eye until it actually had them by the throat.

The United States will not make that fatal mistake.

No act of violence or intimidation will keep us from maintaining intact two bulwarks of defense—first, our line of supply of materiel to the enemies of Hitler; and, second, the freedom of our shipping on the high seas.

No matter what it takes, no matter what it costs, we will keep open the line of legitimate commerce in these defensive waters.

We have sought no shooting war with Hitler. We do not seek it now. But, neither do we want peace so much that we are willing to pay for it by permitting him to attack our naval and merchant ships while they are on legitimate business.

I assume that the German leaders are not deeply concerned by what we Americans say or publish about them. We cannot bring about the downfall of nazi-ism by the use of long-range invectives.

But when you see a rattlesnake poised to strike you do not wait until he has struck before you crush him.

These Nazi submarines and raiders are the rattlesnakes of the Atlantic. They are a menace to the free pathways of the high seas. They are a challenge to our sovereignty. They hammer at our most precious rights when they attack ships of the American flag—symbols of our independence, our freedom, our very life.

It is clear to all Americans that the time has come when

the Americas themselves must now be defended. A continuation of attacks in our own waters, or in waters which could be used for further and greater attacks on us, will inevitably weaken American ability to repel Hitlerism. . . .

If submarines or raiders attack in distant waters, they can attack equally well within sight of our own shores. Their very presence in any waters which America deems vital to its defense constitutes an attack.

In the waters which we deem necessary for our defense American naval vessels and American planes will no longer wait until Axis submarines lurking under the water, or Axis raiders on the surface of the sea, strike their deadly blow first.

Upon our naval and air patrol—now operating in large numbers over a vast expanse of the Atlantic Ocean—falls the duty of maintaining the American policy of freedom of the seas-now. That means very simply and clearly, that our patrolling vessels and planes will protect all merchant ships—not only American ships but ships of any flag—engaged in commerce in our defensive waters. They will protect them from submarines; they will protect them from surface raiders. . . .

My obligation as President is historic; it is clear. Yes, it is inescapable.

It is no act of war on our part when we decide to protect the seas which are vital to American defense. The aggression is not ours. Ours is solely defense.

But let this warning be clear. From now on, if German or Italian vessels of war enter the waters, the protection of which is necessary for American defense, they do so at their own peril.

The orders which I have given as Commander in Chief to the United States Army and Navy are to carry out that policy—at once.

The sole responsibility rests upon Germany. There will be no shooting unless Germany continues to seek it.

That is my obvious duty in this crisis. That is the clear right of this sovereign Nation. That is the only step possible, if we would keep tight the wall of defense which we are pledged to maintain around this Western Hemisphere. . . .

Source: Web site: ibiblio. Available at http://www.ibiblio.org/pha/7–2–188/188–29.html.

107. Text of Basic Japanese Terms of Peace with China: Document Handed by the Japanese Minister for Foreign Affairs (Toyoda) to the U.S. Ambassador in Japan (Grew), 22 September 1941

As lengthy negotiations between the United States and Japan continued, in late September, the Japanese government handed the U.S. ambassador in Tokyo the latest version of the peace terms Japan would be prepared to accept. Japan expected to keep Manzhouguo, to continue stationing some troops in China, and to have the members of its collaborationist puppet administration included in the Chinese government. Predictably, U.S. officials found these unacceptable.

1. Neighborly friendship.
2. Respect for sovereignty and territorial integrity.
3. Cooperative defense between Japan and China.

   Cooperation between Japan and China for the purposes of preventing communistic and other subversive activities which may constitute a menace to the security of both countries and of maintaining the public order in China.

   Stationing of Japanese troops and naval forces in certain areas in the Chinese territory for a necessary period for the purposes referred to above and in accordance with the existing agreements and usages.
4. Withdrawal of Japanese armed forces.

   The Japanese armed forces which have been dispatched to China for carrying out the China Affairs will be withdrawn from China upon the settlement of the said Affairs, excepting those troops which come under point 3.
5. Economic cooperation.
   (a) There shall be economic cooperation between Japan and China, having the development and utilization of essential materials for national defense in China as its principal objective.
   (b) The preceding paragraph does not mean to restrict any economic activities by third Powers in China so long as they are pursued on an equitable basis.

6. Fusion of the Chiang Kai-shek regime and the Wang Chingwei Government.
7. No annexation.
8. No indemnities.

9. Recognition of Manchukuo.

Source: U.S. Department of State, Publication 1983, *Peace and War: United States Foreign Policy, 1931–1941* (Washington, DC: U.S. Government Printing Office, 1943), 744–745.

108. Inter-Allied Council Statement on the Principles of the Atlantic Charter, 24 September 1941

In late September 1941, representatives of those European governments—many of them from countries that were currently under German occupation—fighting Hitler and his allies met in London and endorsed the Atlantic Charter. British Prime Minister Winston Churchill had already promised his Parliament that this agreement's fourth principle would not be allowed to compromise the special economic relationships existing within the British Empire. The Soviet Union made reservations the significance of which would become apparent in the future.

Adherence to the principles set forth in the Roosevelt-Churchill Declarations by the governments allied with Great Britain was formally declared at the second meeting of the Inter-Allied Council, held in London on September 24, 1941.

The position of the Soviet Government was given by its Ambassador, Mr. Maisky, in the following terms: "The Soviet Union defends the right of every nation to the independence and territorial integrity of its country and its right to establish such a social order and to choose such a form of government as it deems opportune and necessary for the better promotion of its economic and cultural prosperity." He added that the Soviet Union advocates the necessity of collective action against aggressors and that "the Soviet Government proclaims its agreement with the fundamental principles of the declaration of Mr. Roosevelt and Mr. Churchill."

The following resolution was then adopted unanimously:

"The Governments of Belgium, Czechoslovakia, Greece, Luxembourg, the Netherlands, Norway, Poland, Union of Soviet Socialist Republics, and Yugoslavia, and representatives of General de Gaulle, leader of Free Frenchmen, having taken note of the declaration recently drawn up by the President of the United States and by the Prime Minister (Mr. Churchill) on behalf of His Majesty's Government in the United Kingdom, now make known their adherence to the common principles of policy set forth in that declaration and their intention to cooperate to the best of their ability in giving effect to them."

[Maisky also added the following reservation:]

"Considering that the practical application of these principles will necessarily adapt itself to the circumstances, needs, and historic peculiarities of particular countries, the Soviet Government can state that a consistent application of these principles will secure the most energetic support on the part of the government and peoples of the Soviet Union."

Source: Foreign Relations of the United States: Diplomatic Papers 1941, Volume 1: *General: The Soviet Union* (Washington, DC: U.S. Government Printing Office, 1958); Arthur M. Schlesinger Jr., ed., *The Dynamics of World Power: A Documentary History of United States Foreign Policy 1945–1973*, 5 vols. Vol. 2: *Eastern Europe and the Soviet Union* (New York: Chelsea House, 1973), 4.

109. Cable from the Japanese Ambassador in Berlin to the Japanese Foreign Ministry, Tokyo, Secret, 1 October 1941

One year after the conclusion of the Tripartite Pact, German officials expressed their dissatisfaction with what they considered to be the very lackluster assistance their country had received from Japan. In a cable intercepted and deciphered by American code-breakers, the Japanese ambassador in Berlin reported this to his Foreign Ministry in Tokyo.

On this the occasion of the first anniversary of the Tripartite Pact, Foreign Minister Ribbentrop has come to Berlin from the Imperial Headquarters especially and I have had several visits with him. Using this opportunity I, and the other members of the staff, have mingled with people from all classes of society and visited with them. I am endeavoring to sum up all these experiences and analyze the present state of feeling toward Japan held by Germany in this report to you.

1. Ribbentrop said that he had absolute proof that, while reports of the content of the Japanese-American negotiations were withheld from Ambassador Ott, America was in secret communication with England in regard to the Japanese-American negotiations. Even Ribbentrop, who is supposed to understand Japan's position, expressed great dissatisfaction regarding Japan's attitude.

2. That the Foreign Office staff from Weizsacker down and also everyone in general were thoroughly disgusted with Japan was very apparent from their attitude toward myself and other members of the staff. Everyone who feels kindly disposed toward Japan is deeply concerned over this state of affairs. Even those who do not come to the same conclusion that Ambassador Ott did in his telegram are outspoken in their dissatisfaction and expression of pessimistic views. I am trying to take the position in interviews with newspaper correspondents and others concerned with the outside that Germany is cognizant of the Japanese-American negotiations and that they are no indication of an alienation between Japan and Germany.

3. Foreign diplomats and newspaper correspondents of third countries show great interest in the Japanese attitude and seem to consider it in a certain sense as a barometer by which the course of the European war can be judged. However we receive the impression that the greater number feel that Japan is avoiding war because of the impoverishment resulting from the China incident and is taking a pessimistic attitude toward the course of the European war.

4. Even though it might be said that Germany is prepared for these machinations of estrangement by third countries and that she is keeping up the pretense that there is no change in her feelings toward Japan, the fact that the feeling of German leaders and the people in general toward Japan is getting bad is one that cannot be covered. Please bear this fact in mind. If Japan takes a wishy-washy attitude and goes ahead with her negotiations without consulting Germany there is no telling what steps Germany may take without consulting Japan.

Please convey this to the army and navy.

Source: United States, 79 Congress, 2nd Session, Joint Committee on the Pearl Harbor Attack, *Hearings,* 39 pts. (Washington, DC: U.S. Government Printing Office, 1946), Pt. 12: 48–49. Exhibits of Joint Committee, Exhibit No. 1, Intercepted Diplomatic Messages Sent by the Japanese Government between 1 July and 8 December 1941. Also available at http://www.ibiblio.org/pha/timeline/411001b.html.

110. Paraphrase of Letter, Franklin D. Roosevelt to Soviet Premier Josef Stalin, 30 October 1941

In October 1941, U.S. and Soviet officials met in Moscow. The U.S. president quickly promised Josef Stalin up to $1 billion worth of supplies for the Russian war effort.

I have examined the record of the Moscow Conference and the members of the mission have discussed the details with me. All of the military equipment and munitions items have been approved and I have ordered that as far as possible the delivery of raw materials be expedited. Deliveries have been directed to commence immediately and to be fulfilled in the largest possible amounts. In an effort to obviate any financial difficulties immediate arrangements are to be made so that supplies up to one billion dollars in value may be effected under the Lend-Lease Act. If approved by the Government of the U.S.S.R. I propose that the indebtedness thus incurred be subject to no interest and that the payments by the Government of the U.S.S.R. do not commence until five years after the war's conclusion and be completed over a ten-year period thereafter.

I hope that special efforts will be arranged by your Government to sell us the available raw materials and commodities which the United States may need urgently under the arrangement that the proceeds thereof be credited to the Soviet Government's account.

At this opportunity I want to tell you of the appreciation of the United States Government for the expeditious handling by you and your associates of the Moscow supply conference, and to send you assurances that we will carry out to the limit all the implications thereof. I hope that you will communicate with me directly without hesitation if you should so wish.

Source: U.S. Department of State Bulletin, 8 November 1941.

111. Notes of Imperial Conference, Government of Japan, 5 November 1941

After lengthy discussions among Japanese military and political leaders, on 5 November a full-dress Imperial Conference met. Its primary function was to ratify the decisions reached at a preceding 1 November meeting of the Liaison Committee of top military and political leaders and to endorse the final version of the document drafted on that occasion. This document, which the conference adopted after lengthy consideration of the probable impact of war upon Japan, set a 1 December deadline for reaching a settlement with the United States that would be acceptable to Japan.

[The conference was convened at 10:30 A.M. and adjourned at 3:15 P.M. with a one-hour recess between 12:30 and 1:30 P.M. The participants were as follows: Tojo Hideki, Prime Minister and War Minister; Hara Yoshimichi, President of the Privy Council; Shimada Shigetaro, Navy Minister; Togo Shigenori, Foreign Minister; Kaya Okinori, Finance Minister; Suzuki Tiichi, Director of the Planning Board; Nagano Osami, Navy Chief of Staff; Sugiyama Gen, Army Chief of Staff; Ito Seiichi, Navy Vice Chief of Staff; Tsukada Ko, Army Vice Chief of Staff. The Secretaries were: Hoshino Naoki, Chief Secretary of the Cabinet; Muto Akira, Chief of the Military Affairs Bureau of the War Ministry; and Oka Takasumi, Chief of the Naval Affairs Bureau of the Navy Ministry.]

Agenda: "Essentials for Carrying Out the Empire's Policies."

I. Our Empire, in order to resolve the present critical situation, assure its self-preservation and self-defense, and establish a New Order in Greater East Asia, decides on this occasion to go to war against the United States and Great Britain and takes the following measures:

1. The time for resorting to force is set at the beginning of December, and the Army and Navy will complete preparations for operations.
2. Negotiations with the United States will be carried out in accordance with the attached document.

3. Cooperation with Germany and Italy will be strengthened.
4. Close military relations with Thailand will be established just prior to the use of force.

II. If negotiations with the United States are successful by midnight of December 1, the use of force will be suspended.

[Attached Document]

Summary of Negotiations with the United States of America:

We will negotiate with the United States and seek to reach an agreement on the basis of attached Proposal A or Proposal B, both of which express, in a more moderate and amended form, important matters that have been pending between both countries.

PROPOSAL A:

We will moderate our position on the most important matters pending in the negotiations between Japan and the United States: (1) stationing and withdrawal of troops in China and French Indochina; (2) nondiscriminatory trade in China; (3) interpretation and execution of the Tripartite Pact; (4) the Four Principles. This will be done as follows:

1. Stationing and withdrawal of troops in China:

We will moderate our position on this point as follows

(in view of the fact that the United States—disregarding for the time being the reason for the stationing of troops—attached importance to the stationing of troops for an indefinite period, disagrees with the inclusion of this item in the terms for peace, and urges us to make a clearer statement of our intentions regarding withdrawal):

Of the Japanese troops sent to China during the China Incident, those in designated sections of North China and Inner Mongolia, and those on Hainan Island, will remain for a necessary period of time after the establishment of peace between Japan and China. The remainder of the troops will begin withdrawal simultaneously with the establishment of peace in accordance with arrangements to be made between Japan and China, and the withdrawal will be completed within two years.

Note: In case the United States asks what the "necessary period of time" will be, we will respond that we have in mind 25 years.

Stationing and withdrawal of troops in French Indochina:

We will moderate our position on this point as follows, since we recognize that the United States is apprehensive that Japan has territorial ambitions in French Indochina and is building a base for military advance into neighboring territories:

Japan respects the sovereignty of French Indochina over her territory. Japanese troops currently stationed in French Indochina will be immediately withdrawn after the settlement of the China Incident or the establishment of a just peace in the Far East.

2. Nondiscriminatory trade in China:

In case there is no prospect of an agreement on the basis of the proposal that was presented on September 25, we will proceed on the basis of the following:

The Japanese Government will recognize the application of the principle of nondiscrimination in the entire Pacific region, including China, if this principle is applied throughout the world.

3. The interpretation and execution of the Tripartite Pact:

On this point we will respond as follows: We do not intend to broaden unreasonably the interpretation of the right of self-defense. Regarding the interpretation and execution of the Tripartite Pact, the Japanese Government, as it has stated on previous occasions, will act independently. Our position will be that we assume that the United States is fully aware of this.

4. Regarding the so-called Four Principles put forward by the United States, we will make every effort to avoid their inclusion in official agreements between Japan and the United States (this includes understandings and other communiqués).

PROPOSAL B:

1. Both Japan and the United States will pledge not to make an armed advance into Southeast Asia and the South Pacific area, except French Indochina.
2. The Japanese and American Governments will cooperate with each other so that the procurement of necessary materials from the Netherlands East Indies will be assured.
3. The Japanese and American Governments will restore trade relations to what they were prior to the freezing of assets. The United States will promise to supply Japan with the petroleum Japan needs.
4. The Government of the United States will not take such actions as may hinder efforts for peace by both Japan and China.

Notes:

1. As occasion demands, it is permissible to promise that with the conclusion of the present agreement Japanese troops stationed in southern Indochina are prepared to move to northern Indochina with the consent of the French Government; and that the Japanese troops will withdraw from Indochina with the settlement of the China Incident or upon the establishment of a just peace in the Pacific area.
2. As occasion demands, we may make insertions in the provision on nondiscriminatory trade and on the interpretation and execution of the Tripartite Pact in the abovementioned proposal (Proposal A).

Statement by Prime Minister Tojo:

The Conference is now opened. With His Majesty's permission I will take charge of the proceedings.

At the Imperial Conference of September 6 "Essentials for Carrying Out the Empire's Policies" was discussed and the following was decided by His Majesty: our Empire, determined not to avoid war with the United States, Great Britain, and the Netherlands in the course of assuring her self-preservation and self-defense, was to complete preparations for war by late October. At the same time it was decided that we would endeavor to attain our demands by using all possible diplomatic measures vis-à-vis the United States and Great Britain; and that in case there was no prospect of our demands being attained through diplomacy by early October, we would decide immediately on war with the United States, Great Britain, and the Netherlands.

Since then, while maintaining close coordination between political and military considerations, we have made a special effort to achieve success in our diplomatic negotiations with the United States. In this interval we have endured what must be endured in our efforts to reach an agreement, but we have not been able to get the United States to reconsider. During the negotiations, there has been a change in the Cabinet.

The Government and the Army and Navy sections of Imperial Headquarters have held eight Liaison Conferences in order to study matters more extensively and deeply on the basis of the "Essentials for Carrying Out the Empire's Policies" adopted on September 6. As a result of this, we have come to the conclusion that we must now decide to go to war, set the time for military action at the beginning of December, concentrate all of our efforts on completing preparations for war, and at the same time try to break the impasse by means of diplomacy. Accordingly, I ask you all to deliberate on the document "Essentials for Carrying Out the Empire's Policies." . . .

Statement by Army Chief of Staff Sugiyama:

I respectfully make my statement.

First I will discuss [enemy] army strength in the several countries in the South.

Army strength in the several countries in the South is gradually being increased. Roughly speaking, Malaya has an army of about 60,000 to 70,000 and about 320 airplanes, the Philippines have about 42,000 men and about 170 airplanes, the Netherlands East Indies have about 85,000 men and about 300 airplanes, and Burma has about 35,000 men and about 60 airplanes. Compared to strength before the outbreak of the war in Europe, enemy strength has been increased about eight times in Malaya, four times in the Philippines, two and one-half times in the Netherlands East Indies, and five times in Burma; it totals well over 200,000 in these countries. It is anticipated that the rate of increase will rise as the situation changes.

The ground forces in these regions, although varying from one region to another, are composed for the most part of native soldiers, with a nucleus of about 30 per cent white, "homeland" soldiers. They do not have sufficient education and training, and their fighting ability is generally inferior. It should be remembered, however, that they are thoroughly acclimatized, and used to tropical conditions. As to the fighting ability of the enemy air force, I assume that it cannot be taken lightly when compared to the ground force, since the ability of the aircraft is excellent and their pilots are comparatively skilled.

I will comment on the following matters: (1) timing of the commencement of war; (2) prospects of the operations in the South; (3) situation in the North resulting from operations in the South; (4) relationship between operations and diplomacy.

1. On the timing of the commencement of war:

From the standpoint of operations, if the time for commencing war is delayed, the ratio of armament between Japan and the United States will become more and more unfavorable to us as time passes; and particularly, the gap in air armament will enlarge rapidly. Moreover, defensive preparations in the Philippines, and other American war preparations, will make rapid progress. Also, the common defense arrangements between the United States, Great Britain, the Netherlands, and China will become all the more close, and their joint defensive capability will be rapidly increased. Finally, if we delay until after next spring, the weather will permit operational activities in the North, and also there will be a high probability that our Empire will have to face simultaneous war in the South and in the North. Thus it would be very disadvantageous for us to delay; and it is to be feared that it might become impossible for us to undertake offensive operations.

In addition, weather conditions in the area where important operations are going to take place are such that no delay is possible. Accordingly, in order to resort to force as soon as preparations for the operations we contemplate are completed, we would like to set the target date in the early part of December.

2. On the prospects of the operation:

Since the principal Army operations in the initial stages in the South will be landing operations against fortified enemy bases, conducted after a long ocean voyage in the intense heat of the sun while repelling attacks from enemy submarines and aircraft, we expect to face considerable difficulties. However, if we take a broad view of the situation, the enemy forces are scattered over a wide area and moreover separated by stretches of water, making coordinated action difficult. We, on the other hand, can concentrate our forces, undertake sudden raids, and destroy the enemy piecemeal. Therefore, we are fully confident of success, given close cooperation between the Army and the Navy. As for operations after we land, we have complete confidence in our victory when we consider the organization, equipment, quality, and strength of the enemy forces.

After the initial stage in our operations has been completed, we will endeavor to shorten greatly the duration of the war, using both political and military strategies, particularly the favorable results from our naval operations. Nevertheless, we must be prepared for the probability that the war will be a protracted one. But since we will seize and hold enemy military and air bases and be able to establish a strategically impregnable position, we think we can frustrate the enemy's plans by one means or another.

We will firmly maintain in general our present posture with respect to defense against the Soviet Union and operations in China while we engage in operations in the South. In this way we will be able to strengthen our invincible position vis-à-vis the North, and there will be no problem carrying on in China as we have been doing. With regard to China, the favorable results of the operations in the South should particularly contribute to the settlement of the China Incident.

3. On the situation in the North resulting from operations in the South:

The Red Army has suffered massive losses at the hands of the German Army; and there has been a marked decline in the productivity of the Soviet armament industry. In addition, the Red Army in the Far East has sent westward to European Russia forces equal to 13 infantry divisions, about 1,300 tanks, and at least 1,300 airplanes since last spring. Its war potential, both militarily and spiritually, is declining. Consequently, the probability of the Soviet Union taking the offensive, so long as the Kwantung Army is firmly entrenched [in Manchuria], is very low.

However, it is possible that the United States may put pressure on the Soviet Union to permit America to utilize a part of the Soviet territory in the Far East for air and submarine bases for use in attacking us; and the Soviet Union would not be in a position to reject these American demands. Hence we must anticipate the possibility that we might see some submarines and aircraft in action against us from the North. Consequently, it cannot be assumed that there is no danger of a war breaking out between Japan and the Soviet Union as a result of such causes and changes in the situation. Thus our Empire must conclude its operations in the South as quickly as possible, and be prepared to cope with this situation.

4. On the relationship between operations and diplomacy:

Up to now, in accordance with the decision of the Imperial Conference of September 6, we have limited our preparations for operations so that they would not impede diplomatic negotiations. But from now on, given the decision for war, we will take all possible measures to be ready to use force at the beginning of December. This will have the effect of goading the United States and Great Britain; but we believe that diplomacy, taking advantage of progress in war preparations, should be stepped up. Needless to say, if diplomatic negotiations succeed by midnight of November 30, we will call off the use of force. If they do not succeed by that time, however, we would like to receive the Imperial Assent to start a war in order not to miss our opportunity, and thereby to fully achieve the objectives of our operations. . . .

Hara [speaking on behalf of the Emperor] . . .

It would not be desirable to fail to get an agreement on Japanese-American negotiations. We have endured hardships for four years because we are a unified nation, under an Imperial family with a history of 2,600 years. It seems that Britain already has war weariness. I wonder about Germany. It also seems that there is an antiwar movement in Italy. I believe that the favorable situation in our country results from our national polity with the Imperial family as its head. Nonetheless, our people want to settle the China Incident quickly. Statesmen must give serious consideration to the wisdom of waging war against a great power like the United States without the prospect of the China Incident being settled quickly. At the last Imperial Conference it was decided that we would go to war if the negotiations failed to lead to an agreement. According to the briefings given today, the present American attitude is not just the same as the previous one, but is even more unreasonable. Therefore, I regret very much that the negotiations have little prospect of success.

It is impossible, from the standpoint of our domestic political situation and our self-preservation, to accept all of the American demands. We must hold fast to our position. As I understand it, the Japanese-Chinese problem is the important point in the negotiations, and there is no suspicion that the United States is acting as spokesman for the Chungking regime. If Chiang, relying on American power, should negotiate with us, I doubt that the negotiations could be completed in two or three months. It would be nice if he would capitulate in the face of Japan's firm determination; but I think there is absolutely no hope for this.

On the other hand, we cannot let the present situation continue. If we miss the present opportunity to go to war, we will have to submit to American dictation. Therefore, I recognize that it is inevitable that we must decide to start a war against the United States. I will put my trust in what I have been told: namely, that things will go well in the early part of the war; and that although we will experience increasing difficulties as the war progresses, there is some prospect of success.

On this occasion I would like to make one comment to the leaders of the Government. Although the China Incident is one cause for war between Japan and the United States and Great Britain, another is the German-British war. I do not believe that the present situation would have developed out of just the China Incident. We have come to where we are because of the war between Germany and Great Britain. What we should always keep in mind here is what would happen to relations between Germany and Great Britain and Germany and the United States, all of them being countries whose population belongs to the white race, if Japan should enter the war. Hitler has said that the Japanese are a second-class race, and Germany has not declared war against the United States. Japan will take positive action against the United States. In that event, will the American people adopt the same attitude toward us psychologically that they do toward the Germans? Their indignation against the Japanese will be stronger than their hatred of Hitler. The Germans in the United States are considering ways of bringing about peace between the United States and Germany. I fear, therefore, that if Japan begins a war against the United States, Germany and Great Britain and Germany and the United States will come to terms, leaving Japan by herself. That is, we must be prepared for the possibility that hatred of the yellow race might shift the hatred now being directed against Germany to Japan, thus resulting in the German-British war's being turned against Japan.

Negotiations with the United States have failed to lead to an agreement. A war against the United States and Great Britain is inevitable if Japan is to survive. However, we must give serious consideration to race relations, exercise constant care to avoid being surrounded by the entire Aryan race—which would leave Japan isolated—and take steps now to strengthen relations with Germany and Italy. Paper agreements will not do. I would like to call the attention of the officials in the Government to the following point: don't let hatred of Japan become stronger than hatred of Hitler, so that everybody will in name and in fact gang up on Japan. I hope that our officials will deal adequately with international affairs in the future.

Tojo: The points of the President of the Privy Council are well taken. Ever since the previous Imperial Conference, the Government has not given up its earnest desire to somehow break the impasse in our negotiations with the United States. It is natural for the Supreme Command to devote itself exclusively to military operations, since it sees little hope for the negotiations' success. However, in the hope that there might be some way to break the impasse, the Government sought a settlement, even though it meant some sacrifice of freedom in military operations. That is, we pursued diplomacy and military planning at the same time. There is still some hope for success. The reason the United States agreed to negotiate with us is that they have some weaknesses: (1) they are not prepared for operations in two oceans; (2) they have not completed strengthening their domestic structure; (3) they are short of materials for national defense (they have only enough for one year); and so on.

They will learn how determined Japan is from the deployment of our troops, which we will carry out on the basis of the present proposal. The United States has from the beginning believed that Japan would give up because of economic pressure; but if they recognize that Japan is determined, then that is the time we should resort to diplomatic measures. I believe this is the only way that is left for us. This is the present proposal. This is the last measure we can take that is in line with what President Hara has called "going by diplomacy." I cannot think of any other way in the present situation.

If we enter into a protracted war, there will be difficulties, as mentioned before. The first stage of the war will not be difficult. We have some uneasiness about a protracted war. But how can we let the United States continue to do as she pleases, even though there is some uneasiness? Two years from now we will have no petroleum for military use. Ships will stop moving. When I think about the strengthening of American defenses in the Southwest Pacific, the expansion of the American fleet, the unfinished China Incident, and so on, I see no end to difficulties. We can talk about austerity and suffering, but can our people endure such a life for a long time? The situation is not the same as it was during the Sino-Japanese War [1894–95]. I fear that we would become a third-class nation after two or three years if we just sat tight. We agreed upon the present proposal as a result of a careful study in the light of the possibility just mentioned. The President should share our views on this point.

I intend to take measures to prevent a racial war once war is started. I should like to prevent Germany and Italy from making peace with Great Britain or with the United States by taking advantage of the results of campaigns in the South. I think the sentiments of the American people are as the President of the Privy Council has indicated, and so I intend to take precautions.

As to what our moral basis for going to war should be, there is some merit in making it clear that Great Britain and the United States represent a strong threat to Japan's self-preservation. Also, if we are fair in governing the occupied areas, attitudes toward us would probably relax. America may be enraged for a while, but later she will come to understand [why we did what we did]. In any case I will be careful to avoid the war's becoming a racial war.

Do you have any other comments? If not, I will rule that the proposals have been approved in their original form.

Source: Nobutaka Ike, ed., *Japan's Decision for War: Records of the 1941 Policy Conferences* (Stanford, CA: Stanford University Press, 1967), 208–239. Reprinted with permission of Stanford University Press.

112. "The Foreign and Domestic Implementation of the 'Essentials for Carrying Out the Empire's Policies' Adopted by the Imperial Conference on November 5," Document Approved by the 67th Liaison Conference, Japanese Government, 12 November 1941

After the 5 November 1941 Imperial Conference, Japanese officials drew up detailed plans for the conduct of the war that now seemed inevitable. Meeting on 12 November, they approved a "Basic Plan for a Wartime Economy," which is not included here, and also a blueprint for the conduct of Japanese diplomacy toward friends, enemies, and neutral powers.

1. Toward Germany and Italy:

In the event that Japanese-American negotiations fail, and it is recognized that war is inevitable (it is assumed that this will be after November 25th), Germany and Italy will be notified without delay that the Empire intends to declare war on Great Britain and the United States as soon as preparations have been completed. As part of the above-mentioned preparations, the following necessary agreements will be negotiated: (a) The participation of Germany and Italy in the war against the United States; (b) neither of the two parties will make peace separately.

Note: In case Germany demands that we participate in the war against the Soviet Union, we will respond that we do not intend to join the war for the time being. Even if this should lead to a situation whereby Germany will delay her entry into the war against the United States, it cannot be helped.

2. Toward Great Britain:

As to those items that might be agreed on as a result of negotiations with the United States that affect Great Britain, we will get Great Britain to accept them; moreover, we will take steps to get her to cooperate immediately in a positive manner by negotiating either directly or through the United States.

In order to keep our plans secret, no other special diplomatic measures will be taken.

3. Toward the Dutch East Indies:

In order that our plans may be kept secret and deceptive, we will gradually begin diplomatic negotiations, ostensibly in the form of continuing our earlier negotiations, for the purpose of acquiring vital materials for our Empire.

4. Toward the Soviet Union:

In general we will continue our negotiations on the basis of Paragraph One of "The Essentials of Diplomatic Negotiations with the Soviet Union," adopted by the Liaison Conference between Supreme Headquarters and the Government on August 4, 1941.

5. Toward Thailand:

(a) Just before we occupy the country we will demand the following and secure Thailand's immediate agreement (even if Thailand does not accept our demands, our troops will enter the country as planned; however, efforts will be made to limit armed clashes between Japan and Thailand); (1) that the transit of Japanese troops and the use of facilities be allowed, and that other aid also be provided; (2) that immediate steps be taken to prevent clashes between Japanese and Thai troops in connection with the transit of Japanese troops; (3) that a mutual defense pact be signed if Thailand wishes it.

Note: There should be no particular change in our approach to Thailand before we enter into these negotiations; great care must be taken to keep secret our plans to begin war.

(b) Immediately after our occupation, agreements will be made on the spot regarding the following points: (1) the transit and stationing of Japanese troops; (2) providing military facilities and building new ones; (3) providing the necessary transportation and communications facilities and factories, etc.; (4) providing billets and provisions for troops in transit and for troops on occupation duty; (5) loaning the necessary military funds.

Note: Negotiations regarding Points (1) and (2) will be on the basis of the "Essentials of Policy toward French Indochina and Thailand" adopted by the Liaison Conference between the Government and the Supreme Headquarters on February 1, 1941. We will promise to respect the sovereignty and territorial integrity of Thailand; in order to facilitate our negotiations and depending on Thailand's attitude, she may be secretly told that in the future she might be given a part of Burma, or perhaps Malaya.

6. Toward China:

The following steps should be taken in order to limit consumption as much as possible so as to prepare for a protracted world war, to assure the preservation of Japan's overall war-making capacity, and to prepare for the possibility that her war-making ability might be reduced in the future:

(a) Eliminate British and American forces in China.

(b) Place enemy Foreign Settlements (including the Foreign Legation Quarter in Peking) under effective Japanese control. However, care should be taken to keep to a minimum the burden placed on Japan's human and material resources. Note: Enemy forces will be removed from the International Settlement and the Peking Legation Quarter, and these areas will be placed under our control; but since the interests of friendly foreign powers are also involved, these areas will not be taken over.

(c) In order to conceal our plans, the foregoing paragraphs will not become effective until war begins with the United States.

(d) The exercise of the rights of a belligerent against Chungking will not take the form of a special declaration, but for practical purposes will go into effect with the opening of hostilities against the United States.

(e) As for enemy rights in China, even those relating to the National Government will, depending on the need, be placed for the time being under the control of Japan. Special steps will be taken to adjust them.

(f) In the occupied areas, the Chinese leaders will be encouraged as much as possible to carry on activities, and efforts will be made to secure the support of the people through Sino-Japanese joint efforts. In this way peace will gradually be restored in local areas wherever possible.

(g) With respect to economic relations with China, emphasis will be placed on the acquisition of vital materials; and for this reason rational adjustments will be made in the restrictions presently in force.

Source: Nobutaka Ike, ed., *Japan's Decision for War: Records of the 1941 Policy Conferences* (Stanford, CA: Stanford University Press, 1967), 241–243. Reprinted with permission of Stanford University Press.

113. "Draft Proposal for Hastening the End of the War against the United States, Great Britain, the Netherlands, and Chiang [Kai-shek]," Approved by the 69th Liaison Conference, Japanese Government, 15 November 1941

Three days after approving a broad plan for the conduct of Japanese diplomacy in the approach to war, the country's top military and civilian officials accepted a policy statement on the strategy to be followed in the impending conflict. Interestingly, not only did Japanese leaders envisage working in close concert with Germany and Italy but they even hoped to negotiate a peace between Germany and the Soviet Union.

POLICY

1. We will endeavor to quickly destroy American, British, and Dutch bases in the Far East, and assure our self-preservation and self-defense. We will endeavor at the same time to hasten the fall of the Chiang regime by taking positive measures, to work for the surrender of Great Britain in co-operation with Germany and Italy, and to destroy the will of the United States to continue the war.

2. We will do our utmost to prevent an increase in the number of countries at war against us; and we will endeavor to influence the countries not presently involved.

SUMMARY

1. Our Empire will engage in a quick war, and will destroy American and British bases in Eastern Asia and in the Southwest Pacific region. At the same time that it secures a strategically powerful position, it will control those areas producing vital materials, as well as important transportation routes, and thereby prepare for a protracted period of self-sufficiency.

At the appropriate time, we will endeavor by various means to lure the main fleet of the United States [near Japan] and destroy it.

2. First of all, Japan, Germany, and Italy will cooperate and work for the surrender of Great Britain.

(a) The Empire will adopt the following policies: (1) the connection between Australia and India and the British mother country will be broken by means of political pressure and the destruction of commerce, and their separation will be achieved; (2) the independence of Burma will be promoted, and this will be used to stimulate the independence of India.

(b) We will endeavor to get Germany and Italy to adopt the following policies: (1) to carry out operations against the Near East, North Africa, and Suez, and at the same time carry out operations against India; (2) strengthen the blockade of Great Britain; (3) if conditions permit, carry out the invasion of the British Isles.

(c) The three countries will cooperate and adopt the following policies: (1) endeavor to establish contact among the three countries through the Indian Ocean; (2) strengthen naval operations; (3) stop the shipment of vital materials from the occupied countries to Great Britain.

3. Japan, Germany, and Italy will cooperate and endeavor to deal with Great Britain, and at the same time endeavor to destroy the will of the United States to fight.

(a) The Empire will adopt the following policies: (1) In dealing with the Philippines, for the time being the present policy will be continued, and thought will be given to how it can hasten the end of the war. (2) An all-out attempt will be made to disrupt commerce to the United States. (3) The flow of materials from China and the South Seas to the United States will be cut off. (4) Strategic propaganda against the United States will be stepped up; emphasis will be placed on enticing the American main fleet to come to the Far East, persuading Americans to reconsider their Far Eastern policy, and pointing out the uselessness of a Japanese-American war; American public opinion will be directed toward opposition to war. (5) Attempts will be made to break the ties between the United States and Australia.

(b) We will endeavor to get Australia and Italy to adopt the following policies: (1) to set up naval attacks against the United States in the Atlantic and Indian Oceans; (2) to step up military, economic, and political offensives against Central and South America.

4. In China we will stop support going to Chiang by uti-

lizing the results of our military operations (especially against the United States, Great Britain, and the Netherlands), and will destroy Chiang's power to resist. We will also work for the collapse of the Chiang regime by vigorously undertaking various strategies—the seizure of the Foreign Settlements, utilization of the overseas Chinese in the South Pacific, stepping up military operations, etc.

5. The Empire will endeavor to the utmost to prevent the outbreak of a war with the Soviet Union while we are engaged in military operations in the South.

We will keep in mind the possibilities of arranging a peace between Germany and the Soviet Union, depending on the wishes of those two countries, and bringing the Soviet Union within the Axis camp; of improving Japanese-Soviet relations; and, depending on circumstances, of encouraging the Soviets to push into Iran and India.

6. We will continue our present policy toward French Indochina. We will persuade Thailand to cooperate with us by restoring to her territory she has lost to the British.

7. While paying full attention to changes in the war situation, the international situation, and popular feelings in enemy countries, we will endeavor to seize the following opportunities in order to bring the war to a close: (a) conclusion of the principal military operations in the South; (b) conclusion of the principal military operations in China, especially the capitulation of the Chiang regime; (c) favorable developments in the war situation in Europe, especially the conquest of the British Isles, the end of the war between Germany and the Soviet Union, and the success of the policy vis-à-vis India.

For this purpose we will step up our diplomatic and propaganda activities directed against Latin America, Switzerland, Portugal, and the Vatican.

The three countries—Japan, Germany, and Italy—agree not to sign a separate peace agreement; at the same time, they will not immediately make peace with Great Britain when she surrenders, but will endeavor to use Great Britain to persuade the United States. In the planning to promote peace with the United States, attention will be paid to supplies of tin and rubber in the South Pacific region, and to the treatment of the Philippines.

Source: Nobutaka Ike, ed., *Japan's Decision for War: Records of the 1941 Policy Conferences* (Stanford, CA: Stanford University Press, 1967), 247–249. Reprinted with permission of Stanford University Press.

114. "The Jews Are to Blame": Article in *Das Reich*, 16 November 1941

By late 1941, German authorities were no longer content simply to impose ever tighter restrictions on Jews in Germany and occupied Europe. They now contemplated more drastic treatment of the Jews: first, their physical removal from Germany by their deportation eastward out of German territory and into ghettos in cities further west, and soon, their elimination by means of mass murder. An article in Das Reich, *the official organ of Josef Goebbels's Ministry of Propaganda, signaled the move toward even harsher German treatment of European Jewry.*

The historical guilt of world Jewry for the outbreak and extension of the war is so clearly proven that there is no point in wasting any words on it. The Jews wanted their war and now they have got it. But now they are feeling the effects of the prophecy which the Führer made on 30 January 1939 in the German Reichstag that, if international finance Jewry should succeed in plunging the nations once again into a world war, the result would not be the Bolshevization of the earth and consequently the victory of Jewry but the annihilation of the Jewish race in Europe.

We are now experiencing the implementation of this prophecy and in the process the Jews are suffering a fate which, while harsh, is more than earned. Sympathy, let alone regret, is entirely inappropriate in this case. In provoking this war, World Jewry has completely miscalculated the forces at its disposal and it is now experiencing a gradual process of annihilation which it intended us to suffer and would inflict on us without any qualms if it had the power to do so. It is now heading for destruction on the basis of its own law: an eye for an eye, a tooth for a tooth.

In this historic confrontation every Jew is our enemy irrespective of whether he is vegetating in a Polish ghetto or is continuing his parasitic existence in Berlin or Hamburg or is blowing a war trumpet in New York or Washington. All Jews are part of an international conspiracy against national socialist Germany on the basis of their birth and race. They desire its defeat and destruction and are doing whatever is in their power to bring this about. The fact that in the Reich itself they have few opportunities to do so is not a result of the fact that they are loyal but is entirely due to the fact that we have taken what seemed to us the appropriate measures to prevent it.

One of these measures is the introduction of the yellow Jewish star which every Jew has to wear so that it is visible. Through this we wanted to mark them out above all so that, in the event of the slightest attempt to offend against the German national community, they could be instantly recognized as Jews. It is an extraordinarily humane regulation, so to speak a hygiene prophylactic measure which is intended

to prevent the Jews from slipping into our ranks unrecognized in order to provoke discord.

When a few weeks ago the Jews appeared on the Berlin street scene adorned with their Jewish star the first impression of the citizens of the Reich capital was one of general surprise. Only very few people knew there were so many Jews in Berlin. Everybody discovered among their acquaintance or in their neighbourhood someone who appeared to be harmless, who may have stood out by their periodic grumbling and complaining, but nobody would have imagined he was Jewish. He had evidently disguised himself, made the right gestures, adapted himself to the milieu in which he lived and awaited his moment. Which of us had the slightest idea that the enemy was standing right next to him, that he was quietly listening in to conversations on the street, in the underground, or in the queues in front of tobacconists or cleverly inciting people? There are Jews who one can hardly recognize as Jews from their outward appearance. Here too they have adapted themselves as far as they can. These are the most dangerous ones. It's typical that every measure that we take against the Jews is reported the following day in the English and American press. So the Jews still have secret contacts with the enemy and make use of them not only in their own interests but in all matters of military importance to the Reich. So the enemy is amongst us. Is it not then obvious that we should make sure that every citizen can recognize him?

The Jews are now gradually finding themselves isolated and are now trying to employ a new trick. They are familiar with the good-natured German *Michel* [a stereotype of a German simpleton] who resides in us, who is always ready to shed a sentimental tear and to forget all the injustice done to us; suddenly one has the impression that the Berlin Jews consist entirely of sweet little helpless babies or infirm old women designed to win our sympathy. The Jews are sending out their sympathy-evoking phalanx. They may disturb a few harmless souls, but not us. We know only too well what they're up to.

If for no other reason we must win the war on their

account. For were we to lose it then those harmless looking Jews would turn into ferocious wolves. They would fall upon our people, on our women and children, in order to take their revenge in a way for which history can show no parallel. This is what they did in Bessarabia and in the Baltic states when Bolshevism took over and in those places they had not even suffered either at the hands of the people or the government; we cannot retreat from our struggle against Jewry—quite apart from the fact that we don't wish to do so. The Jews must be separated off from the German national community since they threaten our national stability.

This is an elementary principle of ethnic, national and social hygiene. They will never cease their activities. If they could they would bring one nation after another into the war against us. What do they care about the suffering that people endure as a result so long as they can force the world to submit to their financial and racial domination. The Jews are a parasitic race which settles on the cultures of nations which are healthy but lack a racial instinct like a putrefying mould. There is only one effective means of combating this: to cut it out and dispose of it. . . .

If we Germans have any fatal flaw in our national character it is our tendency to be too forgetful. Although this flaw demonstrates our human decency and magnanimity, it does not always speak for our political insight or skill. We consider everybody to be as good-natured as ourselves. . . . But [German poet Friedrich Gottlieb] Klopstock gave us the good advice not to be too fair; our enemies were not noble enough to see the good side of our flaw.

If there is any situation where this advice is appropriate then it is vis-à-vis the Jews. Here a concession represents not only weakness but neglect of duty and a crime against the security of the state. For the Jews are only longing for the opportunity to reward our stupidity with blood and terror. It must never come to that. And one of the most effective measures to prevent it is a ruthless, cold toughness towards the destroyers of our nation, towards the people who caused the war, towards those who will profit from it if we lose, and therefore, necessarily towards those who will be its victims if we win. And so let me repeat again for the nth time:

1. The Jews are aiming to destroy us. They have provoked and brought about this war. They want to use it to destroy the German Reich and our people. This plan must be thwarted.
2. There is no difference between Jews. Every Jew is a sworn enemy of the German people. If he does not show his enmity towards us that is only through cow-

ardice or cunning and not because he is not an enemy at heart.
3. The Jews bear the guilt for every German soldier killed in this war. They have him on their conscience and they must therefore pay for it.
4. If someone wears the Jewish star then he is marked out as an enemy of the people. Anyone who maintains social contact with him belongs to him and must be considered and treated as a Jew. He deserves the contempt of the whole nation which he is abandoning in its darkest hour in order to be on the same side as those who hate it.
5. The Jews enjoy the protection of our enemies abroad. There is no further proof needed of their destructive role in our nation.
6. The Jews are the envoys of our enemies among us. Anyone who supports them has gone over to the enemy.
7. The Jews have no right to prance around among us on an equal footing. Wherever they seek to make their views known on the streets, in queues in front of shops, on public transport, they should be told to keep quiet not only because their views are fundamentally wrong but because they are Jews and have no right to a voice in the affairs of the community.
8. If the Jews try to appeal to your sympathy you should be aware that they are relying on your forgetfulness; show them at once that you have seen through them and punish them with your contempt.
9. A decent enemy deserves our magnanimity on defeat. But the Jew is not a decent enemy; he only pretends to be one.
10. The Jews are guilty of the war. They do not suffer an injustice through our treatment of them. They have more than earned it.

It is a matter for the government to deal with them. No one has the right to act off his own bat, but everyone has the duty to respect the state's measures against the Jews, to give them their support and not to allow themselves to be led astray about the threat posed by the Jews by any tricks or subterfuges they may use.

The security of the state requires this of us all.

Source: J. Noakes and G. Pridham, eds., *Nazism 1919–1945,* Volume 3: *Foreign Policy, War and Racial Extermination: A Documentary Reader,* revised ed. (Exeter, UK: University of Exeter Press, 2001), 515–518. Reprinted with permission of University of Exeter Press.

115. The U.S. Congress Repeals the 1939 Neutrality Act: House Joint Resolution No. 237, 17 November 1941

By late 1941, U.S. neutrality legislation had increasingly become a dead letter, as the U.S. government provided military assistance to Great Britain and other belligerents under the new Lend-Lease legislation. In October 1941, Franklin D. Roosevelt requested the repeal of those provisions still in effect, which forbade the arming of American merchant vessels. Less than a month before Pearl Harbor, in November 1941, the U.S. Congress granted his request.

House Joint Resolution No. 237 to repeal Sections 2, 3, and 6 of The Neutrality Act of 1939, and for other purposes.

SECTION I
Resolved by the Senate and House of Representatives of the U.S. of America in Congress assembled, that Section 2 of The Neutrality Act of 1939 (relating to commerce with states engaged in armed conflict), and Section 3 of such act (relating to combat area) are hereby repealed.

SECTION II
Section 6 of The Neutrality Act of 1939 (relating to the arming of American vessels) is hereby repealed; and during the unlimited national emergency, proclaimed by the President on May 27, 1941, the President is authorized, through such agency as he may designate, to arm, or to permit or cause to be armed, any American vessel as defined in such Act. The provision of Section 16 of the Criminal Code (relating to hands from armed vessels on clearing) shall not apply to any such vessel.

Source: Web site: ibiblio. Available at http://www.ibiblio.org/pha/policy/1941/411117b.html.

116. "The Deportation of Jews to the *Reichskommissariat Ostland*": German Gestapo Branch Office, Stuttgart, Directive to the *Landräte* and Police Chiefs of Württemburg, 18 November 1941

In late 1941, the German government began large-scale deportations eastward of Jews living in Germany and territories annexed from the former Austrian and Czechoslovak states. The authorities of the German province of Württemburg each received a "very urgent" directive from the regional Gestapo office in Stuttgart instructing them which Jews had been selected for deportation and how to organize their removal. The state was to confiscate all property and assets of the deportees.

I. Within the framework of the de-jewifying [*Entjudung*] of the whole of Europe, railway transports containing 1,000 Jews each are at present regularly leaving from Germany, the *Ostmark* [formerly Austria] and the Protectorate of Bohemia and Moravia for the *Reichskommissariat Ostland*. Württemburg and Hohenzollern are participating initially with a transport of 1,000 Jews which will leave Stuttgart on 1 December 1941.

II. Those Jews involved have already been selected and registered here. They were selected in accordance with Section 5 of the first supplementary decree of the Reich Citizenship Law of 14 November 1935.... The following were exempted:

1. Jews living in German-Jewish mixed marriages.
2. Jews of foreign nationality.
3. Jews over 65 years of age.

[However, these criteria were breached in individual cases.]

Those Jews scheduled for evacuation from your area are listed in appendix 1. You will be kept informed of alterations which are unavoidable as a result of the resettlement of the remaining Jews in Württemberg, which is continuing simultaneously, and on account of special circumstances, illness etc. I must emphasize that on no account may the number scheduled for your area be deviated from either upwards or downwards. Surplus Jews must be sent back to their previous locations. Absentees (through suicide etc.) must be reported immediately.

III. The train scheduled for transporting the Jews is timetabled to leave Stuttgart on 1 December 1941 between 8 and 9 o'clock.

The Jews who are to be evacuated from Stuttgart itself as well as from the country areas will be concentrated in a transit camp in the grounds of the former Reich Garden Show (Killesberg) in Stuttgart from 27 November onwards.

IV. Each person may take with them:

(a) Money up to 50 RM [reichsmarks] in Reich credit notes. This money will be supplied from here so in practice the Jews should not bring any money with them on their journey here.

(b) 1 or 2 cases (no bulky goods). This luggage must not weigh more than 50 kg.

(c) Bedding, consisting of 1–2 blankets, 2 sheets and 1 mattress for two people (but without a bolster).

(d) A complete set of clothing (particularly warm underwear and decent shoes).

(e) Food for 1–2 days. We have already seen to the further adequate provisioning of all participants in the transport.

(f) Crockery (a plate or pot with a spoon).

The following must not be taken: bonds, foreign exchange, savings books, etc. and valuables of all kinds (gold, silver, platinum with the exception of wedding rings), livestock.

Those ration books valid for the period after 1 December 1941 must be handed in to the local Food Office in return for a receipt. This receipt must be presented in the transit camp.

Work books must be withdrawn and handed over to the local Labour Office.

V. Before the groups which have been assembled for transportation in the various districts are handed over, the local police authority must carry out a thorough search for weapons, ammunition, explosives, poison, foreign exchange, jewellery, etc. Any property seized must be listed and handed over to the local finance office (see further Section VI).

VI. To prevent fraudulent transfers, the entire property of the Jews being deported will be confiscated by the police. I request that this measure is implemented. The Jews have already been sent, via the Jewish Cultural Association, the enclosed property declaration form in which they are obliged to provide a complete declaration of their assets and present the list to their town hall by 25.11.1941 at the latest.

The mayors must carry out sample inspections of the declarations and send them to the local Finance Office.

The entire assets of these Jews will be confiscated. The confiscation orders will be handed over to individuals in the transit camp. The liquidation will be carried out by the President of the Finance Office in Württemberg through the local Finance Offices. You are requested to liaise with them in connection with the sealing of the [Jews'] dwellings and other measures.

VII. Those Jews being evacuated have been informed of my orders today in the enclosed circular. This was done through the Jewish Cultural Association for the sake of administrative convenience and uniformity. In this communication every one of those Jews has been given a transport number which corresponds with the enclosed list. For the sake of convenience, therefore, I suggest that in the event of any queries, and when collecting the group together for transportation, these numbers should be used.

In view of the restricted number of available goods wagons, I request that you pay particular attention to ensuring that the amount of individuals' luggage is kept strictly within the allowance.

I have engaged the firm of Barr, Moering & Co. of Stuttgart to collect the rest of the luggage, some of which is heavy, for the whole area of Württemberg and Hohenzollern. In cooperation with the local authorities, it is responsible for collecting the luggage from the individual districts and transporting it to the station of departure. A representative of this firm will visit you shortly to discuss the procedure in detail.

In addition, I request that you ensure, possibly by employing a Jewish middle man, that a sufficient quantity of building equipment, tools, kitchen equipment for communal feeding, e.g., cauldrons, stoves, buckets, and first aid boxes are provided. For this purpose, the following rough proportions should be adhered to: one bucket for ten persons, one shovel or spade for ten persons, one pickaxe for ten persons, a sharp hatchet or axe for twenty persons, a saw for twenty persons, a stove with chimney and a tray for fifty persons, and a first aid box, a cauldron, and a sewing machine for a hundred persons, a large tool box for twenty persons. However, these materials should not be bought new.

VIII. Your task, therefore, is to collect the Jews together at the proper time, to secure their property in cooperation with the financial authorities, to seal their dwellings and if necessary appoint caretakers, search the Jews' persons and their luggage and, deploying an appropriate number of officials, to deliver the Jews on 27 or 28 November 1941 to the camp in Stuttgart (special instructions will be given concerning the exact time for their delivery to the camp). If the numbers of those involved in the transport to Stuttgart require special railway carriages you must ensure their provision. The transport leader (official) must present a detailed list in quadruplicate containing the transport numbers, the personal details, and the identity numbers.

Any costs arising will be met by the Jewish Cultural Association in Stuttgart and paid from a special fund. . . .

Source: J. Noakes and G. Pridham, eds., *Nazism 1919–1945*, Volume 3: *Foreign Policy, War and Racial Extermination: A Documentary Reader*, revised ed. (Exeter, UK: University of Exeter Press, 2001), 521–523. Reprinted with permission of University of Exeter Press.

117. Memorandum of the Japanese Government to the U.S. Government, Transmitted by Cable from Tokyo to Washington, 6 December 1941

On 6 December 1941, the Japanese government transmitted to its Washington embassy a memorandum breaking off diplomatic relations with the United States. American naval codebreakers intercepted and deciphered this document, which was supposed to be delivered in the near future to the U.S. government. The American government anticipated that, once war began, Japan would attack Western possessions in Asia but did not know precisely when or where this would occur.

1. The Government of Japan, prompted by a genuine desire to come to an amicable understanding with the Government of the United States in order that the two countries by their joint efforts may secure the peace of the Pacific area and thereby contribute toward the realization of world peace, has continued negotiations with the utmost sincerity since April last with the Government of the United States regarding the adjustment and advancement of Japanese-American relations and the stabilization of the Pacific area.

The Japanese Government has the honor to state frankly its views, concerning the claims the American Government has persistently maintained as well as the measures the United States and Great Britain have taken toward Japan during these eight months.

2. It is the immutable policy of the Japanese Government to insure the stability of East Asia and to promote world peace, and thereby to enable all nations to find each its proper place in the world.

Ever since the China Affair broke out owing to the failure on the part of China to comprehend Japan's true intentions, the Japanese Government has striven for the restoration of peace and it has consistently exerted its best efforts to prevent the extension of war-like disturbances. It was also to that end that in September last year Japan concluded the Tripartite Pact with Germany and Italy.

However, both the United States and Great Britain have resorted to every possible measure to assist the Chungking regime so as to obstruct the establishment of a general peace between Japan and China, interfering with Japan's constructive endeavours toward the stabilization of East Asia, exerting pressure on The Netherlands East Indies, or menacing

French Indo-China; they have attempted to frustrate Japan's aspiration to realize the ideal of common prosperity in co-operation with these regions. Furthermore, when Japan in accordance with its protocol with France took measures of joint defense of French Indo-China, both American and British Governments, willfully misinterpreting it as a threat to their own possessions and inducing the Netherlands government to follow suit, they enforced the assets freezing order, thus severing economic relations with Japan. While manifesting thus an obviously hostile attitude, these countries have strengthened their military preparations perfecting an encirclement of Japan, and have brought about a situation which endangers the very existence of the empire.

Nevertheless, to facilitate a speedy settlement, the Premier of Japan proposed, in August last, to meet the President of the United States for a discussion of important problems between the two countries covering the entire Pacific area. However, while accepting in principle the Japanese proposal, insisted that the meeting should take place after an agreement of view had been reached on fundamental and essential questions.

3. Subsequently, on September 25th the Japanese Government submitted a proposal based on the formula proposed by the American government, taking fully into consideration past American claims and also incorporating Japanese views. Repeated discussions proved of no avail in producing readily an agreement of view. The present cabinet, therefore, submitted a revised proposal, moderating still further the Japanese claims regarding the principal points of difficulty in the negotiation and endeavoured strenuously to reach a settlement. But the American Government, adhering steadfastly to its original proposal, failed

to display in the slightest degree a spirit of conciliation. The negotiation made no progress.

Thereupon, the Japanese Government, with a view to doing its utmost for averting a crisis in Japanese-American relations, submitted on November 20th still another proposal in order to arrive at an equitable solution of the more essential and urgent questions which, simplifying its previous proposal, stipulated the following points:

(1) The Governments of Japan and the United States undertake not to dispatch armed forces into any of the regions, excepting French Indo-China, in the Southeastern Asia and the Southern Pacific area.

(2) Both Governments shall cooperate with a view to securing the acquisition in the Netherlands East Indies of those goods and commodities of which the two countries are in need.

(3) Both Governments mutually undertake to restore commercial relations to those prevailing prior to the freezing of assets. The Government of the United States shall supply Japan the required quantity of oil.

(4) The Government of the United States undertakes not to resort to measures and actions prejudicial to the endeavours for the restoration of general peace between Japan and China.

(5) The Japanese Government undertakes to withdraw troops now stationed in French Indo-China upon either the restoration of peace between Japan and China or the establishment of an equitable peace in the Pacific area; and it is prepared to remove the Japanese troops in the southern part of French Indo-China to the northern part upon the conclusion of the present agreement.

As regards China, the Japanese Government, while expressing its readiness to accept the offer of the President of the United States to act as "Introducer" of peace between Japan and China as was previously suggested, asked for an undertaking on the part of the United States to do nothing prejudicial to the restoration of Sino-Japanese peace when the two parties have commenced direct negotiations.

The American government not only rejected the above-mentioned new proposal, but made known its intention to continue its aid to Chiang Kai-shek; and in spite of its suggestion mentioned above withdrew the offer of the President to act as the so-called "Introducer" of peace between Japan and China, pleading that time was not yet ripe for it. Finally, on November 26th, in an attitude to impose upon the Japanese government those principles it has persistently maintained, the American Government made a proposal to-

tally ignoring Japanese claims, which is a source of profound regret to the Japanese Government.

4. From the beginning of the present negotiation the Japanese Government has always maintained an attitude of fairness and moderation, and did its best to reach a settlement, for which it made all possible concessions often in spite of great difficulties.

As for the China question which constituted an important subject of the negotiation, the Japanese Government showed a most conciliatory attitude.

As for the principle of Non-Discrimination in International Commerce, advocated by the American Government, the Japanese Government expressed its desire to see the said principle applied throughout the world, and declared that along with the actual practice of this principle in the world, the Japanese Government would endeavor to apply the same in the Pacific area, including China, and made it clear that Japan had no intention of excluding from China economic activities of third powers pursued on an equitable basis.

Furthermore, as regards the question of withdrawing troops from French Indo-China, the Japanese Government even volunteered, as mentioned above, to carry out an immediate evacuation of troops from Southern French Indo-China as a measure of easing the situation.

It is presumed that the spirit of conciliation exhibited to the utmost degree by the Japanese Government in all these matters is fully appreciated by the American Government.

On the other hand, the American Government, always holding fast to theories in disregard of realities, and refusing to yield an inch on its impractical principles, caused undue delays in the negotiation. It is difficult to understand this attitude of the American Government and the Japanese Government desires to call the attention of the American Government especially to the following points:

1. The American Government advocates in the name of world peace those principles favorable to it and urges upon the Japanese Government the acceptance thereof. The peace of the world may be brought about only by discovering a mutually acceptable formula through recognition of the reality of the situation and mutual appreciation of one another's position.

An attitude such as ignores realities and imposes one's selfish views upon others will scarcely serve the purpose of facilitating the consummation of negotiations.

Of the various principles put forward by the American Government as a basis of the Japanese-American agreement, there are some which the Japanese Government is ready to accept in principle, but in view of the world's actual conditions, it seems only a Utopian ideal, on the part of the American government, to attempt to force their immediate adoption.

Again, the proposal to conclude a multilateral non-aggression pact between Japan, the United States, Great Britain, China, the Soviet Union, The Netherlands, and Thailand, which is patterned after the old concept of collective security, is far removed from the realities of East Asia.

The American proposal contains a stipulation which states: "Both governments will agree that no agreement, which either has concluded with any third powers, shall be interpreted by it in such a way as to conflict with the fundamental purpose of this agreement, the establishment and preservation of peace throughout the Pacific area." It is presumed that the above provision has been proposed with a view to restrain Japan from fulfilling its obligations under the Tripartite Pact when the United States participates in the war in Europe, and, as such, it cannot be accepted by the Japanese Government.

The American Government, obsessed with its own views and opinions, may be said to be scheming for the extension of the war. While it seeks, on the one hand, to secure its rear by stabilizing the Pacific area, it is engaged, on the other hand, in aiding Great Britain and preparing to attack, in the name of self-defense, Germany and Italy, two powers that are striving to establish a new order in Europe. Such a policy is totally at variance with the many principles upon which the American Government proposes to found the stability of the Pacific area through peaceful means.

3. Whereas the American Government, under the principles it rigidly upholds, objects to settling international issues through military pressure, it is exercising in conjunction with Great Britain and other nations pressure by economic power. Recourse to such pressure as a means of dealing with international relations should be condemned as it is at times more inhumane than military pressure.

4. It is impossible not to reach the conclusion that the American Government desires to maintain and strengthen, in collusion with Great Britain and other powers, its dominant position it has hitherto occupied not only in China but in other areas of East Asia. It is a fact of history that the countries of East Asia have for the past two hundred years or more been compelled to observe the status quo under the Anglo-American policy of imperialistic exploitation and to sacrifice themselves to the prosperity of the two nations. The Japanese Government cannot tolerate the perpetuation of such a situation since it directly runs counter to Japan's fundamental policy to enable all nations to enjoy each its proper place in the world.

The stipulation proposed by the American Government relative to French Indo-China is a good exemplification of the above-mentioned American policy. That the six countries—Japan, the United States, Great Britain, The Netherlands, China and Thailand—excepting France, should undertake among themselves to respect the territorial integrity and sovereignty of French Indo-China and equality of treatment in trade and commerce would be tantamount to placing that territory under the joint guarantee of the governments of those six countries. Apart from the fact that such a proposal totally ignores the position of France, it is unacceptable to the Japanese Government in that such an arrangement cannot but be considered as an extension to French Indo-China of a system similar to the Nine Power Treaty structure which is the chief factor responsible for the present predicament of East Asia.

5. All the items demanded of Japan by the American Government regarding China such as wholesale evacuation of troops or unconditional application of the principle of Non-Discrimination in International Commerce ignore the actual conditions of China, and are calculated to destroy Japan's position as the stabilizing factor of East Asia. The attitude of the American Government in demanding Japan not to support militarily, politically or economically any regime other than the regime at Chungking, disregarding thereby the existence of the Nanking Government, shatters the very basis of the present negotiation. This demand of the American Government falling, as it does, in line with its above-mentioned refusal to cease from aiding the Chungking regime, demonstrates clearly the intention of the American Government to obstruct the restoration of normal relations between Japan and China and the return of peace to East Asia.

5 [sic]. In brief, the American proposal contains certain acceptable items such as those concerning commerce, including the conclusion of a trade agreement, mutual removal of the freezing restrictions, and stabilization of the Yen and Dollar exchange, or the abolition of extraterritorial rights in China. On the other hand, however, the proposal in question ignores Japan's sacrifices in the four years of the China Affair, menaces the empire's existence itself and disparages its honour and prestige. Therefore, viewed in its entirety, the Japanese Government regrets that it cannot accept the proposal as a basis of negotiation.

6. The Japanese Government, in its desire for an early conclusion of the negotiation, proposed that simultaneously with the conclusion of the Japanese-American negotiation, agreements be signed with Great Britain and other interested countries. The proposal was accepted by the American Government. However, since the American government has made the proposal of November 26th as a result of frequent consultations with Great Britain, Australia, The Netherlands and Chungking, and presumably by catering to the wishes of the Chungking regime on the question of China, it must be

concluded that all these countries are at one with the United States in ignoring Japan's position.

"VERY IMPORTANT"
7. Obviously it is the intention of the American Government to conspire with Great Britain and other countries to obstruct Japan's efforts toward the establishment of peace through the creation of a New Order in East Asia, and especially to preserve Anglo-American rights and interests by keeping Japan and China at war. This intention has been revealed clearly during the course of the present negotiations. Thus, the earnest hope of the Japanese Government to adjust Japanese-American relations and to preserve and promote the peace of the Pacific through cooperation with the American Government has finally been lost.

The Japanese Government regrets to have to notify hereby the American Government that in view of the attitude of the American Government it cannot but consider that it is impossible to reach an agreement through further negotiations.

Source: United States, 79 Congress, 2nd Session, Joint Committee on the Pearl Harbor Attack, *Hearings,* 39 pts. (Washington, DC: U.S. Government Printing Office, 1946), Pt. 12: 239–245. Exhibits of Joint Committee, Exhibit No. 1, Intercepted Diplomatic Messages Sent by the Japanese Government between 1 July and 8 December 1941. Also available at http://ibiblio.org/pha/timeline/411206d.html.

118. President Franklin D. Roosevelt to Emperor Hirohito of Japan, 6 December 1941

As relations between the United States and Japan appeared to have reached an impasse, the State Department dispatched by cable an urgent message from Presiden Franklin D. Roosevelt to Emperor Hirohito of Japan, making one last appeal for peace.

Almost a century ago the President of the United States addressed to the Emperor of Japan a message extending an offer of friendship of the people of the United States to the people of Japan. That offer was accepted, and in the long period of unbroken peace and friendship which has followed, our respective nations, through the virtues of their peoples and the wisdom of their rulers, have prospered and have substantially helped humanity.

Only in situations of extraordinary importance to our two countries need I address to Your Majesty messages on matters of state. I feel I should now so address you because of the deep and far-reaching emergency which appears to be in formation.

Developments are occurring in the Pacific area which threaten to deprive each of our nations and all humanity of the beneficial influence of the long peace between our two countries. These developments contain tragic possibilities.

The people of the United States, believing in peace and in the right of nations to live and let live have eagerly watched the conversations between our two Governments during these past months. We have hoped for a termination of the present conflict between Japan and China. We have hoped that a peace of the Pacific could be consummated in such a way that nationalities of many diverse peoples could exist side by side without fear of invasion; that unbearable burdens of armaments could be lifted for them all; and that all peoples would resume commerce without discrimination against or in favor of any nation.

I am certain that it will be clear to Your Majesty, as it is to me, that in seeking these great objectives both Japan and the United States should agree to eliminate any form of military threat. This seems essential to the attainment of the high objectives.

More than a year ago Your Majesty's Government concluded an agreement with the Vichy Government by which five or six thousand Japanese troops were permitted to enter into Northern French Indochina for the protection of Japanese troops which were operating against China further north. And this Spring and Summer the Vichy Government permitted further Japanese military forces to enter into Southern French Indochina for the common defense of French Indochina. I think I am correct in saying that no attack has been made upon Indochina, nor that any has been contemplated.

During the past few weeks it has become clear to the world that Japanese military, naval and air forces have been sent to Southern Indochina in such large numbers as to create a reasonable doubt on the part of other nations that this continuing concentration in Indochina is not defensive in its character.

Because these continuing concentrations in Indochina have reached such large proportions and because they extend now to the southeast and the southwest corners of that Peninsula, it is only reasonable that the people of the Philippines, of the hundreds of Islands of the East Indies, of Malaya and of Thailand itself are asking themselves whether these forces of Japan are preparing or intending to make attack in one or more of these many directions.

I am sure that Your Majesty will understand that the fear of all these peoples is a legitimate fear in as much as it involves their peace and their national existence. I am sure that Your Majesty will understand why the people of the United States in such large numbers look askance at the establishment of military, naval and air bases manned and equipped so greatly as to constitute armed forces capable of measures of offense.

It is clear that a continuance of such a situation is unthinkable. None of the peoples whom I have spoken of above can sit either indefinitely or permanently on a keg of dynamite.

There is absolutely no thought on the part of the United States of invading Indochina if every Japanese soldier or sailor were to be withdrawn therefrom.

I think that we can obtain the same assurance from the Governments of the East Indies, the Governments of Malaya and the Government of Thailand. I would even undertake to ask for the same assurance on the part of the Government of China. Thus a withdrawal of the Japanese forces from Indochina would result in the assurance of peace throughout the whole of the South Pacific area.

I address myself to Your Majesty at this moment in the fervent hope that Your Majesty may, as I am doing, give thought in this definite emergency to ways of dispelling the dark clouds. I am confident that both of us, for the sake of the peoples not only of our own great countries but for the sake of humanity in neighboring territories, have a sacred duty to restore traditional amity and prevent further death and destruction in the world. FRANKLIN D. ROOSEVELT

Source: U.S. Department of State, Publication 1983, *Peace and War: United States Foreign Policy, 1931–1941* (Washington, DC: U.S. Government Printing Office, 1943), 828–830.

119. Memorandum of a Conversation, the Secretary of State with Nomura and Kurusu, 7 December 1941

On 7 December 1941, Secretary of State Cordell Hull had his final interview with Ambassadors Kurusu and Nomura, during which they delivered a lengthy memorandum from the Japanese government breaking off diplomatic relations. U.S. code-breakers had already intercepted this document. Since the U.S. government had already received the news of Pearl Harbor, the meeting was notably chilly.

The Japanese Ambassador asked for an appointment to see the Secretary at 1:00 P.M., but later telephoned and asked that the appointment be postponed to 1:45 as the Ambassador was not quite ready. The Ambassador and Mr. Kurusu arrived at the Department at 2:05 P.M. and were received by the Secretary at 2:20.

The Japanese Ambassador stated that he had been instructed to deliver at 1:00 P.M. the document which he handed the Secretary, but that he was sorry that he had been delayed owing to the need of more time to decode the message. The Secretary asked why he had specified one o'clock. The Ambassador replied that he did not know but that that was his instruction.

The Secretary said that anyway he was receiving the message at two o'clock.

After the Secretary had read two or three pages he asked the Ambassador whether this document was presented under instructions of the Japanese Government. The Ambassador replied that it was. The Secretary as soon as he had finished reading the document turned to the Japanese Ambassador and said,

"I must say that in all my conversations with you [the Japanese Ambassador] during the last nine months I have never uttered one word of untruth. This is borne out absolutely by the record. In all my fifty years of public service I have never seen a document that was more crowded with infamous falsehoods and distortions on a scale so huge that I never imagined until today that any Government on this planet was capable of uttering them."

The Ambassador and Mr. Kurusu then took their leave without making any comment.

Source: U.S. Department of State, *Foreign Relations of the United States: Japan, 1931–1941*, 2 vols. (Washington, DC: U.S. Government Printing Office, 1943), II: 830–837.

120. Draft Japanese Declaration of War on the United States, December 1941 (Not Delivered)

The Japanese decision to attack the American fleet without formally declaring war helped to convince U.S. leaders and the general public that their opponent's behavior was beyond the pale. The Japanese Foreign Office did in fact draft a declaration of war, composed in English, for the Japanese ambassador to hand to Secretary of State Cordell Hull, but Admiral Yamamoto's insistence upon delivering the war's first blow unannounced ensured it was never delivered.

Your Excellency:

I have the honour, under instructions from my Government, to inform Your Excellency that as the hostile measures taken by the United States have seriously jeopardized the security, and therefore existence, of Japan, they have been constrained to resort to measures of self-defense and consequently there now exists a state of war between the two countries.

I am also directed to leave with Your Excellency a copy of the Statement of our Government which sets forth their views concerning the rupture of our relations.

I avail myself of this opportunity to renew to Your Excellency the assurances of my highest consideration.

Statement of the Japanese Government

Being earnestly desirous of the peace of the Pacific, the Japanese Government have consistently pursued a policy of promoting friendly relations with Great Britain and the United States. These relations, however, have suffered a progressive deterioration in recent years largely through the unresponsive attitude of these Powers who have failed to understand the realities of the situation prevailing in our part of the world.

Our cardinal policy aims at inaugurating a new order in Greater East Asia throughout which we are striving to ensure and enhance a common prosperity. It is essentially a policy of peace designed to cultivate the friendship among, and increase the welfare of, the peoples of this vast region. It is a policy calculated to serve the interests of these peoples, redounding ultimately to the benefit of the whole mankind.

Great Britain and the United States, however, have willfully misunderstood our aims and aspirations and, in collusion with other hostile countries, have endeavoured, openly and covertly, to oppose and obstruct the peaceful execution of our constructive policy. The Anglo-Saxon Powers have not scrupled to render active assistances to the Chungking régime, a mere pawn in their game of Imperialist politics, prolonging the latter's futile struggle to the untold misery of China's teeming millions who are becoming increasingly anxious for peace with Japan. By aiding the Chungking régime these Powers have greatly impeded the restoration of tranquility in China and by thus opposing our efforts for a speedy settlement of the China Affair, they have more than forfeited the good will of our people. Anxious, however, to maintain amicable relations with them, Japan has, displaying utmost patience, persevered in the face of provocations hoping that they will reconsider and repair their attitude. It is highly regrettable that these Powers should have failed to respond to our policy and should have, on the contrary, resorted to unfriendly measures, some of them very severe and stringent, vis-à-vis this country.

In these circumstances, Japan concluded the Tripartite Pact with Germany and Italy; two leading Powers of Europe who, fully sharing our views, have pledged their willing cooperation in establishing a new order in Greater East Asia. But our association with the Axis Powers has added yet another cause of alienation in our relations with the so-called Democratic Powers who have begun to entertain unwarranted misapprehensions regarding our policy and purposes, despite our repeated assurances that we seek no quarrel with them. Far from harbouring any aggressive design, Japan was, as stated above, bent upon the peaceful initiation of an era of common prosperity throughout the Greater East Asia.

It will be recalled that in August last year Japanese forces were dispatched to Northern French Indo-China in connection with the prosecution of the China Affair. Later on, in summer this year, our forces made a peaceful entry into the Southern region in order to cope with the grave situation developing in the South-western Pacific, due to the rapid augmentation of military measures by the United States, Great Britain and her allies and associates. These Powers chose to regard our peaceful advance into Southern French Indo-China as a menace to their territories and froze our assets in their respective countries, a measure tantamount to a wholesale rupture of economic relations. They have since even gone the length of establishing encircling positions against Japan which, creating an unprecedented tension in the Pacific, has greatly exacerbated their relations with us. The increasing pressure they have brought to bear upon Japan has as its aim no other than our economic strangulation. Sometimes, economic warfare is admittedly more cruel and disastrous than an open resort to arms. Thus the ruthless measures of economic attrition now directed against us constitute a really serious threat, affecting as they deeply do, the very existence of our Empire. In other words, we, as a nation, are faced with the question of life and death. We could not acquiesce in these hostile measures, as it would spell the decline and downfall of our nation.

Finding ourselves in such a predicament, we still patiently endeavoured to find a way out of it. The negotiations at Washington are a case in point.

Our Government have, since April last, conducted protracted negotiations with the American Government with a view to bringing about a friendly and fundamental adjustment of the Japanese-American relations. We were afraid that the steady deterioration of our relations would, if left without a timely check, drift toward an inevitable catastrophe, an awful eventuality entailing immense suffering not only on the countries in the Pacific basin but on the entire mankind as well. We were convinced that, good will animating both sides, there should be no question that is not amenable to amicable settlement. We, therefore, exercised utmost patience and, in the spirit of compromise, proposed many a formula, often involving great sacrifices on our part, to meet the desires of the American Government which were, we much regret to say, not always reasonable nor practicable. In fact, we went to the last possible limit of concessions, short of compromising the honour and prestige as a great Power, in order to satisfy the United States. But the latter has persistently maintained a very rigid attitude, making not the slightest gesture to respond to our sincere efforts to reach a friendly settlement. In short, the American Government were singularly lacking in the spirit of mutual accommodation which is indispensable to a successful conclusion of any international negotiations. They maintained, throughout the course of negotiations lasting more than seven months, their original position from which they stubbornly refused to withdraw even an inch. Thus, it has finally come to the present pass where it can no longer serve any useful purpose by continuing further negotiations. Our untiring and unsparing efforts have been frustrated through the uncompromising attitude of the American Government and we have now been forced, although with great reluctance, to abandon the negotiations and, with that, renounce our cherished desire to come to a friendly understanding with the United States.

With the breakdown of the negotiations, we have thus been led to give up, at last and finally, the hope to find an escape, through peaceful means, from our predicament. At the same time, the hostile ring encircling our Empire is being steadily strengthened day after day, gravely threatening our safety and security. The economic warfare, in its most relentless form, is also being prosecuted with renewed energy against this country. In short, the concerted pressure of the hostile Powers is such that our national existence is now in serious jeopardy. Standing at the cross-roads of her destiny, Japan decided to defend her prime right of existence, a course that offered the only possible way of survival. Our patience finally exhausted and our destiny at stake, the nation has risen, as one man, to meet the challenge. Steeped in the conviction that right always will triumph, our hundred million peoples have girt on the sword of justice, anxious to defend the fatherland and eager to vindicate our glorious cause.

Source: Akira Iriye, *Pearl Harbor and the Coming of the Pacific War: A Brief History with Documents and Essays* (Boston: Bedford/St. Martin's, 1999), 105–108. Originally published in *This Is Yomiuri* (Tokyo: *Yomiuri Shimbun*, 1998), 220–221.

121. Adolf Hitler, Secret "Night-and-Fog Decree" on the Punishment of Offenders in Occupied Territory, 7 December 1941

Resistance efforts were launched in all territories occupied by the German military. Guerrilla and partisan activities were particularly widespread in the Soviet Union. Even when they were not so effective, at the very least such undertakings had considerable nuisance value, and they were also a propaganda liability. In December 1941, Adolf Hitler ordered that in principle the German military should employ the death penalty to punish all such offenses.

The Fuehrer and Supreme Commander of the Armed Forces

Directives for the prosecution of offences committed within the occupied territories against the German State or the occupying power, of December 7th, 1941.

Within the occupied territories, communistic elements and other circles hostile to Germany have increased their efforts against the German State and the occupying powers since the Russian campaign started. The amount and the danger of these machinations oblige us to take severe measures as a deterrent. First of all the following directives are to be applied:

I. Within the occupied territories, the adequate punishment for offences committed against the German State or the occupying power which endanger their security or a state of readiness is on principle the death penalty.

II. The offences listed in paragraph I as a rule are to be dealt with in the occupied countries only if it is probable that sentence of death will be passed upon the offender, at least the principal offender, and if the trial and the execution can be completed in a very short time. Otherwise the offenders, at least the principal offenders, are to be taken to Germany.

III. Prisoners taken to Germany are subjected to military procedure only if particular military interests require this. In case German or foreign authorities inquire about such prisoners, they are to be told that they were arrested, but that the proceedings do not allow any further information.

IV. The Commanders in the occupied territories and the Court authorities within the framework of their jurisdiction, are personally responsible for the observance of this decree.

V. The Chief of the High Command of the Armed Forces determines in which occupied territories this decree is to be applied. He is authorized to explain and to issue executive orders and supplements. The Reich Minister of Justice will issue executive orders within his own jurisdiction.

Source: United States, Office of United States Chief of Counsel for Prosecution of Axis Criminality, *Nazi Conspiracy and Aggression,* 8 vols. and 2 suppl. vols. (Washington, DC: U.S. Government Printing Office, 1946–1948), VII: 873–874 (Doc. No. L-90).

122. "A Date Which Will Live in Infamy": Franklin D. Roosevelt, Address to the U.S. Congress, 8 December 1941

On 8 December 1941, in an address which, though short, was one of the most famous speeches he ever gave, President Franklin D. Roosevelt officially informed Congress of the Japanese attack on Pearl Harbor. Although Japan's behavior put the United States in a de facto state of war, he sought an official declaration of hostilities from Congress. With the exception of one dissenting vote from Congresswoman Jeannette Rankin of Montana, both the Senate and the House voted unanimously in favor of his request.

Yesterday, December 7, 1941—a date which will live in infamy—the United States of America was suddenly and deliberately attacked by naval and air forces of the Empire of Japan.

The United States was at peace with that Nation and, at the solicitation of Japan, was still in conversation with its Government and its Emperor looking toward the maintenance of peace in the Pacific. Indeed, one hour after Japanese air squadrons had commenced bombing in Oahu, the Japanese Ambassador to the United States and his colleague delivered to the Secretary of State a formal reply to a recent American message. While this reply stated that it seemed useless to continue the existing diplomatic negotiations, it contained no threat or hint of war or armed attack.

It will be recorded that the distance of Hawaii from Japan makes it obvious that the attack was deliberately planned many days or even weeks ago. During the intervening time the Japanese Government has deliberately sought to deceive the United States by false statements and expressions of hope for continued peace.

The attack yesterday on the Hawaiian Islands has caused severe damage to American naval and military forces. Very many American lives have been lost. In addition American ships have been reported torpedoed on the high seas between San Francisco and Honolulu.

Yesterday the Japanese Government also launched an attack against Malaya.

Last night Japanese forces attacked Hong Kong.

Last night Japanese forces attacked Guam.

Last night Japanese forces attacked the Philippine Islands.

Last night the Japanese attacked Wake Island.

This morning the Japanese attacked Midway Island.

Japan has, therefore, undertaken a surprise offensive extending throughout the Pacific area. The facts of yesterday speak for themselves. The people of the United States have already formed their opinions and well understand the implications to the very life and safety of our Nation.

As Commander in Chief of the Army and Navy I have directed that all measures be taken for our defense.

Always will we remember the character of the onslaught against us.

No matter how long it may take us to overcome this premeditated invasion, the American people in their righteous might will win through to absolute victory. I believe I interpret the will of the Congress and of the people when I assert that we will not only defend ourselves to the uttermost but will make very certain that this form of treachery shall never endanger us again.

Hostilities exist. There is no blinking at the fact that our people, our territory, and our interests are in grave danger.

With confidence in our armed forces—with the unbounded determination of our people—we will gain the inevitable triumph—so help us God.

I ask that the Congress declare that since the unprovoked and dastardly attack by Japan on Sunday, December 7, a state of war has existed between the United States and the Japanese Empire.

Source: U.S., Department of State, *Peace and War: United States Foreign Policy, 1931–1941* (Washington, DC: U.S. Government Printing Office, 1943), 838–839.

123. China Declares War on Japan, Germany, and Italy: Statement of the Chinese Government, 9 December 1941

An undeclared state of war existed between China and Japan from 7 July 1937 onward. China did not, however, formally declare war on Japan until two days after Pearl Harbor, when, following the example of the United States, the Guomindang government declared that it was at war not just with Japan but also with Germany and Italy. By taking this action China undoubtedly hoped to enhance her chances of receiving assistance from the United States and the other Allied powers.

Japan's national policy has always aimed at the domination of Asia and mastery of the Pacific. For more than four years China has resolutely resisted Japan's aggression, regardless of suffering and sacrifice, in order not only to maintain her national independence and freedom but also to uphold international law and justice and to promote world peace and human happiness.

China is a peace-loving nation. In taking up arms in self-defense, China entertained the hope that Japan might yet realise the futility of her plans of conquest. Throughout the struggle all the other powers have shown the utmost forbearance likewise in the hope that Japan might one day repent and mend her ways in the interest of peace in the entire Pacific region.

Unfortunately Japan's aggressive capacities prove to be incorrigible. After her long and fruitless attempt to conquer China, Japan, far from showing any signs of penitence, has treacherously launched an attack on China's friends, the United States and Great Britain, thus extending the theater of her aggressive activities and making herself the arch-enemy of justice and world peace.

This latest act of aggression on the part of Japan lays bare her insatiable ambitions and has created a situation that no nation which believes in international good faith and human decency can tolerate.

The Chinese Government hereby formally declares war on Japan. The Chinese Government further declares that all treaties, conventions, agreements and contracts regarding relations between China and Japan are and remain null and void.

The Chinese Government's Declaration of War on Germany and Italy

Since the conclusion of the Tripartite Pact of September 1940, Germany, Italy, and Japan have unmistakably banded themselves into a block of aggressor states working closely together to carry out their common program of world conquest and domination. To demonstrate their solidarity Germany and Italy successively accorded recognition to Japan's puppet regimes in northeastern China and at Nanking. As a consequence, China severed her diplomatic relations with Germany and Italy last July. Now the Axis powers have extended the theater of their aggressive activities and thrown the whole Pacific region into turmoil, making themselves the enemies of international justice and world civilization.

This state of affairs can no longer be tolerated by the Chinese Government and people. The Chinese Government hereby declares that as from midnight, December 9, 1941, a state of war exists between China and Germany and between China and Italy. The Chinese Government further declares that all treaties, conventions, agreements, and contracts regarding relations between China and Germany and between China and Italy are and remain null and void.

Source: Contemporary China, Vol. 1, no. 15, 15 December 1941. Web site: ibiblio. Available at www.ibiblio.org/pha/policy/1941/411209b.html.

124. German Declaration of War with the United States: Press Release of the U.S. Department of State, 11 December 1941

Immediately after Pearl Harbor, in cables intercepted by Allied cryptographers, Japan urgently requested both the German and Italian governments to declare war on the United States. Four days after Pearl Harbor, both Axis powers did so. The ranking German diplomat in Washington delivered a formal declaration of war to the United States, a copy of which the German Foreign Office had already presented to the ranking U.S. diplomat left in Berlin. The State Department issued a statement giving the text of the German note in a press release that also described the circumstances of its delivery.

MR. CHARGÉ D'AFFAIRES:

The Government of the United States having violated in the most flagrant manner and in ever increasing measure all rules of neutrality in favor of the adversaries of Germany and having continually been guilty of the most severe provocations toward Germany ever since the outbreak of the European war, provoked by the British declaration of war against Germany on September 3, 1939, has finally resorted to open military acts of aggression.

On September 11, 1941, the President of the United States publicly declared that he had ordered the American Navy and Air Force to shoot on sight at any German war vessel. In his speech of October 27, 1941, he once more expressly affirmed that this order was in force. Acting under this order, vessels of the American Navy, since early September 1941, have systematically attacked German naval forces. Thus, American destroyers, as for instance the Greer, the Kearney and the Reuben James, have opened fire on German sub-marines according to plan. The Secretary of the American Navy, Mr. Knox, himself confirmed that American destroyers attacked German submarines.

Furthermore, the naval forces of the United States, under order of their Government and contrary to international law have treated and seized German merchant vessels on the high seas as enemy ships.

The German Government therefore establishes the following facts:

Although Germany on her part has strictly adhered to the rules of international law in her relations with the United States during every period of the present war, the Government of the United States from initial violations of neutrality has finally proceeded to open acts of war against Germany. The Government of the United States has thereby virtually created a state of war.

The German Government, consequently, discontinues diplomatic relations with the United States of America and declares that under these circumstances brought about by President Roosevelt Germany too, as from today, considers herself as being in a state of war with the United States of America.

Accept, Mr. Chargé d'Affaires, the expression of my high consideration.

December 11, 1941.

RIBBENTROP.

Source: Department of State Bulletin, 13 December 1941 (Washington, DC: U.S. Government Printing Office, 1941).

125. Admiral Yamamoto Isoroku to Admiral Takahashi Sankichi, 19 December 1941

A few days after Pearl Harbor, Admiral Yamamoto described the operation to an eminent colleague, retired Admiral Takahashi Sankichi, a previous naval commander in chief, who had written him a letter of congratulations. He was wrong on one point, that a midget submarine had sunk a battleship unaided, but nonetheless had good reason to feel satisfaction. Yamamoto obviously took great pride in the successful implementation of the strategic plan for which he had argued long and hard in the face of strong opposition.

It was my great honor to have been given your excellency's congratulatory letter upon our early victory in the war. But I think much could not have been done unless the traditional spirit of the Imperial Navy, which my preceding Commanders-in-Chief, including your excellency, had long built up, was fully displayed to save our country's crisis. I think I owe you very much in this respect.

The plan of launching a surprise attack on Pearl Harbor at the outset of a war to give a fatal blow on the enemy fleet was decided in December of last year, when the fleet strategy was revised. Since then, everything possible had been studied or tried to make it possible. Especially in the Nagumo force, which actually undertook the attack, those concerned from Nagumo down to the men exerted themselves to make the plan possible; it was not before the fall that aerial torpedoing in shallow waters of only 10-odd meters was made possible with the great help of the technicians concerned, and it was only in last August and September that the technique of horizontal bombing had been improved so that one hit might be expected from nine attacking bombers. Until then, it had made little progress from the days when your excellency took command of a carrier division.

What made me worry more than anything, however, was the fact that the time of our going to war was called off by one month, a fact which pressed me with intensified fear that refueling in the northern route, the only possible route to take, would no longer be possible to determine the fate of the operation.

As it turned out, however, I should say we were blessed by the War God, since a wide high pressure zone, the last one appearing in that district in this year, prevailed in the district extending as long as 2,000 miles. It was the first such phenomenon since 1928, which enabled refueling at sea. (Though a detailed report on this point is not yet available, I conclude as above.)

Such good luck, together with negligence on the part of the arrogant enemy, enabled us to launch a successful surprise attack. Especially of note is the fact that the actual hit rate of aerial torpedoing and bombing was upped 50 percent compared with that of training. I can't help but conclude that such an achievement was beyond the reach of human beings, and the loyal fliers must have been inspired by the soul of the Emperor, who graciously worried about the outcome of this attempt. I am deeply impressed by this development.

Some of the above apparently should be classed as "confidential," but I dared to write them, believing that you must be glad to hear them, as your excellency, once as C-in-C of the Combined Fleet and also as CO of a carrier division, exerted yourself to improve the skill of the Navy to the present level.

I cannot understand, from the viewpoint of common sense, not to speak of the strategic point of view, why the American Fleet made such a movement. Such a tragic fate ought to have been theirs, since they either made light of our strength and ability or lacked ability to make a correct strategic judgment.

Be that as it may, least expected was the fact that 51 medium land-bombers launched a successful attack on a fully protected enemy fleet without any help from a surface force of fighters, and sustained a minor loss of only three bombers, and even those were shot down after releasing a torpedo. I believe this fact should be taken into serious consideration in planning future war preparations.

On the other hand, I don't think it is time to tell the full account of the midget submarines which penetrated the harbor, but at least it is certain that a radio dispatch saying "successful surprise attack" was received from one of them and also that a battleship was sunk during a time when there was no aerial attack. When thinking of the fact that those daring young men, including young officers who had graduated from the Naval Academy only less than one year before, penetrated an enemy base in spite of darkness and accomplished such a success, I think I should not say such a big word that the youngsters in these days are not a match to. . . . This is another point in which I was deeply impressed by this operation.

I well realize that it will be long before we reach a successful conclusion of the war and there are numerous difficulties lying ahead of us. But, as mentioned, the burning spirit and the skill of those young officers and others are worthy of appreciation and respect. Therefore, I am now thinking that we may be able to meet His Majesty's wish when we exert ourselves to fulfill our mission. . . .

Source: Donald M. Goldstein and Katherine V. Dillon, *The Pearl Harbor Papers: Inside the Japanese Plans* (Washington, DC: Brassey's, 1993), 120–121. Reprinted with permission of Brassey's.

126. Altiero Spinelli and Ernesto Rossi, The Ventotene Manifesto: Towards a Free and United Europe: A Draft Manifesto, 1941

Throughout Europe, the outbreak of war led liberals to turn to the postwar integration of Europe, a measure they now supported as the only means of avoiding future destructive conflicts. The Italian democratic socialists Altiero Spinelli and Ernesto Rossi wrote this manifesto in 1941, while interned on the island of Ventotene. It was initially circulated in mimeographed form, and published clandestinely in Rome in January 1944. This publication also included two lengthy essays by Spinelli, "The United States of Europe and the Various Political Tendencies," and "Marxist Politics and Federalist Politics." This manifesto was regarded as one of the seminal texts that helped to bring about the creation of the European Coal and Steel Community and, eventually, the European Union. It also anticipated the postwar European welfare states—non-Communist and democratic but nonetheless characterized by a substantial element of government direction and control for the general good.

I.

The Crisis of Modern Civilization

Modern civilization has taken the principle of freedom as its basis, a principle which holds that man must not be a mere instrument to be used by others but an autonomous centre of life. With this code at hand, all those aspects of society that have not respected this principle have been placed on trial, a great historical trial.

The equal right of all nations to organize themselves into independent States has been established. Every people, defined by its ethnic, geographical, linguistic and historical characteristics, was expected to find the instrument best suited to its needs within a State organization created according to its own specific concept of political life, and with no outside intervention. The ideology of national independence was a powerful stimulus to progress. It helped overcome narrow-minded parochialism and created a much wider feeling of solidarity against foreign oppression. It eliminated many obstacles hindering the free movement of people and goods. Within the territory of each new State, it brought the institutions and systems of the more advanced societies to more backward ones. But with this ideology came the seeds of capitalist imperialism which our own generation has seen mushroom to the point where totalitarian States have grown up and world wars have been unleashed.

Thus the nation is no longer viewed as the historical product of co-existence between men who, as the result of a lengthy historical process, have acquired greater unity in their customs and aspirations and who see their State as being the most effective means of organizing collective life within the context of all human society. Rather the nation has become a divine entity, an organism which must only consider its own existence, its own development, without the least regard for the damage that others may suffer from this. The absolute sovereignty of national States has led to the desire of each of them to dominate, since each feels threatened by the strength of the others, and considers that its "living space" should include increasingly vast territories that give it the right to free movement and provide self-sustenance without needing to rely on others. This desire to dominate cannot be placated except by the hegemony of the strongest State over all the others.

As a consequence of this, from being the guardian of citizens' freedom, the State has been turned into a master of vassals bound into servitude, and has all the powers it needs to achieve the maximum war-efficiency. Even during peacetime, considered to be pauses during which to prepare for subsequent, inevitable wars, the will of the military class now holds sway over the will of the civilian class in many countries, making it increasingly difficult to operate free political systems. Schools, science, production, administrative bodies are mainly directed towards increasing military strength. Women are considered merely as producers of soldiers and are rewarded with the same criteria as prolific cattle. From the very earliest age, children are taught to handle weapons and hate foreigners. Individual freedom is reduced to nothing since everyone is part of the military establishment and constantly called on to serve in the armed forces. Repeated wars force men to abandon families, jobs, property, and even lay down their lives for goals, the value of which no one really understands. It takes just a few days to destroy the results of decades of common effort to increase the general well-being.

Totalitarian States are precisely those which have unified all their forces in the most coherent way, by implementing the greatest possible degree of centralization and autarky. They have thus shown themselves to be the bodies most suited to the current international environment. It only needs one nation to take one step towards more accentuated totalitarianism for the others to follow suit, dragged down the same groove by their will to survive.

The equal right of all citizens to participate in the process of determining the State's will is well-established. This process should have been the synthesis of the freely expressed and changing economic and ideological needs of all social classes. A political organization of this kind made it possible to correct or at least to minimize many of the most strident injustices inherited from previous regimes. But freedom of the press, freedom of assembly, and the steady extension of suffrage, made it increasingly difficult to defend old privileges, while maintaining a representative system of government. Bit by bit the penniless learned to use these instruments to fight for the rights acquired by the privileged classes. Taxes on unearned income and inheritances, higher taxes levied on larger incomes, tax exemptions for low incomes and essential goods, free public schooling, greater social security spending, land reforms, inspection of factories and manufacturing plants were all achievements that threatened the privileged classes in their well-fortified citadels.

Even the privileged classes who agreed with equality in political rights, could not accept the fact that the underprivileged could use it to achieve a de facto equality that would have created a very real freedom with a very concrete content. When the threat became all too serious at the end of the First World War, it was only natural that these privileged classes should have warmly welcomed and supported the rise of dictatorships that removed their adversaries legislative weapons.

Moreover, the creation of huge industrial, banking conglomerates and trades unions representing whole armies of workers gave rise to forces (unions, employers and financiers) lobbying the government to give them the policies which most clearly favoured their particular interests. This threatened to dissolve the State into countless economic fiefdoms, each bitterly opposed to the others. Liberal and democratic systems increasingly lost their prestige by becoming the tools that these groups will always resort to in order to exploit all of society even more. In this way, the conviction grew up that only a totalitarian State, in which individual liberties were abolished, could somehow resolve the conflicts of interest that existing political institutions were unable to control. Subsequently, in fact, totalitarian regimes consolidated the position of the various social categories at the levels they had gradually achieved. By using the police to control every aspect of each citizen's life, and by violently silencing all dissenting voices, these regimes barred all legal possibility of further correction in the state of affairs. This consolidated the existence of a thoroughly parasitic class of absentee landowners and rentiers who contribute to social productivity only by cutting the coupons off their bonds. It consolidated the position of monopoly holders and the chain stores who exploit the consumers and cause small savers' money to vanish. It consolidated the plutocrats hidden behind the scenes who pull the politicians' strings and run the State machine for their own, exclusive advantage, under the guise of higher national interests. The colossal fortunes of a very few people have been preserved, as has the poverty of the masses, excluded from the enjoyment of the fruits of modern culture. In other words an economic regime has substantially been preserved in which material resources and labour, which ought to be directed to the satisfaction of fundamental needs for the development of essential human energies, are instead channelled towards the satisfaction of the most futile wishes of those capable of paying the highest prices. It is an economic regime in which, through the right of inheritance, the power of money is perpetuated in the same class, and is transformed into a privilege that in no way corresponds to the social value of the services actually rendered. The field of proletarian possibilities is so restricted that workers are often forced to accept exploitation by anyone who offers a job in order to make a living.

In order to keep the working classes immobilized and subjugated, the trade unions, once free organizations of struggle, run by individuals who enjoyed the trust of their members, have been turned into institutions for police surveillance run by employees chosen by the ruling class and responsible only to them. Where improvements are made in this economic regime, they are always solely dictated by military needs which have merged with the reactionary aspirations of the privileged classes in giving rise to and consolidating totalitarian States.

The permanent value of the spirit of criticism has been asserted against authoritarian dogmatism. Everything that is affirmed must prove its worth or disappear. The greatest achievements of human society in every field are due to the scientific method that lies behind this unfettered approach. But this spiritual freedom has not survived the crisis created by totalitarian States. New dogmas to be accepted as articles of faith or simply hypocritically are advancing in all fields of knowledge.

Although nobody knows what a race is, and the most elementary understanding of history brings home the absurdity of the statement, physiologists are asked to believe, demonstrate and even persuade us that people belong to a chosen race, merely because imperialism needs this myth to stir the masses to hate and pride. The most self-evident concepts of economic science have to be treated as anathema so as to enable autarchic policy, trade balance and other old chestnuts of mercantilism to be presented as extraordinary discoveries of our times. Because of the economic interdependence of the entire world, the living space required by any people which wants to maintain a living standard consistent with modern civilization can only be the entire world. But the pseudo-science of geopolitics has been created in an attempt to prove the soundness of theories about living space and to provide a theoretical cloak to the imperialist desire to dominate.

Essential historical facts are falsified, in the interests of the ruling classes. Libraries and bookshops are purged of all works not considered to be orthodox. The shadows of obscurantism once more threaten to suffocate the human spirit. The social ethic of freedom and equality has itself been undermined. Men are no longer considered free citizens who can use the State to achieve collective goals. They are, instead, servants of the State, which decides what their goals must be, and the will of those who hold power becomes the will of the State. Men are no longer subjects with civil rights, but are instead arranged hierarchically and are expected to obey their superiors without argument, the hierarchy culminating in a suitably deified leader. The regime based on castes is reborn from its own ashes, as bullying as it was before.

After triumphing in a series of countries, this reactionary, totalitarian civilization, has finally found in Nazi Germany the power considered strong enough to take the last step. After meticulous preparation, boldly and unscrupulously exploiting the rivalries, egoism and stupidity of others, dragging in its path other European vassal States, primarily Italy, and allying itself with Japan, which follows the very same goals in Asia, Nazi Germany has launched itself on the task of crushing other countries. Its victory would mean the definitive consolidation of totalitarianism in the world. All its characteristics would be exasperated to the utmost degree, and progressive forces would be condemned for many years to the role of simple negative opposition.

The traditional arrogance and intransigence of the German military classes can give us an idea of the nature of their dominance after victory in war. The victorious Germans might even concede a façade of generosity towards other European peoples, formally respecting their territories and their political institutions, and thus be able to command while at the same time satisfying the false patriotic sentiments of those who count the colour of the flag flying at the country's borders and the nationality of prominent politicians as being the major considerations and who fail to appreciate the significance of power relationships and the real content of the State's institutions. However camouflaged, the reality is always the same: a new division of humanity into Spartans and Helots. Even a compromise solution between the two warring sides would be one more step forward for totalitarianism. All those countries which managed to escape Germany's grasp would be forced to adopt the very same forms of political organization to be adequately prepared for the continuation of hostilities.

But while Hitler's Germany has managed to chop down the smaller States one by one, this has forced increasingly powerful forces to join battle. The courageous fighting spirit of Great Britain, even at that most critical moment when it was left to face the enemy alone, had the effect that the Germans came up against the brave resistence of the Russian Army, and gave America the time it needed to mobilize its endless productive resources. This struggle against German imperialism is closely linked to the Chinese people's struggles against Japanese imperialism.

Huge masses of men and wealth are already drawn up against totalitarian powers whose strength has already reached its peak and can now only gradually consume itself. The forces that oppose them have, on the other hand, already survived the worst and their strength is increasing.

With every day that passes, the war the Allies are fighting rekindles the yearning for freedom, even in those countries which were subjected to violence and who lost their way as a result of the blow they received. It has even rekindled this yearning among the peoples in the Axis countries who realize they have been dragged down into a desperate situation, simply to satisfy their rulers' lust for power.

The slow process which led huge masses of men to be meekly shaped by the new regime, who adjusted to it and even contributed to its consolidation, has been halted and the reverse process has started. All the progressive forces can be found in this huge wave, which is slowly gathering momentum: the most enlightened groups of the working classes who have not let themselves be swayed, either by terror or by flattery, from their ambition to achieve a better standard of living, the sharpest members of the intellectual classes, offended by the degradation to which intelligence is subjected, entrepreneurs who, wanting to undertake new initiatives, want to free themselves of the trappings of bureaucracy and national autarky, that bog down all their efforts, and, finally, all those who, with an innate sense of dignity, will not bend one inch when faced with the humiliation of servitude.

Today, the salvation of our civilization is entrusted to these forces.

II.

Post-War Tasks: European Unity

Germany's defeat would not automatically lead to the reorganization of Europe in accordance with our ideal of civilization. In the brief, intense period of general crisis (when the States will lie broken, when the masses will be anxiously waiting for a new message, like molten matter, burning, and easily shaped into new moulds capable of accommodating the guidance of serious internationalist minded men), the most privileged classes in the old national systems will attempt, by underhand or violent methods, to dampen the wave of internationalist feelings and passions and will ostentatiously begin to reconstruct the old State institutions. Most probably, the British leaders, perhaps in agreement with the Americans, will try to push things in this direction, in order to restore balance-of-power politics, in the apparent immediate interests of their empires.

All the reactionary forces can feel the house is creaking around them and are now trying to save their skins: the conservative forces, the administrators of the major institutions of the nation States, the top-ranking officers in the armed forces including, where they still exist, the monarchies, the monopoly capitalist groups whose profits are linked to the fortunes of States, the big landowners and the ecclesiastical hierarchy, whose parasitical income is only guaranteed in a stable, conservative society and, in their wake, the countless band of people who depend on them or who are simply blinded by their traditional power. If the house were to collapse, they would suddenly be deprived of all the privileges they have enjoyed up to now, and would be exposed to the assault of the progressive forces.

The Revolutionary Situation: Old and New Trends

The fall of the totalitarian regimes will, in the feelings of entire populations, mean the coming of "freedom"; all restrictions will disappear and, automatically, very wide freedom of speech and assembly will reign supreme. It will be the triumph of democratic beliefs. These tendencies have countless shades and nuances, stretching from very conservative liberalism to socialism and anarchy. These beliefs place their trust in the "spontaneous generation" of events and institutions and the absolute goodness of drives originating among the grass roots. They do not want to force the hand of "history," or "the people," or "the proletariat," or whatever other name they give their God. They hope for the end of dictatorships, conceiving this as restoring the people's unsuppressible right to self-determination. Their crowning dream is a constituent assembly, elected by the broadest suffrage, which scrupulously respects the rights of the electors, who must decide upon the constitution they want. If the population is immature, the constitution will not be a good one, but to amend it will be possible only through constant efforts of persuasion. Democrats do not refrain from violence on principle but wish to use it only when the majority is convinced it is indispensable, little more, that is, than an almost superfluous "dot" over an "i." They are suitable leaders only in times of ordinary administration, when the overall population is convinced of the validity of the basic institutions and believe that any amendment should be restricted to relatively secondary matters. During revolutionary times, when institutions are not simply to be administered but created, democratic procedures fail miserably. The pitiful impotence of democrats in the Russian, German, Spanish revolutions are the three most recent examples. In these situations, once the old State apparatus had fallen away, along with its laws and its administration, popular assemblies and delegations immediately spring up in which all the progressive socialist forces converge and agitate, either hiding behind the ancient regime, or scorning it. The population does have some fundamental needs to satisfy, but it does not know precisely what it wants and what must be done. A thousand bells ring in its ears. With its millions of minds, it cannot orientate itself, and breaks up into a number of tendencies, currents and factions, all struggling with one another.

At the very moment when the greatest decisiveness and boldness is needed, democrats lose their way, not having the backing of spontaneous popular approval, but rather a gloomy tumult of passions. They think it their duty to form a consensus and they represent themselves as exhortatory preachers, where instead there is a need for leaders who know just what they want. They miss chances favorable to the consolidation of a new regime by attempting to make bodies, which need longer preparation and which are more suited to periods of relative tranquillity, work immediately. They give their adversaries the weapons they need to overthrow them. In their thousand tendencies, they do not represent a will for renewal, but vain and very confused ambitions found in minds that, by becoming paralyzed, actually prepare the terrain for the growth of the reaction. Democratic political methods are a dead weight during revolutionary crises.

As the democrats wear down their initial popularity as

assertors of freedom by their endless polemics, and in the absence of any serious political and social revolution, the pre-totalitarian political institutions would inevitably be re-constituted, and the struggle would again develop along the lines of the old class opposition.

The principle whereby the class struggle is the condition to which all political problems are reduced, has become the fundamental guideline of factory workers in particular, and gave consistency to their politics for as long as the fundamental institutions were not questioned. But this approach becomes an instrument which isolates the proletariat, when the need to transform the entire social organization becomes paramount. The workers, educated in the class system, cannot see beyond the demands of their particular class or even their professional category and fail to concern themselves with how their interests link up with those of other social classes. Or they aspire to a unilateral dictatorship of the proletariat in order to achieve the utopian collectivization of all the material means of production, indicated by centuries of propaganda as the panacea for all evils. This policy attracts no class other than the workers, who thus deprive the other progressive forces of their support, or alternatively leaves them at the mercy of the reaction which skillfully organizes them so as to break up the proletarian movement. Among the various proletarian tendencies, followers of class politics and collectivist ideals, the Communists have recognized the difficulty of obtaining a sufficient following to assure victory so that, unlike the other popular parties, they have turned themselves into a rigidly disciplined movement, exploiting the Russian myth in order to organize the workers, but which does not accept orders from them and uses them in all kinds of political manoeuverings.

This attitude makes the Communists, during revolutionary crises, more efficient than the democrats. But their ability to maintain the workers as far removed from the other revolutionary forces as they can, by preaching that their "real" revolution is yet to come, turns them into a sectarian element that weakens the sum of the progressive forces at the decisive moment. Beside this, their absolute dependence upon the Russian State, which has repeatedly used them in pursuing its national policies, prevents this Party from undertaking political activity with any continuity. They always need to hide behind a Karoly, a Blum, a Negrin, only to fall headlong into ruin with the democratic puppets they used, since power is achieved and maintained, not simply through cunning but with the ability to respond fully and viably to the needs of modern society.

If tomorrow the struggle were to remain restricted within the traditional national boundaries, it would be very difficult to avoid the old contradictions. The nation States, in fact, have so deeply planned their respective economies, that the main question would soon be which group of economic interests, i.e., which class, should be in control of the plan. The progressive front would be quickly shattered in the brawl between economic classes and categories. The most probable result would be that the reactionaries would benefit more than anyone else.

A real revolutionary movement must arise from among those who have been bold enough to criticize the old political approaches and it must be able to collaborate with democratic and with Communist forces; and generally with all those who work for the break-up of totalitarianism, without, however, becoming ensnared by the political practices of any of these. The reactionary forces have capable men and officers who have been trained to command and who will fight tenaciously to preserve their supremacy. In moments of dire need, they know just how to disguise their true nature, saying they stand by freedom, peace, general well-being and the poorer classes.

Already in the past we have seen how they wormed their way into popular movements, paralyzing, deflecting and altering them into precisely the opposite of what they are. They will certainly be the most dangerous force to be faced.

The point they will seek to exploit is the restoration of the nation State. Thus they will be able to latch on to what is, by far the most widespread of popular feelings, so deeply offended by recent events and so easily manipulated to reactionary ends: to patriotic feeling. In this way they can also hope to confound their adversaries' ideas more easily, since for the popular masses, the only political experience acquired to date has been within the national context. It is, therefore, fairly easy to channel them and their more short-sighted leaders towards the reconstruction of the States destroyed in the storm.

If this end is achieved, the forces of reaction will have won. In appearance, these States might well be democratic and socialist on a large scale. It would only be a question of time before power fell into the hands of the reactionaries. National jealousies would be revived, and the State would again seek to fulfil its requirements in its armed strength. In a more or less brief space of time the most important duty would be to convert populations into armies. Generals would again command, the monopoly holders would again draw profits from autarchies, the bureaucracy would continue to swell, the priests would keep the masses docile. All the initial achievements would shrivel into nothing, faced with the need to prepare for war once more.

The question which must be resolved first, failing which progress is no more than mere appearance, is the definitive abolition of the division of Europe into national, sovereign States. The collapse of the majority of the States on the continent under the German steam-roller has already given the people of Europe a common destiny: either they will all submit to Hitler's dominion, or, after his fall, they will all enter a revolutionary crisis and will not find themselves separated by, and entrenched in, solid State structures. Feelings today are already far more disposed than they were in the past to accept a federal reorganization of Europe. The harsh experience of recent decades has opened the eyes even of those who refused to see, and has matured many circumstances favourable to our ideal.

All reasonable men recognize that it is impossible to maintain a balance of power among European States with militarist Germany enjoying equal conditions with other countries, nor can Germany be broken up into pieces or held on a chain once it is conquered. We have seen a demonstration that no country within Europe can stay on the sidelines while the others battle: declarations of neutrality and non-aggression pacts come to nought. The uselessness, even harmfulness, of organizations like the League of Nations has been demonstrated: they claimed to guarantee international law without a military force capable of imposing its decisions and respecting the absolute sovereignty of the member States. The principle of nonintervention turned out to be absurd: every population was supposed to be left free to choose the despotic government it thought best, in other words virtually assuming that the constitution of each individual State was not a question of vital interest for all the other European nations. The multiple problems which poison international life on the continent have proved to be insoluble: tracing boundaries through areas inhabited by mixed populations, defence of alien minorities, seaports for landlocked countries, the Balkan Question, the Irish problem, and so on. All matters which would find easy solutions in the European Federation, just as corresponding problems, suffered by the small States which became part of a vaster national unity, lost their harshness as they were turned into problems of relationships between various provinces.

Moreover, the end of the sense of security inspired and created by an unassailable Great Britain, which led Britain to ["splendid isolation,"] the dissolution of the French army and the disintegration of the French Republic itself at the first serious collision with the German forces (which, it is to be hoped, will have lessened the chauvinistic attitude of absolute Gallic superiority), and in particular the awareness of the risk of total enslavement are all circumstances that will favour the constitution of a federal regime, which will bring an end to the current anarchy. Furthermore, it is easier to find a basis of agreement for a European arrangement of colonial possessions since England has accepted the principle of India's independence and since France has potentially lost its entire empire in recognizing its defeat.

To all of this must be added the disappearance of some of the most important dynasties, and the fragility of the basis which sustains the ones that survive. It must be taken into account that these dynasties, by considering the various countries as their own traditional appanages, together with the powerful interests backing them, represented a serious obstacle to the rational organization of the United States of Europe, which can only be based on the republican constitution of federated countries. And, once the horizon of the old continent is superseded, and all the peoples who make up humanity are included in a single design, it will have to be recognized that the European Federation is the only conceivable guarantee ensuring that relationships with American and Asiatic peoples will work on the basis of peaceful co-operation, waiting for a more distant future when the political unity of the entire world will become possible.

Therefore, the dividing line between progressive and reactionary parties no longer coincides with the formal lines of more or less democracy, or the pursuit of more or less socialism, but the division falls along a very new and substantial line: those who conceive the essential purpose and goal of struggle as being the ancient one, the conquest of national political power, and who, although involuntarily, play into the hands of reactionary forces, letting the incandescent lava of popular passions set in the old moulds, and thus allowing old absurdities to arise once again, and those who see the main purpose as the creation of a solid international State, who will direct popular forces towards this goal, and who, even if they were to win national power, would use it first and foremost as an instrument for achieving international unity.

With propaganda and action, seeking to establish in every possible way the agreements and links among the individual movements which are certainly in the process of being formed in the various countries, the foundation must be built now for a movement that knows how to mobilize all forces for the birth of the new organism which will be the grandest creation, and the newest, that has occurred in Europe for centuries; in order to constitute a steady federal State, that will have at its disposal a European armed service instead of national armies; that will break decisively economic autarkies, the backbone of totalitarian regimes; that will have sufficient means to see that its deliberations for the maintenance of common order are executed in the individual federal States, while each State will retain the autonomy it needs for a plastic articulation and development of political life according to the particular characteristics of the various peoples.

If a sufficient number of men in the main European countries understand this, then victory will soon fall into their hands, since both circumstances and opinion will be favourable to their efforts. They will have before them parties and factions that have already been disqualified by the disastrous experience of the last twenty years. Since it will be the moment for new action, it will also be the moment for new men: the MOVEMENT FOR A FREE AND UNITED EUROPE.

III.

Postwar Duties: Reform of Society

A free and united Europe is the necessary premise to the strengthening of modern civilization as regards which the totalitarian era is only a temporary setback. As soon as this era ends the historical process of struggle against social inequalities and privileges will be restored in full. All the old conservative institutions that have hindered this process will either have collapsed or will be teetering on the verge of collapse. The crisis in these institutions must be boldly and decisively exploited.

In order to respond to our needs, the European revolution must be socialist, i.e., its goal must be the emancipation of the working classes and the creation of more humane conditions for them. The guiding light in determining what steps need to be taken, however, cannot simply be the utterly doctrinaire principle whereby private ownership of the material means of production must in principle be abolished and only temporarily tolerated when dispensing with it entirely. Wholesale nationalization of the economy under State control was the first, utopian form taken by the working classes' concept of their freedom from the yoke of capitalism. But when this State control is achieved, it does not produce the desired results but leads to a regime where the entire population is subservient to a restricted class of bureaucrats who run the economy.

The truly fundamental principle of socialism, vis-à-vis which general collectivization was no more than a hurried and erroneous inference, is the principle which states that, far from dominating man, economic forces, like the forces of nature, should be subject to man, guided and controlled by him in the most rational way, so that the broadest strata of the population will not become their victims. The huge forces of progress that spring from individual interests, must not be extinguished by the grey dullness of routine. Otherwise, the same insoluble problem will arise: how to stimulate the spirit of initiative using salary differentials and other provisions of the same kind. The forces of progress must be extolled and extended, by giving them increasing opportunities for development and employment. At the same time, the tracks guiding these forces towards objectives of greatest benefit for all society must be strengthened and perfected.

Private property must be abolished, limited, corrected, or extended according to the circumstances and not according to any dogmatic principle. This guiding principle is a natural feature in the process of forming a European economic life freed from the nightmares of militarism or national bureaucratism. Rational solutions must replace irrational ones, even in the working class consciousness. With a view to indicating the content of this principle in greater detail, we emphasize the following points while stressing the need to assess the appropriateness of every point in the programme and means of achieving them in relationship to the indispensable premise of European unity:

a) Enterprises with a necessarily monopolistic activity, and in a position to exploit consumers, cannot be left in the hands of private ownership: for example, electricity companies or industries of vital interest to the community which require protective duties, subsidies, preferential orders, etc., if they are to survive (the most visible example of this kind of industry so far in Italy is the steel industry); and enterprises which, owing to the amount of capital invested, the number of workers employed, and the significance of the sector involved can blackmail various State bodies, forcing them to adopt the policies most beneficial to themselves (for example, the mining industries, large banks, large weapons manufacturers). In this field, nationalization must certainly be introduced on a vast scale, without regard for acquired rights.

b) Private property and inheritance legislation in the past was so drawn up as to permit the accumulation of wealth in the hands of a few, privileged members of society. In a revolutionary crisis this wealth must be distributed in an egalitarian way thereby eliminating the parasitic classes and giving the workers the means of production they need to improve their economic standing and achieve greater independence. We are thus proposing an agrarian reform which will increase the number of owners enormously by giving land to those who actually farm it and an industrial reform which will extend workers' ownership in non-nationalized sectors, through co-operative adventures, employee profit-sharing, and so on.

c) The young need to be assisted with all the measures needed to reduce the gap between the starting positions in the struggle to survive to a minimum. In particular, State schools ought to provide a real chance for those who deserve it to continue their studies to the highest level, instead of restricting these opportunities to wealthy students. In each branch of study leading to training in different crafts and the various liberal and scientific professions, State schools should train the number of students which corresponds to the market requirements, so that average salaries will be roughly equal for all the professional categories, regardless of the differing rates of remuneration within each category according to individual skills.

d) The almost unlimited potential of modern technology to mass produce essential goods guarantees, with relatively low social costs, that everyone can have food, lodging, clothing and the minimum of comfort needed to preserve a sense of human dignity. Human solidarity towards those who fall in the economic struggle ought not, therefore, to be manifested with humiliating forms of charity that produce the very same evils they seek to remedy but ought to consist in a series of measures which unconditionally, and regardless of whether a person is able to work or not, guarantee a decent standard of living for all without lessening the stimulus to work and save. In this way, no-one will be forced any longer to accept enslaving work contracts because of their poverty.

e) Working class freedom can only be achieved when the conditions described have been fulfilled. The working classes must not be left to the mercy of the economic policies of monopolistic trade unions who simply apply the overpowering methods characteristic, above all, of great capital to the shop floor. The workers must once again be free to choose their own trusted representatives when collectively establishing the conditions under which they will agree to work, and the State must give them the legal means to guarantee the proper implementation of the terms agreed to. But all monopolistic tendencies can be fought effectively once these social changes have been fulfilled.

These are the changes needed both to create very broad-based support around the new institutional system from a large number of citizens willing to defend its survival and to stamp freedom and a strong sense of social solidarity onto political life in a very marked way. Political freedom with these foundations will not just have a formal meaning but a real meaning for all since citizens will be independent, and will be sufficiently informed as to be able to exert continuous and effective control over the ruling class.

It would be superfluous to dwell at length on constitutional institutions, not knowing at this stage, or being able to foresee, the circumstances under which they will be drawn up and will have to operate. We can do no more than repeat what everyone knows regarding the need for representative bodies, the process of developing legislation, the independence of the courts (which will replace the present system) safeguarding impartial application of legislation and the freedom of the press and right of assembly guaranteeing informed public opinion and the possibility for all citizens to participate effectively in the State's life. Only two issues require further and deeper definition because of their particular significance for our country at this moment: the relationship between Church and State and the nature of political representation.

a) The Treaty which concluded the Vatican's alliance with Fascism in Italy must be abolished so that the purely lay character of the State can be asserted and so that the supremacy of the State in civil matters can be unequivocally established. All religious faiths are to be equally respected, but the State must no longer have earmark funds for religion.

b) The house of cards that Fascism built with its corporativism will collapse together with the other aspects of the totalitarian State. There are those who believe that material for the new constitutional order can be salvaged from this wreck. We disagree. In totalitarian States, the corporative chambers are the crowning hoax of police control over the workers. Even if the corporative chambers were a sincere expression of the will of the various categories of producers, the representative bodies of the various professional categories could never be qualified to handle questions of general policy. In more specifically economic matters, they would become bodies for the accumulation of power and privilege among the categories with the strongest trade union representation. The unions will have broad collaborative functions with State bodies which are appointed to resolve problems directly involving these unions, but they should have absolutely no legislative power, since this would create a kind of feudal anarchy in the economic life of the country, leading to renewed political despotism. Many of those who were ingenuously attracted by the myth of corporativism, can and should be attracted by the job of renewing structures. But they must realize the absurdity of the solution they vaguely desire. Corporativism can only be concretely expressed in the form it was given by totalitarian States regimenting the workers beneath officials who monitored everything they did in the interests of the ruling class The revolutionary party cannot be amateurishly improvised at the decisive moment, but must begin to be formed at least as regards its central political attitude, its upper echelons, the basic directives for action. It must not be a heterogeneous mass of tendencies, united merely negatively and temporarily, i.e., united by their anti-

Fascist past and the mere expectation of the fall of the totalitarian regime, in which all and sundry are ready to go their own separate ways once this goal has been reached. The revolutionary party, on the contrary, knows that only at this stage will its real work begin. It must therefore be made up of men who agree on the main issues for the future.

Its methodical propaganda must penetrate everywhere there are people oppressed by the present regime. Taking as its starting point the problem which is the source of greatest suffering to individuals and classes, it must show how this problem is linked to other problems, and what the real solution will be. But from this gradually increasing circle of sympathizers, it must pick out and recruit into the organization only those who have identified and accepted the European revolution as the main goal in their lives, who carry out the necessary work with strict discipline day in day out, carefully checking up on its continuous and effective safety, even in the most dangerously illegal situations. These recruits will be the solid network that will give consistency to the more ephemeral sphere of the sympathizers.

While overlooking no occasion or sector in which to spread its cause, it must be active first and foremost in those environments which are most significant as centres for the circulation of ideas and recruiting of combative men. It must be particularly active vis-à-vis the working class and intellectuals, the two social groups most sensitive, in the present situation, and most decisive for tomorrow's world. The first group is the one which least gave in to the totalitarian rod and which will be the quickest to reorganize its ranks. The intellectuals, particularly the younger intellectuals, are the group which feels most spiritually suffocated and disgusted with the current despotism. Bit by bit other social groups will gradually be drawn into the general movement.

Any movement which fails in its duty to ally these forces, is condemned to sterility. Because if the movement is made up of intellectuals alone, it will lack the strength to crush reactionary resistance, and it will distrust and be distrusted by the working class and even though inspired by democratic sentiment, when faced with difficulties it will be liable to shift its position, as regards the mobilisation of other classes, against the workers, and thus restore Fascism. If, instead, the movement is backed only by the proletariat, it will be deprived of the clarity of thought which only intellectuals can give and which is so vital in identifying new paths

and new duties: the movement would be a prisoner of the old class structure, looking on everyone as a potential enemy, and will slither towards the doctrinaire Communist solution.

During the revolutionary crisis, this movement will have the task of organizing and guiding progressive forces, using all the popular bodies which form spontaneously, incandescent melting pots in which the revolutionary masses are mixed, not for the creation of plebiscites, but rather waiting to be guided. It derives its vision and certainty of what must be done from the knowledge that it represents the deepest needs of modern society and not from any previous recognition by popular will, as yet inexistent. In this way it issues the basic guidelines of the new order, the first social discipline directed to the unformed masses. By this dictatorship of the revolutionary party a new State will be formed, and around this State new, genuine democracy will grow.

There are no grounds for fearing that such a revolutionary regime will develop into renewed despotism. This arises only when the tendency has been to shape a servile society. But if the revolutionary party continues resolutely from the very outset to create the conditions required for individual freedom whereby every citizen can really participate in the State's life, which will evolve, despite secondary political crises, towards increasing understanding and acceptance of the new order by all—hence towards an increasing possibility of working effectively and creating free political institutions. The time has now come to get rid of these old cumbersome burdens and to be ready for whatever turns up, usually so different from what was expected, to get rid of the inept among the old and create new energies among the young. Today, in an effort to begin shaping the outlines of the future, those who have understood the reasons for the current crisis in European civilization, and who have therefore inherited the ideals of movements dedicated to raising the dignity of humanity, which were shipwrecked either on their inability to understand the goal to be pursued or on the means by which to achieve it, have begun to meet and seek each other.

The road to pursue is neither easy nor certain. But it must be followed and it will be!

Source: Excerpted from *Ventotene, Federalism and Politics: The Ventotene Papers of the Altiero Spinelli Institute for Federalist Studies* (Ventotene, Italy: 1995). Web site: JEF (Young European Federalists). Available at http://www.jef-europe.net/federalism/archives/000937.html. Reprinted with permission.

1942 Documents

127. George C. Marshall, Chief of Staff of the Army, on the Mobilization of U.S. Manpower in World War II: Extract from his Final Biennial Report to the Secretary of War, 1 September 1945

At the end of the war, George C. Marshall, who served as chief of staff of the U.S. Army throughout the war, summarized the Herculean efforts the United States had undertaken to mobilize the greatest army in its history to fight the war.

The process of mobilization for this war reached its peak and immediately started to decline with the surrender of Germany. In the summer of 1943 the firm decision was reached to build up the Army to an effective strength of 7,700,000 enlisted men believed necessary to meet our strategic commitments.

At the close of the European war the operating strength of the Army plus ineffectives was approximately 8,300,000. The ineffectives consisted of 500,000 men undergoing hospitalization, including 100,000 in the process of being discharged because they were no longer fit for either active or limited service, and 100,000 en route overseas as replacements, in all totaling approximately 600,000 men. . . .

The technique for the mobilization of American manpower in this war was unique. The special nature of the war introduced many new factors. Perhaps greater than any other single advantage of the United Nations was the productive capacity of American industry. It was therefore necessary not to cut too deeply into the manpower of the Nation in the process of acquiring the men urgently needed by the Army and the Navy. We had the problems of arming both ourselves and the Allied Nations while, at the same time, we created huge armed forces necessary to the successful prosecution of the war. Furthermore, our lines of communica-

tion were to be extended entirely around the world, requiring large forces of men to work them and absorbing even larger forces in transit over the thousands of miles to and fro without profit to the military enterprise.

Fighting across the oceans, we needed a very powerful Navy and a large merchant fleet to transport and maintain our armies and to carry munitions to our Allies. At the same time, it was our purpose to exploit every possible scientific device and technique to secure victory at the smallest cost in lives of our men. These various efforts demanded large numbers of men and women, and necessitated their allocation among the various programs with exceeding care, so that the right numbers of men would be doing the most important things at the most important time. The mere statement of this requirement fails to indicate the exceeding difficulty involved in its application to the special claims of each industry and the demands of each theater commander. To resolve the conflicting requirements posed a most difficult problem for a democracy at war.

It was estimated that the absolute ceiling on the number of American men physically fit for active war service lay between 15 and 16 million. The requirements of the naval and merchant shipping program had to be given a high order of priority. The Army decided to establish its strength ceiling at 7,700,000. Before we could bring the enemy to battle we had to secure our lines of communication and build our training and service installations. Within this total strength of the Army the minimum requirements of the Service Forces were set at 1,751,000. It was decided at the outset that the first offensive blows we could deliver upon the enemy would be through the air, and anticipated that the heavier and more effective our air assault, the sooner the enemy's capacity to resist would be destroyed. So the Air Forces were authorized to bring their strength to 2,340,000 men and were given the highest priority for the best qualified both physically and by educational and technical ability of the military manpower pool.

Each theater of operations had requirements for men over and above those allocated for its armies, air forces, and service installations. The troop basis allowed 423,000 men for these troops which would be directly attached to theater headquarters and major command installations throughout the world.

This left the Ground Forces with a maximum of 3,186,000 men within the limitations of the 7,700,000 effective troops strength. Yet when we entered the war it was almost impossible to compute accurately how many ground combat troops we would need to win. The precise results to be attained by modern aerial warfare could only be an educated guess.

... [I]n early 1942 we established a troop basis of 3,600,000 men which would permit the organization of 71 divisions: 59 infantry (including 18 National Guard), 10 armored, and two cavalry. This force was the largest we then had the ability to train, equip, and provide a nucleus of trained officers and noncommissioned officers. In mid-1942, when the original build-up in the United Kingdom for the invasion of France and the North African operation began to take shape, we found we needed more and still more service troops. The demand was insatiable. The over-all strength of the Army by the end of the year had increased to 5,397,675 men. Throughout 1942, however, the planners were at work estimating the requirements for 1943 which we believed would carry the Army to its peak of mobilization and would give us the necessary strength to force a victorious decision. At first it was estimated this would provide the Army with 105 divisions. Later it became evident that the men for only 100 divisions could be found with this strength. By the middle of 1943 we determined that this projected mobilization might impose too great a strain on the Nation's manpower, if all of the ambitious efforts planned for the global war were to remain in balance. Fortunately for our dilemma, Stalingrad was now past history and the great Soviet armies were showing a steadily increasing offensive power. The ceiling was therefore reduced to 7,700,000

shortly after the TRIDENT Conference in Washington, the meeting at which the over-all strategy became sufficiently firm to permit more precise planning. This amounted to a reduction of 548,000 men. The projected number of divisions was reduced to 90, including three special or "light" divisions that were being trained for jungle and mountain warfare. Later the 2d Cavalry Division, then in North Africa, was activated to provide urgently required service troops to support the amphibious landing in southern France. At the same time the Air Force mobilization was fixed at 273 combat groups containing five very heavy bombardment (B-29s and 32s), 96 heavy bombardment (Flying Fortresses and Liberators), 26 medium bombardment, 8 light bombardment, 87 fighter, 27 troop carrier, and 24 reconnaissance groups.

On the face of it this appeared to be a critically small ground force for a nation as large as ours. Germany with a prewar population of 80,000,000 was mobilizing 313 divisions. Japan was putting 120 in the field; Italy 70; Hungary 23; Rumania 17; Bulgaria 18. Among the major Allies, the Soviets had a program for more than 550 divisions; the British for more than 50; the Chinese more than 300, though their divisional strength was often little more than regimental according to our method of computation. We were, however, second of the Allies in the mobilization of men and women for military service, third among all the belligerent nations. The Soviet war effort was putting 22,000,000 men and women into the fight. By the time of their defeat, the Germans had mobilized 17,000,000. Our peak mobilization for the military services was 14,000,000. The British Empire mobilized 12,000,000; China 6,000,000.

This war brought an estimated total of 93,000,000 men and women of the Axis and United Nations into the conflict. And fortunately for us the great weight of numbers was on the side of the United Nations. Total Allied mobilization exceeded 62,000,000; total enemy mobilization, 30,000,000. The figures show how heavily the United States was concentrating on aerial warfare, on the production and movement of arms for its own troops and those of its Allies, and the meaning in terms of manpower of waging war from 3,000 to 9,000 miles from our shores.

Our ground strength was, for the size of our population, proportionately much smaller than that of the other belligerents. On the other hand it was, in effect, greater than a simple comparison of figures would indicate, for we had set up a system of training individual replacements that would maintain 89 divisions of ground troops and 273 combat air groups at full effective strength, enabling these units to continue in combat for protracted periods. In past wars it had been the accepted practice to organize as many divisions as manpower resources would permit, fight those divisions until casualties had reduced them to bare skeletons, then withdraw them from the line and rebuild them in a rear area. In 1918 the AEF was forced to reduce the strength of divisions and finally to disband newly arrived divisions in France in order to maintain the already limited strength of those engaged in battle. The system we adopted for this war involved a flow of individual replacements from training centers to the divisions so they would be constantly at full strength. The Air Forces established a similar flow to replace combat casualties and possible relief crews.

This system enabled us to pursue tremendous naval and shipping programs, the air bombardment programs and unprecedented, almost unbelievable, production and supply programs, and at the same time to gather the strength necessary to deliver the knock-out blows on the ground. There were other advantages. The more divisions an Army commander has under his control, the more supporting troops he must maintain and the greater are his traffic and supply problems. If his divisions are fewer in number but maintained at full strength, the power for attack continues while the logistical problems are greatly simplified. . . .

The final manpower crisis occurred during the prolonged and very heavy fighting in the fall of 1944 and the winter of 1944–45, both in Europe and in the Philippines. However, our own tribulations of this nature were much less serious, it is believed, than those of our Allies and certainly of the German enemy, whose divisions at times were reduced below 5,000.

In the Siegfried Line fighting prior to the final advance to the Rhine, the weather was atrocious and most of the troops had been continuously engaged since the landing in Normandy in June. The lack of port facilities prior to the opening of Antwerp to Allied shipping made it impossible to maintain divisions in normal corps reserve and thus permit the rotation of units between the fighting line and comfortable billets in rear areas. Divisions for this purpose were available in England and in northwestern France, but the state of the railroads and the flow of supplies made it impossible to maintain them at the front. All this resulted in a great strain on the fighting troops, and when a shortage in replacements was added, the situation great very serious. It was just at this moment that the Germans launched their final offensive effort in the Ardennes. . . .

To implement the replacement system we had established the Ground and Service Force Replacement Training Centers. It required more than a year to train the many elements of a new division because of the difficulties of teaching men and units the teamwork so essential under the trying conditions of battle. But it was possible and practicable in a much shorter time to train an individual soldier so that he was competent to join a veteran team as a replacement where the battle experienced soldier can quickly fit him into the divisional structure. At the replacement training centers men were made ready to join the divisions and replace casualties in a concentrated training period of 17 weeks. At these training centers they were given six weeks of basic military training and intense physical conditioning. In the remaining period they acquired competence in handling the weapons with which they would fight or the equipment with which they would work and in learning the tactics of squads, platoons, companies, and battalions, the tactical units which actually engaged in combat.

An infantryman, for example, became proficient in his primary weapons and familiarized with the M1 rifle, the carbine, the hand grenade, the rifle grenade, the automatic rifle, the .30 caliber medium machine gun, the 60-mm mortar, and the two-man rocket launcher. These were the weapons that every infantry rifleman might be called upon to use. Not only were men taught to handle their weapons with proficiency in the replacement training centers, but they were taught to take care of themselves personally. There was intensive instruction in personal sanitation, malaria control, processing of contaminated water, cooking, and keeping dry in the open and all the other lore that a good soldier must understand. But most important, our replacements were taught the tricks of survival in battle. As the Army acquired battle veterans, both officers and enlisted men were returned to the United States for duty as instructors in the replacement training centers. These veterans, who learned how to survive in combat, passed on knowledge to new men and thereby increased both their effectiveness and their chances of survival in their first experience of combat. The training of replacements was made as realistic as possible to manage in training. Problems of street fighting, jungle fighting, and close combat were staged in realistic fashion with live ammunition, and men learned to crawl under supporting live artillery barrages just as they must in battle. Although this training cost us a few casualties in this country, it is certain that for every casualty we took in this manner, we saved the lives of many men in battle.

After the completion of their replacement training, men received a furlough at home before reporting to oversea replacement depots where their long journey to the fighting fronts began. In the theaters of operations they again staged through the replacement depots which were established in the rear of each army group, army, and corps. When division commanders needed new men to replace casualties, they called on corps replacement depots and the men moved forward to the line.

Where it was possible, the replacements were absorbed in the division in its inactive periods, or in regiments in reserve positions, and each new man was teamed up with a veteran so that he could learn to know his squadmates before he saw action. But when the battle was moving at a fast pace, replacements at times had to join units engaged with the enemy.

By the spring of 1944, as most of the shortcomings of the replacement system had become evident, the War Department took vigorous corrective action. A directive was sent to every theater requiring the establishment of retraining centers so that every man in the Army would be put to his most efficient use.

Since the early critical days of the mobilization, the Service Forces, the Ground Force training commands, and particularly the Air Forces had acquired great numbers of the best qualified of our men. The shortage of physically qualified men for infantry and artillery became apparent about midway in the activation of the new divisions. Later we started approaching the bottom of the manpower barrel, and it grew increasingly difficult to get men physically fit for combat out of the remaining civilian manpower pools. The only way in which the battle line could be kept firm was with suitable men already in the Army. To do this we speeded up the training program and stripped the divisions training in this country of nearly 90,000 infantrymen. At this same time the overseas divisions were returning increasing numbers of sick, wounded, and injured men to the hospitals as the intensity of the fighting developed and sickness took its toll. It was our purpose to fill up the service units with these hospitalized men who still could serve their country but no longer could endure the extreme hardships of the fox holes, and to send forward fresh men to take their place, after a necessary period of retraining.

In the United States we resolved to move out all physically fit men from the service and training commands and replace them with men who had been wounded or weakened by disease and the hardships of the front, with men who had been overseas so long that they were entitled to return home under the rotation policy, and where possible with civilians. . . .

To keep the overall effective strength of the Army within the troop basis of 7,700,000, the call on Selective Service had been reduced from 160,000 a month in early 1944 to 60,000 in the fall. But when the replacement crisis reached its peak in the winter, there was no remaining alternative but again to call on Selective Service for more men. The call was increased to 80,000 in February of this year and 100,000 a month thereafter to the end of June. . . .

It is remarkable how exactly the mobilization plan fitted the requirements for victory. When Admiral Doenitz surrendered the German Government, every American division was in the operational theaters. All but two had seen action; one had the mission of securing the vital installations in the Hawaiian Islands; the other was an airborne division in SHAEF Reserve. To give General Eisenhower the impetus for final destruction of the German armies of the west, two divisions, already earmarked for future operations in the Pacific, the 86th and 97th, were halted on the West Coast in February, rushed across the United States and onto fast ships for Europe. When these troops left the New York Port of Embarkation there were no combat divisions remaining in the United States. The formed military forces of the nation were completely committed overseas to bring about our victory in Europe and keep sufficient pressure on Japan so that she could not dig in and stave off final defeat.

The significance of these facts should be carefully considered. Even with two-thirds of the German Army engaged by Russia, it took every man the Nation saw fit to mobilize to do our part of the job in Europe and at the same time keep the Japanese enemy under control in the Pacific. What would have been the result had the Red Army been defeated and the British Islands invaded, we can only guess. The possibility is rather terrifying.

Source: George C. Marshall, *General Marshall's Report: The Winning of the War in Europe and the Pacific: Biennial Report of the Chief of Staff of the United States Army July 1, 1943 to June 30, 1945, to the Secretary of War* (New York: Simon and Schuster, 1945), 101–107.

128. Conditions in the Warsaw Ghetto: The Diary of Stanislav Rozycki, 1941 or 1942

As a prelude to embarking on the outright extermination of Jews in Germany and occupied Europe, in 1940, German authorities established ghettos, segregated areas for Jews alone, in most east European cities and towns. Jews from areas farther west were deported to these. The official food allocation for ghetto Jews was 300 calories a day; housing was overcrowded and often unheated in winter, and sanitation was basic. One Polish observer, Stanislav Rozycki, described in his diary conditions in the Warsaw ghetto, ultimately destroyed by German troops in 1943, after fierce fighting from the inhabitants despite their debilitated condition.

. . . . The majority are nightmare figures, ghosts of former human beings, miserable destitutes, pathetic remains of former humanity. One is most affected by the characteristic changes which one sees in their faces: as a result of misery, poor nourishment, the lack of vitamins, fresh air and exercise, the numerous cares, worries, anticipated misfortunes, suffering and sickness, their faces have taken on a skeletal appearance. The prominent bones around their eye sockets, the yellow facial colour, the slack pendulous skin, the alarming emaciation and sickliness. And, in addition, this miserable, frightened, restless, apathetic and resigned expression like that of a hunted animal. I pass my closest friends without recognizing them and guessing their fate. Many of them recognize me, come up to me and ask curiously how things are "over there" behind the walls—there where there is enough bread, fresh air, freedom to move around, and above all freedom. . . .

On the streets children are crying in vain, children who are dying of hunger. They howl, beg, sing, moan, shiver with cold, without underwear, without clothing, without shoes, in rags, sacks, flannel which are bound in strips round the emaciated skeletons, children swollen with hunger, disfigured, half conscious, already completely grown-up at the age of five, gloomy and weary of life. They are like old people and are only conscious of one thing: "I'm cold," "I'm hungry." They have become aware of the most important things in life that quickly. Through their innocent sacrifice and their frightening helplessness the thousands upon thousands of these little beggars level the main accusation against the proud civilization of today. Ten per cent of the new generation have already perished: every day and every night hundreds of these children die and there is no hope that anybody will put a stop to it.

There are not only children. Young and old people, men and women, bourgeois and proletarians, intelligentsia and business people are all being declassed and degraded. . . . They are being gobbled up by the streets on to which they are brutally and ruthlessly thrown. They beg for one month, for two months, for three months—but they all go downhill

and die on the street or in hospitals from cold, or hunger, or sickness, or depression. Former human beings whom no one needs fall by the wayside: former citizens, former "useful members of human society."

I no longer look at people; when I hear groaning and sobbing I go over to the other side of the road; when I see something wrapped in rags shivering with cold, stretched out on the ground, I turn away and do not want to look. . . . I can't. It's become too much for me. And yet only an hour has passed. . . .

For various reasons standards of hygiene are terribly poor. Above all, the fearful population density in the streets with which nowhere in Europe can be remotely compared. The fatal over-population is particularly apparent in the streets: people literally rub against each other, it is impossible to pass unhindered through the streets. And then the lack of light, gas, and heating materials. Water consumption is also much reduced; people wash themselves much less and do not have baths or hot water. There are no green spaces, gardens, parks; no clumps of trees and no lawns to be seen. For a year no one has seen a village, a wood, a field, a river or a mountain: no one has breathed slightly better air for even a few days this year. Bedding and clothing are changed very rarely because of the lack of soap. To speak of food hygiene would be a provocation and would be regarded as mockery. People eat what is available and when it is available. Other principles of nutrition are unknown here. Having said all this, one can easily draw one's own conclusions as to the consequences: stomach typhus and typhus, dysentery, tuberculosis, pneumonia, influenza, metabolic disturbances, the most common digestive illnesses, lack of vitamins and all other illnesses associated with the lack of bread, fresh air, clothing, and heating materials. Typhus is systematically and continually destroying the population. There are victims in every family. On average up to a thousand people are dying each month. In the early morning the corpses of beggars, children, old people, young people and women are lying in every street—the victims of the hunger and the cold. The hospitals are so terribly overcrowded that there are 2–3 patients lying in every bed. Those who do not find a place in a bed lie on the floor in rooms and corridors. The shortage of the necessary medicines in sufficient quantities makes it impossible to treat the sick. Moreover, there is a shortage of food for the sick. There is only soup and tea. . . .

While this cruel struggle for a little bit of bread, for a few metres of living space, for the maintenance of health, energy and life is going on, people are incapable of devoting much energy and strength to intellectual matters. In any case, there are German restrictions and bans. Nothing can be printed, taught or learnt. People are not allowed to organize themselves or exchange cultural possessions. We are cut off from the world and from books. We are not allowed to print anything, neither books nor newspapers; schools, academic institutions etc. are not permitted to open. There are no cinemas, radio, no contacts with world culture. Nothing reaches us, no products of the human spirit reach us. We have to smuggle in not only foodstuffs and manufactured goods, but also cultural products. For that reason everything which we achieve in this respect is worthy of recognition irrespective of how much there is or what it consists of. . . .

Source: J. Noakes and G. Pridham, eds., *Nazism 1919–1945*, Volume 3: *Foreign Policy, War and Racial Extermination: A Documentary Reader* (Exeter, UK: University of Exeter Press, 1988), 460–462. Reprinted with permission of University of Exeter Press.

129. The Final Solution: The Wannsee Protocol, 20 January 1942

In January 1942 top German officials met at Wannsee to discuss the best means for exterminating Jews throughout Europe. They listed not only those Jews then resident in Germany and territories occupied by Germany, but also in countries allied with Germany, neutral, or still unconquered. In their discussion, officials contemplated the initial forcible deportation of Jews to territories in the East, their subsequent employment in labor camps, where many of them were expected to die of "natural causes," and then a "final solution" to remove the remainder permanently from European life. In all, these discussions envisaged disposing of over 11 million Jews throughout Europe. Where persons of mixed blood were concerned, some latitude might be allowed, especially if combined with forcible sterilization. Effectively, the meeting sanctioned genocide on a massive scale, where possible to be implemented by methods adapted from industrial processes designed to handle and process large quantities of raw materials or animals.

TOP SECRET
Minutes of Meeting

This meeting of top German officials with responsibility for Jews under their control was held on 20 January 1942 in Berlin, at Grossen Wannsee No. 56/58. Those present included Gauleiter Dr. Meyer and Reichsamtleiter Dr. Leibbrandt of the Ministry for the Occupied Eastern Territories; Dr. Stuckart, Secretary of State of the Ministry for the Interior; Secretary of State Neumann, Plenipotentiary for the Four Year Plan; Dr. Freisler, Secretary of State of the Ministry of Justice; Dr. Bühler, Secretary of State of the Office of the General Government; Dr. Luther, Under Secretary of State of the Foreign Office; SS-Oberführer Klopfer of the Party Chancellery; Ministerialdirektor Kritzinger of the Reich Chancellery; SS-Gruppenführer Hofmann of the Race and Settlement Main Office; SS-Gruppenführer Müller and SS-Obersturmbannführer Eichmann of the Reich Main Security Office; SS-Oberführer Dr. Schöngarth of the Security Police, Security Department, Commander of the Security Police, Security Department (SD) of the General Government; SS-Sturmbannführer Dr. Lange of the Security Police, Security Department, Commander of the Security Police and the Security Department for the General-District of Latvia, in his capacity as deputy to the Commander of the Security Police and the Security Department for the Reich Commissariat "Eastland" . . .

II.

At the beginning of the discussion Chief of the Security Police and of the SD, SS-Obergruppenführer Heydrich, reported that the Reich Marshal [Hermann Göring] had appointed him delegate for the preparations for the final solution of the Jewish question in Europe and pointed out that this discussion had been called for the purpose of clarifying fundamental questions. The wish of the Reich Marshal to have a draft sent to him concerning organizational, factual and material interests in relation to the final solution of the Jewish question in Europe makes necessary an initial common action of all central offices immediately concerned with these questions in order to bring their general activities into line. The Reichsführer-SS [Heinrich Himmler] and the Chief of the German Police (Chief of the Security Police and the SD) [Reinhard Heydrich] was entrusted with the official central handling of the final solution of the Jewish question without regard to geographic borders. The Chief of the Security Police and the SD then gave a short report of the struggle which has been carried on thus far against this enemy, the essential points being the following:

a) the expulsion of the Jews from every sphere of life of the German people

b) the expulsion of the Jews from the living space of the German people

In carrying out these efforts, an increased and planned acceleration of the emigration of the Jews from Reich territory was started, as the only possible present solution.

By order of the Reich Marshal, a Reich Central Office for Jewish Emigration was set up in January 1939 and the Chief of the Security Police and SD was entrusted with the management. Its most important tasks were

a) to make all necessary arrangements for the preparation for an increased emigration of the Jews

b) to direct the flow of emigration

c) to speed the procedure of emigration in each individual case

The aim of all this was to cleanse German living space of Jews in a legal manner.

All the offices realized the drawbacks of such enforced accelerated emigration. For the time being they had, however, tolerated it on account of the lack of other possible solutions of the problem.

The work concerned with emigration was, later on, not only a German problem, but also a problem with which the authorities of the countries to which the flow of emigrants was being directed would have to deal. Financial difficulties, such as the demand by various foreign governments for increasing sums of money to be presented at the time of the landing, the lack of shipping space, increasing restriction of entry permits, or the cancelling of such, increased extraordinarily the difficulties of emigration. In spite of these difficulties, 537,000 Jews were sent out of the country between the takeover of power and the deadline of 31 October 1941. Of these:

- approximately 360,000 were in Germany proper on 30 January 1933

- approximately 147,000 were in Austria (Ostmark) on 15 March 1939

- approximately 30,000 were in the Protectorate of Bohemia and Moravia on 15 March 1939

The Jews themselves, or their Jewish political organizations, financed the emigration. In order to avoid impoverished Jews remaining behind, the principle was followed that wealthy Jews have to finance the emigration of poor Jews; this was arranged by imposing a suitable tax, i.e., an emigration tax, which was used for financial arrangements in connection with the emigration of poor Jews and was imposed according to income.

Apart from the necessary Reichsmark exchange, foreign currency had to be presented at the time of landing. In order to save foreign exchange held by Germany, the foreign Jewish financial organizations were—with the help of Jewish organizations in Germany—made responsible for arranging an adequate amount of foreign currency. Up to 30 October 1941, these foreign Jews donated a total of around 9,500,000 dollars.

In the meantime the Reichsführer-SS and Chief of the German Police had prohibited emigration of Jews due to the dangers of an emigration in wartime and due to the possibilities of the East.

III.

Another possible solution of the problem has now taken the place of emigration, i.e., the evacuation of the Jews to the East, provided that the Führer gives the appropriate approval in advance.

These actions are, however, only to be considered provisional, but practical experience is already being collected which is of the greatest importance in relation to the future final solution of the Jewish question.

Approximately 11 million Jews will be involved in the final solution of the European Jewish question, distributed as follows among the individual countries:

[The document proceeds to list the number of Jews living not only in states such as France, Hungary, and Rumania already currently under German occupation or control, but also in countries at war with Germany including Britain and Russia; allied with it, such as Italy; sympathetic but neutral, such as Spain and Portugal; and simply neutral, including Ireland, Sweden, and Switzerland.]

Under proper guidance, in the course of the final solution the Jews are to be allocated for appropriate labor in the East.

Able-bodied Jews, separated according to sex, will be taken in large work columns to these areas for work on roads, in the course of which action doubtless a large portion will be eliminated by natural causes.

The possible final remnant will, since it will undoubtedly consist of the most resistant portion, have to be treated accordingly, because it is the product of natural selection and would, if released, act as a the seed of a new Jewish revival (see the experience of history).

In the course of the practical execution of the final solution, Europe will be combed through from west to east. Germany proper, including the Protectorate of Bohemia and Moravia, will have to be handled first due to the housing problem and additional social and political necessities.

The evacuated Jews will first be sent, group by group, to so-called transit ghettos, from which they will be transported to the East.

SS-Obergruppenführer Heydrich went on to say that an important prerequisite for the evacuation as such is the exact definition of the persons involved.

It is not intended to evacuate Jews over 65 years old, but to send them to an old-age ghetto—Theresienstadt is being considered for this purpose.

In addition to these age groups—of the approximately 280,000 Jews in Germany proper and Austria on 31 October 1941, approximately 30% are over 65 years old—severely wounded veterans and Jews with war decorations (Iron Cross I) will be accepted in the old-age ghettos. With this expedient solution, in one fell swoop many interventions will be prevented.

The beginning of the individual larger evacuation actions will largely depend on military developments. Regarding the handling of the final solution in those European countries occupied and influenced by us, it was proposed that the appropriate expert of the Foreign Office discuss the matter with the responsible official of the Security Police and SD.

In Slovakia and Croatia the matter is no longer so difficult, since the most substantial problems in this respect have already been brought near a solution. In Rumania the government has in the meantime also appointed a commissioner for Jewish affairs. In order to settle the question in Hungary, it will soon be necessary to force an adviser for Jewish questions onto the Hungarian government.

With regard to taking up preparations for dealing with the problem in Italy, SS-Obergruppenführer Heydrich considers it opportune to contact the chief of police with a view to these problems.

In occupied and unoccupied France, the registration of Jews for evacuation will in all probability proceed without great difficulty.

Under Secretary of State Luther calls attention in this matter to the fact that in some countries, such as the Scandinavian states, difficulties will arise if this problem is dealt with thoroughly and that it will therefore be advisable to defer actions in these countries. Besides, in view of the small numbers of Jews affected, this deferral will not cause any substantial limitation.

The Foreign Office sees no great difficulties for southeast and western Europe.

SS-Gruppenführer Hofmann plans to send an expert to Hungary from the Race and Settlement Main Office for general orientation at the time when the Chief of the Security Police and SD takes up the matter there. It was decided to assign this expert from the Race and Settlement Main Office, who will not work actively, as an assistant to the police attaché.

IV.

[Intermarriages between Jews and non-Jews could give rise to problems in defining precisely who qualified as a Jew, and here it was proposed to follow the guidelines given in the earlier Nuremberg Laws of the 1930s, though in many cases exceptions and exemptions for meritorious conduct or the reverse were at least theoretically possible, as were forcible sterilization and the forced dissolution of mixed marriages.]

With regard to the issue of the effect of the evacuation of Jews on the economy, State Secretary Neumann stated that Jews who are working in industries vital to the war effort, provided that no replacements are available, cannot be evacuated.

SS-Obergruppenführer Heydrich indicated that these Jews would not be evacuated according to the rules he had approved for carrying out the evacuations then underway.

State Secretary Dr. Bühler stated that the General Government would welcome it if the final solution of this problem could be begun in the General Government, since on the one hand transportation does not play such a large role here nor would problems of labor supply hamper this action. Jews must be removed from the territory of the General Government as quickly as possible, since it is especially here that the Jew as an epidemic carrier represents an extreme danger and on the other hand he is causing permanent chaos in the economic structure of the country through continued black market dealings. Moreover, of the approximately 2.5 million Jews concerned, the majority is unfit for work.

State Secretary Dr. Bühler stated further that the solution to the Jewish question in the General Government is the responsibility of the Chief of the Security Police and the SD and that his efforts would be supported by the officials of the

General Government. He had only one request, to solve the Jewish question in this area as quickly as possible.

In conclusion the different types of possible solutions were discussed, during which discussion both Gauleiter Dr. Meyer and State Secretary Dr. Bühler took the position that certain preparatory activities for the final solution should be carried out immediately in the territories in question, in which process alarming the populace must be avoided.

The meeting was closed with the request of the Chief of the Security Police and the SD to the participants that they afford him appropriate support during the carrying out of the tasks involved in the solution.

Source: Minutes of the Wannsee Protocol, 20 January 1942. Available at Harold B. Lu Library, Brigham Young University, http://lib.byu.edu/rdh/eurodocs/germ/wanneng.html.

130. President Manuel Quezon on Filipino Collaborators: Manuel Quezon to General Douglas MacArthur, 28 January 1942

On 28 January 1942, the Japanese government announced that prominent Filipino government officials had formed a new government under Japanese authority in Manila and gave the names of those Filipinos who had accepted office in it. President Manuel Quezon, sheltering with Douglas MacArthur's forces in Corregidor, heard the news on Japanese radio broadcasts but refused to condemn the behavior of his former colleagues. Indeed, he told MacArthur by letter that such men should not be regarded as traitors to their country.

I have been mortified by the radio broadcast from Tokyo asserting that a new government has been established in the Philippines, which government has pledged its conformity with Japan's New East Asia policy.

I know what the real sentiments of my people are and I am certain that their stand is not changed despite the military reverses of our forces. I am likewise convinced of the loyalty of the men who have accepted positions in the so-called new government.

I want you, therefore, to give publicity to the following statement: "The determination of the Filipino people to continue fighting side by side with the United States until victory is won has in no way been weakened by the temporary reverses suffered by our arms. We are convinced that our sacrifices will be crowned with victory in the end and in that conviction we shall continue to resist the enemy with all our might."

Japanese military forces are occupying sections of the Philippines comprising only one-third of our territory. In the remaining areas constitutional government is still in operation under my authority.

I have no direct information concerning the veracity of the news broadcast from Tokyo that a Commission composed of some well-known Filipinos has been recently organized in Manila to take charge of certain functions of civil government. The organization of such a Commission, if true, can have no political significance not only because it is charged merely with purely administrative functions but also because the acquiescence by its members to serve on the Commission was evidently for the purpose of safeguarding the welfare of the civilian population, and can in no way reflect the sentiments of the Filipinos towards the enemy. Such sentiments are still those I have repeatedly expressed in the past: loyalty to America and resolute resistance against the invasion of our territory and liberties.

At the same time I am going to open my mind and heart to you without attempting to hide anything.

We are before the bar of history and God only knows if this is the last time that my voice will be heard before going to my grave.

My loyalty and the loyalty of the Filipino people has been proven beyond question. Now we are fighting by your side under your command despite overwhelming odds. But, it seems to me questionable whether any government has the right to demand loyalty from its citizens beyond its willingness or ability to render actual protection.

This war is not our making. . . .

Despite all this, we never hesitated for a moment in our stand.

We decided to fight by your side and we have done the best we could and we are still doing as much as could be expected from us under the circumstances. But how long are we going to be left alone? Has it already been decided in Washington that the Philippine front is of no importance as far as the final result of the war is concerned and that, therefore, no help can be expected here in the future, or at least before the power of resistance is exhausted? If so, I want to know, because I have my own responsibility to my countrymen whom, as President of the Commonwealth, I have led into a complete war effort. I am greatly concerned as well regarding the soldiers I have called to the colors and who are now manning the firing line. I want to decide in my own mind whether there is justification for allowing these men to be killed when for the final outcome of the war the shedding of their blood may be wholly unnecessary. It seems that Washington does not fully recognize our situation nor the feelings which the apparent neglect of our safety and welfare have engendered in the hearts of the people here. . . .

In reference to the men who have accepted positions in the Commission established by the Japanese, every one of them wanted to come to Corregidor, but you told me that there was no room for them here. They are not "quislings." The "quislings" are the men who betrayed their country to the enemy. Those men did what they have been asked to do, while they were free, under the protection of their government. Today they are virtually prisoners of the enemy. I am sure they are only doing what they think is their duty. They are not traitors. They are the victims of the adverse fortunes of war and I am sure they have no choice. Besides, it is probable that they accepted their positions in order to safeguard the welfare of the civilian population in the occupied areas. I think, under the circumstances, America should look upon their situation sympathetically and understandingly.

I am confident that you will understand my anxiety about the long-awaited reinforcements and trust you will again urge Washington to insure their early arrival.

Source: Gregorio F. Zaide, ed., *Documentary Sources of Philippine History,* Volume 11 (Metro Manila, Philippines: National Book Store Publishers, 1990), 513–515. Reprinted with permission of the Zaide Foundation.

131. President Franklin D. Roosevelt, Executive Order No. 9066, Authorizing the Secretary of War to Prescribe Military Areas, 19 February 1942

Less than three months after Pearl Harbor, on the urging of the War Department, President Franklin D. Roosevelt issued an executive order permitting the forcible removal of Japanese Americans from areas considered to be important to national defense and their internment for the duration of the war. Although the numbers of German Americans residing in the United States were far greater than those of Japanese origin, they did not face similar restrictions. The order was an example of the manner in which, during the war, the U.S. government frequently disregarded or set aside civil liberties.

WHEREAS the successful prosecution of the war requires every possible protection against espionage and against sabotage to national-defense material, national-defense premises, and national-defense utilities as defined in section 4, Act of April 20, 1918, 40 Stat. 533, as amended by the act of November 30, 1940, 54 Stat. 1220, and the Act of August 21, 1941, 55 Stat. 655 (U. S. C., Title 50, Sec. 104):

NOW, THEREFORE, by virtue of the authority vested in me as President of the United States, and Commander in Chief of the Army and Navy, I hereby authorize and direct the Secretary of War, and the Military Commanders whom he may from time to time designate, whenever he or any designated Commander deems such actions necessary or desirable, to prescribe military areas in such places and of such extent as he or the appropriate Military Commanders may determine, from which any or all persons may be excluded, and with respect to which, the right of any person to enter, remain in, or leave shall be subject to whatever restrictions the Sectary of War or the appropriate Military Commander may impose in his discretion. The Secretary of War is hereby authorized to provide for residents of any such area who are excluded therefrom, such transportation, food, shelter, and other accommodations as may be necessary, in the judgement of the Secretary of War or the said Military Commander, and until other arrangements are made, to accomplish the purpose of this order. The designation of military areas in any region or locality shall supersede designations of prohibited and restricted areas by the Attorney General under the Proclamations of December 7 and 8, 1941, and shall supersede the responsibility and authority of the Attorney General under the said Proclamations in respect of such prohibited and restricted areas. I hereby further authorize and direct the Secretary of War and the said Military Commanders to take such other steps as he or the appropriate Military Commander may deem advisable to enforce compliance with the restrictions applicable to each military area hereinabove authorized to be designated, including the use of Federal troops and other Federal Agencies, with authority to accept assistance of state and local agencies.

I hereby further authorize and direct all Executive Departments, independent establishments and other Federal Agencies, to assist the Secretary of War or the said Military Commanders in carrying out this Executive Order, including the furnishing of medical aid, hospitalization, food, clothing, transportation, use of land, shelter, and other supplies, equipment, utilities, facilities and services.

This order shall not be construed as modifying or limiting in any way the authority heretofore granted under Executive Order No. 8972, dated December 12, 1941, nor shall it be construed as limiting or modifying the duty and responsibility of the Federal Bureau of Investigation, with respect to the investigation of alleged acts of sabotage or the duty and responsibility of the Attorney General and the Department of Justice under the Proclamations of December 7 and 8, 1941, prescribing regulations for the conduct and control of alien enemies, except as such duty and responsibility is superseded by the designation of military areas hereunder.

Source: Web site: War Relocation Authority Camps in Arizona, 1942–1946. Available at http://www.library.arizona.edu/images/jpamer.

132. Anglo-American Mutual Aid Agreement, 23 February 1942

Although all three were Allies, relations between the United States and Great Britain were closer than those of either with the Soviet Union. Their warm relationship was symbolized by the relatively early conclusion of the Anglo-American Mutual Aid Agreement in February 1942, which governed the terms on which the United States provided Lend-Lease aid to Great Britain. Under this agreement, Britain and the United States also secretly pooled their knowledge and expertise on nuclear energy, and leading British scientists crossed the Atlantic to work on the MANHATTAN Project, which developed the first atomic bomb.

Signed in Washington on February 23, 1942, by Sumner Welles, Acting Secretary of State, and Viscount Halifax, British Ambassador

Whereas the Governments of the United States of America and the United Kingdom of Great Britain and Northern Ireland declare that they are engaged in a cooperative undertaking, together with every other nation or people of like mind, to the end of laying the bases of a just and enduring world peace securing order under law to themselves and all nations:

And whereas the President of the United States of America has determined, pursuant to the Act of Congress of March 11, 1941, that the defense of the United Kingdom against aggression is vital to the defense of the United States of America;

And whereas the United States of America has extended and is continuing to extend to the United Kingdom aid in resisting aggression;

And whereas it is expedient that the final determination of the terms and conditions upon which the Government of the United Kingdom receives such aid and of the benefits to be received by the United States of America in return therefore should be deferred until the extent of the defense aid is known and until the progress of events makes clearer and final terms and conditions and benefits which will be in the mutual interests of the United States of America and the United Kingdom and will promote the establishment and maintenance of world peace;

And whereas the Governments of the United States of America and the United Kingdom are mutually desirous of concluding now a preliminary agreement in regard to the provision of defense aid and in regard to certain considerations which shall be taken into account in determining such terms and conditions and the making of such an agreement has been in all respects duly authorized, and all acts, conditions and formalities which it may have been necessary to perform, fulfill or execute prior to the making of such an agreement in conformity with the laws either of the United States of America or of the United Kingdom have been performed, fulfilled or executed as required;

The undersigned, being duly authorized by their respective Governments for that purpose, have agreed as follows:

ARTICLE I

The Government of the United States of America will continue to supply the Government of the United Kingdom with such defense articles, defense services and defense information as the President shall authorize to be transferred or provided.

ARTICLE II

The Government of the United Kingdom will continue to contribute to the defense of the United States of America and the strengthening thereof and will provide such articles, services, facilities or information as it may be in a position to supply.

ARTICLE III

The Government of the United Kingdom will not without the consent of the President of the United States of America transfer title to, or possession of, any defense article or defense information transferred to it under the act or permit the use thereof by any one not an officer, employee, or agent of the Government of the United Kingdom.

ARTICLE IV

If, as a result of the transfer to the Government of the United Kingdom of any defense article or defense information, it becomes necessary for that government to take any action or make any payment in order fully to protect any of the rights of a citizen of the United States of America who has patent rights in and to any such defense article or information, the Government of the United Kingdom will take such action or make such payment when requested to do so by the President of the United States of America.

ARTICLE V

The Government of the United Kingdom will return to the United States of America at the end of the present emergency, as determined by the President, such defense articles transferred under this agreement as shall not have been destroyed, lost, or consumed and as shall be determined by the President to be useful in the defense of the United States of America or of the Western Hemisphere or to be otherwise of use to the United States of America.

ARTICLE VI

In the final determination of the benefits to be provided to the United States of America by the Government of the United Kingdom full cognizance shall be taken of all property, services, information, facilities, or other benefits or considerations provided by the Government of the United Kingdom subsequent to March 11, 1941, and accepted or acknowledged by the President on behalf of the United States of America.

ARTICLE VII

In the final determination of the benefits to be provided to the United States of America by the Government of the United Kingdom in return for aid furnished under the Act of Congress of March 11, 1941, the terms and conditions thereof shall be such as not to burden commerce between the two countries, but to promote mutually advantageous economic relations between them and the betterment of world-wide economic relations. To that end, they shall include provision for agreed action by the United States of America and the United Kingdom, open to participation by all other countries of like mind, directed to the expansion, by appropriate international and domestic measures, of production, employment, and the exchange and consumption of goods, which are the material foundations of the liberty and welfare of all peoples; to the elimination of all forms of discriminatory treatment in international commerce, and to the reduction of tariffs and other trade barriers; and in general, to the attainment of all the economic objectives set forth in the Joint Declaration made on August 12, 1941, by the President of the United States of America and the Prime Minister of the United Kingdom.

At an early convenient date, conversations shall be begun between the two governments with a view to determining, in the light of governing economic conditions, the best means of attaining the above-stated objectives by their own agreed action and of seeking the agreed action of other like-minded governments.

ARTICLE VIII

This agreement shall take effect as from this day's date. It shall continue in force until a date to be agreed upon by the two governments.

Source: Department of State Bulletin, 28 February 1942 (Washington, DC: U.S. Government Printing Office, 1942).

133. The Bataan Death March, April 1942: Recollections of Bill Nolan

In 1942 70,000 starving American and Filipino troops on the Bataan Peninsula in the Philippines surrendered to Japan, ending a hundred-day siege. The horrific sixty-five-mile journey of the weakened survivors, mostly on foot, to Camp O'Donnell, a prisoner-of-war camp, became one of the enduring memories of the Pacific War. A typical account was that of Bill Nolan, one of the American prisoners.

On April 10th, 1942, the Jap guards started us walking from our position at Cabcaben, going north as fast as the guards could walk. Myself with a very sore head, ears hurt, could not hear . . . very thirsty . . . no food or water. The temperature reached 95 degrees and prisoners would faint or pass out on the march. These prisoners that could not get up were shot or bayoneted to death and left along the road. Some were run over by Japanese trucks bringing Jap soldiers for the invasion of Corregidor. As these trucks passed American soldiers, they would hit and club Americans on their head and shoulders. Many fell and died under the wheels of Jap trucks. We walked from 6:00 A.M. until 6:00 or 7:00 P.M. Again no water or food. Calvin Graef, my First Sergeant, and myself both dipped water from the ditch on the side of the road.

This ditch contained water covered with green slime, dead horses, and American soldiers killed by Japs. Everyone suffered from malaria and dysentery. We had no quinine since February, '42. That night we slept on the ground on the side of the road. During these stops, Jap soldiers would strip us for our rings, watches, and pen-and-pencil sets. On dead American soldiers Japs would cut off fingers to get the rings. They took our canteens, gun belts—and left us with shirts and pants. Our helmets were knocked off and left on the road. So no hats for the rest of the march.

These conditions continued for four days until we reached San Fernando. Here we received our first cup of rice and some tea. While waiting in line for food, I passed out. When I came to, I was lying on the ground and had another large bump on the back of my head and was very dizzy.

We stayed here overnight, and the next morning at daybreak, all prisoners were marched to the railway station. At the siding were small, metal box cars. We were pushed by bayonets into those cars. About 100 prisoners in each car . . . could only stand up . . . and no room to sit down. The door was locked by the guards. Again the temperature reached 95 degrees. The metal sides of these box cars became so hot, we could not touch them. The ride lasted until dark when we unloaded. During the ride many prisoners became uncontrollable from the heat with no water or toilet facilities. Everyone had dysentery, and everyone went on the floor and over prisoners lying on the floor. These prisoners had passed out or were dead. I believe 10 or 15 men died in each box car during the eight hour trip.

Source: Adrian R. Martin, Brothers from Bataan: POWs, 1942–1945 (Manhattan, KS: Sunflower University Press, 1992), 78–79. Reprinted with permission of Sunflower University Press.

134. The Internment of Japanese Americans: Recollections of Mary Tsukamoto

Mary Tsukamoto, an American-born Japanese woman, recalls her family's evacuation from Florin, California, after Pearl Harbor, and her efforts, as a member of the Japanese American Citizens League, to help fellow Japanese Americans to follow the government's orders. After the war Tsukamoto became a prominent activist within the Japanese American community, spearheading efforts to preserve and publicize its history. She was also one of the leaders of the ultimately successful campaign by Japanese Americans to obtain financial compensation for their wartime treatment by the U.S. government.

I do remember Pearl Harbor Day. I was about twenty-seven, and we were in church. It was a December Sunday, so we were getting ready for our Christmas program. We were rehearsing and having Sunday School class, and I always played the piano for the adult Issei [Japanese Americans born in Japan] service. Of course, because there were so many Japanese, all of it was in Japanese; the minister was a Japanese, and he preached in Japanese. But after the service started, my husband ran in. He had been home that day and heard on the radio. We just couldn't believe it, but he told us that Japan attacked Pearl Harbor. I remember how stunned we were. And suddenly the whole world turned dark. We started to speak in whispers, and because of our experience [with earlier anti-Japanese sentiment] in Florin, we immediately sensed something terrible was going to happen. We just prayed that it wouldn't, but we sensed that things would be very difficult. The minister and all of the leaders discussed matters, and we knew that we needed to be prepared for the worst.

Then, of course, within a day or two, we heard that the FBI had taken Mr. Tanigawa and Mr. Tsuji. I suppose the FBI had them on their list, and it wasn't long before many of them were taken. We had no idea what they were going through. We should have been more aware. One Issei, Mr. Iwasa, committed suicide. So all of these reports and the anguish and the sorrow made the whole world very dark. Then rumors had it that we were supposed to turn in our cameras and our guns, and they were called in. Every day there was something else about other people being taken by the FBI. Then gradually we just couldn't believe the newspapers and what people were saying. And then there was talk about sending us away, and we just couldn't believe that they would do such a thing. It would be a situation where the whole community would be uprooted. But soon enough we were reading reports of other communities being evacuated from San Pedro and from Puget Sound. After a while we became aware that maybe things weren't going to just stop but would continue to get worse and worse.

We read about President Roosevelt's Executive Order 9066. I remember the Japanese American Citizens League (JACL) people had a convention in San Francisco in March. We realized that we needed to be able to rise to the occasion to help in whatever way we could in our community. We came home trying to figure out just how we could do that. We had many meetings at night and the FBI was always lurking around. We were told we couldn't stay out after eight o'clock in the evening.

Meanwhile, Hakujin [white] neighbors were watching us and reporting to the FBI that we were having secret meetings. We were not supposed to meet after eight o'clock, but often we couldn't cut off our JACL meeting at eight o'clock, and so we would have tea or coffee and keep talking. We would be reported and the police would come. There were so many people making life miserable for us. Then we heard that we had been restricted to traveling five miles from our homes; it was nine miles to Sacramento, and at that time everything was in Sacramento, like doctors, banks, and grocery stores. So it just was a terrible, fearful experience. Every time we went anywhere more than five miles away, we were supposed to go to the Wartime Civilian Control Administration (WCCA) office in Sacramento, nine miles away, to get a permit. It was ridiculous.

A lot of little things just nagged at us and harassed us, and we were frightened, but even in that atmosphere I remember we frantically wanted to do what was American. We were Americans and loyal citizens, and we wanted to do what Americans should be doing. So we were wrapping Red Cross bandages and trying to do what we could to help our country. By May 1942, more than a hundred of our boys were already drafted. We worried about them, and they were worried about what was going to happen to their families. We knew what we wanted to do. We started to buy war bonds, and we took first aid classes with the rest of the Hakujin people in the community. We went out at night to go to these classes, but we worried about being out after eight o'clock. It was a frightening time. Every little rule and regulation was imposed only on the Japanese people. There were Italian and German people in the community, but it was just us that had travel restrictions and a curfew. . . .

I had anxieties for Grandpa and Grandma. They were old and had farmed all their lives, and after more than fifty years here, the thought of uprooting these people and taking them away from their farm and the things they loved was terrible. Grandpa growing tea and vegetables, and Grandma growing her flowers. It was a cruel thing to do to them in their twilight years. But we had to get them ready to leave, anxious for their health and their safety. And my daughter, who was five, had to be ready to go to school. Al [her husband] had had a hemorrhage that winter, so we all had our personal grief as well.

The Farm Security Administration told us that we should work until the very last moment. Yet we had to worry about selling our car and our refrigerator and about what we should do with our chickens and our pets. . . . I wrote to the President of the United States and the principal of the high school and the newspaper editors thanking them for whatever they did for us. I don't know if I was crazy to do this, but I felt that history was happening, and I felt that it was important to say good-bye in a proper way, speaking for the people who were leaving and trying to tell our friends that we were loyal Americans and that we were sorry that this was happening. We needed to say something, and that's what I did.

We left early in the morning on May 29, 1942. Two days earlier we sold our car for eight hundred dollars, which was just about giving it away. We also had to sell our refrigerator. But some wonderful friends came to ask if they could take care of some things we couldn't store. . . .

It happened so suddenly to our community. You know, we grew up together, we went through the hardships of the Depression, and then finally things were picking up. People who had mortgages on their land were beginning to be able to make payments back to the bank. They were going to own the land that they had worked so hard to have. Then we had to evacuate. So there were still some people who owed some money on their property, and they lost the property because, of course, they couldn't make mortgage payments.

These were our people, and we loved them. We wept with them at their funerals and laughed with them and rejoiced at their weddings. And suddenly we found out that the community was going to be split up. The railroad track was one dividing line, and Florin Road the other dividing line. We were going to Fresno; the ones on the other side went to Manzanar; and the ones on the west side went to Tule. The ones on the west and north went to Pinedale and Poston. We never dreamed we would be separated—relatives and close friends, a community. The village people, we were just like brothers and sisters. We endured so much together and never dreamed we would be separated. Suddenly we found out we wouldn't be going to the same place. That was a traumatic disappointment and a great sadness for us. We were just tied up in knots, trying to cope with all of this happening. I can't understand why they had to do this. I don't know why they had to split us up. . . .

I don't know, we had been a very happy family. When we left, we swept our house and left it clean, because that's the way Japanese feel like leaving a place. I can just imagine everyone's emotions of grief and anger when they had to leave, when the military police came and told them, "Get ready right now. You've got two hours to get ready to catch this train."

Early in the morning, Margaret and George File came after us in their car because we no longer had one to move our things. We had taken our luggage the day before on the pick-up. We were very fortunate. Al had a very dear friend, Bob Fletcher, who was going to stay at our place and run our farm, our neighbor's farm, and Al's cousin's farm. So these three adjoining farms would be taken care of, at least the grape vineyards would be. Bob would stay at our place, and we left our dog with him. Nobody could take pets, and this was a sad thing for our daughter. There were tears everywhere; Grandma couldn't leave her flowers, and Grandpa looked at his grape vineyard. We urged him to get into the car and leave. I remember that sad morning when we realized suddenly that we wouldn't be free. It was such a clear, beautiful day, and I remember as we were driving, our tears. We saw the snow-clad Sierra Nevada mountains that we had loved to see so often, and I thought about God and about the prayer that we often prayed.

I remember one scene very clearly: on the train, we were told not to look out the window, but people were peeking out. After a long time on the train somebody said, "Oh, there's some Japanese standing over there." So we all took a peek, and we saw this dust, and rows and rows of barracks, and all these tan, brown Japanese people with their hair all bleached. They were all standing in a huddle looking at us, looking at this train going by. Then somebody on the train said, "Gee, that must be Japanese people in a camp." We didn't realize who they were before, but I saw how terrible it looked: the dust, no trees—just barracks and a bunch of people standing against the fence, looking out. Some children were hanging onto the fence like animals, and that was my first sight of the assembly center. I was so sad and discouraged looking at that, knowing that, before long, we would be inside too.

Source: Mary Tsukamoto, "Jerome," in John Tateishi, ed., *And Justice for All: An Oral History of the Japanese American Detention Camps* (Seattle: University of Washington Press, 1984), 3–13. Permission granted by the University of Washington Press.

135. General Douglas MacArthur, Australia, and the British Empire: Prime Minister's War Conference, Minute 23, 1 June 1942

The experience of war, and the priority that the British—like the American—government gave to winning the war in Europe before that in Asia, severely strained existing ties between Australia and Great Britain, its imperial "mother country." From Pearl Harbor onward Australian Prime Minister John Curtin increasingly turned for aid to the United States, a tendency encouraged by the arrival in Australia in spring 1942 of the dominating American general Douglas MacArthur. Although defeated in the Philippines, MacArthur immediately became Allied supreme commander in the Southwest Pacific area. It was symptomatic of MacArthur's significance to Australia that on 8 April 1942 Curtin created the Prime Minister's War Conference, regular meetings between himself as prime minister and minister for defence and MacArthur, to which other senior ministers were invited on an ad hoc basis. The two men united in sending a barrage of appeals to both London and Washington, urging more assistance to the Pacific theater.

STRATEGICAL POLICY IN THE SOUTHWEST PACIFIC, WITH SPECIAL REFERENCE TO AUSTRALIA AS A BASE

[At the beginning of this meeting MacArthur and his chief of staff, Major Richard K. Sutherland, were handed several highly confidential telegrams on Allied strategy exchanged between Curtin and Australia's minister for external affairs, Herbert V. Evatt, who was then in London.]

2. The Commander-in-Chief [MacArthur] said that, though he had now been in Australia for some time, we were still where we had started insofar as assistance from the United Kingdom was concerned, as we had not obtained an additional ship, soldier or squadron to the forces that were here. He considered these results were distressing.

3. The Commander-in-Chief desired to point out the distinction between the United States and the United Kingdom in their relations and responsibilities to Australia. Australia was part of the British Empire and it was related to Britain and the other Dominions by ties of blood, sentiment and allegiance to the Crown. The United States was an ally whose aim was to win the war, and it had no sovereign interest in the integrity of Australia. Its interest in Australia was from the strategical aspect of the utility of Australia as a base from which to attack and defeat the Japanese. As the British Empire was a Commonwealth of Nations, he presumed that one of its principal purposes was jointly to protect any part that might be threatened. The failure of the United Kingdom and

U.S.A. Governments to support Australia therefore had to be viewed from different angles.

4. The Commander-in-Chief added that, though the American people were animated by a warm friendship for Australia, their purpose in building up forces in the Commonwealth was not so much from an interest in Australia but rather from its utility as a base from which to hit Japan. In view of the strategical importance of Australia in a war with Japan, this course of military action would probably be followed irrespective of the Australian relationship to the people who might be occupying Australia.

5. The Commander-in-Chief said that he had detected a cooling off of the earlier eagerness for offensive action which had been manifested when the Southwest Pacific Area had been created. This was apparently due to the Churchill-Roosevelt agreement to treat Germany as the primary enemy. The directive had provided for preparations for offensive action. Reinforcements had commenced to flow to Australia from the U.S.A. Then they had stopped. The Commander-in-Chief considered that any appeal to the United Kingdom should be not for forces for offensive action, but for those necessary to ensure the security of Australia by adequate defence. The United Kingdom did not admit earlier that the forces were not sufficient for defence. This view had been modified by the promise of reinforcements should Australia be heavily attacked. They now said that they did not believe in the probability of Australia being attacked. The promise of help if Australia were heavily attacked was an extremely weak reed on which to rely, as it would

be impossible to come to the assistance of Australia in sufficient strength and early enough if Japan had air and sea superiority to carry out such an attack. Furthermore, the Commander-in-Chief did not consider that any quid pro quo was being offered for the assistance Australia had rendered overseas with naval, military and air forces. The fact that Britain had carried out a raid on Cologne with 1,000 heavy bombers showed that she must have reserves behind this force of anything up to 4,000 bombers, yet the Commander-in-Chief, Southwest Pacific Area, had a total of 40 heavy bombers, of which a large number were unserviceable.

6. The Commander-in-Chief considered it the fundamental duty of the United Kingdom Government to give aid to Australia, and it was to the strategic advantage of the United States that the security of Australia should be maintained. Therefore, both countries should help.

7. In regard to the future prospects of assistance from the U.S.A., the Commander-in-Chief said that the flow of planes to Australia had been resumed, and he had been promised 107 in June, plus 75% of the requisite personnel. He had been promised that this flow would continue in the quantity based on losses in the South Pacific Area and the estimate of the United States Chiefs of Staff of the situation. The United States authorities are re-considering the amount of assistance by U.S.A. air forces which could be given in the Southwest Pacific Area, and General Arnold's [Henry H. Arnold, Chief of the U.S. Army Air Corps] visit to London was no doubt connected with this. The Commander-in-Chief was hopeful that increases in the United States air forces would be approved in accordance with his request for an increase in the first-line strength from 500 aircraft to 1,000 aircraft. In regard to land forces, the Commander-in-Chief said that the 37th Division was on its way, two-thirds being intended for New Zealand and one-third for Fiji. It would be followed by a United States Marine Division, which would go to New Zealand and be under American and not New Zealand control. It was expected to arrive in July. The Commander-in-Chief stated that he was hopeful of getting the Corps of three divisions for which he had asked. General Richardson, who was the Commanding General of a United States Army Corps, was coming to Australia shortly. The purpose of this mission was not known, but the Commander-in-Chief was hopeful, in view of General Richardson's

command, that it meant that his forces would follow later. . . .

8. In regard to naval forces, the Commander-in-Chief referred to his request for two aircraft carriers for the Southwest Pacific Area. Since the Battle of the Coral Sea the American naval forces in this area had been increased by one 8-inch cruiser and one destroyer. There were therefore now five 8-inch cruisers allotted to the Southwest Pacific Area. The United States authorities had advised the Commander-in-Chief that no carriers were available. At his suggestion, the United States authorities had asked the United Kingdom Government whether they could make any carriers available, but a negative reply was received. The Commander-in-Chief pointed out that Admiral Somerville [U.K. Commander-in-Chief, Far Eastern Fleet] had three aircraft carriers, and he considered that one could be spared in view of the fact that naval action was now centred in the Pacific Ocean, since the Japanese naval forces had withdrawn from the Indian Ocean. The Eastern Fleet was working between the African coast and Ceylon. The Commander-in-Chief suggested that arrangements should be sought whereby part of Admiral Somerville's forces could operate in the Southwest Pacific Area, by special arrangement, in order to exercise joint pressure against Japanese bases to the north of Australia. . . .

11. In regard to the results of Dr. Evatt's mission as shown in the cablegrams, the Commander-in-Chief said that, if he might speak with frankness (which the Prime Minister asked that he should do), he considered that Dr. Evatt was undoubtedly a brilliant advocate who, by the skilful manner in which he had put his case, had aroused a live interest in the English people as to the security of Australia and had achieved a good press for his case. He had no doubt evoked a sympathetic hearing from Mr. Churchill and other Ministers, but from the practical military point of view little had been achieved. He added, however, that probably no one could have done better. As the cables showed, the efforts he had exerted had been those of a great pleader, but the agreement between Mr. Churchill and President Roosevelt on grand strategy was a high hurdle to get over. It was evident that Mr. Churchill was determined that the seat of war should not be in the Pacific Ocean. The Commander-in-Chief agreed that this was good, if Tokyo also agreed. The conception of grand strategy of concentrating against one flank whilst holding the other was quite sound in principle, but he would emphasize that the holding

was as important as the attacking. The United Nations had utterly failed to provide the forces necessary to hold the flank in the Pacific. This was evident from the tragedies that had occurred in Malaya, the Philippines, the Netherlands Indies and Burma. They proved that the United Nations did not have sufficient forces for holding the situation in the Pacific. He emphasized that he was asking for a defensive and not an offensive situation. . . .

12. In regard to what Australia was doing to help itself, the Commander-in-Chief said that the Defence programme was clear and well-defined, and was being executed with reasonable efficiency and speed. It should ultimately provide a first-class Army and also a first-class Air Force by 1943, if the aircraft requested were despatched. Two carriers, however, were required for the naval forces, and a concentration of effort should be made in London to obtain these carriers for [Commander, Allied Naval Forces, Southwest Pacific Area] Admiral Leary's forces, or an arrangement for Admiral Somerville to work in closest contact with the naval forces in the Southwest Pacific Area. The support of Great Britain should also be obtained for the supply to Australia of the aircraft required for the expansion of the R.A.A.F. [Royal Australian Air Force] to 71 squadrons. In regard to the 9th Division of the A.I.F. [Australian Infantry Forces] in the Middle East, the Commander-in-Chief said that he would insist on its return to Australia, but not in too abrupt a manner. . . . The Commander-in-Chief considered that in Australia's hour of peril she was entitled at least to the use of all the forces she could raise herself. If Australian forces were serving overseas and could not be returned, then it was essential that a quid pro quo should be given in the shape of corresponding British forces. In regard to the two R.A.A.F. Spitfire squadrons which were being returned to Australia, the Commander-in-Chief noted that Australia had two permanent R.A.A.F. squadrons abroad and ten squadrons which had been formed under the R.A.A.F. infiltration scheme. Mr. Churchill was only giving back to Australia part of her forces and one R.A.F. [British Royal Air Force] squadron as a gesture.

13. The Commander-in-Chief suggested that a statement be prepared in two columns, the first of which would show what forces Australia has in other theatres and the other what is required for the defence of Australia. He considered that Australia was entitled to have in the Southwest Pacific theatre every unit it could raise, and in his opinion the military situation warranted such a view. . . .

15. Following a general discussion, the Prime Minister stated that he would submit the Commander-in-Chief's suggestions to the next meeting of the Advisory War Council.

Source: Australian Department of Foreign Affairs, *Documents on Australian Foreign Policy 1937–49:* Volume 5: *July 1941–June 1942* (Canberra: Australian Government Publishing Service, 1982), 818–823.

136. Martin Bormann's Confidential Instruction 40/540 on the "Yellow Peril," 5 June 1942

The German military alliance with Japan undercut the racial principles of Aryan supremacy so fiercely espoused by Adolf Hitler and the National Socialist Party. In June 1942, Hitler's secretary found it necessary to issue an order warning that under no circumstances should the German media and public use the term "yellow peril" to refer to the Japanese.

The following item from propaganda themes is issued at the request of the Directorate of Reich Propaganda and the Minister of Propaganda:

It has already been pointed out that particularly stupid people are trying either to belittle the successes of our Japanese allies or to question their significance for Germany by speaking of a "yellow peril" which menaces even Germany.

It must be stated again that any person who does not take exception to such phrases but repeats them thoughtlessly, parrot-fashion, is a traitor to his country and does Germany the gravest harm in the midst of a decisive life and death struggle.

Since discussion of this theme has been taken up in certain intellectual circles, it is necessary to challenge the phrase resolutely wherever it is used and, if necessary, to report the stubborn persons who persist in using it.

Source: Margaret Carlyle, ed., *Documents on International Affairs 1939–1946 Volume II: Hitler's Europe* (London: Oxford University Press, 1954), 84. Reprinted with permission of Chatham House.

137. Agreement between the Governments of Mexico and the United States (The *Bracero* Program), 23 July 1942

In an effort to alleviate the serious labor shortage in the United States and free more young American men for military service, in 1942 the governments of Mexico and the United States signed an agreement admitting Mexicans as temporary guest workers. Most of those Mexicans who entered the United States under this program, which was extended until 1964, worked on farms and railroads. Signed in Mexico City on 23 July 1942, the agreement took effect on 4 August 1942.

Agreement of August 4, 1942, for the Temporary Migration of Mexican Agricultural Workers to the United States as Revised on April 26, 1943, by an Exchange of Notes between the American Embassy at Mexico City and the Mexican Ministry for Foreign Affairs

GENERAL PROVISIONS

1) It is understood that Mexicans contracting to work in the United States shall not be engaged in any military service.

2) Mexicans entering the United States as a result of this understanding shall not suffer discriminatory acts of any kind in accordance with the Executive Order No. 8802 issued at the White House June 25, 1941.

3) Mexicans entering the United States under this understanding shall enjoy the guarantees of transportation, living expenses and repatriation established in Article 29 of the Mexican Federal Labor Law as follows:

Article 29. All contracts entered into by Mexican workers for lending their services outside their country shall be made in writing, legalized by the municipal authorities of the locality where entered into and viséd by the Consul of the country where their services are being used. Furthermore, such contract shall contain, as a requisite of validity of same, the following stipulations, without which the contract is invalid.

I. Transportation and subsistence expenses for the worker, and his family, if such is the case, and all other expenses which originate from point of origin to border points and compliance of immigration requirements, or for any other similar concept, shall be paid exclusively by the employer or the contractual parties.

II. The worker shall be paid in full the salary agreed upon, from which no deduction shall be made in any amount for any of the concepts mentioned in the above sub-paragraph.

III. The employer or contractor shall issue a bond or constitute a deposit in cash in the Bank of Workers, or in the absence of same, in the Bank of Mexico, to the entire satisfaction of the respective labor authorities, for a sum equal to repatriation costs of the worker and his family, and those originated by transportation to point of origin.

IV. Once the employer established proof of having covered such expenses or the refusal of the worker to return to his country, and that he does not owe the worker any sum covering salary or indemnization to which he might have a right, the labor authorities shall authorize the return of the deposit or the cancellation of the bond issued.

It is specifically understood that the provisions of Section III of Article 29 above-mentioned shall not apply to the Government of the United States notwithstanding the inclusion of this section in the agreement, in view of the obligations assumed by the United States government under Transportation (a) and (c) of this agreement.

4) Mexicans entering the United States under this understanding shall not be employed to displace other workers, or for the purpose of reducing rates of pay previously established.

In order to implement the application of the general Principles mentioned above the following specific clauses are established:

(When the word "employer" is used hereinafter it shall be understood to mean the Farm Security Administration of the Department of Agriculture of the United States of America; the word "sub-employer" shall mean the owner or operator of the farm or farms in the United States on which the Mexican will be employed; the word "worker" hereinafter used shall refer to the Mexican Farm laborer entering the United States under this understanding.)

CONTRACTS

a. Contracts will be made between the employer and the worker under the supervision of the Mexican Government. (Contracts must be written in Spanish.)

b. The employer shall enter into a contract with the sub-employer, with a view to proper observance of the principles embodied in this understanding.

ADMISSION

a. The Mexican health authorities will, at the place whence the worker comes, see that he meets the necessary physical conditions.

TRANSPORTATION

a. All transportation and living expenses from the place of origin to destination, and return, as well as expenses incurred in the fulfillment of any requirements of a migratory nature shall be met by the Employer.

b. Personal belongings of the workers up to a maximum of 35 kilos per person shall be transported at the expense of the Employer.

c. In accord with the intent of Article 29 of Mexican Federal Labor Law, quoted under General Provisions (3) above, it is expected that the employer will collect all or part of the cost accruing under (a) and (b) of Transportation from the sub-employer.

WAGES AND EMPLOYMENT

a. (1) Wages to be paid the worker shall be the same as those paid for similar work to other agricultural laborers under the same conditions within the same area, in the respective regions of destination. Piece rates shall be so set as to enable the worker of average ability to earn the prevailing wage. In any case wages for piece work or hourly work will not be less than 30 cents per hour.

b. (2) On the basis of prior authorization from the Mexican Government salaries lower than those established in the previous clause may be paid those emigrants admitted into the United States as members of the family of the worker under contract and who, when they are in the field, are able also to become agricultural laborers but who, by their condition of age or sex, cannot carry out the average amount of ordinary work.

c. The worker shall be exclusively employed as an agricultural laborer for which he has been engaged; any change from such type of employment or any change of locality shall be made with the express approval of the worker and with the authority of the Mexican Government.

d. There shall be considered illegal any collection by reason of commission or for any other concept demanded of the worker.

e. Work of minors under 14 years shall be strictly prohibited, and they shall have the same schooling opportunities as those enjoyed by children of other agricultural laborers.

f. Workers domiciled in the migratory labor camps or at any other place of employment under this understanding shall be free to obtain articles for their personal consumption, or that of their families, wherever it is most convenient for them.

g. The Mexican workers will be furnished without cost to them with hygienic lodgings, adequate to the physical conditions of the region of a type used by a common laborer of the region and the medical and sanitary services enjoyed also without cost to them will be identical with those furnished to the other agricultural workers in the regions where they may lend their services.

h. Workers admitted under this understanding shall enjoy as regards occupational diseases and accidents the same guarantees enjoyed by other agricultural workers under United States legislation.

i. Groups of workers admitted under this understanding shall elect their own representatives to deal with the Employer, but it is understood that all such representatives shall be working members of the group.

The Mexican Consuls, assisted by the Mexican Labor Inspectors, recognized as such by the Employer will take all possible measures of protection in the interest of the Mexican workers in all questions affecting them, within their corresponding jurisdiction, and will have free access to the places of work of the Mexican workers. The Employer will observe that the sub-employer grants all facilities to the Mexican Government for the compliance of all the clauses in this contract.

j. For such time as they are unemployed under a period equal to 75% of the period (exclusive of Sundays) for which the workers have been contracted they shall receive a subsistence allowance at the rate of $3.00 per day.

Should the cost of living rise this will be a matter for reconsideration.

The master contracts for workers submitted to the Mexican government shall contain definite provisions for computation of subsistence and payments under the understanding.

k. The term of the contract shall be made in accordance with the authorities of the respective countries.

l. At the expiration of the contract under this understanding, and if the same is not renewed, the authorities of the United States shall consider illegal, from an immigration point of view, the continued stay of the worker in the territory of the United States, exception made of cases of physical impossibility.

SAVINGS FUND

a. The respective agencies of the Government of the United States shall be responsible for the safekeeping of the sums contributed by the Mexican workers toward the formation of their Rural Savings Fund, until such sums are transferred to *the Wells Fargo Bank and Union Trust Company of San Francisco for the account of the Bank of Mexico, S.A., which will transfer such amounts to the Mexican Agricultural Credit Bank. This last shall assume responsibility for the deposit, for the safekeeping and for the application, or in the absence of these, for the return of such amounts.*

b. The Mexican Government through the Banco de Crédito Agrícola will take care of the security of the savings of the workers to be used for payment of the agricultural implements, which may be made available to the Banco de Crédito Agrícola in accordance with exportation permits for shipment to Mexico with the understanding that the Farm Security Administration will recommend priority treatment for such implements.

NUMBERS

As it is impossible to determine at this time the number of workers who may be needed in the United States for agricultural labor employment, the employer shall advise the Mexican Government from time to time as to the number needed. The Government of Mexico shall determine in each case the number of workers who may leave the country without detriment to its national economy.

GENERAL CONSIDERATIONS

It is understood that, with reference to the departure from Mexico of Mexican workers, who are not farm laborers, there shall govern in understandings reached by agencies to the respective Governments the same fundamental principles which have been applied here to the departure of farm labor.

It is understood that the employers will cooperate with such other agencies of the Government of the United States in carrying this understanding into effect whose authority under the laws of the United States are such as to contribute to the effectuation of the understandings.

Either Government shall have the right to renounce this understanding, given appropriate notification to the other Government 90 days in advance. This understanding may be formalized by an exchange of notes between the Ministry of Foreign Affairs of the Republic of Mexico and the Embassy of the United States of America in Mexico.

[Italicized portions were added in April 1943.]

Source: "Official Bracero Agreement." The Farm Workers Web Site. Available at http://www.farmworkers.org/bpaccord.html.

138. Evan Griffith, "Appeal to Buy War Bonds," 3 August 1942

Although taxes rose in wartime, much of the war's costs were financed by government borrowing. In the Allied countries purchases were voluntary, but much moral pressure was exerted to persuade the general public that it was their patriotic duty to invest in as many war bonds as they could afford. For the first time in over a decade, most people were earning good money in war-related jobs, and due to wartime restrictions there was relatively little on which they could spend their wages. Farmers, too, were enjoying unwonted prosperity after the hardships of the 1930s. The following appeal to Kansas farmers was signed by Evan Griffith, the administrator of that state's War Savings Staff, and sent out on 3 August 1942.

TO THE FARMERS OF KANSAS:

Your own sons and neighbors are fighting on foreign battle fields to hold back the Japs and Hitler. Millions of other American boys are being trained for overseas service. These men cannot fight bare-handed. They must have guns and tanks and ships and planes—which cost a lot of money. We must supply these war implements in a hurry. We must win, and the sooner we win, the fewer American boys will be killed.

Farmers, like all Americans, have obligations to meet and families to support. Crop failures have occurred frequently in recent years. Some sections are just now recovering from the effects of drought and depression years. This year, again, adverse weather conditions have hurt some localities. Farming in Kansas certainly has not been profitable for everyone every year. Still, the Kansas farmer has kept his faith in the "good earth" of Kansas—and that faith now is paying dividends. It appears that farm income for Kansas this year will be more than in any year since 1929—and I am writing to ask you to buy all of the War Bonds you possibly can. You can buy these Bonds through your banker, postmaster, building and loan association and many of our merchants.

You help win the war . . . you're backing the boys in the service . . . when you Buy War Bonds.

War Bonds are the soundest investment on earth . . . you are always guaranteed at least what you pay for them, plus interest . . . War bonds can be cashed in at any time after sixty days . . . they are a liquid asset, like wheat in the bin.

We all realize that we can't buy cars and tires and farm machinery . . . but we can convert Bonds into cash for farm machinery and other necessary articles when the war is over and these articles are available again.

Source: Evan Griffith, "Appeal to Buy War Bonds," 3 August 1942. "Government Material" File, Linda Kuntz Papers, World War II Participants and Contemporaries Collection, Dwight D. Eisenhower Presidential Library. Reprinted in Mark P. Parillo, ed., *We Were in the Big One: Experiences of World War II Generation* (Wilmington, DE: Scholarly Resources, 2002), 14–17.

139. The French Resistance Plans for European Unity and Reform: Extract from Manifesto, "Combat and Revolution," Written by the French Resistance Leaders Henri Frenay, Claude Bourdet, and André Hauriou, and Published in the Southern Resistance Journal *Combat,* July–September 1942

This manifesto, composed in July 1942 in an effort to clarify the long-term aims of the French resistance, called not simply for the overthrow of German rule in France, but also for the establishment of a new republic in France, based on socialist principles, and for the creation of a European federation. Its conclusions summarized this outlook, which was symptomatic of the boost World War II gave to pressures for extensive social reform.

The revolution that we bear within ourselves will be socialist because the moment has come to stop talking and take action to wrest from a powerful oligarchy the control and benefit of the economy, and to restore important sectors of the economy to the nation or, if appropriate, to communities of producers and consumers.

Contrary to Vichy's policy, which has consolidated large-scale capitalism by the Comité d'Organisation, we want to see workers sharing in the life and profits of enterprises. We shall improve their conditions of life by pooling the benefits of technical progress.

The revolution that we bear within ourselves is more than a material revolution—it is a revolution of the mind, of youth and of the people.

The bourgeois Republic was built on narrow selfishness and on fears that were ill-concealed by the rhetoric of goodwill.

The men of the Resistance, hardened by daily trials, will introduce into France a spirit of generosity, greatness and daring.

The path of learning will be genuinely open to all, as part of their education, and will train character as well as the mind. Thus it will bring forth from the heart of the nation a genuine elite which can be constantly renewed. If an elite cannot renew itself, it dies.

We wish to bring about a harmonious synthesis between victorious individualism and a generous awareness of the community.

The revolution that we bear within is the dawn of a new civilization. That is what the worldwide civil war is about.

History teaches us that frontiers are constantly widening.

The United States of Europe—a stage on the road to world union—will soon be a living reality for which we are fighting.

Instead of a Europe which is not united but enslaved under the yoke of a power-intoxicated Germany, we and the other peoples will create a united Europe on the basis of liberty, equality, fraternity and the rule of law.

Frenchmen of town and country, we call on you to fight for the liberation of our territory from dictatorship and for economic and spiritual freedom. Join the ranks of Combat, which is fighting for France from Dunkirk to Bayonne, from Brest to Nice and in the overseas empire.

With General de Gaulle and the Fighting French forces alongside the United Nations we shall win the war and overthrow Fascism. After that we shall remake France.

Source: Henri Frenay, Claude Bourdet, and André Hauriou, "Combat and Revolution," *Combat,* July–September 1942. Excerpted and translated in Walter Lipgens, ed., *Documents on the History of European Integration:* Series B, Vol. I: *Continental Plans for European Union 1939–1945 (*Berlin and New York: de Gruyter, 1984), 291–293. Reprinted with permission of Walter de Gruyter, Co.

140. Soviet Press Release: Josef Stalin to Henry C. Cassidy, Associated Press Representative, Moscow, 3 October 1942

One perennial thorn in Soviet relations with Britain and the United States was the decision of the Western Allies to defer opening a second front in Europe until June 1944. Stalin believed that this hesitancy left his country and its people to absorb the brunt of the German military assault. In response to a question from an American journalist, he wrote a letter complaining of this delay, which the Soviet information services immediately published as a press release.

Henry C. Cassidy, representative of the Associated Press, addressed the Chairman of the Council of People's Commissars of the USSR Josef Stalin with a request to reply orally or in writing to three questions which interest the American public. Mr. Stalin replied with the following letter:

Dear Mr. Cassidy,

Owing to pressure of work and the consequent inability to grant you an interview, I shall confine myself to a brief written answer to your questions.

"1. What place does the possibility of a second front occupy in Soviet estimates of the current situation?"

Answer: A very important place, one might say, a place of first-rate importance.

"2. To what extent is Allied aid to the Soviet Union proving effective and what could be done to amplify and improve this aid?"

Answer: As compared with the aid which the Soviet Union is giving to the Allies by drawing upon itself the main forces of the German fascist armies, the aid of the Allies to the Soviet Union has so far been little effective. In order to amplify and improve this aid, only one thing is required: that the Allies fulfill their obligations fully and on time.

"3. What remains of the Soviet capacity for resistance?"

Answer: I think that the Soviet capacity of resisting the German brigands is in strength not less, if not greater, than the capacity of fascist Germany or of any other aggressive power to secure for itself world domination.

With respect,

J. STALIN.

Source: Information Bulletin, Embassy of the U.S.S.R., 6 October 1942.

141. President Franklin D. Roosevelt, Executive Order Providing for the Stabilizing of the National Economy, White House News Release, 4 October 1942

Wartime conditions often generated inflation, as wages and prices both spiraled out of control. In most countries, governments responded with interventionist measures and controls. In October 1942, President Franklin D. Roosevelt established an agency to stabilize the U.S. economy insofar as possible, through wage and price controls. This was only one of a wide array of government controls imposed during the war, ranging from conscription and higher taxes to rationing and the supervision of labor practices.

By virtue of the authority vested in me by the Constitution and the statutes, and particularly by the Act of October 2, 1942, entitled "An Act to Amend the Emergency Price Control Act of 1942, to Aid in Preventing Inflation, and for Other Purposes," as President of the United States and Commander in Chief of the Army and Navy, and in order to control so far as possible the inflationary tendencies and the vast dislocations attendant thereon which threaten our military effort and our domestic economic structure, and for the more effective prosecution of the war, it is hereby ordered as follows:

TITLE I

Establishment of an Office of Economic Stabilization

1. There is established in the Office for Emergency Management of the Executive Office of the President an Office of Economic Stabilization at the head of which shall be an Economic Stabilization Director (hereinafter referred to as the Director).

2. There is established in the Office of Economic Stabilization an Economic Stabilization Board with which

the Director shall advise and consult. The Board shall consist of the Secretary of the Treasury, the Secretary of Agriculture, the Secretary of Commerce, the Secretary of Labor, the Chairman of the Board of Governors of the Federal Reserve System, the Director of the Bureau of the Budget, the Price Administrator, the Chairman of the National War Labor Board, and two representatives each of labor, management, and farmers to be appointed by the President. The Director may invite for consultation the head of any other department or agency. The Director shall serve as Chairman of the Board.

3. The Director, with the approval of the President, shall formulate and develop a comprehensive national economic policy relating to the control of civilian purchasing power, prices, rents, wages, salaries, profits, rationing, subsidies, and all related matters—all for the purpose of preventing avoidable increases in the cost of living, cooperating in minimizing the unnecessary migration of labor from one business, industry, or region to another, and facilitating the prosecution of the war. To give effect to this comprehensive national economic policy the Director shall have power to issue directives on policy to the Federal departments and agencies concerned.

4. The guiding policy of the Director and of all departments and agencies of the Government shall be to stabilize the cost of living in accordance with the Act of October 2, 1942; and it shall be the duty and responsibility of the Director and of all departments and agencies of the Government to cooperate in the execution of such administrative programs and in the development of such legislative programs as may be necessary to that end. The administration of activities related to the national economic policy shall remain with the departments and agencies now responsible for such activities, but such administration shall conform to the directives on policy issued by the Director.

TITLE II
Wage and Salary Stabilization Policy

1. No increases in wage rates, granted as a result of voluntary agreement, collective bargaining, conciliation, arbitration, or otherwise, and no decreases in wage rates, shall be authorized unless notice of such increases or decreases shall have been filed with the National War Labor Board, and unless the National War Labor Board has approved such increases or decreases.

2. The National War Labor Board shall not approve any increase in the wage rates prevailing on September 15, 1942, unless such increase is necessary to correct maladjustments or inequalities, to eliminate substandards of living, to correct gross inequities, or to aid in the effective prosecution of the war.

   Provided, however, that where the National War Labor Board or the Price Administrator shall have reason to believe that a proposed wage increase will require a change in the price ceiling of the commodity or service involved, such proposed increase, if approved by the National War Labor Board, shall become effective only if also approved by the Director.

3. The National War Labor Board shall not approve a decrease in the wages for any particular work below the highest wages paid therefor between January 1, 1942 and September 15, 1942, unless to correct gross inequities and to aid in the effective prosecution of the war.

4. The National War Labor Board shall, by general regulation, make such exemptions from the provisions of this title in the case of small total wage increases or decreases as it deems necessary for the effective administration of this Order.

5. No increases in salaries now in excess of $5,000 per year (except in instances in which an individual has been assigned to more difficult or responsible work) shall be granted until otherwise determined by the Director.

6. No decrease shall be made in the salary for any particular work below the highest salary paid therefor between January 1, 1942 and September 15, 1942, unless to correct gross inequities and to aid in the effective prosecution of the war.

7. In order to correct gross inequities and to provide for greater equality in contributing to the war effort, the Director is authorized to take the necessary action, and to issue the appropriate regulations, so that, insofar as practicable, no salary shall be authorized until Title III, Section 4 to the extent that it exceeds $25,000 after the payment of taxes allocable to the sum in excess of $25,000. Provided, however, that such regulations shall make due allowance for the payment of life insurance premiums on policies heretofore issued, and required payments on fixed obligations heretofore incurred, and shall make provision to prevent undue hardship.

8. The policy of the Federal Government, as established in Executive Order No. 9017 of January 12, 1942, to encourage free collective bargaining between employers and employees is reaffirmed and continued.

9. Insofar as the provisions of Clause (1) of section 302(c) of the Emergency Price Control Act of 1942 are inconsistent with this Order, they are hereby suspended.

TITLE III
Administration of Wage and Salary Policy

1. Except as modified by this Order, the National War Labor Board shall continue to perform the powers, functions, and duties conferred upon it by Executive Order No. 9017, and the functions of said Board are hereby extended to cover all industries and all employees. The National War Labor Board shall continue to follow the procedures specified in said Executive Order.
2. The National War Labor Board shall constitute the agency of the Federal Government authorized to carry out the wage policies stated in this Order, or the directives on policy issued by the Director under this Order. The National War Labor Board is further authorized to issue such rules and regulations as may be necessary for the speedy determination of the propriety of any wage increases or decreases in accordance with this Order, and to avail itself of the services and facilities of such State and Federal departments and agencies as, in the discretion of the National War Labor Board, may be of assistance to the Board.
3. No provision with respect to wages contained in any labor agreement between employers and employees . . . which is inconsistent with the policy herein enunciated or hereafter formulated by the Director shall be enforced except with the approval of the National War Labor Board within the provisions of this Order. . . .

TITLE IV
Prices of Agricultural Commodities

1. The prices of agricultural commodities and of commodities manufactured or processed in whole or substantial part from any agricultural commodity shall be stabilized, so far as practicable, on the basis of levels which existed on September 15, 1942 and in compliance with the Act of October 2, 1942. . . .

TITLE V
Profits and Subsidies

1. The Price Administrator in fixing, reducing, or increasing prices, shall determine price ceilings in such a manner that profits are prevented which in his judgment are unreasonable or exorbitant.
2. The Director may direct any Federal department or agency including, but not limited to, the Department of Agriculture (including the Commodity Credit Corporation and the Surplus Marketing Administration), the Department of Commerce, the Reconstruction Finance Corporation, and other corporations organized pursuant to Section 5d of the Reconstruction Finance Corporation Act, as amended, to use its authority to subsidize and to purchase for resale, if such measures are necessary to insure the maximum necessary production and distribution of any commodity, or to maintain ceiling prices, or to prevent a price rise inconsistent with the purposes of this Order. . . .

Source: Web site: ibiblio. Available at http://www.ibiblio.org/pha/policy/1942/421003a.html.

142. The New Order in East Asia: Speech of Lieutenant Colonel Nagatomo, 28 October 1942

In 1942, Japanese Lieutenant Colonel Nagatomo, chief of the No. 3 Branch of the Thailand Prisoner of War Administration, delivered the following speech to Allied prisoners of war at Thanbyuzayat, Burma. His audience, most of whom went on to work on the notorious Burma Railroad, were expected to remain smiling while listening to the speech, an attitude perhaps facilitated by the fact that very few of them understood Japanese.

It is a great pleasure to me to see you at this place as I am appointed Chief of the war prisoner camp obedient to the Imperial Command issued by His Majesty the Emperor. The great East Asiatic war has broken out due to the rising of the East Asian Nations whose hearts were burnt with the desire to live and preserve their nations on account of the intrusion of the British and Americans for many years past.

There is, therefore, no other reason for Japan to drive out the Anti-Asiatic powers of the arrogant and insolent British and Americans from East Asia in cooperation with our neighbors of China and other East Asiatic Nations and establish the Greater East Asia Co-Prosperity Sphere for the benefit of all human beings and establish lasting great peace in the world. During the past few centuries, Nippon [Japan] has made great sacrifices and extreme endeavors to become the leader of the East Asiatic Nations, who were mercilessly and pitilessly treated by the outside forces of the British and Americans, and the Nippon Army, without disgracing anybody, has been doing her best until now for fostering Nippon's real power.

You are only a few remaining skeletons after the invasion of East Asia for the past few centuries, and are pitiful victims. It is not your fault, but until your governments do not [sic] wake up from their dreams and discontinue their resistance, all of you will not be released. However, I shall not treat you badly for the sake of humanity as you have no fighting power left at all.

His Majesty the Emperor has been deeply anxious about all prisoners of war, and has ordered us to enable the operating of war prisoner camps at almost all the places in the SW countries.

The Imperial Thoughts are unestimable and the Imperial Favors are infinite and, as such, you should weep with gratitude at the greatness of them. I shall correct or mend the misleading and improper Anti-Japanese ideas. I shall meet with you hereafter and at the beginning I shall require of you the four following points:

(1) I heard that you complain about the insufficiency of various items. Although there may be lack of materials it is difficult to meet your requirements. Just turn your eyes to the present conditions of the world. It is entirely different from the prewar times. In all lands and countries materials are considerably short and it is not easy to obtain even a small piece of cigarette, and the present position is such that it is not possible even for needy women and children to get sufficient food. Needless to say, therefore, at such inconvenient places even our respectable Imperial Army is also not able to get mosquito nets, foodstuffs, medicines, and cigarettes. As conditions are such, how can you expect me to treat you better than the Imperial Army? I do not prosecute according to my own wishes and it is not due to the expense but due to the shortage of materials at such difficult places. In spite of our wishes to meet their requirements, I cannot do so with money. I shall supply you, however, if I can do so with my best efforts and I hope you will rely upon me and render your wishes before me. We will build the railroad if we have to build it over the white man's

body. It gives me great pleasure to have a fast-moving defeated nation in my power. You are merely rubble, but I will not feel bad because it is your rulers. If you want anything you will have to come through me for same and there will be many of you who will not see your homes again. Work cheerfully at my command.

(2) I shall strictly manage all of your going out, coming back, meeting with friends, communications. Possessions of money shall be limited, living manners, deportment, salutation, and attitude shall be strictly according to the rules of the Nippon Army, because it is only possible to manage you all, who are merely rabble, by the order of military regulations. By this time I shall issue separate pamphlets of house rules of war prisoners and you are required to act strictly in accordance with these rules and you shall not infringe on them by any means.

(3) My biggest requirement from you is escape. The rules of escape shall naturally be severe. This rule may be quite useless and only binding to some of the war prisoners, but it is most important for all of you in the management of the camp. You should, therefore, be contented accordingly. If there is a man here who has at least 1 percent of a chance of escape, we shall make him face the extreme penalty. If there is one foolish man who is trying to escape, he shall see big jungles toward the East which are impossible for communication. Towards the West he shall see boundless ocean and, above all, in the main points of the North, South, our Nippon Armies are guarding. You will easily understand the difficulty of complete escape. A few such cases of ill-omened matters which happened in Singapore (execution of over a thousand Chinese civilians) shall prove the above and you should not repeat such foolish things although it is a lost chance after great embarrassment.

(4) Hereafter, I shall require all of you to work as nobody is permitted to do nothing and eat at the present. In addition, the Imperial Japanese have great work to promote at the places newly occupied by them, and this is an essential and important matter. At the time of such shortness of materials your lives are preserved by the military, and all of you must award them with your labor. By the hand of the Nippon Army Railway Construction Corps to connect Thailand and Burma, the work has started to the great interest of the world. There are deep jungles where no man ever came to clear them by cutting the trees.

There are also countless difficulties and suffering, but you shall have the honor to join in this great work which was never done before, and you shall also do your best effort. I shall investigate and check carefully about your coming back, attendance so that all of you except those who are unable to work shall be taken out for labor. At the same time I shall expect all of you to work earnestly and confidently henceforth you shall be guided by this motto.

Source: Robert S. La Forte and Ronald E. Marcello, eds., *Building the Death Railway: The Ordeal of American POWs in Burma, 1942–1945* (Wilmington, DE: Scholarly Resources, 1993), 287–289.

143. Mohandas Gandhi, "Message to America," 31 October 1942

Although the Congress Party in India supported the Allied war effort, it also continued to call upon the withdrawal of British rule from India as soon as possible. In autumn 1942, Mohandas Gandhi, who spearheaded the movement for Indian independence, appealed to Americans to support the demands of Indian nationalists as an important war measure.

As I am supposed to be the spirit behind the much discussed and equally well abused resolution of the Working Committee of the Indian National Congress on independence, it has become necessary for me to explain my position, for I am not unknown to you.

I have in America perhaps the largest number of friends in the West—not even excepting Great Britain. . . .

Moreover, you have given me a teacher in Thoreau, who furnished me through his essay on the "Duty of Civil Disobedience" scientific confirmation of what I was doing in South Africa. . . .

I invite you to read my formula of withdrawal or as it has been popularly called "Quit India" with this background. . . .

. . . . I assert that I would not have asked my country to invite Great Britain to withdraw her rule over India irrespective of any demand to the contrary, if I had not seen at once that for the sake of Great Britain and the Allied cause it was necessary for Britain boldly to perform the duty of freeing India from bondage.

By that supreme act of justice Britain would have taken away all cause for the seething discontent of India. She will turn the growing ill will into active good will. I submit that it is worth all the battleships and airships that your wonder working engineers and financial resources can produce.

I know that interested propaganda has filled your ears and eyes with distorted visions of the Congress position. I have been painted as a hypocrite and enemy of Britain under disguise. My demonstrable spirit of accommodation has been described as my inconsistency, proving me to be an utterly unreliable man. I am not going to burden this letter with proof in support of my assertions. If the credit which I have enjoyed in America will not stand me in good stead, nothing I may argue in self defense will carry conviction.

You have made common cause with Great Britain. You cannot therefore disown responsibility for anything that her representatives do in India. You will do a grievous wrong to the Allied cause, if you do not sift the Truth from the chaff whilst there is yet time. Just think of it. Is there anything wrong in the Congress demanding unconditional recognition of India's independence? It is being said: "But this is not the time." We say: This is the psychological moment for that recognition. For then and then only can there be irresistible opposition to Japanese aggression. It is of immense value to the Allied cause if it is also of equal value to India.

I want you to look upon the immediate recognition of India's independence as a war measure of first class magnitude.

Source: Mohandas Gandhi, "Message to America," *India Today,* October 1942. Web site: ibiblio. Available at http://www.ibiblio.org/pha/policy/1942/421031a.html.

144. White House News Release, President Franklin D. Roosevelt, Statement Announcing the Opening of a Second Front in French North and West Africa, 7 November 1942

In November 1942, Anglo-American forces under the overall command of U.S. General Dwight D. Eisenhower opened a second front against French colonies in North Africa, including Morocco, Tunisia, and Algeria. Although these areas were under the control of officials supposedly loyal to the collaborationist Vichy government in France, Allied leaders hoped that they would quickly come over to the Allied side. Roosevelt made a radio broadcast to the French people, appealing to them to support the invasion. He followed up these appeals with personal messages seeking support from the head of the French government, Marshal Henri Philippe Pétain, and the governors general and commanders of the French colonies. He also sought the continued neutrality of the dictator of Spain, General Francisco Franco.

In order to forestall an invasion of Africa by Germany and Italy, which if successful, would constitute a direct threat to America across the comparatively narrow sea from Western Africa, a powerful American force equipped with adequate weapons of modern warfare and under American Command is today landing on the Mediterranean and Atlantic Coasts of the French Colonies in Africa.

The landing of this American Army is being assisted by the British Navy and air forces and it will, in the immediate future, be reinforced by a considerable number of divisions of the British Army.

This combined allied force, under American Command, in conjunction with the British campaign in Egypt is designed to prevent an occupation by the Axis armies of any part of Northern or Western Africa, and to deny to the aggressor nations a starting point from which to launch an attack against the Atlantic Coast of the Americas.

In addition, it provides an effective second front assistance to our heroic allies in Russia.

The French Government and the French people have been informed of the purpose of this expedition, and have been assured that the allies seek no territory and have no intention of interfering with friendly French Authorities in Africa.

The Government of France and the people of France and the French Possessions have been requested to cooperate with and assist the American expedition in its effort to repel the German and Italian international criminals, and by so doing to liberate France and the French Empire from the Axis yoke.

This expedition will develop into a major effort by the Allied Nations and there is every expectation that it will be successful in repelling the planned German and Italian invasion of Africa and prove the first historic step to the liberation and restoration of France.

Source: Web site: ibiblio. Available at http://www.ibiblio.org/pha/policy/1942/421107b.html.

145. Enigma Codebreaking in World War II: Recollections of Edward Thomas

The Allies' ability to intercept and decrypt German, Italian, and Japanese military codes was a major advantage to them in World War II. Beginning in spring 1940, the British gradually broke those of Germany (Enigma) and Italy (Fish), while the Americans received a steady stream of intelligence from Japanese (MAGIC) intercepts. The overall codebreaking operations were known as Ultra. The headquarters of British operations of the Government Code and Cypher School was Bletchley Park, where teams of British and, eventually, American cryptographers lived in great seclusion and secrecy, working in huts in the mansion's spacious grounds. One of them was Edward Thomas, a young naval officer who joined Hut 3 at Bletchley Park in early 1942, after eighteen months in Iceland as a naval intelligence officer.

In early 1942 some half-dozen naval officers knowing German were summoned to Bletchley's Naval Section. Current gossip at the Park had it that there were two explanations for this. One was that the Section's head, observing that Hut 3 boasted several individuals in RAF and Army uniform, wished to have some navy-clad folk about the place to impress visiting VIPs. The other was that officers with first-hand experience of the naval war might be able to add a touch of verismo to the interpretation and analysis of the German naval Enigma decrypts then being done in Hut 4, mainly by men and women in civilian garb. We naval folk were soon to learn the supererogatory character of this second explanation. There was precious little that Hut 4's civilians did not know about how navies worked. Most of what I ever knew about the German navy came from those who had been working on the naval Enigma since it was first broken a year earlier.

I vividly remember the sense of shock produced on my first arrival at the Park by the grimness of its barbed-wire defences, by the cold and dinginess of its hutted accommodation, and by the clerk-work we were first set to do. But this was soon swept aside by the much greater shock of discovering the miracles that were being wrought at the Park. In Iceland I had been interrogating the survivors of the many merchant ships sunk in the, at first, highly successful offensive against the Atlantic convoys launched by the U-boats in March 1941. I had spent many hours trying to analyse their strength and tactics. I could have spared my pains. For I now discovered that all this, and everything else about the U-boats, was known with precision by those privy to the Enigma decrypts. Leafing through the files of past messages—for the dreaded Shark key for U-boats, that had been introduced a week before my arrival, was to defeat Hut 8's cryptographers for another ten months—I shivered at seeing the actual words of the signals passing between Admiral Dönitz and the boats under his command whose terrible work I had seen at first hand. . . .

I can place the date of my arrival in Hut 4 pretty exactly. It was shortly before 11 February 1942, the day of the famous "Channel Dash" of the *Scharnhorst, Gneisenau,* and *Prinz Eugen.* There was great commotion in the hut and cries of "Where's Harry? Harry will be furious!" Indeed he was. Harry Hinsley, whom we naval newcomers had already pin-pointed as perhaps the most knowledgeable of all those in Hut 4, flew in late in the afternoon scattering smiles, scarves, and stimulus in every direction, exclaiming, "It's happened again: whenever I take a day off something big blows up." There had, indeed, been good indications that the ships were about to move; but the Enigma settings of 10, 11, and 12 February, by a stroke of the ill luck which precipitated tragedy from time to time, were not solved until three days later.

Hinsley was a key figure in Hut 4. His uncanny ability to sense, from tiny clues in the decrypts or the externals of the radio traffic, that something unusual was afoot was already legendary in the Park. He was well versed in the ways of navies, having more than once visited the Home Fleet in Scapa Flow to explain the workings of the Enigma to the Commander-in-Chief. He was a popular figure there and was known, as I later discovered when I joined the Home Fleet, as "the Cardinal." He was the chief channel for the exchange of ideas between the Naval Section and the Admiralty's Operational Intelligence Centre (OIC). This capable—but not infallible—organization had already in 1940 rejected a suggestion by Hinsley which, if adopted, might have saved the aircraft carrier *Glorious.* On the other hand, during the "Channel Dash" it was smart work done in the OIC which contrived to use the decrypts to have the *Scharnhorst* and the *Gneisenau* mined off the Dutch coast with resounding strategic consequences. . . .

This episode coincided with the onset of Hut 8's ten-month-long inability to break into the newly introduced Shark. Severe losses of merchant ships were to follow, largely in consequence of this. But already by the end of 1941 a turning-point had been reached in the battle of the Atlantic. The evasive routing of convoys made possible by Hut 8's breaking of the naval Enigma in the spring of 1941 had, according to some historians' calculations, spared some three hundred merchant ships and so provided a cushion against the heavy losses yet to come. It also defeated Dönitz's offensive, which was intended to knock out Britain while the German armies disposed of Russia, so avoiding a two-front war. The six-months' long decline in sinkings also provided a crucial breathing-space during which the Allies could develop anti-submarine weapons and tactics, and get on with building more merchant ships. This victory, which saved Britain, was based entirely on the work of Bletchley Park. It was also responsible, though I did not know it at the time, for the great reduction in the number of survivors who passed through my hands in Iceland, reducing my work-load and making it possible for me to be released to Bletchley....

We naval newcomers were at once impressed by the easy relations and lack of friction between those in, and out of, uniform. Despite the high tension of much of the work, a spirit of relaxation prevailed. Anyone of whatever rank or degree could approach anyone else, however venerable, with any idea or suggestion, however crazy. This was partly because those in uniform had mostly been selected from the same walks of life as the civilians—scholarship, journalism, publishing, linguistics, and so forth—and partly because these were the people who saw most clearly what stood to be lost by a Hitler victory. All at the Park were determined to give their all to see this did not happen. Service officers gladly served under civilians, and vice versa. Dons from Oxford and Cambridge worked smoothly together....

... Hut 3 [was] responsible for translating and elucidating the German Air Force and Army decrypts from Hut 6, for supporting its cryptanalysts, and for signalling the gist of the decrypts to operational Commands in the Mediterranean and, later, in other theatres.... New, fascinating, and exciting work was found for us. [German General Erwin] Rommel, fighting in Africa, depended on shipments of fuel, ammunition, and other supplies sent across the Mediterranean in convoys controlled by the Italians. His fortunes waxed or waned with the adequacy, or inadequacy, of his supplies. His most notable victories came when his logistic position was good; and his defeats when he was weakened through want of supplies. They were adequate when the fortunes of war permitted his convoys to arrive safely and in sufficient number: but he faltered when the RAF and Navy contrived to prevent this. His final defeat owed much

to the sustained sinking of his supply ships. Bletchley played a big part in bringing this about.

Hut 6's decrypts told us a great deal about these convoy movements. One source was the Air Force Enigma which throughout 1941 had been revealing, albeit somewhat spasmodically, the instructions for their air escort. This intelligence had, for example, resulted in considerable disruption of the transport to Africa of the first of Rommel's armoured formations. The second and more important source was the Italian administration machine cipher, C38m, broken by Hut 8 in the summer of 1941. This yielded, amongst other things, advance warning of the sailing dates, routes, and composition of virtually all trans-Mediterranean supply convoys. It also threw occasional light on Italian main-fleet movements. During 1941 the gist of the relevant Enigma decrypts had been signalled by Hut 3 to the Mediterranean authorities by the SCU/SLU channel, while that of the C38m decrypts had been sent by a part-naval, part-civilian processing watch in Hut 4 separately to Malta and elsewhere. An outstanding result of these messages had been a spate of sinkings in late 1941 which played a big part in Rommel's retreat to El Agheila at that time.

It was probably a coincidence that, at the time of the Hut 3 reorganization of early 1942, a twenty-four-hour watch of naval officers—one of them a regular—was set up and became an integral part of that hut. Called 3N, one of its jobs was to provide advice, hitherto lacking, to the watch on naval problems arising from the Army-Air Force decrypts. Its other and more important task was to co-ordinate the shipping intelligence from these decrypts with what came out of the C38m. To bring this about 3N and Hut 4's Italian watch became virtually a single team, the former being responsible for the final shape of the outgoing signals—and for taking on the chin any riposte from bewildered recipients at the other end (which was seldom). This development came at a bad time for the British in the Mediterranean. The Axis had greatly strengthened its convoy defences and Malta was all but immobilized by the attacks of the newly arrived Luftflotte 2. Axis convoys were getting through wholesale, and opportunities for attacking them were much reduced. Rommel's recovery in January 1942 was made possible by these developments. Every scrap of intelligence became doubly valuable. The co-ordination of the two sources came at the right moment....

The Air Force Enigma, unlike the C38m, would sometimes indicate the importance—to the German Air Force, of course—of a given convoy, occasionally specifying that it carried urgent supplies of fuel or ammunition. Though these indications were made only in general terms, they were invaluable to the attack planners. From about August 1942 Hut 6 regularly broke the Chaffinch key of the German Army in

Africa and this provided, as well as much else of the highest importance, precise details of cargoes. Ships carrying operationally urgent supplies could now be distinguished from those with routine shipments. This made selective attack possible and greatly increased the effectiveness of the anti-ship campaign. An example of its effectiveness may be found in the Allies' ability, which came as a surprise to some historians, to feed the 250,000 prisoners trapped in Cape Bon during the final phase of the war in Africa. Ships known from the decrypts to be carrying rations had been spared; while those with cargoes of tanks, fuel, and ammunition had been selected for attack.

The arrival of Chaffinch, supplementing the former sources, coincided with that of Rommel on the Egyptian frontier. It now became doubly urgent to deprive him of supplies. It also coincided, to our great good fortune, with the recovery of Malta as a base for anti-shipping operations, and with the breaking by Hut 8 of the naval Enigma key used by the Germans in the Mediterranean. Its yield made for much more efficient attacks on coastal supply shipping, on which Rommel, far from his supply bases and convoy terminals, now largely depended. All this sharply increased the pace of our work. Rommel clamoured for fuel, and attacks on tanker convoys were now given highest priority. Many were successful. Those during August 1942 were largely responsible for his failure at Alam Haifa. After the war I found my initials at the bottom of the signals giving details of the three supremely important tanker movements at the time of the October battle of El Alamein. Their sinking was largely responsible for Rommel's long and halting retreat westwards. I well remember the frustration that exploded from our Hut 3 colleagues at Montgomery's failure to overtake and destroy him. I had not seen such a demonstration since the Knightsbridge fighting six months earlier, when the Eighth Army advanced against an anti-tank trap at the so-called "Cauldron" position and lost heavily. Hut 3 believed that it had provided full details of Rommel's intentions on this occasion.

The Hut 4/3N routine continued until the final victory at Cape Bon. It seemed scarcely credible that the Axis could have sufficient ships left unsunk to succour the fighting in Tunisia. But they did. And the pressure continued right up to the end.

Source: Edward Thomas, "A Naval Officer in Hut 3." Reprinted in F. H. Hinsley and A. Stripp, eds. *Codebreakers: The Inside Story of Bletchley Park* (Oxford, UK: Oxford University Press, 1993), pp. 42–49. Reprinted by permission of Oxford University Press.

146. A. Philip Randolph, "Why Should We March?" November 1942

Even after Franklin D. Roosevelt issued Executive Order 8802, supposedly banning racial discrimination by any business in receipt of government wartime contracts, discriminatory practices and segregation remained entrenched in employment and the armed services. Black protests and the March on Washington Movement continued until March 1946. In late 1942 A. Philip Randolph, head of the Congress on Racial Equality and the group's chief spokesperson, justified his activist tactics.

Though I have found no Negroes who want to see the United Nations lose this war, I have found many who, before the war ends, want to see the stuffing knocked out of white supremacy and of empire over subject peoples. American Negroes, involved as we are in the general issues of the conflict, are confronted not with a choice but with the challenge both to win democracy for ourselves at home and to help win the war for democracy the world over.

There is no escape from the horns of this dilemma. There ought not to be escape. For if the war for democracy is not won abroad, the fight for democracy cannot be won at home. If this war cannot be won for the white peoples, it will not be won for the darker races.

Conversely, if freedom and equality are not vouchsafed the peoples of color, the war for democracy will not be won. Unless this double-barreled thesis is accepted and applied, the darker races will never wholeheartedly fight for the victory of the United Nations. That is why those familiar with the thinking of the American Negro have sensed his lack of enthusiasm, whether among the educated or uneducated, rich or poor, professional or nonprofessional, religious or secular, rural or urban, north, south, east or west.

That is why questions are being raised by Negroes in church, labor union, and fraternal society; in poolroom, barbershop, schoolroom, hospital, hair-dressing parlor; on college campus, railroad, and bus. One can hear such questions asked as these: What have Negroes to fight for? What's the difference between Hitler and that "cracker" [Governor Eugene] Talmadge of Georgia? Why has a man got to be Jim Crowed to die for democracy? If you haven't got democracy yourself, how can you carry it to somebody else?

What are the reasons for this state of mind? The answer

is: discrimination, segregation, Jim Crow. Witness the navy, the army, the air corps; and also government services at Washington. In many parts of the South, Negroes in Uncle Sam's uniform are being put upon, mobbed, sometimes even shot down by civilian and military police, and on occasion lynched. Vested political interests in race prejudice are so deeply entrenched that to them winning the war against Hitler is secondary to preventing Negroes from winning democracy for themselves. This is worth many divisions to Hitler and Hirohito. While labor, business, and farm are subjected to ceilings and floors and not allowed to carry on as usual, these interests trade in the dangerous business of race hate as usual.

When the defense program began and billions of the taxpayers' money were appropriated for guns, ships, tanks and bombs, Negroes presented themselves for work only to be given the cold shoulder. North as well as South, and despite their qualifications, Negroes were denied skilled employment. Not until their wrath and indignation took the form of a proposed protest march on Washington, scheduled for July 1, 1941, did things begin to move in the form of defense jobs for Negroes. The march was postponed by the timely issuance (June 25, 1941) of the famous Executive Order No. 8802 by President Roosevelt. But this order and the President's Committee on Fair Employment Practice, established thereunder, have as yet only scratched the surface by way of eliminating discriminations on account of race or color in war industry. Both management and labor unions in too many places and in too many ways are still drawing the color line.

It is to meet this situation squarely with direct action that the March on Washington Movement launched its present program of protest mass meetings. Twenty thousand were in attendance at Madison Square Garden, June 16; sixteen thousand in the Coliseum in Chicago, June 26; nine thousand in the City Auditorium of St. Louis, August 14. Meetings of such magnitude were unprecedented among Negroes. The vast throngs were drawn from all walks and levels of Negro life—businessmen, teachers, laundry workers, Pullman porters, waiters, and red caps; preachers, crapshooters, and social workers; jitterbugs and Ph.D's. They came and sat in silence, thinking, applauding only when they considered the truth was told, when they felt strongly that something was going to be done about it.

The March on Washington is essentially a movement of the people. It is all Negro and pro-Negro, but not for that reason anti-white or anti-Semitic, or anti-Catholic, or anti-foreign, or anti-labor. Its major weapon is the non-violent demonstration of Negro mass power. Negro leadership has united back of its drive for jobs and justice. "Whether Negroes should march on Washington, and if so, when?" will be the focus of a forthcoming national conference. For the

plan of a protest march has not been abandoned. Its purpose would be to demonstrate that American Negroes are in deadly earnest, and all out for their full rights. No power on earth can cause them today to abandon their fight to wipe out every vestige of second class citizenship and the dual standards that plague them.

A community is democratic only when the humblest and weakest person can enjoy the highest civil, economic, and social rights that the biggest and most powerful possess. To trample on these rights of both Negroes and poor whites is such a commonplace in the South that it takes readily to anti-social, anti-labor, anti-Semitic, and anti-Catholic propaganda. It was because of laxness in enforcing the Weimar constitution in republican Germany that Nazism made headway. Oppression of the Negroes in the United States, like suppression of the Jews in Germany, may open the way for a fascist dictatorship.

By fighting for their rights now, American Negroes are helping to make America a moral and spiritual arsenal of democracy. Their fight against the poll tax, against lynch law, segregation, and Jim Crow, their fight for economic, political, and social equality, thus becomes part of the global war for freedom.

PROGRAM OF THE MARCH ON WASHINGTON MOVEMENT

1. We demand, in the interest of national unity, the abrogation of every law which makes a distinction in treatment between citizens based on religion, creed, color, or national origin. This means an end to Jim Crow in education, in housing, in transportation, and in every other social, economic, and political privilege; and especially, we demand, in the capital of the nation, an end to segregation in public places and in public institutions.

2. We demand legislation to enforce the Fifth and Fourteenth Amendments guaranteeing that no person shall be deprived of life, liberty or property without due process of law, so that the full weight of the national government may be used for the protection of life and thereby may end the disgrace of lynching.

3. We demand the enforcement of the Fourteenth and Fifteenth Amendments and the enactment of the Pepper Poll Tax bill so that all barriers in the exercise of the suffrage are eliminated.

4. We demand the abolition of segregation and discrimination in the army, navy, marine corps, air corps, and all other branches of national defense.

5. We demand an end to the discrimination in jobs and job training. Further, we demand that the FEPC be made a permanent administrative agency of the U.S.

Government and that it be given power to enforce its decisions based on its findings.

6. We demand that federal funds be withheld from any agency which practices discrimination in the use of such funds.

7. We demand colored and minority group representation on all administrative agencies so that these groups may have recognition of their democratic right to participate in formulating policies.

8. We demand representation for the colored and mi-nority racial groups on all missions, political and technical, which will be sent to the peace conference so that the interests of all people everywhere may be fully recognized and justly provided for in the post-war settlement.

Source: A. Philip Randolph. "Why Should We March?" *Survey Graphic* (November 1942). Reprinted in William L. Van Deburg, ed., *Modern Black Nationalism: From Marcus Garvey to Louis Farrakhan* (New York: New York University Press, 1997), 74–77. Reprinted with kind permission of the A. Philip Randolph Institute, Washington, D.C.

147. Elizabeth Gurley Flynn, *Women in the War*, 1942

The left-wing American activist Elizabeth Gurley Flynn was an energetic member of the American Communist Party, which published her 1942 pamphlet urging women to contribute to the American war effort. Flynn's exhortations exemplified not only the new demands the war made on women but also the united front against fascism which, after Hitler's invasion of the Soviet Union in June 1941, the international Communist movement urged upon its members. Flynn also urged that both women and American blacks should permanently increase their participation in the labor force and that the American labor movement make a concerted effort to unionize women and blacks and drop its discrimination against them. After the war, neither of these hopes would be entirely fulfilled.

We American women, like the Chinese, British, and Soviet women, will work till we drop and fight till we die to defend our beautiful country and our democratic liberties from the brutish ideology of the Nazis. We are not called upon to engage in actual combat. . . .

Today it is more useful and just as heroic to *make arms* for our fighting forces and our brave allies. Our main tasks are on the home front. Eighteen people are required at work to keep one fighter on the field at sea, or in the air. Women's work is manifold today. It includes industry, civilian defense, politics, the labor unions, and as trained auxiliaries to the armed forces. General H. H. Kitchener said in the last war: "If the women of either side should stop their war work, that side would lose." This is even more evident today. The women of the nation are essential to winning the war. They are the reservoir of labor. In ever-increasing numbers women will be called out of the kitchen onto the assembly line. It is a matter of patriotism, necessity, and arithmetic. Women are cheerfully answering the call.

Our armed forces are expected to reach ten million in 1943. They are drawn mainly out of production. Their needs take precedence. They must be fed, clothed, shod, trained, transported, given tanks, guns, airplanes, bullets, bombs, Jeeps, ships, parachutes, and myriad other essentials. Civilian needs must also be adequately met to keep our home-front forces healthy and efficient. It is estimated that fifty-eight million workers will be required in 1943. War Chief [Paul V. McNutt, head of the War Production Board] announces that eighteen million must be women or five million more than are employed today. *One out of six able-bodied women, over eighteen years old, will be in war jobs within the next year. . . .*

Prejudices break down in a national crisis. Women and the Negro people must be given the right to show their mettle as workers. Work is not man's versus women's, any more than it is white's versus Negro's, or native-born's versus foreign-born's, or Christian's versus Jew's. Such a characterization as "male, white, Christian, native born" is typically Nazi, repugnant to American concepts of democracy. Women's role in industry, like that of the Negro people, is not of a temporary nature. War emergency accelerates the entry of women into industry. But there were ten million employed in 1930, two and a half million more than in 1920. Many more will remain in industry after this war than were there before, especially in new industries. . . .

The Negro people and women must have permanent access to all jobs and professions. This is democracy. To deny it is to disrupt national unity and cripple production in a critical war period. Victory is at stake. . . .

When women delegates at auto, steel, and other conventions insist that women's problems are today the concern of the whole labor movement, they are absolutely right. *There are over twelve million unorganized women workers in America today. This figure nearly equals the total membership of all existing trade unions put together.* In other words, organized labor could double its strength and influence by organizing all the women workers now outside its ranks. . . .

If women workers remain unorganized, the labor unions will have themselves to blame. The dire results of neglect will most directly affect the women. It will lower their standards, deprive them of strength to defend themselves, and weaken their morale as workers in a war period—and after. It will make them ready prey for anti-union schemes such as company unionism. In addition to the disastrous effects upon the women workers, labor unions must face the reality that the security of already established standards, the guarantee of hard-fought gains, the very existence of some unions depend upon enlisting these new workers. As the labor composition changes, it must either be absorbed in the union or the union is thereby weakened. Several million male trade unionists are away in our armed forces. More will follow. Not only the jobs they vacate but the unions they build will depend upon the women they leave behind them. . . .

It is likewise a disgrace that some A. F. of L. [American Federation of Labor] and independent unions adhere stubbornly to their bars against Negroes as members. This automatically excludes them from occupations where a closed shop or union contract exists. Or they are denied equal status, discouraged from joining, or "Jim Crowed" into separate locals, deprived of the right to hold office or to be delegates to conventions. Jurisdictional rights are invoked by the offending unions to resist efforts of the A. F. of L. Council to remedy the situation—just as Southern states invoke "state's rights" to resist abolition of poll-tax restrictions on voting and national antilynching legislation. The C.I.O. [Committee on Industrial Organization] has taken a strong position opposing all forms of discrimination against Negro workers. It encourages Negro membership on an equal basis and has many Negro organizers and officials. C.I.O. contracts in iron and steel, maritime and mining industries, among others, have eliminated wage differentials between Negroes and whites on similar jobs. The result is that the C.I.O. has a large Negro membership, and Negroes have proven themselves efficient workers, loyal and intelligent members, and capable leaders.

Eternal vigilance is the price of democracy. The best resolutions and declarations of principle must be put in practice or they are empty words, "full of sound and fury—signifying nothing." The doubly shameful and un-American discrimination against Negro women, as Negroes and as women, is widespread. It demands the most emphatic protest and actions by women's organizations, by trade unions, and by government agencies. Despicable and widespread discrimination still prevails in spite of President Roosevelt's Order No. 8802, which specifically bars discrimination against Negroes in plants working on war orders. . . .

To summarize—the vital needs of American women workers to help win the war are as follows:

1. Equal opportunity to work for all women (Negro and white) at all occupations.
2. Adequate training for jobs, under government and union supervision.
3. Equal pay for equal work.
4. Safe and sanitary shop conditions.
5. Equal membership, protection by and participation in labor unions.
6. Child-care centers, with federal funds and supervision.
7. Adequate modern housing. . . .

The voice of women must be heard in the highest councils of the trade union movement and the government. Let us overcome our past shortcomings now in the white heat of a war for human liberation. There should be more than 6 women out of 531 in Congress. England has 13 women members in a Parliament of 615. The Supreme Soviet has 50 percent women, from all regions and occupations. Labor, as the vanguard of progressive forces in our country, can blaze a trail, set an example.

Source: Judy Barrett Litoff and David C. Smith, eds., *American Women in a World at War: Contemporary Accounts from World War II* (Wilmington, DE: Scholarly Resources, 1997), 16–24; original Elizabeth Gurley Flynn, *Women in the War* (New York: Workers Library Publishers, 1942). Reprinted with permission of the Communist Party of the United States, International Publishers Company.

148. Oral History of Fanny Christina Hill

World War II opened new opportunities for all women, black and white alike. Fanny Christina Hill was a Texas-born black woman, aged twenty-four in 1940, who worked as a domestic servant in California until she took a job at the North American Aircraft plant. Although she stopped work late in the war to have a child, she returned to North American Aircraft in 1946, where she remained until she retired in 1980.

Most of the men was gone, and they wasn't hiring too many men unless they had a good excuse. Most of the women was in my bracket, five or six years younger or older. I was twenty-four. There was a black girl that hired in with me. I went to work the next day, sixty cents an hour.

I think I stayed at the school for about four weeks. They only taught you shooting and bucking rivets and how to drill the holes and to file. You had to use a hammer for certain things. After a couple of whiles, you worked on the real thing. But you were supervised so you didn't make a mess. . . .

I was a good student, if I do say so myself. But I have found out through life, sometimes even if you're good, you just don't get the breaks if the color's not right. I could see where they made a difference in placing you in certain jobs. They had fifteen or twenty departments [in the factory], but all the Negroes went to Department 17 because there was nothing but shooting and bucking rivets. You stood on one side of the panel and your partner stood on this side, and he would shoot the rivets with a gun and you'd buck them with the bar. That was about the size of it. I just didn't like it. I didn't think I could stay there with all this shooting and a'bucking and a'jumping and a'bumping. I stayed in it about two or three weeks and then I decided I did *not* like that. I went and told my foreman and he didn't do anything about it, so I decided I'd leave.

While I was standing out on the railroad track, I ran into somebody else out there fussing also. I went over to the union and they told me what to do. I went back inside and they sent me to another department where you did bench work and I liked that much better. You had a little small jig that you would work on and you just drilled out holes. Sometimes you would rout them or you would scribe them and then you'd cut them with a cutters.

I must have stayed there nearly a year, and then they put me over in another department, "Plastics." It was the tail section of the B-Bomber, the Billy Mitchell Bomber. I put a little part in the gun sight. You had a little ratchet set and you would screw it in there. Then I cleaned the top of the glass off and put a piece of paper over it to seal it off to go to the next section. I worked over there until the end of the war. Well, not quite the end, because I got pregnant, and while I was off having the baby the war was over. . . .

I started working in April and before Thanksgiving, my sister and I decided we'd buy a house instead of renting this room. The people was getting a little hanky-panky with you; they was going up on the rent. So she bought the house in her name and I loaned her some money. The house only cost four thousand dollars with four hundred dollars down. It was two houses on the lot, and we stayed in the little small one-bedroom house in the back. I stayed in the living room part before my husband came home and she stayed in the bedroom. I bought the furniture to go in the house, which was the stove and the refrigerator, and we had our old bedroom sets shipped from Texas [where they had grown up]. I worked the day shift and my sister worked the night shift. I worked ten hours a day for five days a week. Or did I work on a Saturday? I don't remember, but know it was ten hours a day. I'd get up in the morning, take a bath, come to the kitchen, fix my lunch—I always liked a fresh fixed lunch— get my breakfast, and then stand outside for the ride to come by. I always managed to get someone that liked to go to work slightly early. I carried my crocheting and knitting with me.

You had a spot where you always stayed around, close to where you worked, because when the whistle blew, you wanted to be ready to get up and go to where you worked. The leadman always come by and give you a job to do or you already had one that was a hangover from the day before. So you had a general idea what you was going to do each day. . . .

Some weeks I brought home twenty-six dollars, some weeks sixteen dollars. Then it gradually went up to thirty dollars, then it went up a little bit more and a little bit more. And I learned somewhere along the line that in order to make a good move you gotta make some money. You don't make the same amount everyday. You have some days good, sometimes bad. Whatever you make you're supposed to save some. I was also getting that fifty dollars a month from my husband and that I saved straight away. I was planning on buying a home and a car. And I was going to go back to school. My husband came back, but I never was laid off, so I just never found it necessary to look for another job or to go to school for another job.

I was still living over on Compton Avenue with my sister

in this small little back house when my husband got home. Then, when Beverly [her daughter] was born, my sister moved in the front house and we stayed in the back house. . . .

I worked up until the end of March [1945] and then I took off. Beverly was born the twenty-first of June. I'd planned to come back somewhere in the last of August. I went to verify the fact that I did come back, so that did not go on my record that I didn't just quit. But they laid off a lot of people, most of them, because the war was over.

It didn't bother me much—not thinking about it job-wise. I was just glad that the war was over. I didn't feel bad because my husband had a job and he also was eligible to go to school with his GI bill. So I really didn't have too many plans—which I wish I had had. I would have tore out page one and fixed it differently; put my version of page one in there.

I went and got me a job doing day work. That means you go to a person's house and clean up for one day out of the week and then you go to the next one and clean up. I did that a couple of times and I discovered I didn't like that so hot.

Then I got me a job downtown working in a little factory where you do weaving—burned clothes and stuff like that. I learned to do that real good. It didn't pay too much but it paid enough to get me going, seventy-five cents or about like that.

When North American called me back, was I a happy soul! I dropped that job and went back. That was a dollar an hour. So, from sixty cents an hour, when I first hired in there, up to one dollar. That wasn't traveling fast, but it was better than anything else because you had hours to work by and you had benefits and you come home at night with your family. So it was a good deal.

It made me live better. I really did. We always say that Lincoln took the [cotton] bale off the Negroes. I think there is a statue up there in Washington, D.C., where he's lifting something off the Negro. Well, my sister always said—that's why you can't interview her because she's so radical—"Hitler was the one that got us out of the white folks' kitchen."

Source: Sherna Berger Gluck, ed., *Rosie the Riveter Revisited* (Boston: Twayne Publishers, 1987), 37–42. Reprinted by permission of Sherna Berger Gluck.

149. Extract from the Beveridge Report, December 1942

In all European countries, the experience of fighting the war and the sacrifices that ordinary people were obliged to make for that objective encouraged the perspective that, after the war, states must provide for the welfare of all citizens. The presence of labor representatives in the coalition governments fighting the war reinforced this view. In 1942 the British government published the Beveridge Report, written by Sir William Beveridge, head of the London School of Economics, which laid the foundations of the postwar British welfare state.

THREE GUIDING PRINCIPLES OF RECOMMENDATIONS

6. In proceeding from this first comprehensive survey of social insurance to the next task—of making recommendations—three guiding principles may be laid down at the outset.

7. The first principle is that any proposals for the future, while they should use to the full the experience gathered in the past, should not be restricted by consideration of sectional interests established in the obtaining of that experience. Now, when the war is abolishing landmarks of every kind, is the opportunity for using experience in a clear field. A revolutionary moment in the world's history is a time for revolutions, not for patching.

8. The second principle is that organisation of social insurance should be treated as one part only of a comprehensive policy of social progress. Social insurance fully developed may provide income security; it is an attack upon Want. But Want is one only of five giants on the road of reconstruction and in some ways the easiest to attack. The others are Disease, Ignorance, Squalor and Idleness.

9. The third principle is that social security must be achieved by co-operation between the State and the individual. The State should offer security for service and contribution. The State in organising security should not stifle incentive, opportunity, responsibility; in establishing a national minimum, it should leave room and encouragement for voluntary action by each individual to provide more than that minimum for himself and his family.

10. The Plan for Social Security set out in this Report is built upon these principles. It uses experience but is not tied by experience. It is put forward as a limited contribution to a wider social policy, though as something that could be achieved now without wait-

ing for the whole of that policy. It is, first and foremost, a plan of insurance—of giving in return for contributions benefits up to subsistence level, as of right and without means test, so that individuals may build freely upon it.

THE WAY TO FREEDOM FROM WANT

11. The work of the Inter-departmental Committee began with a review of existing schemes of social insurance and allied services. The Plan for Social Security, with which that work ends, starts from a diagnosis of want—of the circumstances in which, in the years just preceding the present war families and individuals in Britain might lack the means of healthy subsistence. During those years impartial scientific authorities made social surveys of the conditions of life in a number of principal towns in Britain, including London, Liverpool, Sheffield, Plymouth, Southampton, York and Bristol. They determined the proportions of the people in each town whose means were below the standard assumed to be necessary for subsistence, and they analysed the extent and causes of that deficiency. From each of these social surveys the same broad result emerges. Of all the want shown by the surveys, from three-quarters to five-sixths, according to the precise standard chosen for want, was due to interruption or loss of earning power. Practically the whole of the remaining one-quarter to one-sixth was due to failure to relate income during earning to the size of the family. These surveys were made before the introduction of supplementary pensions had reduced the amount of poverty amongst old persons. But this does not affect the main conclusion to be drawn from these surveys: abolition of want requires a double redistribution of income, through social insurance and by family needs.

12. Abolition of want requires, first, improvement of State insurance, that is to say provision against interruption and loss of earning power. All the principal causes of interruption or loss of earnings are now the subject of schemes of social insurance. If, in spite of these schemes, so many persons unemployed or sick or old or widowed are found to be without adequate income for subsistence according to the standards adopted in the social surveys, this means that the benefits amount to less than subsistence by those standards or do not last as long as the need, and that the assistance which supplements insurance is either insufficient in amount or available only on terms which make men unwilling to have recourse to it.

None of the insurance benefits provided before the war were in fact designed with reference to the standards of the social surveys. Though unemployment benefit was not altogether out of relation to those standards, sickness and disablement benefit, old age pensions and widows' pensions were far below them, while workmen's compensation was below subsistence level for anyone who had family responsibilities or whose earnings in work were less than twice the amount needed for subsistence. To prevent interruption or destruction of earning power from leading to want, it is necessary to improve the present schemes of social insurance in three directions: by extension of scope to cover persons now excluded, by extension of purposes to cover risks now excluded, and by raising the rates of benefit.

13. Abolition of want requires, second, adjustment of incomes, in periods of earning as well as in interruption of earning, to family needs, that is to say, in one form or another it requires allowances for children. Without such allowances as part of benefit or added to it, to make provision for large families, no social insurance against interruption of earnings can be adequate. But, if children's allowances are given only when earnings are interrupted and are not given during earning also, two evils are unavoidable. First, a substantial measure of acute want will remain among the lower paid workers as the accompaniment of large families. Second, in all such cases, income will be greater during unemployment or other interruptions of work than during work.

14. By a double re-distribution of income through social insurance and children's allowances, want, as defined in the social surveys, could have been abolished in Britain before the present war. As is shown in para. 445, the income available to the British people was ample for such a purpose. The Plan for Social Security set out in Part V of this Report takes abolition of want after this war as its aim. It includes as its main method compulsory social insurance, with national assistance and voluntary insurance as subsidiary methods. It assumes allowances for dependent children, as part of its background. The plan assumes also establishment of comprehensive health and rehabilitation services and maintenance of employment, that is to say avoidance of mass unemployment, as necessary conditions of success in social insurance. These three measures—of children's allowances, health and rehabilitation and maintenance of employment—are described as assumptions A, B and C of the plan; they fall partly within and partly

without the plan extending into other fields of social policy. . . .

15. The plan is based on a diagnosis of want. It starts from facts, from the condition of the people as revealed by social surveys between the two wars. It takes account of two other facts about the British community, arising out of past movements of the birth rate and the death rate, which should dominate planning for its future. . . . The first of the two facts is the age constitution of the population, making it certain that persons past the age that is now regarded as the end of working life will be a much larger proportion of the whole community than at any time in the past. The second fact is the low reproduction rate of the British community today: unless this rate is raised very materially in the near future, a rapid and continuous decline of the population cannot be prevented. The first fact makes it necessary to seek ways of postponing the age of retirement from work rather than of hastening it. The second fact makes it imperative to give first place in social expenditure to the care of childhood and to the safeguarding of maternity.

16. The provision to be made for old age represents the largest and most growing element in any social insurance scheme. . . . Briefly, the proposal is to introduce for all citizens adequate pensions without means test by stages over a transition period of twenty years, while providing immediate assistance pensions for persons requiring them. . . .

SUMMARY OF PLAN FOR SOCIAL SECURITY

17. The main feature of the Plan for Social Security is a scheme of social insurance against interruption and destruction of earning power and for special expenditure arising at birth, marriage or death. The scheme embodies six fundamental principles: flat rate of subsistence benefit; flat rate of contribution; unification of administrative responsibility; adequacy of benefit; comprehensiveness; and classification. . . . Based on [these principles] and in combination with national assistance and voluntary insurance as subsidiary methods, the aim of the Plan for Social Security is to make want under any circumstances unnecessary.

Source: Sir William Beveridge, *Social Insurance and Allied Services: Report by Sir William Beveridge Presented to Parliament by Command of His Majesty, November 1942* (London: His Majesty's Stationery Office, 1942), 6–9.

1943 Documents

150. General Douglas MacArthur, Communiqué Announcing the End of the Papuan Campaign, 24 January 1943

After six months of heavy fighting, in January 1943, Allied forces commanded by U.S. General Douglas MacArthur recaptured Papua from the Japanese. This event represented the first significant Allied land victory in the Pacific war. At the end of the campaign, MacArthur issued a communiqué summing up the operations of the previous six months.

The destruction of the remnants of the enemy forces in the Sanananda area concludes the Papuan campaign. The Horii Army has been annihilated. The outstanding military lesson of this campaign was the continuous calculated application of air power, inherent in the potentialities of every component of the Air Forces, employed in the most intimate tactical and logistical union with ground troops. The effect of the modern instrumentality was sharply accentuated by the geographical limitations of the theater. For months on end, air transport with constant fighter coverage moved complete infantry regiments and artillery battalions across the almost impenetrable mountains and jungles of Papua, and the reaches of the sea; transported field hospitals and other base installations to the front; supplied the troops and evacuated casualties. For hundreds of miles bombers provided all-around reconnaissance, protected the coast from hostile naval intervention, and blasted the way for the infantry as it drove forward. A new form of campaign was tested which points the way to the ultimate defeat of the enemy in the Pacific. The offensive and defensive power of the air and the adaptability, range and capacity of its transport in an effective combination with ground forces, represent tactical and strategical elements of a broadened conception of warfare that will permit the application of offensive power in swift, massive strokes, rather than the dilatory and costly island advance that some have assumed to be necessary in a theater where the enemy's far-flung strongholds are dispersed throughout a vast expense of archipelagos. Air forces and ground forces were welded together in Papua and when in sufficient strength with proper naval support, their indissoluble union points the way to victory through new and broadened strategic and tactical conceptions.

Source: Charles E. Willoughby et al., eds., *Reports of General MacArthur: The Campaigns of MacArthur in the Pacific,* 2 vols. (Washington, DC: U.S. Government Printing Office, 1966), 1: 98.

151. An American Bombing Raid on Düsseldorf: Robert S. Raymond to His (Future) Fiancée, 27 January 1943

In spring 1940 Robert S. Raymond, a young American from Kansas City, volunteered to serve in the French Army. During the fall of France he was evacuated to Great Britain, where he joined the Royal Air Force and trained as a bomber pilot, flying thirty missions on Lancaster bombers. He then transferred to the U.S. Army Air Force, where he remained until the war ended. This letter to Betty, a friend who later became his wife, describes a major bombing raid over the German city of Düsseldorf from which he had just returned. It was written at midnight, when Raymond, though tired, was still too keyed up to sleep.

Have just returned from Düsseldorf, and sitting here in my quiet room, with Griffiths sleeping peacefully, it seems incredible that I was there only 4 hours ago. Griffiths's curly blonde head is little troubled by the experience of another bombing raid, but I am not yet sleepy and shall tell you about it, for memory, particularly mine, is a transient thing, and inevitably softens the clear-cut lines of any experience, however impressive.

Düsseldorf is a great industrial city situated in the Ruhr on the Rhine River, producing great quantities of vital war materials so badly needed by the Wehrmacht on all fronts. It is vulnerable in that the great river is an outstanding landmark, enabling easy identification, and because it is less than 400 miles from England, making it possible for us to carry a much greater weight of bombs than, for instance, to Italy.

We took off under low cloud with the promise of better weather over the target and on our return. Climbed up through several cloud layers just as the sun was tinting them with the last red colours of the day, and so up over the North Sea with George flying. Some flak over the Dutch coast was sent up to our height through a solid layer of cloud, and from then on we were never entirely free from it until we had arrived within a few minutes of the target, when I remarked to Watt that, although we were quite sure of our position, it looked too quiet to be entirely healthy. But we were evidently the first to arrive, and the defenses were lying doggo in the hope that we would either pass over and not bother them or, being uncertain of our position, fail to locate the city. Neither happened; being quite sure of where we were even above the scattered cloud, we ran straight in and planted our cookie and incendiaries (more than 1000 of them) and, since, the scattered cloud below made a good photo of the result improbable, I turned away immediately.

Watt said, "Bomb's gone."

Immediately after the cookie blossomed into a great red mushroom glow and the string of incendiaries began to sprinkle on the ground, more than 50 searchlights concentrated on the place where we should have been after dropping that load, and the flak was bursting right at the apex of the searchlight cone. The ground defenses had been quietly plotting our track all the while, and now that they knew they were to be the "Target for tonight," they threw up everything they had. I'm afraid we left our companions a hard row to hoe, but we have faced the same situation elsewhere.

Flak all the way to the coast, and finally the blessed emptiness of the lonely North Sea, where we found ice forming on our wings when we attempted to descend through the cloud, and so stayed upstairs at lower temperatures until we were over England and Price could get us the latest weather report from our Base.

An hour before we arrived the cloud ceiling was 4,000 feet and closing down rapidly. By the time we got there, it was down to 800 feet with rain falling and the air gusty and full of pockets (air currents) that tossed us around like peas in an empty sack between 300 and 1,200 feet. Having just [censored] just before setting course from Base earlier in the evening, we were even more cautious than usual. Discipline in the air is absolutely essential, for only the W.A.A.F. in the control tower knows where everyone is. Reviewing the situation now, I know that six months ago under such conditions I would most certainly have been listed as missing with my crew from this night's operations. But somewhere during my training I learned to fly confidently by instruments alone, and only that accuracy enabled me to maintain contact and land on the flarepath as smoothly and easily in darkness as it is possible to do during the day. All members of air-crew are trained, not born, for their jobs, and only hard work and practice enable any crew to live through an Operational tour. I've known so many who trusted to instinct, luck and fortune to carry them through. Each serves in more or less marginal situations, but eventually there can be no substitute. For that reason an Operational Crew of proven ability is a premium product and a valuable unit. They can be developed from average material, but somehow the sum of their abilities must be so integrated that the whole is something greater than the sum of its parts. And that is one of the reasons why I still enjoy flying a bomber.

Primarily, I suppose, it's based on vanity. We live a life of comparative life and leisure, are fed, clothed, housed and paid more than others, but when the chips are down, it's up to small units of 7 men each, to do in a few hours what would otherwise cost the lives of many thousands to accomplish. Our capacity for destruction is tremendous. God grant that in the days of peace to come we shall work as hard and be as zealous to rebuild and re-create the brave new world.

Several bursts of flak were so near tonight that the gunners still think we were hit, since we could not examine the plane adequately in the dark when we had parked it at the dispersal point, but we shall see tomorrow. . . .

My letters inevitably taper off to unconnected inconsequentials. Just remembered some sounds I would like to hear—the long, hollow whistle of a train—you, singing—birds on a spring morning—frogs at midnight—traffic on Main Street—the smooth patter of a salesman (with the goods)—wind in a pine forest—the K.C. [Kansas City] Philharmonic—a church choir—the clatter of a mowing machine—the rustle of tall corn—the drowsy hum of bees around a hive—the crackle of a wood fire—carpenters sawing and hammering—and many others, but most of all your voice.

Source: "Diary (4)" File, World War II Participants and Contemporaries Collection, Dwight D. Eisenhower Presidential Library, Abilene, Kansas. Reprinted in Mark P. Parillo, ed., *We Were in the Big One: Experiences of World War II Generation* (Wilmington, DE: Scholarly Resources, 2002), 70–72. Courtesy Elizabeth Raymond.

152. Final Declaration of the Casablanca Conference, 12 February 1943

From 14–24 January 1943, British Prime Minister Winston Churchill and American President Franklin D. Roosevelt met at Casablanca, Morocco, a gathering also attended by the Free French leader Charles de Gaulle and General Henri Giraud, who represented the Vichy government. Josef Stalin, the Soviet president, was invited but, in view of his country's critical wartime situation, declined to leave Russia. The Casablanca Conference first set the Allied war objective of demanding the unconditional surrender of Germany, Italy, and Japan—a policy intended in part to allay the fears of both Stalin and the Chinese President Jiang Jieshi (Chiang Kai-shek) that their allies might desert them and make a separate peace. The conference's final declaration was not released until the following month, by which time all nations whose representatives had absented themselves from the conference were already familiar with its terms.

The decisions reached and the actual plans made at Casablanca were not confined to any one theater of war or to any one continent or ocean or sea. Before this year is out, it will be made known to the world—in actions rather than words—that the Casablanca Conference produced plenty of news; and it will be bad news for the Germans and Italians—and the Japanese.

We have lately concluded a long, hard battle in the Southwest Pacific and we have made notable gains. That battle started in the Solomons and New Guinea last summer. It has demonstrated our superior power in planes and, most importantly, in the fighting qualities of our individual soldiers and sailors.

American armed forces in the Southwest Pacific are receiving powerful aid from Australia and New Zealand and also directly from the British themselves.

We do not expect to spend the time it would take to bring Japan to final defeat merely by inching our way forward from island to island across the vast expanse of the Pacific.

Great and decisive actions against the Japanese will be taken to drive the invader from the soil of China. Important actions will be taken in the skies over China—and over Japan itself.

The discussions at Casablanca have been continued in Chungking with the Generalissimo [Chiang Kai-shek or Jiang Jieshi] by General Arnold and have resulted in definite plans for offensive operations.

There are many roads which lead right to Tokyo. We shall neglect none of them.

In an attempt to ward off the inevitable disaster, the Axis propagandists are trying all of their old tricks in order to divide the United Nations. They seek to create the idea that if we win this war, Russia, England, China, and the United States are going to get into a cat-and-dog fight.

This is their final effort to turn one nation against another, in the vain hope that they may settle with one or two at a time—that any of us may be so gullible and so forgetful as to be duped into making "deals" at the expense of our Allies.

To these panicky attempts to escape the consequences of their crimes we say—all the United Nations say—that the only terms on which we shall deal with an Axis government or any Axis factions are the terms proclaimed at Casablanca: "Unconditional Surrender." In our uncompromising policy we mean no harm to the common people of the Axis nations. But we do mean to impose punishment and retribution in full upon their guilty, barbaric leaders . . .

In the years of the American and French revolutions the fundamental principle guiding our democracies was established. The cornerstone of our whole democratic edifice was the principle that from the people and the people alone flows the authority of government.

It is one of our war aims, as expressed in the Atlantic Charter, that the conquered populations of today be again the masters of their destiny. There must be no doubt anywhere that it is the unalterable purpose of the United Nations to restore to conquered peoples their sacred rights.

Source: Web site: The Avalon Project at the Yale Law School. Available at http://www.yale.edu/lawweb/avalon/wwii/casablan.htm.

153. "The Four Policemen": Harry L. Hopkins, Special Assistant to President Roosevelt, Memorandum of Conversation during a Meeting with Anthony Eden, 27 March 1943

In 1943, President Franklin D. Roosevelt described his concept of the future world order to visiting British Foreign Secretary Anthony Eden. The president envisaged that the greatest powers, the United States, Great Britain, Soviet Russia, and China, would act as the "four policemen" and, between them, organize and dominate the rest of the world. Roosevelt was reluctant to permit the automatic return of the European powers to their former Asian colonies.

Subject: Eden Visit—Conference with the President, Anthony Eden, Cordell Hull, Sumner Welles, Viscount Halifax, Mr. Wm. Strang

1. . . . There was a general discussion about the organization of the United Nations after the war. The President and Welles were very emphatic that the United States could not be a member of any independent regional body such as a European Council; they felt that all the United Nations should be members of one body for the purposes of recommending policy; that this body should be world-wide in scope.
2. That there would be under this body regional councils with similar advisory powers made up of the nations geographically located in the regions; but, finally, that the real decisions should be made by the United States, Great Britain, Russia and China, who would be the powers for many years to come that would have to police the world.

The President was very insistent with Eden that China

should be a member, altho it was clear to me that Eden still was not convinced of the wisdom of the procedure. The President feels that China, in any serious conflict of policy with Russia, would undoubtedly line up on our side.

I said that Churchill's speech in which he advocated a purely European Council of Nations, had a very unfortunate effect over here. Eden said he was sure Churchill had not meant to exclude the United States and that he rather felt that Churchill spoke on the spur of the moment and that he, Eden, agreed that the United Nations should be organized on a global basis.

The whole idea of the trusteeship of mandated islands, etc. was discussed and the President and Eden seemed to be much closer together than they were at the beginning of their conferences on this policy.

The President made it clear that he did not want a commitment made in advance that all those colonies in the Far East should go back to the countries which owned or controlled them prior to the war. He specifically mentioned Timor, Portugal, Indo-China and France. He suggested that all the specific problems which Mr. Eden had raised in his visit here be referred to the State Department and they be asked to start exploratory discussions with the British or with any other country in regard to all of them.

I said I thought it would have a very bad effect, both in England and the United States, if the world got the impression that the United States and England were, together, planning the future of the world without consulting anyone else. Eden agreed to this and said the British were conducting direct conferences on matters that concerned them and Russia and he assumed we would do the same thing.

Source: Web site: PBS: The American Experience. Available at http://www.pbs.org/wgbh/amex/holocaust/filmmore/reference/primary/presmemorandum.html.

154. German Security Department, Report on Adolf Hitler's Disappearance from Public View, 19 April 1943

As the German war news became less favorable, Adolf Hitler, Germany's supreme leader, made dramatically fewer public appearances. A report from the German Security Department commented on the detrimental impact of his reclusive habits on German public opinion and the opportunity his absence from popular view gave for damaging rumors to spread.

It has been emphasized in some reports that the whole population has appreciated the fact that recently they have heard more of the Führer. Judicious and positive-minded citizens have remarked that it is not a good idea for the Führer to remain "out of sight" for too long. The nation wants to have its close personal relationship with the Führer confirmed by frequently receiving news of him. But in the course of the war it has become rare for a picture of the Führer to appear in the newspapers or in the newsreels; the same is true of speeches by the Führer. A picture of the Führer in which one could see that his hair had not gone completely white, as rumour once had it, would have a more positive effect on the population than many fighting slogans. In order to keep alive the contact between leader and nation, it was frequently suggested that the Führer should be shown not only at highly official occasions and at military conferences, but more often in his personal life, as was done before, at the field kitchen or while having a walk, and that there should be reports on his daily routine, and his remarks and comments should be published.

Source: Jeremy Noakes, ed., *Nazism 1919–1945, Volume 4: The Home Front in World War II* (Exeter, UK: University of Exeter Press, 1998), 547. Reprinted with permission of University of Exeter Press.

155. Soviet President Josef Stalin, Reuter's Interview on the Dissolution of the Comintern, May 1943

In May 1943, Soviet President Josef Stalin decided to dissolve the Comintern, the Moscow-based central Communist International that for more than 20 years had sought to direct the efforts of non-Soviet Communist parties. As early as 1940, Stalin contemplated this move on the grounds that the Comintern's existence made it easier to depict Communist parties in other countries as Soviet-controlled subversive organizations. At the time he took this action, he may also have hoped to ingratiate himself with his Allies, the United States and Great Britain. On his instructions, Secretary General Georgi Dimitrov of the Comintern and his assistant, Dmitry Zakharovich Manuilsky, drew up a draft resolution that, with minor modifications—some of them inserted at Stalin's behest after the fact—the presidium of the organization accepted. After the dissolution of the Comintern, Soviet President Josef Stalin granted the chief Reuter's news agency correspondent in Moscow an interview. He justified the dissolution of the Comintern on the grounds that this demonstrated the independence of the various national Communist parties, something that, given their heavy involvement in many resistance movements throughout Europe and elsewhere, he may have been particularly eager to emphasize at this time.

The dissolution of the Communist International is proper and timely because it facilitates the organization of the common onslaught of all freedom-loving nations against the common enemy—Hitlerism. The dissolution of the Communist International is proper because:

(a) It exposes the lie of Hitlerites to the effect that "Moscow" allegedly intends to intervene in the life of other nations and to "Bolshevise" them. An end is now being put to this lie.

(b) It exposes the calumny of the adversaries of Communism within the Labour movement to the effect that Communist Parties in various countries are allegedly acting not in the interests of their people but on orders from outside. An end is now being put to this calumny too.

(c) It facilitates the work of patriots of all countries for uniting the progressive forces of their respective countries, regardless of party or religious faith, into a single camp of national liberation—for unfolding the struggle against Fascism.

(d) It facilitates the work of patriots of all countries for uniting all freedom-loving peoples into a single international camp for the fight against the menace of world domination by Hitlerism, thus clearing the way to the future organization of a companionship of nations based on their equality.

I think that all these circumstances taken together will result in a further strengthening of the United Front of the Allies and other united nations in their fight for victory over Hitlerite tyranny. I feel that the dissolution of the Communist International is perfectly timely—because it is exactly now, when the Fascist beast is exerting its last strength, that it is necessary to organize the common onslaught of freedom-loving countries to finish off this beast and to deliver the people from Fascist oppression.

Source: Jane Degras, ed., *The Communist International 1919–1943: Documents,* 3 vols. (London: Frank Cass, 1971), 3: 476–477. Reprinted with permission of Chatham House.

156. The Zoot-Suit Riots, Los Angeles, June 1943: Report of Warren Committee

In a week-long rampage in early June 1943, hundreds of servicemen clashed with "zoot-suited" young Mexican Americans in East Los Angeles, stripping them of their distinctive clothing and beating them up. Mexican Americans were generally impoverished; lived in substandard housing; were subjected to disease, malnutrition, and discrimination; were forced to attend segregated schools; and had few economic oppportunities open to them. Young Mexican American men tended to join "pachuco" gangs that were often at violent odds with each other, as well as the white community. Governor Earl Warren of California established a committee to investigate the zoot-suit riots, which eventually issued a report strongly condemning the involvement of the police and armed forces in these events. Little further action, however, was taken on it.

There are approximately 250,000 persons of Mexican descent in Los Angeles County. Living conditions among the majority of these people are far below the general level of the community. Housing is inadequate; sanitation is bad and is made worse by congestion. Recreational facilities for children are very poor; and there is insufficient supervision of the playgrounds, swimming pools and other youth centers. Such conditions are breeding places for juvenile delinquency. . . .

Mass arrests, dragnet raids, and other wholesale classifications of groups of people are based on false premises and tend merely to aggravate the situation. Any American citizen suspected of crime is entitled to be treated as an individual, to be indicted as such, and to be tried, both at law and in the forum of public opinion, on his merits or errors, regardless of race, color, creed, or the kind of clothes he wears.

Group accusations foster race prejudice, the entire group accused want revenge and vindication. The public is led to believe that every person in the accused group is guilty of crime.

It is significant that most of the persons mistreated during the recent incidents in Los Angeles were either persons of Mexican descent or Negroes. In undertaking to deal with the cause of these outbreaks, the existence of race prejudice cannot be ignored. . . .

On Monday evening, June seventh, thousands of Angelenos, in response to twelve hours' advance notice in the press, turned out for a mass lynching. Marching through the streets of downtown Los Angeles, a mob of several thousand soldiers, sailors, and civilians, proceeded to beat up every zoot-suiter they could find. Pushing its way into the important motion picture theaters, the mob ordered the management to turn on the house lights and then ranged up and down the aisles dragging Mexicans out of their seats. Street cars were halted while Mexicans, and some Filipinos and Negroes, were jerked out of their seats, pushed into the streets, and beaten with sadistic frenzy. If the victims wore zoot-suits, they were stripped of their clothing and left naked or half-naked on the streets, bleeding and bruised. Proceeding down Main Street from First to Twelfth, the mob stopped on the edge of the Negro district. Learning that the Negroes planned a warm reception for them, the mobsters turned back and marched through the Mexican east side spreading panic and terror.

Throughout the night the Mexican communities were in the wildest possible turmoil. Scores of Mexican mothers were trying to locate their youngsters and several hundred Mexicans milled around each of the police substations and the Central Jail trying to get word of missing members of their families. Boys came into the police stations saying: "Charge me with vagrancy or anything, but don't send me out there!" pointing to the streets where other boys, as young as twelve and thirteen years of age, were being beaten and stripped of their clothes . . . not more than half of the victims were actually wearing zoot-suits. A Negro defense worker, wearing a defense-plant identification badge on his workclothes, was taken from a street car and one of his eyes was gouged out with a knife. Huge half-page photographs, showing Mexican boys stripped of their clothes, cowering on the pavement, often bleeding profusely, surrounded by jeering mobs of men and women, appeared in all the Los Angeles newspapers. . . .

At midnight on June seventh, the military authorities decided that the local police were completely unable or unwilling to handle the situation, despite the fact that a thousand reserve officers had been called up. The entire downtown area of Los Angeles was then declared "out of bounds" for military personnel. This order immediately slowed down the pace of the rioting. The moment the Military Police and Shore Patrol went into action, the rioting quieted down.

Source: Governor's Citizens' Committee, Report on Los Angeles Riots, 1943. Digital History Web Site. Available at http://www.gliah.uh.edu/mexican_voices/voices_display.cfm?id=104 (Gilder Lehrman Resource Guides).

157. Earl Brown, "The Detroit Race Riots of [June] 1943"

In June 1943 serious race riots took place in the American industrial city of Detroit, Michigan. Over the previous three years, Detroit's population had swollen from 1.6 million to 1.8 million, as around 50,000 blacks and 150,000 largely Southern whites emigrated to the city in response to the demands of the industrial war effort. Tensions between blacks and whites and between newcomers and older residents were fierce. In the hot summer of 1943 Detroit erupted in race riots. In the course of two days 34 people—25 of them black—were killed, 461 were injured, and extensive looting took place. Less extensive riots also occurred in Los Angeles, New York, Beaumont (Texas), and Newark (New Jersey). Earl Brown, then the only black individual on the editorial staff of Life *magazine, wrote an account of the Detroit riots.*

On Sunday, June 20, 1943, one of the most serious race riots in American history broke out in the city of Detroit. Before it was brought under control some thirty hours later, twenty-five Negroes and nine white persons were killed and property worth several hundreds of thousands of dollars had been destroyed.

The forces which led to the outbreak in that city exist, to a greater or lesser degree, in most of our cities. Similar outbreaks have occurred elsewhere. A study of the factors leading to the outbreak in Detroit is important because it can show us how to avoid similar outbreaks, not only in Detroit, but in other cities. . . .

My first visit to wartime Detroit occurred in July, 1942. I found that although Detroit is the munitions capital of the United Nations and its war production is essential to victory, there was a disturbing lack of unity of effort. The atmosphere was tense, and the tension was increasing. There were sudden gusts of strikes for unimportant reasons—a strike occurred at the Chrysler Tank Arsenal because the men were not allowed to smoke during work.

But racial feeling was the most alarming of all. Groups of Negro zoot-suiters were brawling with gangs of young white toughs; the determination of Negroes to hold the war jobs they had won was matched by the determination of numerous white groups to oust them. There were many signs of trouble. . . .

One of the features of Detroit that in many ways sets it off from many other cities is the presence of great numbers of religious and political fanatics. Even before the last war Detroit was known as the city of "jazzed-up religion." Today all shades of opinion are to be found in the city, all races, all creeds, all political attitudes and beliefs. The first figure to attract national attention was Father Charles Coughlin. Railing against Hoover and Wall Street from his radio pulpit, he soon attracted a great following in Detroit and through the Middle West. Next came the Black Legion, an organization of native white Americans and an offshoot of the Ku Klux

Klan—with hoods, grips, and passwords. It was organized originally for the purpose of getting and holding jobs for Southern whites, but it quickly developed into an elaborate "hate" organization—its enmity directed against Catholics, Jews, Negroes, and "radicals." . . .

By the middle 30s, Detroit had a representation of every kind of panacea, political nostrum, and agitation. There were the Anglo-Saxon Federation and an anti-Negro organization called the National Workers League. But the most steady, day-in and day-out exhortation came from the sensational preachers. Of these the best known are the Reverend Frank J. Norris and the Reverend Gerald L. K. Smith. . . .

These three men—Coughlin, Norris, and Smith—are the best known of the Detroit religious-political demagogues, but there are thousands of others. Some have been in Detroit for years; others came during the recent migrations. It is estimated that there are more than 2,500 Southern-born evangelists of one kind or another in Detroit alone, not counting those in near-by communities. This war has caused an upheaval among the little shouting sects in the South; they have split and split again, and new sects have been formed. . . .

There is a connection between the apocalyptic doctrine of these sects and religious and racial intolerance. The appeal is not only highly emotional but is grounded on old traditions—which in the South mean White Protestant Supremacy. . . . Many of these exhorters are members of the Klan off-shoot organizations, defiantly "American," suspecting "radicals," and completely at home with White Supremacy. For more than a decade—and increasingly during the past three years—these rustic preachers have been spreading their brand of the Word. As feeling in Detroit became more aroused over the race issue, the effect of this kind of preaching was like pouring gasoline on a bonfire. . . .

It is interesting to note that despite the racial collisions and the frequent enforcement of Jim Crow practices in Detroit, Negroes have succeeded in getting some political preferment. There are two Negro assistant prosecuting attorneys, the State Labor Commissioner is a Negro, and one of the State Senators is a Negro. The Detroit Street Railway Company, which is owned by the city, employs about a thousand Negroes—both men and women—as motormen, bus drivers, conductors, and workers of other kinds. With the police it is another matter, and this has been a burning issue. Out of 3,600 policemen, only forty are Negroes. In addition, Southern whites have been taken into the force freely, and they have frequently shown a hostile attitude toward Negroes.

The local political machine was perfectly happy to cooperate with Negro gamblers, but they had no interest whatever in the fact that most of Detroit's Negroes lived in two wretched slum areas. The two principal Negro districts in Detroit cover about thirty square blocks on the West Side and a larger district on the East Side called Paradise Valley. . . . Here—on the East Side—live most of Detroit's Negroes. Almost everybody now has plenty of war wages to pay for lodging, but decent houses simply do not exist. The only recourse the Negroes have is to cram themselves into the filthy valley tenements. . . .

The war naturally aggravated Detroit's underlying instability. Anti-Negro sentiment was particularly strong in the Polish districts of Hamtramck, a suburb. As early as July, 1941, gangs of Polish youths provoked a series of minor riots. An editor of a Polish paper reports that anti-Negro handbills were distributed on the steps of St. Florian's Church in Hamtramck during the Sojourner Truth riots.

For many months the Negro press in Detroit and elsewhere busily promoted a "Double-V" campaign for victory at home as well as abroad. This campaign was based on the assumption that victory in the war against the fascists abroad did not mean much if there was Jim Crow at home. Colored soldiers had told a thousand bitter stories of discrimination and lack of respect for the uniform. The killings of colored soldiers at Alexandria, Louisiana, and in other Southern communities were taken to heart. The hopes roused by President Roosevelt's Executive Order 8802, issued June 25, 1941, forbidding job discrimination in plants with war contracts slowly faded. The Committee on Fair Employment Practice, set up by the President shortly after the issuance of the Executive Order, was left to pine away without money or authority and was finally placed under the War Manpower Commission. If the government would do nothing, there was nothing left but the union and the determination of the Negroes themselves. Colored workers who had been promoted to more skilled jobs were ready to hold on for dear life to their new jobs, and the brimstone

evangelists, viewing with alarm this resolution of the Negroes, whipped up resentment.

Shortly after the beginning of 1943 a series of anti-Negro strikes broke out in the plants. Aside from fights between individuals, there was no violence in the plants, but much bitterness was aroused. The U.S. Bureau of Labor Statistics lists anti-Negro strikes in the following plants from mid-March until the end of May: United States Rubber Company; Vickers, Incorporated; Hudson Motor Car Company; Hudson Naval Arsenal; and the Packard Motor Car Company. In the Packard strike, which brought the climax, 26,883 men left work when three Negroes were upgraded. The circumstances of this strike were so peculiar that union leaders were convinced that it had been engineered by one of the anti-Negro groups in the city, but nothing was ever proved.

Shortly after the Packard strike Mayor Jeffries called together the editors of the three local dailies, the *Free Press,* the *News,* and the *Times,* to take counsel. The conference over, nothing was done. A procession of Negro leaders and a few prominent white citizens besought the Mayor to take heed and act before the explosion. The Mayor listened, but appeared to be more confused after these visits than before. Then everyone relaxed to await the inevitable. It came on the evening of June 24, 1943.

Belle Isle lies in the Detroit River, connected with the city and Grand Boulevard by a bridge. There were probably a hundred thousand persons in the park that hot, humid Sunday, and the greater number seem to have been Negroes. The atmosphere was anything but peaceful. Tension had increased to the breaking point. An argument between a Negro and a white man became a fist fight and the fighting spread.

A hurry call was made for the police, but by the time they arrived the brawl, involving some two hundred white sailors by this time, was eddying across the bridge into the riverside park on the mainland near the Naval Armory. The news that fighting had broken out traveled like the wind. A young man in a colored night club on Hastings Street is supposed to have grabbed the microphone about 11:30 and urged the five hundred customers present to "come on and take care of a bunch of whites who have killed a colored woman and her baby at Belle Isle Park." This rumor was, of course, false. It was matched by another story, which spread through the white districts, that Negroes had raped and killed a white woman on the park bridge. By midnight fighting and looting had spread into a dozen different districts and Paradise Valley was going crazy. By two o'clock that morning a crowd of Negroes stopped an East Side street car and stoned white factory workers who were passengers. White men coming from work at the Chevrolet Gear and Axle plant, three miles away from the center of Paradise Valley, were attacked by a Negro mob.

Alfred McClung Lee, chairman of the Sociology Department of Wayne University, and Norman Humphrey, Assistant Professor of Sociology at the same institution, have pieced together a remarkable timetable of the violence in *Race Riot* (New York: Dryden Press, 1943), a report on the riot. Both the authors were present and moved about the city while the fighting was in progress. Their report shows that:

At four o'clock in the morning (Monday, June 21) there was a meeting in the office of Police Commissioner Witherspoon to determine action. Mayor Jeffries, Colonel Krech (the U.S. Army commander of the Detroit area), Captain Leonard of the Michigan State Police, John Bugas (in charge of the local office of the F.B.I.), and Sheriff Baird were present. Colonel Krech told the Mayor that the military police could be on duty in Detroit in forty-nine minutes after a request from the Mayor had been cleared through the Governor and the proper U.S. Army officials. Nothing was done about this at the time, and by 6:30 A.M. Commissioner Witherspoon decided that there was a let-up in "serious rioting."

But there was no let-up. At 8:30 in the morning a Negro delegation asked the Mayor to send for troops. At nine o'clock Commissioner Witherspoon asked the Mayor for troops. Mayor Jeffries telephoned to the Governor, who transmitted the request by telephone to the Sixth Service Command Headquarters in Chicago. By eleven o'clock it was known that troops could not come unless martial law was declared. Governor Kelly hesitated to do so. By this time gangs of white hoodlums were roaming the streets burning Negro cars.

The police had already shown themselves to be helpless or negligent. On the previous night, police had been stationed outside the all-night Roxy movie theater. A witness reported that a threatening white crowd assembled at the entrance and every time a Negro came out of the theater the mob went for him. When the witness asked the police to get Negroes a safe-conduct through the mob, the officers replied, "See the chief about it!"

At four o'clock on Monday afternoon Major General Aurand arrived from Chicago. By that time, according to Lee and Humphrey, "the crowds of whites were increasing in size on Woodward Avenue. Milling packs of human animals hunted and killed any of the easily visible black prey which chanced into the territory."

At 6:30 Monday night, just as Mayor Jeffries was going on the air with a plea for a return to sanity, four white boys, aged 16 to 20, shot down Moses Kiska, a middle-aged Negro, "because we didn't have anything to do." Still no troops, and all through the evening, after even the Mayor had admitted that the city administration and police were unable to deal with the situation, there went on an endless amount of official confusion until, at last, it was discovered precisely what had to be done to get federal intervention. Just before midnight President Roosevelt proclaimed a state of emergency, and by Tuesday morning 6,000 troops in trucks and jeeps were patrolling the city. The hold of the city authorities had so completely collapsed that it took the United States Army to get twenty-nine Negro members of the graduating class of Northeastern High School away from the closing exercises in safety.

Two days later Governor Kelly decided to ease restrictions a little, and by degrees the city began to breathe again....

Source: Earl Brown, *Why Race Riots?: Lessons from Detroit,* Public Affairs Pamphlet No. 87, (New York: 1944), 1–3, 14–15, 18–24. Reprinted in Herbert Aptheker, ed., *A Documentary History of the Negro People of the United States,* Vol. 4: *From the New Deal to the End of World War II* (New York: Citadel Press, 1992), 443–453. Used with permission of the Manuscripts, Archives, and Rare Books Division, Schomburg Center for Research in Black Culture, The New York Public Library, Astor, Lenox, and Tilden Foundations.

158. Minister of Justice Dino Grandi, Order of the Day, Submitted to the Fascist Grand Council, Demanding the Restoration of the Functions of Various Organs of the Constitution, 24 July 1943

As Allied forces invaded Italy, where major cities had already been subjected to heavy Allied bombing, and closed in on Rome, its capital, the Italian dictator called what would become the last meeting of the Fascist Grand Council, Italy's highest governing body. Mussolini hoped to use this occasion to eliminate any remaining vestiges of opposition to him within his government. Instead, Count Dino Grandi, minister of justice and former ambassador to Great Britain, proposed a motion to restore the king of Italy to power. The motion passed by 18 votes to 9, with 1 abstention. Mussolini was overthrown, arrested, and imprisoned; and the king of Italy and his new prime minister, Marshal Pietro Badoglio, opened negotiations with the Allies for an armistice, which was signed on 8 September 1943. German forces in Italy nonetheless continued to fight fiercely against the Allies until spring 1945.

The Grand Council,

Assembled in these days of supreme trial, turns its thought first of all to the heroic fighters of every branch of the forces, who side by side with the proud people of Sicily, among whom the single-minded faith of the Italian people shines most brightly, are renewing the noble traditions of arduous courage and the indomitable spirit of self sacrifice of our glorious armed forces; proclaims it to be the sacred duty of all Italians to defend at all costs the unity, independence, and liberty of the country, the fruits of the sacrifices and efforts of four generations from the Risorgimento till today, and the life and future of the Italian people;

Affirms the need for the moral and physical union of all Italians at this serious moment which is decisive for the destiny of the nation;

Declares that to achieve this unity it is necessary to restore immediately all functions belonging to the state, ascribing to the Crown, the Grand Council, the Government, Parliament, and the Corporations the tasks and responsibilities laid down for them by our state and constitutional laws;

Invites the Head of the Government to pray His Majesty the King, to whom the faithful and trusting heart of the whole Nation turns, that for the honour and safety of the country he now assumes effective command of the armed forces on land, on sea, and in the air, in accordance with Article 5 of the Statute of the Kingdom, and therewith the supreme initiative of decision which our institutions attribute to him, and which have always been throughout our national history the glorious appendage of our august dynasty of the House of Savoy.

Source: Margaret Carlyle, ed., *Documents on International Affairs 1939–1946 Volume II: Hitler's Europe* (London: Oxford University Press, 1954), 118. Reprinted with permission of Chatham House.

159. The Kreisau Circle, "Basic Principles for a New Order in Germany," 9 August 1943

The Kreisau Circle was a cosmopolitan group of anti-Hitler Christians, politicians, aristocratic lawyers, and intellectuals who gathered around two distinguished Prussian noblemen, Count Peter Yorck von Wartenburg and Count Helmuth James von Moltke, at the latter's Kreisau estate. Several held office within the Foreign Ministry and the military bureaucracy. They developed extensive plans for postwar Germany, envisaging a Christian democratic nation in which the state would have a major economic and social role and power would be divided between the central and provincial governments. They also advocated the integration of the various European countries into a federal system. Much of what they suggested eventually came to pass after 1945, but few of them survived to see this transpire. Following the discovery of their implication in a military plot to overthrow Hitler in 1943, most of the Kreisau Circle members were arrested and executed.

The Government of the German Reich sees in Christianity the basis for the moral and religious revival of our people, for the overcoming of hatred and lies, for the reconstruction of the European community of nations.

The starting point is man's commitment to the divine order on which his inner and outer existence depends. Only when one has succeeded in making this the criterion for relations between people and nations can the disorder of our time be overcome and a genuine state of peace be created. The internal reorganization of the Reich is the basis for the achievement of a just and lasting peace.

In view of the collapse of a power structure which no longer feels any obligations and which is based solely on its command of technology, European humanity is faced above all with this task. The way to its solution lies in the determined and active realization of Christian values. The Reich Government is therefore determined to realize the following indispensable requirements, which cannot be renounced inwardly, with all available means:

1. Justice which has been trampled underfoot must be raised again and made predominant over all areas of human life. Under the protection of conscientious, independent judges free from the fear of men, it is the foundation for all future plans for peace.

2. Freedom of faith and conscience will be safeguarded. Existing laws and regulations which violate these principles will be repealed at once.

3. Totalitarian moral constraint must be broken and the inviolable dignity of the human person must be recognized as the basis for the order of justice and peace which is to be striven for. Everybody will partake in the responsibility of the various social, political and international spheres of life. The right to work and to hold property will be under public protection, irrespective of race, nationality or faith.

4. The basic unit of peaceful social life is the family. It will be under public protection which, apart from education, will also secure its material needs: food, clothing, a dwelling, garden and health.

5. Work must be organized in such a way that it promotes personal responsibility and does not let it wither. Apart from creating the material conditions of work and further professional training this requires everyone's effective co-responsibility in the factory and further in the general economic context to which his work contributes. Through this he will contribute to the growth of a healthy and durable structure of life in which the individual, his family, and the community can achieve organic development in a balanced economic system. Those who manage the economy must safeguard these basic requirements.

6. The political responsibility of every individual demands his cooperation in the self-government of small communities which are to be revived. Rooted and tested in these, his co-determination in the state and in the community of nations must be secured by elected representatives and in this way he must be convinced of his co-responsibility for political events.

7. The special responsibility and loyalty of every individual to his national origin, to his language and to the intellectual and historical traditions of his people must be guarded and respected. But it must not be misused for the concentration of political power or for the degrading persecution or suppression of foreign races. The free and peaceful development of na-

tional culture can no longer be reconciled with the claim to absolute sovereignty of national states. Peace requires the creation of an arrangement comprising individual states. As soon as the free agreement of all nations concerned is guaranteed, those responsible for this arrangement must have the right to demand obedience, reverence, if necessary even the risking of life and property for the highest political authority of the community of nations. . . .

The Reich will remain the supreme authority of the German nation. Its political constitution should be supported by the true authority, cooperation and co-responsibility of the nation. It is based on the natural subdivisions of the nation: family, local community and province [*land*]. The Reich will be structured on the principle of self-administration. It will combine freedom and personal responsibility with the requirements of order and leadership.

This structure is intended to facilitate the unity and the combined leadership of the Reich and its integration in the community of the European nations.

The political activity of the nation will occur within a context which is easily comprehensible for the individual. Provinces which are geographically, economically and culturally homogeneous will be formed on the basis of the natural subdivisions of local communities and districts. In order to achieve effective self-administration the provinces should contain between 3 and 5 million inhabitants.

The distribution of tasks will be based on the principle that every corporate body is responsible for the carrying out all those tasks which it makes sense for it to carry out itself. . . .

IV. *The Reich*
The Reich parliament will be elected by the provincial parliaments. Every male Reich citizen who has reached the age of 27 is entitled to be elected. Political officials and members of the armed forces are electable. The electoral law will ensure that, for the time being, at least half of those elected do not belong to one of the corporate bodies involved in the election. . . .

Source: Jeremy Noakes, ed., *Nazism 1919–1945, Volume 4: The Home Front in World War II* (Exeter, UK: University of Exeter Press, 1998), 614–616. Reprinted with permission of University of Exeter Press.

160. General Headquarters, Southwest Pacific Area, Press Release: Statement of General Douglas MacArthur on the Capture of Munda, New Georgia, 9 August 1943

In the Pacific theater, Allied forces under General Douglas MacArthur waged a succession of hard-fought but ultimately successful campaigns. On 5 August 1943, during the New Georgia campaign, Allied troops took the stronghold of Munda, a prelude to victory in the entire campaign, which was achieved on 10 October 1943. MacArthur issued a communiqué marking Munda's capture, shrewdly taking the opportunity to highlight what he considered to be the continuing shortfall of men and equipment in his command.

We are doing what we can with what we have. Our resources are still very limited, but the results of our modest but continuous successes in campaigns have been cumulative to the point of being vital. A measure of their potentiality can be obtained by imagining the picture to have been reversed, with the enemy capturing Guadalcanal and besieging Port Moresby rather than we in possession of Munda and at the gates of Salamaua. Such a contrast might well have meant defeat for us in the war for the Pacific.

The margin was close but it was conclusive. Although for many reasons our victories may have lacked in glamorous focus, they have been decisive of the final result in the Pacific. I make no predictions as to time or detail, but Japan on the Pacific fronts has exhausted the fullest resources of concentrated attack of which she was capable, has failed, and is now on a defensive which will yield just in proportion as we gather force and definition. When that will be I do not know, but it is certain.

Source: Charles A. Willoughby et al., eds., *Reports of General MacArthur: The Campaigns of MacArthur in the Pacific*, 2 vols. (Washington, DC: U.S. Government Printing Office, 1966), 1: 118–120.

161. The Quebec Conference, 17–24 August 1943: Joint Statement by Prime Minister Winston Churchill and President Franklin D. Roosevelt, 24 August 1943

In August 1943, Roosevelt and Churchill and their staffs met at Quebec, to coordinate Anglo-American military and diplomatic strategy. The two leaders announced that they intended to do more to assist China and had also considered the question of relations with the Free French government in exile.

The Anglo-American war conference, which opened at Quebec on August 17, under the hospitable auspices of the Canadian Government, has now concluded its work.

The whole field of world operations has been surveyed in the light of the many gratifying events which have taken place since the meeting of the President and the Prime Minister in Washington at the end of May, and the necessary decisions have been taken to provide for the forward action of the fleets, armies, and air forces of the two nations.

Considering that these forces are intermingled in continuous action against the enemy in several quarters of the globe, it is indispensable that entire unity of aim and method should be maintained at the summit of the war direction.

Further conferences will be needed, probably at shorter intervals than before, as the war effort of the United States and British Commonwealth and Empire against the enemy spreads and deepens.

It would not be helpful to the fighting troops to make any announcement of the decisions which have been reached. These can only emerge in action.

It may, however, be stated that the military discussions of the chiefs of staff turned very largely upon the war against Japan and the bringing of effective aid to China. Dr. T. V. Soong, representing the Generalissimo Kai-shek, was a party to the discussions. In this field, as in the European, the President and the Prime Minister were able to receive and approve the unanimous recommendation of the Combined Chiefs of Staff. Agreements were also reached upon the political issues underlying or arising out of the military operations.

It was resolved to hold another conference before the end of the year between the British and American authorities, in addition to any tri-partite meeting which it may be possible to arrange with Soviet Russia. Full reports of the decisions so far as they affect the war against Germany and Italy will be furnished to the Soviet Government.

Consideration has been given during the Conference to the question of relations with the French Committee of Liberation, and it is understood that an announcement by a number of governments will be made in the latter part of the week.

Source: U.S. Department of State, *A Decade of American Foreign Policy: Basic Documents, 1941–49* (Washington, DC: U.S. Government Printing Office, 1950), 7–8.

162. Military Armistice between the Allied Powers and the Italian Government, Signed at Fairfield Camp, Sicily, 3 September 1943

After lengthy negotiations, in September 1943, the king of Italy and his new prime minister, Marshal Pietro Badoglio, signed an armistice with the invading Anglo-American forces under General Dwight D. Eisenhower. This agreement did not mark the end of fighting in Italy. German troops in Italy doggedly refused to surrender and continued to oppose the Allies fiercely until spring 1945.

The following conditions of an Armistice are presented by General Dwight D. Eisenhower, Commander-in-Chief of the Allied Forces, acting by authority of the Governments of the United States and Great Britain and in the interest of the United Nations, and are accepted by Marshal Pietro Badoglio, Head of the Italian Government

1. Immediate cessation of all hostile activity by the Italian armed forces.

2. Italy will use its best endeavors to deny, to the Germans, facilities that might be used against the United Nations.

3. All prisoners or internees of the United Nations to be

immediately turned over to the Allied Commander in Chief, and none of these may now or at any time be evacuated to Germany.

4. Immediate transfer of the Italian Fleet and Italian aircraft to such points as may be designated by the Allied Commander in Chief, with details of disarmament to be prescribed by him.

5. Italian merchant shipping may be requisitioned by the Allied Commander in Chief to meet the needs of his military-naval program.

6. Immediate surrender of Corsica and of all Italian territory, both islands and mainland, to the Allies, for such use as operational bases and other purposes as the Allies may see fit.

7. Immediate guarantee of the free use by the Allies of all airfields and naval ports in Italian territory, regardless of the rate of evacuation of the Italian territory by the German forces. These ports and fields to be protected by Italian armed forces until this function is taken over by the Allies.

8. Immediate withdrawal to Italy of Italian armed forces from all participation in the current war from whatever areas in which they may be now engaged.

9. Guarantee by the Italian Government that if necessary it will employ all its available armed forces to insure prompt and exact compliance with all the provisions of this Armistice.

10. The Commander in Chief of the Allied Forces reserves to himself the right to take any measure which in his opinion may be necessary for the protection of the interests of the Allied Forces for the prosecution of the war, and the Italian Government binds itself to take such administrative or other action as the Commander in Chief may require, and in particular the Commander in Chief will establish Allied Military Government over such parts of Italian territory as he may deem necessary in the military interests of the Allied Nations.

11. The Commander in Chief of the Allied Forces will have a full right to impose measures of disarmament, demobilization, and demilitarization.

12. Other conditions of a political, economic, and financial nature with which Italy will be bound to comply will be transmitted at a later date.

The conditions of the present Armistice will not be made public without prior approval of the Allied Commander in Chief. The English will be considered the official text.

Source: Treaties and Other International Agreements of the United States of America 1776–1949, Volume 3: Multilateral 1931–1945, Department of State Publication 8484 (Washington, DC: U.S. Government Printing Office, 1969), 769–770.

163. General Douglas MacArthur's Strategy of Highly Selective "Island-Hopping": General Headquarters, Southwest Pacific Area, Press Release, 21 September 1943

General Douglas MacArthur, commander of Allied forces in the Southwest Pacific, is generally regarded as one of the greatest and most successful exponents of the Pacific War "island-hopping" strategy. He himself, however, wished to make it clear that the policy he favored was more of a leapfrogging strategy and that he had no wish to take every island dividing American forces and the Japanese homeland.

My strategic conception for the Pacific Theater, which I outlined after the Papuan Campaign and have since consistently advocated, contemplates massive strokes against only main strategic objectives, utilizing surprise and air-ground striking power supported and assisted by the fleet. This is the very opposite of what is termed "island-hopping" which is the gradual pushing back of the enemy by direct frontal pressure with the consequent heavy casualties which will certainly be involved. Key points must of course be taken but a wise choice of such will obviate the

need for storming the mass of islands now in enemy possession. "Island-hopping" with extravagant losses and slow progress . . . is not my idea of how to end the war as soon and as cheaply as possible. New conditions require for solution and new weapons require for maximum application new and imaginative methods. Wars are never won in the past.

Source: Charles A. Willoughby et al., eds., Reports of General MacArthur: The Campaigns of MacArthur in the Pacific, 2 vols. (Washington, DC: U.S. Government Printing Office, 1966), 1: 100.

164. The Fulbright and Connally Resolutions, September–November 1943

After World War I, Senate opposition had blocked U.S. entry into the League of Nations, the international organization established to mediate and settle future disputes between states. After Pearl Harbor, many Americans held their country's failure to join the League at least partly responsible for the occurrence of World War II. By large majorities, in 1943, the Senate and the House both passed resolutions demanding that the United States help to create and participate in a new international organization, which it was hoped would be more successful than its predecessor. The Senate resolution was sponsored by Senator Tom Connally of Texas, and its House counterpart by Congressman J. William Fulbright of Arkansas.

The Fulbright Resolution: House Concurrent Resolution 25, Seventy-Eighth Congress, 21 September 1943

. . . . *Resolved by the House of Representatives (the Senate concurring),* That the Congress hereby expresses itself as favoring the creation of appropriate international machinery with power adequate to establish and to maintain a just and lasting peace, among the nations of the world, and as favoring participation by the United States therein through its constitutional processes.

Source: U.S. Department of State, *A Decade of American Foreign Policy: Basic Documents, 1941–49* (Washington, DC: U.S. Government Printing Office, 1950), 11.

The Connally Resolution: Senate Resolution 192, Seventy-Eighth Congress, 5 November 1943

Resolved, that the war against all our enemies be waged until complete victory is achieved.

That the United States cooperate with its comrades-in-arms in securing a just and honorable peace.

That the United States, acting through its constitutional processes, join with free and sovereign nations in the establishment and maintenance of international authority with power to prevent aggression and to preserve the peace of the world.

That the Senate recognizes the necessity of there being established at the earliest practicable date a general international organization, based on the principle of the sovereign equality of all peace-loving states, and open to membership by all such states, large and small, for the maintenance of international peace and security.

That, pursuant to the Constitution of the United States, any treaty made to effect the purposes of this resolution, on behalf of the Government of the United States with any other nation or any association of nations, shall be made only by and with the advice and consent of the Senate of the United States, provided two-thirds of the Senators present concur.

Source: U.S. Department of State, *A Decade of American Foreign Policy: Basic Documents, 1941–49* (Washington, DC: U.S. Government Printing Office, 1950), 15.

165. Joint Declarations of the Moscow Conference, 18 October–1 November 1943

In October 1943, the foreign ministers of the "Big Four" Allied powers—Great Britain, the United States, China, and the Soviet Union—met in Moscow to discuss future policy on the war. At the conference's end, they declared their intention of continuing their collaboration after the war, in order to establish a postwar international organization to maintain order and security. Britain, the United States, and the Soviet Union also jointly issued more specific declarations on policy toward Italy, Austria, and the prosecution of war crimes. On Italy, they declared their intention of overthrowing the fascist system of government. Their declaration on Austria was couched in terms designed to encourage that country to separate itself from Germany, in the hope of receiving better postwar treatment from the victorious Allies. They announced their intention of prosecuting those responsible for wartime atrocities. These meetings and the announcements that followed were the preliminaries to summit meetings late the next month of U.S. President Franklin D. Roosevelt, British Prime Minister Winston Churchill, and Chinese President Jiang Jieshi (Chiang Kai-shek) at Cairo, followed immediately by a similar meeting of Churchill, Roosevelt, and Soviet President Josef Stalin in Tehran.

JOINT FOUR-NATION DECLARATION

The governments of the United States of America, United Kingdom, the Soviet Union, and China;

United in their determination, in accordance with the declaration by the United Nations of January, 1942, and subsequent declarations, to continue hostilities against those Axis powers with which they respectively are at war until such powers have laid down their arms on the basis of unconditional surrender;

Conscious of their responsibility to secure the liberation of themselves and the peoples allied with them from the menace of aggression;

Recognizing the necessity of insuring a rapid and orderly transition from war to peace and of establishing and maintaining international peace and security with the least diversion of the world's human and economic resources for armaments;

Jointly declare:

1. That their united action, pledged for the prosecution of the war against their respective enemies, will be continued for the organization and maintenance of peace and security.
2. That those of them at war with a common enemy will act together in all matters relating to the surrender and disarmament of that enemy.
3. That they will take all measures deemed by them to be necessary to provide against any violation of the terms imposed upon the enemy.
4. That they recognize the necessity of establishing at the earliest practicable date a general international organization, based on the principle of the sovereign equality of all peace-loving states, and open to membership by all such states, large and small, for the maintenance of international peace and security.
5. That for the purpose of maintaining international peace and security pending the re-establishment of law and order and the inauguration of a system of general security they will consult with one another and as occasion requires with other members of the United Nations, with a view to joint action on behalf of the community of nations.
6. That after the termination of hostilities they will not employ their military forces within the territories of other states except for the purposes envisaged in this declaration and after joint consultation.
7. That they will confer and cooperate with one another and with other members of the United Nations to bring about a practicable general agreement with respect to the regulation of armaments in the post-war period.

DECLARATION REGARDING ITALY

The Foreign Secretaries of the United States, the United Kingdom and the Soviet Union have established that their three governments are in complete agreement that Allied policy toward Italy must be based upon the fundamental principle that Fascism and all its evil influence and configuration shall be completely destroyed and that the Italian people shall be given every opportunity to establish governmental and other institutions based on democratic principles.

The Foreign Secretaries of the United States and the

United Kingdom declare that the action of their governments from the inception of the invasion of Italian territory, in so far as paramount military requirements have permitted, has been based upon this policy.

In furtherance of this policy in the future the Foreign Secretaries of the three governments are agreed that the following measures are important and should be put into effect:

1. It is essential that the Italian Government should be made more democratic by inclusion of representatives of those sections of the Italian people who have always opposed Fascism.
2. Freedom of speech, of religious worship, of political belief, of press and of public meeting, shall be restored in full measure to the Italian people, who shall be entitled to form anti-Fascist political groups.
3. All institutions and organizations created by the Fascist regime shall be suppressed.
4. All Fascist or pro-Fascist elements shall be removed from the administration and from institutions and organizations of a public character.
5. All political prisoners of the Fascist regime shall be released and accorded full amnesty.
6. Democratic organs of local government shall be created.
7. Fascist chiefs and army generals known or suspected to be war criminals shall be arrested and handed over to justice.

In making this declaration the three Foreign Secretaries recognize that so long as active military operations continue in Italy the time at which it is possible to give full effect to the principles stated above will be determined by the Commander-in-Chief on the basis of instructions received through the combined chiefs of staff.

The three governments, parties to this declaration, will, at the request of any one of them, consult on this matter. It is further understood that nothing in this resolution is to operate against the right of the Italian people ultimately to choose their own form of government.

DECLARATION ON AUSTRIA

The governments of the United Kingdom, the Soviet Union and the United States of America are agreed that Austria, the first free country to fall a victim to Hitlerite aggression, shall be liberated from German domination.

They regard the annexation imposed on Austria by Germany on March 15, 1938, as null and void. They consider themselves as in no way bound by any charges effected in Austria since that date. They declare that they wish to see re-established a free and independent Austria and thereby to open the way for the Austrian people themselves, as well as those neighboring States which will be faced with similar problems, to find that political and economic security which is the only basis for lasting peace. Austria is reminded, however that she has a responsibility, which she cannot evade, for participation in the war at the side of Hitlerite Germany, and that in the final settlement account will inevitably be taken of her own contribution to her liberation.

STATEMENT ON ATROCITIES, Signed by President Roosevelt, Prime Minister Churchill and Premier Stalin.

The United Kingdom, the United States and the Soviet Union have received from many quarters evidence of atrocities, massacres and cold-blooded mass executions which are being perpetrated by Hitlerite forces in many of the countries they have overrun and from which they are now being steadily expelled. The brutalities of Nazi domination are no new thing, and all peoples or territories in their grip have suffered from the worst form of government by terror. What is new is that many of the territories are now being redeemed by the advancing armies of the liberating powers, and that in their desperation the recoiling Hitlerites and Huns are redoubling their ruthless cruelties. This is now evidenced with particular clearness by monstrous crimes on the territory of the Soviet Union which is being liberated from Hitlerites, and on French and Italian territory.

Accordingly, the aforesaid three Allied powers, speaking in the interest of the thirty-two United Nations, hereby solemnly declare and give full warning of their declaration as follows:

At the time of granting of any armistice to any government which may be set up in Germany, those German officers and men and members of the Nazi party who have been responsible for or have taken a consenting part in the above atrocities, massacres and executions will be sent back to the countries in which their abominable deeds were done in order that they may be judged and punished according to the laws of these liberated countries and of free governments which will be erected therein. Lists will be compiled in all possible detail from all these countries having regard especially to invaded parts of the Soviet Union, to Poland and Czechoslovakia, to Yugoslavia and Greece including Crete and other islands, to Norway, Denmark, Netherlands, Belgium, Luxembourg, France and Italy.

Thus, Germans who take part in wholesale shooting of Polish officers or in the execution of French, Dutch, Belgian or Norwegian hostages or Cretan peasants, or who have shared in slaughters inflicted on the people of Poland or in territories of the Soviet Union which are now being swept clear of the enemy, will know they will be brought back to the scene of their crimes and judged on the spot by the peoples whom they have outraged.

Let those who have hitherto not imbrued their hands with innocent blood beware lest they join the ranks of the guilty, for most assuredly the three Allied powers will pursue them to the uttermost ends of the earth and will deliver them to their accusors in order that justice may be done.

The above declaration is without prejudice to the case of German criminals whose offenses have no particular geographical localization and who will be punished by joint decision of the government of the Allies.

Source: U.S. Department of State, *A Decade of American Foreign Policy: Basic Documents, 1941–49* (Washington, DC: U.S. Government Printing Office, 1950), 11–15.

166. Joint Declaration of the Greater East Asia Congress, Tokyo, 6 November 1943

In early November 1943 representatives of seven Asian nations—Japan, China, Thailand, Manzhouguo, the Philippines, Burma, and Free India, a government established by the breakaway Indian nationalist Subhas Chandra Bose—met at Tokyo on the invitation of the Japanese government to establish the Greater East Asia Co-Prosperity Sphere. On 6 November the meeting issued a declaration expressing the participants' intention of working together against Great Britain and the United States to drive Western powers completely out of Asia.

It is a basic principle for the establishment of world peace that the nations of the world each have its proper place and enjoy prosperity in common through mutual aid and assistance. The United States of America and the British Empire have, in seeking their own prosperity, oppressed other nations and peoples. Especially in East Asia, they indulged in insatiable aggression and exploitation, sought to satisfy their incredible ambition of enslaving the entire region and finally came to menace seriously the stability of East Asia. Herein lies the cause of the present war.

The countries of Greater East Asia, with a view of contributing to the cause of world peace, undertake to cooperate toward prosecuting the War of Greater East Asia to a successful conclusion, liberating their region from the yoke of British-American domination, ensuring their self-existence and self-defense and constructing a Greater East Asia in accordance with the following principles:

1. The countries of Greater East Asia, through mutual cooperation, will ensure the stability of their region and construct an order of common prosperity and well-being based upon justice.

2. The countries of Greater East Asia will ensure the fraternity of the nations in their region by respecting one another's sovereignty and independence and practising mutual assistance and amity.

3. The countries of Greater East Asia, by respecting one another's traditions and developing the faculties of each race, will enhance the culture and civilization of Greater East Asia.

4. The countries of Greater East Asia will endeavor to accelerate their economic development through close cooperation upon a basis of reciprocity and promote thereby the general prosperity of their region.

5. The countries of Greater East Asia will cultivate friendly relations with all the countries of the world and work for the abolition of racial discrimination, the promotion of cultural intercourse throughout the world and contribute thereby to the progress of mankind.

Source: Gregorio F. Zaide, ed., *Documentary Sources of Philippine History,* Vol. 12 (Metro Manila, Philippines: National Book Store Publishers, 1990), 43–45. Courtesy Zaide Foundation.

167. Agreement for United Nations Relief and Rehabilitation Administration, 9 November 1943

The war created millions of refugees, the care of whom could not be left until the war had ended. In late 1943, the Allied governments therefore established an agency for this purpose. Inevitably, the United States provided the bulk of the new organization's funding, one reason why its first director was former Governor Herbert Lehman of New York. Lehman's Jewish origins and prewar involvement in efforts to help European Jews escape the Nazis also made him an appropriate choice, as did his executive ability.

The Governments or Authorities whose duly authorized representatives have subscribed hereto,

[Australia, Belgium, Bolivia, the United States of Brazil, Canada, Chile, China, Colombia, Costa Rica, Cuba, Czechoslovakia, Dominican Republic, Ecuador, Egypt, El Salvador, Ethiopia, French Committee of National Liberation, Greece, Guatemala, Haiti, Honduras, Iceland, India, Iran, Iraq, Liberia, Luxembourg, United Mexican States, Netherlands, New Zealand, Nicaragua, Norway, Panama, Paraguay, Peru, Philippine Commonwealth, Poland, Union of South Africa, Union of Soviet Socialist Republics, United Kingdom of Great Britain and Northern Ireland, United States of America, Uruguay, Venezuela, and Yugoslavia]

Being United Nations or being associated with the United Nations in this war,

Being determined that immediately upon the liberation of any area by the armed forces of the United Nations or as a consequence of retreat of the enemy the population thereof shall receive aid and relief from their sufferings, food, clothing and shelter, aid in the prevention of pestilence and in the recovery of the health of the people, and that preparation and arrangements shall be made for the return of prisoners and exiles to their homes and for assistance in the resumption of urgently needed agricultural and industrial production and the restoration of essential services,

Have agreed as follows:

ARTICLE I

There is hereby established the United Nations Relief and Rehabilitation Administration.

1. The Administration shall have power to acquire, hold and convey property, to enter into contracts and undertake obligations, to designate or create agencies and to review the activities of agencies as created, to manage undertakings and in general to perform any legal act appropriate to its objects and purposes.

2. Subject to the provisions of Article VII, the purposes and functions of the Administration shall be as follows:

(a) To plan, coordinate, administer or arrange for the administration of measures for the relief of victims of war in any area under the control of any of the United Nations through the provision of food, fuel, clothing, shelter and other basic necessities, medical and other essential services; and to facilitate in such areas, so far as necessary to the adequate provision of relief, the production and transportation of these articles and the furnishing of these services. The form of activities of the Administration within the territory of a member government wherein that government exercises administrative authority and the responsibility to be assumed by the member government for carrying out measures planned by the Administration therein shall be determined after consultation with and with the consent of the member government.

(b) To formulate and recommend measures for individual or joint action by any or all of the member governments for the coordination of purchasing, the use of ships and other procurement activities in the period following the cessation of hostilities, with a view to integrating the plans and activities of the Administration with the total movement of supplies, and for the purpose of achieving an equitable distribution of available supplies. The Administration may administer such coordination measures as may be authorized by the member governments concerned.

(c) To study, formulate and recommend for individual or joint action by any or all of the member governments measures with respect to such related matters, arising out of its experience in planning and performing the work of relief and rehabilitation, as may be proposed by any of the member governments. Such proposals shall be studied and recommendations formulated if the proposals are supported by a vote of the Council, and the recommendations shall be referred to any or all of the member governments for individual or joint action if approved by unanimous vote of the Central Committee and by the vote of the Council.

ARTICLE II. MEMBERSHIP

The members of the United Nations Relief and Rehabilitation Administration shall be the governments or authorities signatory hereto and such other governments or authorities as may upon application for membership be admitted thereto by action of the Council. The Council may, if it desires, authorize the Central Committee to accept new members between sessions of the Council. . . .

ARTICLE III. THE COUNCIL

1. Each member government shall name one representative, and such alternates as may be necessary, upon the Council of the United Nations Relief and Rehabilitation Administration, which shall be the policy-making body of the Administration. The Council shall, for each of its sessions, select one of its members to preside at the session. The Council shall determine its own rules of procedure. Unless otherwise provided by the Agreement or by action of the Council, the Council shall vote by simple majority.

2. The Council shall be convened in regular session not less than twice a year by the Central Committee. It may be convened in special session whenever the Central Committee shall deem necessary, and shall be convened within thirty days after request therefor by one-third of the members of the Council.

3. The Central Committee of the Council shall consist of the representatives of China, the Union of Soviet Socialist Republics, the United Kingdom, and the United States of America, with the Director General presiding, without vote. Between sessions of the Council it shall when necessary make policy decisions of an emergency nature. All such decisions shall be recorded in the minutes of the Central Committee which shall be communicated promptly to each member government. Such decisions shall be open to reconsideration by the Council at any regular session or at any special session called in accordance with Article III, paragraph 2. The Central Committee shall invite the participation of the representative of any member government at those of its meetings at which action of special interest to such government is discussed. It shall invite the participation of the representative serving as Chairman of the Committee on Supplies of the Council at those of its meetings at which policies affecting the provision of supplies are discussed.

4. The Committee on Supplies of the Council shall consist of the members of the Council, or their alternates, representing those member governments likely to be principal suppliers of materials for relief and rehabilitation. The members shall be appointed by the Council, and the Council may authorize the Central Committee to make emergency appointments between sessions of the Council, such appointments to continue until the next session of the Council. The Committee on Supplies shall consider, formulate and recommend to the Council and the Central Committee policies designed to assure the provision of required supplies. The Central Committee shall from time to time meet with the Committee on Supplies to review policy matters affecting supplies.

5. The Committee of the Council for Europe shall consist of all the members of the Council, or their alternates, representing member governments or territories within the European area and such other members of the Council representing other governments directly concerned with the problems of relief and rehabilitation in the European area as shall be appointed by the Council; the Council may authorize the Central Committee to make these appointments in cases of emergency between sessions of the Council, such appointments to continue until the next session of the Council. The Committee of the Council for the Far East shall consist of all members of the Council, or their alternates, representing member governments of territories within the Far Eastern area and such other members of the Council representing other governments directly concerned with the problems of relief and rehabilitation in the Far Eastern area as shall be appointed by the Council; the Council may authorize the Central Committee to make these appointments in cases of emergency between sessions of the Council, such appointments to continue until the next session of the Council. The regional committees shall normally meet within their respective areas. They shall consider and recommend to the Council and the Central Committee policies with respect to relief and rehabilitation within their respective areas. The Committee of the Council for Europe shall replace the Inter-Allied Committee on European post-war relief established in London on September 24, 1941 and the records of the latter shall be made available to the Committee for Europe.

6. The Council shall establish such other standing regional committees as it shall consider desirable, the

functions of such committees and the method of appointing their members being identical to that provided in Article III, paragraph 5 with respect to the Committees of the Council for Europe and for the Far East. The Council shall also establish such other standing committees as it considers desirable to advise it, and, in intervals between sessions of the Council, to advise the Central Committee. For such standing technical committees as may be established, in respect of particular problems such as nutrition, health, agriculture, transport, repatriation, and finance, the members may be members of the Council or alternates nominated by them because of special competence in their respective fields of work. The members shall be appointed by the Council, and the Council may authorize the Central Committee to make emergency appointments between sessions of the Council, such appointments to continue until the next session of the Council. Should a regional committee so desire, subcommittees of the standing technical committees shall be established by the technical committees in consultation with the regional committees, to advise the regional committees.

7. The travel and other expenses of members of the Council and of members of its committees shall be borne by the governments which they represent.

8. All reports and recommendations of committees of the Council shall be transmitted to the Director General for distribution to the Council and the Central Committee by the secretariat of the Council established under the provisions of Article IV, paragraph 4.

ARTICLE IV. THE DIRECTOR GENERAL

1. The executive authority of the United Nations Relief and Rehabilitation Administration shall be in the Director General, who shall be appointed by the Council on the nomination by unanimous vote of the Central Committee. The Director General may be removed by the Council on recommendation by unanimous vote of the Central Committee.

2. The Director General shall have full power and authority for carrying out relief operations contemplated by Article I, paragraph 2 (a), within the limits of available resources and the broad policies determined by the Council or its Central Committee. Immediately upon taking office he shall in conjunction with the military and other appropriate authorities of the United Nations prepare plans for the emergency relief of the civilian population in any area occupied by the armed forces of any of the United Nations, arrange for the procurement and assembly of the necessary supplies and create or select the emergency organization required for this purpose. In arranging for the procurement, transportation, and distribution of supplies and services, he and his representatives shall consult with the appropriate authorities of the United Nations and shall, wherever practicable, use the facilities made available by such authorities. Foreign voluntary relief agencies may not engage in activity in any area receiving relief from the Administration without the consent and unless subject to the regulation of the Director General. The powers and duties of the Director General are subject to the limitations of Article VII.

3. The Director General shall also be responsible for the organization and direction of the functions contemplated by Article I, paragraphs 2 (b) and 2 (c)....

ARTICLE V. SUPPLIES AND RESOURCES

1. In so far as its appropriate constitutional bodies shall authorize, each member government will contribute to the support of the Administration in order to accomplish the purposes of Article I, paragraph 2 (a). The amount and character of the contributions of each member government under this provision will be determined from time to time by its appropriate constitutional bodies. All such contributions received by the Administration shall be accounted for.

2. The supplies and resources made available by the member governments shall be kept in review in relation to prospective requirements by the Director General, who shall initiate action with the member governments with a view to assuring such additional supplies and resources as may be required....

ARTICLE VI. ADMINISTRATIVE EXPENSES

The Director General shall submit to the Council an annual budget, and from time to time such supplementary budgets as may be required, covering the necessary administrative expenses of the Administration. Upon approval of a budget by the Council the total amount approved shall be allocated to the member governments in proportions to be determined by the Council.

Each member government undertakes, subject to the requirements of its constitutional procedure, to contribute to the Administration promptly its share of the administrative expenses so determined.

ARTICLE VII

Notwithstanding any other provision herein contained, while hostilities or other military necessities exist in any area, the Administration and its Director General shall not undertake activities therein without the consent of the military command of that area, and unless subject to such control as the command may find necessary. The determination that such hostilities or military necessities exist in any area shall be made by its military commander. . . .

Source: Pamphlet No. 4, *Pillars of Peace: Documents Pertaining to American Interest in Establishing a Lasting World Peace: January 1941–February 1946* (Carlisle Barracks, PA: Book Department, Army Information School, May 1946), 18–26.

168. The Cairo Conference Declaration, 23–25 November 1943

In late November 1943 Churchill and Roosevelt met at Cairo with China's leader, Jiang Jieshi (Chiang Kai-shek), before proceeding to Tehran, where the two joined Stalin. At the conclusion of the Tehran meeting, they issued a public declaration that they sought the unconditional surrender of Japan, independence for Korea, and the expulsion of Japan from all the territories it had seized.

The several military missions have agreed upon future military operations against Japan. The Three Great Allies expressed their resolve to bring unrelenting pressure against their brutal enemies by sea, land, and air. This pressure is already mounting.

The Three Great Allies are fighting this war to restrain and punish the aggression of Japan. They covet no gain for themselves and have no thought of territorial expansion.

It is their purpose that Japan shall be stripped of all the islands in the Pacific which she has seized or occupied since the beginning of the first World War in 1914, and that all the territories Japan has stolen from the Chinese, such as Manchuria, Formosa, and the Pescadores, shall be restored to the Republic of China.

Japan will also be expelled from all other territories which she has taken by violence and greed. The aforesaid three great powers, mindful of the enslavement of the people of Korea, are determined that in due course Korea shall become free and independent.

With these objects in view the three Allies, in harmony with those of the United Nations at war with Japan, will continue to persevere in the serious and prolonged operations necessary to procure the unconditional surrender of Japan.

Source: Declaration of the Cairo Conference, 23–25 November 1943, Released 1 December 1943. In U.S. Department of State, *A Decade of American Foreign Policy: Basic Documents, 1941–1949* (Washington, DC: U.S. Government Printing Office, 1950), 20.

169. Declarations of the Tehran Conference, 28 November–1 December 1943

From 28 November to 1 December 1943 Churchill, Stalin, and Roosevelt met at Tehran, to discuss the future prosecution of the war. When the conference ended, the three leaders issued various public declarations on the prosecution and objectives of the war and their future treatment of Iran. Privately, they agreed to provide support for the Communist partisans in Yugoslavia, and to launch Operation OVERLORD, the invasion of Western Europe, in May—a date later deferred to June—1944.

(i) DECLARATION OF THE THREE POWERS, 1 DECEMBER 1943

We the President of the United States, the Prime Minister of Great Britain, and the Premier of the Soviet Union, have met these four days past, in this, the Capital of our Ally, Iran, and have shaped and confirmed our common policy.

We express our determination that our nations shall work together in war and in the peace that will follow.

As to war—our military staffs have joined in our round table discussions, and we have concerted our plans for the destruction of the German forces. We have reached com-

plete agreement as to the scope and timing of the operations to be undertaken from the east, west and south.

The common understanding which we have here reached guarantees that victory will be ours.

And as to peace—we are sure that our concord will win an enduring Peace. We recognize fully the supreme responsibility resting upon us and all the United Nations to make a peace which will command the goodwill of the overwhelming mass of the peoples of the world and banish the scourge and terror of war for many generations.

With our Diplomatic advisors we have surveyed the

problems of the future. We shall seek the cooperation and active participation of all nations, large and small, whose peoples in heart and mind are dedicated, as are our own peoples, to the elimination of tyranny and slavery, oppression and intolerance. We will welcome them, as they may choose to come, into a world family of Democratic Nations.

No power on earth can prevent our destroying the German armies by land, their U Boats by sea, and their war plants from the air.

Our attack will be relentless and increasing.

Emerging from these cordial conferences we look with confidence to the day when all peoples of the world may live free lives, untouched by tyranny, and according to their varying desires and their own consciences.

We came here with hope and determination. We leave here, friends in fact, in spirit and in purpose.

(ii) DECLARATION OF THE THREE POWERS REGARDING IRAN, 1 DECEMBER 1943

The President of the United States, the Premier of the U.S.S.R., and the Prime Minister of the United Kingdom, having consulted with each other and with the Prime Minister of Iran, desire to declare the mutual agreement of their three Governments regarding their relations with Iran.

The Governments of the United States, the U.S.S.R., and the United Kingdom recognize the assistance which Iran has given in the prosecution of the war against the common enemy, particularly by facilitating the transportation of supplies from overseas to the Soviet Union.

The Three Governments realize that the war has caused special economic difficulties for Iran, and they are agreed that they will continue to make available to the Government of Iran such economic assistance as may be possible, having regard to the heavy demands made upon them by their world-wide military operations, and to the world-wide shortage of transport, raw materials, and supplies for civilian consumption.

With respect to the post-war period, the Governments of the United States, the U.S.S.R., and the United Kingdom are in accord with the Government of Iran that any economic problems confronting Iran at the close of hostilities should receive full consideration, along with those of other members of the United Nations, by conferences or international agencies held or created to deal with international economic matters.

The Governments of the United States, the U.S.S.R., and the United Kingdom are at one with the Government of Iran in their desire for the maintenance of the independence, sovereignty, and territorial integrity of Iran. They count upon the participation of Iran, together with all other peace-loving nations, in the establishment of international peace, security, and prosperity after the war, in accordance with the principles of the Atlantic Charter, to which all four Governments have subscribed.

(iii) MILITARY CONCLUSIONS OF THE TEHRAN CONFERENCE, 1 DECEMBER 1943

The Conference:

(1) Agreed that the Partisans in Yugoslavia should be supported by supplies and equipment to the greatest possible extent, and also by commando operations:

(2) Agreed that, from the military point of view, it was most desirable that Turkey should come into the war on the side of the Allies before the end of the year:

(3) Took note of Marshal Stalin's statement that if Turkey found herself at war with Germany, and as a result Bulgaria declared war on Turkey or attacked her, the Soviet Union would immediately be at war with Bulgaria. The Conference further took note that this fact could be explicitly stated in the forthcoming negotiations to bring Turkey into the war:

(4) Took note that Operation OVERLORD would be launched during May 1944, in conjunction with an operation against Southern France. The latter operation would be undertaken in as great a strength as availability of landing-craft permitted. The Conference further took note of Marshal Stalin's statement that the Soviet forces would launch an offensive at about the same time with the object of preventing the German forces from transferring from the Eastern to the Western Front:

(5) Agreed that the military staffs of the Three Powers should henceforward keep in close touch with each other in regard to the impending operations in Europe. In particular it was agreed that a cover plan to mystify and mislead the enemy as regards these operations should be concerted between the staffs concerned.

Source: U.S. Department of State, *A Decade of American Foreign Policy: Basic Documents, 1941–49* (Washington, DC: U.S. Government Printing Office, 1950), 21–22.

170. Declarations and Statements of the Anti-Fascist Council of National Liberation, Jajce, Bosnia, Yugoslavia, 29 November 1943

In Yugoslavia, which was occupied by German troops during the war, Communist partisans led by Josip Broz Tito came to dominate the anti-German guerrilla movement and rejected the monarchical government-in-exile of King Peter II. The Yugoslav case was an example of the manner in which fierce anti-German resistance won European Communists new credibility in various occupied countries. On occasion, the Communists treated royalist and non-Communist rivals at least as savagely as they did their German enemies, and fierce internecine feuding divided the guerrilla movement. In November 1943, Communist partisans met at Jajce, Bosnia, where they asserted their claims to represent the Yugoslav people and their vision of the Communist government that would take power after the war. The monarchist government was declared illegitimate.

Declaration of the Second Session of the Anti-Fascist Council of the People's Liberation of Yugoslavia, Jajce, Bosnia, Yugoslavia, 29 November 1943

In the course of two and a half years of continuous people's liberation struggle against the occupier and his collaborators, the peoples of Yugoslavia have achieved big and decisive successes, both in internal and in foreign policy affairs. After each attempt of the enemy to atomize our People's Liberation Army, the military strength of our Army has increased, consolidated its ranks and raised them to a higher military and technical level. The more pressure the enemy put in an effort to suppress the liberation movement of our peoples, the closer became the ranks of the people in this movement around the Supreme Headquarters and Comrade Tito, the celebrated leader of the people, around the Anti-Fascist Council of the People's Liberation of Yugoslavia and around the national political representatives of the individual nations of Yugoslavia. Our liberated territory has steadily increased, our material reserves and sources of supply of our People's Liberation Army and the population have increased also.

Simultaneously, organs of people's authority and various economic and management organs in service of this authority have developed.

The recognition of the big successes of our People's Liberation War abroad on the one side and the complete unmasking of the role and high treason of the Yugoslavia "government"-in-exile on the other side have set entirely new tasks before the leading organs of our peoples' liberation movement. It was necessary systematically to consolidate all these successes and to exploit them for a further successful continuation of our People's Liberation War.

In view of these facts, the Anti-Fascist Council of the People's Liberation of Yugoslavia at its Second Session, held on November 29, 1943,

Establishes:

I

1. The two and a half years of our People's Liberation War have offered proof to the whole world that the peoples of Yugoslavia have set off, firmly and with determination, on a path of armed resistance to the occupier, on a path indicated to our people by the Communist Party of Yugoslavia, which all truly patriotic forces and political groups of our peoples have been pursuing with it. The enormous majority of the peoples of Yugoslavia have joined the ranks of the liberation movement, and extended active support to its People's Liberation Army. Also all patriotic and honest functionaries from all political parties, groups and patriotic organizations, have, together with the people, actively participated in the peoples' liberation movement. All this is equally true of all the Yugoslav nations. By their activity in the peoples' liberation movement, the peoples of Yugoslavia have spoken up publicly in protest against traitors, reactionaries and speculators in the country and abroad who stayed in power in old Yugoslavia by means of violence and deceit and are now once again trying—by depending on the most reactionary circles—to regain power with the help of treason, deceit and speculation. But all these endeavours cannot conceal the fact that an entirely new relation of political forces has been created in our country during the People's Liberation War and that this new relation must be adequately expressed also in its management and state leadership . . .

III

Bearing in mind all these facts, the Anti-Fascist Council of the People's Liberation of Yugoslavia, which is the supreme and only true representation of the will and feelings of all peoples of Yugoslavia,

Decides

1. To constitute the Anti-Fascist Council of the People's Liberation of Yugoslavia as the supreme legislative and executive representative organ of Yugoslavia, as the supreme representative of the sovereignty of the peoples and state of Yugoslavia as a whole, and to set up a National Committee of the Liberation of Yugoslavia as an organ with all the characteristics of a peoples' government, through which the Anti-Fascist Council of the People's Liberation of Yugoslavia will exercise its executive function.

2. To deprive the Yugoslav "traitor" government-in-exile of all the rights of a legal government of Yugoslavia and especially of the right to represent the peoples of Yugoslavia—anywhere and before anyone.

Source: Snezana Trifunovska, *Yugoslavia through Documents: From Its Creation to Its Dissolution* (Dordrecht, Holland: Martinus Nijhoff, 1994), 202–210. Reprinted with permission of Martinus Nijhoff.

Decision to Create Yugoslavia on Federal Principles, Jajce, 29 November 1943

On the basis of the right of every people to self-determination, including the right to secession or to unification with other peoples, and in accordance with the true will of all the peoples of Yugoslavia, made certain during the three-year joint people's liberation struggle which praised the inseparable fraternity of the peoples of Yugoslavia, the Anti-Fascist Council of the People's Liberation of Yugoslavia passes the following

Decision

1. The peoples of Yugoslavia do not recognize and have never recognized the partition of Yugoslavia by the fascist imperialists and they have proved, during the joint armed struggle, their firm will to remain further united in Yugoslavia;

2. In order to carry out the principles of the sovereignty of the peoples of Yugoslavia, and in order for Yugoslavia to present a true homeland for all its peoples

and never again to become a domain of any other hegemonistic clique, Yugoslavia is building and will be built along the lines of the federal principle which will provide for full equality of the Serbs, Croats and Slovenes, Macedonians and Montenegrins, respectively the peoples of Serbia, Croatia, Slovenia, Macedonia, Montenegro and Bosnia and Herzegovina. . . .

4. All rights will be guaranteed to the national minorities in Yugoslavia. . . .

Source: Snezana Trifunovska, *Yugoslavia through Documents: From Its Creation to Its Dissolution* (Dordrecht, Holland: Martinus Nijhoff, 1994), 202–210. Reprinted with permission of Martinus Nijhoff.

Decision on the Supreme Legislative and Executive People's Representative Body of Yugoslavia and the National Committee of Liberation of Yugoslavia, as Temporary Organs of the Supreme People's Authority in Yugoslavia during the People's Liberation War, Jajce, 29 November 1943

1. In accordance with the firm will of the peoples of Yugoslavia, their harmony and unity in the struggle against the occupying forces, to build a new national fraternity and equality based upon Yugoslavia as the joint homeland of all its peoples, and thanks to the successes of the unified People's Liberation Army and Partisan Detachments of Yugoslavia, which, under the leadership of the Supreme Headquarters, have united in the very struggle all people's-liberation movements in Yugoslavia, the Anti-Fascist Council of the People's Liberation Army of Yugoslavia has developed—during the liberation war—into the supreme representative of the sovereignty of the peoples and state of Yugoslavia as the whole.

2. Relating to that fact and to the degree of the people's liberation struggle in Yugoslavia, in accordance with the principles of the federal system of the fraternally-built Yugoslavia, the Anti-Fascist Council of the People's Liberation of Yugoslavia constitutes itself as the supreme legislative and executive people's representative body of Yugoslavia during the people's liberation war. . . .

Source: Snezana Trifunovska, *Yugoslavia through Documents: From Its Creation to Its Dissolution* (Dordrecht, Holland: Martinus Nijhoff, 1994), 202–210. Reprinted with permission of Martinus Nijhoff.

171. The "Death Railway" from Burma to Thailand: Experiences of Roy M. "Max" Offerle

The Japanese generally sent their prisoners of war to labor camps, working on a variety of industrial, construction, mining, and agricultural enterprises. Although working conditions varied, they were generally poor, with food increasingly short as the war progressed, clothing inadequate, and medical facilities poor and sometimes virtually nonexistent. Camps were primitive and overcrowded, with dangerously poor sanitation and mechanical equipment conspicuous by its absence. One of the most notorious of these work projects was the construction of the railway linking the Burmese capital, Rangoon, to Thailand's capital, Bangkok, on which 50,000 Australian, British, Dutch, and American prisoners of war and around 250,000 local Asian slave laborers worked. Perhaps a third of the Western prisoners and almost one-half of the Asian laborers died while working on the "death railway," many from horrific tropical ulcers, cholera, dysentery, malaria, or other diseases. Working conditions were worst fom February to October 1943, when Japanese officials launched a campaign to expedite completion of the railway, and those supervising its construction demanded still more work from men whose health and strength were rapidly declining.

[Roy M. "Max" Offerle, born in Texas in 1921, was one of 668 American soldiers of the Second Battalion captured on the Indonesian island of Java in March 1942. Recovering from amoebic dysentery, he was set to work on constructing the Burma-Thailand Railway, and sent to 18 Kilo(meter) Camp, where his elder brother Oscar, who later died of a tropical ulcer, was also working.]

Basically, 18 Kilo was like one of the many camps we were to be in in the future. You're talking about, like, maybe three, four, five thousand men in these camps, a lot of men. They had long huts made out of bamboo frames tied together with atap, which are leaves wrapped over thin pieces of bamboo about three feet long. They'd leave the walls open, and they had atap leaf roofs that were then overhanging. My brother was working in the cookhouse and then on the wood detail, cutting wood for the kitchen. Anybody related to the kitchen got a little better food. When I got there, he started bringing me some extra food, and it helped me get well fast. The quality wasn't too good, but the quantity was fair.

The first job we had was a fill about three blocks long. It was forty meters across the top of the depression; there was a natural slope to it, which went about twenty feet deep. It took four or five thousand men working a month or two to build this fill. . . . The men worked hard because they knew they were off as soon as they moved a meter of dirt. After we got accustomed to pick-and-shovel work and carrying dirt, we would finish at three or four o'clock in the afternoon.

Well, then the Japs just gave us a larger quota. So we went to a meter-and-a-tenth, a meter-and-a-quarter, a meter-and-a-half per man per day. Later on up country, they went to two meters of dirt. When they went to one-and-a-half meters of dirt, you'd get in about dark. Two meters of dirt would get you in at about ten or eleven o'clock at night. They eventually went to this, and by then, too, we got food that didn't have all of your vitamins. You weren't keeping your strength up. The men's physical strength gradually wore down and our quotas gradually went up, which set us up for disease and sickness and a lot of the things that were to follow.

At this time, our group, which was one of the largest groups of Americans working on the railroad, hadn't yet experienced real hardship. We were getting a little sickness, some malaria, maybe a few people hurt. From 18 Kilo we went to 80 Kilo Camp. Now, we had larger quotas to meet. We were up in a lot more jungle. Conditions were not so good. We were farther away, so supplies were harder to get up there. We got away from canteens and extra food that you could buy.

From 80 Kilo, which was a smaller camp, we went to 100 Kilo, which was a larger camp. Incidentally, we were at 85 Kilo Camp for a while—80, 85, 100. But 100 Kilo Camp seemed to be a larger camp. I believe it was in 100 Kilo Camp where we got the full brunt of the rainy season. When you talk about rainy season in Burma, you're talking about three or four months where it comes out like you're pouring it from a bucket, day in and day out. It's possibly three or four hundred inches of rain in a season. Actually, creeks and rivers form, and you can almost watch vegetation grow. The rainy or monsoon season turned everything to soup or mud. They couldn't get supplies up there easily. Then the speedup on work came. We went from one meter, to a meter-and-a-half, to two meters of dirt per day. Well, the men's health broke down. We started getting lots of malaria, beriberi, dysentery, and tropical ulcers, because it seemed that the germ that causes tropical ulcers was more prevalent in the rainy season. We started getting a multitude of diseases.

The more people that got sick, the less the Japs had for working parties, so more sick people had to work. They'd set a quota of men every day that had to go out, and they'd fill it. I worked all this time. I hadn't been sick, although I lost weight. I didn't have malaria, beriberi, or any diseases. So I worked. This *kumi* of fifty men that I was in was originally all sergeants, and it was down after the rainy season started to thirteen or fourteen men. That didn't mean they were all dead; some of them were, but most of them were just sick. They were sick enough that if they had been in the United States, they'd have been in an isolation ward with a nurse twenty-four hours a day. Yet here they were in a bamboo hut in the rainy season eating a little rice and water stew; no medication and no one to take care of them, except our own medics and doctor who had no medicine.

This developed into a situation where we started losing men fast. The Japs would force the sick out. If they wanted a *kumi* of twenty-five to go out, and had fourteen healthy there, that meant eleven sick had to go out. So they would come down through the sick barracks. The first time I stayed in, I had malaria and was sick as a dog. I was shaking and felt terrible and had a high fever and chills. I asked the doctor if I could stay in, and he said, "Yes, you haven't been in, so stay in." So here come the Japs down for extra men to go to work. Well, I got off the heavy-duty job, but they said they had to send me out on light duty. The doctor said, "There are some men sicker than you. Can you go out on light duty?" I said, "Well, if I have to, I will." He said, "Yes, you'd better go out." These Japs raised Cain, and they started beating everybody and giving the doctors and medics a hard time. So, light duty was busting rocks with a sledgehammer—putting rocks on the roads—because they were just a sea of mud, and they were trying to fix the roads enough to get trucks up them with supplies.

Source: Robert S. La Forte and Ronald E. Marcello, eds., *Building the Death Railway: The Ordeal of American POWs in Burma, 1942–1945* (Wilmington, DE: Scholarly Resources, 1993), 171–173.

172. The British Home Front: Recollections of Pamela Lazarus

When World War II began, Pamela Lazarus, a young Jewish girl, lived in the East End of London, which suffered worst in the Blitz. Her memories of the war focus on themes common to many recollections: the shortage of food, the blackout, the horrors of bombing, the dramatic impact of American soldiers upon the British population, and the absence of her father in the armed forces.

It wasn't much fun being a small kid at that time. It was too scary. London was a smoggy city, filled with gray skies, gray fog, rainy days and one seldom saw a blue sky or sunshine. Or so it seemed. And indoors, it always seemed to be night. Everyone had black curtains on the windows so that no light would escape into the street, and more importantly, be seen from the German airplanes flying overhead. Lights could show them a good place to drop a bomb. Besides, electricity was expensive, and not to be used if not necessary.

My Dad was away in the army, somewhere in Europe and my mother was very nervous. She was a young woman in her mid 20s, with a little girl (me) and a new baby, and she wanted someone to look after her, and there wasn't anyone to do it. So she cried a lot, and when the siren would go off to warn of an air-raid, she would scream in fear. I always felt responsible for her, like I should be her mother and take care of her. But I was only three and four and five and six and didn't know how, except by not being a burden.

In the beginning, the bombing was at night. She would tell me to quickly! quickly! put on a sweater or coat and shoes and run downstairs. I would hide under the kitchen table until she had dressed herself and wrapped up the baby. Then we would run through the long, narrow garden to the air-raid shelter. It seemed always to be night, and dark, with sirens screaming and wailing.

The shelter was simply some corrugated steel sheets made into a shed against the brick, garden wall, with a sloping roof. It had a dirt floor and two wooden benches inside on which to sit. No heat, no light. Mother brought candles if she remembered, or else we sat in the dark. If a stranger was on the street when the sirens began, they could knock at any house door and be taken in to the shelter, and spend the night in the shelter.

Mother was always complaining about the rations. She wasn't a good cook and didn't know how to make exotic things like puddings or any treats, so our food was very simple. Mostly something boiled or fried. There was often nothing—nothing at all—to eat and we got used to being hungry. . . .

The City Authorities would regularly send people (women with small children) out of the City, into the country for safety. Mother would go with much grumbling and complaining. She was a City person.

The train would be packed to the limit with American soldiers coming and going somewhere. Every seat was taken, every foot of ground had someone crammed into it. As a small child, I could not step over the rucksacks or around the people, so the soldiers would pass me down the corridor, from hand to hand, with my mother trying to keep up. And they gave me chewing gum! I learned to say "Any gum, chum?" for a stick of Wrigley's Spearmint gum.

Those yanks! I thought they were the grandest, most glamorous people in the world.

Easy smiling, handsome, glamorous looking, movie-star sounding, generous and friendly.

Yanks! With oranges and chocolate bars in their backpacks, silk stockings in their hip pocket, chewing gum (Wrigley's Juicy Fruit) in their hands. All to be given away, to us, if only we can get to talk to them. If only your young and pretty aunt will go dancing with one, and then invite him home for tea.

They aren't like us English. To be proper we must be standoffish, serious, and quiet. (Children should be seen and not heard.) And we shouldn't want or take more than one of anything.

But the Yanks! Their uniforms are smooth and beautiful; their movements are relaxed, spacious. They take up lots of space, just standing there. They have wonderful accents. Sometimes hard to understand, but wonderful to hear when they draaawl their words. It sounds soft, unthreatening, friendly. They talk easily, loudly to each other—they laugh easily, out loud, even in public places!

They like children! How astonishing—they actually like children! Talk to us, tousle our hair, sit us on their laps, tell us we're cute (what's cute??), give us sticks of gum. And we don't have to save it—we can eat it. Before dinner! And they don't get angry if we ask for more. Or if we hang around them, stay close, touch them. This must be what having a father is like.

Age 5—in love. Head-over-heels madly in love—with Yanks. . . .

During one of these exits from the city, we were staying with a woman and her four daughters in a big farm house. These pretty girls were being dated by American soldiers and one day one of the soldiers brought an extraordinary treat to the house. It was something I had never seen before

and that the girls had not seen in 4 or 5 years—a fresh orange! The orange was peeled, with everyone standing around the table watching. Then, it was carefully divided into segments, and each person got one segment. First we licked it, so no drop of juice could escape. Then, we took tiny nibbles, letting the juice come slowly into our mouths, and held it there. Don't swallow too fast! Then take another tiny nibble, until finally, the whole slice was gone. How terrible that there was no more. Seeing what a great success the gift had been, the soldier decided he had to be a hero to the nth degree.

A few days later he came back with his friend, and a carton, a whole carton of cans of sliced peaches. 12 cans. 12 CANS! Wow! What to do with such booty? Urgent conversations took place. Suggestions made and discarded. Finally, with everyone watching, the carton, less one can, was taken down into the cellar, and buried under the heap of coal.

Then, everyone was sworn to secrecy. No one must tell what was hidden there.

Some time passed, and one day there was a knock at the door. Military police. They wanted to search the house for stolen contraband from the PX. My heart was racing . . . would we go to jail? Would the soldiers be arrested? What would happen? They searched everywhere, but did not want to get dirty moving the heap of black, sooty coal, and so the peaches were undiscovered. But we all felt horribly guilty whenever a can was opened, and it spoiled the pleasure in eating those sweet slices. . . .

Back in London, one day my Zaida (Grandfather) and Mum were pushing the baby carriage along the High Street of our neighborhood, in the middle of the day, when the siren began its up and down wailing. Mother wanted to run to the tube station shelter because it was closer. But Zaida said "No, we cannot leave Booba (Grandmother) alone. She would be too frightened." Mother insisted on going to the station. . . . But Zaida grabbed hold of the baby carriage and began pushing it, running, toward home. Mother and I had no choice but to follow him.

We spent the rest of the day and all the night in the dark, in the shelter. In the morning, when it was quiet, we came out, only to hear on the news that the subway station we had almost gone to had been bombed. All the people down there on the subway platform had died.

When the war was over, there was a party on the street. And some time later the soldiers began coming home.

I begged my mother to allow me to run down the stairs and answer the door when my daddy came home. And she said yes.

It seemed a long time later that the doorbell rang, and I remember very well the excitement of that moment. I ran to the door, opened it, and a giant stood there. A tall, tall man in uniform, with a backpack. A total stranger. I don't remember him at all after that moment for many years. My mother told me that I kept asking her when he was going away again, because I didn't like this stranger telling me what to do.

Source: Web site: Timewitnesses: Memories of the Last Century. Available at http://timewitnesses.org/english/%7Epamelay.html. Reprinted with permission of Pamela Lazarus.

173. Susan B. Anthony II on Women's Rights in the Postwar World, 1943

Feminist activists demanded that women not simply revert to prewar roles after the war, but that, as part of the war's objectives, they should gain full equality with men. In 1943 Susan B. Anthony II, niece of the prominent nineteenth-century American woman activist who had likewise taken the lead in fighting for women's rights, articulated these concerns. She warned that, if women did not obtain adequate guarantees of their future rights and status, they would be discouraged from devoting themselves wholeheartedly to the war effort.

What assurance have the women of America that maximum exertion of their energies now will give them not only a place in the war today but a place in the world tomorrow? . . .

If we are to win the war it is clear that nursery schools, public cafeterias, housing projects, medical services, recreation facilities, and special services for maternity cases are vital necessities. But they are more than that—they are the key to the postwar position of women and a promise to men and women of a standard of living that will enable *three-thirds of a nation* to be well-housed, well fed, and well cared for.

If we do not obtain nursery schools, if we do not obtain adequate health programs, school lunch, and milk for our children *now, when they are desperately needed as wartime measures,* you can be sure of a reversion in the postwar world to substandards of living. . . .

Victory can no longer be regarded as separate from the assurance to our people of a future that will hold a place for them. To arouse the spirit of victory the people must be given a demonstration of what democracy means, what full employment means, what public services mean.

We are in a death struggle against fascism—a system whose ideology and practice reduces men and women to slaves, living on starvation levels. What better proof could we offer the American people of our absolute irreconcilability with Hitler's methods than to start *now* to provide employment and security for all. . . .

America has limped along for too many centuries utilizing half the productive forces of the nation. Only in wartime does our vast industrial and agricultural machine become nearly fully used. Only in wartime does the vast energy and talent of the American woman begin to be unleashed. It has been said that women are the margin for victory in this war.

I would add that women are the margin for victory for the economic life of the peace. The kind of war we wage determines the kind of peace. The kind of peace we have will be determined largely by the kind of use we make of our labor potential.

If we plan a nation producing enough food, housing, clothing, for all of our people, then we will need the labor of all of the adult men and women to staff the factories, farms, and offices. Energies going into the weapons of war today should be used for the essentials and for the luxuries of life tomorrow. Unless we envisage a return to the economy of scarcity of prewar America, we are going to need our women as well as our men in production. Unless we envisage losing the war, we need community services *now* to release women for the big wartime tasks of production.

With them America will be on the road to victory, both in war and peace. Without them America cannot mobilize its labor forces either for war or peace. If we provide these services now, they will be a means to victory. They can then be utilized as a means of raising the peacetime standards of living of *all our people.*

Yet women need more than the mere extension of community services to give them a real stake in the war. They need the assurance that *never again will they be deprived of the right to work, and the right to hold top positions.* Temporary orders permitting equal pay for equal work, transitory demands of employers for their services, are not enough. . . .

When women formed only one-quarter of the productive forces of the nation, it was easy to push aside their claims to equal participation in governing the nation. The right to vote has been relied upon as the complete answer to our demands for a voice in the highest councils of the Government.

In almost doubling the number of women workers this war doubles the justice of our demands for an equal place in the legislatures, on the court benches, and in law enforcement.

No longer can women be satisfied with a backseat in Congress, with one seat in the President's circle of advisers and administrators, *with no seat on the Supreme Court Bench.* Wherever people are governed, representatives of these people should be amongst the governors. That is part of the fundamental democratic principle for which we are now fighting. Women, being governed, must logically be among the governors. We would be but a poor pretender to democracy if, after having worked our women to the utmost to win the war, we barred them from a meaningful role in the peace. How can we claim to be purified of fascist tendencies in our own nation if we permit a fascist concept of women to prevail?

As we know, the fascist concept of woman is that her life's work is to breed and feed. She breeds a dozen years and feeds for a lifetime. After breeding—after having fulfilled her biological function—she is then, according to the fascists, only useful to brood over the kitchen stove. The boundary for women, under fascism, is the home; and beyond that boundary she must not go. Democracy's task is to elevate woman so that the world is her home—not the home her world.

Fascism is determined to make women servants of the house. Democracy must encourage women to be servants of the world. The conditions of war are definitely pulling women out of the house into the world. The peace must not push them back into the house, unless they wish to go there.

We must recognize that woman's place is in the world as much as man's is. Woman's place is in the factory, in the office, in the professions, in the fields, and at the council table—wherever human labor, human effort, is needed to produce and create. In the postwar world there must be an abolition of the fatal distinctions between men and women—between "men's jobs" and "women's jobs." Personal ability, not choice, must determine the job-holder. Present discriminations must be done away with, for they work against men as well as women.

The greatest distinction between men's and women's work is that jobs at the top are tacitly regarded as being "For Men Only." The menial and the semiskilled jobs are thought to be ideal for women. Wartime necessity will to some degree wipe out this distinction; but extreme vigilance will be needed in the postwar period if we are to maintain any of the higher positions we reach now as an expedient because the men are fighting.

The hopeful thing is that each major American war has resulted in the extension of democracy to a group that was formerly underprivileged. The American Revolution extended to white men the right to vote, the right to elect the world's first republican form of Government. The Civil War extended to black men the right to vote. The First World War extended to white and black women the right to vote.

This extension of democracy in past wars has not come easily. It has not been handed down generously from above. It has been wrenched from the hands and against the prejudices of those in power; it has been reluctantly granted, after great pressures and bloody battles.

In these wars of American history, the Government has had to extend democracy to new sections of the population for a specific reason of winning the war. Each war in our history has demanded the lives and the sweat of larger and larger sections of the population.

Today, we are engaged in the greatest war of our history. More men, more machines, more material are being used against the enemy. Today, for the first time, whole populations, men and women, are involved as active belligerents.

And out of the necessities of our struggle against fascism, this nation is being forced to mobilize that great reservoir of anti-fascist fighters—the American women. As in the Civil War when the Union freed the Negroes to fight to win the war, so today our Government is being forced to free women to win this war. America must unlock the doors that have imprisoned millions of women. Women must be let out—liberated from the homes, so that they can take their place in the war of the world today—and in the work of the world tomorrow.

Source: Susan B. Anthony II, *Out of the Kitchen—Into the War: Woman's Winning Role in the Nation's Drama* (New York: Stephen Daye, 1943). Reprinted in Judy Barrett Litoff and David C. Smith, eds., *American Women in a World at War: Contemporary Accounts from World War II* (Wilmington, DE: Scholarly Resources, 1997), 214–218.

1944 Documents

174. General Joseph W. Stilwell on China, 1942–1944

Relations between General Joseph W. Stilwell, commander of United States forces in China and Burma from 1942 to 1944, and Jiang Jieshi (Chiang K'ai-shek), the leader of China's Nationalist Guomindang government, were poor. In his diary Stilwell jotted caustic comments on Jiang and his government, assailing its inefficiency and corruption, which he contrasted with the austerity of the regime's Communist rivals. Jiang's reluctance to take the offensive and his eagerness to conserve his resources for the postwar battle against the Communists he already anticipated also irked Stilwell, whom the Roosevelt administration withdrew at Jiang's request in 1944 after his relations with the Guomindang leader had deteriorated to the point where they had become unworkable.

General Joseph W. Stilwell on China, Excerpts from *The Stilwell Papers*

[Undated Diary Note]

CHIANG K'AI-SHEK. I never heard Chiang K'ai-shek say a single thing that indicated gratitude to the President or to our country for the help we were extending to him. Invariably, when anything was promised, he would want more. Invariably, he would complain about the small amount of material that was being furnished. He would make comparisons between the huge amounts of Lend-Lease supplies going to Great Britain and Russia with the meagre trickle going to China. He would complain that the Chinese had been fighting for six or seven years and yet we gave them practically nothing. It would of course have been undiplomatic to go into the nature of the military effort Chiang K'ai-shek had made since 1938. It was practically zero.

Whether or not he was grateful was a small matter. The regrettable part of it was that there was no quid pro quo. We did what we could, furnished what was available, without being allowed to first ask what he would do, etc. The result was that we were continuously on the defensive and he could obstruct and delay any of our plans without being penalized. . . .

[Undated Diary Note]

[I have] faith in Chinese soldiers and Chinese people; fundamentally great, democratic, misgoverned. No bars of caste or religion. . . . Honest, frugal, industrious, cheerful, independent, tolerant, friendly, courteous.

I judge Kuomintang and Kungchangtang [Communist Party] by what I saw:

[KMT] Corruption, neglect, chaos, economy, taxes, words and deeds. Hoarding, black market, trading with enemy.

Communist programme . . . reduce taxes, rents, interest. Raise production, and standard of living. Participate in government. Practice what they preach. . . .

[Excerpts from an Undated Paper on the Dominant Military Doctrine of the Chinese Army]

In time of war you have to take your allies as you find them. We are fighting Germany to tear down the Nazi system—one-party government, supported by the Gestapo and headed by an unbalanced man with little education. We had plenty to say against such a system. China, our ally, was being run by a one-party government (the Kuomintang), supported by a Gestapo (Tai Li's organization) and headed by an unbalanced man with little education. This government, however, had the prestige of the possession of power—it was opposing Japan, and its titular head had been built up by propaganda in America out of all proportion to his desserts and accomplishments. We had to back the existing regime in order to have any chance of getting China to pull her weight. To change the structure during the emergency would have been next to impossible. All through the Chinese machinery of government there are interlocking ties of interest . . . family, financial, political, etc. No man, no matter how efficient, can hope for a position of authority on account of being the man best qualified for the job: he simply must have other backing. To reform such a system, it must be torn to pieces. You build a framework to grow grape-vines on: in the course of time, the vines grow all over it, twisting in and out and around and pretty soon the frame is so tightly held by the vines that if you start pulling them out, you will tear the frame to pieces. We could not risk it, we had to take the instrument as we found it and do the best we could. But because it was expedient to back this government to get action against Japan, it was not necessarily advisable to endorse its methods and policies. We could have required some return for our help.

Chiang K'ai-shek made a great point of how badly the U.S.A. had neglected China, who had been fighting desperately for so long, while Lend-Lease materials had been poured into Great Britain and Russia by the billion. His case was that we owed him a great debt and that it was a crying shame we didn't do more to discharge it. This attitude met with sympathy in the U.S. It was true that large quantities of Lend-Lease materials were going to Russia and Great Britain. It was also true that Russia and Great Britain, particularly Russia, were making good use of this material against Germany. It was also true that there was no possible way of delivering the goods to Chiang K'ai-shek unless he made an effort on his part to break the blockade. It seemed reasonable to expect Great Britain to use the huge Indian Army for the purpose. The U.S. was fighting Germany in Europe, and Japan in the Pacific. She was supplying enormous quantities of munitions and food to all the Allies. Under the circumstances it seemed reasonable for somebody else to display a little energy in Burma.

To keep the show going, I had to overlook some of these incongruities and pretend, like the other players. If not, the critics would say it was a bum show, and we are very much afraid of the critics in our show.

[This paper was never finished.]

[Notes, Probably July 1944]

SOLUTION IN CHINA

The cure for China's trouble is the elimination of Chiang K'ai-shek. The only thing that keeps the country split is his fear of losing control. He hates the Reds and will not take any chances on giving them a toehold in the government. The result is that each side watches the other and neither gives a damn about the war [against Japan]. If this condition persists, China will have civil war immediately after Japan is out. If Russia enters the war before a united front is formed in China, the Reds, being immediately accessible, will naturally gravitate to Russia's influence and control. The condition will directly affect the relations between Russia and China, and therefore indirectly those between Russia and [the] U.S.

If we do not take action, our prestige in China will suffer seriously. China will contribute nothing to our effort against Japan, and the seed will be planted for chaos in China after the war. . . .

[Undated Notes]

Chiang K'ai-shek is the head of a one-party government supported by a Gestapo and a party secret service. He is now organizing an S.S. of 100,000 members.

[He] hates the so-called Communists. He intends to crush them by keeping any munitions furnished him and by occupying their territory as the Japs retire.

[He] will not make an effort to fight seriously. He wants to finish the war coasting, with a big supply of material, so as to perpetuate his regime. He has blocked us for three years and will continue to do so. He has failed to keep his agreements.

[He] has spoken contemptuously of American efforts and has never said one word to express gratitude for our help, except in one message to the President, in which he attacked me.

[He] is responsible for major disasters of the war. Nanking. Lan Fang. Changsha and Hengyang. Kweilin and Liuchow. Red blockade.

But [he] is the titular head of China and has marked me as *persona non grata*.

Therefore I cannot operate in the China theatre while he is in power. . . .

Source: Joseph Stilwell, *The Stilwell Papers,* ed. Theodore H. White (New York: Sloan Associates, 1948), pp. 291–296, 311–312. Courtesy heirs of Winifred Stilwell.

175. The Economic Bill of Rights: President Franklin D. Roosevelt, State of the Union Message to Congress, 11 January 1944

Franklin D. Roosevelt had won fame as a reformist president who was responsible for the New Deal of the 1930s, a major program of social and economic measures intended to help poorer Americans weather the Great Depression. In his State of the Union address to Congress in January 1944, the president made it clear that he hoped to revitalize reform at home. He proposed the passage of an Economic Bill of Rights, a major domestic-reform program, to accompany American victories overseas. Roosevelt's thinking reflected that of many other liberals in numerous countries, who shared the hope that the war would force the implementation of measures that would bring substantially greater social justice to the working classes and the poor.

Franklin D. Roosevelt on the Economic Bill of Rights, State of the Union Message to Congress, 11 January 1944

This Nation in the past two years has become an active partner in the world's greatest war against human slavery.

We have joined with like-minded people in order to defend ourselves in a world that has been gravely threatened with gangster rule.

But I do not think that any of us Americans can be content with mere survival. Sacrifices that we and our Allies are making impose upon us all a sacred obligation to see to it that out of this war we and our children will gain something better than mere survival.

We are united in determination that this war shall not be followed by another interim which leads to new disaster—that we shall not repeat the tragic errors of ostrich isolationism.

When Mr. Hull went to Moscow in October, and when I went to Cairo and Tehran in November, we knew that we were in agreement with our Allies in our common determination to fight and win this war. But there were many vital questions concerning the future peace, and they were discussed in an atmosphere of complete candor and harmony. . . .

The one supreme objective for the future, which we discussed for each nation individually, and for all the United Nations, can be summed up in one word: Security.

And that means not only physical security which provides safety from attacks by aggressors. It means also economic security, social security, moral security—in a family of nations.

In the plain down-to-earth talks that I had with the Generalissimo [Jiang Jieshi or Chiang Kai-shek] and Marshal Stalin and Prime Minister Churchill, it was abundantly clear that they are all most deeply interested in the resumption of peaceful progress by their own peoples—progress toward a better life.

All our Allies have learned by experience—bitter experience—that real development will not be possible if they are to be diverted from their purpose by repeated wars—or even threats of war.

The best interests of each nation, large and small, demand that all freedom-loving nations shall join together in a just and durable system of peace. In the present world situation, evidenced by the actions of Germany, Italy, and Japan, unquestioned military control over the disturbers of the peace is as necessary among nations as it is among citizens in any community. And an equally basic essential to peace—permanent peace—is a decent standard of living for all individual men and women and children in all nations. Freedom from fear is eternally linked with freedom from want.

There are people who burrow through our nation like unseeing moles, and attempt to spread the suspicion that if other nations are encouraged to raise their standards of living, our own American standard of living must of necessity be depressed.

The fact is the very contrary. It has been shown time and again that if the standard of living of any country goes up, so does its purchasing power—and that such a rise encourages a better standard of living in neighboring countries with whom it trades. That is just plain common sense—and it is the kind of plain common sense that provided the basis for our discussions at Moscow, and Cairo and Teheran. . . .

The overwhelming majority of our people have met the demands of this war with magnificent courage and a great deal of understanding. They have accepted inconveniences; they have accepted hardships; they have accepted tragic sacrifices.

However, while the majority goes on about its great work without complaint, we all know that a noisy minority maintains an uproar, an uproar of demands for special favors for special groups. . . .

2012 World War II Documents: 1944

Such selfish agitation can be and is highly dangerous in wartime. It creates confusion. It damages morale. It hampers our national effort. It prolongs the war. . . .

If ever there was a time to subordinate individual or group selfishness to the national good, that time is now. Disunity at home, and bickering, self-seeking partisanship, stoppages of work, inflation, business as usual, politics as usual, luxury as usual—and sometimes a failure to tell the whole truth—these are the influences which can undermine the morale of the brave men ready to die at the front for us here. . . .

Therefore, in order to concentrate all of our energies, all of our resources on winning this war, and to maintain a fair and stable economy at home, I recommend that the Congress adopt:

First, (1) A realistic and simplified tax law which will tax all unreasonable profits, both individual and corporate, and reduce the ultimate cost of the war to our sons and our daughters. The tax bill now under consideration by the Congress does not begin to meet this test.

Second, (2) A continuation of the law for the renegotiations of war contracts which will prevent exorbitant profits and assure fair prices to the Government. For two long years I have pleaded with the Congress to take undue profits out of war.

Third, (3) A cost of food law which will enable the Government (a) to place a reasonable floor under the prices the farmer may expect for his production; and (b) to place a ceiling on the prices the consumer will have to pay for the necessary food he buys. This should apply, as I have intimated, to necessities only; and this will require public funds to carry it out. It will cost in appropriations about one percent of the present annual cost of the war.

Fourth, (4) An early re-enactment of the stabilization statute of October, 1942. This expires this year, June 30th, 1944, and if it is not extended well in advance, the country might just as well expect price chaos by summertime. We cannot have stabilization by wishful thinking. We must take positive action to maintain the integrity of the American dollar.

And Fifth, (5) A national service law which, for the duration of the war, will prevent strikes, and, with certain appropriate exceptions, will make available for war production or for any other essential services every able-bodied adult in this whole Nation.

These five measures together form a just and equitable whole. I would not recommend a national service law unless the other laws were passed to keep down the cost of living, to share equitably the burdens of taxation, to hold the stabilization line, and to prevent undue profits.

The Federal Government already has the basic power to draft capital and property of all kinds for war purposes on a basis of just compensation.

And, as you know, I have for three years hesitated to recommend a national service act. Today, however, with all the experience we have behind us and with us, I am convinced of its necessity. Although I believe that we and our Allies can win the war without such a measure, I am certain that nothing less than total mobilization of all our resources of manpower and capital will guarantee an earlier victory, and reduce the toll of suffering and sorrow and blood. . . .

National service is the most democratic way to wage a war. Like selective service for the armed forces, it rests on the obligation of each citizen to serve his nation to his utmost where he is best qualified. . . .

It is our duty now to begin to lay the plans and determine the strategy. More than the winning of the war, it is time to begin plans and determine the strategy for the winning a lasting peace and the establishment of an American standard of living higher than ever known before.

This Republic had its beginning, and grew to its present strength, under the protection of certain inalienable political rights—among them the right of free speech, free press, free worship, trial by jury, freedom from unreasonable searches and seizures. They were our rights to life and liberty.

We have come to a clear realization of the fact, however, that true individual freedom cannot exist without economic security and independence. "Necessitous men are not free men." People who are hungry, people who are out of a job are the stuff of which dictatorships are made.

In our day these economic truths have become accepted as self-evident. We have accepted, so to speak, a second Bill of Rights under which a new basis of security and prosperity can be established for all—regardless of station, or race or creed.

Among these are:

- The right to a useful and remunerative job in the industries or shops or farms or mines of the nation;
- The right to earn enough to provide adequate food and clothing and recreation;
- The right of farmers to raise and sell their products at a return which will give them and their families a decent living;
- The right of every business man, large and small, to trade in an atmosphere of freedom from unfair competition and domination by monopolies at home or abroad;

- The right of every family to a decent home;
- The right to adequate medical care and the opportunity to achieve and enjoy good health;
- The right to adequate protection from the economic fears of old age, and sickness, and accident and unemployment;
- And finally, the right to a good education.

All of these rights spell security. And after this war is won we must be prepared to move forward, in the implementation of these rights, to new goals of human happiness and well-being.

America's own rightful place in the world depends in large part upon how fully these and similar rights have been carried into practice for all our citizens. For unless there is security here at home there cannot be lasting peace in the world. . . .

I ask the Congress to explore the means for implementing this economic bill of rights—for it is definitely the responsibility of the Congress so to do, and the country knows it. Many of these problems are already before committees of the Congress in the form of proposed legislation. I shall from time to time communicate with the Congress with respect to these and further proposals. In the event that no adequate program of progress is evolved, I am certain that the Nation will be conscious of the fact.

Our fighting men abroad—and their families at home—expect such a program and have the right to insist on it. It is to their demands that this Government should pay heed, rather than to the whining demands of selfish pressure groups who seek to feather their nests while young Americans are dying. . . .

Each and every one of us has a solemn obligation under God to serve this Nation in its most critical hour—to keep this Nation great—to make this Nation greater in a better world.

Source: Franklin D. Roosevelt on the Economic Bill of Rights, State of the Union Message to Congress, 11 January 1944. Fireside Chat Files: State Department, 1944, Franklin D. Roosevelt Digital Archives. Available at http://www.fdrlibrary.marist.edu/011144.html.

176. Anglo-American Combined Chiefs of Staff, Directive to Supreme Commander Allied Expeditionary Force, 12 February 1944

In early 1944, the Anglo-American chiefs of staff issued a directive formally appointing General Dwight D. Eisenhower, who had previously led the North African and Italian campaigns, commander of the Allied forces that would undertake Operation OVERLORD, the long-awaited Western invasion of Germany. The original invasion date was set for May, though it was later deferred until 6 June 1944.

1. You are hereby designated as Supreme Allied Commander of the forces placed under your orders for operations for liberation of Europe from Germans. Your title will be Supreme Commander Allied Expeditionary Force.
2. *Task.* You will enter the continent of Europe and, in conjunction with the other United Nations, undertake operations aimed at the heart of Germany and the destruction of her armed forces. The date for entering the Continent is the month of May, 1944. After adequate Channel ports have been secured, exploitation will be directed towards securing an area that will facilitate both ground and air operations against the enemy.
3. Notwithstanding the target date above you will be prepared at any time to take immediate advantage of favorable circumstances, such as withdrawal by the enemy on your front, to effect a reentry into the Continent with such forces as you have available at the time; a general plan for this operation when approved will be furnished for your assistance.
4. *Command.* You are responsible to the Combined Chiefs of Staff and will exercise command generally in accordance with the diagram at Appendix. Direct communication with the United States and British Chiefs of Staff is authorized in the interest of facilitating your operations and for arranging necessary logistic support.
5. *Logistics.* In the United Kingdom the responsibility for logistics organization, concentration, movement, and supply of forces to meet the requirements of your plan will rest with British Service Ministries so far as British Forces are concerned. So far as United States Forces are concerned, this responsibility will rest with the United States War and Navy Departments. You will be responsible for the coordination

of logistical arrangements on the Continent. You will also be responsible for coordinating the requirements of British and United States forces under your command.

6. *Coordination of operations of other Forces and Agencies.* In preparation for your assault on enemy occupied Europe, Sea and Air Forces, agencies of sabotage, subversion, and propaganda, acting under a variety of authorities, are now in action. You may recommend any variation in these activities which may seem to you desirable.

7. *Relationship to United Nations Forces in other areas.* Responsibility will rest with the Combined Chiefs of Staff for supplying information relating to operations of the Forces of the U.S.S.R. for your guidance in timing your operations. It is understood that the Soviet Forces will launch an offensive at about the same time as OVERLORD with the object of preventing the German forces from transferring from the Eastern to the Western front. The Allied Commander in Chief, Mediterranean Theater, will conduct operations de-

signed to assist your operation, including the launching of an attack against the south of France at about the same time as OVERLORD. The scope and timing of his operations will be decided by the Combined Chiefs of Staff. You will establish contact with him and submit to the Combined Chiefs of Staff your views and recommendations regarding operations from the Mediterranean in support of your attack from the United Kingdom. The Combined Chiefs of Staff will place under your command the forces operating in Southern France as soon as you are in a position to assume such command. You will submit timely recommendations compatible with this regard.

8. *Relationship with Allied Governments—the re-establishment of Civil Governments and Liberated Allied Territories and the administration of enemy territories.* Further instructions will be issued to you on these subjects at a later date.

Source: Web site: ibiblio. Available at http://www.ibiblio.org/pub/academic/history/marshall/military/wwii/D-Day/eisenhower_dir.txt.

177. General Headquarters, Southwest Pacific Area, Communiqué No. 677, Statement of General Douglas MacArthur on the Seizure of the Northern Solomon Islands, New Georgia, 16 February 1944

In February 1944, General Douglas MacArthur issued a press statement marking the Allied capture of the Northern Solomon Islands, which brought the Solomon Campaign to a close. This event also represented a further setback for Japan in the Pacific.

We have seized the northern end of the Solomons Archipelago. New Zealand and American ground troops, covered by naval and air forces, landed and occupied the Green Islands. Enemy ground resistance was negligible and his air reaction weak. This culminates the successful series of flank movements commencing in the New Georgia group which has gradually enveloped all enemy forces in the Solomons. These forces, estimated at 22,000 strong, dispersed through Choiseul, Shortland, Bougainville and Buka Islands, are now isolated from their source of supply at

Rabaul. Starvation and disease, certain to ensue from military blockade, render their position hopeless. With their airfields destroyed and their barge traffic paralyzed, the relief of these scattered garrisons is no longer practicable and their ultimate fate is sealed. For all strategic military purposes this completes the campaign for the Solomon Islands.

Source: Charles A. Willoughby et al., eds., *Reports of General MacArthur: The Campaigns of MacArthur in the Pacific,* 2 vols. (Washington, DC: U.S. Government Printing Office, 1966), 1: 136.

178. General Headquarters, Southwest Pacific Area, Communiqué No. 691, Statement of General Douglas MacArthur on the Bismarck Campaign, 1 March 1944

At the end of February 1944, Allied forces under General Douglas MacArthur's command in the Southwest Pacific theater undertook a risky series of landings on the Admiralty Islands in the Bismarck Sea. MacArthur, who personally supervised this operation, issued a communiqué highlighting its military significance.

We have landed in the Admiralty Islands which stand at the northern entrance to the Bismarck Sea almost due south of Guam and 1,300 miles from the Philippines. . . . This marks a final stage in the great swinging move pivoting on New Guinea which has been the basic purpose of the operations initiated on June 29, 1943, when the Southwest Pacific area and South Pacific Area were united under General MacArthur's command. The axis of advance has thereby been changed from the north to the west. This relieves our supply line of the constant threat of flank attack which has been present since the beginning of the Papuan Campaign. This line, previously so precariously exposed, is now firmly secured not only by air cover, but by our own front to which it is perpendicular. Tactically it tightens the blockade of the enemy's remaining bases. Their supply lines are definitely and conclusively severed and only a minimum of blockade running, by submarine or individual surface craft, is now possible. In addition to the troops trapped in the Solomons, some fifty thousand of the enemy, largely in New Britain and at Rabaul, are now inclosed. Their situation has become precarious and their ultimate fate is certain under blockade, bombardment and the increasing pressure of besieging ground forces. The end of the Bismarck Campaign is now clearly in sight with a minimum of loss to ourselves.

Source: Charles A. Willoughby et al., eds., *Reports of General MacArthur: The Campaigns of MacArthur in the Pacific*, 2 vols. (Washington, DC: U.S. Government Printing Office, 1966), 1:140.

179. General Headquarters, Southwest Pacific Area, Communiqué No. 745, Statement of General Douglas MacArthur on the Hollandia Landings, 25 April 1944

Continuing their policy of chipping away at Japanese conquests in the Pacific, in April 1944, Allied forces commanded by General Douglas MacArthur landed at Hollandia and Aitape in Dutch New Guinea. MacArthur marked the occasion, as usual, with a communiqué setting forth the significance of this new development.

We have seized the Humboldt Bay area on the northern coast of Dutch New Guinea, approximately 500 miles west of Saidor. Our ground troops have landed at Aitape, Hollandia, and Tanahmerah Bay, covering a front of about 150 miles. The landings were made under cover of naval and air bombardment and followed neutralizing attacks by our air forces, and planes from carriers of the Pacific Fleet. Complete surprise and effective support, both surface and air, secured our initial landings with slight losses. We are pushing forward to secure the local airfields. Our feints over the past week towards Madang and Wewak apparently deceived the enemy into concentrating the mass of his forces forward into those areas, thus leaving the vital sector of Hollandia vulnerable and making possible our surprise movement to his rear. The operation throws a loop of envelopment around the enemy's Eighteenth Army, dispersed along the coast of New Guinea in the Madang, Alexishafen, Hansa Bay, Wewak sectors, similar to the Solomons and Bismarck loops of envelopment. To the east are the Australians and the Americans; to the west the Americans; to the north the sea controlled by our Allied naval forces; to the south untraversed jungle mountain ranges; and over all our Allied air mastery. This enemy army is now completely isolated. With its communication and supply lines severed, its condition becomes similar to that of the beleaguered Seventeenth and Eighteenth Armies in the Bismarck and Solomon Archipelagos. Its present strength is 60,000. The total remaining forces of these two armies, which are now themselves surrounded, are estimated at 140,000: 50,000 in New Britain, 10,000 in New Ireland, 20,000 in Bougainville, and 60,000 in New Guinea. Since the start of the campaign they have lost 110,000 men, 44 percent of their original strength of a quarter of a million, and the remainder is now neutralized and strategically impotent. The enemy's maritime and air losses have been proportionately heavy. His invested garrisons can be expected to strike desperately to free themselves and time and combat will be required to accomplish the annihilation, but their ultimate fate is now certain. Their situation reverses Bataan. The present operation when completed frees British New Guinea from enemy control, and is the first recapture of Dutch territory in the war.

Source: Charles A. Willoughby et al., eds., *Reports of General MacArthur: The Campaigns of MacArthur in the Pacific*, 2 vols. (Washington, DC: U.S. Government Printing Office, 1966), 1:147–148.

180. Georgios Papandreou, Prime Minister of Greece, the Lebanon Charter, 20 May 1944

In several Balkan countries, most notably Greece and Yugoslavia, the anti-German guerrilla resistance movement was bitterly split between left-wing and Communist forces and their right-wing and centrist, often monarchist, counterparts. The rival groupings frequently fought each other as bitterly as they did the Germans, and in both countries civil war ensued toward the end of the war. On 29 February 1944, the forces of left-wing ELAS (the Greek People's Liberation Army) and center-right EDES (the National Republican Greek League) signed the Plaka agreement, an armistice which supposedly brought to an end the civil war that had erupted between them the previous October. Ten days later, a new democratic umbrella organization to govern Greece was established, around which all anti-German forces could supposedly unite. Two months after the putative establishment of this Government of National Unity, the Greek prime minister, Georgios Papandreou, a moderate democrat, summoned a meeting of representatives of all Greek political groupings in Lebanon. In his final speech, Papandreou listed eight points on which all Greeks could agree, and the rest of the delegates promised to unite around these in future. At the end of the year, with the defeat of Germany in sight, civil war began once again.

1. The reorganization and re-establishment of discipline in the Greek armed forces in the Middle East under the Greek national flag must be carried out exclusively on a national and military basis, not on a political basis. The army will carry out the orders of the Government, and cannot possess political opinions.

2. All guerilla bands in free Greece must be unified and disciplined under the orders of a single Government. The guerilla principle of military organization cannot be a permanent one; but no change should be made at the moment which will lead to a reduction of resistance. Consequently the present situation must be regarded as a transitional one, and the initiative in settling it can only be taken by the Government in consultation with GHQ, MEF [General Headquarters, Middle East Force].

3. The reign of terror in the Greek countryside must cease and the personal security and political liberty of the people must be firmly established when and where the invader has been driven out. Outbreaks of terrorism must also cease in the towns. Ministers of the Government will be in office in Greece to administer the armed forces and the liberated Greek population. As soon as the presence of the Government in Greece is possible, it must not lose a minute in proceeding there.

4. Adequate supplies of food and medicines must be sent to enslaved and mountain Greece.

5. Greece, when liberated, must be secured to the state of order and liberty necessary to enable the people to decide, freely and without pressure, both on their constitution and their régime and Government:
   (a) The special task of the Government of National Unity will be to secure order and liberty.
   (b) The people must be enabled to make its decision as soon as possible.

(c) On the question of the sovereign power, the political leaders who have joined the Government of National Unity are understood to retain such views as they have already expressed.

6. Severe punishment will be imposed on traitors and those who have exploited the misfortunes of the people. Since this problem concerns the post-liberation period, it is necessary to make it clear that the Government of National Unity will continue beyond the date of liberation for such period as the conscience of the nation and its own political judgment may decide.

7. Arrangements will be made in advance in concert with the Allies, for the satisfaction of Greece's material needs in the way of reconstruction, including such necessities as the provision of outlets for Greek products and freedom of emigration.

8. Full satisfaction of Greece's national claims is called for by the past services and sacrifices of the Greek people. This must include the security of our new frontiers.

Source: Margaret Carlyle, ed., *Documents on International Affairs 1939–1946 Volume II: Hitler's Europe* (London: Oxford University Press, 1954), 348–349. Reprinted with permission of Chatham House.

181. General Headquarters, Southwest Pacific Area, Communiqué No. 780, Statement of General Douglas MacArthur on the Biak Island Landing, 28 May 1944

Just one month after landing on Hollandia, American and Australian forces landed on Biak Island, Dutch New Guinea. This operation developed into a particularly bloody campaign, as Japanese defenders took refuge in the caves that honeycombed the island and fought bitterly and tenaciously, often to the death. Allied troops faced particularly difficult conditions in terms of food shortages, illness, and foul wet weather.

We have landed on Biak Island.... The capture of this stronghold will give us command domination of Dutch New Guinea except for isolated enemy positions. For strategic purposes this marks the practical end of the New Guinea campaign. The final stage has also been reached in the offensive initiated in this theater on 29 June 1943, by the combined forces of the Southwest Pacific and the South Pacific Areas. It has resulted in the reconquest or neutralization of the Solomons, the Bismarcks, the Admiralties, and New Guinea. From the forward point reached by the Japanese we have advanced our front approximately 1,800 statute miles westward and approximately 700 miles to the north....

Compared with the enemy our offensive employed only modest forces and through the maximum use of maneuver and surprise has incurred only light losses. The operations have effected a strategic penetration of the conquered empire Japan was attempting to consolidate in the Southwestern Pacific and have secured bases of departure for the advance to its vital areas in the Philippines and the Netherlands East Indies.

Source: Charles A. Willoughby et al., eds., *Reports of General MacArthur: The Campaigns of MacArthur in the Pacific,* 2 vols. (Washington, DC: U.S. Government Printing Office, 1966), 1:152.

182. General Dwight D. Eisenhower, Order of the Day and Letter to Troops, 6 June 1944

After long months of planning, on 6 June 1944 the Allies launched their Western offensive against German forces in France and Western Europe. Before the invasion began, General Dwight D. Eisenhower, commander of the Allied Expeditionary Force, issued an order of the day to his troops. Each soldier also received a letter detailing how the Allied troops should conduct themselves in the areas they liberated. In marked contrast to German looting of the conquered areas of Europe, Eisenhower warned soldiers that they must treat the inhabitants generously and respect their rights and property.

TO TROOPS OF A.E.F.

Soldiers, Sailors and Airmen of the Allied Expeditionary Forces!: You are about to embark upon the Great Crusade, toward which we have striven these many months. The eyes of the world are upon you. The hopes and prayers of liberty-loving people everywhere march with you. In company with our brave Allies and brothers-in-arms on other Fronts you will bring about the destruction of the German war machine, the elimination of Nazi tyranny over oppressed peoples in Europe, and security for ourselves in a free world.

Your task will not be an easy one. Your enemy is well trained, well equipped and battle-hardened. He will fight savagely.

But this is the year 1944! Much has happened since the Nazi triumphs of 1940–41. The United Nations have inflicted upon the Germans great defeats, in open battle, man-to-man. Our air offensive has seriously reduced their strength in the air and their capacity to wage war on the ground. Our Home Fronts have given us an overwhelming superiority in weapons and munitions of war, and placed at our disposal great reserves of trained fighting men. The tide has turned! The free men of the world are marching together to Victory!

I have full confidence in your courage, devotion to duty and skill in battle. We will accept nothing less than full victory!

Good Luck! And let us all beseech the blessing of Almighty God upon this great and noble undertaking.

TO TROOPS OF THE A.E.F.

You are soon to be engaged in a great undertaking—the invasion of Europe. Our purpose is to bring about, in company with our Allies, and our comrades on other fronts, the total defeat of Germany. Only by such a complete victory can we free ourselves and our homelands from the fear and threat of the Nazi tyranny.

A further element of our mission is the liberation of those people of Western Europe now suffering under German oppression.

Before embarking on this operation, I have a personal message for you as to your own individual responsibility, in relation to the inhabitants of our Allied countries.

As a representative of this country, you will be welcomed with deep gratitude by the liberated peoples, who for years have longed for this deliverance. It is of the utmost importance that this feeling of friendliness and goodwill be in no way impaired by careless or indifferent behavior on your part. By a courteous and considerate demeanor, you can on the other hand do much to strengthen that feeling.

The inhabitants of Nazi-occupied Europe have suffered great privations, and you will find that many of them lack even the barest necessities. You, on the other hand, have been, and will continue to be, provided adequate food, clothing, and other necessities. You must not deplete the already meager local stocks of food and other supplies by indiscriminate buying, thereby fostering the "Black Market," which can only increase the hardship of the inhabitants.

The rights of individuals, as to their persons and property, must be scrupulously respected, as though in your own country. You must remember, always, that these people are our friends and Allies.

I urge each of you to bear constantly in mind that by your actions not only you as an individual, but your country as well, will be judged. By establishing a relationship with the liberated peoples, based on mutual understanding and respect, we shall enlist their wholehearted assistance in the defeat of our common enemy. Thus shall we lay the foundations for a lasting peace, without which our great effort will have been in vain.

Source: Papers of Dwight D. Eisenhower, Eisenhower Presidential Library, Abilene, KS; reprinted in Alfred D. Chandler, ed., *The Papers of Dwight David Eisenhower: The War Years,* 5 vols. (Baltimore, MD: Johns Hopkins University Press, 1970), 3:1913–1914.

183. Forrest C. Pogue on D-Day, 6–7 June 1944

Forrest C. Pogue, then a young official army combat historian, was present at the D-Day landings. His group of five combat historians was attached to part of the 175th Infantry, which was supposed to land on the afternoon of 6 June 1944, D-Day itself. Congestion on the invasion beaches meant that the 175th did not land until 7 June 1944, while the historical personnel remained on board ship until the following day. From this vantage point Pogue could see very little because "everything was obscured by smoke from the firing, fires that had been started by shells, and by the demolition of mines." He later wrote rather skeptically that he had never "been able to understand how correspondents, who watched the D-Day attack from ten miles out, ever got such vivid pictures of the shore." Beginning on 7 June, when various wounded men came aboard his ship, over the next six weeks Pogue conducted numerous interviews with officers and men who had taken part in the D-Day fighting, enabling him to form a composite picture of these events.

Naval craft off the beaches fired sporadically. Everyone seemed pleased that the French ships were joining in the attack on shore positions. Destroyers lay near the shore and fired on shore positions several miles in. The Germans replied occasionally to the fire, but without effect, and as for German air, we saw only one enemy plane, a reconnaissance aircraft, during the day. British and American planes were over in force all day. In one fifteen-minute period we counted five flights of eighteen Marauders each.

After three o'clock the skies cleared except for a few clouds over the fighting area and it turned hot, to our great discomfort. We wanted to go ashore, but orders came out that only people with rifles, who were prepared to use them, were to go in. So we parasites, armed for the most part with pistols, stayed aboard as spectators of the second act. Standing on jeeps and trucks, we watched developments off Omaha Beach as if we were at a fair. Actually, we could make out very little on the shore. Signs of movement were obscured by smoke from the firing, fires that had been started by shells, and by the demolition of mines. I did not see how it was possible for troops to have recognized any landmarks, nor have I been able to understand how correspondents, who watched the D-Day attack from ten miles out, ever got such vivid pictures of the shore. . . .

My own picture of D-Day was gleaned from dozens of interviews with officers and men who went in during the morning of 6 June. Some I talked to shortly after they were wounded, others I interviewed as they rested near the front lines, and some gave their stories weeks later. A short outline of that morning is given below.

The ships that took the assault elements to Normandy had been loaded, much like ours, in many coves and inlets in Wales, southern England, and the eastern counties. On the evening of 5 June they had proceeded from the rendezvous area near the Isle of Wight southward toward France. Shortly after midnight, minesweepers of the Allied fleet began to clear channels through the minefields for the ships. British and American airborne units took off from English fields and flew overhead to drop over their objectives—the British east of the Orne and the Americans in the Cotentin Peninsula. The British reached their bridgehead early and secured it, while the American forces, scattered to a considerable degree, had a tough job of assembling for concerted action.

Toward daylight the planes and ships took up their task of softening up the enemy, the chief change in plan being that . . . the air force struck a few miles inland instead of at the beaches. On the western limit of Omaha Beach, the Rangers scrambled ashore to find that the six guns they were to knock out were pulled back out of their way.

By daylight, ship channels had been cleared to the beaches and the small landing craft had been filled with men from the LSTs and larger transports and were on their way in from rendezvous points some ten miles out. The floating tanks were started in, as were guns in small craft. Only five out of thirty-two DDs survived of those that tried to float in under their own power, while most of those in the other tank battalion, sent in at the last minute by boat, got in safely. In one field artillery battalion all but one gun was lost when the craft carrying them capsized.

The accounts of the early landings tend to follow the same pattern. Heavy seas threatened to swamp the smaller craft and made many of the soldiers seasick. Enemy fire struck numerous craft or forced navy crews to unload in deep water. Poor visibility, obstacles, and inexperience led other navy crews to land on the wrong beaches. Many of the soldiers in the first waves had to wade ashore carrying heavy equipment, which they often disposed of in deep water. At the extreme ends of the beaches, the cliffs interfered to some extent with the enemy fire and gave our troops some protection. In front of Vierville, the men hid behind the seawall that ran along the beach, and near Saint-Laurent-sur-Mer they found mounds of shingles to use as cover. Accounts of the first hours on the beaches speak of efforts of officers and non-coms [non-commissioned officers] to organize their units and get them off the beaches, but often those who tried to direct the attack fell as soon as they exposed themselves to the enemy. In some cases, platoons stuck together, but in others sections landed some distance apart—and there were instances where dispersed elements attached themselves to entirely different regiments and divisions and did not return to their parent organization for two or three days.

The first real effort to give direction to the attack came after the regimental commanders landed. The command group of the 116th Regimental Combat Team, which included Brigadier General Norman D. Cota, the assistant division commander, and Colonel C. D. W. Canham, the regimental commander, came in at about 7.30 A.M. The S-4 of the regiment was killed near the water's edge and other members of the command group were hit. Colonel Canham was wounded as he tried to organize the attack, but after receiving first aid he returned to his task. One of the most active commanders was General Cota, who, according to the accounts of the soldiers, was apparently everywhere that morning. Some spoke of his handling the bangalore torpedo that breached the wire at one of the exits, and others had him handling a Browning automatic rifle. His activities in the first weeks ashore made him almost a legendary figure. Non-coms were also called on to give leadership, as heavy casualties were inflicted on the junior officers. In one case, a private who had worked until a short time before in the regimental Post Exchange rallied the men of his unit by calling them by name and persuading them to follow him over the seawall.

On the 16th Infantry's beaches, Colonel George Taylor, the RCT commander, gained lasting fame by saying to his officers and men: "The only people on the beach are the dead and those who are going to die—now let's get the hell out of here." In a short time he had the men in his sector moving. He and Colonel Canham were promoted to the rank of brigadier general for their work on D-Day.

The manner of the advance up the bluffs differed somewhat among the various units. Some stayed behind the seawall until units in the second and third waves came in through them and went up the cliffs. Others, after being reorganized, pressed forward and by noon were on top of the bluffs.

By midnight on 6 June all of the regiments in the 1st Division (the 16th, the 18th, and 26th) and two from the 29th (the 116th and 115th) had been landed on Omaha Beach. The 2d and 5th Ranger Battalions were in position to their right. Heavy seas, landings on the wrong beaches, intense fire from well-entrenched positions, the foundering of DD tanks and artillery pieces, abnormally high casualties among officers, failure to open all the beach exits, beach congestion, the slowness of some of the assault waves to move forward from the seawall, the difficulty of using the full force of naval gunfire because of the fear of inflicting losses on the infantrymen, the lack of sufficient gaps in underwater obstacles and beach obstacles, and the failure, for various reasons, of air bombardment to take out beach fortifications all placed V Corps a considerable distance from its D-Day objectives, and, as a result of the presence of the German 352d Division in the area, in danger of a counterattack before the time estimated. In the face of this situation, the regiments were reorganized, defenses were set up for the night, and preparations made for a vigorous offensive to attain the D-Day objectives as quickly as possible.

Source: Forrest C. Pogue, *Pogue's War: Diaries of a WWII Combat Historian* (Lexington: University Press of Kentucky, 2001), 51–54. Reprinted with permission of University Press of Kentucky.

184. President Franklin D. Roosevelt, Statement on Signing the GI Bill of Rights (The Servicemen's Readjustment Act of 1944, S. 1767, Public Law 346, Chapter 268), 22 June 1944

Although Congress remained unresponsive to President Franklin D. Roosevelt's call for an "economic bill of rights" for all Americans, politicians were, by contrast, eager to provide an extensive package of benefits for each returning U.S. serviceman. In summer 1944, Congress therefore passed an act providing World War II veteran soldiers with a cash bonus, access to subsidized medical care, higher education, and substantial housing benefits, including subsidized mortgages. Many returning soldiers were able to use these assorted facilities to become the first members of their families to enter the American middle class. The program also set the precedent that the U.S. government would provide a similar range of benefits to all future veterans of its wars.

This bill, which I have signed today, substantially carries out most of the recommendations made by me in a speech on July 28, 1943, and more specifically in messages to the Congress dated October 27, 1943, and November 23, 1943:

1. It gives servicemen and women the opportunity of resuming their education or technical training after discharge, or of taking a refresher or retrainer course, not only without tuition charge up to $500 per school year, but with the right to receive a monthly living allowance while pursuing their studies.
2. It makes provision for the guarantee by the Federal Government of not to exceed 50 percent of certain loans made to veterans for the purchase or construction of homes, farms, and business properties.
3. It provides for reasonable unemployment allowances payable each week up to a maximum period of one year, to those veterans who are unable to find a job.
4. It establishes improved machinery for effective job counseling for veterans and for finding jobs for returning soldiers and sailors.
5. It authorizes the construction of all necessary additional hospital facilities.
6. It strengthens the authority of the Veterans Administration to enable it to discharge its existing and added responsibilities with promptness and efficiency.

With the signing of this bill a well-rounded program of special veterans' benefits is nearly completed. It gives emphatic notice to the men and women in our armed forces that the American people do not intend to let them down.

By prior legislation, the Federal Government has already provided for the armed forces of this war: adequate dependency allowances; mustering-out pay; generous hospitalization, medical care, and vocational rehabilitation and training; liberal pensions in case of death or disability in military service; substantial war risk life insurance, and guaranty of premiums on commercial policies during service; protection of civil rights and suspension of enforcement of certain civil liabilities during service; emergency maternal care for wives of enlisted men; and reemployment rights for returning veterans.

This bill therefore and the former legislation provide the special benefits which are due to the members of our armed forces—for they "have been compelled to make greater economic sacrifice and every other kind of sacrifice than the rest of us, and are entitled to definite action to help take care of their special problems." While further study and experience may suggest some changes and improvements, the Congress is to be congratulated on the prompt action it has taken.

There still remains one recommendation which I made on November 23, 1943, which I trust that the Congress will soon adopt—the extension of social security credits under the Federal Old-Age and Survivors' Insurance Law to all servicemen and women for the period of their service.

I trust that the Congress will also soon provide similar opportunities for postwar education and unemployment insurance to the members of the merchant marine, who have risked their lives time and again during this war for the welfare of their country.

But apart from these special benefits which fulfill the special needs of veterans, there is still much to be done. . . .

As a related problem the Congress has had under consideration the serious problem of economic reconversion and readjustment after the war, so that private industry will be able to provide jobs for the largest possible number. . . .

A sound postwar economy is a major present responsibility.

Source: Web site: The Franklin D. Roosevelt Presidential Library and Museum. Available at http://www.fdrlibrary.marist.edu/odgist.html.

185. Report on Conditions in the Concentration Camps of Oswieczim (Auschwitz) and Birkenau: Summary of the Auschwitz Escapees Report by Gerhart Riegner, World Jewish Congress, Geneva, Sent under Cover of R. E. Shoenfeld, U.S. Chargé to Czech Government in London, to Cordell Hull, Secretary of State, 5 July 1944

Throughout the war, German concentration and extermination camps continued to murder millions of Jews. They were also used to provide slave labor for German industry and agriculture. In summer 1944, the U.S. government received a graphic account of the horrifying conditions in the Auschwitz and Birkenau concentration camps.

The Czechoslovak Government has received through its representative in a neutral country an extract from the document drawn up regarding the fate of the Jews in the German camp at Birkenau. This document was drawn up at Bratislava by two Slovak Jews who had managed to escape from the camps at Oswieczim and Birkenau in April. It contains an urgent request for the Allies to be informed of the frightful conditions in these camps. The Czechoslovak Government considers it its duty to comply with this request and the following is a literal translation of the extract as received from the neutral country.

The information contained in the document has been further considerably supplemented by reports which a Polish major who escaped from Oswieczim furnished to the underground organization in Slovakia.

OSWIECZIM AND BIRKENAU

The concentration camp at Oswieczim was originally intended for political prisoners, and about 15,000 Germans, Czechoslovaks, Poles and Russians were there in "protective detention." Besides this, professional criminals were sent there and asocial elements, homosexuals, Bible students, and later Jews from the occupied countries. Over the entrance is the inscription in German "Arbeit macht frei."

The Birkenau labour camp, which lies 4 km. from Oswieczim, and the agricultural work of the Harmense camps are both under the control of the governor of the Oswieczim camp. Inside Oswieczim camp are work-shops of the German armaments concerns Siemens and Krupp. The huts in the camp are in three rows covering an area of 500 x 300 metres. They are surrounded by a double fence 3 metres high charged with high tension electricity. At every 500 metres is a watch-tower 5 metres high with machine-guns and search-lights. This is the "kleine Postenkette" [little post chain]. Another line of watch-towers runs in a circle of 2 kilometres and the work-shops are between the two rows of watch-towers.

Birkenau camp is formed of three blocks covering an area 1,600 x 850 metres and is also surrounded by two rings of watch-towers. The outer ring is connected with the outer ring of watch-towers of Oswieczim camp and they are only separated by the railway-lines. Birkenau camp is called after the small forest of Birkenwald (in Polish Brzezinky) nearby. The local population used to call this place "Rajsko."

Working conditions at Birkenau and Oswieczim are unimaginable. Work is carried on either in the camp or in the neighbourhood. Roads are built. Reinforced concrete buildings are put up. Gravel is quarried. Houses in the neighbourhood are knocked down. New buildings are put up in the camps and in the work-shops. Work is also done in the neighbouring coal mines or in the factory for synthetic rubber. Some persons also work in the administration of the camps. Any person who does not carry out his work to the satisfaction of the overseer is flogged or beaten to death. The food is 300 grammes of bread per head every evening, or 1 litre per head of turnip soup and a little coffee. That is for the Jews. Non-Jews receive rather more. Anyone who cannot work and has a temperature of at least 38.6 degrees is sent to the "Krankenbau," the hut for the sick. The German doctor divides sick persons into two groups: curable and seriously ill. The seriously ill are disposed of by a phenol injection in the region of the heart. Among non-Jews this is done only to those who are really seriously ill, while among the Jews 80 to 90 percent of all those ill receive it. 15,000 to 20,000 persons have already been got rid of in this way by injections. Particularly inhuman scenes took place when the sick were killed wholesale during the process of delousing when a typhus epidemic broke out. Near the "Krankenbau" is the "hygiene institute" where sterilisation and artificial insemination of the women are carried out and blood tests are made for blood transfusion. For these experiments chiefly Jews are used. Since March, 1942 enormous transports of Jews have come to Oswieczim and Birkenau. A very small number of them have been sent to the labour camp, while an average of 90 percent of those who have come have been taken straight from the train and killed. These executions took place at the beginning in the forest of Birkenwald by gas suffocation in a special building constructed for the purpose. After the suffocation by gas the dead bodies were burnt. At the end of February, 1943, four new crematoria were built, two large and two small, in the camp of Birkenau itself. The crematorium contains a large hall, a gas chamber and a furnace. People are assembled in the hall which holds 2,000 and gives the impression of a swimming-bath. They have to undress and are given a piece of soap and a towel as if they were going to the baths. Then they are crowded into the gas chamber which is hermetically sealed. Several S.S. men in gas-masks then pour into the gas chamber through three openings in the ceiling a preparation of the poison gas megacyklon, which is made in Hamburg. At the end of three minutes all the persons are dead. The dead bodies are then taken away in carts to the furnace to be burnt. The furnace has nine chambers, each of them with four openings. Each opening will take three bodies at once. They are completely burnt after 1.5 hours. Thus each crematorium can burn 1,500 bodies daily. The crematoria can be recognized from outside by their lofty chimneys.

On principle only Jews are put to death by gas, this is only done to Aryans in exceptional cases. Aryans are shot with pistols on a special execution ground which lies between blocks 10 and 11 of Oswieczim camp. The first executions took place there in the summer of 1941 and reached their peak a year later when they were carried out by hundreds. Later when this aroused attention a large number of non-Jews who were condemned to death, were taken straight from the train to the execution ground and not entered on the lists of the camp. According to careful calculations during the period from April, 1942, to April, 1944, from 1.5 to 1.75 million Jews were put to death by gas or in some other way, half of these being Polish Jews, others [being] Jews from Holland, Greece, France, Belgium, Germany, Yugoslavia, Czechoslovakia, Italy, Norway, Lithuania, Austria and Jews of various other nationalities who were brought to Oswieczim from other camps in Poland. About 90 percent of the members of the transports arriving in Birkenau and Oswieczim were taken straight from the train to be put to death and about 10 percent became inmates of the camp. Each of the new inmates was registered and received a number. In April, 1944, 180,000 persons in all had been registered as inmates of the camp, counting Jews and non-Jews together. Of the whole number who had arrived before there were only 34,000 in the camp at the beginning of April this year, 18,000 of them being non-Jews. (In both the sources that we have quoted this number includes the membership of both camps together.)

The remainder had been killed by hard work, illness, especially epidemics of typhus and malaria, ill treatment, and finally "selection." Twice a week the camp doctor indicated persons destined for selection. Those selected were all gassed. In a single block of Birkenau camp the average number of deaths a week was as much as 2,000, 1,200 of these being natural deaths and 800 "selection." A special book entitled "S.B. Sonderbehandelte" is kept dealing with the "selected." Notice of the deaths of the others is sent to the supreme commander of the camp at Oranienburg. At the beginning of 1943 the "political section" (camp Gestapo) at Oswieczim received 500,000 forms for release. The governor had them all made out in the names of persons who had already been gassed and lodged them in the archives of the camp.. . .

The above is the contents of the two documents. The persons who have managed to secure the transmission of the documents to a neutral country added

(a) the following information:

"12,000 Jews are being deported daily from the territories of Carpathian Ruthenia, Transylvania and the district of Kosice where there used to be 320,000 Jews. Those deported are sent to Oswieczim, 5,000 going by train via Slovakia daily and 7,000 via Carpathian Ruthenia."

and (b) the following suggestions:

1. The Allied Governments, especially those whose citizens are suffering in both these camps, should jointly address to the Germans and Hungarians a threat of reprisals directed at the Germans in the hands of these governments.
2. The crematoria in both camps, which are recognisable by their high chimneys and watch-towers, should be bombed and so should the main railway-lines connecting Slovakia and Carpathian Ruthenia with Poland which are also of military importance, (especially the bridge at Cop).
3. Public warnings to the Germans and Hungarians should be repeated.
4. The Vatican should be requested to pronounce a severe public condemnation.

Source: PBS: The American Experience. Available at http://www.pbs.org/wgbh/amex/holocaust/filmmore/reference/primary/bombsummary.html.

186. General Dwight D. Eisenhower to General George C. Marshall, 5 July 1944

Supreme Commander of the Allied Forces in Europe General Dwight D. Eisenhower supplemented his official reports with regular personal letters to General George C. Marshall, chief of staff of the U.S. Army. One month after the Normandy landings, American forces faced fierce and difficult fighting in France, in conditions which Eisenhower graphically described.

. . . . I spent four days in the beachhead. We began attacking southward with the VIII Corps on the 3rd and the VII Corps joined in with one Division on July 4th. I was particularly anxious to visit these Corps and their Divisions during actual operations. The going is extremely tough, with three main causes responsible. The first of these, as always, is the fighting quality of the German soldier. The second is the nature of the country. Our whole attack has to fight its way out of very narrow bottlenecks flanked by marshes and against an enemy who has a double hedgerow and an intervening ditch almost every fifty yards as ready-made strong points. The third cause is the weather. Our air has been unable to operate at maximum efficiency and on top of this the rain and mud were so bad during my visit that I was reminded of Tunisian wintertime. It was almost impossible to locate artillery targets although we have plenty of guns available. Even with clear weather it is extraordinarily difficult to point out a target that is an appropriate one for either air or artillery.

Source: Joseph Patrick Hobbs, ed., *Dear General: Eisenhower's Wartime Letters to Marshall* (Baltimore, MD: Johns Hopkins University Press, 1971), 194–195. Reprinted with permission of the Eisenhower Library.

187. General Erwin Rommel, Teletype Message to Hitler, 15 July 1944

Six weeks after the Normandy Invasion began, Field Marshal Erwin Rommel, commander of German forces in France, sent Hitler a teletype message warning that Germany faced defeat by the Allies and should withdraw from France. Ignoring this advice, Hitler ordered what became a disastrous German counterattack against advancing Allied units around Caen. On 17 July, Rommel was severely injured when British fighter planes strafed his car. In company with other like-minded German generals, Rommel had intended that, if Hitler ignored his advice, he would open negotiations with Allied commanders in France for an armistice and a separate peace in the West, a move he hoped would spare Germany from invasion by Russian forces from the east. Rommel had also met with a representative of another group of German military officers who intended to assassinate Hitler, though he himself apparently knew little or nothing of these plans. He had, however, stated that he believed Hitler should be removed from power, albeit without bloodshed. On 20 July, the planned coup failed, and the conspirators, who were arrested and tortured, eventually implicated Rommel. In order not to embarrass the German government, he was given the opportunity to commit suicide, which he accepted. After his death, he received a hero's funeral, with full military honors.

The situation on the Normandy front is growing worse every day and is now approaching a grave crisis.

Due to the severity of the fighting, the enemy's enormous use of material—above all, artillery and tanks—and the effect of his unrestricted command of the air over the battle area, our casualties are so high that the fighting power of our divisions is rapidly diminishing. Replacements from home are few in number and, with the difficult transport situation, take weeks to get to the front. As against 97,000 casualties (including 2,360 officers)—i.e., an average of 2,500 to 3,000 a day—replacements to date number 10,000, of whom about 6,000 have actually arrived at the front.

Material losses are also huge and have so far been replaced on a very small scale; in tanks, for example, only 17 replacements have arrived to date as compared with 225 losses.

The newly arrived infantry divisions are raw and, with their small establishment of artillery, anti-tank guns and close-combat anti-tank weapons, are in no state to make a lengthy stand against major enemy attacks coming after hours of drum-fire and heavy bombing. The fighting has shown that with this use of material by the enemy, even the bravest army will be smashed piece by piece, losing men, arms and territory in the process.

Due to the destruction of the railway system and the threat of the enemy air force to roads and tracks up to 90 miles behind the front, supply conditions are so bad that only the barest essentials can be brought to the front. It is consequently now necessary to exercise the greatest economy in all fields, and especially in artillery and mortar ammunition. These conditions are unlikely to improve, as enemy action is steadily reducing the transport capacity available. Moreover, this activity in the air is likely to become even more effective as the numerous air-strips in the bridgehead are taken into use.

No new forces of any consequence can be brought up to the Normandy front except by weakening Fifteenth Army's front on the Channel, or the Mediterranean front in southern France. Yet Seventh Army's front, taken over all, urgently requires two fresh divisions, as the troops in Normandy are exhausted.

On the enemy's side, fresh forces and great quantities of war material are flowing into his front every day. His supplies are undisturbed by our air force. Enemy pressure is growing steadily stronger.

In these circumstances we must expect that in the foreseeable future the enemy will succeed in breaking through our thin front, above all, Seventh Army's, and thrusting deep into France. Apart from the Panzer Group's sector reserves, which are at present tied down by the fighting on their own front and—due to the enemy's command of the air—can only move by night, we dispose of no mobile reserve for defence against such a break-through. Action by our air force will, as in the past, have little effect.

The troops are everywhere fighting heroically, but the unequal struggle is approaching its end. It is urgently necessary for the proper conclusion to be drawn from this situation. As C.-in-C. of the Army Group I feel myself in duty bound to speak plainly on this point.

Source: B. H. Liddell Hart, ed., *The Rommel Papers* (New York: Harcourt, Brace and Company, 1953), 486–487.

188. Gestapo Interrogation Record of Captain Kaiser on Count von Stauffenberg's Assassination Plot of 20 July 1944

From 1943 onward, a substantial number of German military officers, many of them former supporters who felt that both Hitler's conduct of the war on the Eastern Front and his refusal to seek a negotiated peace settlement were misguided, made plans to assassinate Hitler. On 20 July 1944, these plans culminated in an unsuccessful attempt, spearheaded by Colonel Claus Schenk von Stauffenberg, to kill the Führer at a meeting by means of a bomb hidden in a briefcase. The plotters were quickly arrested, interrogated under torture, and brutally executed. Gestapo interrogations soon revealed the extent of their plans, including the terms on which they hoped to make peace with the Allies. By the time of the assassination attempt, the Normandy invasion had already made some of these terms a dead letter, and even before then, the plotters undoubtedly overestimated the concessions the Allies were likely to grant.

The recent interrogation of Captain Kaiser has produced several indications that Stauffenberg had two channels to the English via middlemen. The details are currently being investigated. Already on 25 May, Kaiser produced a note for Stauffenberg to serve as the basis for negotiations with the enemy:

1. To cease the air war immediately.
2. To give up plans for invasion.
3. To avoid further sacrifice of blood.
4. To maintain a permanent defence capability in the east, withdraw from all occupied territories in the north, west and south.
5. To avoid any occupation.
6. A freely elected government as part of an independently formulated constitution.
7. Total participation in the implementation of armistice conditions and in the preparation of peace.
8. The Reich frontiers of 1914 in the east. Austria and the Sudetenland to remain with the Reich. Autonomy for Alsace-Lorraine. The acquisition of South Tyrol down to Bolzano, Merano.

9. Energetic reconstruction with participation in the reconstruction of Europe.
10. The right to deal with the enemies of the people ourselves.
11. The reacquisition of honour, self-respect and the respect of others.

At the end of June 1944 Kaiser learned from [former mayor of Leipzig Carl] Goerdeler that inquiries were being made at the highest level in England about the clique of conspirators. Stauffenberg sent over a list of the men who would be the future negotiation partners, expressing the wish that Austria should remain with the Reich and that the settlement of accounts with the war criminals should be left to the future German government.

Source: Jeremy Noakes, ed., *Nazism 1919–1945,* Volume 4: *The Home Front in World War II* (Exeter, UK: University of Exeter Press, 1998), 617. Reprinted with permission of University of Exeter Press.

189. The Bretton Woods Agreements: United Nations Monetary and Financial Conference at Bretton Woods: Summary of Agreements, 22 July 1944

The Allies recognized that the postwar world would require new international organizations to perform not just political but also economic functions. In summer 1944, Allied representatives met in the United States at Bretton Woods, New Hampshire, to devise plans for the International Monetary Fund and the International Bank for Reconstruction and Development. These two bodies were expected to play major roles in reestablishing stable currencies and financing postwar economic reconstruction. Although professional bankers would be recruited to run them, they were organized and funded by governments and represented a great departure from the more ad hoc arrangements among private bankers for reconstruction and recovery that had characterized the post–World War I period.

This Conference at Bretton Woods, representing nearly all the peoples of the world, has considered matters of international money and finance which are important for peace and prosperity. The Conference has agreed on the problems needing attention, the measures which should be taken, and the forms of international cooperation or organization which are required. The agreements reached on these large and complex matters are without precedent in the history of international economic relations.

I. THE INTERNATIONAL MONETARY FUND

Since foreign trade affects the standard of life of every people, all countries have a vital interest in the system of exchange of national currencies and the regulations and conditions which govern its working. Because these monetary transactions are international exchanges, the nations must agree on the basic rules which govern the exchanges if the system is to work smoothly. When they do not agree, and when single nations and small groups of nations attempt by special and different regulations of the foreign exchanges to gain trade advantages, the result is instability, a reduced volume of foreign trade, and damage to national economies.

This course of action is likely to lead to economic warfare and to endanger the world's peace.

The Conference has therefore agreed that broad international action is necessary to maintain an international monetary system which will promote foreign trade. The nations should consult and agree on international monetary changes which affect each other. They should outlaw practices which are agreed to be harmful to world prosperity, and they should assist each other to overcome short-term exchange difficulties.

The Conference has agreed that the nations here represented should establish for these purposes a permanent international body, The International Monetary Fund, with powers and resources adequate to perform the tasks assigned to it. Agreement has been reached concerning these powers and resources and the additional obligations which the member countries should undertake. Draft Articles of Agreement on these points have been prepared.

II. THE INTERNATIONAL BANK FOR RECONSTRUCTION AND DEVELOPMENT

It is in the interest of all nations that post-war reconstruction should be rapid. Likewise, the development of the resources of particular regions is in the general economic interest. Programs of reconstruction and development will speed economic progress everywhere, will aid political stability and foster peace.

The Conference has agreed that expanded international investment is essential to provide a portion of the capital necessary for reconstruction and development.

The Conference has further agreed that the nations should cooperate to increase the volume of foreign investment for these purposes, made through normal business channels. It is especially important that the nations should cooperate to share the risks of such foreign investment, since the benefits are general.

The Conference has agreed that the nations should establish a permanent international body to perform these functions, to be called The International Bank for Reconstruction and Development. It has been agreed that the Bank should assist in providing capital through normal channels at reasonable rates of interest and for long periods for projects which will raise the productivity of the borrowing country. There is agreement that the Bank should guarantee loans made by others and that through their subscriptions of capital in all countries should share with the borrowing country in guaranteeing such loans. The Conference has agreed on the powers and resources which the Bank must have and on the obligations which the member countries must assume, and has prepared draft Articles of Agreement accordingly.

The Conference has recommended that in carrying out the policies of the institutions here proposed special consideration should be given to the needs of countries which have suffered from enemy occupation and hostilities.

The proposals formulated at the Conference for the establishment of the Fund and the Bank are now submitted, in accordance with the terms of the invitation, for consideration of the governments and people of the countries represented.

Source: Pamphlet No. 4, *Pillars of Peace: Documents Pertaining to American Interest in Establishing a Lasting World Peace: January 1941–February 1946* (Carlisle Barracks, PA: Book Department, Army Information School, May 1946), 30–31. Also available at http://www.ibiblio.org/pha/policy/1944/440722a.html.

190. General Headquarters, Southwest Pacific Area, Communiqué No. 845, Statement of General Douglas MacArthur on the Capture of Sansapor, New Guinea, 1 August 1944

The Allied landing on and capture of Sansapor effectively marked the end of the New Guinea Campaign. As always, Allied Commander General Douglas MacArthur issued a communiqué to mark the occasion.

We have seized the coastal area of Sansapor and the nearby islands of Amsterdam and Middelburg, at the western tip of Dutch New Guinea, nearly 200 miles beyond Noemfoor and slightly more than 600 miles southeast of the Philippines. . . . The operation was an amphibious one, the ground troops acting in coordination with naval and air forces. The enemy base at Manokwari, the pivot of the defense of the Vogelkop Peninsula, is now bypassed and useless. Its garrison, 15,000 strong . . . is now isolated with its only possible escape route to the south over hazardous terrain of swamp and jungle.

Our air bases are now established from Milne Bay along the entire coast of New Guinea. The enemy is no longer able to operate in this area, either by air or sea, beyond the Halmahera-Philippine line which is the main defense cover for his conquered empire in the Southwest Pacific. Should this line go, all of his conquests south of China will be imperiled and in grave danger of flank envelopment.

Source: Charles A. Willoughby et al., eds., *Reports of General MacArthur: The Campaigns of MacArthur in the Pacific,* 2 vols. (Washington, DC: U.S. Government Printing Office, 1966), 1:160.

191. The Morgenthau Plan, August 1944

Within the U.S. government, opinions differed over the future treatment of Germany. Some, especially members of the War Department, believed that it would be necessary to reintegrate Germany into the broader European economy and that Germany should therefore be treated relatively leniently. Others, notably Henry Morgenthau Jr., the U.S. secretary of the treasury, took a more punitive approach, envisaging the breakup of Germany and its "pastoralization," namely, the permanent destruction of the country's industrial capabilities. In August 1944, Morgenthau put forward a plan encapsulating his views on the desirability of harsh postwar treatment of Germany.

TOP SECRET: PROGRAM TO PREVENT GERMANY FROM STARTING A WORLD WAR III

1. Demilitarization of Germany. It should be the aim of the Allied Forces to accomplish the complete demilitarization of Germany in the shortest possible period of time after surrender. This means completely disarming the German Army and people (including the removal or destruction of all war material), the total destruction of the whole German armament industry, and the removal or destruction of other key industries which are basic to military strength.

2. New Boundaries of Germany.

(a) Poland should get that part of East Prussia which doesn't go to the U.S.S.R. and the southern portion of Silesia.

(b) France should get the Saar and the adjacent territories bounded by the Rhine and the Moselle Rivers.

(c) As indicated in 4 below an International Zone should be created containing the Ruhr and the surrounding industrial areas.

3. Partitioning of New Germany. The remaining portion of Germany should be divided into two autonomous, independent states, (a) a South German state comprising Bavaria, Wuerttemberg, Baden and some smaller areas and (b) a North German state comprising a large part of the old state of Prussia, Saxony, Thuringia and several smaller states.

There shall be a custom union between the new South German state and Austria, which will be restored to her pre-1938 political borders.

4. The Ruhr Area. (The Ruhr, surrounding industrial areas, including the Rhineland, the Kiel Canal, and all German territory north of the Kiel Canal.)

Here lies the heart of German industrial power. This area should not only be stripped of all presently existing industries; but so weakened and controlled that it can not in the foreseeable future become an industrial area. The following steps will accomplish this:

(a) Within a short period, if possible not longer than 6 months after the cessation of hostilities, all industrial plants and equipment not destroyed by military action shall be completely dismantled and transported to Allied Nations as restitution. All equipment [shall] be removed from the mines and the mines closed.

(b) The area should be made an international zone to be governed by an international security organization to be established by the United Nations. In governing the area the international organization should be guided by policies designed to further the above stated objective.

5. Restitution and Reparation. Reparations, in the form of future payments and deliveries, should not be demanded. Restitution and reparation shall be effected by the transfer of existing German resources and territories, e.g.,

(a) by restitution of property looted by the Germans in territories occupied by them;

(b) by transfer of German territory and German private rights in industrial property situated in such territory to invaded countries and the international organization under the program of partition;

(c) by the removal and distribution among devastated countries of industrial plants and equipment situated within the International Zone and the North and South German states delimited in the section on partition;

(d) by forced German labor outside Germany; and

(e) by confiscation of all German assets of any character whatsoever outside of Germany.

6. Education and Propaganda.

(a) All schools and universities will be closed until an Allied commission of Education has formulated an effective reorganization program. It is contemplated that it may require a considerable period of time before any institutions of higher education are reopened. Meanwhile the education of German students in foreign universities will not be prohibited. Elementary schools will be reopened as quickly as appropriate teachers and textbooks are available.

(b) All German radio stations and newspapers, magazines, weeklies, etc. shall be discontinued until adequate controls are established and an appropriate program formulated.

7. Political Decentralization. The military administration in Germany in the initial period should be carried out with a view toward the eventual partitioning of Germany. To facilitate partitioning and to assure its permanence the military authorities should be guided by the following principles:

(a) Dismiss all policy-making officials of the Reich government and deal primarily with local governments.

(b) Encourage the reestablishment of state governments in each of the states (Lander) corresponding to 18 states into which Germany is presently divided and in addition make the Prussian provinces separate states.

(c) Upon the partition of Germany, the various state governments should be encouraged to organize a federal government for each of the newly partitioned areas. Such new governments should be in the form of a large degree of local autonomy.

8. Responsibility of Military for Local German Economy. The sole purpose of the military in control of the German economy shall be to facilitate military operations and military occupation. The Allied Military Government shall not assume responsibility for such economic problems as price controls, rationing, unemployment, production, reconstruction, distribution, consumption, housing, or transportation, or take any measures designed to maintain or strengthen the German economy, except those which are essential to military operations. The responsibility for sustaining the German people rests with the German people with such facilities as may be available under the circumstances.

9. Controls Over Development of German Economy. During a period of at least twenty years after surrender ade-

quate controls, including controls over foreign trade and tight restrictions on capital imports, shall be maintained by the United Nations designed to prevent in the newly-established states the establishment or expansion of key industries basic to the German military potential and to control other key industries.

10. Agrarian Program. All large estates should be broken up and divided among the peasants and the system of primogeniture and entail should be abolished.

11. Punishment of War Crimes and Treatment of Special Groups. A program for the punishment of certain war crimes and for the treatment of Nazi organizations and other special groups is contained in section 11 [not printed].

12. Uniforms and Parades.

(a) No German shall be permitted to wear, after an appropriate period of time following the cessation of hostilities, any military uniform or any uniform of any quasi military organizations.

(b) No military parades shall be permitted anywhere in Germany and all military bands shall be disbanded.

13. Aircraft. All aircraft (including gliders), whether military or commercial, will be confiscated for later disposition. No German shall be permitted to operate or to help operate any aircraft, including those owned by foreign interests.

14. United States Responsibilities. Although the United States would have full military and civilian representation on whatever international commission or commissions may be established for the execution of the whole German program, the primary responsibility for the policing of Germany and for civil administration in Germany should be assumed by the military forces of Germany's continental neighbors. Specifically, these should include Russian, French, Polish, Czech, Yugoslav, Norwegian, Dutch and Belgian soldiers.

Under this program United States troops could be withdrawn within a relatively short time.

Source: W. Lafeber, ed., *Origins of the Cold War: A Historical Problem with Interpretations and Documents* (New York and Chichester, UK: John Wiley and Sons, 1971), 107–111.

192. The Warsaw Uprising: Telegrams among the Allied Leaders, 20–22 August 1944

In August 1944, Soviet troops advanced across Polish territory toward the capital city of Warsaw, still occupied by German forces. Anticipating the speedy arrival of Russian forces and encouraged by broadcasts from refugee Communist compatriots based in Moscow, Poles in Warsaw launched a desperate uprising against the occupying Nazis. For several weeks, however, the Soviet army halted its advance not far from Warsaw, enabling the Nazis savagely to repress the revolt before Soviet troops took the city. Soviet officials also refused to permit Britain or the United States to airlift supplies to the beleaguered Poles of Warsaw, an attitude against which British and American leaders protested. Many believed that the underlying reason for Soviet nonassistance to the Polish uprising was the political calculation that by the time Soviet troops entered Warsaw, Nazi forces would have eliminated many non-Communist Poles who might otherwise have spearheaded resistance to future Soviet domination. Winston Churchill and Franklin D. Roosevelt begged Josef Stalin to permit his troops to assist the rebels, but he refused. The episode marked the beginning a definite downturn in Soviet relations with the Western Allies.

Telegram from President Franklin D. Roosevelt and Prime Minister Winston Churchill to Josef Stalin, 20 August 1944

We are thinking of world opinion if the anti-Nazis in Warsaw are in effect abandoned. We believe that all three of us should do the utmost to save as many of the patriots there as possible. We hope that you will drop immediate supplies and munitions to the patriot Poles in Warsaw, or you will agree to help our planes in doing it very quickly. We hope you will approve. The time element is of extreme importance.

Source: U.S. Department of State. *Foreign Relations of the United States 1944,* Volume III (Washington, DC: U.S. Government Printing Office, 1965), 1383.

Telegram from Josef Stalin to Franklin D. Roosevelt and Winston Churchill, 22 August 1944

I have received the message from you and Mr. Roosevelt about Warsaw. I wish to express my opinions.

Sooner or later the truth about the group of criminals, who have embarked on the Warsaw adventure in order to seize power, will become known to everybody. These people have exploited the good faith of the citizens of Warsaw, throwing many almost unarmed people against the German guns, tanks and aircraft. A situation has arisen in which each new day serves not only the Poles for the liberation of Warsaw but the Hitlerites who are inhumanly shooting down the inhabitants of Warsaw.

From the military point of view, the situation which has arisen, by increasingly directing the attention of the Germans to Warsaw, is just as unprofitable for the Red Army as for the Poles. Meanwhile the Soviet troops who have recently encountered new and notable efforts by the Germans to go over to the counter attack, are doing everything possible to smash these counter attacks of the Hitlerites and to go over to a new wide-scale attack in the region of Warsaw. There can be no doubt that the Red Army is not sparing its efforts to break the Germans round Warsaw and to free Warsaw for the Poles. That will be the best and most effective help for the Poles who are anti-Nazis.

Source: U.S. Department of State. *Foreign Relations of the United States 1944,* Volume III (Washington, DC: U.S. Government Printing Office, 1965), 1391.

193. David K. E. Bruce Describes the Liberation of Paris, 24–25 August 1944

Like its fall to German forces in June 1940, the liberation of Paris, the French capital city, by Allied forces represented one of the great symbolic moments of the war. From the first landings on D-Day, Colonel David K. E. Bruce, the European head of the Office of Strategic Services, the wartime U.S. overseas intelligence agency, accompanied the invading Allied forces. He and his compatriot, the novelist and foreign correspondent Ernest Hemingway, were the first two Americans to enter Paris in the vanguard of the liberating forces. By the afternoon of 24 August 1944, their unit was on the outskirts of the city, the center of which Allied troops entered the next day.

DAVID K. E. BRUCE, DIARY ENTRY, 24 AUGUST 1944
We got up at six o'clock, and waited around for a couple of hours before joining one of [Free French General Jacques] Le Clerc's [Second Armored Division] columns . . .

As we went down the hill toward the Seine about five o'clock in the afternoon, the streets were lined with people. All houses were gay with flags, and the population was almost hysterical with joy. Our progress was extremely slow, and there were many long halts as road blocks were cleared, or small pockets of enemy resistance eliminated. During these stops we were mobbed by the bystanders. They gave us fruit and flowers, they kissed us on both cheeks, men, women, and children throwing their arms around us and saying, "Merci, Messieurs" (often adding: "We have waited for you four years.") When they knew we were Americans that often seemed to increase their enthusiasm. Although we were passing through a tenement district, the people, on the whole, appeared to be moderately well dressed and fed. The French flag was everywhere—often it had the Cross of Lorraine [emblem of the Free French] imprinted on it. There were a good many American and British flags, and a few Russian, in evidence. We yelled ourselves hoarse, shouting "Vive la France" as we passed through the crowds. Everyone thrust drinks at us that they had been hoarding for this occasion. It was impossible to refuse them, but the combination was enough to wreck one's constitution. In the course of the afternoon, we had beer, cider, white and red Bordeaux, white and red Burgundy, champagne, rum, whiskey, cognac, armagnac, and Calvados.

As night fell, we were still a mile short of the Pont de Sèvres, and there was determined resistance in a factory below the bridge at which our tanks were cutting loose. The vehicles were drawn up along the sidewalks. Mouthard found a house in which we distributed ourselves, and we had our rations there. We could cook nothing, since there is no gas or coal, but the electricity, they told us, is turned on for several hours each day and night.

The people all complain of the high cost of food. For six weeks most of the railroads operating into Paris have been inactive as a result of bombing, sabotage, or for other causes, and the transport of produce to the city from other parts of France has been almost completely suspended.

DAVID K. E. BRUCE, DIARY ENTRY, 25 AUGUST 1944
There had been some fighting during the night and this morning. We did not get under way until 12:30 P.M. when we crossed the bridge. Tanks had preceded us some time before. The Artillery halted two kilometers from the bridge and shelled Mont Valérien thoroughly.

As we drove into a large square near the Bois de Boulogne, we were suddenly halted in front of a café, and it was said that snipers were firing with machine guns from some of the upstairs windows of a larger apartment house. In any event, everyone turned loose at the building. I did see flashes several times near the roof as if someone were shooting from there, although I could not actually distinguish a weapon. Ernest [Hemingway], Gravey and I, sheltered in a doorway, Lester and Mac [his driver] more bravely lay under the jeep. Finally, a tank sent a few shells into the unfortunate house, and we were told to move on. From that point forward, we were surrounded continually by surging masses of cheering people. Kissing and shouting were general and indiscriminate. It was a wonderful sunny day and a wonderful scene. The women were dressed in their best clothes, and all wore somewhere the tricolor—on their blouses, in their hair, and even as earrings.

We stopped once when three German tanks were signalled ahead. We then turned off and, under the guidance of a Spahis lieutenant raced through the side streets until we emerged, just behind the Arc de Triomphe, on Avenue Foch where we parked the cars. The Majestic Hotel, which had been German headquarters, was on fire. At the end of the Champs Elysées a vehicle was burning in the Place de la Concorde, and behind, in the Tuileries Gardens, it looked as if a tank was on fire. Smoke was issuing from the Crillon Hotel, and across the river, from the Chamber of Deputies. Snipers were firing steadily into the area around the Arc de Triomphe, and the French were firing back at them.

We walked across to the Tomb of the Unknown Soldier. It was being guarded by six veterans, standing at attention, and a mutilated ex-soldier, seated in a wheel chair. They had been there all during the fracas at the Majestic. The French Captain in charge asked us if we wanted to ascend to the roof of the Arc. We did so and were greeted by a squadron of Pompiers standing at attention. For some reason, their Commander presented me with a pompier's medal. The view was breathtaking. One saw the golden dome of the Invalides, the green roof of the Madeleine, Sacré-Coeur, and other familiar landmarks. Tanks were firing in various streets. Part of the Arc was under fire from snipers. A shell from a German 88 nicked one of its sides.

When we descended, Mouthard led us back toward our car. Seven or eight German soldiers lay dead in a heap on the street. As we made our way forward there was a burst of fire. We found the head of the street, where our car stood, barricaded, while shots were interchanged with a Gestapo headquarters there. As we sheltered beneath a tank, a man drove in alongside of us and asked if we would like to drink a bottle of champagne at his house. The Spahis lieutenant, Lester, Gravey and I accepted. As we started down Avenue Foch, firing became general again. Every side street seemed enfiladed. There was enthusiastic confusion. Almost every civilian had a weapon and wanted to shoot it. People on roofs were being shot at, and in many of the top stories of buildings. Some of them were, no doubt, German snipers dressed in civilian clothes, and some of them the hated French Milice [collaborationist militia]. We finally made our way to our host's, not without fear.

Arrived there, we found a most beautiful apartment, with very fine furniture and Chinese porcelains, his lovely wife, and a magnum of iced champagne. His name was Robert Lalou, 40, Avenue Foch. He said he had been an aviator in the French Army in 1940. After another couple of bottles of champagne, our Spahis friend announced he must return to his squadron. We crossed the Avenue and parted with him. On the corner, we found a retired French Lieutenant-Colonel entertaining some of our men with champagne, which was continually renewed by a servant bringing hampers of it from a nearby apartment. We dallied there for a while and decided to push on. Hemingway, Red (Hemingway's driver) and myself, finding the Champs Elysées absolutely bare of traffic, passed down it at racing speed to the Travellers Club. When we entered, we found the rooms all closed with the exception of the bar. There a number of the Old Guard had collected, including the President of the Club. We were the first outsiders to come there since the taking of Paris. They celebrated by opening champagne. In the midst of this festivity a sniper began to fire from an adjoining roof. Red shouldered his musket and made for the roof, but was balked.

We next collected our gang and not knowing what was ahead except for the usual indiscriminate popping of small arms, dashed to the Café de la Paix. The Place de l'Opéra was a solid mass of cheering people, and, after kissing several thousand men, women, and babies, and losing a carbine by theft, we escaped to the Ritz. Except for the manager, the imperturbable Ausiello, the Ritz was completely deserted, so we arranged to quarter there as well as to take lodging for the Private Army. This was done. Ausiello asked what he could immediately do for us, and we answered we would like fifty martini cocktails. They were not very good, as the bartender had disappeared, but they were followed by a superb dinner. During the night, there was almost incessant shooting. The French Forces of the Interior are well out of hand, and draw on anybody whom they consider suspicious.

Source: Nelson Lankford, ed., *OSS against the Reich: The World War II Diaries of Colonel David K. E. Bruce* (Kent, OH: Kent State University Press, 1991), 170–174. Reprinted with the permission of the family of David K. E. Bruce.

194. General Douglas MacArthur, Radiogram to Commander, Allied Air Forces, and Commander in Chief, Pacific Ocean Areas, 2 September 1944

Like Supreme Commander Dwight D. Eisenhower in Europe, Douglas MacArthur sought to win the hearts and minds of those people whom he was liberating. Just before launching the Allied campaign to retake the Philippines, he therefore insisted to the air and naval commanders that the invading forces must make every effort to respect the lives and property of the Philippine inhabitants.

One of the purposes of the Philippine campaign is to liberate the Filipinos; they will not understand liberation if accomplished by indiscriminate destruction of their homes, their possessions, their civilization and their own lives; humanity and our moral standing throughout the Far East dictate that the destruction of lives and property in the Philippines be held to a minimum, compatible with the assurance of a successful military campaign; indications are that in some localities the Japanese are evacuating cities, leaving Filipinos in residence, either failing to warn them or compelling them to stay; aerial bombing causes the greatest destruction; our objective in areas we are to occupy is to destroy totally hostile effort in order to insure our own success; in other areas we neutralize, to weaken any hostile effort which may tend to increase resistance to our occupation objectives; in the latter areas, our attack objectives are primarily airfields and shipping, not metropolitan areas or villages or barrios; to the extent possible, we must preserve port facilities that we plan to use. The Commander Allied Air Forces will, and CINC-POA [the Commander-in-Chief of the Pacific Ocean Areas] is requested, to issue general instructions in consonance with the above objective of minimizing destruction of life and property of Filipinos. . . .

Source: Charles A. Willoughby et al., eds., *Reports of General MacArthur: The Campaigns of MacArthur in the Pacific*, 2 vols. (Washington, DC: U.S. Government Printing Office, 1966), 1:191–193.

195. General Douglas MacArthur to Major General John Hilldring, 2 September 1944

Besides taking steps to safeguard Philippine lives and property, General Douglas MacArthur also wrote to the director of the Civil Affairs Department of the War Department in Washington, urging that, once liberated, the Philippines be granted at least the same degree of independence from U.S. control the islands had enjoyed before the war began.

It is essential . . . in any plans for the control of civil affairs that the measure of freedom and liberty given to the Filipino people be at least comparable to that enjoyed under the Commonwealth Government before Japanese occupation. . . . It would be a matter of gravest concern if restrictions were imposed, whether by direct or by individual means, in excess of those existing before the war. If any impressions were created that the United States is curtailing rather than expanding liberties, the most unfortunate repercussions might be expected. The only restrictions which should be imposed are the minimum required by military necessity and these should be removed as quickly as possible. . . .

I repeat, utmost care should be taken that an imperialistic attitude not be introduced into the situation under the guise of military operations and necessity. This would be entirely alien to the spirit of recent legislation passed by Congress and the announced purposes of the President of the United States.

Source: Charles A. Willoughby et al., eds., *Reports of General MacArthur: The Campaigns of MacArthur in the Pacific*, 2 vols. (Washington, DC: U.S. Government Printing Office, 1966), 1:193.

196. General Dwight D. Eisenhower to General George C. Marshall, 14 September 1944

As the Normandy Invasion progressed, Supreme Commander of the Allied Forces General Dwight D. Eisenhower reported regularly to General George C. Marshall, the Army's chief of staff in Washington. After three months of fighting, he already found it necessary to discourage British efforts to rush to take Berlin ahead of Soviet forces. Eisenhower rightly anticipated that his troops faced at least one more major battle before they could overcome the desperate German resistance.

I think that by forwarding to the Combined Chiefs of Staff periodic appreciations as well as copies of principal directives you are kept fairly well acquainted with our situation. The fact is that we are stretched to the absolute limit in maintenance both as to intake and as to distribution after supplies are landed.

From the start we have always known that we would have to choose, after breaking out of the original bridgehead, some line which would mark a relative slackening in offensive operations while we improved maintenance facilities and prepared for an offensive operation that could be sustained for another indefinite period. At first it seemed to me that the German would try to use some one of the number of lines available to him in France on which to make a rather determined stand, but due to the decisiveness of our victory below the Seine I determined to go all out in effort and in risk to continue the drive beyond the German border, up to and including the Rhine before we began the process of regrouping and re-fitting.

While this was going on [British Commander Field Marshal Bernard] Montgomery suddenly became obsessed with the idea that his Army Group could rush right on into Berlin provided we gave him all the maintenance that was in the theater—that is, immobilize all other divisions and give their transport and supplies to his Army Group, with some to Hodges. Examination of this scheme exposes it as a fantastic idea. First of all, it would have to be done with the ports we now have, supplemented possibly by Calais and Ostend. The attack would be on such a narrow front that flanking threats would be particularly effective and no other troops in the whole region would be capable of going to its support. Actually I doubt that the idea was proposed in any conviction that it could be carried through to completion; it was based merely on wishful thinking, and in an effort to induce me to give to 21st Army Group and to [U.S. General Omar] Bradley's left every ounce of maintenance there is in the theater.

As opposed to this the only profitable plan is to hustle all our forces up against the Rhine, including Devers's forces, build up our maintenance facilities and our reserves as rapidly as possible and then put on one sustained and unremitting advance against the heart of the enemy country. Supporting this great attack will probably be subsidiary operations against the German ports on the left and against his southern industrial areas on the right.

I have sacrificed a lot to give Montgomery the strength he needs to reach the Rhine in the north and to threaten the Ruhr. That is, after all, our main effort for the moment. The great Airborne attack which will go in support of this operation will be Sunday the 17th, unless weather prevents. It should be successful in carrying Montgomery up and across the Rhine; thereafter it is absolutely imperative that he quickly capture the approaches to Antwerp so that we may use that port. The port facilities themselves are practically undamaged and we have there ample storage for bulk oil, something that we critically need.

Le Havre will be developed for utilization by U.S. forces.

During the early and middle summer, I was always ready to defer capture of ports in favor of bolder and more rapid movement to the front. But now approaches the season of the year when we can no longer afford this, especially in view of the resistance the German is ready to offer in Fortress defense, as demonstrated both at St. Malo and at Brest. Every day I thank my stars that I held out for ANVIL in the face of almost overwhelming pressure. Marseilles may yet be a Godsend to us.

My own belief is that, assuming continuation of the Russian pressure at its present scale, we will have to fight one more major battle in the West. This will be to break through the German defenses on the border and to get started on the invasion. Thereafter the advance into Germany will not be as rapid as it was in France, because we won't have the F.F.I. [French Forces of the Interior] in the German rear, but I doubt that there will be another full-dress battle involved. The big crash to start that move may prove to be a rather tough affair.

Recently Spaatz received a message from Arnold suggesting the desirability of moving a lot of our heavy bombers to France immediately. This is simply beyond the realm of feasibility at the moment. Big bombers can still operate effectively from England and we need every ton of space and every bit of port capacity to get in the things that the ground troops and their shorter range air support units require. This will continue to be true for an indefinite period.

Source: Papers of Dwight D. Eisenhower, Eisenhower Presidential Library, Abilene, KS; printed in Joseph Patrick Hobbs, ed., *Dear General: Eisenhower's Wartime Letters to Marshall* (Baltimore, MD: Johns Hopkins University Press, 1971), 202–203. Reprinted with permission of the Eisenhower Library.

197. Winston Churchill, The Percentages Agreement, 9 October 1944

In his wartime memoirs, British Prime Minister Winston Churchill gave the following account of how he reached agreement with Soviet leader Josef Stalin over the division of much of Eastern Europe and the Balkans into British and Soviet spheres of influence.

We [the British party] alighted at Moscow on the afternoon of October 9, and were received very heartily and with full ceremonial by [Russian Foreign Minister V. I.] Molotov and many high Russian personages. This time we were lodged in Moscow itself, with every care and comfort. I had one small, perfectly appointed house, and Anthony [Eden, the British Foreign Secretary] another near by. We were glad to dine together and rest. At ten o'clock that night we held our first important meeting in the Kremlin. There were only Stalin, Molotov, Eden, [United States Ambassador to the Soviet Union W. Averell] Harriman, and I, with Major Birse and Pavlov as interpreters. . . .

The moment was apt for business, so I said, "Let us settle about our affairs in the Balkans. Your armies are in Rumania and Bulgaria. We have interests, missions, and agents there. Don't let us get at cross-purposes in small ways. So far as Britain and Russia are concerned, how would it do for you to have ninety per cent predominance in Rumania, for us to have ninety per cent of the say in Greece, and go fifty-fifty about Yugoslavia?" While this was being translated I wrote out on a half-sheet of paper:

Rumania	
Russia	90%
The others	10%
Greece	
Great Britain	90%
(in accord with U.S.A.)	
Russia	10%
Yugoslavia	50–50%
Hungary	50–50%
Bulgaria	
Russia	75%
The others	25%

I pushed this across to Stalin, who had by then heard the translation. There was a slight pause. Then he took his blue pencil and made a large tick upon it, and passed it back to us. It was all settled in no more time than it takes to set down.

Of course we had long and anxiously considered our point, and were only dealing with immediate war-time arrangements. All larger questions were reserved on both sides for what we then hoped would be a peace table when the war was won.

After this there was a long silence. The pencilled paper lay in the centre of the table. At length I said, "Might it not be thought rather cynical if it seemed we had disposed of these issues, so fateful to millions of people, in such an offhand matter? Let us burn the paper." "No, you keep it," said Stalin. . . .

After our first meeting I reflected on our relations with Russia throughout Eastern Europe, and, in order to clarify my ideas, drafted a letter to Stalin on the subject, enclosing a memorandum stating our interpretation of the percentages which we had accepted across the table. In the end I did not send this letter, deeming it wiser to let well alone. I print it only as an authentic account of my thought.

MOSCOW, OCTOBER 11, 1944

I deem it profoundly important that Britain and Russia should have a common policy in the Balkans which is also acceptable to the United States. The fact that Britain and Russia have a twenty year alliance makes it especially important for us to be in broad accord and to work together easily and trustfully and for a long time. I realise that nothing we can do here can be more than preliminary to the final decisions that we shall have to take when all three of us are gathered together at the table of victory. Nevertheless I hope that we may be able to reach understandings, and in some cases agreements, which will help us through immediate emergencies, and will afford a solid foundation for long-enduring world peace.

These percentages which I have put down are no more than a method by which in our thoughts we can see how near we are together, and then decide upon the necessary steps to bring us into full agreement. As I said, they would be considered crude, and even callous, if they were exposed to the scrutiny of the Foreign Offices and diplomats all over the world. Therefore they could not be the basis of any public document, certainly not at the present time. They might however be a good guide for the conduct of our affairs. If we manage these affairs well we shall perhaps prevent several civil wars and much bloodshed and strife in the small countries concerned. Our broad principle should be to let every country have the form of government which its people desire. We certainly do not wish to force on any Balkan State monarchic or republican institutions. We have however established certain relations of faithfulness with the Kings of Greece and Yugoslavia. They have sought our shelter from the Nazi foe, and we think that when normal tranquility is re-established and the enemy has been driven out the peoples of these countries should have a free and fair chance of choosing. It might even be that Commissioners of the three Great Powers should be stationed there at the time of the elections so as to see that the people have a genuine free choice. There are good precedents for this.

However, besides the institutional question there exists in all these countries the ideological issue between totalitarian forms of government and those we call free enterprise controlled by universal suffrage. We are very glad that you have declared yourselves against trying to change by force or by Communist propaganda the established systems in the various Balkan countries. Let them work out their own fortunes during the years that lie ahead. One thing however we cannot allow—Fascism or Nazism in any of their forms, which give to the toiling masses neither the securities offered by your system nor those offered by ours, but, on the contrary, lead to the build-up of tyrannies at home and aggression abroad. In principle I feel that Great Britain and Russia should feel easy about the internal government of these countries, and not worry about them or interfere with them once conditions of tranquillity are restored after this terrible blood-bath which they, and indeed we, have all been through.

It is from this point of view that I have sought to adumbrate the degrees of interest which each of us takes in these countries with the full assent of the other, and subject to the approval of the United States, which may go far away for a long time and then come back again unexpectedly with giant strength.

In writing to you, with your experience and wisdom, I do not need to go through a lot of arguments. Hitler has tried to exploit the fear of an aggressive, proselytising Communism which exists throughout Western Europe, and he is being decisively beaten to the ground. But, as you know well, this fear exists in every country, because, whatever the merits of our different systems, no country wishes to go through the bloody revolution which will certainly be necessary in nearly every case before so drastic a change could be made in the life, habits, and outlook of their society. We feel we were right in interpreting your dissolution of the Comintern as a decision by the Soviet Government not to interfere in the internal political affairs of other countries. The more this can be established in people's minds the smoother everything will go. We, on the other hand, and I am sure the United States as well, have Governments which stand on very broad bases, where privilege and class are under continual scrutiny and correction. We have the feeling that, viewed from afar and on a grand scale, the differences between our systems will tend to get smaller, and the great common ground which we share of making life richer and happier for the mass of the people is growing every year. Probably if there were peace for fifty years the differences which now might cause such grave troubles to the world would become matters for academic discussion.

At this point, Mr. Stalin, I want to impress upon you the great desire there is in the heart of Britain for a long, stable friendship and co-operation between our two countries, and that with the United States we shall be able to keep the world engine on the rails.

To my colleagues at home I sent the following:

Prime Minister to Colleagues in London 12 Oct. 44

The system of percentages is not intended to prescribe the numbers sitting on commissions for the different Balkan countries, but rather to express the interest and sentiment with which the British and Soviet Governments approach the problems of these countries, and so that they might reveal their minds to each other in some way that could be comprehended. It is not intended to be more than a guide, and of course in no way commits the United States, nor does it attempt to set up a rigid system of spheres of interest. It may however help the United States to see how their two principal Allies feel about these regions when the picture is presented as a whole.

2. Thus it is seen that quite naturally Soviet Russia has vital interests in the countries bordering on the Black Sea, by one of whom, Rumania, she has been most wantonly attacked with twenty-six divisions, and with the other of whom, Bulgaria, she has ancient ties. Great Britain feels it right to show particular respect to Russian views about these two countries, and to the Soviet desire to take the lead in a practical way in guiding them in the name of the common cause.

3. Similarly, Great Britain has a long tradition of friendship with Greece, and a direct interest as a Mediterranean Power in her future. In this war Great Britain lost 30,000 men in trying to resist the German-Italian invasion of Greece, and wishes to play a leading part in guiding Greece out of her present troubles, maintaining that close agreement with the United States which has hitherto characterised Anglo-American policy in this quarter. Here it is understood that Great Britain will take the lead in a military sense and try to help the existing Royal Greek Government to establish itself in Athens upon as broad and united a basis as possible. Soviet Russia would be ready to concede this position and function to Great Britain in the same sort of way as Britain would recognise the intimate relationship between Russia and Rumania. This would prevent in Greece the growth of hostile factions waging civil war upon each other and involving the British and Russian Governments in vexatious arguments and conflict of policy.

4. Coming to the case of Yugoslavia, the numerical symbol 50–50 is intended to be the foundation of joint action and an agreed policy between the two Powers now closely involved, so as to favour the creation of a united Yugoslavia after all elements there have been joined together to the utmost in driving out the Nazi invaders. It is intended to prevent, for instance, armed strife between Croats and Slovenes on the one hand and powerful and numerous elements in Serbia on the other, and also to produce a joint and friendly policy towards Marshal Tito, while ensuring that weapons furnished to him are used against the common Nazi foe rather than for internal purposes. Such a policy, pursued in common by Britain and Soviet Russia, without any thought of special advantages to themselves, would be of real benefit.

5. As it is the Soviet armies which are obtaining control

of Hungary, it would be natural that a major share of influence should rest with them, subject of course to agreement with Great Britain and probably the United States, who, though not actually operating in Hungary, must view it as a Central European and not a Balkan State.

6. It must be emphasised that this broad disclosure of Soviet and British feelings in the countries mentioned above is only an interim guide for the immediate war-time future, and will be surveyed by the Great Powers when they meet at the armistice or peace table to make a general settlement of Europe.

Source: Winston Churchill, *The Second World War: Triumph and Tragedy* (Boston: Houghton Mifflin, 1953), 226–228, 231–235. Reprinted with permission of Churchill Archives, Churchill College, Cambridge, and HMSO.

198. General Headquarters, Southwest Pacific Area, Special Communiqué, Statement of General Douglas MacArthur on the Leyte Island Landings in the Philippines, 20 October 1944

In October 1944, General Douglas MacArthur's forces launched the Philippine Campaign, the beginning of a nine-month effort to retake the former U.S. dependency. On this occasion, MacArthur's headquarters issued a special press release, noting that the campaign marked yet another step in the gradual dismantling of the Japanese Empire.

In a major amphibious operation we have seized the eastern coast of Leyte Island in the Philippines, 600 miles north of Morotai and 2,500 miles from Milne Bay from whence our offensive started nearly 16 months ago. This point of entry in the Visayas is midway between Luzon and Mindanao and at one stroke splits in two the Japanese forces in the Philippines. The enemy's anticipation of attack in Mindanao caused him to be caught unawares in Leyte and beachheads in the Tacloban area were secured with small casualties. The landing was preceded by heavy naval and air bombardments which were devastating in effect. Our ground troops are rapidly extending their positions and supplies and heavy equipment are already flowing out in great volume. The troops comprise elements of the 6th U.S. Army, to which are attached units from the Central Pacific, with supporting elements.

The naval forces consist of the 7th U.S. Fleet, the Australian Squadron, and supporting elements of the 3rd U.S. Fleet. Air support was given by naval carrier forces, the Far East Air Force, and the RAAF [Royal Australian Air Force].

The enemy's forces of an estimated 225,000 include the 14th Army Group under command of Field Marshal Count Terauchi, of which seven divisons have already been identified: 16th, 26th, 30th, 100th, 102nd, 103rd, and 105th.

The strategic result of capturing the Philippines will be decisive. The enemy's so-called Greater East Asia Co-Prosperity Sphere will be cut in two. His conquered empire to the south comprising the Dutch East Indies, and the British possessions of Borneo, Malaya, and Burma will be severed from Japan proper. The great flow of transportation and supply upon which Japan's vital war industry depends will be cut as will the counter supply of his forces to the south. A half million men will be cut off without hope of support and with ultimate destruction at the leisure of the Allies a certainty. In broad strategical conception the defensive line of the Japanese which extends along the coast of Asia from the Japan Islands through Formosa, the Philippines, the East Indies, to Singapore and Burma will be pierced in the center permitting an envelopment to the south and to the north. Either flank will be vulnerable and can be rolled up at will.

Source: Charles A. Willoughby et al., eds., *Reports of General MacArthur: The Campaigns of MacArthur in the Pacific*, 2 vols. (Washington, DC: U.S. Government Printing Office, 1966), 1: 202.

199. General Dwight D. Eisenhower to General George C. Marshall, 11 November 1944

In November 1944, Supreme Commander of the Allied forces in Europe General Eisenhower described to the U.S. Army chief of staff, General George C. Marshall, in Washington the delays to which bad weather was subjecting the Allies' Western offensive against Germany.

I am getting exceedingly tired of the weather. Every day we have some report of weather that has broken records existing anywhere from twenty-five to fifty years. The latest case is that of the floods in [US General George C.] Patton's area. His attack got off exactly as planned and with an extraordinarily fine example of cooperation between the Eighth Air Force and the ground troops. Then the floods came down the river and not only washed out two fixed bridges, but destroyed his principal floating bridge and made others almost unusable. It was so bad that in one case where we had installed a fixed bridge, the approaches to it were under three feet of water. At one point the Moselle is more than one mile wide, with a current of from seven to ten feet a second. Nevertheless, the peak of the flood should be passed in a day or so—provided rain in that basin is not too great—and Patton will get ahead all along his front.

The attack of the First and Ninth Armies was scheduled anywhere between the 11th and the 16th, depending upon the weather necessary to get the desired air support. The jump-off had to be postponed this morning even after a rather favorable prediction yesterday. The predictions now give us a sorry outlook, and it appears that we will have to go, eventually, without the planned air support. The weather is apt to prevent even our fighter-bombers from rendering the help that they otherwise could.

Within the last three days [US General Omar] Bradley and I have visited every division of the First and Ninth Armies. Morale is surprisingly high and the men have succeeded in making themselves rather comfortable. There are no signs of exhaustion and the sick rate is not nearly as high as we would have a reasonable right to expect.

All of us keep hoping that some little spell will come along in which we can have a bit of relief from mud, rain, and fog so that tanks and infantry can operate more easily on the offensive and so that we can use our great air asset. In spite of difficulties, no one is discouraged and we will yet make the German wish that he had gone completely back of the Rhine at the end of his great retreat across France. . . .

Source: Papers of Dwight D. Eisenhower, Eisenhower Presidential Library, Abilene, KS; printed in Joseph Patrick Hobbs, ed., *Dear General: Eisenhower's Wartime Letters to Marshall* (Baltimore, MD: Johns Hopkins University Press, 1971), 209–210. Reprinted with permission of the Eisenhower Library.

200. The United States Government Refuses to Bomb Auschwitz: John J. McCloy, Assistant Secretary of War, to John W. Pehle, Director, War Refugee Board, 18 November 1944

In August 1944 Jewish representatives requested the United States War Department to authorize the bombing of Auschwitz. To the distress of the Jewish community John J. McCloy, then assistant secretary of war, refused on the ground that to do so would require the diversion of scarce military resources from other missions and that it might provoke further German reprisals against the Jews. In November 1944 McCloy, facing renewed requests to this effect, again refused to permit American airplanes to undertake the bombing of the concentration camps at Auschwitz and Birkenau. German officials continued to operate these facilities for several additional months, until invading Allied ground forces finally liberated the camps and their inmates.

I refer to your letter of November 8th, in which you forwarded the report of two eye-witnesses on the notorious German concentration and extermination camps of Auschwitz and Birkenau in Upper Silesia.

The Operation Staff of the War Department has given careful consideration to your suggestion that the bombing of these camps be undertaken. In consideration of this proposal the following points were brought out:

a. Positive destruction of these camps would necessitate precision bombing, employing heavy or medium bombardment, or attack by low flying or dive bombing aircraft, preferably the latter.
b. The target is beyond the maximum range of medium bombardment, dive bombers and fighter bombers located in United Kingdom, France or Italy.
c. Use of heavy bombardment from United Kingdom bases would necessitate a hazardous round trip flight unescorted of approximately 2,000 miles over enemy territory.
d. At the present critical stage of the war in Europe, our strategic air forces are engaged in the destruction of industrial target systems vital to the dwindling war potential of the enemy, from which they should not be diverted. The positive solution to this problem is the earliest possible victory over Germany, to which end we should exert our entire means.
e. This case does not at all parallel the Amiens mission because of the location of the concentration and extermination camps and the resulting difficulties encountered in attempting to carry out the proposed bombing.

Based on the above, as well as the most uncertain, if not dangerous effect such a bombing would have on the object to be attained, the War Department has felt that it should not, at least for the present, undertake these operations.

I know that you have been reluctant to press this activity on the War Department. We have been pressed strongly from other quarters, however, and have taken the best military opinion on its feasibility, and we believe the above conclusion is a sound one.

Source: John J. McCloy, Assistant Secretary of War, to John W. Pehle, Director, War Refugee Board, 18 November 1944. Available at Public Broadcasting Service: The American Experience. http://www.pbs.org/wgbh/amex/holocaust/filmmore/reference/primary/bombworld.html.

201. General Dwight D. Eisenhower to General George C. Marshall, 5 December 1944

From France, General Dwight D. Eisenhower continued his informal reports to Marshall on the conditions facing the Allied forces. At the end of the year, German resistance still remained strong.

Much now depends on the date and scale of the anticipated winter offensive of the Russians. I say "anticipated" although we have nothing except conjecture on which to base our ideas as to Russia's intentions. At present we have newly formed Divisions arriving on our front, and have attracted several Divisions directly from Hungary and East Prussia. In spite of all this, the enemy is badly stretched on this front and is constantly shifting units up and down the line to reinforce his most threatened points. G-2 studies show that he is more frightened of our operations in the First and Ninth Armies than anywhere else. He is assisted in that area, however, by the flooded condition of the Roer River and the capability he has of producing a sudden rush of water by blowing the dams near Schmidt. [US General Omar] Bradley has about come to the conclusion that we must take that area by a very difficult attack from the west and southwest.

There can be no question of the value of our present operations. The German is throwing in the line some Divisions with only six weeks' training, a fact that contributes materially to his high casualty rate. As explained in my most recent appreciation to the Combined Chiefs of Staff, our problem is to continue our attacks as long as the results achieved are so much in our favor, while at the same time preparing for a full-out, heavy offensive when weather conditions become favorable, assuming the enemy holds out. Unless some trouble develops from within Germany, a possibility of which there is now no real evidence, he should be able to maintain a strong defensive front for some time, assisted by weather, floods and muddy ground. . . .

Source: Papers of Dwight D. Eisenhower, Eisenhower Presidential Library, Abilene, KS; printed in Joseph Patrick Hobbs, ed., *Dear General: Eisenhower's Wartime Letters to Marshall* (Baltimore, MD: Johns Hopkins University Press, 1971), 210–211. Reprinted with permission of the Eisenhower Library.

202. The Comfort Women of World War II: Reminiscences of "Ms. K"

During World War II thousands of attractive young Korean, Chinese, Indonesian, and Dutch women were virtually enslaved and forced to become prostitutes or "comfort women" serving the Japanese forces. Many were so ashamed that only decades later were they prepared even to tell of their experiences. The following is the story of Ms. K, a Korean woman who wished to remain anonymous.

I was born in Ulsan, a small town in the southern part of Korea, in 1928. I was the oldest among several children in my family.

My Japanese name was Kikuko Kanazima. Under the Japanese colonial rule at the time, we were forbidden to use our own Korean names or language. I finished elementary school under the direction of a Japanese principal. Twice a day, at the beginning and the end of school, we were instructed to bow to the picture of Emperor Hirohito placed at the top of the classroom blackboard. We were also ordered to bow to soldiers whenever they passed.

I was about 15 years old when a tragic fate took hold of me. A town clerk and policeman visited my home and told me that I had to appear at the county office by a certain date. I was told that young girls had to join "*Jungshindae,*" the women's labor corps, to fight for the Emperor so that the war would soon be won. They also told me that I would work at a military factory and that I would be paid wages.

My mother resisted this order. However, at the end of September, a policeman came again and took me to the county office by force. When I arrived, there were about 30 girls of my age there. The police put us on a truck that took us to a military cargo train. On the train I could see 30 or 40 Korean men who were drafted as laborers. We were put into a boxcar which had no windows, with lighting only from a dim candle. Two soldiers guarded us.

After about one week's ride, we arrived at Uonkil Station in Manchuria. They separated us into different groups and put us into military trucks. After riding quite a while through the night, I and a few other girls were discharged at a military camp. Some young girls, including those of Chinese origin, were already at the camp. Each girl received two blankets, one towel, and a military-type uniform. Then guards took us to a wooden warehouse surrounded by barbed wire. They put one girl into each of the small cubicles. Our supervisors were Japanese soldiers or men wearing militia uniform. They told us to obey them.

For the first three days, only officers visited me. After that I was forced to have sex with 20 to 40 soldiers a day. I worked from eight in the morning till ten at night, but there were many nights I had to sleep overnight with an officer. A military doctor inspected us on a regular basis, but we all ended up having venereal diseases. Some girls died from these and other illnesses. Some girls became hysterical and crazy. In exchange for sex, soldiers apparently paid some kind of military money, but our supervisors took the money, saying that they would save it for us. In any case, I never received a penny from them.

During this horrifying enslavement, I was moved to three different military camps. The last unit was called "Koyabashi 8000" stationed near Jijiharu. Whenever we were moved, we were guarded by military policemen and kept under constant watch. I tried to escape several times, but I was caught each time by the soldiers and severely beaten by the supervisors. On one occasion, I jumped off a truck and tried to run away in the dark. But they caught me and my supervisor beat me savagely all over my body and then cut off my three left fingers with a knife.

Life in the camp became devastating toward the end of the war. We were starving. Those who were sick had no medical treatment. Then, one day, the camp became completely silent. I went outside. There were no soldiers in the camp. Finally, a Chinese told me that the war was over.

It took me about two months to walk back to Korea. I had to beg food from the Chinese on the way. I was glad to have survived, but very ashamed and angry about my past life. I decided not to go back to my home because of the shame and potential harm to my family.

I settled down in Pusan and worked as a waitress in restaurants and as a house maid. Eventually, I contacted an aunt who arranged a meeting with my mother. My mother asked me to come back to her, but I decided to live by myself. As time passed, I became sick and had to undergo a hysterectomy.

In 1979, my younger sister who was living in New York City invited me to live with her. So I came to America. At present, I live alone with financial assistance from my sister, the U.S. government, and the South Korean government. I wait for death.

If I were to speak to the Japanese government, there is one question I would ask: Is it right to ignore me like this as if they did nothing to me? Are they justified after trampling an innocent and fragile teenage girl and making her suffer for the rest of her life? How would you feel if your own daughter met the same fate as mine?

This should never happen again in the world. I hope the Japanese people will also join mankind's march for justice and peace.

Source: Sangmie Choi Schellstede, ed., *Comfort Women Speak: Testimony of Sex Slaves of the Japanese Military* (New York: Holmes and Meier, 2000), 102–105. Reprinted with permission of Holmes and Meier.

203. Reminiscences of Arnold Brown, 1944–1945

The burden of the hardest fighting and highest casualties fell upon the infantry. Arnold Brown, a company commander in the 90th Infantry Division, enlisted as a private in 1936 and gradually won promotion. His unit fought through the Normandy campaign and into Germany, and he was awarded a British Military Cross. His recollections highlight the brutal and wasteful aspects of war.

The first thing, here comes old General Patton walking across the stage. He walks from one end of the stage to the other, then he walks back and stops. And he says, "Men, this is it!"

I'm not going to quote all his curse words. He said, "We're going to cross that damn Moselle River at 2 o'clock in the morning."

He said, "I want to tell you a little bit about the enemy over there. Now, in these fortress battalions, the Germans don't have their best troops. Their armored forces, their crack troops, are back in reserve. Some of the fillers in these fortress battalions are old men."

He said, "Kill the sonofabitches."

He said, "Some of them have been slightly wounded in combat, or maybe they've got a crippled leg or one arm missing, but they can man those machine guns in these forts. Kill the sonofabitches."

Then he said, "There's this business about taking prisoners. When you accept an enemy as a prisoner, and you've searched him and disarmed him and he's in your possession, you treat him according to the Geneva Convention.

"But there's nothing that says you can't shoot the sonofabitch before you've accepted him as a prisoner. Some of those snipers will take camouflage in a tree, and some of them are going to let you pass and are camouflaged behind you, and they'll kill a few of your men. Then, when you locate his position, he wants to come out and surrender. Don't accept that sonofabitch. Kill him." . . .

One other incident took place that I think is of interest. I had my company command post in Oberwampach set up in the home of the Schilling family. When the Germans were shelling us, a five-year-old boy got excited and dashed out the front door, right into the impact area of the artillery. A 20-year-old soldier dashed out to rescue the little boy.

They were both mortally wounded.

The soldier asked someone to rub his left arm; he claimed it hurt him. I rubbed his arm, and he turned blue and died.

The little boy died slowly in his mother's arms, and to see this—you read about these things—but to see the grief this mother was going through of her son being killed by something she had no control over, it really brings some strong lessons to you.

This soldier's name was Sergeant Whitfield. I recommended him for a Distinguished Service Cross and he got it. Now he was a true hero. He gave his life trying not to defend his own life, but to rescue an innocent little boy, and truly he earned his decoration.

After the battle, we picked up a German soldier who had been wounded. He had been shot in the leg with a .50-caliber bullet, and he laid out overnight in this freezing, subzero weather. Both of his arms and both of his legs were frozen stiff as a board. He begged us to shoot him.

I couldn't do it. I asked for a volunteer. Even if he survived, he'd have to have both arms and both legs amputated, and this could have been a mercy killing. But these battle hardened soldiers that had been fighting Germans a few minutes before would not volunteer. One soldier, out of sympathy for the suffering and bravery of this soldier, lit a cigarette and held it to his lips. Another soldier brought him a hot cup of coffee and held it so he could get coffee until we got the litter jeep up there and sent him to the rear.

I've always been curious to know what happened to him, but I believe he would have died before they got him back to the aid station.

Source: Aaron Elson, *9 Lives: An Oral History* (2000). Available at http://www.tankbooks.com/Ninelives/chap1page3.htm. Reprinted with permission of Aaron Elson.

1945 Documents

204. General Dwight D. Eisenhower to General George C. Marshall, 12 January 1945

In January 1945, Supreme Commander of the Allied Forces in Europe General Eisenhower confidentially informed the U.S. Army's chief of staff, General George C. Marshall, of the weaknesses of the Free French forces fighting with the Allies.

At the moment our most worrisome area is the south. While there is nothing vital in the region that we should not be able to cover easily if we could solve all of our problems from the purely tactical viewpoint, the great danger is that [US General Jacob] Devers will be caught out of position and some of his troops manhandled. The French were so completely upset over my plan to pull out of the Alsace Plain, that obviously the problem became, in its larger sense, a military one. I could not have the weakened French forces trying to fight a battle by themselves and, more serious than this, I could not have the French government getting in extremely bad position with its population, a consequence which it was apparent de Gaulle thought would follow upon a voluntary evacuation of Alsace.

When Devers turned his complete Seventh Army northward, he was badly mistaken in the ability of the French Army to finish off the Colmar pocket. At that time he had been directed to turn part of the 15th Corps northward, west of the Vosges, in order to support Patton's right but it was expected that his first concern east of the mountains would be to clean up his own rear. I must say that he can hardly be blamed for making a miscalculation with respect to the French, because the forces opposing them in the pocket were at that time estimated at not over 12,000 to 14,000 fighting men. Nevertheless, it is a very bad thorn in our side today.

Tomorrow morning the attacks on the northerly side of the Ardennes salient are being extended. [General Matthew B.] Ridgway's 18th [Airborne] Corps will come in, attacking in the direction of St. Vith. As our lines shorten in the salient I will be able to get a reserve out of refitting divisions, and these will be so stationed as to support our right. . . .

The weather is abominable. It seems to me that I have fought weather for two years and a half. Right now, at my base headquarters, a foot of snow is on the ground. Flying conditions in the battle zone have been almost impossible for several days now. A week of good weather would be nothing less than a godsend. . . .

Source: Papers of Dwight D. Eisenhower, Eisenhower Presidential Library, Abilene, KS; printed in Joseph Patrick Hobbs, ed., *Dear General: Eisenhower's Wartime Letters to Marshall* (Baltimore, MD: Johns Hopkins University Press, 1971), 212–213. Reprinted with permission of the Eisenhower Library.

205. The Yalta Accords, 11 February 1945

The most controversial of the wartime summit meetings of Churchill, Stalin, and Roosevelt was that held in the Crimea at Yalta in February 1945, which discussed questions relating to the future government of many states in both Europe and Asia. Hard and sometimes inconclusive bargaining took place on several issues, including the future status of Germany, Eastern Europe and the Balkans, Poland, German reparations, and the nature of the United Nations organization. Although portions on "Liberated Europe," "Poland," and "Meetings of the Three Foreign Secretaries" were published on 13 February 1945, the remaining text of the Yalta agreements signed by the Russian, British, and American foreign ministers was not released until 24 March 1945. Churchill, Stalin, and Roosevelt themselves personally signed accords on the prosecution of the war in Asia and the postwar status and rights of various Asian nations, including the Soviet Union.

Washington, 24 March [1945].—The text of the agreements reached at the Crimea (Yalta) Conference between President Roosevelt, Prime Minister Churchill and Generalissimo Stalin, as released by the State Department today, follows:

PROTOCOL OF PROCEEDINGS OF CRIMEA CONFERENCE
The Crimea Conference of the heads of the Governments of the United States of America, the United Kingdom, and the Union of Soviet Socialist Republics, which took place from Feb. 4 to 11, came to the following conclusions:

I. WORLD ORGANIZATION
It was decided:

1. That a United Nations conference on the proposed world organization should be summoned for Wednesday, 25 April, 1945, and should be held in the United States of America.

2. The nations to be invited to this conference should be:

(a) the United Nations as they existed on 8 Feb., 1945; and

(b) Such of the Associated Nations as have declared war on the common enemy by 1 March, 1945. (For this purpose, by the term "Associated Nations" was meant the eight Associated Nations and Turkey.) When the conference on world organization is held, the delegates of the United Kingdom and United States of America will support a proposal to admit to original membership two Soviet Socialist Republics, i.e., the Ukraine and White Russia.

3. That the United States Government, on behalf of the three powers, should consult the Government of China and the French Provisional Government in regard to decisions taken at the present conference concerning the proposed world organization.

4. That the text of the invitation to be issued to all the nations which would take part in the United Nations conference should be as follows:

"The Government of the United States of America, on behalf of itself and of the Governments of the United Kingdom, the Union of Soviet Socialist Republics and the Republic of China and of the Provisional Government of the French Republic invite the Government of————to send representatives to a conference to be held on 25 April, 1945, or soon thereafter, at San Francisco, in the United States of America, to prepare a charter for a general international organization for the maintenance of international peace and security.

"The above-named Governments suggest that the conference consider as affording a basis for such a Charter the proposals for the establishment of a general international organization which were made public last October as a result of the Dumbarton Oaks conference and which have now been supplemented by the following provisions for Section C of Chapter VI:

C. Voting

"1. Each member of the Security Council should have one vote.

"2. Decisions of the Security Council on procedural matters should be made by an affirmative vote of seven members.

"3. Decisions of the Security Council on all matters should be made by an affirmative vote of seven members, including the concurring votes of the permanent members; provided that, in decisions under Chapter VIII, Section A and under the second sentence of Paragraph 1 of Chapter VIII, Section C, a party to a dispute should abstain from voting.

"Further information as to arrangements will be transmitted subsequently.

"In the event that the Government of————desires in advance of the conference to present views or comments concerning the proposals, the Government of the United

States of America will be pleased to transmit such views and comments to the other participating Governments."

Territorial trusteeship:

It was agreed that the five nations which will have permanent seats on the Security Council should consult each other prior to the United Nations conference on the question of territorial trusteeship.

The acceptance of this recommendation is subject to its being made clear that territorial trusteeship will only apply to

(a) existing mandates of the League of Nations;
(b) territories detached from the enemy as a result of the present war;
(c) any other territory which might voluntarily be placed under trusteeship; and
(d) no discussion of actual territories is contemplated at the forthcoming United Nations conference or in the preliminary consultations, and it will be a matter for subsequent agreement which territories within the above categories will be placed under trusteeship.

[Beginning of first section published Feb. 13, 1945.]

II. DECLARATION OF LIBERATED EUROPE
The following declaration has been approved:

The Premier of the Union of Soviet Socialist Republics, the Prime Minister of the United Kingdom and the President of the United States of America have consulted with each other in the common interests of the people of their countries and those of liberated Europe. They jointly declare their mutual agreement to concert during the temporary period of instability in liberated Europe the policies of their three Governments in assisting the peoples liberated from the domination of Nazi Germany and the peoples of the former Axis satellite states of Europe to solve by democratic means their pressing political and economic problems.

The establishment of order in Europe and the rebuilding of national economic life must be achieved by processes which will enable the liberated peoples to destroy the last vestiges of nazism and fascism and to create democratic institutions of their own choice. This is a principle of the Atlantic Charter—the right of all people to choose the form of government under which they will live—the restoration of sovereign rights and self-government to those peoples who have been forcibly deprived of them by the aggressor nations.

To foster the conditions in which the liberated people may exercise these rights, the three governments will jointly assist the people in any European liberated state or former Axis state in Europe where, in their judgment conditions require,

(a) to establish conditions of internal peace;
(b) to carry out emergency relief measures for the relief of distressed peoples;
(c) to form interim governmental authorities broadly representative of all democratic elements in the population and pledged to the earliest possible establishment through free elections of Governments responsive to the will of the people; and
(d) to facilitate where necessary the holding of such elections.

The three Governments will consult the other United Nations and provisional authorities or other Governments in Europe when matters of direct interest to them are under consideration.

When, in the opinion of the three Governments, conditions in any European liberated state or former Axis satellite in Europe make such action necessary, they will immediately consult together on the measures necessary to discharge the joint responsibilities set forth in this declaration.

By this declaration we reaffirm our faith in the principles of the Atlantic Charter, our pledge in the Declaration by the United Nations and our determination to build in cooperation with other peace-loving nations world order, under law, dedicated to peace, security, freedom and general well-being of all mankind.

In issuing this declaration, the three powers express the hope that the Provisional Government of the French Republic may be associated with them in the procedure suggested.

[End of first section published Feb. 13, 1945.]

III. DISMEMBERMENT OF GERMANY
It was agreed that Article 12 (a) of the Surrender terms for Germany should be amended to read as follows:

"The United Kingdom, the United States of America and the Union of Soviet Socialist Republics shall possess supreme authority with respect to Germany. In the exercise of such authority they will take such steps, including the complete dismemberment of Germany as they deem requisite for future peace and security."

The study of the procedure of the dismemberment of Germany was referred to a committee consisting of Mr. Anthony Eden, Mr. John Winant, and Mr. Fedor T. Gusev. This body would consider the desirability of associating with it a French representative.

IV. ZONE OF OCCUPATION FOR THE FRENCH AND CONTROL COUNCIL FOR GERMANY
It was agreed that a zone in Germany, to be occupied by the French forces, should be allocated to France. This zone

would be formed out of the British and American zones and its extent would be settled by the British and Americans in consultation with the French Provisional Government.

It was also agreed that the French Provisional Government should be invited to become a member of the Allied Control Council for Germany.

V. REPARATION

The following protocol has been approved:

Protocol On the Talks Between the Heads of Three Governments at the Crimean Conference on the Question of the German Reparations in Kind

1. Germany must pay in kind for the losses caused by her to the Allied nations in the course of the war. Reparations are to be received in the first instance by those countries which have borne the main burden of the war, have suffered the heaviest losses and have organized victory over the enemy.

2. Reparation in kind is to be exacted from Germany in three following forms:

(a) Removals within two years from the surrender of Germany or the cessation of organized resistance from the national wealth of Germany located on the territory of Germany herself as well as outside her territory (equipment, machine tools, ships, rolling stock, German investments abroad, shares of industrial, transport and other enterprises in Germany, etc.), these removals to be carried out chiefly for the purpose of destroying the war potential of Germany.
(b) Annual deliveries of goods from current production for a period to be fixed.
(c) Use of German labor.

3. For the working out on the above principles of a detailed plan for exaction of reparation from Germany an Allied reparation commission will be set up in Moscow. It will consist of three representatives—one from the Union of Soviet Socialist Republics, one from the United Kingdom and one from the United States of America.

4. With regard to the fixing of the total sum of the reparation as well as the distribution of it among the countries which suffered from the German aggression, the Soviet and American delegations agreed as follows:

"The Moscow reparation commission should take in its initial studies as a basis for discussion the suggestion of the Soviet Government that the total sum of the reparation in accordance with the points (a) and (b) of the Paragraph 2 should be 22 billion dollars and that 50 per cent should go to the Union of Soviet Socialist Republics."

The British delegation was of the opinion that, pending consideration of the reparation question by the Moscow

reparation commission, no figures of reparation should be mentioned.

The above Soviet-American proposal has been passed to the Moscow reparation commission as one of the proposals to be considered by the commission.

VI. MAJOR WAR CRIMINALS

The conference agree that the question of the major war criminals should be the subject of inquiry by the three Foreign Secretaries for report in due course after the close of the conference.

[Beginning of second section published Feb. 13, 1945.]

VII. POLAND

The following declaration on Poland was agreed by the conference:

"A new situation has been created in Poland as a result of her complete liberation by the Red Army. This calls for the establishment of a Polish Provisional Government which can be more broadly based than was possible before the recent liberation of the western part of Poland. The Provisional Government which is now functioning in Poland should therefore be reorganized on a broader democratic basis with the inclusion of democratic leaders from Poland itself and from Poles abroad. This new Government should then be called the Polish Provisional Government of National Unity.

"[Soviet Foreign Minister] M. Molotov, [U.S. Ambassador to the Soviet Union] Mr. Harriman and [British Ambassador to the Soviet Union] Sir A. Clark Kerr are authorized as a commission to consult in the first instance in Moscow with members of the present Provisional Government and with other Polish democratic leaders from within Poland and from abroad, with a view to the reorganization of the present Government along the above lines. This Polish Provisional Government of National Unity shall be pledged to the holding of free and unfettered elections as soon as possible on the basis of universal suffrage and secret ballot. In these elections all democratic and anti-Nazi parties shall have the right to take part and to put forward candidates.

"When a Polish Provisional Government of National Unity has been properly formed in conformity with the above, the Government of the U.S.S.R., which now maintains diplomatic relations with the present Provisional Government of Poland, and the Government of the United Kingdom and the Government of the United States of America will establish diplomatic relations with the new Polish Provisional Government of National Unity, and will exchange Ambassadors by whose reports the respective Governments will be kept informed about the situation in Poland.

"The three heads of Government consider that the eastern frontier of Poland should follow the Curzon Line with digressions from it in some regions of five to eight kilometers in favor of Poland. They recognize that Poland must receive substantial accessions in territory in the north and west. They feel that the opinion of the new Polish Provisional Government of National Unity should be sought in due course of the extent of these accessions and that the final delimitation of the western frontier of Poland should thereafter await the peace conference."

[Provisions on Yugoslavia, Italy, Bulgaria, Southeastern Europe, Iran, Turkey, the Dardanelles Straits, and Regular Meetings of Foreign Ministers omitted.]

[End of third section published Feb. 13, 1945.]

[The following agreement on the war in Asia was signed by the three principals at the meeting, Churchill, Roosevelt, and Stalin.]

AGREEMENT REGARDING JAPAN, 11 FEBRUARY 1945
The leaders of the three great powers—the Soviet Union, the United States of America and Great Britain—have agreed that in two or three months after Germany has surrendered and the war in Europe is terminated, the Soviet Union shall enter into war against Japan on the side of the Allies on condition that:

1. The status quo in Outer Mongolia (the Mongolian People's Republic) shall be preserved.

2. The former rights of Russia violated by the treacherous attack of Japan in 1904 shall be restored, viz:

(a) The southern part of Sakhalin as well as the islands adjacent to it shall be returned to the Soviet Union;

(b) The commercial port of Dairen shall be internationalized, the pre-eminent interests of the Soviet Union in this port being safeguarded, and the lease of Port Arthur as a naval base of the U.S.S.R. restored; and

(c) The Chinese-Eastern Railroad and the South Manchurian Railroad, which provide an outlet to Dairen, shall be jointly operated by the establishment of a joint Soviet-Chinese company, it being understood that the pre-eminent interests of the Soviet Union shall be safeguarded and that China shall retain sovereignty in Manchuria.

3. The Kurile Islands shall be handed over to the Soviet Union.

It is understood that the agreement concerning Outer Mongolia and the ports and railroads referred to above will require concurrence of Generalissimo Chiang Kai-shek. The President will take measures in order to maintain this concurrence on advice from Marshal Stalin.

The heads of the three great powers have agreed that these claims of the Soviet Union shall be unquestionably fulfilled after Japan has been defeated.

For its part, the Soviet Union expresses it readiness to conclude with the National Government of China a pact of friendship and alliance between the U.S.S.R. and China in order to render assistance to China with its armed forces for the purpose of liberating China from the Japanese yoke.

Source: U.S. Department of State, *A Decade of American Foreign Policy: Basic Documents, 1941–49* (Washington, DC: U.S. Government Printing Office, 1950), 23–28.

206. Lothar Metzger, Eyewitness Account of the Firebombing of Dresden, 13–14 February 1945

In 1944 and 1945, most major German cities were subjected to fire raids. In a raid that lasted two days, from 13 to 14 February 1945, more than 1,200 British and American bombers poured incendiary bombs over the German city of Dresden, the population of which, swollen by numerous refugees, amounted to close to 1 million. It was later estimated that 35,000 Germans died in the attack, though some sources put the number closer to 100,000.

It was February 13th, 1945. I lived with my mother and sisters (13, 5 and 5 months old twins) in Dresden and was looking forward to celebrating my 10th birthday February 16th. My father, a carpenter, had been a soldier since 1939 and we got his last letter in August 1944. My mother was very sad to receive her letters back with the note: "Not to be found." We lived in a 3 room flat on the 4th floor in a working class region of our town. I remember celebrating Shrove Tuesday (February 13th) together with other children. The activities of the war in the east came nearer and nearer. Lots of soldiers went east and lots of refugees went west through our town or stayed there, also in the air raid night February 13th/14th.

About 9:30 PM the alarm was given. We children knew that sound and got up and dressed quickly, to hurry downstairs into our cellar which we used as an air raid shelter. My older sister and I carried my baby twin sisters, my mother carried a little suitcase and the bottles with milk for our babies. On the radio we heard with great horror the news: "Attention, a great air raid will come over our town!" This news I will never forget.

Some minutes later we heard a horrible noise—the bombers. There were nonstop explosions. Our cellar was filled with fire and smoke and was damaged, the lights went out and wounded people shouted dreadfully. In great fear we struggled to leave this cellar. My mother and my older sister carried the big basket in which the twins were lain. With one hand I grasped my younger sister and with the other I grasped the coat of my mother.

We did not recognize our street any more. Fire, only fire wherever we looked. Our 4th floor did not exist anymore. The broken remains of our house were burning. On the streets there were burning vehicles and carts with refugees, people, horses, all of them screaming and shouting in fear of death. I saw hurt women, children, old people searching a way through ruins and flames.

We fled into another cellar overcrowded with injured and distraught men, women and children shouting, crying and praying. No light except some electric torches. And then suddenly the second raid began. This shelter was hit too, and so we fled through cellar after cellar. Many, so many, desperate people came in from the streets. It is not possible to describe! Explosion after explosion. It was beyond belief, worse than the blackest nightmare. So many people were horribly burnt and injured. It became more and more difficult to breathe. It was dark and all of us tried to leave this cellar with inconceivable panic. Dead and dying people were trampled upon, luggage was left or snatched up out of our hands by rescuers. The basket with our twins covered with wet cloths was snatched up out of my mother's hands and we were pushed upstairs by the people behind us. We saw the burning street, the falling ruins and the terrible firestorm. My mother covered us with wet blankets and coats she found in a water tub.

We saw terrible things: cremated adults shrunk to the size of small children, pieces of arms and legs, dead people, whole families burnt to death, burning people ran to and fro, burnt coaches filled with civilian refugees, dead rescuers and soldiers, many were calling and looking for their children and families, and fire everywhere, everywhere fire, and all the time the hot wind of the firestorm threw people back into the burning houses they were trying to escape from.

I cannot forget these terrible details. I can never forget them.

Now my mother possessed only a little bag with our identity papers. The basket with the twins had disappeared and then suddenly my older sister vanished too. Although my mother looked for her immediately it was in vain. The last hours of this night we found shelter in the cellar of a hospital nearby surrounded by crying and dying people. In the next morning we looked for our sister and the twins but without success. The house where we lived was only a burning ruin. The house where our twins were left we could not go in. Soldiers said everyone was burnt to death and we never saw my two baby sisters again.

Totally exhausted, with burnt hair and badly burnt and wounded by the fire we walked to the Loschwitz bridge where we found good people who allowed us to wash, to eat and to sleep. But only a short time because suddenly the second air raid began (February 14th) and this house too was bombed and my mother's last identity papers burnt. Completely exhausted we hurried over the bridge (river Elbe) with many other homeless survivors and found another family ready to help us, because somehow their home survived this horror.

In all this tragedy I had completely forgotten my 10th birthday. But the next day my mother surprised me with a piece of sausage she begged from the "Red Cross." This was my birthday present.

In the next days and weeks we looked for my older sister but in vain. We wrote our present address on the last walls of our damaged house. In the middle of March we were evacuated to a little village near Oschatz and on March 31st, we got a letter from my sister. She was alive! In that disastrous night she lost us and with other lost children she was taken to a nearby village. Later she found our address on the wall of our house and at the beginning of April my mother brought her to our new home.

You can be sure that the horrible experiences of this night in Dresden led to confused dreams, sleepless nights and disturbed our souls, me and the rest of my family. Years later I intensively thought the matter over, the causes, the political contexts of this night. This became very important for my whole life and my further decisions.

Source: Web site: Timewitnesses: Memories of the Last Century. Available at http://timewitnesses.org/english/lothar.html. Reprinted with permission of Tim Holloway, webmaster.

207. General Dwight D. Eisenhower to General George C. Marshall, 20 February 1945

By late February 1945, Eisenhower could report to Marshall in Washington that, though hampered by floods and difficulties with the French, Allied forces on the Western Front were making steady progress.

The Germans handled the Roer dams in the one way that was most detrimental to us. Rather than blow out the dams completely, they jammed the flood gates in such a way as to create flood conditions throughout the length of the Roer river and to prolong the flood period to the greatest possible extent. We have already reported that we believe we can attack on the 23rd. I sincerely hope that we will not be longer delayed. [US General John Edwin] Hull will have told you that all our preparations are made, the troops are in fine fettle and there is no question in my mind that if we get off to a good start over the river, the operations will be a complete success.

Throughout the front the German has thinned out very much indeed. If we had only a few extra divisions we could put on a very worthwhile attack anywhere between Karlsruhe and the Ardennes.

The French continue to be difficult. I must say that next to the weather I think they have caused me more trouble in this war than any other single factor. They even rank above landing craft. Right now they want three divisions released from the line to assist in the development of new divisions and to exhibit armed might throughout the countryside. Of course there is some merit in their contentions but I suspect also that they are showing a bit of pique at what they consider the slight that [Free French leader] General de Gaulle suffered in not being invited to [the Yalta Conference of Big Three Allied leaders in the] Crimea. As usual we will work out something that will cause us as little damage as possible, but the most popular note in the French press these days is expression of dissatisfaction with the Allies, including this Command, for failing to bring in more foodstuffs and rolling stock for the French, and lack of political deference to their government.

Hull has probably given you the sequence of our projected operations. If the weather improves with the advancing spring I feel that matters will work out almost exactly as projected. I get terribly impatient during periods such as we are now forced to undergo, but I never forget the situation of the German and consequently never lose my basic optimism.

Source: Papers of Dwight D. Eisenhower, Eisenhower Presidential Library, Abilene, KS; printed in Joseph Patrick Hobbs, ed., *Dear General: Eisenhower's Wartime Letters to Marshall* (Baltimore, MD: Johns Hopkins University Press, 1971), 215–216. Reprinted with permission of the Eisenhower Library.

208. Refugees on the Eastern Front: A Teenage Girl Describes the Flight from East Prussia, January–February 1945

As the Eastern Front moved into German territory when Russian troops entered East Prussia in January 1945, millions of Germans fled west before the advancing army. Some were physically expropriated from their homes, as Russia had already determined that postwar Poland would receive much of this area, and Germans were unlikely to remain welcome residents. During this forcible evacuation and flight, in the depths of winter, at least 1 million Germans died, most of them civilians, experiencing the kind of treatment that, earlier in the war, their own forces had inflicted on occupied countries. A teenage German girl later described her family's flight eastward, which lasted more than a month.

On 21 January 1945 Lyck had to be evacuated. With a heavy heart my mother, my sister and I parted from my father, who had been conscripted into the Volkssturm, and from my grandparents. My grandfather intended to take as much of our movable property as possible and join a trek going in the direction of Arys.

With the last trains that were running we reached Rastenburg, where we stayed the night with relatives. Radio reports which we heard indicated that East Prussia was in a hopeless position. In the meantime, the bad news had reached us that trains to the Reich had stopped running. Now we had only one thought: to leave Rastenburg as quickly as possible. My grandmother stayed behind with her maid because she was determined to wait for her husband. We were never to see her or my grandfather again.

At the goods depot in Rastenburg we three found refuge in a goods wagon which was carrying soldiers in the direction of Königsberg. We had to leave the train at Korschen but had the good fortune to get another goods train which was full of refugees. Babies died of hunger on the way.

On 26 January 1945 we reached Bartenstein. In their fear of falling into the hands of the Russians many refugees had managed, despite the extreme cold, to attach themselves to the transport in open coal wagons. On arrival in Bartenstein many had already frozen to death.

We stayed the night in our wagon. At first light, we left the goods train and looked for lodgings in Bartenstein. A female acquaintance from Lyck joined us with her son, who had been caught out by the flight in the middle of his convalescence. It was minus 25 degrees centigrade. While we were going along we heard the dull grumble of artillery fire in the distance.

We found lodgings and rested for two days. But then the approaching artillery fire drove us out of the town of Bartenstein. With the sound of endless explosions as our own troops blew up the Wehrmacht installations in Bartenstein, we found our way out of the town amidst a headless mass of fleeing people. We soon realized that we could not make any progress along the roads. We went back to the goods depot and again had the incredible luck of finding a wagon which was only partly full. Our acquaintance got hold of a railwayman who, after much persuasion, agreed to couple this wagon onto a hospital train which was going to Braunsberg. The railwaymen looked after the refugees in a very touching way and provided them with food and drink.

On 1 February the transport arrived at Braunsberg. Here we received the latest bad news. Allenstein had fallen. Elbing was occupied by the Russians. We were in a huge trap!

The Russian planes endlessly attacked Braunsberg with bombs and gunfire. A friend of my mother's took us in. Many refugees had to camp in cellars. We stayed in Braunsberg until 10 February 1945. Every day we had to queue for food and coal. The drone of the Stalin organs [Katyusha rockets] was getting nearer and nearer. Electricity and gas had packed up. There were ten of us living in a single room. We decided to leave the town. We left our domicile in the dark with a few other fellow-sufferers and groped our way forward in a pitch black night along a road covered with human and animal corpses. Behind us was Braunsberg in flames; to the left of us—around Frauenberg—bitter fighting was going on.

Around midnight—completely filthy and muddy—we reached the little town of Passarge on the Frische Haff. We awaited the new day in a barn. Hein P., our convalescent soldier, could go no further. We had to leave them behind as we continued on foot to the Frische Haff. In the meantime, the icy cold had been replaced by constant rain. We reached the banks of the Frische Haff, paused for a few minutes and then began the walk to the opposite spit of land.

The ice was brittle and in many places we had to wade through water 25 cm. deep. We kept testing the surface in front of us with sticks. Numerous bomb craters forced us to make detours. Often one slipped and thought one had had it. Our clothes, which were soaked through, only allowed us to move clumsily. But fear of death made us forget the shivering which shook our bodies.

I saw women performing superhuman feats. As leaders of the treks they instinctively found the safest paths for their wagons. Household goods were strewn all over the ice; wounded people crept up to us with pleading gestures, hobbling on sticks; others were carried on small sledges by their comrades.

Our journey through this valley of death took us six hours. We reached the Frische Haff. We sank into a fitful sleep in a tiny chicken coop. Our stomachs grumbled with hunger.

On the next day we walked in the direction of Danzig. On the way we saw gruesome scenes. Mothers in a fit of madness threw their children into the sea. People hanged themselves; others fell upon dead horses, cutting out bits of flesh and roasting them on open fires. Women gave birth in the wagons. Everyone thought only of himself—no one could help the sick and the weak.

In Kahlberg we placed ourselves at the disposal of the Red Cross and cared for the wounded in the Beach Hall. On 13 February 1945 we went on board a ship as nursing personnel. On the next day we reached Danzig-Neufahrwasser and disembarked.

On 15 February 1945 we were assigned accommodations in Zoppot. My mother, sister and I could barely keep upright. Nevertheless, we dragged ourselves to the goods depot in Gotenhafen where, for the third time, by a stroke of luck we managed to get a military postal wagon to take us to Stolp (Pomerania). On 19 February as nursing personnel on a hospital train, we arrived via Hanover in Gera in Thuringia, where we were put up by relatives. It was 28 February 1945. On that day our flight from East Prussia was over.

Source: Jeremy Noakes, ed., *Nazism 1919–1945*, Volume 4: *The Home Front in World War II* (Exeter, UK: University of Exeter Press, 1998), 664–666. Reprinted with permission of University of Exeter Press.

209. The Restoration of the Philippine Commonwealth: Douglas MacArthur, Address at Malacañang Palace, Manila, 27 February 1945

After brutally heavy fighting, on 23 February 1945, American and Filipino forces took Manila, the Philippine capital, from the Japanese defenders. On behalf of the United States, General Douglas MacArthur, the Allied commander in chief, made a rather grandiloquent official declaration that the government of the Philippines was now restored to civilian administration under the Commonwealth government headed by Philippine President Sergio Osmeña.

More than three years have elapsed—years of bitterness, struggle and sacrifice—since I withdrew our forces and installations from this beautiful city that, open and undefended, its churches, monuments and cultural centers might, in accordance with the rules of warfare, be spared the violence of military ravage. The enemy would not have it so and much that I sought to preserve has been unnecessarily destroyed by his desperate action at bay but by these ashes he has wantonly fixed the future pattern of his doom.

Then we were but a small force struggling to stem the advance of overwhelming hordes treacherously hurled against us, behind the mask of professed friendship and international goodwill. That struggle was not in vain! God has indeed blessed our arms! The girded and unleashed power of America supported by our Allies turned the tide of battle in the Pacific and resulted in an unbroken series of crushing defeats upon the enemy culminating in the redemption of your soil and the liberation of your people. My country has kept the faith.

These soldiers have come here as an army of free men, dedicated, with your people, to the cause of human liberty and committed to the task of destroying those evil forces that have sought to suppress it by brutality of the sword. An army of free men that has brought your people once again under democracy's banner, to rededicate their churches, long desecrated, to the glory of God and public worship; to reopen their schools to liberal education; to till the soil and reap its harvest without fear of confiscation; to reestablish their industries that they may again enjoy the profit from the sweat of their own toil; and to restore the sanctity and happiness of their homes unafraid of violent intrusion.

Thus to millions of your now liberated people comes the opportunity to pledge themselves—their hearts, their minds, and their hands—to the task of building a new and stronger nation—a nation consecrated in the blood boldly shed that this day might be—a nation dedicated to making imperishable those sacred liberties for which we have fought and many have died.

On behalf of my Government I now solemnly declare, Mr. President, the full powers and responsibilities under the Constitution restored to the Commonwealth whose seat is here reestablished as provided by law.

Your country thus is again at liberty to pursue its destiny to an honored position in the family of free nations. Your capital city, cruelly punished though it be, has regained its rightful place—Citadel of Democracy in the Far East.

Source: Gregorio F. Zaide, ed., *Documentary Sources of Philippine History,* Volume 12 (Metro Manila, Philippines: National Book Store Publishers, 1990), 107–108. Reprinted with permission of the Zaide Foundation.

210. President Jiang Jieshi (Chiang Kai-shek), Speech before the Preparatory Commission for Constitutional Government, Chongqing, China, 1 March 1945

In China, the prospect of victory against Japan in the relatively near future did little to bring peace. The Chinese Nationalist leader, President Jiang Jieshi, announced his intention of summoning a national assembly to reestablish constitutional government in China. He also took the opportunity to assert the Guomindang Party's status as the sole legitimate government, appeal for national unity, and demand that Chinese Communist forces lay down their arms as a precondition for their inclusion in the forthcoming assembly. The Chinese Communists, who already controlled substantial parts of the country, were highly unlikely to do so, as they feared—with some justification—that any such move would put them at the mercy of the Guomindang's own forces. Their refusal to do so after the Japanese surrender would become one major cause of the lengthy and bitter civil war that by late 1945 had broken out in China.

You will recall that in 1936 the Government decided to summon a National Assembly on November 12, 1937, for the inauguration of constitutional government and the termination of the period of political tutelage under the Kuomintang. On July 7, 1937, Japan suddenly made war on us, and the plan had to be shelved. However, the determination of the Kuomintang to realize constitutional government remained as strong as ever. Had it not been for the recommendation of further postponement by the People's Political Council, the National Assembly would have been convened during 1940 in accordance with another Government decision. This year, on the first of January, on behalf of the Government, I announced that the National Assembly will be summoned before the close of the year, unless untoward and unexpected military developments should in the meanwhile intervene.

The Kuomintang is the historical party of national revolution; it overthrew the Manchu dynasty; it destroyed Yuan Shih-kai who would be emperor; it utterly defeated the militarists that succeeded Yuan Shih-kai; it brought about national unification; it achieved the removal of the unequal treaties; and it led the country into the eight-year-old struggle against Japan. It is we who are the party of liberation and progress. In summoning the National Assembly and returning the rule to the people in conformity with the sacred will of Dr. Sun Yat-sen, the Kuomintang is performing its historical role.

We must emerge from this war a united nation. Only a united nation can effectively perform the tasks of political and economic reconstruction to raise the lot of our toiling masses and handle the problems of external relations in a new, uncharted world. Before the Japanese invasion, we were a united nation. Today, but for the Communists and their armed forces, we are a united nation. There are no independent warlords or local governments challenging the central authority.

I have long held the conviction that the solution of the Communist question must be through political means. The Government has labored to make the settlement a political one. As the public is not well informed on our recent efforts to reach a settlement with the Communists, the time has come for me to clarify the atmosphere.

As you know, negotiations with the Communists have been a perennial problem for many years. It has been our unvarying experience that no sooner is a demand met than fresh ones are raised. The latest demand of the Communists is that the Government should forthwith liquidate the Kuomintang rule, and surrender all power to a coalition of various parties. The position of the Government is that it is ready to admit other parties, including the Communists as well as non-partisan leaders, to participate in the Government without, however, relinquishment by the Kuomintang of its power of ultimate decision and final responsibility until the convocation of the National Assembly. We have even offered to include the Communists and other parties in an organ to be established along the line of what is known abroad as a "war cabinet." To go beyond this and to yield to the Communist demand would not only place the Government in open contravention of the political program of Dr. Yat-sen, but also create insurmountable practical difficulties for the country.

During the past eight years, the country has withstood all the vicissitudes of military reverses and of unbelievable privation and has ridden through the storm for the simple reason that it has been led by a stable and strong Government. The war remains to be won, the future is still fraught with peril. If the Government shirks its responsibility and surrenders its power of ultimate decision to a combination of political parties, the result would be unending friction and fears, leading to a collapse of the central authorities. Bear in mind that in such a contingency, unlike in other countries, there exists in our country at present no responsible body representing the people for the government to appeal to.

I repeat, whether by accident or design, the Kuomintang has had the responsibility of leading the country during the turbulent last decade and more. It will return the supreme power to the people through the instrumentality of the National Assembly, and in the meanwhile, it will be ready to admit other parties to a share in the government, but it definitely cannot abdicate to a loose combination of parties. Such a surrender would not mean returning power to the people.

We must emerge from the war with a united army. The Communists should not keep a separate army. Here allow me to digress a little. The Chinese Communist propaganda abroad has tried to justify this private army on the ground that if it becomes incorporated in the National Army, it will be in danger of being destroyed or discriminated against. Their propaganda also magnify, out of all proportion, the actual military strength of the Communists. To you, I need hardly say that Government forces have always without exception borne the brunt of Japanese attack and will continue to do so. Today, with the wholehearted co-operation of our Allies, powerful armies are being equipped and conditioned to assume the offensive. We are synchronizing our efforts with those of our Allies in expelling Japan from the Asiatic mainland. . . .

To meet any fear the Communists may have the Government has expressed its willingness for the duration of the war to place an American general in command of the Communist forces under my over-all command as supreme commander—again if the United States Government could agree to the appointment of an American officer. The Communists have, however, rejected all those offers. If the Communists are sincere in their desire to fight the Japanese alongside us and our Allies, they have indeed been given every opportunity to do so.

No one mindful of the future of our 450,000,000 people and conscious of standing at the bar of history, would wish to plunge the country into a civil war. The Government has shown its readiness and is always ready to confer with the Communists to bring about a real and lasting settlement with them. . . .

I have explained the Government's position on the Communist problem at length, because today that is the main problem to unity and constitutional government. . . .

Upon the inauguration of constitutional government, all political parties will have legal status and enjoy equality. The Government has offered to give legal recognition to the Communist party as soon as the latter agrees to incorporate their army and local administration in the National Army and Government. The offer still stands. . . .

I am optimistic of national unification and the future of democratic government in our country. The torrent of public opinion demanding national unity and reconstruction is mounting ever stronger and will soon become an irresistible force. No individual or political party can afford to disregard this force any longer. Let all of us, regardless of party affiliations, work together for the twin objectives of our people—national unity and reconstruction.

Source: Chinese News Service. Web site: ibiblio. Available at http://www.ibiblio.org/pha/policy/1945/450301b.html.

211. The Firebombing of Tokyo, 10 March 1945: Reminiscences of Shinoda Tomoko

As the end of the war came closer, most major Japanese cities, like those in Germany, were subjected to intense firebombing raids. In 1945, Shinoda Tomoko was a schoolgirl of 16. She recalled her experiences in the major raid on Tokyo.

We were among those surrounded by flames on 10 March 1945. My mother, older sister, and I tried to make our escape. Wherever I went, a wave of fire rushed toward me. Finally I made it to Oshiage station. There were thousands of people there. It was so hot and suffocating that I pressed my cheek to the ground. The air was cool and clean down there. I saw the legs of all sorts of people in front of me. Occasionally on my way a man I didn't know would splash ditch water from a bucket on us and urge us on, say-

ing it was just a little further. Behind me a man sat covered with a large quilt. My back pressed against his, I waited for day to break, fearful and worried about the heat.

With the coming of the pale dawn, people started heading for home. Several military trucks came by around that time. Thinking they had come to help us, I stood up, and the man behind me toppled over. I shook him, but he was dead. They said he died from smoke and the heat of the flames.

On the way home, I thought I saw some black work

gloves. When I took a closer look, they were hands that had been torn off. Many red fire trucks were burned out on the major road next to the streetcar tracks, with firemen dead on their vehicles. The dead were blackened and had shrunk to the size of children. It was impossible to tell if they were men or women.

I finally made it back to the charred remains of our house. My mother and sister were there. We hugged each other, weeping. We dug up the crockery, furniture, and food that we had buried in our yard. The rice that had been washed and in our pot was now charred, but we ate it. The tin cans of food that had been stored in the basement of the school building, which had been spared, had burst open due to the tremendous heat of the surrounding fires. I had two younger brothers in first and second grade, but they had been evacuated and were not in Tokyo, so they were safe.

Source: Frank Gibney, ed., *Senso: The Japanese Remember the Pacific War: Letters to the Editor of* Asahi Shimbun (Armonk, NY: M. E. Sharpe, 1995), 204–205. Reprinted with permission of M. E. Sharpe.

212. General Dwight D. Eisenhower to General George C. Marshall, 26 March 1945

In March 1945, American forces crossed the Rhine River into German territory. Supreme Commander General Eisenhower reported informally to Chief of Staff George C. Marshall on the move, which marked the beginning of the final stage of the war in Europe. He ascribed much of the final campaign's success to his own earlier insistence that the Allies engage German forces west of the Rhine in battle, which had helped to exhaust them.

I have just finished a rapid tour of the battle front. Yesterday and the day before I was with the 9th Army to witness its jumpoff and the early stages of the Rhine crossing. [General William Hood] Simpson performed in his usual outstanding style. Our losses in killed, during the crossing, were 15 in one assault division and 16 in the other. I stayed up most of one night to witness the preliminary bombardment by 1250 guns. It was an especially interesting sight because of the fact that all the guns were spread out on a plain so that the flashes from one end of the line to the other were all plainly visible. It was a real drum-fire. . . .

Naturally I am immensely pleased that the campaign west of the Rhine that [U.S. General Omar Bradley] and I planned last summer and insisted upon as a necessary preliminary to a deep penetration east of the Rhine, has been carried out so closely in accordance with conception. You possibly know that at one time the C.I.G.S. [Chief of the (British) Imperial General Staff Sir Alan Brooke] thought I was wrong in what I was trying to do and argued heatedly upon the matter. Yesterday I saw him on the banks of the Rhine and he was gracious enough to say that I was right, and that my current plans and operations are well calculated to meet the current situation. The point is that the great defeats, in some cases almost complete destruction, inflicted on the German forces west of the Rhine, have left him with very badly depleted strength to man that formidable obstacle. It was those victories that made possible the bold and relatively easy advances that both First and Third Armies are now making toward Kassel. I hope this does not sound boastful, but I must admit to a great satisfaction that the things that Bradley and I have believed in from the beginning and have carried out in the face of some opposition both from within and without, have matured so splendidly.

Source: Papers of Dwight D. Eisenhower, Eisenhower Presidential Library, Abilene, KS; printed in Joseph Patrick Hobbs, ed., *Dear General: Eisenhower's Wartime Letters to Marshall* (Baltimore, MD: Johns Hopkins University Press, 1971), 219–220. Reprinted with permission of the Eisenhower Library.

213. Winston Churchill and Berlin, 1–3 April 1945

Increasingly concerned that Soviet influence would dominate much of central and eastern Europe when the war ended, in March and April 1945, British Prime Minister Winston Churchill dispatched a barrage of telegrams in which he sought to persuade the American General Dwight D. Eisenhower, the supreme commander of Allied forces in Europe, U.S. Army Chief of Staff George C. Marshall, and President Franklin D. Roosevelt to follow a strategy of striking directly for the German capital of Berlin. His final appeal was addressed to Roosevelt. Roosevelt's reply, possibly drafted by Marshall, ignored the implications for dealings with the Soviets raised by Churchill and focused entirely on the tactical military questions involved.

Winston Churchill to Franklin D. Roosevelt, Telegram No. C-931, 1 April 1945

. . . I venture to put to you a few considerations upon the merits of the changes in our original plans now desired by General Eisenhower. It seems to me the differences are small and as usual not of principle but of emphasis. Obviously, laying aside every impediment and shunning every diversion, the allied armies of the north and centre should now march at the highest speed towards the Elbe. Hitherto the axis has been upon Berlin. General Eisenhower on his estimate of the enemy's resistance, to which I attach the greatest importance, now wishes to shift the axis somewhat to the southward and strike through Leipzig, even perhaps as far south as Dresden. He withdraws the Ninth U.S. Army from the northern group of armies and in consequence stretches its front southwards. I should be sorry if the resistance of the enemy was such as to destroy the weight and momentum of the advance of the British Twenty First Army Group and to leave them in an almost static condition along the Elbe when and if they reach it. I say quite frankly that Berlin remains of high strategic importance. Nothing will exert a psychological effect of despair upon all German forces of resistance equal to that of the fall of Berlin. It will be the supreme signal of defeat to the German people. On the other hand, if left to itself to maintain a siege by the Russians among its ruins and as long as the German flag flies there, it will animate the resistance of all Germans under arms.

There is moreover another aspect which it is proper for you and me to consider. The Russian armies will no doubt overrun all Austria and enter Vienna. If they also take Berlin, will not their impression that they have been the overwhelming contributor to our common victory be unduly imprinted in their minds, and may this not lead them into a mood which will raise grave and formidable difficulties in the future? I therefore consider that from a political standpoint we should march as far east into Germany as possible and that should Berlin be in our grasp we should certainly take it. This also appears sound on military grounds.

To sum up, the difference that might exist between General Eisenhower's new plans and those we advocated, and which were agreed upon beforehand, would seem to be the following, viz, whether the emphasis should be put on an axis directed on Berlin or on one directed upon Leipzig and Dresden. This is surely a matter upon which a reasonable latitude of discussion should be allowed to our two Chiefs of Staff Committees before any final commitment involving the Russians is entered into.

Source: Warren F. Kimball, ed., *Roosevelt and Churchill: Their Complete Correspondence,* 3 vols. (Princeton, NJ: Princeton University Press, 1985), 3: 603–605, 607–609. Reprinted with permission of the Churchill Archives, Churchill College, Cambridge, and HMSO.

Franklin D. Roosevelt to Winston Churchill, Telegram No. R-733, 4 April 1945

I have given your personal message No. 931 a very careful reading and have gone over the various papers involved, some of which I had not previously read. Further, I have just received a copy of Eisenhower's directive to his Army Group Commanders, dated April 2. . . .

As to the "far-reaching changes desired by General Eisenhower in the plans that had been concerted by the Combined Chiefs of Staff at Malta and had received your and my joint approval," I do not get the point. For example, the strength and all the resources agreed upon for the northern Group of Armies were made available to Montgomery. Following the unexpected Remagen Bridgehead and the destruction of the German Armies in the Saar Basin there developed so great a weakness on those fronts that the secondary efforts realized an outstanding success. This fact must have a very important relation to the further conduct of the battle. However, General Eisenhower's directive of April 2, it seems to me, does all and possibly a little more to the north than was anticipated at Malta. Leipzig is not far removed from Berlin which is well within the center of the combined effort. At the same time the British Army is given what seems to me very logical objectives on the northern flank. . . .

I appreciate your generous expression of confidence in Eisenhower and I have always been deeply appreciative of the backing you have given him and the fact that you yourself proposed him for this command. I regret that the phrasing of a formal discussion should have so disturbed you but I regret even more that at the moment of a great victory by our combined forces we should become involved in such unfortunate reactions.

It appears reasonable to expect that under Eisenhower's present plans the great German Army will in the very near future be completely broken up into separate resistance groups, while our forces will remain tactically intact and in a position to destroy in detail the separated parts of the Nazi Army.

You have my assurance of every cooperation.

Source: Warren F. Kimball, ed., *Roosevelt and Churchill: Their Complete Correspondence,* 3 vols. (Princeton, NJ: Princeton University Press, 1985), 3: 603–605, 607–609. Reprinted with permission of the Churchill Archives, Churchill College, Cambridge, and HMSO.

214. Statement of Truman K. Gibson Jr., Civilian Aide to the Secretary of War, at Press Conference, Monday, 9 April 1945

Faced with rising African American pressure, the United States army sought—somewhat inaccurately—to depict the wartime American military as a haven of racial tolerance and integration. In spring 1945, as the war in Europe was ending, Truman K. Gibson, Jr., an African American aide in the Press Branch of the War Department Bureau of Public Relations, issued a somewhat anodyne statement on the subject. Although undoubtedly something of a whitewash effort designed to placate American and international public opinion, Gibson's statement did illustrate the United States army's perceived need and wish to portray itself as strongly opposed to racial discrimination.

The press has already reported that Negro and White Infantrymen are now fighting side by side in Germany. In France I visited some of the Negro platoons before they left for the front and talked with the men being trained at the Reinforcement Training Center. What I saw and heard was evidence that the Supreme Command in SHAEF was following in racial matters what must be the basic policy of any Army, in any way, namely, that of utilizing most efficiently all available resources of men and materiel to defeat the enemy.

Such a policy is working. At the Training Center a white noncommissioned veteran, who was assisting in the training program, said graphically, if ungrammatically, about the Negro trainees: "Sure they'll get along all right. It don't matter whose [sic] firing next to you when you're both killing Krauts." The Texas-born, battle-scarred Commanding Officer of the Center was confident that the trainees, all of whom volunteered for the training course with all noncommissioned officers, taking a reduction to the grade of private, would do well in combat. He said, "These men will fight because they have been trained and treated just like the other soldiers here and they know they are going to be used in the same manner. In the same Divisions. They want to fight. When the first group went out we had only two cases of AWOL [Absent Without Leave] among all the Negro soldiers in the Center. We found out where the two men were when we received a wire from a front line Division Commander informing us that they had reported to him to fight."

The estimate of this officer has been confirmed by the report of an official observer who spent time with some of the platoons in the fighting around Remagen where the first of the units was committed to combat. He reported that the Negro soldiers fought as well as any others and that the mistakes they made were the same as those made by other troops lacking battle experience.

This policy of making the best use of all soldiers is further evidenced in the excellent performance of the Service of Supply troops throughout the theater. These troops, a large percentage of whom are Negroes, regard themselves as soldiers performing vital jobs. They had a very real identification with the fighting front. In one Quartermaster Depot, manned by Negro personnel, the first sergeant when questioned as to why the men were working voluntarily around the clock, replied: "We have got to keep the supplies moving and we all want to do our part." The officers in this unit were white and were enthusiastic about their men and their work. Discussing their men, Negro officers in a Quartermaster Truck Company said that on many occasions their drivers had insisted on delivering white Infantrymen into dangerous territory late at night far in advance of the debarkation points because "they hated to see the 'Doughs' walk."

In the European Theater of Operations are the first units of Negro nurses and Wacs to go overseas. The nurses, stationed at a hospital in the north of England, are busy treating American soldiers who have been wounded in action. They are described by their Commanding Officer as being the equals professionally of any nurses in the area. The Wacs officer and man the Central Postal Directory for the entire European Theater of Operations. Their efficiency has drawn repeated praise from the Commanding Officer of the United Kingdom Base Section. They have adjusted exceptionally well in the short time they have been overseas to their work and the community in which they are situated.

Generally, on both the Continent and in England, it was apparent that the attitude of the Supreme Command that there should be no discrimination against any soldier on account of his race had reached all elements of the Command. Discriminatory acts and incidents that have occurred were regarded by the soldiers as being individual in nature. As a result of my trip to the Mediterranean and European Theaters I am impressed that such differences as exist between soldiers are not due to racial characteristics but to such factors as training, motivation, and environment. The fact that the Commands in these theaters believe this is encouraging. Certainly the record being made by Negro soldiers gives the lie to any charge that Negroes cannot and will not fight.

Source: Statement of Truman K. Gibson Jr., Civilian Aide to the Secretary of War, at Press Conference, 9 April 1945. Available at Harry S. Truman Presidential Library Web Site. Desegregation of the Armed Forces Folder, 1945, http://www.trumanlibrary.org/whistlestop/study_collections/desegregation/.

215. General Dwight D. Eisenhower to General George C. Marshall, 15 April 1945

By mid-April 1945, Allied forces were moving into the Ruhr, Germany's industrial heartland. Supreme Commander Dwight D. Eisenhower wrote to Chief of Staff George C. Marshall in Washington, laying out his strategy for the rest of the war. Eisenhower defended his decision, in which Marshall concurred, to ignore British suggestions that British and American forces should take Berlin before Soviet troops arrived there. He also described the horrific experience of visiting a German internment camp, which had clearly shaken him.

Today I forwarded to the Combined Chiefs of Staff the essentials of my future plans. In a word, what I am going to do now that the western enemy is split into two parts, is to take up a defensive line in the center (along a geographical feature that will tend to separate our forces physically from the advancing Russians) and clean up the important jobs on our flanks. A mere glance at the map shows that one of these is to get Lubeck and then clear up all the areas west and north of there. The other job is the so-called "redoubt." I deem both of these to be vastly more important than the capture of Berlin—anyway, to plan for making an immediate effort against Berlin would be foolish in view of the relative situation of the Russians and ourselves at this moment. We'd get all coiled up for something that in all probability would never come off. While true that we have seized a small bridgehead over the Elbe, it must be remembered that only our spearheads are up to that river; our center of gravity is well back of there.

[British Commander Field Marshal Sir Bernard] Montgomery anticipates that he will need no help from the Americans other than that involved in an extension of [General William Hood] Simpson's left. However, I rather think that he will want possibly an American Airborne Division and maybe an Armored Division. I have enough in reserve to give him this much if he needs it. But assuming that he needs no American help, that job will be performed by the 17 divisions of the 21st Army Group.

In the center, extending all the way from Newhouse on the Elbe down to the vicinity of Selb on the border of Czechoslovakia, will be the Ninth and First Armies, probably with about 23 to 24 divisions, including their own reserves. This will be enough to push on to Berlin if resistance is light, and the Russians do not advance in that sector. [US General Omar] Bradley's main offensive effort will be the thrust along the line Wurzburg-Nuremberg-Linz, carried out by the Third Army with about 12 divisions. [US General Jacob] Devers, with another 12 U.S. divisions and 6 French divisions, will capture Munich and all of the German territory lying within his zone of advance.

About 8 divisions at that time will be on strictly occupational duties, largely under Fifteenth Army. This will leave about 5 divisions, including Airborne, in my Reserve.

The intervention of the British Chiefs of Staff in my military dealings with the Soviet has thrown quite a monkey-wrench into our speed of communication. If you will note from [Acting Soviet Chief of Staff of the Russian Army

General Alexei] Antonov's reply to the telegram that we finally sent (as revised on recommendations of the BCOS [British Chiefs of Staff]) the point he immediately raised is whether our message implies an attempt, under the guise of military operations, to change the occupational boundaries already agreed upon by our three governments. Frankly, if I should have forces *in the Russian occupational zone* and be faced with an order or "request" to retire so that they may advance to the points they choose, I see no recourse except to comply. To do otherwise would probably provoke an incident, with the logic of the situation all on the side of the Soviets. I cannot see exactly what the British have in mind for me to do, under such circumstances. It is a bridge that I will have to cross when I come to it but I must say that I feel a bit lost in trying to give sensible instructions to my various commanders in the field.

On a recent tour of the forward areas in First and Third Armies, I stopped momentarily at the salt mines to take a look at the German treasure. There is a lot of it. But the most interesting—although horrible—sight that I encountered during the trip was a visit to a German internment camp near Gotha. The things I saw beggar description. While I was touring the camp I encountered three men who had been inmates and by one ruse or another had made their escape. I interviewed them through an interpreter. The visual evidence and the verbal testimony of starvation, cruelty and bestiality were so overpowering as to leave me a bit sick. In one room, where they [there] were piled up twenty or thirty naked men, killed by starvation, [US General] George Patton would not even enter. He said he would get sick if he did so. I made the visit deliberately, in order to be in position to give *first-hand* evidence of these things if ever, in the future, there develops a tendency to charge these allegations merely to "propaganda."

If you could see your way clear to do it, I think you should make a visit here at the earliest possible moment, while we are still conducting a general offensive. You would be proud of the Army you have produced. . . .

Source: Papers of Dwight D. Eisenhower, Eisenhower Presidential Library, Abilene, KS; printed in Joseph Patrick Hobbs, ed., *Dear General: Eisenhower's Wartime Letters to Marshall* (Baltimore, MD: Johns Hopkins University Press, 1971), 221–223. Reprinted with permission of the Eisenhower Library.

216. President Harry S Truman, First Message to Congress, 16 April 1945

On 12 April 1945, President Franklin D. Roosevelt, who had led the United States since 1933, died suddenly of a cerebral hemorrhage. His successor, Harry S Truman of Missouri, quickly reaffirmed his intention of carrying on the policies of Franklin D. Roosevelt, including the prosecution of the war to victory and the formulation of a lasting peace settlement. When he became president, many considered Truman a mediocrity, but he became one of the major architects of American involvement in the Cold War that would very soon pit the Soviet Union against the Western powers.

It is with heavy heart that I stand before you, my friends and colleagues, in the Congress of the United States.

Only yesterday, we laid to rest the mortal remains of our beloved President, Franklin Delano Roosevelt. At a time like this, words are inadequate. The most eloquent tribute would be a reverent silence.

Yet, in this decisive hour, when world events are moving so rapidly, our silence might be misunderstood and might give comfort to our enemies.

In His infinite wisdom, Almighty God has seen fit to take from us a great man who loved, and was beloved by, all humanity.

No man could possibly fill the tremendous void left by the passing of that noble soul. No words can ease the aching hearts of untold millions of every race, creed, and color. The world knows it has lost a heroic champion of justice and freedom.

Tragic fate has thrust upon us grave responsibilities. We must carry on. Our departed leader never looked backward. He looked forward and moved forward. That is what he would want us to do. That is what America will do.

So much blood has already been shed for the ideals which we cherish, and for which Franklin Delano Roosevelt lived and died, that we dare not permit even a momentary pause in the hard fight for victory.

Today, the entire world is looking to America for enlightened leadership to peace and progress. Such a leadership requires vision, courage, and tolerance. It can be provided only by a united nation deeply devoted to the highest ideals.

I call upon all Americans to help me keep our Nation united in defense of those ideals which have been so eloquently proclaimed by Franklin Roosevelt.

I want in turn to assure my fellow Americans and all of those who love peace and liberty throughout the world that

I will support and defend those ideals with all my strength and with all my heart. That is my duty and I shall not shirk it.

So that there can be no possible misunderstanding, both Germany and Japan can be certain, beyond any shadow of doubt, America will confine to fight for freedom until no vestige of resistance remains!

We are deeply conscious of the fact that much hard fighting is still ahead of us.

Having to pay such a heavy price to make complete victory certain, America will never become a party to any plan for partial victory!

To settle for merely another temporary respite would surely jeopardize the future security of all the world.

Our demand has been, and it remains, unconditional surrender!

We will not traffic with the breakers of the peace on the terms of the peace.

The responsibility for the making of the peace—and it is a very grave responsibility—must rest with the defenders of the peace, the United Nations. We are not unconscious of the dictates of humanity. We do not wish to see unnecessary or unjustified suffering. But the laws of God and of man have been violated and the guilty must not go unpunished. Nothing shall shake our determination to punish the war criminals even though we must pursue them to the end of the earth.

Lasting peace can never be secured if we permit our dangerous opponents to plot future wars with impunity at any mountain retreat—however distant. In this shrinking world, it is futile to seek safety behind geographical barriers. Real security will be found only in law and in justice.

Here in America, we have labored long and hard to achieve a social order worthy of our great heritage. In our time, tremendous progress has been made toward a really democratic way of life. Let me assure the forward-looking people of America that there will be no relaxation in our efforts to improve the lot of the common people.

In the difficult days ahead, unquestionably we shall face problems of staggering proportions. However, with the faith of our fathers in our hearts, we fear no future.

On the battlefields, we have frequently faced overwhelming odds—and won! At home, Americans will not be less resolute!

We shall never cease our struggle to preserve and maintain our American way of life.

At this very moment, America, along with her brave Allies, is paying again a heavy price for the defense of our freedom. With characteristic energy, we are assisting in the liberation of entire nations. Gradually, the shackles of slavery are being broken by the forces of freedom.

All of us are praying for a speedy victory. Every day peace is delayed costs a terrible toll.

The armies of liberation today are bringing to an end Hitler's ghastly threat to dominate the world. Tokyo rocks under the weight of our bombs.

The grand strategy of a United Nations' war has been determined—due in no small measure to the vision of our departed Commander in Chief. We are now carrying out our part of that strategy under the able direction of Admiral Leahy, General Marshall, Admiral King, General Arnold, General Eisenhower, Admiral Nimitz, and General MacArthur.

I want the entire world to know that this direction must and will remain—unchanged and unhampered!

Our debt to the heroic men and valiant women in the service of our country can never be repaid. They have earned our undying gratitude. America will never forget their sacrifices. Because of these sacrifices, the dawn of justice and freedom throughout the world slowly casts its gleam across the horizon.

Our forefathers came to our rugged shores in search of religious tolerance, political freedom, and economic opportunity. For those fundamental rights, they risked their lives. We know today that such rights can be preserved only by constant vigilance, the eternal price of liberty! Within an hour after I took the oath of office, I announced that the San Francisco Conference would proceed. We will face the problems of peace with the same courage that we have faced and mastered the problems of war. In the memory of those who have made the supreme sacrifice—in the memory of our fallen President—we shall not fail!

It is not enough to yearn for peace. We must work and, if necessary, fight for it. The task of creating a sound international organization is complicated and difficult. Yet, without such organization, the rights of man on earth cannot be protected. Machinery for the just settlement of international differences must be found. Without such machinery, the entire world will have to remain an armed camp. The world will be doomed to deadly conflict, devoid of hope for real peace.

Fortunately, people have retained hope for a durable peace. Thoughtful people have always had faith that ultimately justice must triumph. Past experience surely indicates that, without justice, an enduring peace becomes impossible.

In bitter despair, some people have come to believe that wars are inevitable.

With tragic fatalism, they insist that, as wars have always been, of necessity wars will always be. To such defeatism, men and women of good-will must not and cannot yield. The outlook for humanity is not so hopeless.

During the darkest hours of this horrible war, entire nations were kept going by something intangible—hope! When warned that abject submission offered the only salvation against overwhelming power, hope showed the way to victory.

Hope has become the secret weapon of the forces of liberation!

Aggressors could not dominate the human mind. As long as hope remains, the spirit of man will never be crushed.

But hope alone was not and is not sufficient to avert war. We must not only have hope but we must have faith enough to work with other peace-loving nations to maintain the peace. Hope was not enough to beat back the aggressors as long as the peace-loving nations were unwilling to come to each other's defense. The aggressors were beaten back only when the peace-loving nations united to defend themselves.

If wars in the future are to be prevented, the peace-loving nations must be united in their determination to keep the peace under law. The breaking of the peace anywhere is the concern of peace-loving nations everywhere.

Nothing is more essential to the future peace of the world than continued cooperation of the nations which had to muster the force necessary to defeat the conspiracy of the Fascist powers to dominate the world.

While these great states have a special responsibility to enforce the peace, their responsibility is based upon the obligations resting upon all states, large and small, not to use force in international relations except in the defense of law. The responsibility of the great states is to serve and not dominate the peoples of the world.

To build the foundation of enduring peace we must not only work in harmony with our friends abroad but we must have the united support of our own people.

Even the most experienced pilot cannot bring a ship safely into harbor unless he has the full cooperation of the crew. For the benefit of all, every individual must do his duty.

I appeal to every American, regardless of party, race, creed, or color, to support our efforts to build a strong and lasting United Nations Organization.

You, the members of Congress, surely know how I feel.

Only with your help can I hope to complete one of the greatest tasks ever assigned to a public servant. With Divine guidance, and your help, we will find the new passage to a far better world, a kindly and friendly world, with just and lasting peace.

With confidence, I am depending upon all of you.

To destroy greedy tyrants with plans of world domination, we cannot continue in successive generations to sacrifice our finest youth.

In the name of human decency and civilization, a more rational method of deciding national differences must and will be found!

America must assist suffering humanity back along the path of peaceful progress. This will require time and tolerance. We shall need also an abiding faith in the people, the kind of faith and courage which Franklin Delano Roosevelt always had!

Today, America has become one of the most powerful forces for good on earth. We must keep it so. We have achieved a world leadership which does not depend solely upon our military and naval might.

We have learned to fight with other nations in common defense of our freedom We must now learn to live with other nations for our mutual good. We must learn to trade more with other nations so that there may be—for our mutual advantage—increased production, increased employment, and better standards of living throughout the world.

May we Americans live up to our glorious heritage.

In that way, America may well lead the world to peace and prosperity.

At this moment, I have in my heart a prayer. As I assume my heavy duties, I humbly pray to Almighty God, in the words of Solomon:

"Give therefore thy servant an understanding heart to judge thy people, that I may discern between good and bad: for who is able to judge this thy so great a people?"

I ask only to be a good and faithful servant of my Lord and my people.

Source: United States Department of State Bulletin. Web site: ibiblio. Available at http://www.ibiblio.org/pha/policy/1945/450416a.html.

217. Henry L. Stimson, Memorandum Discussed with President Harry S Truman, 25 April 1945

By spring 1945, it seemed likely that the United States would succeed in its massive MANHATTAN *Project to develop atomic weapons. At the end of April, Secretary of War Henry L. Stimson suggested to the new president, Harry S Truman, then only a fortnight into his tenure of the presidency, that it might be desirable to place both the military and peaceful uses of atomic energy under some form of international control.*

1. Within four months we shall in all probability have completed one of the most terrible weapons ever known in human history, one bomb of which could destroy a whole city.

2. Although we have shared its development with the U.K., physically the U.S. is at present in the position of controlling the resources with which to construct and use it and no other nation could reach this position for some years.

3. Nevertheless it is practically certain that we could not remain in this position indefinitely.

   a. Various segments of its discovery and production are widely known among many scientists in many countries, although few scientists are now acquainted with the whole process which we have developed.

   b. Although its construction under present methods requires great scientific and industrial effort and raw materials, which are temporarily mainly within the possession and knowledge of U.S. and U.K., it is extremely probable that much easier and cheaper methods of production will be discovered by scientists in the future, together with the use of materials of much wider distribution. As a result, it is extremely probable that the future will make it possible for atomic bombs to be constructed by smaller nations or even groups, or at least by a larger nation in a much shorter time.

4. As a result, it is indicated that the future may see a time when such a weapon may be constructed in secret and used suddenly and effectively with devastating power against an unsuspecting nation or group of much greater size and material power. With its aid even a very powerful unsuspecting nation might be conquered within a very few days by a very much smaller one....

5. The world in its present state of moral advancement compared with its technical development would be eventually at the mercy of such a weapon. In other words, modern civilization might be completely destroyed.

6. To approach any world peace organization of any pattern now likely to be considered, without an appreciation by the leaders of our country of the power of the new weapon, would seem to be unrealistic. No system of control heretofore considered would be adequate to control this menace. Both inside any particular country and between the nations of the world, the control of this weapon will undoubtedly be a matter of the greatest difficulty and would involve such thoroughgoing rights of inspection and internal controls as we have never heretofore contemplated.

7. Furthermore, in the light of our present position with reference to this weapon, the question of sharing it with other nations and, if so shared, upon what terms, becomes a primary question of our foreign relations. Also our leadership in the war and in the development of this weapon has placed a certain moral responsibility upon us which we cannot shirk without very serious responsibility for any disaster to civilization which it would further.

8. On the other hand, if the problem of the proper use of this weapon can be solved, we would have the opportunity to bring the world into a pattern in which the peace of the world and our civilization can be saved.

9. As stated in General Groves's report, steps are under way looking towards the establishment of a select committee of particular qualifications for recommending action to the executive and legislative branches of our government when secrecy is no longer in full effect. The committee would also recommend the actions to be taken by the War Department prior to that time in anticipation of the postwar problems. All recommendations would of course be first submitted to the President.

Source: Henry L. Stimson with McGeorge Bundy, *On Active Service in Peace and War* (New York: Harper and Row, 1948). Reprinted with permission of Yale Archives (for Stimson Papers), 635–636.

218. The Private and Political Testaments of Adolf Hitler, 29 April 1945

Shortly before committing suicide in Berlin, together with his longtime companion Eva Braun, whom he married at this time, Adolf Hitler wrote a will and testament. By killing himself, he avoided trial by the Allies. Hitler's will made it clear that, despite Germany's crushing defeat, he retained all his faith in the political principles he had proclaimed for a quarter of a century. He blamed the outbreak of war and Germany's defeat upon an international Jewish conspiracy and expelled from the party Hermann Göring and Heinrich Himmler, who had tried to open peace negotiations with the Allies.

MY PRIVATE WILL AND TESTAMENT

As I did not consider that I could take responsibility, during the years of struggle, of contracting a marriage, I have now decided, before the closing of my earthly career, to take as my wife that girl who, after many years of faithful friendship, entered, of her own free will, the practically besieged town in order to share her destiny with me. At her own desire she goes as my wife with me into death. It will compensate us for what we both lost through my work in the service of my people.

What I possess belongs—insofar as it has any value—to the Party. Should this no longer exist, to the State; should the State also be destroyed, no further decision of mine is necessary.

My pictures, in the collections which I have bought over the course of years, have never been collected for private purposes, but only for the extension of a gallery in my home town of Linz a.d. Donau.

It is my most sincere wish that this bequest may be duly executed.

I nominate as my Executor my most faithful Party comrade, Martin Bormann.

He is given full legal authority to make all decisions. He is permitted to take out everything that has a sentimental value or is necessary for the maintenance of a modest simple life, for my brothers and sisters, also above all for the mother of my wife and my faithful co-workers who are well known to him, principally my old Secretaries Frau Winter, etc. who have for many years aided me by their work.

I myself and my wife—in order to escape the disgrace of deposition or capitulation—choose death. It is our wish to be burnt immediately on the spot where I have carried out the greatest part of my daily work in the course of twelve years' service to my people.

Given in Berlin, 29th April 1945, 4:00 o'clock
(Signed) A. HITLER

MY POLITICAL TESTAMENT

More than thirty years have now passed since I in 1914 made my modest contribution as a volunteer in the first world war that was forced upon the Reich.

In these three decades I have been actuated solely by love and loyalty to my people in all my thoughts, acts, and life. They gave me the strength to make the most difficult decisions which have ever confronted mortal man. I have spent my time, my working strength, and my health in these three decades.

It is untrue that I or anyone else in Germany wanted the war in 1939. It was desired and instigated exclusively by those international statesmen who were either of Jewish descent or worked for Jewish interests. I have made too many offers for the control and limitation of armaments, which posterity will not for all time be able to disregard, for the responsibility for the outbreak of this war to be laid on me. I have further never wished that after the first fatal world war a second against England, or even against America, should break out. Centuries will pass away, but out of the ruins of our towns and monuments the hatred against those finally responsible whom we have to thank for everything, international Jewry and its helpers, will grow.

Three days before the outbreak of the German-Polish war I again proposed to the British ambassador in Berlin a solution to the German-Polish problem—similar to that in the case of the Saar district, under international control. This offer also cannot be denied. It was only rejected because the leading circles in English politics wanted the war, partly on account of the business hoped for and partly under influence of propaganda organized by international Jewry.

I have also made it quite plain that, if the nations of Europe are again to be regarded as mere shares to be bought and sold by these international conspirators in money and finance, then that race, Jewry, which is the real criminal of this murderous struggle, will be saddled with the responsibility. I further left no one in doubt that this time not only would millions of children of Europe's Aryan peoples die of hunger, not only would millions of grown men suffer death, and not only would hundreds of thousands of women and children be burnt and bombed to death in the towns, without the real criminal having to atone for this guilt, even if by more humane means.

After six years of war, which in spite of all setbacks will go down one day in history as the most glorious and valiant demonstration of a nation's life purpose, I cannot forsake the city which is the capital of this Reich. As the forces are too small to make any further stand against the enemy attack at this place, and our resistance is gradually being weakened by men who are as deluded as they are lacking in initiative, I should like, by remaining in this town, to share my fate with those, the millions of others, who have also taken upon themselves to do so. Moreover I do not wish to fall into the hands of an enemy who requires a new spectacle organized by the Jews for the amusement of their hysterical masses.

I have decided therefore to remain in Berlin and there of my own free will to choose death at the moment when I believe the position of the Fuehrer and Chancellor itself can no longer be held.

I die with a happy heart, aware of the immeasurable deeds and achievements of our soldiers at the front, our women at home, the achievements of our farmers and workers and the work, unique in history, of our youth who bear my name.

That from the bottom of my heart I express my thanks to you all, is just as self-evident as my wish that you should, because of that, on no account give up the struggle but rather continue it against the enemies of the Fatherland, no matter where, true to the creed of great Clausewitz. From the sacrifice of our soldiers and from my own unity with them unto death, will in any case spring up in the history of Germany, the seed of a radiant renaissance of the National-Socialist movement and thus of the realization of a true community of nations.

Many of the most courageous men and women have decided to unite their lives with mine until the very last. I have begged and finally ordered them not to do this, but to take part in the further battle of the Nation. I beg the heads of the Armies, the Navy, and the Air Force to strengthen by all possible means the spirit of resistance of our soldiers in the National-Socialist sense, with special reference to the fact that also I myself, as founder and creator of this movement, have preferred death to cowardly abdication or even capitulation.

May it, at some future time, become part of the code of honour of the German officer—as is already the case in our Navy—that the surrender of a district or of a town is impossible, and that above all the leaders here must march ahead as shining examples, faithfully fulfilling their duty unto death.

SECOND PART OF THE POLITICAL TESTAMENT

Before my death I expel the former Reichsmarschall Hermann Goering from the party and deprive him of all rights which he may enjoy by virtue of the decree of June 29th, 1941; and also by virtue of my statement in the Reichstag on September 1st, 1939, I appoint in his place Grossadmiral Doenitz, President of the Reich and Supreme Commander of the Armed Forces.

Before my death I expel the former Reichsfuehrer-SS and Minister of the Interior, Heinrich Himmler, from the party and from all offices of State. In his stead I appoint Gauleiter Karl Hanke as Reichsfuehrer-SS and Chief of the German Police, and Gauleiter Paul Giesler as Reich Minister of the Interior.

Goering and Himmler, quite apart from their disloyalty to my person, have done immeasurable harm to the country and the whole nation by secret negotiations with the enemy, which they conducted without my knowledge and against my wishes, and by illegally attempting to seize power in the State for themselves.

In order to give the German people a government composed of honourable men,—a government which will fulfill its pledge to continue the war by every means—I appoint the following members of the new Cabinet as leaders of the nation:

President of the Reich: DOENITZ
Chancellor of the Reich: DR. GOEBBELS
Party Minister: BORMANN
Foreign Minister: SEYSS-INQUART

[Here follow fifteen other names.]

Although a number of these men, such as Martin Bormann, Dr. Goebbels, etc., together with their wives, have joined me of their own free will and did not wish to leave the capital of the Reich under any circumstances, but were willing to perish with me here, I must nevertheless ask them to obey my request, and in this case set the interests of the nation above their own feelings. By their work and loyalty as comrades they will be just as close to me after death, as I hope that my spirit will linger among them and always go with them. Let them be hard, but never unjust, above all let them never allow fear to influence their actions, and set the honour of the nation above everything in the world. Finally, let them be conscious of the fact that our task, that of continuing the building of a National Socialist State, represents the work of the coming centuries, which places every single person under an obligation always to serve the common interest and to subordinate his own advantage to this end. I demand of all Germans, all National Socialists, men, women, and all the men of the Armed Forces, that they be faithful and obedient unto death to the new government and its President.

Above all I charge the leaders of the nation and those under them to scrupulous observance of the laws of race and to merciless opposition to the universal poisoner of all peoples, international Jewry.

Given in Berlin, this 29th day of April 1945. 4:00 A.M.
ADOLF HITLER

Source: U.S. Office of United States Chief of Counsel for Prosecution of Axis Criminality, *Nazi Conspiracy and Aggression,* 8 vols. and 2 suppl. vols. (Washington, DC: U.S. Government Printing Office, 1946–1948), VI: 259–263, Doc. No. 3569-PS. Web site: ibiblio. Available at http://www.ibiblio.org/pha/policy/1945/450429a.html.

219. "Mussolini and Other Fascist Leaders Shot: The Scene in the Square," Report "From Our Special Correspondent," Dateline 29 April 1945; Published in the *Manchester Guardian,* 30 April 1945

As the war drew to its end, mob justice was sometimes brutal. Driven from power in 1943 and rescued by the German military, who thereafter used him as a puppet head of government, by spring 1945, the Italian dictator Benito Mussolini sought escape. A British newspaper reported on his capture and murder by Italian partisans, a move that many rather cynically felt spared Italy the embarrassment of a lengthy and divisive trial.

Mussolini, with mistress, Clara Petacci, and twelve members of his Cabinet, were executed by partisans in a village on Lake Como yesterday afternoon, after being arrested in an attempt to cross the Swiss frontier. The bodies were brought to Milan last night. A partisan knocked at my door early this morning to tell me the news.

We drove out to the working-class quarter of Loreto and there were the bodies heaped together with ghastly promiscuity in the open square under the same fence against which one year ago fifteen partisans had been shot by their own countrymen.

Mussolini's body lay across that of Petacci. In his dead hand had been placed the brass ensign of the Fascist Arditi. With these fourteen were also the bodies of Farinacci and Starace, two former general secretaries of the Fascist party, and Teruzzo, formerly Minister of Colonies who had been caught elsewhere and executed by partisans.

Mussolini was caught yesterday at Dongo, Lake Como, driving by himself in a car with his uniform covered by a German greatcoat. He was driving in a column of German cars to escape observation but was recognised by an Italian Customs guard.

The others were caught in a neighbouring village. They include Pavolini, Barracu, and other lesser lights in Fascist world on whom Mussolini had to call in later days to staff his puppet Government.

This is the first conspicuous example of mob justice in liberated Italy. Otherwise the partisans have been kept well under control by their leaders. The opinion expressed this morning by the partisan C.-in-C., General Cadorna, son of the former field marshal, was that such incidents in themselves were regrettable. Nevertheless, in this case he considered the execution a good thing, since popular indignation against the Fascists demanded some satisfaction. The risk of protracted trials, such as has been taking place in Rome, was thus avoided.

Source: Manchester Guardian, 30 April 1945. Reprinted with permission.

220. Grand Admiral Karl Dönitz, Broadcast Informing the German People of Their Unconditional Surrender, 8 May 1945

One week after telling the German people of Hitler's death, Grand Admiral Karl Dönitz, his successor, spoke again on the radio, to give them the news that Germany had signed an unconditional surrender, which would come into effect at 11 P.M. on 8 May 1945. He appealed to his countrymen to conduct themselves with dignity and to hope that ultimately they would be able to find a respected place in Europe.

GERMAN MEN AND WOMEN:

When I addressed the German nation on May 1 telling it that the Fuehrer had appointed me his successor, I said that my foremost task was to save the lives of the German people. In order to achieve this goal, I ordered the German High Command during the night of May 6–7 to sign the unconditional surrender for all fronts.

On May 8 at 23 hours (11 P.M.) the arms will be silent.

German soldiers, veterans of countless battles, are now treading the bitter path of captivity, and thereby making the last sacrifice for the life of our women and children, and for the future of our nation.

We bow to all who have fallen. I have pledged myself to the German people that in the coming times of want I will help courageous women and children, as far as I humanly can, to alleviate their conditions. Whether this will be possible I do not know.

We must face facts squarely. The unity of state and party does not exist any more. The party has left the scene of its activities.

With the occupation of Germany, the power has been transferred to the occupying authorities. It is up to them to confirm me in my function and the Government I have appointed or decide whether to appoint a different one.

Should I be required to help our Fatherland, I will remain at my post.

Should the will of the German people express itself in the appointment of a head of state, or should the powers of occupation make it impossible for me to continue in my office remains to be seen.

Duty keeps me in my difficult post for the sake of Germany. I will not remain one hour more than can be reconciled with the dignity of the Reich. I will disregard my person in this matter.

All of us have to face a difficult path. We have to walk it with dignity, courage and discipline which those demand of us who sacrificed their all for us. We must walk it by making the greatest efforts to create a firm basis for our future lives.

We will walk it unitedly. Without this unity we shall not be able to overcome the misery of the times to come. We will walk it in the hope that one day our children may lead a free and secure existence in a peaceful Europe. On this thorny path, which we all will have to tread, I will try to help you as much as is possible, should I remain at my post. Should we succeed in going this way together, this step will be a service to the nation and to the Reich.

Source: New York Times, 9 May 1945. Web site: ibiblio. Available at http://www.ibiblio.org/pha/policy/1945/450508b.html.

221. Supreme Allied Commander General Dwight D. Eisenhower, Victory Order of the Day and Proclamation on Germany's Defeat, 8 May 1945

With Germany defeated, General Dwight D. Eisenhower, the supreme Allied commander in Europe, issued a triumphant but sober order of the day and victory proclamation, acknowledging the millions who had suffered and fought for this moment. He proclaimed that the objectives the Allies had set for themselves in Europe had now been attained.

VICTORY ORDER OF THE DAY

The crusade on which we embarked in the early summer of 1944 has reached its glorious conclusion. It is my especial privilege, in the name of all nations represented in this theatre of war, to commend each of you for the valiant performance of duty.

Though these words are feeble, they come from the bottom of a heart overflowing with pride in your loyal service and admiration for you as warriors. Your accomplishments at sea, in the air, on the ground and in the field of supply have astonished the world.

Even before the final week of the conflict you had put 5,000,000 of the enemy permanently out of the war. You have taken in stride military tasks so difficult as to be classed by many doubters as impossible. You have confused, defeated and destroyed your savagely fighting foe. On the road to victory you have endured every discomfort and privation and have surmounted every obstacle that ingenuity and desperation could throw in your path. You did not pause until our front was firmly joined up with the great Red Army coming from the east and other Allied forces coming from the south.

Full victory in Europe has been attained. Working and fighting together in single and indestructible partnership you have achieved a perfection in the unification of air, ground and naval power that will stand as a model in our time.

The route you have traveled through hundreds of miles is marked by the graves of former comrades. From them have been exacted the ultimate sacrifice. The blood of many nations—American, British, Canadian, French, Polish and others—has helped to gain the victory. Each of the fallen died as a member of a team to which you belong, bound together by a common love of liberty and a refusal to submit to enslavement. No monument of stone, no memorial of whatever magnitude could so well express our respect and veneration for their sacrifice as would the perpetuation of the spirit of comradeship in which they died.

As we celebrate victory in Europe let us remind ourselves that our common problems of the immediate and distant future can be best solved in the same conceptions of cooperation and devotion to the cause of human freedom as have made this Expeditionary Force such a mighty engine of righteous destruction. Let us have no part in the profitless quarrels in which other men will inevitably engage as to what country and what service won the European war.

Every man and every woman of every nation here represented has served according to his or her ability and efforts and each has contributed to the outcome. This we shall remember and in doing so we shall be revering each honored grave and be sending comfort to the loved ones of comrades who could not live to see this day.

COMMANDER'S PROCLAMATION

In 1943 the late President Roosevelt and Premier Churchill met in Casablanca. There they pronounced the formula of unconditional surrender for the Axis Powers.

In Europe that formula has now been fulfilled. The Allied force which invaded Europe on June 6, 1944, has, with its great Russian Ally and the forces advancing from the south, utterly defeated the Germans on land, sea and air.

This unconditional surrender has been achieved by team-work, team-work not only among all the Allies participating but among all the services, land, sea and air.

To every subordinate that has been in this command of almost 5,000,000 Allies I owe a debt of gratitude that can never be repaid. The only repayment that can be made to them is the deep appreciation and lasting gratitude of all the free citizens of all the United Nations.

Source: New York Times, 9 May 1945. Web site: ibiblio. Available at www/ibiblio.org/pha/policy/1945/450508h.html.

222. Marquis Koichi Kido, "Analysis of and Plan for the War Situation," 8 June 1945

Although Japanese military leaders were determined to fight to the bitter end, other officials were less committed to their country's destruction. Immediately after a meeting of the Imperial Conference, attended by the emperor, approved the military plans for the anticipated American invasion of the Japanese homeland, the eminent Marquis Koichi Kido, a relative of Emperor Hirohito, drafted a memorandum that he handed to the latter. Kido recommended opening peace negotiations with the Allies, using the then-still-neutral Soviets as intermediaries, a suggestion to which the emperor agreed. These discussions proved inconclusive, especially after the Soviet Union itself declared war on Japan the following month. Given the intransigence of the Japanese military and their reluctance to consider any negotiated settlement, it is by no means certain that, even if Japan and the Allies had reached some agreement on surrender terms, Kido and like-minded colleagues would have been able to obtain its acceptance by the Japanese government.

(1) The progress of the war in Okinawa, to my regret, makes me believe that it is destined inevitably to result in a miserable fiasco. Moreover, it is almost certain that this result will come about in the very near future.

(2) After a careful scrutiny of reports on our national strength, attached for reference to the agenda of the conference in the imperial presence, I can see that, by the latter part of this year, we will be all but incapable of conducting the war on all fronts.

(3) Although it is very likely that I, a nonexpert in this field, would be unable to estimate accurately the enemy's strategy for the future, I can say that, judging from his air force at present and the tremendous effect of his mass incendiary bombing, it would not be a difficult task to sweep away, one after another, all the cities and towns, down to villages in the country. He would not require much time for it either. If the enemy were to adopt the tactics of destroying residential quarters, this would at the same time bring about the loss of stored clothing and foodstuffs. Especially in farming villages, since they are not accustomed to air raids or to confronting this type of attack, it would be almost impossible to enforce the dispersal of supplies beforehand. So it has to be observed that most of these supplies will have to be lost, especially in small towns and villages all over the country, since their antiaircraft defense has hardly amounted to anything.

(4) If this is correct, the extreme shortage of provisions and foodstuffs that will sweep the country in the latter part of this year and thereafter—in light of the approaching chilly season—will cause serious unrest among the people at large. And, in consequence, the situation will be beyond salvation.

(5) Therefore, I believe it is most urgent that resolute steps be taken. By what means and measures should we attain this objective? That is what must be most carefully worked out.

(6) Judging from various announcements and articles indicating the enemy's so-called peace offensive, it is well nigh certain that he looks upon the overthrowing of the so-called militarist clique as his chief objective.

(7) Although I believe it is a proper course to start negotiations after the military proposed peace, this is almost impossible at present, considering the current condition of our country. Also, we are most likely to lose a good chance should we wait until the opportunity matures. As a result, we cannot be sure we will not share the fate of Germany and be reduced to adverse circumstances under which we will not attain even our supreme object of safeguarding the Imperial Household and preserving the national polity.

(8) Although to do so may be very much out of usage according to past precedents, and although it is regrettable to have to ask for His Majesty's approval concerning this monumental proposal, I believe we have no alternative but to solicit an imperial resolution for the sake of all the people and exert our wholehearted efforts to saving the war situation as follows: (a) Negotiate with a mediating country by means of His Majesty the Emperor's personal message. Though it would perhaps be a good idea to initiate direct negotiations with the Anglo-Americans, who are our opponents, it would be more appropriate to have Soviet Russia, which is observing neutrality at present, act as

our intermediary. (b) The chief point in the prospective message by His Majesty would be to make it known that the Throne, who had always been interested in peace—citing the imperial rescript on the declaration of war—has decided, in view of the impossibly heavy war damages we have sustained, to bring the war to a close on "very generous terms." (c) The terms would have limits: If a guarantee for making the Pacific Ocean literally "a pacific ocean" in the true sense were obtained, Japan would give up her position of occupation and direction in the Pacific, inasmuch as we would be allowed to help various nations and races achieve independence in their respective

countries and sectors. The army and navy forces stationed in the occupied areas would be evacuated on our own initiative. Though it is possible that they might be forced by pressing circumstances to give up their arms on the spot, this would have to depend on the outcome of negotiations. In regard to the reduction of armaments, we must be prepared for pretty strong demands being forced on us. There will be no choice for us but to be content with a minimum defense.

Source: The Diary of Marquis Kido, 1931–45: Selected Translations into English (Frederick, MD: University Publications of America, 1984), 434–436.

223. Charter of the United Nations, San Francisco, 26 June 1945

In June 1945, the great powers finally completed their negotiations over the creation of the United Nations, the new international organization designed to prevent future wars. Its charter represented a compromise between the idea that all nations should be equal, with all entitled to vote in the General Assembly, and President Franklin D. Roosevelt's "four policemen" vision of a concert of the great powers running the world between them. Five member states, Great Britain, the United States, the Soviet Union, China, and France, the coalition that had won the war, each had a permanent seat and veto power on the Security Council, which had to approve all executive action taken by the United Nations. In conjunction with the new United Nations, the Allies also created an international court of justice. A lineal descendant of the prewar international court of justice, its function was to rule on and settle disputes between states.

WE THE PEOPLES OF THE UNITED NATIONS DETERMINED to save succeeding generations from the scourge of war, which twice in our lifetime has brought untold sorrow to mankind, and to reaffirm faith in fundamental human rights, in the dignity and worth of the human person, in the equal rights of men and women and of nations large and small, and to establish conditions under which justice and respect for the obligations arising from treaties and other sources of international law can be maintained, and to promote social progress and better standards of life in larger freedom, AND FOR THESE ENDS to practice tolerance and live together in peace with one another as good neighbours, and to unite our strength to maintain international peace and security, and to ensure, by the acceptance of principles and the institution of methods, that armed force shall not be used, save in the common interest, and to employ international machinery for the promotion of the economic and social advancement of all peoples, HAVE RESOLVED TO COMBINE OUR EFFORTS TO ACCOMPLISH THESE AIMS.

Accordingly, our respective Governments, through representatives assembled in the city of San Francisco, who have exhibited their full powers found to be in good and due form, have agreed to the present Charter of the United Nations and do hereby establish an international organization to be known as the United Nations.

CHAPTER I
PURPOSES AND PRINCIPLES
Article 1
The Purposes of the United Nations are:

1. To maintain international peace and security, and to that end: to take effective collective measures for the prevention and removal of threats to the peace, and for the suppression of acts of aggression or other breaches of the peace, and to bring about by peaceful means, and in conformity with the principles of justice and international law, adjustment or settlement

of international disputes or situations which might lead to a breach of the peace;

2. To develop friendly relations among nations based on respect for the principle of equal rights and self-determination of peoples, and to take other appropriate measures to strengthen universal peace;

3. To achieve international co-operation in solving international problems of an economic, social, cultural, or humanitarian character, and in promoting and encouraging respect for human rights and for fundamental freedoms for all without distinction as to race, sex, language, or religion; and

4. To be a centre for harmonizing the actions of nations in the attainment of these common ends.

Article 2

The Organization and its Members, in pursuit of the Purposes stated in Article 1, shall act in accordance with the following Principles.

1. The Organization is based on the principle of the sovereign equality of all its Members.

2. All Members, in order to ensure to each of them the rights and benefits resulting from membership, shall fulfil in good faith the obligations assumed by them in accordance with the present Charter.

3. All Members shall settle their international disputes by peaceful means in such a manner that international peace and security, and justice, are not endangered.

4. All Members shall refrain in their international relations from the threat or use of force against the territorial integrity or political independence of any state, or in any other manner inconsistent with the Purposes of the United Nations.

5. All Members shall give the United Nations every assistance in any action it takes in accordance with the present Charter, and shall refrain from giving assistance to any state against which the United Nations is taking preventive or enforcement action.

6. The Organization shall ensure that states which are not Members of the United Nations act in accordance with these Principles so far as may be necessary for the maintenance of international peace and security.

7. Nothing contained in the present Charter shall authorize the United Nations to intervene in matters which are essentially within the domestic jurisdiction of any state or shall require the Members to submit such matters to settlement under the present Charter; but this principle shall not prejudice the application of enforcement measures under Chapter VII.

CHAPTER II
MEMBERSHIP

Article 3

The original Members of the United Nations shall be the states which, having participated in the United Nations Conference on International Organization at San Francisco, or having previously signed the Declaration by United Nations of 1 January 1942, sign the present Charter and ratify it in accordance with Article 110.

Article 4

1. Membership in the United Nations is open to other peace-loving states which accept the obligations contained in the present Charter and, in the judgment of the Organization, are able and willing to carry out these obligations.

2. The admission of any such state to membership in the United Nations will be effected by a decision of the General Assembly upon the recommendation of the Security Council.

Article 5

A Member of the United Nations against which preventive or enforcement action has been taken by the Security Council may be suspended from the exercise of the rights and privileges of membership by the General Assembly upon the recommendation of the Security Council. The exercise of these rights and privileges may be restored by the Security Council.

Article 6

A Member of the United Nations which has persistently violated the Principles contained in the present Charter may be expelled from the Organization by the General Assembly upon the recommendation of the Security Council.

CHAPTER III
ORGANS

Article 7

1. There are established as the principal organs of the United Nations: a General Assembly, a Security Council, an Economic and Social Council, a Trusteeship Council, an International Court of Justice, and a Secretariat.

2. Such subsidiary organs as may be found necessary may be established in accordance with the present Charter.

Article 8

The United Nations shall place no restrictions on the

eligibility of men and women to participate in any capacity and under conditions of equality in its principal and subsidiary organs.

CHAPTER IV
THE GENERAL ASSEMBLY
Composition
Article 9

1. The General Assembly shall consist of all the Members of the United Nations.
2. Each Member shall have not more than five representatives in the General Assembly.

Functions and Powers
Article 10

The General Assembly may discuss any questions or any matters within the scope of the present Charter or relating to the powers and functions of any organs provided for in the present Charter, and, except as provided in Article 12, may make recommendations to the Members of the United Nations or to the Security Council or to both on any such questions or matters.

Article 11

1. The General Assembly may consider the general principles of co-operation in the maintenance of international peace and security, including the principles governing disarmament and the regulation of armaments, and may make recommendations with regard to such principles to the Members or to the Security Council or to both.
2. The General Assembly may discuss any questions relating to the maintenance of international peace and security brought before it by any Member of the United Nations, or by the Security Council, or by a state which is not a Member of the United Nations in accordance with Article 35, paragraph 2, and, except as provided in Article 12, may make recommendations with regard to any such questions to the state or states concerned or to the Security Council or to both. Any such question on which action is necessary shall be referred to the Security Council by the General Assembly either before or after discussion.
3. The General Assembly may call the attention of the Security Council to situations which are likely to endanger international peace and security.
4. The powers of the General Assembly set forth in this Article shall not limit the general scope of Article 10.

Article 12

1. While the Security Council is exercising in respect of any dispute or situation the functions assigned to it in the present Charter, the General Assembly shall not make any recommendation with regard to that dispute or situation unless the Security Council so requests.
2. The Secretary-General, with the consent of the Security Council, shall notify the General Assembly at each session of any matters relative to the maintenance of international peace and security which are being dealt with by the Security Council and similarly notify the General Assembly, or the Members of the United Nations if the General Assembly is not in session, immediately if the Security Council ceases to deal with such matters.

Article 13

1. The General Assembly shall initiate studies and make recommendations for the purpose of:
   a. promoting international co-operation in the political field and encouraging the progressive development of international law and its codification;
   b. promoting international co-operation in the economic, social, cultural, educational, and health fields, and assisting in the realization of human rights and fundamental freedoms for all without distinction as to race, sex, language, or religion.
2. The further responsibilities, functions and powers of the General Assembly with respect to matters mentioned in paragraph 1 above are set forth in Chapters IX and X.

Article 14

Subject to the provisions of Article 12, the General Assembly may recommend measures for the peaceful adjustment of any situation, regardless of origin, which it deems likely to impair the general welfare or friendly relations among nations, including situations resulting from a violation of the provisions of the present Charter setting forth the Purposes and Principles of the United Nations.

Article 15

1. The General Assembly shall receive and consider annual and special reports from the Security Council; these reports shall include an account of the measures that the Security Council has decided upon or taken to maintain international peace and security.
2. The General Assembly shall receive and consider reports from the other organs of the United Nations.

Article 16

The General Assembly shall perform such functions with respect to the international trusteeship system as are assigned to it under Chapters XII and XIII, including the approval of the trusteeship agreements for areas not designated as strategic.

Article 17

1. The General Assembly shall consider and approve the budget of the Organization.
2. The expenses of the Organization shall be borne by the Members as apportioned by the General Assembly.
3. The Assembly shall consider and approve any financial and budgetary arrangements with specialized agencies referred to in Article 57 and shall examine the administrative budgets of such specialized agencies with a view to making recommendations to the agencies concerned.

Voting

Article 18

1. Each member of the General Assembly shall have one vote.
2. Decisions of the General Assembly on important questions shall be made by a two-thirds majority of the members present and voting. These questions shall include: recommendations with respect to the maintenance of international peace and security, the election of the non-permanent members of the Security Council, the election of the members of the Economic and Social Council, the election of members of the Trusteeship Council in accordance with paragraph 1 of Article 86, the admission of new Members to the United Nations, the suspension of the rights and privileges of membership, the expulsion of Members, questions relating to the operation of the trusteeship system, and budgetary questions.
3. Decisions on other questions, including the determination of additional categories of questions to be decided by a two-thirds majority, shall be made by a majority of the members present and voting.

Article 19

A Member of the United Nations which is in arrears in the payment of its financial contributions to the Organization shall have no vote in the General Assembly if the amount of its arrears equals or exceeds the amount of the contributions due from it for the preceding two full years.

The General Assembly may, nevertheless, permit such a Member to vote if it is satisfied that the failure to pay is due to conditions beyond the control of the Member.

Procedure

Article 20

The General Assembly shall meet in regular annual sessions and in such special sessions as occasion may require. Special sessions shall be convoked by the Secretary-General at the request of the Security Council or of a majority of the Members of the United Nations.

Article 21

The General Assembly shall adopt its own rules of procedure. It shall elect its President for each session.

Article 22

The General Assembly may establish such subsidiary organs as it deems necessary for the performance of its functions.

CHAPTER V
THE SECURITY COUNCIL

Composition

Article 23

1. The Security Council shall consist of fifteen Members of the United Nations. The Republic of China, France, the Union of Soviet Socialist Republics, the United Kingdom of Great Britain and Northern Ireland, and the United States of America shall be permanent members of the Security Council. The General Assembly shall elect ten other Members of the United Nations to be non-permanent members of the Security Council, due regard being specially paid, in the first instance to the contribution of Members of the United Nations to the maintenance of international peace and security and to the other purposes of the Organization, and also to equitable geographical distribution.
2. The non-permanent members of the Security Council shall be elected for a term of two years. In the first election of the non-permanent members after the increase of the membership of the Security Council from eleven to fifteen, two of the four additional members shall be chosen for a term of one year. A retiring member shall not be eligible for immediate re-election.
3. Each member of the Security Council shall have one representative.

Functions and Powers
Article 24

1. In order to ensure prompt and effective action by the United Nations, its Members confer on the Security Council primary responsibility for the maintenance of international peace and security, and agree that in carrying out its duties under this responsibility the Security Council acts on their behalf.

2. In discharging these duties the Security Council shall act in accordance with the Purposes and Principles of the United Nations. The specific powers granted to the Security Council for the discharge of these duties are laid down in Chapters VI, VII, VIII, and XII.

3. The Security Council shall submit annual and, when necessary, special reports to the General Assembly for its consideration.

Article 25

The Members of the United Nations agree to accept and carry out the decisions of the Security Council in accordance with the present Charter.

Article 26

In order to promote the establishment and maintenance of international peace and security with the least diversion for armaments of the world's human and economic resources, the Security Council shall be responsible for formulating, with the assistance of the Military Staff Committee referred to in Article 47, plans to be submitted to the Members of the United Nations for the establishment of a system for the regulation of armaments.

Voting
Article 27

1. Each member of the Security Council shall have one vote.

2. Decisions of the Security Council on procedural matters shall be made by an affirmative vote of nine members.

3. Decisions of the Security Council on all other matters shall be made by an affirmative vote of nine members including the concurring votes of the permanent members; provided that, in decisions under Chapter VI, and under paragraph 3 of Article 52, a party to a dispute shall abstain from voting.

Procedure
Article 28

1. The Security Council shall be so organized as to be able to function continuously. Each member of the Security Council shall for this purpose be represented at all times at the seat of the Organization.

2. The Security Council shall hold meetings at which each of its members may, if it so desires, be represented by a member of the government or by some other specially designated representative.

3. The Security Council may hold meetings at such places other than the seat of the Organization as in its judgment will best facilitate its work.

Article 29

The Security Council may establish such subsidiary organs as it deems necessary for the performance of its functions.

Article 30

The Security Council shall adopt its own rules of procedure, including the method of selecting its President.

Article 31

Any Member of the United Nations which is not a member of the Security Council may participate, without vote, in the discussion of any question brought before the Security Council whenever the latter considers that the interests of that Member are specially affected.

Article 32

Any Member of the United Nations which is not a member of the Security Council or any state which is not a Member of the United Nations, if it is a party to a dispute under consideration by the Security Council, shall be invited to participate, without vote, in the discussion relating to the dispute. The Security Council shall lay down such conditions as it deems just for the participation of a state which is not a Member of the United Nations.

CHAPTER VI
PACIFIC SETTLEMENT OF DISPUTES
Article 33

1. The parties to any dispute, the continuance of which is likely to endanger the maintenance of international peace and security, shall, first of all, seek a solution by negotiation, enquiry, mediation, conciliation, arbitration, judicial settlement, resort to regional agencies or arrangements, or other peaceful means of their own choice.

2. The Security Council shall, when it deems necessary, call upon the parties to settle their dispute by such means.

Article 34

The Security Council may investigate any dispute, or any situation which might lead to international friction or give rise to a dispute, in order to determine whether the continuance of the dispute or situation is likely to endanger the maintenance of international peace and security.

Article 35

1. Any Member of the United Nations may bring any dispute, or any situation of the nature referred to in Article 34, to the attention of the Security Council or of the General Assembly.

2. A state which is not a Member of the United Nations may bring to the attention of the Security Council or of the General Assembly any dispute to which it is a party if it accepts in advance, for the purposes of the dispute, the obligations of pacific settlement provided in the present Charter.

3. The proceedings of the General Assembly in respect of matters brought to its attention under this Article will be subject to the provisions of Articles 11 and 12.

Article 36

1. The Security Council may, at any stage of a dispute of the nature referred to in Article 33 or of a situation of like nature, recommend appropriate procedures or methods of adjustment.

2. The Security Council should take into consideration any procedures for the settlement of the dispute which have already been adopted by the parties.

3. In making recommendations under this Article the Security Council should also take into consideration that legal disputes should as a general rule be referred by the parties to the International Court of Justice in accordance with the provisions of the Statute of the Court.

Article 37

1. Should the parties to a dispute of the nature referred to in Article 33 fail to settle it by the means indicated in that Article, they shall refer it to the Security Council.

2. If the Security Council deems that the continuance of the dispute is in fact likely to endanger the maintenance of international peace and security, it shall decide whether to take action under Article 36 or to recommend such terms of settlement as it may consider appropriate.

Article 38

Without prejudice to the provisions of Articles 33 to 37,
the Security Council may, if all the parties to any dispute so request, make recommendations to the parties with a view to a pacific settlement of the dispute.

CHAPTER VII
ACTION WITH RESPECT TO THREATS TO THE PEACE, BREACHES OF THE PEACE, AND ACTS OF AGGRESSION

Article 39

The Security Council shall determine the existence of any threat to the peace, breach of the peace, or act of aggression and shall make recommendations, or decide what measures shall be taken in accordance with Articles 4 and 42, to maintain or restore international peace and security.

Article 40

In order to prevent an aggravation of the situation, the Security Council may, before making the recommendations or deciding upon the measures provided for in Article 39, call upon the parties concerned to comply with such provisional measures as it deems necessary or desirable. Such provisional measures shall be without prejudice to the rights, claims, or position of the parties concerned. The Security Council shall duly take account of failure to comply with such provisional measures.

Article 41

The Security Council may decide what measures not involving the use of armed force are to be employed to give effect to its decisions, and it may call upon the Members of the United Nations to apply such measures. These may include complete or partial interruption of economic relations and of rail, sea, air, postal, telegraphic, radio, and other means of communication, and the severance of diplomatic relations.

Article 42

Should the Security Council consider that measures provided for in Article 41 would be inadequate or have proved to be inadequate, it may take such action by air, sea, or land forces as may be necessary to maintain or restore international peace and security. Such action may include demonstrations, blockade, and other operations by air, sea, or land forces of Members of the United Nations.

Article 43

1. All Members of the United Nations, in order to contribute to the maintenance of international peace and security, undertake to make available to the Security Council, on its request and in accordance with a special agreement or agreements, armed forces, assis-

tance, and facilities, including rights of passage, necessary for the purpose of maintaining international peace and security.

2. Such agreement or agreements shall govern the numbers and types of forces, their degree of readiness and general location, and the nature of the facilities and assistance to be provided.

3. The agreement or agreements shall be negotiated as soon as possible on the initiative of the Security Council. They shall be concluded between the Security Council and Members or between the Security Council and groups of Members and shall be subject to ratification by the signatory states in accordance with their respective constitutional processes.

Article 44

When the Security Council has decided to use force it shall, before calling upon a Member not represented on it to provide armed forces in fulfilment of the obligations assumed under Article 43, invite that Member, if the Member so desires, to participate in the decisions of the Security Council concerning the employment of contingents of that Member's armed forces.

Article 45

In order to enable the Nations to take urgent military measures, Members shall hold immediately available national air-force contingents for combined international enforcement action. The strength and degree of readiness of these contingents and plans for their combined action shall be determined, within the limits laid down in the special agreement or agreements referred to in Article 43, by the Security Council with the assistance of the Military Staff Committee.

Article 46

Plans for the application of armed force shall be made by the Security Council with the assistance of the Military Staff Committee.

Article 47

1. There shall be established a Military Staff Committee to advise and assist the Security Council on questions relating to the Security Council's military requirements for the maintenance of international peace and security, the employment and command of forces placed at its disposal, the regulation of armaments, and possible disarmament.

2. The Military Staff Committee consists of the Chiefs of Staff of the permanent members of the Security

Council or their representatives. Any Member of the United Nations not permanently represented on the Committee shall be invited by the Committee to be associated with it when the efficient discharge of the Committee's responsibilities requires the participation of that Member its work.

3. The Military Staff Committee shall be responsible under the Security Council for the strategic direction of any armed forces placed at the disposal of the Security Council. Questions relating to the command of such forces shall be worked out subsequently.

4. The Military Staff Committee, with the authorization of the Security Council and after consultation with appropriate regional agencies, may establish subcommittees.

Article 48

1. The action required to carry out the decisions of the Security Council for the maintenance of international peace and security shall be taken by all the Members of the United Nations or by some of them, as the Security Council may determine.

2. Such decisions shall be carried out by the Members of the United Nations directly and through their action in the appropriate international agencies of which they are members.

Article 49

The Members of the United Nations shall join in affording mutual assistance in carrying out the measures decided upon by the Security Council.

Article 50

If preventive or enforcement measures against any state are taken by the Security Council, any other state, whether a Member of the United Nations or not, which finds itself confronted with special economic problems arising from the carrying out of those measures shall have the right to consult the Security Council with regard to a solution of those problems.

Article 51

Nothing in the present Charter shall impair the inherent right of individual or collective self-defence if an armed attack occurs against a Member of the United Nations, until the Security Council has taken measures necessary to maintain international peace and security. Measures taken by Members in the exercise of this right of self-defence shall be immediately reported to the Security Council and shall not in any way affect the authority and responsibility of the Security Council under the present Charter to take at any time such action as it deems necessary in order to maintain or restore international peace and security.

CHAPTER VIII
REGIONAL ARRANGEMENTS

Article 52

1. Nothing in the present Charter precludes the existence of regional arrangements or agencies for dealing with such matters relating to the maintenance of international peace and security as are appropriate for regional action, provided that such arrangements or agencies and their activities are consistent with the Purposes and Principles of the United Nations.

2. The Members of the United Nations entering into such arrangements or constituting such agencies shall make every effort to achieve pacific settlement of local disputes through such regional arrangements or by such regional agencies before referring them to the Security Council.

3. The Security Council shall encourage the development of pacific settlement of local disputes through such regional arrangements or by such regional agencies either on the initiative of the states concerned or by reference from the Security Council.

4. This Article in no way impairs the application of Articles 34 and 35.

Article 53

1. The Security Council shall, where appropriate, utilize such regional arrangements or agencies for enforcement action under its authority. But no enforcement action shall be taken under regional arrangements or by regional agencies without the authorization of the Security Council, with the exception of measures against any enemy state, as defined in paragraph 2 of this Article, provided for pursuant to Article 107 or in regional arrangements directed against renewal of aggressive policy on the part of any such state, until such time as the Organization may, on request of the Governments concerned, be charged with the responsibility for preventing further aggression by such a state.

2. The term enemy state as used in paragraph 1 of this Article applies to any state which during the Second World War has been an enemy of any signatory of the present Charter.

Article 54

The Security Council shall at all times be kept fully informed of activities undertaken or in contemplation under regional arrangements or by regional agencies for the maintenance of international peace and security.

CHAPTER IX
INTERNATIONAL ECONOMIC AND SOCIAL CO-OPERATION

Article 55

With a view to the creation of conditions of stability and well-being which are necessary for peaceful and friendly relations among nations based on respect for the principle of equal rights and self-determination of peoples, the United Nations shall promote:

a. higher standards of living, full employment, and conditions of economic and social progress and development;

b. solutions of international economic, social, health, and related problems; and international cultural and educational co-operation; and

c. universal respect for, and observance of, human rights and fundamental freedoms for all without distinction as to race, sex, language, or religion.

Article 56

All Members pledge themselves to take joint and separate action in co-operation with the Organization for the achievement of the purposes set forth in Article 55.

Article 57

1. The various specialized agencies, established by intergovernmental agreement and having wide international responsibilities, as defined in their basic instruments, in economic, social, cultural, educational, health, and related fields, shall be brought into relationship with the United Nations in accordance with the provisions of Article 63.

2. Such agencies thus brought into relationship with the United Nations are hereinafter referred to as specialized agencies.

Article 58

The Organization shall make recommendations for the co-ordination of the policies and activities of the specialized agencies.

Article 59

The Organization shall, where appropriate, initiate negotiations among the states concerned for the creation of any new specialized agencies required for the accomplishment of the purposes set forth in Article 55.

Article 60

Responsibility for the discharge of the functions of the Organization set forth in this Chapter shall be vested in the General Assembly and, under the authority of the General Assembly, in the Economic and Social Council, which shall have for this purpose the powers set forth in Chapter X.

CHAPTER X

THE ECONOMIC AND SOCIAL COUNCIL

Composition

Article 61

1. The Economic and Social Council shall consist of fifty-four Members of the United Nations elected by the General Assembly.

2. Subject to the provisions of paragraph 3, eighteen members of the Economic and Social Council shall be elected each year for a term of three years. A retiring member shall be eligible for immediate re-election.

3. At the first election after the increase in the membership of the Economic and Social Council from twenty-seven to fifty-four members, in addition to the members elected in place of the nine members whose term of office expires at the end of that year, twenty-seven additional members shall be elected. Of these twenty-seven additional members, the term of office of nine members so elected shall expire at the end of one year, and of nine other members at the end of two years, in accordance with arrangements made by the General Assembly.

4. Each member of the Economic and Social Council shall have one representative.

Functions and Powers

Article 62

1. The Economic and Social Council may make or initiate studies and reports with respect to international economic, social, cultural, educational, health, and related matters and may make recommendations with respect to any such matters to the General Assembly, to the Members of the United Nations, and to the specialized agencies concerned.

2. It may make recommendations for the purpose of promoting respect for, and observance of, human rights and fundamental freedoms for all.

3. It may prepare draft conventions for submission to the General Assembly, with respect to matters falling within its competence.

4. It may call, in accordance with the rules prescribed by the United Nations, international conferences on matters falling within its competence.

Article 63

1. The Economic and Social Council may enter into agreements with any of the agencies referred to in Article 57, defining the terms on which the agency concerned shall be brought into relationship with the United Nations. Such agreements shall be subject to approval by the General Assembly.

2. It may co-ordinate the activities of the specialized agencies through consultation with and recommendations to such agencies and through recommendations to the General Assembly and to the Members of the United Nations.

Article 64

1. The Economic and Social Council may take appropriate steps to obtain regular reports from the specialized agencies, may make arrangements with the Members of the United Nations and with the specialized agencies to obtain reports on the steps taken to give effect to its own recommendations and to recommendations on matters falling within its competence made by the General Assembly.

2. It may communicate its observations on these reports to the General Assembly.

Article 65

The Economic and Social Council may furnish information to the Security Council and shall assist the Security Council upon its request.

Article 66

1. The Economic and Social Council shall perform such functions as fall within its competence in connection with the carrying out of the recommendations of the General Assembly.

2. It may, with the approval of the General Assembly, perform services at the request of Members of the United Nations and at the request of specialized agencies.

3. It shall perform such other functions as are specified elsewhere in the present Charter or as may be assigned to it by the General Assembly.

Voting

Article 67

1. Each member of the Economic and Social Council shall have one vote.

2. Decisions of the Economic and Social Council shall be made by a majority of the members present and voting.

Procedure

Article 68

The Economic and Social Council shall set up commissions in economic and social fields and for the promotion of human rights, and such other commissions as may be required for the performance of its functions.

Article 69

The Economic and Social Council shall invite any Member of the United Nations to participate, without vote, in its deliberations on any matter of particular concern to that Member.

Article 70

The Economic and Social Council may make arrangements for representatives of the specialized agencies to participate, without vote, in its deliberations and in those of the commissions established by it, and for its representatives to participate in the deliberations of the specialized agencies.

Article 71

The Economic and Social Council may make suitable arrangements for consultation with non-governmental organizations which are concerned with matters within its competence. Such arrangements may be made with international organizations and, where appropriate, with national organizations after consultation with the Member of the United Nations concerned.

Article 72

1. The Economic and Social Council shall adopt its own rules of procedure, including the method of selecting its President.
2. The Economic and Social Council shall meet as required in accordance with its rules, which shall include provision for the convening of meetings on the request of a majority of its members.

CHAPTER XI

DECLARATION REGARDING NON-SELF-GOVERNING TERRITORIES

Article 73

Members of the United Nations which have or assume responsibilities for the administration of territories whose peoples have not yet attained a full measure of self-government recognize the principle that the interests of the inhabitants of these territories are paramount, and accept as a sacred trust the obligation to promote to the utmost, within the system of international peace and security established by the present Charter, the well-being of the inhabitants of these territories, and, to this end:

a. to ensure, with due respect for the culture of the peoples concerned, their political, economic, social, and educational advancement, their just treatment, and their protection against abuses;
b. to develop self-government, to take due account of the political aspirations of the peoples, and to assist them in the progressive development of their free political institutions, according to the particular circumstances of each territory and its peoples and their varying stages of advancement;
c. to further international peace and security;
d. to promote constructive measures of development, to encourage research, and to co-operate with one another and, when and where appropriate, with specialized international bodies with a view to the practical achievement of the social, economic, and scientific purposes set forth in this Article; and
e. to transmit regularly to the Secretary-General for information purposes, subject to such limitation as security and constitutional considerations may require, statistical and other information of a technical nature relating to economic, social, and educational conditions in the territories for which they are respectively responsible other than those territories to which Chapters XII and XIII apply.

Article 74

Members of the United Nations also agree that their policy in respect of the territories to which this Chapter applies, no less than in respect of their metropolitan areas, must be based on the general principle of good-neighourliness, due account being taken of the interests and well-being of the rest of the world, in social, economic, and commercial matters.

CHAPTER XII

INTERNATIONAL TRUSTEESHIP SYSTEM

Article 75

The United Nations shall establish under its authority an international trusteeship system for the administration and supervision of such territories as may be placed thereunder by subsequent individual agreements. These territories are hereinafter referred to as trust territories.

Article 76

The basic objectives of the trusteeship system, in accordance with the Purposes of the United Nations laid down in Article 1 of the present Charter, shall be:

a. to further international peace and security;
b. to promote the political, economic, social, and educational advancement of the inhabitants of the trust territories, and their progressive development towards self-government or independence as may be appropriate to the particular circumstances of each territory and its peoples and the freely expressed wishes of the peoples concerned, and as may be provided by the terms of each trusteeship agreement;
c. to encourage respect for human rights and for fundamental freedoms for all without as to race, sex, language, or religion, and to encourage recognition of the interdependence of the peoples of the world; and
d. to ensure equal treatment in social, economic, and commercial matters for all Members of the United Nations and their nationals, and also equal treatment for the latter in the administration of justice, without prejudice to the attainment of the foregoing objectives and subject to the provisions of Article 80.

Article 77

1. The trusteeship system shall apply to such territories in the following categories as may be placed thereunder by means of trusteeship agreements:
    a. territories now held under mandate;
    b. territories which may be detached from enemy states as a result of the Second World War; and
    c. territories voluntarily placed under the system by states responsible for their administration.
2. It will be a matter for subsequent agreement as to which territories in the foregoing categories will be brought under the trusteeship system and upon what terms.

Article 78

The trusteeship system shall not apply to territories which have become Members of the United Nations, relationship, among which shall be based on respect for the principle of sovereign equality.

Article 79

The terms of trusteeship for each territory to be placed under the trusteeship system, including any alteration or amendment, shall be agreed upon by the states directly concerned, including the mandatory power in the case of territories held under mandate by a Member of the United Nations, and shall be approved as provided for in Articles 83 and 85.

Article 80

1. Except as may be agreed upon in individual trustee-

ship agreements, made under Articles 77, 79, and 81, placing each territory under the trusteeship system, and until such agreements have been concluded, nothing in this Chapter shall be construed in or of itself to alter in any manner the rights whatsoever of any states or any peoples or the terms of existing international instruments to which Members of the United Nations may respectively be parties.
2. Paragraph 1 of this Article shall not be interpreted as giving grounds for delay or postponement of the negotiation and conclusion of agreements for placing mandated and other territories under the trusteeship system as provided for in Article 77.

Article 81

The trusteeship agreement shall in each case include the terms under which the trust territory will be administered and designate the authority which will exercise the administration of the trust territory. Such authority, hereinafter called the administering authority, may be one or more states or the Organization itself.

Article 82

There may be designated, in any trusteeship agreement, a strategic area or areas which may include part or all of the trust territory to which the agreement applies, without prejudice to any special agreement or agreements made under Article 43.

Article 83

1. All functions of the United Nations relating to strategic areas, including the approval of the terms of the trusteeship agreements and of their alteration or amendment, shall be exercised by the Security Council.
2. The basic objectives set forth in Article 76 shall be applicable to the people of each strategic area.
3. The Security Council shall, subject to the provisions of the trusteeship agreements and without prejudice to security considerations, avail itself of the assistance of the Trusteeship Council to perform those functions of the United Nations under the trusteeship system relating to political, economic, social, and educational matters in the strategic areas.

Article 84

It shall be the duty of the administering authority to ensure that the trust territory shall play its part in the maintenance of international peace and security. To this end the administering authority may make use of volunteer forces, facilities, and assistance from the trust territory in carrying out the obligations towards the Security Council undertaken in this regard by the administering authority, as well as for local defence and the maintenance of law and order within the trust territory.

Article 85

1. The functions of the United Nations with regard to trusteeship agreements for all areas not designated as strategic, including the approval of the terms of the trusteeship agreements and of their alteration or amendment, shall be exercised by the General Assembly.
2. The Trusteeship Council, operating under the authority of the General Assembly, shall assist the General Assembly in carrying out these functions.

CHAPTER XIII
THE TRUSTEESHIP COUNCIL

Composition
Article 86

1. The Trusteeship Council shall consist of the following Members of the United Nations:
   a. those Members administering trust territories;
   b. such of those Members mentioned by name in Article 23 as are not administering trust territories; and
   c. as many other Members elected for three-year terms by the General Assembly as may be necessary to ensure that the total number of members of the Trusteeship Council is equally divided between those Members of the United Nations which administer trust territories and those which do not.
2. Each member of the Trusteeship Council shall designate one specially qualified person to represent it therein.

Functions and Powers
Article 87

The General Assembly and, under its authority, the Trusteeship Council, in carrying out their functions, may:

a. consider reports submitted by the administering authority;
b. accept petitions and examine them in consultation with the administering authority;
c. provide for periodic visits to the respective trust territories at times agreed upon with the administering authority; and
d. take these and other actions in conformity with the terms of the trusteeship agreements.

Article 88

The Trusteeship Council shall formulate a questionnaire on the political, economic, social, and educational advancement of the inhabitants of each trust territory, and the administering authority for each trust territory within the competence of the General Assembly shall make an annual report to the General Assembly upon the basis of such questionnaire.

Voting
Article 89

1. Each member of the Trusteeship Council shall have one vote.
2. Decisions of the Trusteeship Council shall be made by a majority of the members present and voting.

Procedure
Article 90

1. The Trusteeship Council shall adopt its own rules of procedure, including the method of selecting its President.
2. The Trusteeship Council shall meet as required in accordance with its rules, which shall include provision for the convening of meetings on the request of a majority of its members.

Article 91

The Trusteeship Council shall, when appropriate, avail itself of the assistance of the Economic and Social Council and of the specialized agencies in regard to matters with which they are respectively concerned.

CHAPTER XIV
THE INTERNATIONAL COURT OF JUSTICE
Article 92

The International Court of Justice shall be the principal judicial organ of the United Nations. It shall function in accordance with the annexed Statute, which is based upon the Statute of the Permanent Court of International Justice and forms an integral part of the present Charter.

Article 93

1. All Members of the United Nations are de facto parties to the Statute of the International Court of Justice.
2. A state which is not of the United Nations may become a party to the Statute of the International Court of Justice on conditions to be determined in each case by the General Assembly upon the recommendation of the Security Council.

Article 94

1. Each Member of the United Nations undertakes to comply with the decision of the International Court of Justice in any case to which it is a party.
2. If any party to a case fails to perform the obligations incumbent upon it under a judgment rendered by the Court, the other party may have recourse to the Security Council, which may, if it deems necessary, make recommendations or decide upon measures to be taken to give effect to the judgment.

Article 95

Nothing in the present Charter shall prevent Members of the United Nations from entrusting the solution of their differences to other tribunals by virtue of agreements already in existence or which may be concluded in the future.

Article 96

1. The General Assembly or the Security Council may request the International Court of Justice to give an advisory opinion on any legal question.
2. Other organs of the United Nations and specialized agencies, which may at any time be so authorized by the General Assembly, may also request advisory opinions of the Court on legal questions arising within the scope of their activities.

CHAPTER XV
THE SECRETARIAT

Article 97

The Secretariat shall comprise a Secretary-General and such staff as the Organization may require. The Secretary-General shall be appointed by the General Assembly upon the recommendation of the Security Council. He shall be the chief administrative officer of the Organization.

Article 98

The Secretary-General shall act in that capacity in all meetings of the General Assembly, of the Security Council, of the Economic and Social Council, and of the Trusteeship Council, and shall perform such other functions as are entrusted to him by these organs. The Secretary-General shall make an annual report to the General Assembly on the work of the Organization.

Article 99

The Secretary-General may bring to the attention of the Security Council any matter which in his opinion may threaten the maintenance of international peace and security.

Article 100

1. In the performance of their duties the Secretary-General and the staff shall not seek or receive instructions from any government or from any other authority external to the Organization. They shall refrain from any action which might reflect on their position as international officials responsible only to the Organization.
2. Each Member of the United Nations undertakes to respect the exclusively international character of the responsibilities of the Secretary-General and the staff and not to seek to influence them in the discharge of their responsibilities.

Article 101

1. The staff shall be appointed by the Secretary-General under regulations established by the General Assembly.
2. Appropriate staffs shall be permanently assigned to the Economic and Social Council, the Trusteeship Council, and, as required, to other organs of the United Nations. These staffs shall form a part of the Secretariat.
3. The paramount consideration in the employment of the staff and in the determination of the conditions of service shall be the necessity of securing the highest standards of efficiency, competence, and integrity. Due regard shall be paid to the importance of recruiting the staff on as wide a geographical basis as possible.

CHAPTER XVI
MISCELLANEOUS PROVISIONS

Article 102

1. Every treaty and every international agreement entered into by any Member of the United Nations after the present Charter comes into force shall as soon as possible be registered with the Secretariat and published by it.
2. No party to any such treaty or international agreement which has not been registered in accordance with the provisions of paragraph 1 of this Article may invoke that treaty or agreement before any organ of the United Nations.

Article 103

In the event of a conflict between the obligations of the Members of the United Nations under the present Charter and their obligations under any other international agreement, their obligations under the present Charter shall prevail.

Article 104

The Organization shall enjoy in the territory of each of its Members such legal capacity as may be necessary for the exercise of its functions and the fulfilment of its purposes.

Article 105

1. The Organization shall enjoy in the territory of each of its Members such privileges and immunities as are necessary for the fulfilment of its purposes.

2. Representatives of the Members of the United Nations and officials of the Organization shall similarly enjoy such privileges and immunities as are necessary for the independent exercise of their functions in connection with the Organization.

3. The General Assembly may make recommendations with a view to determining the details of the application of paragraphs 1 and 2 of this Article or may propose conventions to the Members of the United Nations for this purpose.

CHAPTER XVII
TRANSITIONAL SECURITY ARRANGEMENTS

Article 106

Pending the coming into force of such special agreements referred to in Article 43 as in the opinion of the Security Council enable it to begin the exercise of its responsibilities under Article 42, the parties to the Four-Nation Declaration, signed at Moscow, 30 October 1943, and France, shall, in accordance with the provisions of paragraph 5 of that Declaration, consult with one another and as occasion requires with other Members of the United Nations with a view to such joint action on behalf of the Organization as may be necessary for the purpose of maintaining international peace and security.

Article 107

Nothing in the present Charter shall invalidate or preclude action, in relation to any state which during the Second World War has been an enemy of any signatory to the present Charter, taken or authorized as a result of that war by the Governments having responsibility for such action.

CHAPTER XVIII
AMENDMENTS

Article 108

Amendments to the present Charter shall come into force for all Members of the United Nations when they have been adopted by a vote of two-thirds of the members of the General Assembly and ratified in accordance with their respective constitutional processes by two-thirds of the Members

of the United Nations, including all the permanent members of the Security Council.

Article 109

1. A General Conference of the Members of the United Nations for the purpose of reviewing the present Charter may be held at a date and place to be fixed by a two-thirds vote of the members of the General Assembly and by a vote of any nine members of the Security Council. Each Member of the United Nations shall have one vote in the conference.

2. Any alteration of the present Charter recommended by a two-thirds vote of the conference shall take effect when ratified in accordance with their respective constitutional processes by two-thirds of the Members of the United Nations including the permanent members of the Security Council.

3. If such a conference has not been held before the tenth annual session of the General Assembly following the coming into force of the present Charter, the proposal to call such a conference shall be placed on the agenda of that session of the General Assembly, and the conference shall be held if so decided by a majority vote of the members of the General Assembly and by a vote of any seven members of the Security Council.

CHAPTER XIX
RATIFICATION AND SIGNATURE

Article 110

1. The present Charter shall be ratified by the signatory states in accordance with their respective constitutional processes.

2. The ramifications shall be deposited with the Government of the United States of America, which shall notify all the signatory states of each deposit as well as the Secretary-General of the Organization when he has been appointed.

3. The present Charter shall come into force upon the deposit of ramifications by the Republic of China, France, the Union of Soviet Socialist Republics, the United Kingdom of Great Britain and Northern Ireland, and the United States of America, and by a majority of the other signatory states. A protocol of the deposited ramifications shall thereupon be drawn up by the Government of the United States of America which shall communicate copies thereof to all the signatory states.

4. The states signatory to the present Charter which ratify it after it has come into force will become original Members of the United Nations on the date of the deposit of their respective ratifications.

Article 111

The present Charter, of which the Chinese, French, Russian, English, and Spanish texts are equally authentic, shall remain deposited in the archives of the Government of the United States of America. Duly certified copies thereof shall be transmitted by that Government to the Governments of the other signatory states.

IN FAITH WHEREOF the representatives of the Governments of the United Nations have signed the present Charter.

DONE at the city of San Francisco the twenty-sixth day of June, one thousand nine hundred and forty-five.

Source: U.S. Department of State, *A Decade of American Foreign Policy: Basic Documents, 1941–49* (Washington, DC: U.S. Government Printing Office, 1950), 95–110.

224. The Berlin (Potsdam) Conference, 17 July–2 August 1945

After the German surrender but before that of Japan, the "Big Three" Allied leaders met at Potsdam in Berlin, Germany. They decided to establish a council of the foreign ministers of the major Allied powers to meet at regular intervals and discuss questions arising out of the war. They agreed on temporary arrangements for the administration of Germany, in principle on the transfer of German territory in the east to Poland, and on the consequent need for the transfer of populations from country to country.

PROTOCOL OF THE PROCEEDINGS, 1 AUGUST 1945

The Berlin Conference of the Three Heads of Government of the U.S.S.R., U. S. A., and U. K., which took place from July 17 to August 2, 1945, came to the following conclusions:

I. ESTABLISHMENT OF A COUNCIL OF FOREIGN MINISTERS.

A. The Conference reached the following agreement for the establishment of a Council of Foreign Ministers to do the necessary preparatory work for the peace settlements:

(1) There shall be established a Council composed of the Foreign Ministers of the United Kingdom, the Union of Soviet Socialist Republics, China, France, and the United States.

(2) (i) The Council shall normally meet in London which shall be the permanent seat of the joint Secretariat which the Council will form. Each of the Foreign Ministers will be accompanied by a high-ranking Deputy, duly authorized to carry on the work of the Council in the absence of his Foreign Ministers, and by a small staff of technical advisers.

(ii) The first meeting of the Council shall be held in London not later than September 1st 1945. Meetings may be held by common agreement in other capitals as may be agreed from time to time.

(3) (i) As its immediate important task, the Council shall be authorized to draw up, with a view to their submission to the United Nations, treaties of peace with Italy, Rumania, Bulgaria, Hungary and Finland, and to propose settlements of territorial questions outstanding on the termination of the war in Europe. The Council shall be utilized for the preparation of a peace settlement for Germany to be accepted by the Government of Germany when a government adequate for the purpose is established.

(ii) For the discharge of each of these tasks the Council will be composed of the Members representing those States which were signatory to the terms of surrender imposed upon the enemy State concerned. For the purposes of the peace settlement for Italy, France shall be regarded as a signatory to the terms of surrender for Italy. Other Members will be invited to participate when matters directly concerning them are under discussion.

(iii) Other matters may from time to time be referred to the Council by agreement between the Member Governments.

(4) (i) Whenever the Council is considering a question of direct interest to a State not represented thereon, such State should be invited to send representatives to participate in the discussion and study of that question.

(ii) The Council may adapt its procedure to the particular problems under consideration. In some cases it may hold its own preliminary discussions prior to the participation of other interested States. In other cases, the Council may convoke a formal conference of the States chiefly interested in seeking a solution of the particular problem.

B. It was agreed that the three Governments should each address an identical invitation to the Governments of China and France to adopt this text and to join in establishing the Council. . . .

C. It was understood that the establishment of the Council of Foreign Ministers for the specific purposes named in the text would be without prejudice to the agreement of the Crimea Conference that there should be periodical consultation between the Foreign Secretaries of the United States, the Union of Soviet Socialist Republics and the United Kingdom.

D. The Conference also considered the position of the European Advisory Commission in the light of the Agreement to establish the Council of Foreign Ministers. It was noted with satisfaction that the Commission had ably discharged its principal tasks by the recommendations that it had furnished for the terms of surrender for Germany, for the zones of occupation in Germany and Austria and for the inter-Allied control machinery in those countries. It was felt that further work of a detailed character for the coordination of Allied policy for the control of Germany and Austria would in future fall within the competence of the Control Council at Berlin and the Allied Commission at Vienna. Accordingly it was agreed to recommend that the European Advisory Commission be dissolved.

II. THE PRINCIPLES TO GOVERN THE TREATMENT OF GERMANY IN THE INITIAL CONTROL PERIOD.
A. POLITICAL PRINCIPLES.

1. In accordance with the Agreement on Control Machinery in Germany, supreme authority in Germany is exercised, on instructions from their respective Governments, by the Commanders-in-Chief of the armed forces of the United States of America, the United Kingdom, the Union of Soviet Socialist Republics, and the French Republic, each in his own zone of occupation, and also jointly, in matters affecting Germany as a whole, in their capacity as members of the Control Council.

2. So far as is practicable, there shall be uniformity of treatment of the German population throughout Germany.

3. The purposes of the occupation of Germany by which the Control Council shall be guided are:

(i) The complete disarmament and demilitarization of Germany and the elimination or control of all German industry that could be used for military production. To these ends:

(a) All German land, naval and air forces, the SS., SA., SD., and Gestapo, with all their organizations, staffs and institutions, including the General Staff, the Officers' Corps, Reserve Corps, military schools, war veterans' organizations and all other military and semi-military organizations, together with all clubs and associations which serve to keep alive the military tradition in Germany, shall be completely and finally abolished in such manner as permanently to prevent the revival or reorganization of German militarism and Nazism;

(b) All arms, ammunition and implements of war and all specialized facilities for their production shall be held at the disposal of the Allies or destroyed. The maintenance and production of all aircraft and all arms, ammunition and implements of war shall be prevented.

(ii) To convince the German people that they have suffered a total military defeat and that they cannot escape responsibility for what they have brought upon themselves, since their own ruthless warfare and the fanatical Nazi resistance have destroyed German economy and made chaos and suffering inevitable.

(iii) To destroy the National Socialist Party and its affiliated and supervised organizations, to dissolve all Nazi institutions, to ensure that they are not revived in any form, and to prevent all Nazi and militarist activity or propaganda.

(iv) To prepare for the eventual reconstruction of German political life on a democratic basis and for eventual peaceful cooperation in international life by Germany.

4. All Nazi laws which provided the basis of the Hitler regime or established discriminations on grounds of race, creed, or political opinion shall be abolished. No such discriminations, whether legal, administrative or otherwise, shall be tolerated.

5. War criminals and those who have participated in planning or carrying out Nazi enterprises involving or resulting in atrocities or war crimes shall be arrested and brought to judgment. Nazi leaders, influential Nazi supporters and high officials of Nazi organizations and institutions and any other persons dangerous to the occupation or its objectives shall be arrested and interned.

6. All members of the Nazi Party who have been more than nominal participants in its activities and all other persons hostile to Allied purposes shall be removed from public and semi-public office, and from positions of responsibility in important private undertakings. Such persons shall be replaced by persons who, by their political and moral qualities, are deemed capable of assisting in developing genuine democratic institutions in Germany.

7. German education shall be so controlled as completely to eliminate Nazi and militarist doctrines and to make possible the successful development of democratic ideas.

8. The judicial system will be reorganized in accordance with the principles of democracy, of justice under law, and of equal rights for all citizens without distinction of race, nationality or religion.

9. The administration in Germany should be directed towards the decentralization of the political structure and the development of local responsibility. To this end:

(i) local self-government shall be restored throughout Germany on democratic principles and in particular through elective councils as rapidly as is consistent with military security and the purposes of military occupation;

(ii) all democratic political parties with rights of assembly and of public discussion shall be allowed and encouraged throughout Germany;

(iii) representative and elective principles shall be introduced into regional, provincial and state (land) administration as rapidly as may be justified by the successful application of these principles in local self-government;

(iv) for the time being, no central German Government shall be established. Notwithstanding this, however, certain essential central German administrative departments, headed by State Secretaries, shall be established, particularly in the fields of finance, transport, communications, foreign trade and industry. Such departments will act under the direction of the Control Council.

10. Subject to the necessity for maintaining military security, freedom of speech, press and religion shall be permitted, and religious institutions shall be respected. Subject likewise to the maintenance of military security, the formation of free trade unions shall be permitted.

B. ECONOMIC PRINCIPLES.

11. In order to eliminate Germany's war potential, the production of arms, ammunition and implements of war as well as all types of aircraft and sea-going ships shall be prohibited and prevented. Production of metals, chemicals, machinery and other items that are directly necessary to a war economy shall be rigidly controlled and restricted to Germany's approved post-war peacetime needs to meet the objectives stated in paragraph 15. Productive capacity not needed for permitted production shall be removed in accordance with the reparations plan recommended by the Allied Commission on Reparations and approved by the Governments concerned or if not removed shall be destroyed.

12. At the earliest practicable date, the German economy shall be decentralized for the purpose of eliminating the present excessive concentration of economic power as exemplified in particular by cartels, syndicates, trusts and other monopolistic arrangements.

13. In organizing the German Economy, primary emphasis shall be given to the development of agriculture and peaceful domestic industries.

14. During the period of occupation Germany shall be treated as a single economic unit. To this end common policies shall be established in regard to:

(a) mining and industrial production and its allocation;
(b) agriculture, forestry and fishing;
(c) wages, prices and rationing;
(d) import and export programs for Germany as a whole;
(e) currency and banking, central taxation and customs;
(f) reparation and removal of industrial war potential;
(g) transportation and communications.

In applying these policies account shall be taken, where appropriate, of varying local conditions.

15. Allied controls shall be imposed upon the German economy but only to the extent necessary:

(a) to carry out programs of industrial disarmament, demilitarization, of reparations, and of approved exports and imports.
(b) to assure the production and maintenance of goods and services required to meet the needs of the occupying forces and displaced persons in Germany and essential to maintain in Germany average living standards not exceeding the average of the standards of living of European countries. (European countries means all European countries excluding the United Kingdom and the U.S.S.R.)
(c) to ensure in the manner determined by the Control Council the equitable distribution of essential commodities between the several zones so as to produce a balanced economy throughout Germany and reduce the need for imports.
(d) to control German industry and all economic and financial international transactions including exports and imports, with the aim of preventing Germany from developing a war potential and of achieving the other objectives named herein.
(e) to control all German public or private scientific bodies, research and experimental institutions, laboratories, et cetera connected with economic activities.

16. In the imposition and maintenance of economic controls established by the Control Council, German administrative machinery shall be created and the German authorities shall be required to the fullest extent practicable to proclaim and assume administration of such controls. Thus it should be brought home to the German people that the responsibility for the administration of such controls and any break-down in these controls will rest with themselves. Any German controls which may run counter to the objectives of occupation will be prohibited.

17. Measures shall be promptly taken:

(a) to effect essential repair of transport;
(b) to enlarge coal production;
(c) to maximize agricultural output; and
(d) to erect emergency repair of housing and essential utilities.

18. Appropriate steps shall be taken by the Control Council to exercise control and the power of disposition over German-owned external assets not already under the con-

trol of United Nations which have taken part in the war against Germany.

19. Payment of Reparations should leave enough resources to enable the German people to subsist without external assistance. In working out the economic balance of Germany the necessary means must be provided to pay for imports approved by the Control Council in Germany. The proceeds of exports from current production and stocks shall be available in the first place for payment for such imports.

The above clause will not apply to the equipment and products referred to in paragraphs 4 (a) and 4 (b) of the Reparations Agreement.

III. REPARATIONS FROM GERMANY.

1. Reparation claims of the U.S.S.R. shall be met by removals from the zone of Germany occupied by the U.S.S.R., and from appropriate German external assets.

2. The U.S.S.R. undertakes to settle the reparation claims of Poland from its own share of reparations.

3. The reparation claims of the United States, the United Kingdom and other countries entitled to reparations shall be met from the Western Zones and from appropriate German external assets.

4. In addition to the reparations to be taken by the U.S.S.R. from its own zone of occupation, the U.S.S.R. shall receive additionally from the Western Zones:

(a) 15 per cent of such usable and complete industrial capital equipment, in the first place from the metallurgical, chemical and machine manufacturing industries as is unnecessary for the German peace economy and should be removed from the Western Zones of Germany, in exchange for an equivalent value of food, coal, potash, zinc, timber, clay products, petroleum products, and such other commodities as may be agreed upon.

(b) 10 per cent of such industrial capital equipment as is unnecessary for the German peace economy and should be removed from the Western Zones, to be transferred to the Soviet Government on reparations account without payment or exchange of any kind in return.

Removals of equipment as provided in (a) and (b) above shall be made simultaneously.

5. The amount of equipment to be removed from the Western Zones on account of reparations must be determined within six months from now at the latest.

6. Removals of industrial capital equipment shall begin as soon as possible and shall be completed within two years from the determination specified in paragraph 5. The delivery of products covered by 4 (a) above shall begin as soon as possible and shall be made by the U.S.S.R. in agreed installments within five years of the date hereof. The determination of the amount and character of the industrial capital equipment unnecessary for the German peace economy and therefore available for reparation shall be made by the Control Council under policies fixed by the Allied Commission on Reparations, with the participation of France, subject to the final approval of the Zone Commander in the Zone from which the equipment is to be removed.

7. Prior to the fixing of the total amount of equipment subject to removal, advance deliveries shall be made in respect to such equipment as will be determined to be eligible for delivery in accordance with the procedure set forth in the last sentence of paragraph 6.

8. The Soviet Government renounces all claims in respect of reparations to shares of German enterprises which are located in the Western Zones of Germany as well as to German foreign assets in all countries except those specified in paragraph 9 below.

9. The Governments of the U.K. and U.S.A. renounce all claims in respect of reparations to shares of German enterprises which are located in the Eastern Zone of occupation in Germany, as well as to German foreign assets in Bulgaria, Finland, Hungary, Rumania and Eastern Austria.

10. The Soviet Government makes no claims to gold captured by the Allied troops in Germany.

IV. DISPOSAL OF THE GERMAN NAVY AND MERCHANT MARINE.

A. The following principles for the distribution of the German Navy were agreed:

(1) The total strength of the German surface navy, excluding ships sunk and those taken over from Allied Nations, but including ships under construction or repair, shall be divided equally among the U.S.S.R., U.K., and U.S.A.

(2) Ships under construction or repair mean those ships whose construction or repair may be completed within three to six months, according to the type of ship. Whether such ships under construction or repair shall be completed or repaired shall be determined by the technical commission appointed by the Three Powers and referred to below, subject to the principle that their completion or repair must be achieved within the time limits above provided, without any increase of skilled employment in the German

shipyards and without permitting the reopening of any German ship building or connected industries. Completion date means the date when a ship is able to go out on its first trip, or, under peacetime standards, would refer to the customary date of delivery by shipyard to the Government.

(3) The larger part of the German submarine fleet shall be sunk. Not more than thirty submarines shall be preserved and divided equally between the U.S.S.R., U.K., and U.S.A. for experimental and technical purposes.

(4) All stocks of armament, ammunition and supplies of the German Navy appertaining to the vessels transferred pursuant to paragraphs (1) and (3) hereof shall be handed over to the respective powers receiving such ships.

(5) The Three Governments agree to constitute a tripartite naval commission comprising two representatives for each government, accompanied by the requisite staff, to submit agreed recommendations to the Three Governments for the allocation of specific German warships and to handle other detailed matters arising out of the agreement between the Three Governments regarding the German fleet. The Commission will hold its first meeting not later than 15th August, 1945, in Berlin, which shall be its headquarters. Each Delegation on the Commission will have the right on the basis of reciprocity to inspect German warships wherever they may be located.

(6) The Three Governments agreed that transfers, including those of ships under construction and repair, shall be completed as soon as possible, but not later than 15th February, 1946. The Commission will submit fortnightly reports, including proposals for the progressive allocation of the vessels when agreed by the Commission.

B. The following principles for the distribution of the German Merchant Marine were agreed:

(1) The German Merchant Marine, surrendered to the Three Powers and wherever located, shall be divided equally among the U.S.S.R., the U.K., and the U.S.A. The actual transfers of the ships to the respective countries shall take place as soon as practicable after the end of the war against Japan. The United Kingdom and the United States will provide out of their shares of the surrendered German merchant ships appropriate amounts for other Allied States whose merchant marines have suffered heavy losses in the common cause against Germany, except that the Soviet Union shall provide out of its share for Poland.

(2) The allocation, manning, and operation of these ships during the Japanese War period shall fall under the cognizance and authority of the Combined Shipping Adjustment Board and the United Maritime Authority.

(3) While actual transfer of the ships shall be delayed until after the end of the war with Japan, a Tripartite Shipping Commission shall inventory and value all available ships and recommend a specific distribution in accordance with paragraph (1).

(4) German inland and coastal ships determined to be necessary to the maintenance of the basic German peace economy by the Allied Control Council of Germany shall not be included in the shipping pool thus divided among the Three Powers.

(5) The Three Governments agree to constitute a tripartite merchant marine commission comprising two representatives for each Government, accompanied by the requisite staff, to submit agreed recommendations to the Three Governments for the allocation of specific German merchant ships and to handle other detailed matters arising out of the agreement between the Three Governments regarding the German merchant ships. The Commission will hold its first meeting not later than September 1st, 1945, in Berlin, which shall be its headquarters. Each delegation on the Commission will have the right on the basis of reciprocity to inspect the German merchant ships wherever they may be located.

V. CITY OF KOENIGSBERG AND THE ADJACENT AREA.

The Conference examined a proposal by the Soviet Government to the effect that pending the final determination of territorial questions at the peace settlement, the section of the western frontier of the Union of Soviet Socialist Republics which is adjacent to the Baltic Sea should pass from a point on the eastern shore of the Bay of Danzig to the east, north of Braunsberg-Goldap, to the meeting point of the frontiers of Lithuania, the Polish Republic and East Prussia.

The Conference has agreed in principle to the proposal of the Soviet Government concerning the ultimate transfer to the Soviet Union of the City of Koenigsberg and the area adjacent to it as described above subject to expert examination of the actual frontier.

The President of the United States and the British Prime Minister have declared that they will support the proposal of the Conference at the forthcoming peace settlement.

VI. WAR CRIMINALS.

The Three Governments have taken note of the discussions which have been proceeding in recent weeks in London between British, United States, Soviet and French representatives with a view to reaching agreement on the methods of trial of those major war criminals whose crimes under the Moscow Declaration of October, 1943 have no particular geographical localization. The Three Governments reaffirm their intention to bring these criminals to swift and sure justice. They hope that the negotiations in London will result in speedy agreement being reached for this purpose, and they regard it as a matter of great importance that the trial of these major criminals should begin at the earliest possible date. The first list of defendants will be published before 1st September.

VII. AUSTRIA.

The Conference examined a proposal by the Soviet Government on the extension of the authority of the Austrian Provisional Government to all of Austria.

The three governments agreed that they were prepared to examine this question after the entry of the British and American forces into the city of Vienna.

It was agreed that reparations should not be exacted from Austria.

VIII. POLAND.

A. DECLARATION.

We have taken note with pleasure of the agreement reached among representative Poles from Poland and abroad which has made possible the formation, in accordance with the decisions reached at the Crimea Conference, of a Polish Provisional Government of National Unity recognized by the Three Powers. The establishment by the British and United States Governments of diplomatic relations with the Polish Provisional Government of National Unity has resulted in the withdrawal of their recognition from the former Polish Government in London, which no longer exists.

The British and United States Governments have taken measures to protect the interests of the Polish Provisional Government of National Unity as the recognized government of the Polish State in the property belonging to the Polish State located in their territories and under their control, whatever the form of this property may be. They have further taken measures to prevent alienation to third parties of such property. All proper facilities will be given to the Polish Provisional Government of National Unity for the exercise of the ordinary legal remedies for the recovery of any property belonging to the Polish State which may have been wrongfully alienated.

The Three Powers are anxious to assist the Polish Provisional Government of National Unity in facilitating the return to Poland as soon as practicable of all Poles abroad who wish to go, including members of the Polish Armed Forces and the Merchant Marine. They expect that those Poles who return home shall be accorded personal and property rights on the same basis as all Polish citizens.

The Three Powers note that the Polish Provisional Government of National Unity, in accordance with the decisions of the Crimea Conference, has agreed to the holding of free and unfettered elections as soon as possible on the basis of universal suffrage and secret ballot in which all democratic and anti-Nazi parties shall have the right to take part and to put forward candidates, and that representatives of the Allied press shall enjoy full freedom to report to the world upon developments in Poland before and during the elections.

B. WESTERN FRONTIER OF POLAND.

In conformity with the agreement on Poland reached at the Crimea Conference the three Heads of Government have sought the opinion of the Polish Provisional Government of National Unity in regard to the accession of territory in the north and west which Poland should receive. The President of the National Council of Poland and members of the Polish Provisional Government of National Unity have been received at the Conference and have fully presented their views. The three Heads of Government reaffirm their opinion that the final delimitation of the western frontier of Poland should await the peace settlement.

The three Heads of Government agree that, pending the final determination of Poland's western frontier, the former German territories cast of a line running from the Baltic Sea immediately west of Swinamunde, and thence along the Oder River to the confluence of the western Neisse River and along the Western Neisse to the Czechoslovak frontier, including that portion of East Prussia not placed under the administration of the Union of Soviet Socialist Republics in accordance with the understanding reached at this conference and including the area of the former free city of Danzig, shall be under the administration of the Polish State and for such purposes should not be considered as part of the Soviet zone of occupation in Germany.

IX. CONCLUSION OF PEACE TREATIES AND ADMISSION TO THE UNITED NATIONS ORGANIZATION.

The Three Governments consider it desirable that the present anomalous position of Italy, Bulgaria, Finland, Hungary and Rumania should be terminated by the conclusion of Peace Treaties. They trust that the other interested Allied Governments will share these views.

For their part the Three Governments have included the preparation of a Peace Treaty for Italy as the first among the immediate important tasks to be undertaken by the new Council of Foreign Ministers. Italy was the first of the Axis Powers to break with Germany, to whose defeat she has made a material contribution, and has now joined with the Allies in the struggle against Japan. Italy has freed herself from the Fascist regime and is making good progress towards reestablishment of a democratic government and institutions. The conclusion of such a Peace Treaty with a recognized and democratic Italian Government will make it possible for the three Governments to fulfill their desire to support an application from Italy for membership of the United Nations.

The Three Governments have also charged the Council of Foreign Ministers with the task of preparing Peace Treaties for Bulgaria, Finland, Hungary and Rumania. The conclusion of Peace Treaties with recognized democratic governments in these States will also enable the Three Governments to support applications from them for membership of the United Nations. The Three Governments agree to examine each separately in the near future, in the light of the conditions then prevailing, the establishment of diplomatic relations with Finland, Rumania, Bulgaria, and Hungary to the extent possible prior to the conclusion of peace treaties with those countries.

The Three Governments have no doubt that in view of the changed conditions resulting from the termination of the war in Europe, representatives of the Allied press will enjoy full freedom to report to the world upon developments in Rumania, Bulgaria, Hungary and Finland.

As regards the admission of other States into the United Nations Organization, Article 4 of the Charter of the United Nations declares that:

1. Membership in the United Nations is open to all other peace-loving States who accept the obligations contained in the present Charter and, in the judgment of the organization, are able and willing to carry out these obligations.
2. The admission of any such State to membership in the United Nations will be effected by a decision of the General Assembly upon the recommendation of the Security Council.

The Three Governments, so far as they are concerned, will support applications for membership from those States which have remained neutral during the war and which fulfill the qualifications set out above.

The Three Governments feel bound however to make it clear that they for their part would not favour any application for membership put forward by the present Spanish Government, which, having been founded with the support of the Axis Powers, does not, in view of its origins, its nature, its record and its close association with the aggressor States, possess the qualifications necessary to justify such membership.

X. TERRITORIAL TRUSTEESHIP.

The Conference examined a proposal by the Soviet Government on the question of trusteeship territories as defined in the decision of the Crimea Conference and in the Charter of the United Nations Organization.

After an exchange of views on this question it was decided that the disposition of any former Italian colonial territories was one to be decided in connection with the preparation of a peace treaty for Italy and that the question of Italian colonial territory would be considered by the September Council of Ministers of Foreign Affairs.

XI. REVISED ALLIED CONTROL COMMISSION PROCEDURE IN RUMANIA, BULGARIA, AND HUNGARY.

The Three Governments took note that the Soviet Representatives on the Allied Control Commissions in Rumania, Bulgaria, and Hungary, have communicated to their United Kingdom and United States colleagues proposals for improving the work of the Control Commissions, now that hostilities in Europe have ceased.

The Three Governments agreed that the revision of the procedures of the Allied Control Commissions in these countries would now be undertaken, taking into account the interests and responsibilities of the Three Governments which together presented the terms of armistice to the respective countries, and accepting as a basis, in respect of all three countries, the Soviet Government's proposals for Hungary as annexed hereto. (Annex I)

XII. ORDERLY TRANSFER OF GERMAN POPULATIONS.

The Three Governments, having considered the question in all its aspects, recognize that the transfer to Germany of German populations, or elements thereof, remaining in Poland, Czechoslovakia and Hungary, will have to be undertaken. They agree that any transfers that take place should be effected in an orderly and humane manner.

Since the influx of a large number of Germans into Germany would increase the burden already resting on the occupying authorities, they consider that the Control Council in Germany should in the first instance examine the problem, with special regard to the question of the equitable distribution of these Germans among the several zones of occupation. They are accordingly instructing their respective representatives on the Control Council to report to their Governments as soon as possible the extent to which such persons have already entered Germany from Poland, Czechoslovakia and Hungary, and to submit an estimate of the time and rate at which further transfers could be carried out having regard to the present situation in Germany.

The Czechoslovak Government, the Polish Provisional Government and the Control Council in Hungary are at the same time being informed of the above and are being requested meanwhile to suspend further expulsions pending an examination by the Governments concerned of the report from their representatives on the Control Council.

XIII. OIL EQUIPMENT IN RUMANIA.

The Conference agreed to set up two bilateral commissions of experts, one to be composed of United Kingdom and Soviet Members and one to be composed of United States and Soviet Members, to investigate the facts and examine the documents, as a basis for the settlement of questions arising from the removal of oil equipment in Rumania. It was further agreed that these experts shall begin their work within ten days, on the spot.

XIV. IRAN.

It was agreed that Allied troops should be withdrawn immediately from Tehran, and that further stages of the withdrawal of troops from Iran should be considered at the meeting of the Council of Foreign Ministers to be held in London in September, 1945.

XV. THE INTERNATIONAL ZONE OF TANGIER.

A proposal by the Soviet Government was examined and the following decisions were reached:

Having examined the question of the Zone of Tangier, the three Governments have agreed that this Zone, which includes the City of Tangier and the area adjacent to it, in view of its special strategic importance, shall remain international.

The question of Tangier will be discussed in the near future at a meeting in Paris of representatives of the Governments of the Union of Soviet Socialist Republics, the United States of America, the United Kingdom and France.

XVI. THE BLACK SEA STRAITS.

The Three Governments recognized that the Convention concluded at Montreux should be revised as failing to meet present-day conditions.

It was agreed that as the next step the matter should be the subject of direct conversations between each of the three Governments and the Turkish Government. . . .

XXI. MILITARY TALKS.

During the Conference there were meetings between the Chiefs of Staff of the Three Governments on military matters of common interest. . . .

Source: U.S. Department of State, *A Decade of American Foreign Policy: Basic Documents, 1941–49* (Washington, DC: U.S. Government Printing Office, 1950), 28–29.

225. Allied Proclamation Defining Terms for Japanese Surrender, Potsdam, 26 July 1945

At the Potsdam Conference, the leaders of China, the United States, and Great Britain agreed upon the wording of a proclamation calling upon Japan to surrender or otherwise face devastation. Although the atomic bomb had just been tested, they did not specifically describe the impact that the new weapon would be likely to have on Japan. This step was taken in large part on the suggestion of Henry L. Stimson, the influential American secretary of war, who hoped thereby to avoid the use of atomic weapons against Japan.

(1) We—The President of the United States, the President of the National Government of the Republic of China, and the Prime Minister of Great Britain, representing the hundreds of millions of our countrymen, have conferred and agree that Japan shall be given an opportunity to end this war.

(2) The prodigious land, sea and air forces of the United States, the British Empire and of China, many times reinforced by their armies and air fleets from the west, are poised to strike the final blows upon Japan. This military power is sustained and inspired by the determination of all the Allied Nations to prosecute the war against Japan until she ceases to resist.

(3) The result of the futile and senseless German resistance to the might of the aroused free peoples of the world stands forth in awful clarity as an example to the people of Japan. The might that now converges

on Japan is immeasurably greater than that which, when applied to the resisting Nazis, necessarily laid waste to the lands, the industry and the method of life of the whole German people. The full application of our military power, backed by our resolve, *will* mean the inevitable and complete destruction of the Japanese armed forces and just as inevitably the utter devastation of the Japanese homeland.

(4) The time has come for Japan to decide whether she will continue to be controlled by those self-willed militaristic advisers whose unintelligent calculations have brought the Empire of Japan to the threshold of annihilation, or whether she will follow the path of reason.

(5) Following are our terms. We will not deviate from them. There are no alternatives. We shall brook no delay.

(6) There must be eliminated for all time the authority and influence of those who have deceived and misled the people of Japan into embarking on world conquest, for we insist that a new order of peace, security and justice will be impossible until irresponsible militarism is driven from the world.

(7) Until such a new order is established and until there is convincing proof that Japan's war-making power is destroyed, points in Japanese territory to be designated by the Allies shall be occupied to secure the achievement of the basic objectives we are here setting forth.

(8) The terms of the Cairo Declaration shall be carried out and Japanese sovereignty shall be limited to the islands of Honshu, Hokkaido, Kyushu, Shikoku and such minor islands as we determine.

(9) The Japanese military forces, after being completely disarmed, shall be permitted to return to their homes with the opportunity to lead peaceful and productive lives.

(10) We do not intend that the Japanese shall be enslaved as a race or destroyed as a nation, but stern justice shall be meted out to all war criminals, including those who have visited cruelties upon our prisoners. The Japanese Government shall remove all obstacles to the revival and strengthening of democratic tendencies among the Japanese people. Freedom of speech, of religion, and of thought, as well as respect for the fundamental human rights shall be established.

(11) Japan shall be permitted to maintain such industries as will sustain her economy and permit the exaction of just reparations in kind, but not those [industries] which would enable her to re-arm for war. To this end, access to, as distinguished from control of, raw materials shall be permitted. Eventual Japanese participation in world trade relations shall be permitted.

(12) The occupying forces of the Allies shall be withdrawn from Japan as soon as these objectives have been accomplished and there has been established in accordance with the freely expressed will of the Japanese people a peacefully inclined and responsible government.

(13) We call upon the government of Japan to proclaim now the unconditional surrender of all Japanese armed forces, and to provide proper and adequate assurances of their good faith in such action. The alternative for Japan is prompt and utter destruction.

Source: U.S. Department of State, *A Decade of American Foreign Policy: Basic Documents, 1941–49* (Washington, DC: U.S. Government Printing Office, 1950), 49–50.

226. President Harry S Truman Recalls the Decision to Drop the Atomic Bomb

In his memoirs, President Truman later described his reasons for using atomic weapons, a decision he claimed he never subsequently regretted. He focused upon his desire to save American lives that would otherwise have been lost in the impending invasion of Japan. Truman's account has since been challenged by claims that Japan would in any case have surrendered, a hypothesis that is itself questionable. Although by this time the emperor and moderate politicians in Japan apparently wished to negotiate peace, even after the bomb had been used militarists within the Japanese cabinet and army were determined to continue fighting. It remains dubious whether, absent the impact of the explosions over Hiroshima and Nagasaki, the emperor would have been able to prevail in seeking peace.

A month before the test explosion of the atomic bomb the service Secretaries and the Joint Chiefs of Staff had laid their detailed plans for the defeat of Japan before me for approval. . . .

The Army plan envisaged an amphibious landing in the fall of 1945 on the island of Kyushu, the southernmost of the Japanese home islands. This would be accomplished by our Sixth Army, under the command of General Walter Krueger. The first landing would then be followed approximately four months later by a second great invasion, which would be carried out by our Eighth and Tenth Armies, followed by the First Army transferred from Europe, all of which would go ashore in the Kanto plains area near Tokyo. In all, it had been estimated that it would require until the late fall of 1946 to bring Japan to her knees.

This was a formidable conception, and all of us realized fully that the fighting would be fierce and the losses heavy. But it was hoped that some of Japan's forces would continue to be preoccupied in China and others would be prevented from reinforcing the home islands if Russia were to enter the war.

There was, of course, always the possibility that the Japanese might choose to surrender sooner. Our air and fleet units had begun to inflict heavy damage on industrial and urban sites in Japan proper. Except in China, the armies of the Mikado had been pushed back everywhere in relentless successions of defeats.

Acting Secretary of State Grew had spoken to me in late May about issuing a proclamation that would urge the Japanese to surrender but would assure them that we would permit the emperor to remain as head of the state. Grew backed this with arguments taken from his ten years' experience as our Ambassador in Japan, and I told him that I had already given thought to this matter myself and that it seemed to me a sound idea. Grew had a draft of a proclamation with him, and I instructed him to send it by the customary channels to the Joint Chiefs and the State-War-Navy Coordinating Committee in order that we might get the opinions of all concerned before I made my decision.

On June 18 Grew reported that the proposal had met with the approval of his Cabinet colleagues and of the Joint Chiefs. The military leaders also discussed the subject with me when they reported the same day. Grew, however, favored issuing the proclamation at once, to coincide with the closing of the campaign on Okinawa, while the service chiefs were of the opinion that we should wait until we were ready to follow a Japanese refusal with the actual assault of our invasion forces.

It was my decision then that the proclamation to Japan should be issued from the forthcoming conference at Potsdam. This, I believed, would clearly demonstrate to Japan and to the world that the Allies were united in their purpose. By that time, also, we might know more about two matters of significance for our future effort: the participation of the Soviet Union and the atomic bomb. We knew that the bomb would receive its first test in mid-July. If the test of the bomb was successful, I wanted to afford Japan a clear chance to end the fighting before we made use of this newly gained power. If the test should fail, then it would be even more important to us to bring about a surrender before we had to make a physical conquest of Japan. General Marshall told me that it might cost half a million American lives to force the enemy's surrender on his home grounds.

But the test was now successful. . . .

[At Secretary of War Henry L. Stimson's suggestion, shortly after becoming president in April 1945 Truman had] set up a committee of top men and had asked them to study with great care the implications the new weapon might have for us.

Secretary Stimson headed this group as chairman, and the other members were George L. Harrison, president of the New York Life Insurance Company, who was then serving as a special assistant to the Secretary of War; James F. Byrnes, as my personal representative; Ralph A. Bard,

Under Secretary of the Navy; Assistant Secretary William L. Clayton for the State Department; and three of our most renowned scientists—Dr. Vannevar Bush, president of the Carnegie Institution of Washington and Director of the Office of Scientific Research and Development; Dr. Karl T. Compton, president of the Massachusetts Institute of Technology and Chief of Field Service in the Office of Scientific Research and Development; and Dr. James B. Conant, president of Harvard University and chairman of the National Defense Research Committee.

This committee was assisted by a group of scientists, of whom those most prominently connected with the development of the atomic bomb were Dr. Oppenheimer, Dr. Arthur H. Compton, Dr. E. O. Lawrence, and the Italian-born Dr. Enrico Fermi. The conclusions reached by these men, both in the advisory committee of scientists and in the larger committee, were brought to me by Secretary Stimson on June 1.

It was their recommendation that the bomb be used against the enemy as soon as it could be done. They recommended further that it should be used without specific warning and against a target that would clearly show its devastating strength. I had realized, of course, that an atomic bomb explosion would inflict damage and casualties beyond imagination. On the other hand, the scientific advisers of the committee reported, "We can see no acceptable alternative to direct military use." It was their conclusion that no technical demonstration such as they might propose, such as over a deserted island, would be likely to bring the war to an end. It had to be used against an enemy target.

The final decision of where and when to use the atomic bomb was up to me. Let there be no mistake about it. I regarded the bomb as a military weapon and never had any doubt that it should be used. The top military advisers to the President recommended its use, and when I talked to Churchill he unhesitatingly told me that he favored the use of the atomic bomb if it might aid to end the war.

In deciding to use this bomb I wanted to make sure that it would be used as a weapon of war in the manner prescribed by the laws of war. That meant that I wanted it dropped on a military target. I had told Stimson that the bomb should be dropped as nearly as possibly upon a war production center of prime military importance.

Stimson's staff had prepared a list of cities in Japan that might serve as targets. Kyoto, though favored by [Head of the Army Air Force] General Arnold as a center of military activity, was eliminated when Secretary Stimson pointed out that it was a cultural and religious shrine of the Japanese.

Four cities were finally recommended as targets: Hiroshima, Kokura, Niigata, and Nagasaki. They were listed in that order as targets for the first attack. The order of selection was in accordance with the military importance of these cities, but allowance would be given for weather conditions at the time of the bombing. . . .

On July 28 Radio Tokyo announced that the Japanese government would continue to fight. There was no formal reply to the joint ultimatum of the United States, the United Kingdom, and China. There was no alternative now. The bomb was scheduled to be dropped after August 3 unless Japan surrendered before that day.

On August 6, the fourth day of the journey home from Potsdam, came the historic news that shook the world. . . . Shortly afterward I called a press conference. . . . My statements on the atomic bomb . . . read in part. . . .

"We are now prepared to obliterate more rapidly and completely every productive enterprise the Japanese have above ground in any city. We shall destroy their docks, their factories, and their communications. Let there be no mistake; we shall completely destroy Japan's power to make war.

"It was to spare the Japanese people from utter destruction that the ultimatum of July 26 was issued at Potsdam. Their leaders promptly rejected that ultimatum. If they do not now accept our terms, they may expect a rain of ruin from the air, the like of which has never been seen on this earth." . . .

Still no surrender offer came. An order was issued to General Spaatz [commander of U.S. air forces in Asia] to continue operations as planned unless otherwise instructed. . . .

On August 9 the second atom bomb was dropped, this time on Nagasaki. We gave the Japanese three days in which to make up their minds to surrender, and the bombing would have been held off another two days had weather permitted. During those days we indicated that we meant business. On August 7 the 20th Air Force sent out a bomber force of some one hundred and thirty B-29s, and on the eighth it reported four hundred and twenty B-29s in day and night attacks. The choice of targets for the second atom bomb was first Kokura, with Nagasaki second. The third city on the list, Niigata, had been ruled out as too distant. By the time Kokura was reached the weather had closed in, and after three runs over the spot without a glimpse of the target, with gas running short, a try was made for the second choice, Nagasaki. There, too, the weather had closed in, but an opening in the clouds gave the bombardier his chance, and Nagasaki was successfully bombed.

This second demonstration of the power of the atomic bomb apparently threw Tokyo into a panic, for the next morning brought the first indication that the Japanese Empire was ready to surrender.

Source: Harry S Truman, *Memoirs: Year of Decisions* (Garden City, NY: Doubleday, 1955), 416–426. Reprinted courtesy Ms. Margaret Truman Daniel.

227. The Effects of the Atomic Bombs: Excerpt from United States Strategic Bombing Survey Summary Report (Pacific War), Washington, D.C., 1 July 1946

Less than a year after the Pacific war ended, the U.S. government sought to assess the effects upon Japan of the major bombing campaign mounted in the later years of the war. The survey covered both the physical impact and casualties and the effect on morale. It provided a graphic account of the explosions of nuclear devices over both Hiroshima and Nagasaki. It was too soon, however, to assess the long-term impact of the nuclear explosions upon the health of the survivors.

EFFECTS OF THE ATOMIC BOMBS

On 6 August and 9 August 1945, the first two atomic bombs to be used for military purposes were dropped on Hiroshima and Nagasaki respectively. One hundred thousand people were killed, 6 square miles or over 50 percent of the built-up areas of the two cities were destroyed. The first and crucial question about the atomic bomb thus was answered practically and conclusively; atomic energy had been mastered for military purposes and the overwhelming scale of its possibilities had been demonstrated. A detailed examination of the physical, economic, and morale effects of the atomic bombs occupied the attention of a major portion of the Survey's staff in Japan in order to arrive at a more precise definition of the present capabilities and limitations of this radically new weapon of destruction.

Eyewitness accounts of the explosion all describe similar pictures. The bombs exploded with a tremendous flash of blue-white light, like a giant magnesium flare. The flash was of short duration and accompanied by intense glare and heat. It was followed by a tremendous pressure wave and the rumbling sound of the explosion. This sound is not clearly recollected by those who survived near the center of the explosion, although it was clearly heard by others as much as fifteen miles away. A huge snow-white cloud shot rapidly into the sky and the scene on the ground was obscured first by a bluish haze and then by a purple-brown cloud of dust and smoke.

Such eyewitness accounts reveal the sequence of events. At the time of the explosion, energy was given off in the forms of light, heat, radiation, and pressure. The complete band of radiations, from X- and gamma-rays, through ultraviolet and light rays to the radiant heat of infra-red rays, travelled with the speed of light. The shock wave created by the enormous pressures built up almost instantaneously at the point of explosion but moved out more slowly, that is at about the speed of sound. The superheated gases constituting the original fire ball expanded outward and upward at a slower rate.

The light and radiant heat rays accompanying the flash travelled in a straight line and any opaque object, even a single leaf of a vine, shielded objects lying behind it. The duration of the flash was only a fraction of a second, but it was sufficiently intense to cause third degree burns to exposed human skin up to a distance of a mile. Clothing ignited, though it could be quickly beaten out, telephone poles charred, thatchroofed houses caught fire. Black or other dark-colored surfaces of combustible material absorbed the heat and immediately charred or burst into flames; white or light-colored surfaces reflected a substantial portion of the rays and were not consumed. Heavy black clay tiles which are an almost universal feature of the roofs of Japanese houses bubbled at distances up to a mile. Test of samples of this tile by the National Bureau of Standards in Washington indicates that temperatures in excess of 1,800° C. must have been generated in the surface of the tile to produce such an effect. The surfaces of granite blocks exposed to the flash scarred and spoiled at distances up to almost a mile. In the immediate area of ground zero (the point on the ground immediately below the explosion), the heat charred corpses beyond recognition.

Penetrating rays such as gamma-rays exposed X-ray films stored in the basement of a concrete hospital almost a mile from ground zero. Symptoms of their effect on human beings close to the center of the explosion, who survived other effects thereof, were generally delayed for two or three days. The bone marrow and as a result the process of blood formation were affected. The white corpuscle count went down and the human processes of resisting infection were destroyed. Death generally followed shortly thereafter.

The majority of radiation cases who were at greater distances did not show severe symptoms until 1 to 4 weeks after the explosion. The first symptoms were loss of appetite, lassitude and general discomfort. Within 12 to 48 hours, fever became evident in many cases, going as high as 104° to 105° F., which in fatal cases continued until death. If the fever subsided, the patient usually showed a rapid disappearance of other symptoms and soon regained his feeling of good health. Other symptoms were loss of white blood corpuscles, loss of hair, and decrease in sperm count.

Even though rays of this nature have great powers of penetration, intervening substances filter out portions of them. As the weight of the intervening material increases the percentage of the rays penetrating goes down. It appears that a few feet of concrete, or a somewhat greater thickness of earth, furnished sufficient protection to humans, even those close to ground zero, to prevent serious after effects from radiation.

The blast wave which followed the flash was of sufficient force to press in the roofs of reinforced concrete structures and to flatten completely all less sturdy structures. Due to the height of the explosion, the peak pressure of the wave at ground zero was no higher than that produced by a near miss of a high-explosive bomb, and decreased at greater distances from ground zero. Reflection and shielding by intervening hills and structures produced some unevenness in the pattern. The blast wave, however, was of far greater extent and duration than that of a high-explosive bomb and most reinforced-concrete structures suffered structural damage or collapse up to 700 feet at Hiroshima and 2,000 feet at Nagasaki. Brick buildings were flattened up to 7,300 feet at Hiroshima and 8,500 feet at Nagasaki. Typical Japanese houses of wood construction suffered total collapse up to approximately 7,300 feet at Hiroshima and 8,200 feet at Nagasaki. Beyond these distances structures received less serious damage to roofs, wall partitions, and the like. Glass windows were blown out at distances up to 5 miles. The blast wave, being of longer duration than that caused by high-explosive detonations, was accompanied by more flying debris. Window frames, doors, and partitions which would have been shaken down by a near-miss of a high-explosive bomb were hurled at high velocity through those buildings which did not collapse. Machine tools and most other production equipment in industrial plants were not directly damaged by the blast wave, but were damaged by collapsing buildings or ensuing general fires.

The above description mentions all the categories of the destructive action by the atomic-bomb explosions at Hiroshima and Nagasaki. There were no other types of action. Nothing was vaporized or disintegrated; vegetation is growing again immediately under the center of the explosions; there are no indications that radio-activity continued after the explosion to a sufficient degree to harm human beings.

Let us consider, however, the effect of these various types of destructive action on the cities of Hiroshima, and Nagasaki and their inhabitants.

Hiroshima is built on a broad river delta; it is flat and little above sea level. The total city area is 26 square miles but only 7 square miles at the center were densely built up. The principal industries, which had been greatly expanded during the war, were located on the periphery of the city. The population of the city had been reduced from approximately 340,000 to 245,000 as a result of a civilian defense evacuation program. The explosion caught the city by surprise. An alert had been sounded but in view of the small number of planes the all-clear had been given. Consequently, the population had not taken shelter. The bomb exploded a little northwest of the center of the built-up area. Everyone who was out in the open and was exposed to the initial flash suffered serious burns where not protected by clothing. Over 4 square miles in the center of the city were flattened to the ground with the exception of some 50 reinforced concrete buildings, most of which were internally gutted and many of which suffered structural damage. Most of the people in the flattened area were crushed or pinned down by the collapsing buildings or flying debris. Shortly thereafter, numerous fires started, a few from the direct heat of the flash, but most from overturned charcoal cooking stoves or other secondary causes. These fires grew in size, merging into a general conflagration fanned by a wind sucked into the center of the city by the rising heat. The civilian-defense organization was overwhelmed by the completeness of the destruction, and the spread of fire was halted more by the air rushing toward the center of the conflagration than by efforts of the fire-fighting organization.

Approximately 60,000 to 70,000 people were killed, and 50,000 were injured. Of approximately 90,000 buildings in the city, 65,000 were rendered unusable and almost all the remainder received at least light superficial damage. The underground utilities of the city were undamaged except where they crossed bridges over the rivers cutting through the city. All of the small factories in the center of the city were destroyed. However, the big plants on the periphery of the city were almost completely undamaged and 94 percent of their workers unhurt.

These factories accounted for 74 percent of the industrial production of the city. It is estimated that they could have resumed substantially normal production within 30 days of the bombing, had the war continued. The railroads running through the city were repaired for the resumption of through traffic on 8 August, 2 days after the attack.

Nagasaki was a highly congested city built around the harbor and up into the ravines and river valleys of the surrounding hills. Spurs of these hills coming down close to the head of the bay divide the city roughly into two basins. The built-up area was 3.4 square miles of which 0.6 square miles was given over to industry. The peak wartime population of 285,000 had been reduced to around 230,00 by August 1945, largely by pre-raid evacuations. Nagasaki had been attacked sporadically prior to 9 August by an aggregate of 136 planes which dropped 270 tons of high explosives and 53 tons of incendiary bombs. Some 2 percent of the residential buildings had been destroyed or badly damaged; three of the large industrial plants had received scattered damage. The city was thus comparatively intact at the time of the atomic bombing.

The alarm was improperly given and therefore few persons were in shelters. The bomb exploded over the northwest portion of the city; the intervening hills protected a major portion of the city lying in the adjoining valley. The heat radiation and blast actions of the Nagasaki bomb were more intense than those of the bomb dropped over Hiroshima. Reinforced-concrete structures were structurally damaged at greater distances; the heavy steel-frame industrial buildings of the Mitsubishi steel works and the arms plant were pushed at crazy angles away from the center of the explosion. Contrary to the situation at Hiroshima, the majority of the fires that started immediately after the explosion resulted from direct ignition by the flash.

Approximately 40,000 persons were killed or missing and a like number injured. Of the 52,000 residential buildings in Nagasaki 14,000 were totally destroyed and a further 5,400 badly damaged. Ninety-six percent of the industrial output of Nagasaki was concentrated in the large plants of the Mitsubishi Co. which completely dominated the town. The arms plant and the steel works were located within the area of primary damage. It is estimated that 58 percent of the yen value of the arms plant and 78 percent of the value of the steel works were destroyed. The main plant of the Mitsubishi electric works was on the periphery of the area of greatest destruction. Approximately 25 percent of its value was destroyed. The dockyard, the largest industrial establishment in Nagasaki and one of the three plants previously damaged by high-explosive bombs, was located down the bay from the explosion. It suffered virtually no new damage. The Mitsubishi plants were all operating, prior to the attack, at a fraction of their capacity because of a shortage of raw materials. Had the war continued, and had the raw material situation been such as to warrant their restoration, it is estimated that the dockyard could have been in a position to produce at 80 percent of its full capacity within 3 to 4 months; that the steel works would have required a year to get into substantial production; that the electric works could have resumed some production within 2 months and been back at capacity within 6 months; and that restoration of the arms plant to 60 to 70 percent of former capacity would have required 15 months.

Some 400 persons were in the tunnel shelters in Nagasaki at the time of the explosion. The shelters consisted of rough tunnels dug horizontally into the sides of hills with crude, earth-filled blast walls protecting the entrances. The blast walls were blown in but all the occupants back from the entrances survived, even in those tunnels almost directly under the explosion. Those not in a direct line with the entrance were uninjured. The tunnels had a capacity of roughly 100,000 persons. Had the proper alarm been sounded, and these tunnel shelters been filled to capacity, the loss of life in Nagasaki would have been substantially lower.

The Survey has estimated that the damage and casualties caused at Hiroshima by the one atomic bomb dropped from a single plane would have required 220 B-29s carrying 1,200 tons of incendiary bombs, 400 tons of high-explosive bombs, and 500 tons of anti-personnel fragmentation bombs, if conventional weapons, rather than an atomic bomb, had been used. One hundred and twenty-five B-29s carrying 1,200 tons of bombs would have been required to approximate the damage and casualties at Nagasaki. This estimate pre-supposed bombing under conditions similar to those existing when the atomic bombs were dropped and bombing accuracy equal to the average attained by the Twentieth Air Force during the last 3 months of the war.

As might be expected, the primary reaction of the populace to the bomb was fear, uncontrolled terror, strengthened by the sheer horror of the destruction and suffering witnessed and experienced by the survivors. Prior to the dropping of the atomic bombs, the people of the two cities had fewer misgivings about the war than people in other cities and their morale held up after it better than might have been expected. Twenty-nine percent of the survivors interrogated indicated that after the atomic bomb was dropped they were convinced that victory for Japan was impossible. Twenty-four percent stated that because of the bomb they felt personally unable to carry on with the war. Some 40 percent testified to various degrees of defeatism. A greater number (24 percent) expressed themselves as being impressed with the power and scientific skill which underlay the discovery and production of the atomic bomb than expressed anger at its use (20 percent). In many instances, the reaction was one of resignation.

The effect of the atomic bomb on the confidence of the Japanese civilian population outside the two cities was more restricted. This was in part due to the effect of distance, lack of understanding of the nature of atomic energy, and the impact of other demoralizing experiences. . . .

Source: Web site: The Anesi Web site. Available at http://www.anesi. com/ussbs01.htm.

228. Paul Fussell, "Thank God for the Atom Bomb"

On only two occasions have atomic weapons ever been detonated in a combat situation—in August 1945, over the cities of Hiroshima and Nagasaki. Many have since questioned the need for their use, especially against cities that contained many civilians. The literary critic Paul Fussell, who had already seen heavy fighting in the European theater, later took issue with those who suggested that American soldiers deprecated these bombings. He recalled the very different reaction of himself and his fellow soldiers, who felt that the employment of atomic weapons was amply justified if it meant that no further American soldiers died in combat.

On Okinawa, only weeks before Hiroshima, 123,000 Japanese and Americans *killed* each other. (About 140,000 Japanese died at Hiroshima.) "Just awful" was the comment on the Okinawa slaughter not of some pacifist but of General MacArthur. On July 14, 1945, General Marshall sadly informed the Combined Chiefs of Staff—he was not trying to scare the Japanese—that it's "now clear . . . that in order to finish with the Japanese quickly, it will be necessary to invade the industrial heart of Japan." The invasion was definitely on, as I know because I was to be in it.

When the atom bomb ended the war, I was in the Forty-fifth Infantry Division, which had been through the European war so thoroughly that it had needed to be reconstituted two or three times. We were in a staging area near Rheims, ready to be shipped back across the United States for refresher training at Fort Lewis, Washington, and then sent on for final preparation in the Philippines. My division, like most of the ones transferred from Europe, was to take part in the invasion of Honshu. (The earlier landing on Kyushu was to be carried out by the 700,000 infantry already in the Pacific, those with whom James Jones has sympathized.) I was a twenty-one-year-old second lieutenant of infantry leading a rifle platoon. Although still officially fit for combat, in the German war I had already been wounded in the back and the leg badly enough to be adjudged, after the war, 40 percent disabled. But even if my leg buckled and I fell to the ground whenever I jumped out of the back of a truck, and even if the very idea of more combat made me breathe in gasps and shake all over, my condition was held to be adequate for the next act. When the atom bombs were

dropped and news began to circulate that "Operation Olympic" would not, after all, be necessary, when we learned to our astonishment that we would not be obliged in a few months to rush up the beaches near Tokyo assault-firing while being machine-gunned, mortared, and shelled, for all the practiced phlegm of our tough façades we broke down and cried with relief and joy. We were going to live. We were going to grow to adulthood after all. The killing was all going to be over, and peace was actually going to be the state of things. When the *Enola Gay* dropped its package, "There were cheers," says John Toland, "over the intercom; it meant the end of the war." . . .

Experience whispers that the pity is not that we used the bomb to end the Japanese war but that it wasn't ready in time to end the German one. If only it could have been rushed into production faster and dropped at the right moment on the Reich Chancellery or Berchtesgaden or Hitler's military headquarters in East Prussia (where Colonel Stauffenberg's July 20 [1944] bomb didn't do the job because it wasn't big enough), much of the Nazi hierarchy could have been pulverized immediately, saving not just the embarrassment of the Nuremberg trials but the lives of around four million Jews, Poles, Slavs, and gypsies, not to mention the lives and limbs of millions of Allied soldiers. If the bomb had only been ready in time, the young men of my infantry platoon would not have been so cruelly killed and wounded.

Source: Paul Fussell, *Thank God for the Atom Bomb and Other Essays* (New York: Ballantine Books, 1988), 13–18. Reprinted with permission of Paul Fussell.

229. Mao Zedong, "Chiang Kai-shek Is Provoking Civil War," Commentary Written for the Xinhua News Agency, 13 August 1945

In August 1945 the Chinese Communist leader Mao Zedong condemned the order of Generalissimo Jiang Jieshi (Chiang Kai-shek), head of the Guomindang nationalist government, that only Guomindang representatives could accept the surrender of Japanese forces in China. Mao feared that, if Communist officials accepted this ruling, Guomindang officials would augment their existing weaponry with surrendered Japanese arms, putting the Chinese Communists in a disadvantageous position should, as seemed increasingly likely, fighting break out between them and the Guomindang. Within a few months civil war had indeed begun between the Guomindang and its Communist opponents, a conflict that lasted until October 1949, when Jiang's forces fled to the island of Taiwan and the victorious Communists established the People's Republic of China.

A spokesman for the Propaganda Department of the Kuomintang Central Executive Committee has made a statement describing as "a presumptuous and illegal act" the order setting a time-limit for the surrender of the enemy and the puppets, which was issued by Chu Teh, Commander-in-Chief of the Eighteenth Group Army, on August 10 from the General Headquarters in Yenan. This comment is absolutely preposterous. Its logical implication is that it was wrong of Chu Teh to act in accordance with the Potsdam Declaration and with the enemy's declared intention of surrendering and to order his troops to effect the surrender of the enemy and the puppets, and that on the contrary it would have been right and legitimate to advise the enemy and puppets to refuse to surrender. No wonder that even before the enemy's actual surrender, Chiang Kai-shek, China's fascist ringleader, autocrat and traitor to the people, had the audacity to "order" the anti-Japanese armed forces in the Liberated Areas to "stay where they are, pending further orders," that is, to tie their own hands and let the enemy attack them. No wonder this selfsame fascist ringleader dared to "order" the so-called underground forces (who are, in fact, puppet troops "saving the nation by a devious path" and Tai Li's secret police collaborating with the Japanese and puppets) as well as other puppet troops to "be responsible for maintaining local order," while forbidding the anti-Japanese armed forces in the Liberated Areas to "take presumptuous action on their own" against enemy and puppet forces. This transposition of the enemy and the Chinese is in truth a confession by Chiang Kai-shek; it gives a vivid picture of his whole psychology, which is one of consistent collusion with the enemy and puppets and of liquidation of all those not of his ilk. However, the people's anti-Japanese armed forces in China's Liberated Areas will never be taken in by this venomous scheme. . . .

Both the comment by the spokesman for the Propaganda Department of the Kuomintang Central Executive Committee and Chiang Kai-shek's "orders" are from beginning to end provocations to civil war; at this moment, when attention at home and abroad is focused on Japan's unconditional surrender, their aim is to find a pretext for switching to civil war as soon as the War of Resistance ends. . . . So now they are saying that the Eighth Route Army and the New Fourth Army should not demand that the enemy and puppet troops surrender their guns. In the eight years of the War of Resistance, the Eighth Route Army and the New Fourth Army have suffered enough from the attacks and encirclements of both Chiang Kai-shek and the Japanese. And now, with the War of Resistance coming to an end, Chiang Kai-shek is hinting to the Japanese (and to his beloved puppet troops) that they should not surrender their guns to the Eighth Route Army and the New Fourth Army but "only to me, Chiang Kai-shek." One thing, however, Chiang Kai-shek has left unsaid, " . . . so that I can use these guns to kill the Communists and wreck the peace of China and the world." Isn't this the truth? What will be the result of telling the Japanese to hand over their guns to Chiang Kai-shek and telling the puppet troops to "be responsible for maintaining local order"? The result can only be that a merger of the Nanking and Chungking regimes and co-operation between Chiang Kai-shek and the puppets will take the place of "Sino-Japanese collaboration" and of co-operation between the Japanese and the puppets, and that Chiang Kai-shek's "anti-communism and national reconstruction" will take the place of the "anti-communism and national reconstruction" of the Japanese and [the collaborationist Japanese-backed wartime President of China] Wang Ching-wei. Isn't this a violation of the Potsdam Declaration? Can there be any doubt that the grave danger of civil war will confront the people of the whole country the moment the War of Resistance is over? We now appeal to all our fellow-countrymen and to the Allied countries to take action, together with the people of the Liberated Areas, resolutely to prevent a civil war in China, which would endanger world peace.

After all, who has the right to accept the surrender of the Japanese and puppets? Relying solely on their own efforts and the support of the people, the anti-Japanese armed forces in China's Liberated Areas, to whom the Kuomintang government refused all supplies and recognition, have succeeded by themselves in liberating vast territories and more than 100 million people and have resisted and pinned down 56 per cent of the invading enemy troops in China and 95 per cent of the puppet troops. If not for these armed forces, the situation in China would never have been what it is today! To speak plainly, in China only the anti-Japanese armed forces of the Liberated Areas have the right to accept the surrender of the enemy and puppet troops. As for Chiang Kai-shek, his policy has been to look on with folded arms and sit around and wait for victory; indeed he has no right at all to accept the surrender of the enemy and the puppets.

We declare to all our fellow-countrymen and to the people of the whole world: The Supreme Command in Chungking cannot represent the Chinese people and those Chinese armed forces which have really fought Japan; the Chinese people demand the right of the anti-Japanese armed forces of China's Liberated Areas under Commander-in-Chief Chu Teh to send their representatives directly in order to participate in the acceptance of Japan's surrender and in the military control over Japan by the four Allied Powers and also to participate in the future peace conference. If this is not done, the Chinese people will deem it most improper.

Source: Mao Zedong, "Chiang Kai-Shek Is Provoking Civil War, 13 August 1945," in *Selected Works of Mao Tse-tung,* Vol. 4 (Beijing: Foreign Language Press), 27–29. Also available at Maoist Documentation Project, http://www.maoism.org/msw/vol4/mswv4_02.htm. Used by permission of the Foreign Language Press, Beijing.

230. Emperor Hirohito, Radio Broadcast Accepting the Potsdam Declaration, 14 August 1945

On 14 August 1945, Japanese Emperor Hirohito (the Shōwa emperor) transmitted a message to his people informing them that the Japan government had decided to accept the terms of the previous month's Potsdam declaration and surrender to the Allies. He called upon his subjects to resolve to bear the unbearable, an appeal widely credited with preventing last-ditch military opposition to the Allied occupation.

To our good and loyal subjects: After pondering deeply the general trends of the world and the actual conditions obtaining in our empire today, we have decided to effect a settlement of the present situation by resorting to an extraordinary measure.

We have ordered our Government to communicate to the Governments of the United States, Great Britain, China and the Soviet Union that our empire accepts the provisions of their joint declaration.

To strive for the common prosperity and happiness of all nations as well as the security and well-being of our subjects is the solemn obligation which has been handed down by our imperial ancestors and which we lay close to the heart.

Indeed, we declared war on America and Britain out of our sincere desire to insure Japan's self-preservation and the stabilization of East Asia, it being far from our thought either to infringe upon the sovereignty of other nations or to embark upon territorial aggrandizement.

But now the war has lasted for nearly four years. Despite the best that has been done by everyone—the gallant fighting of our military and naval forces, the diligence and assiduity of out servants of the State and the devoted service of our 100,000,000 people—the war situation has developed not necessarily to Japan's advantage, while the general trends of the world have all turned against her interest.

Moreover, the enemy has begun to employ a new and most cruel bomb, the power of which to do damage is, indeed, incalculable, taking the toll of many innocent lives. Should we continue to fight, it would not only result in an ultimate collapse and obliteration of the Japanese nation, but also it would lead to the total extinction of human civilization.

Such being the case, how are we to save the millions of our subjects, nor to atone ourselves before the hallowed spirits of our imperial ancestors? This is the reason why we have ordered the acceptance of the provisions of the joint declaration of the powers.

We cannot but express the deepest sense of regret to our allied nations of East Asia, who have consistently cooperated with the Empire toward the emancipation of East Asia.

The thought of those officers and men as well as others who have fallen in the fields of battle, those who died at their posts of duty, or those who met death [otherwise] and all their bereaved families, pains our heart night and day.

The welfare of the wounded and the war sufferers and of those who lost their homes and livelihood is the object of our profound solicitude. The hardships and sufferings to which our nation is to be subjected hereafter will be certainly great.

We are keenly aware of the inmost feelings of all of you, our subjects. However, it is according to the dictates of time and fate that we have resolved to pave the way for a grand peace for all the generations to come by enduring the unendurable and suffering what is unsufferable. Having been able to save and maintain the structure of the Imperial State, we are always with you, our good and loyal subjects, relying upon your sincerity and integrity.

Beware most strictly of any outbursts of emotion that may engender needless complications, of any fraternal contention and strife that may create confusion, lead you astray and cause you to lose the confidence of the world.

Let the entire nation continue as one family from generation to generation, ever firm in its faith of the imperishableness of its divine land, and mindful of its heavy burden of responsibilities, and the long road before it. Unite your total strength to be devoted to the construction for the future. Cultivate the ways of rectitude, nobility of spirit, and work with resolution so that you may enhance the innate glory of the Imperial State and keep pace with the progress of the world.

Source: Web site: Mount Holyoke College International Relations Program. Available at http://www.mtholyoke.edu/acad/intrel/hirohito. htm.

231. William J. Donovan to Harold D. Smith, Director, Bureau of the Budget, 25 August 1945

In August 1945 President Harry S Truman disbanded the Office of Strategic Services (OSS), the United States wartime foreign intelligence agency. OSS Director General William J. Donovan remained convinced that the United States needed a permanent overseas intelligence agency, to conduct overseas espionage operations. In a coordinated lobbying campaign, as he gradually liquidated his operations, Donovan expressed these views to the influential director of the Bureau of the Budget and numerous other Washington officials. Within two years, his efforts succeeded, as the burgeoning Cold War resulted in the creation of the Central Intelligence Agency.

It is our estimate . . . the effectiveness of OSS as a War Agency will end as of January 1, or at latest February 1946, at which time liquidation should be completed. At that point I wish to return to private life. Therefore, in considering the disposition to be made of the assets created by OSS, I speak as a private citizen concerned with the future of his country.

In our government today there is no permanent agency to take over the functions which OSS will have then ceased to perform. These functions while carried on as incident to the war are in reality essential in the effective discharge by this nation of its responsibilities in the organization and maintenance of the peace.

Since last November I have pointed out the immediate necessity of setting up such an agency to take over valuable assets created by OSS. Among these assets was the establishment for the first time in our nation's history of a foreign secret intelligence service which reported information as seen through American eyes. As an integral and inseparable part of this service there is a group of specialists to analyze and evaluate the material for presentation to those who determine national policy.

It is not easy to set up a modern intelligence system. It is more difficult to do so in time of peace than in time of war.

It is important therefore that it be done before the War Agency has disappeared so that profit may be made of its experience and "know how" in deciding how the new agency may best be conducted.

I have already submitted a plan for the establishment of a centralized system. However, the discussion of that proposal indicated the need of an agreement upon certain fundamental principles before a detailed plan is formulated. If those concerned could agree upon the principles with which such a system should be established, acceptance of a common plan would be more easily achieved.

Accordingly, I attach a statement of principles, the soundness of which I believe has been established by study and by practical experience.

PRINCIPLES—THE SOUNDNESS OF WHICH IT IS BELIEVED HAS BEEN ESTABLISHED BY OUR OWN EXPERIENCE AND FIRST-HAND STUDY OF THE SYSTEMS OF OTHER NATIONS—WHICH SHOULD GOVERN THE ESTABLISHMENT OF A CENTRALIZED UNITED STATES FOREIGN INTELLIGENCE SYSTEM.

The formulation of a national policy both in its political and military aspects is influenced and determined by knowledge (or ignorance) of the aims, capabilities, intentions, and policies of other nations.

All major powers except the United States have had for a long time past permanent world-wide intelligence services, reporting directly to the highest echelons of their governments. Prior to the present war, the United States had no foreign secret intelligence service. It never has had and does not now have a coordinated intelligence system.

The defects and dangers of this situation have been generally recognized. Adherence to the following would remedy this defect in peace as well as war so that American policy could be based upon information obtained through its own sources on foreign intentions, capabilities, and developments as seen and interpreted by Americans.

1. That each department of Government should have its own intelligence bureau for the collection and processing of such informational material as it finds necessary in the actual performance of its functions and duties. Such a bureau should be under the sole control of the department head and should not be encroached upon or impaired by the functions granted any other governmental intelligence agency.

Because secret intelligence covers all fields and because of possible embarrassment, no executive department should be permitted to engage in secret intelligence but in a proper case should call upon the central agency for service.

2. That in addition to the intelligence unit for each department there should be established a national centralized foreign intelligence agency which should have the authority:

A. To serve all departments of the Government.
B. To procure and obtain political, economic, psychological, sociological, military, and other information which may bear upon the national interest and which has been collected by the different Governmental departments or agencies.
C. To collect when necessary supplemental information either at its own instance or at the request of any Governmental departments or agencies.
D. To integrate, analyze, process, and disseminate, to authorized Governmental agencies and officials, intelligence in the form of strategic interpretive studies.

3. That such an agency should be prohibited from carrying on clandestine activities within the United States and should be forbidden the exercise of any police functions at home or abroad.

4. That since the nature of its work requires it to have status, it should be independent of any department of the government (since it is obliged to serve all and must be free of the natural bias of an operating department). It should be under a director, appointed by the President, and be administered under Presidential direction, or in the event of a General Manager being appointed, should be established in the Executive Office of the President, under his direction.

5. That subject to the approval of the President or the General Manager the policy of such a service should be determined by the Director with the advice and assistance of a Board on which the Secretaries of State, War, Navy, and Treasury should be represented.

6. That this agency, as the sole agency for secret intelligence, should be authorized, in the foreign field only, to carry on services such as espionage, counterespionage, and those special operations (including morale and psychological) designed to anticipate and counter any attempted penetration and subversion of our national security by enemy action.

7. That such a service should have an independent budget granted directly by the Congress.

8. That such a service should have its own system of codes and should be furnished facilities by departments of Government proper and necessary for the performance of its duties.

9. That such a service should include in its staff specialists (within Governmental departments, civil and military, and in private life) professionally trained in analysis of information and possessing a high degree of linguistic, regional, or functional competence, to analyze, coordinate, and evaluate incoming information, to make special intelligence reports, and to provide guidance for the collecting branches of the agency.

10. That in time of war or unlimited national emergency, all programs of such agency in areas of actual and projected military operations shall be coordinated with military plans, and shall be subject to the approval of the Joint Chiefs of Staff, or if there be consolidation of the armed services, under the supreme commander. Parts of such programs which are to be executed in the theater of military operations shall be subject to control of the military commander.

Source: "General Donovan's Letter to the Director of the Bureau of Budget, Harold D. Smith," *Counterintelligence in World War II* on the National Counterintelligence Center's Web site. Available at http://www.fas.org/irp/ops/ci/docs/ci2/2ch3_c.htm.

232. George C. Marshall, "Price of Victory": American Casualties in World War II: Extract from Final Biennial Report to the Secretary of War, 1 September 1945

American leaders were well aware of the human cost the war exacted. In his final report to the secretary of war, Army Chief of Staff George C. Marshall gave detailed figures on American military casualties. These did not include the numbers of those killed or invalided out as the result of disease, exposure, or accident rather than in combat.

Even with our overwhelming concentration of air power and fire power, this war has been the most costly of any in which the Nation has been engaged. The victory in Europe alone cost us 772,626 battle casualties of which 160,045 are dead. The price of victory in the Pacific was 170,596 including 41,322 dead. Army battle deaths since 7 December 1941 were greater than the combined losses, Union and Confederate, of the Civil War. . . .

Army casualties in all theaters from 7 December 1941 until the end of the period of this report [30 June 1945] total 943,222, including 201,367 killed, 570,732 wounded, 114,205 prisoners, 56,867 missing; of the total wounded, prisoners, or missing more than 633,200 have returned to duty, or have been evacuated to the United States.

The great strategic bombardment strikes on Germany and the inauguration of the Mediterranean campaign pushed our total casualty rate above 5,000 a month in 1943. In the first five months of 1944 the increasing tempo of the air attack and the fighting in Italy drove our losses, killed, wounded, missing, and prisoners, to 13,700 men a month. Once ashore in Western Europe, the casualty rate leaped to 48,000 a month and increased to 81,000 by December. The average for the last seven months of the year was 59,000.

Out in the Pacific the advance on Japan cost 3,200 men a month throughout 1944. In the first seven months of this year the rate increased to 12,750 as we closed on the Japanese Islands.

The heaviest losses have been on the ground where the fighting never ceases night or day. Disregarding their heavy losses to disease and exposure, the combat divisions have taken more than 81 percent of all our casualties. However, though the percentage of the total is small, the casualties among the combat air crews have been very severe. By the end of July the Army Air Forces had taken nearly 120,000 casualties. Of this total 36,698 had died. The air raids over enemy territory gave Air Force casualties the heaviest weighting of permanency. The wounded of the Ground Forces drove their total casualties high, but with the exceptional medical care the Army has had in this war, the wounded had good chances to recover. . . .

In the Army at large, the infantry comprises only 20.5 percent of total strength overseas, yet it has taken 70 percent of the total casualties. Enemy fire is no respecter of rank in this war; 10.2 percent of the casualties have been officers, a rate slightly higher than that for enlisted men.

The improvement of battle surgery and medical care, on the other hand, reduced the rate of death from wounds to less than one-half the rate in World War I, and permitted more than 58.8 percent of men wounded in this war to return to duty in the theaters of operations.

As staggering as our casualties have been, the enemy forces opposing us suffered many time more heavily; 1,592,600 Germans, Italians, and Japanese troops were killed for the 201,367 American soldiers who died. It is estimated that permanently disabled enemy total 303,700. We captured and disarmed 8,150,447 enemy troops.

Source: George C. Marshall, *General Marshall's Report: The Winning of the War in Europe and the Pacific: Biennial Report of the Chief of Staff of the United States Army July 1, 1943 to June 30, 1945, to the Secretary of War* (New York: Simon and Schuster, 1945), 107–108.

233. George C. Marshall, "For the Common Defense," Extract from Final Biennial Report to the Secretary of War, 1 September 1945

As the war ended, George C. Marshall, army chief of staff, put forward proposals for a "peacetime security policy" for the United States. He envisaged a relatively small permanent standing army, buttressed by a citizen soldiery who could be called to arms in case of need. The latter he hoped to create through a program of universal military training, required of all young American men. Marshall expected the regular army to be "a strategic force, heavy in air power, partially deployed in the Pacific and the Caribbean ready to protect the Nation against a sudden hostile thrust and immediately available for emergency action wherever required." In addition, he called for the creation of substantial national stockpiles of arms, ammunition, and other military equipment, and a heavy emphasis on the promotion of scientific research and development in the defense field. Largely due to popular opposition, the United States did not introduce universal military training, but most of Marshall's other recommendations were put into effect.

Our present national policies require us to: Maintain occupation forces in Europe and the Pacific; prepare for a possible contribution of forces to a world security organization; maintain national security while the world remains unstable and later on a more permanent or stable basis.

These policies require manpower. Yet at the same time it is the policy of the nation to completely demobilize the wartime army as rapidly as possible. Unless hundreds of thousands of men of the wartime forces are to remain in service at home and overseas, more permanent decisions must be made.

The War Department recommends that the occupation forces and the U.S. complement in the International security force be composed as much as possible of volunteers. This can be accomplished by establishing now a new permanent basis for the regular military establishment. If this recommendation and those which I will now discuss in detail for establishing a peacetime security policy are now adopted by the Congress, demobilization can proceed uninterrupted until all men now in temporary service have returned to their homes.

FOR THE COMMON DEFENSE

To fulfill its responsibility for protecting this Nation against foreign enemies, the Army must project its planning beyond the immediate future. In this connection I feel that I have a duty, a responsibility, to present publicly at this time my conception, from a military point of view, of what is required to prevent another international catastrophe.

For years men have been concerned with individual security. Modern nations have given considerable study and effort to the establishment of social security systems for those unable or unwise enough to provide for themselves.

But effective insurance against the disasters which have slaughtered millions of people and leveled their homes is long overdue.

We finish each bloody war with a feeling of acute revulsion against this savage form of human behavior, and yet on each occasion we confuse military preparedness with the causes of war and then drift almost deliberately into another catastrophe. . . .

We must start, I think, with a correction of the tragic misunderstanding that a security policy is a war policy. War has been defined by a people who have thought a lot about it—the Germans. They have started most of the recent ones. The German soldier-philosopher Clausewitz described war as a special violent form of political action. Frederic of Prussia, who left Germany the belligerent legacy which has now destroyed her, viewed war as a device to enforce his will whether he was right or wrong. He held that with an invincible offensive military force he could win any political argument. This is the doctrine Hitler carried to the verge of complete success. It is the doctrine of Japan. It is a criminal doctrine, and like other forms of crime, it has cropped up again and again since man began to live with his neighbors in communities and nations. There has long been an effort to outlaw war for exactly the same reason that man has outlawed murder. But the law prohibiting murder does not of itself prevent murder. It must be enforced. The enforcing power, however, must be maintained on a strictly democratic basis. There must not be a large standing army subject to the behest of a group of schemers. The citizen-soldier is the guarantee against such a misuse of power.

In order to establish an international system for preventing wars, peace-loving peoples of the world are demonstrating an eagerness to send their representatives to such conferences as those at Dumbarton Oaks and San Francisco with the fervent hope that they may find a practical solution. Yet, until it is proved that such a solution has been found to prevent wars, a rich nation which lays down its arms as we have done after every war in our history, will court disaster. The existence of the complex and fearful instruments of destruction now available make this a simple truth which is, in my opinion, undebatable.

So far as their ability to defend themselves and their institutions was concerned, the great democracies were sick nations when Hitler openly massed his forces to impose his will on the world. As sick as any was the United States of America. We had no field army. There were the bare skeletons of three and one-half divisions scattered in small pieces over the entire United States. It was impossible to train even these few combat troops as divisions because motor transportation and other facilities were lacking and funds for adequate maneuvers were not appropriated. The Air Forces consisted of a few partially equipped squadrons serving continental United States, Panama, Hawaii, and the Philippines; their planes were largely obsolescent and could hardly have survived a single day of modern aerial combat. We lacked modern arms and equipment. When President Roosevelt proclaimed, on 8 September 1939, that a limited emergency existed for the United States we were, in terms of available strength, not even a third-rate military power. Some collegians had been informing the world and evidently convincing the Japanese that the young men of America would refuse to fight in defense of their country.

The German armies swept over Europe at the very moment we sought to avoid war by assuring ourselves that there could be no war. The security of the United States of America was saved by sea distance, by Allies, and by the errors of a prepared enemy. For probably the last time in the history of warfare those ocean distances were a vital factor in our defense. We may elect again to depend on others and the whim and error of potential enemies, but if we do we will be carrying the treasure and freedom of this great Nation in a paper bag.

Returning from France after the last war, with General Pershing [commander in chief of the American Expeditionary Force in World War I], I participated in his endeavors to persuade the Nation to establish and maintain a sound defense policy. Had his recommendations been accepted, they might have saved this country the hundreds of billions of dollars and the more than a million casualties it has cost us again to restore the peace. We might even have been spared this present world tragedy. . . .

Twice in recent history the factories and farms and people of the United States have foiled aggressor nations; conspirators against the peace would not give us a third opportunity.

Between Germany and America in 1914 and again in 1939 stood Great Britain and the USSR, France, Poland, and the other countries of Europe. Because the technique of destruction had not progressed to its present peak, these nations had to be eliminated and the Atlantic Ocean crossed by ships before our factories could be brought within the range of the enemy guns. At the close of the German war in Europe they were just on the outer fringes of the range of fire from an enemy in Europe. [German Field Marshall Hermann] Goering stated after his capture that it was a certainty that the eastern Americas would have been under rocket bombardment had Germany remained undefeated for two more years. The first attacks would have started much sooner. The technique of war has brought the United States, its homes and factories into the front line of world conflict. They escaped destructive bombardment in the second World War. They would not in a third.

It no longer appears practical to continue what we once conceived as hemispheric defense as a satisfactory basis for our security. We are now concerned with the peace of the entire world. And the peace can only be maintained by the strong.

What then must we do to remain strong and still not bankrupt ourselves on military expenditures to maintain a prohibitively expensive professional army even if one could be recruited? President Washington answered that question in recommendations to the first Congress to convene under the United States Constitution. He proposed a program for the peacetime training of a citizen army. At that time the conception of a large professional Regular Army was considered dangerous to the liberties of the Nation. It is still so today. But the determining factor in solving this problem will inevitably be the relation between the maintenance of military power and the cost in annual appropriations. No system, even if actually adopted in the near future, can survive the political pressure to reduce the military budget if the costs are high—and professional armies are very costly.

There is now another disadvantage to a large professional standing army. Wars in the twentieth century are fought with the total resources, economic, scientific, and human of entire nations. Every specialized field of human knowledge is employed. Modern war requires the skill and knowledge of the individuals of a nation.

Obviously we cannot all put on uniforms and stand ready to repel invasion. The greatest energy in peacetime of any successful nation must be devoted to productive and gainful labor. But all Americans can, in the next generations, prepare themselves to serve their country in maintaining the peace or against the tragic hour when peace is broken, if such a misfortune again overtakes us. This is what is meant by Universal Military *Training*. It is not universal military *service*—the actual induction of men into the combatant forces. Such forces would be composed during peacetime of volunteers. The trainees would be in separate organizations maintained for training purposes only. Once trained, young men would be freed from further connection with the Army unless they chose, as they now may, to enroll in the National Guard or an organized reserve unit, or to volunteer for service in the small professional army. When the Nation is in jeopardy they could be called, just as men are now called, by a committee of local neighbors, in an order of priority and under such conditions as directed at that time by the Congress.

The concept of universal military training is not founded, as some may believe, on the principle of a mass Army. The Army has been accused of rigidly holding to this doctrine in the face of modern developments. Nothing, I think, could be farther from the fact, as the record of the mobilization for this war demonstrates. Earlier in this report I explained how we had allocated manpower to exploit American technology. Out of our entire military mobilization of 14,000,000 men, the number of infantry troops was less than 1,500,000 Army and Marine.

The remainder of our armed forces, sea, air, and ground, was largely fighting a war of machinery. Counting those engaged in war production there were probably 75 to 80,000,000 Americans directly involved in prosecution of the war. To technological warfare we devoted 98 percent of our entire effort.

Nor is it proposed now to abandon this formula which has been so amazingly successful. The harnessing of the basic power of the universe will further spur our efforts to use brain for brawn in safeguarding the United States of America.

However, technology does not eliminate the need for men in war. The Air Forces, which were the highest developed technologically of any of our armed forces in this war, required millions of men to do their job. Every B-29 that winged over Japan was dependent on the efforts of 12 officers and 73 men in the immediate combat area alone. . . .

This war has made it clear that the security of the Nation, when challenged by an armed enemy, requires the services of virtually all able-bodied male citizens within the effective military group.

In war the Nation cannot depend on the numbers of men willing to volunteer for active service; nor can our security in peace.

In another national emergency, the existence of a substantial portion of the Nation's young manpower already trained or in process of training, would make it possible to fill out immediately the peacetime ranks of the Navy, the Regular Army, the National Guard, and the Organized Reserve. As a result our Armed Forces would be ready for almost immediate deployment to counter initial hostile moves, ready to prevent an enemy from gaining footholds from which he could launch destructive attack against our industries and our homes. By this method we would establish, for the generations to come, a national military policy: (1) which is entirely within the financial capabilities of our peacetime economy and is absolutely democratic in its nature, and (2) which places the military world and therefore the political world on notice that this vast power, linked to our tremendous resources, wealth, and production, is immediately available. There can be no question that all the nations of the world will respect our views accordingly, creating at least a probability of peace on earth and of good will among men rather than disaster upon disaster in a tormented world where the very processes of civilization itself are constantly threatened. . . .

The terms of the final peace settlement will provide a basis for determining the strength of the regular or permanent postwar military forces of the United States, air, ground, and naval, but they cannot, in my opinion, alter the necessity for a system of Universal Military Training.

The yardstick by which the size of the permanent force must be measured is maximum security with minimum cost in men, matériel, and maintenance. So far as they can foresee world conditions a decade from now, War Department planners, who have taken every conceivable factor into consideration, believe that our position will be sound if we set up machinery which will permit the mobilization of an Army of 4,000,000 men within a period of 1 year following any international crisis resulting in a national emergency for the United States.

The Regular Army must be comprised largely of a strategic force, heavy in air power, partially deployed in the Pacific and the Caribbean ready to protect the Nation against a sudden hostile thrust and immediately available for emergency action wherever required. It is obvious that another war would start with a lightning attack to take us unaware. The pace of the attack would be at supersonic speeds of rocket weapons closely followed by a striking force which would seek to exploit the initial and critical advantage. We must be sufficiently prepared against such a threat to hold the enemy at a distance until we can rapidly mobilize our strength. The Regular Army, and the National Guard, must be prepared to meet such a crisis.

Another mission of the Regular Army is to provide the security garrisons for the outlying bases. We quickly lost the Philippines, Guam, and Wake Islands at the beginning of this war and are still expending lives and wealth in recovering them.

The third mission of the permanent Army is to furnish the overhead, the higher headquarters which must keep the machine and the plans up to date for whatever national emergency we may face in the future. This overhead includes the War Department, the War College, the service schools, and the headquarters of the military area into which continental United States is subdivided to facilitate decentralized command and coordination of the peacetime military machine. This was about all we had on the eve of this war, planners and a small number of men who had little to handle in practice but sound ideas on how to employ the wartime hosts that would be gathered in the storm. Had it not been for the time the British Empire and the Soviets bought us, those plans and ideas would have been of little use.

The fourth and probably the most important mission of the Regular Army is to provide the knowledge, the expert personnel, and the installations for training the citizen-soldier upon whom, in my view, the future peace of the world largely depends. . . .

Only by Universal Military Training can full vigor and life be instilled into the Reserve system. It creates a pool of well-trained men and officers from which the National Guard and the Organized Reserve can draw volunteers; it provides opportunities for the Guard and Reserve units to participate in corps and Army maneuvers, which are vital preparations to success in military campaigns. Without these trained men and officers, without such opportunities to develop skill through actual practice in realistic maneuvers, neither the Regular Army, the National Guard, nor the Reserve can hope to bring efficiency to their vital missions. . . .

An unbroken period of 1 year's training appears essential to the success of a sound security plan based on the concept of a citizen army.

It is possible to train individual soldiers as replacements for veteran divisions and air groups as we now do in a comparatively short period of time. The training of the unit itself cannot be accomplished at best in less than a year; air units require even more time. The principle is identical to that of coaching a football team. A halfback can quickly learn how to run with the ball, but it takes time and much practice and long hours of team scrimmage before he is proficient at carrying the ball through an opposing team. So it is with an army division or combat air group. Men learn to fire a rifle or machine gun quickly, but it takes long hours of scrimmage, which the army calls maneuver, before the firing of the rifle is coordinated with the activities of more than 14,000 other men on the team.

All men who might someday have to fight for their Nation must have this team training. The seasoned soldiers of our present superb divisions will have lived beyond the age of military usefulness. The situation will be similar in the peacetime army to that which was obtained when we began to mobilize for this war and all men had to have at least a year of unit training before we had divisions even fit for shipment overseas.

The training program would be according to the standards which have made the American soldier in this war the equal of the finest fighting men. It would be kept abreast of technical developments and the resulting modification of tactics. . . .

The peacetime army must not only be prepared for immediate mobilization of an effective war army, but it must have in reserve the weapons needed for the first months of the fighting and clear-cut plans for immediately producing the tremendous additional quantities of matériel necessary in total war. We must never again face a great national crisis with ammunition lacking to serve our guns, few guns to fire, and no decisive procedures for procuring vital arms in sufficient quantities.

The necessity for continuous research into the military ramifications of man's scientific advance is now clear to all and it should not be too difficult to obtain the necessary appropriations for this purpose in peacetime. There is, however, always much reluctance to expenditure of funds for improvement of war-making instruments, particularly where there is no peacetime usefulness in the product.

The development of combat airplanes is closely allied with development of civil aeronautics; the prototypes of many of our present transport planes and those soon to come were originally bombers. Many of the aeronautical principles that helped give this Nation the greatest Air Force in the world grew out of commercial development and our production know-how at the start of this war was partially the fruit of peacetime commercial enterprise. Since many vital types of weapons have no commercial counterpart, the peacetime development of these weapons has been grossly neglected. Antiaircraft weapons are a good example. The highly efficient antiaircraft of today did not materialize until long after the fighting began. The consequent cost in time, life, and money of this failure to spend the necessary sums on such activity in peacetime has been appalling.

There is another phase of scientific research which I think has been somewhat ignored—the development of expeditious methods for the mass production of war matériel. This is of great importance since it determines how quickly we can mobilize our resources if war comes and how large and costly our reserve stocks of war matériel must be. Serious thought and planning along this line can save millions of tax dollars.

We can be certain that the next war, if there is one, will be even more total than this one. The nature of war is such that once it now begins it can end only as this one is ending, in the destruction of the vanquished, and it should be assumed that another reconversion from peace to war production will take place initially under distant enemy bombardment. Industrial mobilization plans must be founded on these assumptions and so organized that they will meet them and any other situation that may develop. Yet they must in no way retard or inhibit the course of peacetime production.

If this Nation is to remain great it must bear in mind now and in the future that war is not the choice of those who wish passionately for peace. It is the choice of those who are willing to resort to violence for political advantage. We can fortify ourselves against disaster, I am convinced, by the measures I have here outlined. In these protections we can face the future with a reasonable hope for the best and with quiet assurance that even though the worst may come, we are prepared for it.

Source: George C. Marshall, *General Marshall's Report: The Winning of the War in Europe and the Pacific: Biennial Report of the Chief of Staff of the United States Army July 1, 1943 to June 30, 1945, to the Secretary of War* (New York: Simon and Schuster, 1945), 116–123.

234. Kase Toshikazu, Account of the Japanese Surrender Ceremony, 2 September 1945

Eleven Japanese delegates attended the ceremony of surrender to the Allied powers, on board the USS Missouri *in Tokyo Bay. Kase Toshikazu, one of three Foreign Ministry representatives, gave a vivid account of what was for Japan its moment of utmost humiliation.*

It was a surprisingly cool day for early September. The sky was dull gray with clouds hanging low. We left Tokyo at about five o'clock in the morning. There were nine of us, three each from the Foreign Office, and the War and Navy Departments, besides the two delegates, Shigemitsu, the Foreign Minister representing the government, and General Umedzu, the Chief of Staff of the Army representing the Supreme Command. With the two delegates leading the procession, our cars sped at full speed on the battered and bumpy road to Yokohama. Along the highway, we could see nothing but miles and miles of debris and destruction where there had once flourished towns containing a great number of munitions factories. The ghastly sight of death and desolation was enough to freeze my heart. These hollow ruins, however, were perhaps a fit prelude to the poignant drama in which we were about to take part for were we not sorrowing men come to seek a tomb for a fallen Empire? They were also a grim reminder that a nation was snatched from an impending annihilation. For were not the scenes of havoc the atomic bomb wrought a sufficient warning? The waste of war and the ignominy of surrender were put on my mental loom and produced a strange fabric of grief and sorrow. There were few men on the road and none probably recognized us. Our journey was kept in utmost secrecy in order to avoid publicity lest extremists might attempt to impede us by violence.

To begin with, there was much ado in selecting the delegates. Nobody wanted to volunteer for the odious duty. The Prime Minister, Prince Higashikuni, was the Emperor's uncle and was considered unsuitable on that account. Next choice fell on Prince Konoye, who was Vice Premier and the real power in the government, but he shunned the ordeal. Finally the mission was assigned to Shigemitsu, the Foreign Minister. On accepting the imperial command to sign the surrender document as principal delegate, he confided to me what an honor he felt it, since it was the mark of the sovereign's confidence in him. Shigemitsu, who had served twice before as Foreign Minister—namely, in the latter period of the Tojo Cabinet and through the duration of the succeeding Koiso Cabinet—is a man of confirmed peaceful views and during his twelve months' term of office did his utmost to prepare for an early termination of the war. His efforts, in which I assisted him to the best of my ability, were in fact, powerfully instrumental in expediting the restoration of peace. Such being the case, there was reason to believe that unlike others who evaded the mission, hating it as unbearably onerous, Shigemitsu regarded it as a painful but profitable task. In his mind he was determined to make this day of national mortification the starting day for a renewed pilgrimage onward toward the goal, though dim and distant, of a peaceful state. If this day marked a journey's end it must also signify a journey's beginning. Only the traveler to grief must be replaced by the traveler to glory.

Not so with General Umedzu, who reluctantly accepted the appointment as the second delegate. He had opposed the termination of hostilities to the last moment and was, moreover, a soldier born to command and not to sue. When he was recommended for the mission he grew, so it is reported, pale with anger and laconically remarked that if it was forced upon him, he would instantly commit hara-kiri in protest. It required the Emperor's personal persuasion to make him execute the duties with good grace.

It may sound somewhat silly, but as precautions were then deemed necessary, the appointment of two delegates was not intimated to the press until the last moment. The names of nine persons who accompanied them were not published at all as the service officers were against this, though these names had been communicated to and approved by the Allied authorities. Such, indeed, was the temper of the times.

This party arrived in Yokohama in less than an hour's time. It was on this day that the spearhead of the Eighth Army landed at the same port. Sentries with gleaming bayonets were heavily guarding the streets through which we rode slowly to the port area. All the cars had removed the flags on the bonnet and officers had left their swords behind. We had thus furled the banner and ungirt the sword. Diplomats without flag and soldiers without sword—sullen and silent we continued the journey till we reached the quay.

There were four destroyers with white placards hung on the mast marked A to D. We boarded the one marked B, which was the *Lansdown,* a ship which saw much meritorious service in the battle of the Pacific. As the destroyer pushed out of the harbor, we saw in the offing lines on lines of gray warships, both heavy and light, anchored in majestic array. This was the mighty pageant of the Allied navies that so lately belched forth their crashing battle, now holding in their swift thunder and floating like calm sea birds on the subjugated waters. A spirit of gay festivity pervaded the atmosphere.

After about an hour's cruise the destroyer stopped in full view of the battleship *Missouri,* which lay anchored some eighteen miles off the shore. The huge 45,000 tonner towered high above the rest of the proud squadron. High on the mast there fluttered in the wind the Stars and Stripes. It was this flag that had lighted the marching step of America's destiny on to shining victory. Today this flag of glory was raised in triumph to mark the Big Day. As we approached the battleship in a motor launch, our eyes were caught by rows of sailors massed on her broadside lining the rails, a starry multitude, in their glittering uniforms of immaculate white.

Soon the launch came alongside the battleship, and we climbed its gangway, Shigemitsu leading the way, heavily limping on his cane. For he walks on a wooden leg, having had his leg blown off by a bomb outrage in Shanghai some fifteen years ago. It was as if he negotiated each step with a groan and we, the rest of us, echoed it with a sigh. As we, eleven in all, climbed onto the veranda deck on the starboard side, we gathered into three short rows facing the representatives of the Allied powers across a table covered with green cloth, on which were placed the white documents of surren-

der. The veranda deck was animated by a motley of sparkling colors, red, gold, brown, and olive, as decorations and ribbons decked the uniforms of different cut and color worn by the Allied representatives. There were also row upon row of American admirals and generals in somber khaki; but what added to the festive gayety of the occasion was the sight of the war correspondents who, monkey-like, hung on to every cliff-like point of vantage in most precarious postures. Evidently scaffolding had been specially constructed for the convenience of the cameramen, who were working frantically on their exciting job. Then there was a gallery of spectators who seemed numberless, overcrowding every bit of available space on the great ship, on the mast, on the chimneys, on the gun turrets—on everything, and everywhere.

They were all thronged, packed to suffocation, representatives, journalists, spectators, an assembly of brass, braid, and brand. As we appeared on the scene we were, I felt, being subjected to the torture of the pillory. There were a million eyes beating us in the million shafts of a rattling storm of arrows barbed with fire. I felt their keenness sink into my body with a sharp physical pain. Never have I realized that the glance of glaring eyes could hurt so much.

We waited for a few minutes standing in the public gaze like penitent boys awaiting the dreaded schoolmaster. I tried to preserve with the utmost sangfroid the dignity of defeat, but it was difficult and every minute seemed to contain ages. I looked up and saw painted on the wall nearby several miniature Rising Suns, our flag, evidently in numbers corresponding to the planes and submarines shot down or sunk by the crew of the battleship. As I tried to count these markings, tears rose in my throat and quickly gathered to my eyes, flooding them. I could hardly bear the sight now. Heroes of unwritten stories, they were young boys who defied death gaily and gallantly, manning the daily thinning ranks of the suicide corps. They were just like cherry blossoms, emblems of our national character, all of a sudden blooming into riotous beauty and just as quickly going away. What do they see today, their spirit, the glorious thing, looking down on the scene of surrender.

MacArthur walks quietly from the interior of the ship and steps to the microphones:

"We are gathered here, representatives of the major warring powers," he said, "to conclude a solemn agreement whereby peace may be restored. The issues, involving divergent ideals and ideologies, have been determined on the battlefields of the world and hence are not for our discussion or debate. Nor is it for us here to meet, representing as we do a majority of the people of the earth, in a spirit of distrust, malice or hatred. But rather it is for us, both victors and vanquished, to rise to that higher dignity which alone befits the sacred purposes we are about to serve, committing all our people unreservedly to faithful compliance with the obligation that they are here formally to assume.

"It is my earnest hope and indeed the hope of all mankind that from this solemn occasion a better world shall emerge out of the blood and carnage of the past—a world founded upon faith and understanding—a world dedicated to the dignity of man and the fulfillment of his most cherished wish—for freedom, tolerance and justice.

"The terms and conditions upon which the surrender of the Japanese Imperial Forces is here to be given and accepted are contained in the instrument of surrender now before you.

"As Supreme Commander for the Allied Powers, I announce it my firm purpose, in the tradition of the countries I represent, to proceed in the discharge of my responsibilities with justice and tolerance, while taking all necessary dispositions to insure that the terms of surrender are fully, promptly and faithfully complied with."

In a few minutes' time the speech was over and the Supreme Commander invited the Japanese delegates to sign the instrument of surrender. Shigemitsu signed first followed by Umedzu. It was eight minutes past nine when MacArthur put his signature to the documents. Other representatives of the Allied Powers followed suit in the order of the United States, China, the United Kingdom, the Soviet Union, Australia, Canada, France, the Netherlands and New Zealand.

When all the representatives had finished signing, MacArthur announced slowly: "Let us pray that peace be now restored to the world and that God will preserve it always. These proceedings are closed."

At that moment, the skies parted and the sun shone brightly through the layers of clouds. There was a steady drone above and now it became a deafening roar and an armada of airplanes paraded into sight, sweeping over the warships. Four hundred B-29's and 1,500 carrier planes joined in the aerial pageant in a final salute. It was over.

Source: Kase Toshikazu, *Eclipse of the Rising Sun,* ed. David Nelson Rowe (London: Jonathan Cape, 1951), 4–10, reprinted in Douglas MacArthur, *Reminiscences* (New York: McGraw-Hill, 1964), 272–275.

235. First Instrument of Japanese Surrender, 2 September 1945

On 2 September 1945, representatives of the Allied powers met with Japanese delegates on the USS Missouri, *moored in Tokyo Bay, to accept the Japanese surrender. A brief document, it called upon all Japanese military forces to lay down their arms and cease fighting and represented Japan's acceptance of the unconditional surrender terms demanded by the Allies. It also ceded ultimate authority over the government of Japan to Supreme Commander of the Allied Powers in the Pacific General Douglas MacArthur, who was the foremost American representative at the ceremony.*

We, acting by command of and in behalf of the Emperor of Japan, the Japanese Government and the Japanese Imperial General Headquarters, hereby accept the provisions set forth in the declaration issued by the Heads of the Governments of the United States, China, and Great Britain on 26 July 1945 at Potsdam, and subsequently adhered to by the Union of Soviet Socialist Republics, which four powers are hereafter referred to as the Allied Powers.

We hereby proclaim the unconditional surrender to the Allied Powers of the Japanese Imperial General Headquarters and of all Japanese armed forces and all armed forces under the Japanese control wherever situated.

We hereby command all Japanese forces wherever situated and the Japanese people to cease hostilities forthwith, to preserve and save from damage all ships, aircraft, and military and civil property and to comply with all requirements which may be imposed by the Supreme Commander for the Allied Powers or by agencies of the Japanese Government at his direction.

We hereby command the Japanese Imperial Headquarters to issue at once orders to the Commanders of all Japanese forces and all forces under Japanese control wherever situated to surrender unconditionally themselves and all forces under their control.

We hereby command all civil, military and naval officials to obey and enforce all proclamations, and orders and directives deemed by the Supreme Commander for the Allied Powers to be proper to effectuate this surrender and issued by him or under his authority, and we direct all such officials to remain at their posts and to continue to perform their non-combatant duties unless specifically relieved by him or under his authority.

We hereby undertake for the Emperor, the Japanese Government and their successors to carry out the provisions of the Potsdam Declaration in good faith, and to issue whatever orders and take whatever actions may be required by the Supreme Commander for the Allied Powers or by any other designated representative of the Allied Powers for the purpose of giving effect to that Declaration.

We hereby command the Japanese Imperial Government and the Japanese Imperial General Headquarters at once to liberate all allied prisoners of war and civilian internees now under Japanese control and to provide for their protection, care, maintenance and immediate transportation to places as directed.

The authority of the Emperor and the Japanese Government to rule the state shall be subject to the Supreme Commander for the Allied Powers who will take such steps as he deems proper to effectuate these terms of surrender.

Signed at TOKYO BAY, JAPAN at 0904 on the SECOND day of SEPTEMBER, 1945

MAMORU SHIGEMITSU

By Command and on Behalf of the Emperor of Japan and the Japanese Government

YOSHIJIRO UMEDZU

By Command and on Behalf of the Japanese Imperial General Headquarters

Accepted at TOKYO BAY, JAPAN at 0903 on the SECOND day of SEPTEMBER, 1945, for the United States, Republic of China, United Kingdom and the Union of Soviet Socialist Republics, and in the interests of the other United Nations at war with Japan.

DOUGLAS MACARTHUR
Supreme Commander for the Allied Powers
C.W. NIMITZ
United States Representative
HSU YUNG-CH'ANG
Republic of China Representative
BRUCE FRASER
United Kingdom Representative
KUZMA DEREVYANKO
Union of Soviet Socialist Republics Representative
THOMAS BLAMEY
Commonwealth of Australia Representative
L. MOORE COSGRAVE
Dominion of Canada Representative
JACQUES LE CLERC
Provisional Government of the French Republic Representative
C.E.L. HELFRICH
Kingdom of the Netherlands Representative
LEONARD M. ISITT
Dominion of New Zealand Representative

Source: Surrender by Japan: Terms between the United States of America and the Other Allied Powers and Japan. Department of State Publication 2504, Executive Agreement Series 493. Web site: Taiwan Documents Project website. Available at www.taiwandocuments.org/surrender01.htm.

236. Declaration of Independence of the Democratic Republic of Vietnam, 2 September 1945

On 2 September 1945, as Vietnam waited for the defeated Japanese forces to leave, Ho Chi Minh, the Vietnamese Communist and nationalist leader, declared in Hanoi that an independent state now existed in Vietnam, which until taken over by Japan during the war had been under French colonial rule. Hoping to secure United States support, Ho deliberately modeled his statement on the American Declaration of Independence. Although French forces returned to Indochina in fall 1945 and temporarily ousted Ho, he continued to lead the Vietnamese battle for independence, driving out the French in 1954. Subsequent American attempts to maintain the southern portion of Vietnam as an independent non-Communist state and prevent its unification with the Communist north ruled by Ho ultimately embroiled the United States in the lengthy and divisive Vietnam War.

"All men are created equal. They are endowed by their Creator with certain inalienable rights, among these are Life, Liberty, and the pursuit of Happiness."

This immortal statement was made in the Declaration of Independence of the United States of America in 1776. In a broader sense, this means: All the peoples on the earth are equal from birth, all the peoples have a right to live, to be happy and free.

The Declaration of the French Revolution made in 1791 on the Rights of Man and the Citizen also states: "All men are born free and with equal rights, and must always remain free and have equal rights."

Those are undeniable truths.

Nevertheless, for more than eighty years, the French imperialists, abusing the standard of Liberty, Equality, and Fraternity, have violated our Fatherland and oppressed our fellow-citizens. They have acted contrary to the ideals of humanity and justice.

In the field of politics, they have deprived our people of every democratic liberty. They have enforced inhuman laws; they have set up three distinct political regimes in the North, the Center and the South of Viet-Nam in order to wreck our national unity and prevent our people from being united.

They have built more prisons than schools. They have mercilessly slain our patriots—they have drowned our uprisings in rivers of blood.

They have fettered public opinion; they have practised obscurantism against our people.

To weaken our race they have forced us to use opium and alcohol.

In the fields of economics, they have fleeced us to the backbone, impoverished our people, and devastated our land.

They have robbed us of our rice fields, our mines, our forests, and our raw materials. They have monopolised the issuing of bank-notes and the export trade.

They have invented numerous unjustifiable taxes and reduced our people, especially our peasantry, to a state of extreme poverty.

They have hampered the prospering of our national bourgeoisie; they have mercilessly exploited our workers.

In the autumn of 1940, when the Japanese Fascists violated Indochina's territory to establish new bases in their fight against the Allies, the French imperialists went down on their bended knees and handed over our country to them.

Thus, from that date, our people were subjected to the double yoke of the French and the Japanese. Their sufferings and miseries increased. The result was that from the end of last year to the beginning of this year, from Quang Tri province to the North of Viet-Nam, more than two million of our fellow-citizens died from starvation. On March 9 [1945], the French troops were disarmed by the Japanese. The French colonialists either fled or surrendered, showing that not only were they incapable of "protecting" us, but that, in the span of five years, they had twice sold our country to the Japanese.

On several occasions before March 9, the Viet Minh League urged the French to ally themselves with it against the Japanese. Instead of agreeing to this proposal, the French colonialists so intensified their terrorist activities against the Viet Minh members that before fleeing they massacred a great number of our political prisoners detained at Yen Bay and Cao Bang.

Notwithstanding all this, our fellow-citizens have always manifested toward the French a tolerant and humane attitude. Even after the Japanese putsch of March 1945, the Viet Minh League helped many Frenchmen to cross the frontier, rescued some of them from Japanese jails, and protected French lives and property.

From the autumn of 1940, our country had in fact ceased to be a French colony and had become a Japanese possession.

After the Japanese had surrendered to the Allies, our whole people rose to regain our national sovereignty and to found the Democratic Republic of Viet-Nam.

The truth is that we have wrested our independence from the Japanese and not from the French.

The French have fled, the Japanese have capitulated, Emperor Bao Dai has abdicated. Our people have broken the chains which for nearly a century have fettered them and have won independence for the Fatherland. Our people at the same time have overthrown the monarchic regime that has reigned supreme for dozens of centuries. In its place has been established the present Democratic Republic.

For these reasons, we, members of the Provisional Government, representing the whole Vietnamese people, declare that from now on we break off all relations of a colonial character with France; we repeal all the international obligation that France has so far subscribed to on behalf of Viet-Nam and we abolish all the special rights the French have unlawfully acquired in our Fatherland.

The whole Vietnamese people, animated by a common purpose, are determined to fight to the bitter end against any attempt by the French colonialists to reconquer their country.

We are convinced that the Allied nations which at Tehran and San Francisco have acknowledged the principles of self-determination and equality of nations, will not refuse to acknowledge the independence of Viet-Nam.

A people who have courageously opposed French domination for more than eighty years, a people who have fought side by side with the Allies against the Fascists during these last years, such a people must be free and independent.

For these reasons, we, members of the Provisional Government of the Democratic Republic of Viet-Nam, solemnly declare to the world that Viet-Nam has the right to be a free and independent country and in fact it is so already. The entire Vietnamese people are determined to mobilise all their physical and mental strength, to sacrifice their lives and property in order to safeguard their independence and liberty.

Source: Bernard B. Fall, ed., *Ho Chi Minh on Revolution: Selected Writings, 1920–66* (London: Pall Mall Press, 1967), 143–145. Courtesy Dorothy Fall.

237. General H. H. Arnold, "Air Power and the Future," 12 November 1945

As the war came to an end, General Henry H. "Hap" Arnold, head of the Army Air Forces and a long-time advocate of the establishment of a large American air force, set forth his vision of the future of American air power. Not only did he call for a major enhancement of American air capabilities, he also believed it should be backed up by overseas bases, active governmental encouragement of scientific research and development, the development of civil aviation capacities, the creation of a permanent U.S. foreign intelligence agency, and the integration of American defense services. Arnold also argued that for the indefinite future, the existence of atomic weapons made it advisable for the United States to seek overwhelming air superiority over all other nations. In what was undoubtedly part of a coordinated campaign, the following July, the U.S. Strategic Bombing Survey reinforced Arnold's message when it submitted a report repeating the same conclusions.

MANY DEFINITE CONCLUSIONS CAN BE DRAWN FROM OUR EXPERIENCE IN WORLD WAR II. WHAT PRACTICAL STEPS WE SHOULD TAKE TO MAINTAIN OUR NATIONAL SECURITY IN THE YEARS THAT LIE AHEAD OF US.

This is a final report on the war activities of the Army Air Forces. I would also like to make it a document of some help to those entrusted with the future security of our country, as well as to the leaders of our Air Forces in the future. It is not possible to cover all the causes and effects from which timely lessons from the war may be drawn. A number of indicated steps, however, may be taken in the near future. Many of them are not so clear, and will require years of study and evaluation before they become apparent. Meanwhile, I offer herewith in both categories some of the personal conclusions which I have reached after my many years of service, and as a result of my experience in command of the Army Air Forces during World War II. It must be borne in mind that these conclusions are my own and may or may not reflect the views of the War Department. . . .

Air superiority . . . is the first essential for effective offense as well as defense. A modern, autonomous, and thoroughly trained Air Force in being at all times will not alone be sufficient, but without it there can be no national security.

AIR POWER AND AIR FORCE

Air Power includes a nation's ability to deliver cargo, people, destructive missiles and war-making potential through the air to a desired destination to accomplish a desired purpose.

Air Power is not composed alone of the war-making components of aviation. It is the total aviation activity—civilian and military, commercial and private, potential as well as existing.

Military Air Power—or Air Force—is dependent upon the air potential provided by industry which, in turn, thrives best in an atmosphere of individual initiative and private enterprise. Government can do much to increase this air potential by judicious use of its coordinating and planning powers.

An Air Force is always verging on obsolescence and, in time of peace, its size and replacement rate will always be inadequate to meet the full demands of war. Military Air Power should, therefore, be measured to a large extent by the ability of the existing Air Force to absorb in time of emergency the increase required by war together with new ideas and techniques.

National safety would be endangered by an Air Force whose doctrines and techniques are tied solely to the equipment and processes of the moment. Present equipment is but a step in progress, and any Air Force which does not keep its doctrines ahead of its equipment, and its vision far into the future, can only delude the nation into a false sense of security.

Further, our concept of the implements of Air Power should not be confined to manned vehicles. Controlled or directed robots will be of increasing importance, and although they probably will never preclude some form of human guidance, reliance upon direct manual skills in pilotage will gradually decrease.

In practical terms for the immediate future, the doctrine of Air Force growing out of the larger concept of Air Power can be expressed as a determination:

1. To maintain a striking air arm in being.
2. To keep the AAF and the aviation industry able to expand harmoniously as well as rapidly.
3. To maintain well-equipped overseas bases.
4. To support an alert and aggressive system of commercial air transportation—one of the foundations of American Air Power.

5. To remember that it is the team of the Army, Navy and Air Force working in close cooperation that gives strength to our armed services in peace or war.

6. To make available to the United Nations Organization, in accordance with the provisions of its Charter, adequate and effective Air Force contingents for possible use by the Security Council in maintaining international peace and security.

7. To promote scientific research and development, and to maintain a close contact with industry. . . .

Our Air Force must be flexible in its basic structure and capable of successfully adapting itself to the vast changes which are bound to come in the foreseeable future. Whatever its numerical size may be, it must be second to none in range and striking power. . . .

SCIENTIFIC RESEARCH AND DEVELOPMENT

. . . [T]he spectacular innovations in technological warfare which appeared with ever-increasing momentum in World War II and culminated with the atomic bomb demand continuous scientific research to insure the maintenance of our national security and world peace. In the past, the United States has shown a dangerous willingness to be caught in a position of having to start a war with equipment and doctrines used at the end of a preceding war. We have paid heavily for this error. A repetition of this error in the future could mean annihilation. No war will be started unless the aggressor considers that he has sufficient supremacy in weapons to leave his adversaries in a state of ineffective warmaking capacity. . . .

In the accomplishment of its fundamental responsibility for insuring that the nation is prepared to wage effective warfare, the Air Force must be able to call on all talents and facilities existing in the nation and sponsor further development of the facilities and creative work of science and industry. The Air Force must also be authorized to expand existing research facilities and to make such facilities available to scientists and industrial concerns working on problems for the Air Force. Further, the Air Force must have the means of recruiting and training personnel who have full understanding of the scientific facts necessary to procure and use the most advanced equipment. Although basic scientific research should not be undertaken by the Air Force in its own organization, it must encourage and sponsor such basic research as may be deemed necessary for the defense of the nation.

During this war the Army, the Army Air Forces and the Navy have made unprecedented use of scientific and industrial resources. When the countless aspects of Air Force operations requiring scientific and technological talent are considered, the conclusion is inescapable that we have not yet established the balance necessary to insure the continuance of teamwork among the military, other government agencies, industry and the universities. The Legislative and Executive branches of the Government should determine the best form of organization and the most efficient scheme for uniting all efforts to create the best scientific facilities and utilize all available scientific talents.

It is in the national interest to establish a national research foundation composed of the most highly qualified scientists in the United States and charged with the responsibility of furthering basic research and development in all fields of science and the scientific training of adequate numbers of highly qualified men. Scientific planning must be years in advance of the actual research and development work. The Air Force must be advised continuously on the progress of scientific research and development in view of the new discoveries and improvements in aerial warfare.

INTEGRATION OF AIR POWER INTO NATIONAL DEFENSE

The greatest lesson of this war has been the extent to which air, land and sea operations can and must be coordinated by joint planning and united command. The attainment of better coordination and balance than now exists between services is an essential of national security. . . .

The Joint Chiefs of Staff organization presided over by the Chief of Staff to the President, as developed during World War II, proved itself sound, and made coordination of effort possible not only among our own armed services but with the Allies. This organization should be continued in time of peace when the absence of the compulsions of war make cooperation and coordination of effort much more difficult to achieve.

The following requirements, in my opinion, must accordingly be met:

A. Organization

(1) One integrated, balanced United States military organization that will establish, develop, maintain and direct at the minimum expense the forces, including the mobile striking forces, required for peace enforcement and for national security with the capability for the most rapid expansion in case of all-out war.

(2) Retention of the Joint Chiefs of Staff organization with a Chief of Staff to the President.

(3) The size and composition of our striking forces to be based on:

(a) Capabilities and limitations of possible enemies.

(b) Effectiveness and employment of modern weapons of war.

(c) The geographical position of the United States, its outlying bases and such other bases as it might control or use.

(4) Maximum economy and efficiency to be secured by:

(a) Ruthless elimination of all arms, branches, services, weapons, equipment or ideas whose retention might be indicated only by tradition, sentiment or sheer inertia.

(b) Ruthless elimination of duplication throughout the entire organization.

B. Principles

(1) The above organization, to attain its objectives, must adhere rigidly to the following principles:

(a) Development of the Intelligence necessary for the effective application of our military force to whatever job it may be called upon to do.

(b) Continuous planning for both offensive and defensive operations against all potential enemies, taking into account their capabilities and possible intentions.

(c) Planning for, and direction of technical research to ensure that the most modern weapons are being developed, tested and service tested in order to retain for the United States military equipment its present preeminent position.

(d) Development and application of the most effective tactics and techniques.

(e) Realistic recommendations for Congressional appropriations for military purposes and for the distribution of these appropriations where they will produce the maximum benefit to the national security.

The Air Forces must also assume their full responsibility, under the provisions of the Charter of the United Nations Organization, to hold immediately available national Air Force contingents for combined enforcement action. These forces must be of sufficient strength, and their degree of readiness must be such as to make effective use of their inherent striking power and mobility.

World War II brought unprecedented death and destruction to war-making and peace-loving nations alike, and as any future war will be vastly more devastating, the mission of the armed forces of the United States should be not to prepare for war, but to prevent war—to insure that peace be perpetuated.

Source: H. H. Arnold, *Third Report of the Commanding General of the Air Forces to the Secretary of War* (Washington, DC: U.S. Government Printing Office, 1945), 452–470.

238. Soviet Espionage during World War II: Robert J. Lamphere to Meredith Gardner, "EMIL JULIUS KLAUS FUCHS aka Karl Fuchs," 26 September 1949

Espionage activities continued unabated during World War II, as each side spied on its enemies and also on its (then) allies. In 1949 United States authorities discovered that during the war Klaus Fuchs, a German-born British scientist with Communist sympathies who had worked since the early 1940s in the joint Anglo-American program to develop an atomic bomb, had passed on vital information to the Soviet Union, thereby speeding up the postwar development of Soviet atomic weapons. In the late 1940s Robert J. Lamphere, the Federal Bureau of Investigations operative entrusted with liaison duties with other agencies on Soviet espionage, consulted with Meredith Gardner, a highly trained cryptographer in the Army Security Agency, in an effort to identify one of the Soviet sources in the atomic-energy project, whom decoded Soviet communications had codenamed "Rest." The two men eventually succeeded in pinpointing Fuchs, who stood trial for espionage and was convicted and sentenced to fourteen years in prison.

REST

On June 15, 1944, Rest furnished to a representative of Soviet intelligence (M.G.B.), Part III of a document now identified as MSN-12. This document dated June 6, 1944, is on file with the Atomic Energy Commission and is entitled "Fluctuations and the Efficiency of a Diffusion Plant," and Part III specifically refers to "The Effect of Fluctuations in the Flow of N2." The designation MSN stands for documents prepared by British scientists who were in New York City working on Atomic Energy research. The author of this document is K. Fuchs, who is actually Emil Julius Klaus Fuchs, who is usually known as Karl Fuchs. He is a top ranking British Atomic scientist.

Information available concerning Rest indicated that he was a British scientist, inasmuch as he had also furnished to the Soviet Intelligence information concerning British participation in the Atomic Energy development. It was also indicated that he had a sister in the United States. There are indications that Rest was actually the author of the document.

Emil Julius Klaus Fuchs also known as Karl Fuchs, was born December 19, 1911, at Russelsheim, Germany. His father, Emil Fuchs was born May 13, 1874, and was a professor in Germany. Emil Julius Klaus Fuchs entered the United Kingdom in 1933, and from 1941 to 1943, was a medical physicist at the University of Birmingham, England. In November 1943, he was designated by the British Government to come to the United States as a part of the British Atomic Energy Commission. He arrived at New York City on December 3, 1943, and went to Los Alamos in August 1944. While in the United States, Fuchs worked with a group of British scientists in the period of March to June 1944, on the development of diffusional operational processes working particularly with the Kellex Corporation, which was working under the Manhattan Engineering District. Fuchs left for England from Montreal, Canada, on June 28, 1946.

In November 1947, Fuchs was back in the United States and visiting the Chicago Operations Office of the Atomic Energy Commission. At that time, he attended discussions regarding unclassified and declassified aspects of neutron spectroscopy. He also participated in declassification conferences which were being held between the United States, Great Britain and Canada. Fuchs is presently the senior research worker at the Atomic Energy Commission project at Harwell, England.

Fuchs has a sister, Kristal Fuchs Heineman, who prior to January 1941, resided at 55 Carver Road, Watertown, Massachusetts. From approximately 1941, until about 1945, she resided with her husband, Robert Block Heineman at 144 Lakeview Avenue, Cambridge, Massachusetts. They presently reside at 94 Lakeview Avenue, Cambridge, Massachusetts. Robert Block Heineman has been reliably reported as a member of the Communist Party, United States of America in 1947.

The address book of Israel Halperin implicated in the Canadian Espionage network contained the following: "Klaus Fuchs, Asst. to M. Born, 84 Grange Lane, University

of Edinburgh, Scotland Camp (possibly comp) N.—Camp L., Internment Operations—Kristal Heineman, 55 Carvel Road, Watertown." The phrase Camp L is encircled.

In addition to the foregoing a captured German document prepared presumably by German Counter Intelligence and which relates to Communist Party members in Germany contains the following:

"Klaus Fuchs, student of philosophy, December 29, 1911, Russelsheim, RSHA-IVA2, Gestapo Field Office Kiel.

"Gerhard Fuchs, October 30, 1909, Russelsheim, student RSHA-IVA2, Gestapo Field Office Kiel."

It is to be noted that Gerhard Fuchs is the brother of Emil Julius Klaus Fuchs.

GUS (GOOSE)

In connection with Rest, who furnished the document MSN-12 and who is thought to be Emil Julius Klaus Fuchs, it is also known that Rest's sister was a contact of Gus (Goose), who has presumably a scientific background. You will recall, Gus contemplated preparing a work on the production method with respect to the thermal diffusion of gases.

You will also recall, Gus, who has not been identified, was also a contact of Abraham Brothman, a Consulting Engineer in New York City, who furnished espionage information to Elizabeth Bentley in 1940.

It is thought that Gus may possibly be identical with Arthur Phineas Weber, who is presently an employee of the Kellex Corporation which is engaged in work under the Atomic Energy Commission. Weber was born March 10, 1920, in Brooklyn, New York, and is a chemical engineer. From 1941 to 1942, he worked with Brothman for the Henderick Manufacturing Company. From June 1942 to June 1944, he worked with Brothman in the Chemurgy Design Corporation, and according to some information during a part of this period he was also working for the Kellex Corporation. Weber lists employment with Kellex Corporation as a chemical engineer from July 1944 to March 29, 1946, and again from April 8, 1946, to the present. It should be noted that the Kellex Corporation was closely working in 1944 with the British Scientist group which included Fuchs.

Source: Robert Louis Benson and Michael Warner, eds., *Venona: Soviet Espionage and the American Response, 1939–1957* (Washington, DC: National Security Agency: Central Intelligence Agency, 1996), 141–143. Reprinted in Robert Louis Benson and Michael Warner, eds., *Venona: Soviet Espionage and the American Response, 1939–1957* (Laguna Hills, CA: Aegean Park Press, 1997).

Index

Page ranges for main entries appear in boldface type. Pages for documents are followed by "D."